Fifth Edition

TEACHING IN THE MIDDLE AND SECONDARY SCHOOLS

Joseph F. Callahan

Leonard H. Clark

Richard D. Kellough
California State University, Sacramento

Merrill,
an imprint of Prentice Hall

Englewood Cliffs, New Jersey   Columbus, Ohio

Library of Congress Cataloging-in-Publication Data

Teaching in the middle and secondary schools / [edited by] Joseph F. Callahan, Leonard H. Clark, Richard D. Kellough.—5th ed.
      p.   cm.
      Includes bibliographical references and index.
      ISBN 0-02-318272-5 (pbk.)
      1. High school teaching—United States. 2. Middle schools—United States.   I. Callahan, Joseph F. II. Clark, Leonard H. III. Kellough, Richard D. (Richard Dean)
   LB1737.U6T43   1995
     373.11'02—dc20   94-16330
                     CIP

Cover art: © Jane Sterrett
Editor: Debbie Stollenwerk
Production Editor: Laura Messerly, Julie Anderson Tober
Text Designer: Thomas Mack
Cover Designer: Thomas Mack
Production Buyer: Patricia A. Tonneman
Electronic Text Management: Marilyn Wilson Phelps, Matthew Williams, Jane Lopez, Karen L. Bretz
Illustrations: Steve Botts

This book was set in New Baskerville by Prentice Hall and was printed and bound by Semline, Inc., a Quebecor America Book Group Company. The cover was printed by Phoenix Color Corp.

© 1995 by Prentice-Hall, Inc.
A Simon & Schuster Company
Englewood Cliffs, New Jersey 07632

Earlier edition entitled *Teaching in the Secondary School: Planning for Competence* © 1977 by Macmillan Publishing Co., Inc. Earlier edition entitled *Teaching in the Middle and Secondary Schools,* © 1982 by Macmillan Publishing Co., Inc. Earlier edition entitled *Teaching in the Middle and Secondary Schools: Planning for Competence,* © 1988 by Macmillan Publishing Co., Inc.

Portions of this text were adapted from Kellough, *A Resource Guide for Teaching: K-12*; Kellough, Kellough, and Hough, *Middle School Teaching: Methods and Resources*; Kim and Kellough, *A Resource Guide for Secondary School Teaching: Planning for Competence*, all published by Merrill/Prentice Hall.

Printed in the United States of America

10 9 8 7 6 5 4 3 2 1

ISBN: 0-02-318272-5

Prentice-Hall International (UK) Limited, *London*
Prentice-Hall of Australia Pty. Limited, *Sydney*
Prentice-Hall of Canada, Inc., *Toronto*
Prentice-Hall Hispanoamericana, S. A., *Mexico*
Prentice-Hall of India Private Limited, *New Delhi*
Prentice-Hall of Japan, Inc., *Tokyo*
Simon & Schuster Asia Pte. Ltd., *Singapore*
Editora Prentice-Hall do Brasil, Ltda., *Rio de Janeiro*

Preface

Recent trends in education have caused much rethinking about teaching and learning in today's schools. Consider modern development in cognitive learning theory and its perspective on intelligence, the increasing prominence of the constructivist approach to conceptual understanding, and the greater use of social-interactive learning as an important instructional practice. Think of the renewed interest in discovery learning and the concomitant involvement of students in metacognition and problem solving. Finally, contemplate development in the reorganization and restructuring of schools, the successes of the middle school movement, and the continuing exploration of multicultural education. These and other trends have prompted us to make major changes for this 5th edition of our text. From a sound research base, revisions have been meticulously integrated throughout. In essence, the book has been completely reorganized and rewritten for this edition. We have tried to provide a work that is as current, accurate, complete, and practical as possible for college and university students who are in the process of becoming competent teachers at the middle school, junior high school, and high school levels.

We continue to provide a basically self-instructional text on the methods of teaching of students of grades 7 through 12. To promote mastery learning we employ a competency-based modular format as our mode of presentation. Consistent with a competency-based approach, each module contains: (1) an opening list of specific learning objectives for that module; (2) a presentation of content as related to those objectives; (3) an integration of practice and reinforcement in each module; and (4) an assessment of the learning of the opening objectives at the completion of the module.

While preparing this edition we kept in mind the rationale for including each of the topics by attempting to illustrate how each of the methods presented can be implemented in today's classroom. As you progress toward conceptual mastery, we expect that considerable self-confidence will develop and self-motivation will increase. There should be a gradual development in confidence as you master the concepts of each module, and that confidence should result in a desire to do further investigation. For that purpose, footnotes at the bottom of relevant pages and a list of readings at the end of each module augment the main flow of the text.

Of course, expertise in methods and techniques of instruction comes from practice, particularly guided practice and experience. No one has ever become truly expert simply by studying a book and carrying out learning activities. These modules, however, provide the necessary background and fundamental knowledge that make early teaching practice a successful experience. The modules should serve as effective springboards for your laboratory experiences in teaching. We believe that teachers of methods courses can depend on the modules to provide enough basic instruction that they can individualize their instruction and devote their time and attention to specific learning activities.

Reorganization of This Edition

In preparing this 5th edition, we carefully heeded the recommendations made by users and reviewers of the previous edition. We would like to acknowledge and offer a sincere thank you for the cogent reviews and recommendations made by:

Frank D. Adams, Wayne State University

Kenneth M. Ahrendt, Oregon State University

Leigh Chiarelott, Bowling Green State University

Noble R. Corey, Indiana State University

Nedra A. Crow, University of Utah

Karen Kusiak, Colby College

Jennifer Nelson, Gonzaga University

Ronald E. Peake, University of West Florida

The result was this 5th edition, a largely reorganized and rewritten book, including the module objectives and posttest questions. Posttest questions, for example, were rewritten to better reflect today's emphasis on higher-level thinking and performance. The result, we think, is a book that is clear and succinct, is organized sensibly, and has as current a research base as is possible.

The modules are now organized into five parts. Part I, Introduction to Teaching in Middle and Secondary Schools, consists of two modules. This part is designed to bridge the theoretical foundations of education courses with the practical information contained in the rest of the modules of this methods book. We have tried to make sure that the content of Part I accurately reflects today's understanding of how young people learn and develop intellectually.

Part II, Planning for Instruction, consists of three modules. It covers various aspects of the preactive phase of instruction (i.e., instructional planning), including the planning necessary to affect and maintain a safe and effective classroom environment. Effective classroom management is not something that just happens—it needs thoughtful and thorough planning. Thoughtful and thorough preparation of a *written* classroom management system is every bit as important as is giving the same attention to other aspects of planning, such as preparing a course outline and writing objectives. Too many beginning teachers fail to comprehend this.

Part III, Selecting and Implementing Instruction Strategies, consists of two modules. It is about the interactive phase of instruction, (the teaching phase). The first module focuses on student-centered, or indirect, instructional strategies; the second module focuses on teacher-centered, or direct, instructional strategies. Central to our revision of these two modules is our belief in the important of your: (1) using an eclectic style of instruction, (2) using interactive teaching strategies, (3) ensuring equality in the classroom, (4) using the most authentic learning possible, and (5) believing that all students can learn. Your job, to our way of thinking, is to help students to believe in themselves and well as to develop their conceptual understandings and intellectual skills. We trust you will find that these beliefs underlie the material of both modules of Part III—and, indeed, throughout the book.

Part IV, Instructional Aids and Resources, consists of two modules. The first covers the use of nonprojected instructional aids; the second covers the use of projected and recorded instructional aids. Finally, Part V, Assessment of Teaching and Learning, also consists of two modules. The first deals principally with the Reflective phase of instruction (analyzing and evaluating your teaching). The second (the last module of this text) was designed to help you continue your professional development and get your first teaching job.

As we prepared this 5th edition, the exercises of the previous edition were reviewed and their clarity improved, with some deleted and new ones added. Although teaching in middle schools and secondary schools has become increasingly complex—with many new and exciting things happening as schools restructure their efforts to provide learning that is more authentic for today's youth—we strive to keep the size of the book from becoming too large. We hope the book remains "user friendly." We thank all of those who helped in its development. In addition to the reviewers acknowledged earlier, we would like to thank those who have contributed to the book and are acknowledged at appropriate places throughout; our friends and efficient professionals at Prentice Hall and Merrill Publishing Company, who have maintained their belief in and support for this book; and especially Dan Duffee, for his brilliant editing of the original manuscript of two consecutive editions of this book.

Although this edition is the result of contributions of many professionals, we, as always, assume full responsibility for its shortcoming. Our aspiration for this 5th edition is that it will spark reflective thinking about your teaching, and that you will find it stimulating and professional rewarding.

Contents

PART I
INTRODUCTION TO TEACHING IN MIDDLE AND SECONDARY SCHOOLS   1

Module 1
Today's Middle and Secondary Schools   2

Module 2
Middle and Secondary School Students: Meeting the Challenge   30

PART II
PLANNING FOR INSTRUCTION   73

Module 3
Selecting Content and Preparing Objectives   75

Module 4
Preparing Unit and Lesson Plans   124

Module 5
Planning and Maintaining a Supportive Classroom Environment   194

PART III
SELECTING AND IMPLEMENTING INSTRUCTIONAL STRATEGIES   245

Module 6
Student-centered Instructional Strategies   247

Module 7
Teacher-centered Instructional Strategies   301

PART IV
INSTRUCTIONAL AIDS AND RESOURCES   347

Module 8
Nonprojected Instructional Aids   348

Module 9
Projected and Recorded Instructional Aids   368

PART V
ASSESSMENT OF TEACHING AND LEARNING   399

Module 10
Assessing and Reporting Student Achievement   400

Module 11
Assessment of Teaching and Becoming a Professional   446

Part I

INTRODUCTION TO TEACHING IN MIDDLE AND SECONDARY SCHOOLS

The school in which you may soon be teaching may bear little resemblance to the school from which you graduated, in its curriculum, its student body, its methods of instruction, or its physical appearance.

—Callahan, Clark, and Kellough

Today's concept of effective teaching and learning emphasizes the importance of learning as being a personal process, through which each learner builds on his or her personal knowledge and experiences.

—Callahan, Clark, and Kellough

Personal experience is all the experience we ever have.

—Anonymous

The two modules of Part I provide an orientation to middle and secondary school teaching by:

- Discussing the teacher as a decision maker.
- Introducing important principles of learning.
- Introducing the concept of mastery learning.
- Introducing today's concept of teaching and learning.
- Preparing you for the challenge of middle school and secondary school teaching today.
- Presenting a five-step model for effective teaching.
- Presenting information about teaching and learning styles.
- Presenting specific guidelines for working with students of diversity and differences.
- Presenting the characteristics of intelligent behavior.
- Reviewing important contributions of leading learning theorists.
- Reviewing the characteristics of middle level and high school students.
- Reviewing the differences between schools that are called secondary schools, namely, the middle school, the junior high school, and the high school.

Module 1

Today's Middle and Secondary Schools

RATIONALE

Although this book is designed to explain the *know-how* of teaching more than the *why*, to use teaching methods well requires an understanding of the *whys*. Consequently, the two modules of Part I review fundamental concepts that serve as a foundation for the selection of instructional strategies. Module 1 focuses on your understanding about middle schools and secondary schools; Module 2 concentrates on your understanding of students of those schools and how they best learn.

Our reason for reviewing these concepts is simple: to be a competent teacher, you must not only know how to teach but also understand why one approach is likely to be more effective than another for a given purpose or situation. To best accomplish your instructional goals, you need to understand your options and use the best strategies and techniques. The material in Part I will provide a basis for selecting the instructional strategies and techniques presented in subsequent modules.

SPECIFIC OBJECTIVES

At the completion of this module, you should be able to:

1. Define *secondary school*.
2. Describe the similarities and differences among the middle school, junior high school, and senior high school.
3. Describe the various schools and grade configurations that are common to middle and secondary schools.
4. Describe the difference between the schedules of a school that follows a conventional pattern and of one that uses a year-round pattern.
5. Describe the difference between team teaching and a teaching team.
6. Describe how the nature of learning influences the selection of effective instructional methods.
7. Describe the characteristics of the school-within-a-school concept.
8. Describe the various daily scheduling patterns used by middle and secondary schools.
9. Define *school restructuring* and identify the common purpose of school restructuring efforts.
10. Describe differences between the exemplary middle school and the traditional junior high school.
11. Describe the differences between direct and indirect instruction and their effects on learning.
12. Identify the philosophy behind the middle school movement.
13. Describe today's concept of teaching and learning and how it differs from the traditional concept.
14. Describe the meaning and purpose of minds-on and hands-on learning.
15. Define *mastery learning*.
16. Identify the basic premise upon which such restructuring approaches as outcome-based education and the Coalition of Essential Schools are based.
17. Identify the basic assumptions of any mastery learning model.
18. Identify the elements of a mastery learning model.
19. Explain the characteristics and importance of an eclectic teaching style.
20. Identify and distinguish the thought-processing phases of instruction and explain how each is related to effective decision making.
21. Explain the importance of the concept of locus of control and its relationship to teacher accountability.
22. Define *teaching style*.
23. Describe the elements that are involved in evolving a teaching style.

MODULE TEXT

Today's Middle and Secondary Schools

The rapid and dramatic changes occurring throughout modern society, as well as what has been learned in recent years about teaching and learning, are reflected in the equally rapid and dramatic changes occurring in today's middle and secondary schools. The school in which you soon will be teaching may bear little resemblance to the secondary school from which you graduated—in its curriculum, its student body, its methods of instruction, or its physical appearance.

Definition of *Secondary School*

A *secondary school* is any school that houses students in some combination of what traditionally have been known as grades 7 through 12. However, as we discuss later, some middle schools, which may have students through eighth grade level, also house children in grade 6 and even grade 5. (That is why we have used both terms—*middle schools* and *secondary schools*—in the title for this book.) Let's begin your quest for understanding by considering some of the more significant characteristics of today's middle and secondary schools, beginning with descriptions of the calendar year.

Calendar Year Operation: Conventional and Year-Round

School-year schedules vary from state to state, from district to district, and from school to school. Most school years begin in late August or early September and continue through late May or mid-June, though some schools operate on a year-round schedule. With year-round operation, a teacher might teach for three-quarters of the year and be off for one-quarter or teach in a 45/15 program, which means nine weeks of school (45 days) "on track" followed by three weeks of school (15 days) "off track" throughout the year. Most schools operate 5 days a week, though some are open for just 4 days. Whether school follows a year-round schedule or not, for teachers and students the school year still approximates 180 days.

Later in your teacher preparation, and also when you get your first teaching contract, you will want to pay attention to the various school schedules, including schedules for special programs and special days, as well as for different tracks. Figure 1.1 provides a sample junior high school schedule with different schedules for Monday, for Tuesday through Friday, and for minimum days, days when students attend for less than the usual length of time. In year-round schools, teachers and students are on tracks, referred to as A Track, B Track, and so on, with starting and ending times that vary depending on the track and time of year. Figure 1.2 shows a sample middle school schedule that operates on a year-round schedule.

The school day usually begins at about 8:00 A.M. and lasts until about 3:00 or 4:00 P.M. You will notice in Figure 1.2 that during the summer months the day begins and ends earlier (7:15 and 2:24). In schools that are crowded, beginning and ending times of the school day may be staggered. With a staggered start, some students and teachers start as early as 7:15 A.M. and end at about 2:30 P.M., while others begin at 9:00 A.M. and continue until 4:00 P.M. In many schools, the first and last periods of the day are scheduled with classes that are optional for students; those periods are often called *0 periods*. District and state laws vary, but generally they require that teachers be in the classroom no less than 15 minutes prior to the start of school and remain in their classrooms no less than 15 minutes after dismissal of students.

Teaching Teams

Traditionally, teachers have taught their subjects five or six times each day, in their own classrooms and fairly isolated from other teachers and school activities—not unlike the parallel play of preschool children. In many schools that is still the case. Increasingly, however, middle school teachers—and junior high and high school teachers, too—are finding themselves mem-

MONDAY SCHEDULE

7th Grade

First Bell	8:15
Core #1	8:20 – 9:35
Core #2	9:40 – 11:00
Lunch	11:00 – 11:35
Resource	11:40 – 11:50
Period 5	11:55 – 12:40
Period 6	12:45 – 1:30

8th Grade

First Bell	7:55
Period 1	8:00 – 8:45
Period 2	8:50 – 9:35
Core #1	9:40 – 11:15
Lunch	11:15 – 11:50
Core #2	11:55 – 1:30

9th Grade

First Bell	7:55
Period 1	8:00 – 8:45
Period 2	8:50 – 9:35
Period 3	9:40 – 10:25
Period 4	10:30 – 11:15
Lunch	11:15 – 11:50
Period 5	11:55 – 12:40
Period 6	12:45 – 1:30

TUESDAY – FRIDAY

7th Grade

First Bell	8:25
Core #1	8:30 – 10:05
Core #2	10:10 – 11:45
Lunch	11:45 – 12:20
Resource	12:25 – 12:50
Period 5	12:55 – 1:50
Period 6	1:55 – 2:55

8th Grade

First Bell	7:55
Period 1	8:00 – 9:00
Period 2	9:05 – 10:05
Core #1	10:10 – 12:00
Lunch	12:00 – 12:35
Core #2	12:40 – 2:30

9th Grade

First Bell	7:55
Period 1	8:00 – 9:00
Period 2	9:05 – 10:05
Period 3	10:10 – 11:10
Period 4	11:15 – 12:15
Lunch	12:15 – 12:50
Period 5	12:55 – 1:50
Period 6	1:55 – 2:55

MINIMUM DAY

7th Grade

First Bell	7:55
Core #1	8:00 – 9:15
Core #2	9:20 – 10:35
Period 5	10:40 – 11:15
Period 6	11:20 – 11:55

8th Grade

First Bell	7:55
Period 1	8:00 – 8:35
Period 2	8:40 – 9:15
Core #1	9:20 – 10:35
Core #2	10:40 – 11:55

9th Grade

First Bell	7:55
Period 1	8:00 – 8:35
Period 2	8:40 – 9:15
Period 3	9:20 – 9:55
Period 4	10:00 – 10:35
Period 5	10:40 – 11:15
Period 6	11:20 – 11:55

Figure 1.1   A Sample Junior High School Schedule Showing Different Schedules for Monday, for Tuesday through Friday, and for Minimum Days

Figure 1.2 A Sample Middle School Schedule that Operates on a Year-round Schedule

Period	July–August	September–June	Minimum Days
0		8:25	8:25
1	7:15	9:20	9:20
2	8:12	10:17	9:55
3	9:09	11:14	10:25
4			10:55
Early class	10:06	12:11	
Late lunch	10:58	1:03	No lunch period
Early lunch	10:01	12:06	
Late class	10:41	12:45	
5	11:38	1:43	11:25
6	12:35	2:40	11:55
0	1:32		
School out	2:24	3:32	12:20

bers of a collaborative teaching team in which several teachers from different subject areas work together to plan the curriculum for a common group of students.

The team may comprise only a few teachers, such as high school teachers who teach the same group of eleventh grade students in English and in world history; they may meet periodically to plan a curriculum and activities around a common theme, such as the Elizabethan era. Often, especially in middle schools, **teaching teams** comprise one teacher each from English/language arts, mathematics, science, and history/social studies.[1] These four subject areas are known as the **core curriculum**. In addition to the core subjects, specialty-area teachers may be part of the teaching team, including teachers of physical education, art, and music, and even special education teachers and at-risk specialty personnel. Because a growing number of middle-level students are those identified as being "at risk" (that is, at risk of dropping out of school), some teams may ask a school counselor or a community-resource person to be a member. Because the core and specialty subjects cross different disciplines of study, they are commonly called interdisciplinary teaching teams or simply interdisciplinary teams.

Block Scheduling and the School within a School

Some schools may have teams of teachers that meet together with a group of students, in contrast to the traditional pattern of separate subject-centered courses.[2] The interdisciplinary team will meet the same group of students for a block of time—perhaps two hours or even all day—working with the students as a team. For example, in California's Partnership Academies, which are three-year high schools, the interdisciplinary team consists of four teachers—representing English, mathematics, either science or social studies, and a vocational/technical teacher.[3] The teaching team is an integral part of a concept known as a **school within a school** (an important concept in today's school restructuring, a topic considered later in this module).

[1] A distinction must be made between teaching teams and team teaching. *Team teaching* refers to two or more teachers simultaneously providing instruction to students in the same classroom. Members of a teaching team may participate in team teaching.

[2] For example, at Addison, Illinois, Trail High School, a heterogeneous group of forty-five eleventh grade students meets for a time block of two periods each day in an integrated English and social studies course that focuses on American history and literature. The course is team taught by two teachers, an English teacher and a social studies teacher. For an account of their approach, see Kathy Smith, "Becoming the 'Guide on the Side,'" *Educational Leadership* 51(2):35–36 (October 1993). For a discussion of other types of breaks from the traditional six- or seven-period schedule, see Robert Lynn Canady and Michael D. Rettig, "Unlocking the Lockstep High School Schedule," *Phi Delta Kappan* 75(4):310–314 (December 1993).

[3] The California Partnership Academies have been developing since the early 1980s and consist of at least fifty high schools designed especially to provide education for at-risk students and a productive relationship between the schools and the business community; see Charles Dayton, Marilyn Raby, David Stern, and Alan Weisbert, "The California Partnership Academies: Remembering the 'Forgotten Half,'" *Phi Delta Kappan* 73(7):539–545 (March 1992). For a discussion of high school academy programs sponsored by the National Academy Foundation, see N. S. Rosenfeld, "The Career Connection: These Students Don't Have to be Reminded Why They're in School," *American Educator: The Professional Journal of the American Federation of Teachers* 15(2):24–29, 42 (Fall 1991).

Such an interdisciplinary teaching team and its students are sometimes referred to variously as a "house," "village," "pod," or "family"—a school within a school—where each team of teachers is assigned each day to the same group of up to 150 students for a common block of time. Within this time block, teachers on the team are responsible for the many professional decisions necessary, such as how to make school meaningful to students' lives, what specific responsibilities each teacher has each day, what the guidance activities are to be implemented, what special attention is needed by individual students, and how students will be grouped for instruction. Members of such a team become "students of their students," and thereby build the curriculum and instruction around their students' interests, perspectives, and perceptions. Their classrooms become exciting places because they "turn on" learning.[4]

This school-within-a-school concept helps students make important and meaningful connections among disciplines—that is, to make bridges within their learning—and provides them with peer and adult group identification with an important and concomitant sense of belonging. In some schools members of the "village" remain together throughout a student's years at that school. Teaching in this kind of environment has these advantages:

- The combined thinking of several teachers creates an expanded pool of ideas, enhances individual capacities for handling complex problems, and provides intellectual stimulation and emotional support. The synergism of talents produces an energy that has a positive impact on the instructional program.
- The beginning teacher has the benefit of support from more experienced teammates.
- When a team member is absent, other members of the team work closely with the substitute, resulting in less loss of instructional time for students.
- More and better planning for students occurs as teachers discuss, argue, and reach agreement on behavioral expectations, curriculum emphasis, instructional approaches, and materials.[5]

Common planning time.   For a team of teachers to plan a common curriculum, members must meet frequently. This is best accomplished when they have a common planning time. Instead of each teacher's having a different preparation period, the members of the team share the same preparation time, using this common time to plan curriculum and to discuss the progress and needs of individual students.

Lead teacher.   Each teaching team, especially when there are four or more members, may assign a member to be the **lead teacher**, also known as the teacher leader or team leader; the lead teacher may instead be appointed by the principal, or leadership may be rotated from year to year. The lead teacher facilitates discussions during the planning time, organizes the meetings, and acts as liaison with the school principal and, sometimes, district office personnel, making sure the team has the necessary resources to put its plans into action.

Classroom location.   "Proximity of team members' classrooms can facilitate coordination of instruction, allow more flexibility in scheduling, and promote productive collaboration between colleagues. Classrooms scattered about the school are less likely to facilitate a cohesive learning environment."[6]

School leadership team.   Often a team's lead teachers (or another member designated by the team) serves on the school leadership team, a group of teachers and administrators designated

---

[4]The phrases "students of their students" and "turn on learning" are borrowed from Carl A. Grant and Christine E. Sleeter, *Turning on Learning* (New York: Merrill/Macmillan, 1989), p. 2. In contrast, "symptoms of turned-off learning include students' seeming inabilities to grasp concepts, to exert effort, or to display enthusiasm; repeated lateness or absence; boredom; and work that is sloppy or of poor quality."

[5]Robert J. McCarthy, *Initiating Restructuring at the School Site*, Fastback 324 (Bloomington, IN: Phi Delta Kappa Educational Foundation, 1991), p. 11.

[6]Jerry Valentine et al., *Leadership in Middle Level Education* (Reston, VA: National Association of Secondary School Principals, 1993), p. 53.

by the principal or elected by the faculty to assist in the leadership operation of the school.[7] In some schools however, membership in the leadership team is not always so clearly established or well defined.

Block scheduling. To accommodate common planning time for members of a teaching team and to allow for more instructional flexibility, some schools use "block scheduling" to achieve horizontal articulation—assigning students to teachers for instruction. Blocks of time ranging from 70 to 90 minutes replace the traditional structure of 45- to 60-minute-long class periods. The sample block schedule of Figure 1.3 illustrates the assignment of teachers to different classes. The sample student schedule of Figure 1.4 shows how a student might be assigned to different classes on different days.

Other Examples of Nonconventional Scheduling.
Most schools use a specific number of daily periods—usually six, seven, or eight—and some use a form of block scheduling. But that does not exhaust the possibilities. One alternative—

[7] Valentine et al., p. 28.

Teacher	Advisor–Advisee	Block 1 M W F	Block 1 T Th	Block 2 M W F	Block 2 T Th	Block 3 M W F	Block 3 T Th	Block 4 M W F	Block 4 T Th
A	yes	Sci–6	Sci–6	Plan time	Plan time	Sci–6	Sci–6	Reading–6	Exploratory–6
B	yes	Eng–6	Eng–6	Plan time	Plan time	Eng–6	Eng–6	Reading–6	Exploratory–6
C	yes	SS–6	SS–6	Plan time	Plan time	SS–6	SS–6	Reading–6	Exploratory–6
D	yes	Mth–6	Mth–6	Plan time	Plan time	Mth–6	Mth–6	Reading–6	Exploratory–6
E	yes	Eng–7	Eng–7	Eng–7	Eng–7	Plan time	Plan time	Speech	Exploratory–6
F	yes	Sci–7	Sci–7	Sci–7	Sci–7	Plan time	Plan time	Reading–7	Exploratory–6
G	yes	SS–7	SS–7	SS–7	SS–7	Plan time	Plan time	Reading–7	Exploratory–6
H	yes	Pre Alg–7	Mth–7	Mth–7	Mth–7	Plan time	Plan time	Reading–7	Exploratory–6
I	yes	Plan time	Plan time	SS–8	SS–8	SS–8	SS–8	Reading–7	Exploratory–7
J	yes	Plan time	Plan time	Alg I–8	Pre Alg –7	Pre Alg–8	Mth–8	Mth–8	Pre Alg-8
K	yes	Plan time	Plan time	Sci–8	Sci–8	Sci–8	Sci–8	Intramurals	Sci-8
L	yes	Plan time	Plan time	Eng–8	Eng–8	Eng–8	Speech	Eng–8	Eng–8
M	yes	Computer	Computer	Home Ec–8	Home Ec–8	Plan time	Plan time	Home Ec–8	Exploratory–7
N	yes					Shop–8	Shop–8	Shop–8	Exploratory–7
O	yes							Spanish–8	Exploratory–7
P	yes	Plan time	Plan time	Art–6	Art–6	Art–7	Art–7	Art–8	Exploratory–7
Q	no						Art–8		
R	no	LD	LD	LD	LD	LD	LD	Plan time	Plan time

Figure 1.3 Sample Block Schedule

Figure 1.4 Sample Student Schedule

WEEK SCHEDULE A

		Mon Wed Fri	Tu Thur
7:45–8:10		Advisor-advisee	Advisor-advisee
8:10–9:35	1st Block	Social studies	Mathematics
9:35–11:35	2nd Block	English	Science
11:35–1:00	3rd Block	General music (1/2) P.E./Health (1/2)	Art (1/2) P.E./Health (1/2)
1:00–2:25	4th Block	Reading	Exploratory

WEEK SCHEDULE B

		Mon Wed Fri	Tu Thur
7:45–8:10		Advisor-advisee	Advisor-advisee
8:10–9:35	1st Block	Mathematics	Social studies
9:35–11:35	2nd Block	Science	English
11:35–1:00	3rd Block	Art (1/2) P.E./Health (1/2)	General music (1/2) P.E./Health (1/2)
1:00–2:25	4th Block	Exploratory	Reading

more popular in the 1950s and 1960s than today—is a modular schedule in which each module is 15–22 minutes. A teacher in a school that uses modular scheduling might meet a certain class for only one or two modules on one day, whereas on another day that teacher might meet the same class for several modules. Administrators of schools that use this flexible modular scheduling often felt stymied by the rigidity of the six- or seven-period day, concluding that the usual 45- to 60-minute periods are both too short and too long. Such periods may provide more minutes for instruction than are reasonably usable for the teaching goals of a particular day. Yet, at other times, such periods are too short to accomplish goals, as when a group needs to do research, work on projects, do a simulation, take a field trip, or view a video or film.

In contrast, schools with modular scheduling establish as a base period an amount of time that represents the smallest number of minutes that can be effectively utilized. For example, a period can be as short as one module (15 minutes), during which students can meet for such things as homebase activities, attendance taking, and other school business. Periods can be extended by linking as many "mods" as the instructional goals seem to indicate as being necessary. In a similar fashion, the size of the student group can be modified from 3 to 10 students (known as a small group) or 10 to 20 students (middle-size group) to perhaps 120 students (large group), such as the school-within-a-school program might provide or the entire student population of the life science program might include. The size of the group is determined by the nature of the instruction planned. During the day, or during the week, periods have different lengths. And the sequence of periods can change over time.

In a more recent restructuring effort, some schools have changed the traditional schedule to periods as long as 95 minutes each, called macroperiods. Macroperiods allow additional time for the teacher to supervise and coach students as they work on homework assignments and to help them with their reading, writing, thinking, and study skills. Learning activities that might be otherwise difficult to accomplish in traditional class periods of 45 to 60 minutes can be accommodated in a macroperiod.

Some schools have lengthened the time students are in a course while simultaneously reducing the number of courses taken at one time. For example, at the Mount Everett Regional School in Sheffield, Massachusetts (grades 7–12), students take three 90-minute courses per semester.[8]

---

[8]Scott Willis, "Are Longer Classes Better?" *ASCD Update* 35(3):1–3 (March 1993).

Under another plan, students take only one class (for 30 days) or two classes (for 60 days) at a time. Called macroclasses, these classes last four or two hours each.[9] Those participating in a macroclass plan report these advantages: students become better known by their teachers, are responded to with more care, do more writing, pursue issues in greater depth, enjoy classes more, feel more challenged, and gain deeper understandings.[10]

School Restructuring

Sometimes, it may appear that more energy has recently been devoted to organizational change (*how* the curriculum is delivered) than to school curriculum (*what* is taught). Note, however, that the two are not inseparable. School organization has a direct effect on what students learn; if it didn't, educators wouldn't be spending so much valuable time trying to restructure their schools to effect the most productive delivery of the curriculum—both the planned or formal curriculum and the "hidden" or informal curriculum.[11]

Organizational changes are referred to today as *school restructuring*, a term that has a variety of connotations, including site-based management, collaborative decision making, school choice, personalized learning, integrated curricula, and collegial staffing. School restructuring has been defined as "activities that change fundamental assumptions, practices, and relationships, both within the organization and between the organization and the outside world, in ways leading to improved learning outcomes."[12] No matter how it is defined, educators agree on this point: the design and functions of schools should reflect the needs of young people who will be in the work force in the twenty-first century, rather than the needs of the nineteenth century. As emphasized by Villars, too many schools are still designed like factories, organized like factories, and run like factories. The purpose of school restructuring is to move from that factory model to a more personalized redesign that better reflects the needs of all students.[13] Experimentation with scheduling, for instance, is part of the effort to restructure schools.

Exemplified by California's Partnership Academies, the redesigning of schools into "houses" of 125 to 150 students, each with an interdisciplinary team of four or five teachers (plus additional support personnel), represents a movement that is becoming increasingly common across the country.[14] In general, this movement is from what Villars refers to as a "system of schooling" rooted in the "Industrial Age" toward a design more in touch with the emerging demands of the twenty-first century, or the "Information Age."[15] With this redesign, schools would perhaps better address the needs and capabilities of each unique student. A number of specific needed changes are shown in Figure 1.5. As a teacher in the twenty-first century, you will undoubtedly help accomplish many of those changes.

Middle Schools and Junior High Schools

When you receive your state teaching credentials, you may or may not be certified to teach at the middle school level. In some states a secondary school credential certifies a person to teach a particular subject at any grade level, K through 12. In other states such a credential qualifies a person to teach only grades 7 through 12. In yet other states a middle school teaching cre-

[9]See Joseph M. Carroll, *The Copernican Plan: Restructuring the American High School*, available from The Regional Laboratory for Educational Improvement of the Northeast and Islands, 300 Brickstone Square, Ste. 900, Andover, MA 01810.

[10]Willis, p. 3.

[11]The hidden curriculum comprises the "tacit values, attitudes, and unofficial rules of behavior students must learn to participate and succeed in school." See Chapter 3 of Hilda Hernández, *Multicultural Education: A Teacher's Guide to Content and Process* (New York: Merrill/Macmillan, 1989), pp. 45–76. See also Kevin Ryan, "Mining the Values in the Curriculum," *Educational Leadership* 51(3):16–18 (November 1993).

[12]David T. Conley, "Restructuring: In Search of a Definition," *Principal* 72(3):12–16 (January 1993), p. 12.

[13]Jerry Villars, *Restructuring Through School Design*, Fastback 322 (Bloomington, IN: Phi Delta Kappa Educational Foundation, 1991), pp. 12–13.

[14]See, for example, the entire theme issue "new roles, new relationships," of *Educational Leadership* 51(2) (October 1993).

[15]Villars, p. 41.

School Emphases of the Industrial Age	School Emphases Needed for the Information Age
1. Top-down organizational structure at state, district levels.	1. Decentralization of decision making; participative management; reduction of federal/state regulations; decisions made closest to where action is carried out; clear accountability.
2. Conventional K–12 curriculum (ages 6–18); proliferation of course titles and fragmented curricula; textbook oriented.	2. Earlier, more flexible entry ages (entry on one's birthday at age 4, 5, or 6); age clustering for instruction (4–7, 8–12, 12–15); simplified core curriculum (less is more); integrative/transdisciplinary approaches; continuing education options; global emphasis on world as interdependent community.
3. Fragmented learning time.	3. Flexible scheduling; variable time blocks.
4. Teacher isolation in planning and instruction; limited planning time.	4. Staff organized as teams for planning and instruction; block of time for team/individual planning.
5. Community involvement in school activities.	5. Community/school shared ownership and accountability for carrying out school's purposes.
6. Classroom (cell) model of organization, by age-grade level.	6. House model design, learning task spaces, multi-age and multiyear student cohort families; school as experiential place.
7. Tracking and ability grouping.	7. Personalized programming for every student; varied groupings based on task demands and student interests.
8. Minimal teacher expectations and parental aspirations for disadvantaged/at-risk students.	8. High expectations for optimal learning of every student.
9. Promotion based on time spent in school, with little evidence of true accomplishment.	9. Promotion based on performance, using obtainable outcomes with agreed-on standards.
10. Teaching emphasis on low cognitive skills, short-term memory tasks.	10. Teaching emphasis on higher-order reasoning, problem-solving skills.
11. Student as passive consumer of information.	11. Students as active participants in formulating and accomplishing relevant (real life) objectives.
12. Impersonal student-teacher relationships; emotional flatness of classroom.	12. Teacher as mentor, coach, learning facilitator, providing timely feedback to improve student performance; concern for affective needs of students.
13. Flatness in teachers' salary, few professional growth options.	13. Differential staffing; salary based on roles and responsibilities.
14. Piecemeal tinkering of present structure; focus on maintaining status quo.	14. Systemic approach to organizational change that transforms school.

Figure 1.5 Today's Changes in School Emphasis.

Source: Jerry Villars, *Restructuring Through School Design*, Fastback 322 (Bloomington, IN: Phi Delta Kappa Educational Foundation, 1991), pp. 16–18. By permission of Phi Delta Kappa Educational Foundation.

dential is received only after successfully completing a teacher preparation program specifically designed to prepare teachers for that level. Although thirty-three of the fifty states have middle school certification, only about 11 percent of middle school teachers have that certification. Sixty-three percent have secondary credentials, and 26 percent hold elementary credentials. These 1992 data compare with 1981 data that showed that 80 percent of middle level teachers held secondary credentials, 11 percent held middle level credentials, and only 9 percent held elementary credentials. The trend toward the holding of elementary credentials by middle-level teachers is probably reflective of the increase in the number of middle schools housing grades 5 and 6.[16]

[16]Valentine et al., p. 30–31.

At this point you should note that there are two sometimes quite different types of schools, both of which are called middle schools. One is the traditional junior high school with perhaps a few minor changes, such as changing its name to "middle school." The second is the exemplary middle school, which is, as shown in Table 1.1, quite different from the traditional junior high school. To understand the significance of the middle school, certain background information may prove helpful.

Origin and Evolution of the Middle School

The first middle school was established in 1950, in Bay City, Michigan.[17] The middle school movement, however, began its growth in the 1960s with the publication of Donald Eichhorn's *The Middle School* and William Alexander's *The Emergent Middle School*.[18] The middle school, founded on many of the same principles as the traditional junior high school, developed from the notion that greater and more specific attention should be given to the special needs of young adolescents. The middle school can generally be described as a school of some three to five years between the elementary school and the high school that is focused on the educational needs of students in these in-between years and designed to promote continuous educational progress for all students.[19] A survey of the United States Department of Education, National Center for Education Statistics, Statistics of State School Systems and Common Core of Data, defines a middle school as one beginning with grade 4, 5, or 6 and ending with grade 6, 7, or 8.

Sixth graders, and even fifth graders, are increasingly becoming a part of middle schools, whereas ninth graders are continuing to be excluded.[20] The perception that sixth graders belong in a middle school while ninth graders do not is echoed by the National Middle School Association in its official position paper titled *This We Believe*.[21] From 1981 to 1992, the pattern

[17]Harvey A. Allen, Fred L. Splittgerber, and M. Lee Manning, *Teaching and Learning in the Middle School* (New York: Merrill/Macmillan, 1993), p. 30.

[18]Donald Eichhorn, *The Middle School* (New York: The Center for Applied Research in Education, 1966); William M. Alexander et al. *The Emergent Middle School* (New York: Holt, Rinehart and Winston, 1969).

[19]William M. Alexander and Paul S. George, *The Exemplary Middle School* (New York: Holt, Rinehart, and Winston, 1981), p. 3.

[20]See Valentine et al., p. 19.

[21]National Middle School Association, *This We Believe* (Columbus, OH: Author, 1982 and reissued in 1992).

Table 1.1 Summary of Differences between Middle and Junior High Schools

	Junior High School	**Middle School**
Most common grade span	7–8 or 7–9	6–8
Scheduling	Traditional	Flexible, usually block
Subject organization	Departmentalized	Integrated and thematic; interdisciplinary, usually language arts, math, science, and social studies
Guidance/counseling	Separate advising by full-time counselor on individual or "as needed" basis	Advisor-advisee relation between teacher and student within a home base or homeroom
Exploratory curriculum	Electives by individual choice	Common "wheel" of experiences for all students
Teachers	Subject-centered; grades 7–12 certification	Interdisciplinary teams; student-centered; grades K–8 or 6–8 certification
Instruction	Traditional; lecture; skills and repetition	Thematic units; discovery techniques; "learning how to learn" study skills
Athletics	Interscholastic sports emphasizing competition	Intramural programs emphasizing participation

of grades 5 through 8 for middle schools increased threefold. The rationale is this: the onset of puberty occurs for many youngsters near or during the sixth grade, the same grade in which they must adjust to a new school, new teachers, friends, programs, and so on. Beginning middle-level schooling at the fifth grade enables students to make those adjustments before they must deal with the challenges of puberty.[22]

Youngsters of middle school and junior high school age have been given various nomenclatures, including, "transescent," "preadolescent," "preteen," "prepubescent," "in-betweenager," and "tweenager." Although the term used is, perhaps, inconsequential, some understanding of various developmental stages associated with this group of youngsters is essential if an educational program and its instruction are to be appropriately tailored to address their needs. These students may be as young as ten (the youngsters enrolled in the fifth grade), or as old as fourteen or more (the students you will find in an eight grade class).

Donald Eichhorn called this developmental phase transescence, defining it as:

> The stage of development which begins before the onset of puberty and extends through the early stages of adolescence. Since puberty does not occur for all precisely at the same chronological age in human development, the transescent designation is based on the many physical, social, emotional, and intellectual changes in body chemistry that appear before the time which the body gains a practical degree of stabilization over these complex pubescent changes.[23]

Organizational Provisions for Student Differences

Schools have traditionally tried to provide for the differences among students through organizational means, such as by providing different types of schools for persons with different goals. For example, in medieval Europe, the clerk-to-be was educated in a monastery or church school, whereas the would-be knight was apprenticed as a page to an influential knighted lord. In seventeenth-century Massachusetts, the minister-to-be went to Harvard for academic training, whereas the tradesman was schooled in a private venture school or as an apprentice.

Differentiated Schools

Today, there continues to be an attempt to provide different types of schools for persons with different needs or aspirations. The secondary level includes magnet schools, academies, middle schools, junior high schools, comprehensive high schools, private secondary schools, church-affiliated schools, vocational schools, continuation and alternative high schools, and so on. The practice of providing different routes for students with different needs and different vocational and academic aspirations continues.

Curriculum Tracks

Some school systems provide different schools for youths planning for different vocations. In most school systems, though, these differences are accommodated by offering a variety of curricula in comprehensive high schools. By a judicious selection of curriculum offerings (courses), students can prepare themselves for entrance to a four-year college or for a specific vocation. If students wish neither four-year college nor vocational preparation, they can select a general program of high school studies. Such a choice of curricula is probably the most common administrative or organizational means of providing for individual differences at the high school level. Although a student's choice of a curriculum may begin in middle school or junior high school, it usually begins or becomes apparent at the high school. Such choice is infrequent at lower grade levels.

Some high schools are organized on the basis of the demonstrated ability of students. For instance, a school may provide one sequence for honors students, a second sequence for college-preparatory students, a third sequence for general students, and a fourth sequence for

[22]Valentine et al., p. 19.

[23]Eichhorn, p. 3.

academically slower or seemingly unmotivated students. These different sequences—sometimes called tracks or streams—may differ from one another in difficulty and complexity of subject content, rate of student progress, and methods of instruction. Thus, the students in a mathematics honors group may move to the study of calculus in the twelfth grade, while a slow group might never go beyond the development of basic computational skills.

Homogeneous Grouping

Tracks or streams are, in effect, a type of homogeneous grouping. Homogeneous groups are formed by dividing students into class sections, according to some criterion or a combination of criteria. Usually the criteria include a combination of ability, desire, and prior academic success. Other criteria are educational-vocational goals (e.g., business English or college-preparatory English) or just interest. In any case, the reasons for forming homogeneous groups are to provide for the differences in students and to make teaching more efficient and perhaps easier. Theoretically, when classes are grouped homogeneously, teachers can more easily select content and methods that are suitable for all students in that group.

In some instances, and to some degree, homogeneous grouping (i.e., ability grouping) works. For example, when all the students in an advanced mathematics class are interested, motivated, and self-confident (and have similar styles of learning and modality preferences), teaching them is no doubt easier. And finding content, textbooks, and methods suitable for everyone in a class is also easier if the group is homogeneous. Nevertheless, homogeneous grouping is not necessarily the answer to the problem of addressing individual student differences.[24]

In the first place, homogeneous groups are not truly homogeneous; they are merely attempts to make groups similar, according to certain criteria. All that homogeneous grouping does is to reduce the heterogeneity of classes, making certain aspects of the problem of providing for individual differences in students a bit more manageable.

Whatever the advantages of homogeneous grouping, this organizational scheme also has several built-in problems. One occurs when the teacher assumes that the class is truly homogeneous. In classes grouped according to ability and academic history, the range of proven academic ability may be reduced, but the range of interest, ambitions, motivations, and goals is probably just as wide as in any other class. No matter how much a school attempts to homogenize classes—and no matter what plan of grouping is used—you as the teacher will always face the necessity of attending to and providing for differences in individual students.

Another problem of ability grouping is that students of the "less academically rigorous" courses may, due to poor teaching, get short-changed, with little expected of them and with little for them to do. For example, "students in low groups generally have quantitatively fewer and qualitatively inferior opportunities to learn than those in higher levels."[25] Furthermore, these students have little opportunity to interact with and to learn from their "brighter" or more motivated peers. Students can learn a great deal from one another. Consequently, slower learners benefit from associating with their more talented and motivated peers, who in turn can learn from the slower students. When this opportunity for interaction is not provided, classes for the slower, less-motivated students become educational ghettos—simply a continuation of the educationally deprived environments in which they often live outside school. If there is anything that has been learned well in recent years it is that there is no student in a public school who cannot learn if given the proper classroom environment, opportunity, and

[24]Ability grouping, or tracking, is the assignment of students to classes based upon academic ability. Grouping and tracking do not seem to increase overall achievement in schools, but they do promote inequity. Although most research studies conclude that tracking should be discontinued because of its discriminatory and damaging effects on students, many secondary schools continue using it, either directly, by counseling students into classes according to student ability and the degree of academic rigor of the classes, or indirectly, by designating certain classes as "college prep" and others as "non–college prep" and allowing students some degree of freedom to choose. For a strong research-based argument for the elimination or severe reduction in the use of tracking and ability grouping, see Adam Gamoran, "Is Ability Grouping Equitable?" *Educational Leadership* 50(2):11–17 (October 1992); see also other articles in that theme issue of *Educational Leadership*. For current patterns of grouping children in middle schools and junior high schools, see Jerry W. Valentine, *Leadership in Middle Level Education* (Reston, VA: National Association of Secondary School Principals, 1993), pp. 56–60.

[25]Hilda Hernández, *Multicultural Education: A Teacher's Guide to Content and Process* (New York: Merrill/Macmillan, 1989), p. 57.

encouragement. (The value of using heterogeneous cooperative-learning groups within a class is discussed in Module 6.)

Promotion Schemes

The strategies of grade skipping and retaining students in the same grade for another year are other devices that have traditionally been used to provide for differences in student achievement. Years ago, in order that the period skipped or repeated might not be too long, city systems instituted half-year courses. Under this sort of plan, students were promoted every half year. Today, some systems schedule half-year and quarterly courses and even short minicourses.

A relatively newer promotion strategy, called continuous progress (or continuous promotion) consists of dividing the course work into modules. When a student completes one module, he or she goes on to the next. Theoretically, continuous progress plans are an excellent means of providing for individual differences. This strategy is most commonly found in continuation or alternative high schools where promotion is based on mastery and readiness.

The difficulty that prevents a wider use of continuous progress is that schools are usually graded. At the end of one school year, students go on to the next grade, often whether they are ready or not. A continuous progress plan works better with the concept of a nongraded school. In a nongraded school, students are placed in courses not because they are in a certain grade but because they have reached a certain level of academic proficiency or achievement.[26]

Students at Risk of Not Finishing School

In practice, the undisciplined, academically disengaged, and lesser-motivated students are those who seem to have the most difficulty with nonconventional schedules and organizational patterns. Yet these academically **at-risk** students are the same ones who have the most difficulty with conventional school schedules as well.[27] A nonconventional schedule or organization alone—without concomitant changes in teaching and curriculum approaches and without quality attention to the individual needs of all students—seems to be of no value in addressing the needs of students who are at risk of not finishing school.

School restructuring, then, is just one way of helping students who are at risk. Other ways that can also affect the schedules of teachers who are involved in the efforts include:

- Special literacy programs before school, after school, or as pullout (where the student is pulled out of the regular program for a portion of the day, and placed in special classes).
- Teacher mentors and community or business mentors to encourage positive adult role models.
- Private business and industry contributing technology and work-study programs.
- Appointment of at-risk program coordinators within school districts and at-risk counselors at the school campus.
- Establishment of school-home connections.

School–Home–Community Connections

During the 1990s educators have been embracing the idea of rekindled partnerships among the home, school, and community in order to promote the learning and achievement of all students. Many teachers do effectively involve parents and guardians in their children's school work, but most families still have little positive interaction with the schools their children attend. Some of the ways that teachers attempt to involve parents and guardians are by making time for parent conferences, writing positive notes home, calling parents and guardians to involve them in their child's school work, and including parents in reviewing student portfolios.

[26]See, for example, Robert H. Anderson, "The Return of the Nongraded Classroom," *Principal* 72(3):9–12 (January 1993).

[27]Since the 1983 publication of *A Nation At Risk* (Washington, DC: National Commission on Excellence in Education), the term *at risk* has become commonly used to identify students who have a high probability of not finishing school, and has been defined variously. For example, the Austin (Texas) Independent School District defines a student who is at risk in grades 7 through 12 on the basis of the student's age, achievement, failing grades, and scores on the TEAMS test. See Linda Frazer and Todd Nichols, *At-Risk Report: 1990–91: Executive Summary* (Austin, TX: Office of Research and Evaluation, Austin Independent School District, 1991).

Some states, districts, and local schools have adopted formal policies about home and school partnerships. Any school can become more successful if parents are productively active in their children's education. And any student can become more successful at school if the school links curricula to comprehensive programs of parent and guardian involvement.[28] School and administrative efforts to foster parent involvement include:

- Student-teacher-parent contracts.
- Weekly calendars and folders that include the student's record and that are sent home each week.
- Home visitor programs.
- Workshops for parents.

Some schools have initiated homework-hotline programs in which students and parents can get help by phone for homework difficulties.[29]

As should be obvious, to generalize about middle and secondary schools is not easy, but perhaps you have been given sufficient information and examples to arouse your curiosity about the many variations that can and do exist. Later, you will visit schools to learn firsthand about schools, curricula, teachers, and schedules.

Today's Concept of Teaching and Learning

Teaching is *not* telling something to a group of listeners, or explaining some concept, or demonstrating a mastery of an important skill or topic. Rather, teaching is the facilitation of student learning. Of course, when you are helping students learn, you may tell, explain, or demonstrate, but you do these only as a means to accomplish an end. In the final analysis your success as a teacher is determined by how well your students have learned.

For better or worse, however, teaching constitutes more than just helping students learn. Teachers must ensure that students learn designated material—the content that comprises the planned curriculum—and do this in such a way that each student builds her or his confidence and self-esteem.

An understanding of students—how they develop intellectually, how they think, what they think about, and how they learn—is essential to becoming an effective teacher. To the content of this book you bring your knowledge and opinions, which are derived from your experiences and your perceptions of those experiences. The framework of theoretical and practical knowledge presented in this text was designed to cause you to examine those perceptions. Through that process, you will deepen your understanding about the way students learn and develop intellectually and about how you, as their teacher, will facilitate that learning and development.

In essence, your task as a teacher is the same—to cause your students to examine their perceptions and build deeper and broader frameworks of understanding. Remember that students do not come to your classroom as blank slates. Because of individual personal experiences, each student comes with his or her own perceptions about almost everything related to the subject content. To cause students to examine or change some of those perceptions is anything but an easy task—but that is your job. Anyone who ever said that to become an effective teacher is an easy job didn't know the first thing about teaching.

Constructing Knowledge

Today's concept of effective teaching and learning emphasizes the importance of learning as being a personal process, through which each learner builds on his or her personal knowledge and experiences.[30] Like constructing a skyscraper, the process of teaching and learning is grad-

---

[28]Zelma P. Solomon, "California's Policy on Patent Involvement," *Phi Delta Kappan* 72(5):359–362 (January 1991), p. 362.

[29]For a description of such partnership programs, see the special section "Parent Involvement" in *Phi Delta Kappan* 72 (5) (January 1991).

[30]In many respects, today's view of teaching and learning is similar to that advanced more than thirty years ago by Arthur L. Combs and other perceptual psychologists of that time. For example, see Arthur L. Combs (ed), *Perceiving, Behaving, and Becoming*, 1962 ASCD Yearbook (Alexandria, VA: Association for Supervision and Curriculum Development, 1962).

ual and sometimes painstaking. This modern view stands in opposition to the older view of teaching as "covering the material." Today's view of learning is learn less but learn well. Today's concept of competent teaching is to start where the students are (with their perceptions) and build upon that base, helping them make connections from their knowledge and experiences. The methodology uses what is often referred to as a **hands-on** (doing it) and **minds-on** (thinking about it) approach to constructing—and often, reconstructing—the learner's perceptions. When compared with the traditional behaviorist mode of instruction, teaching in this constructivist mode is slower, involving discussion, debate, cooperative learning, and the re-creation of ideas. Rather than following previously established steps, the curriculum evolves, with a heavy dependence on materials and student manipulation of those materials. The details of the curriculum is primarily determined by the student's interests and questions. Less content is covered, fewer facts are remembered for a test, and progress is sometimes exceedingly slow.[31]

Social Interaction and Collaborative Learning

Today's concept of effective teaching emphasizes the social nature of learning. From that perspective, the more traditional instruction—in which students sat quietly, listened to an instructor, and worked alone most of the time—is of dubious value. These days, perhaps more than at any other time, you are likely to find student learning being facilitated, as students (and teachers) learn together and develop their respect for one another in heterogeneous groups. Teachers model the same behavior, collaborating as members of teaching teams and working together with other members of the faculty, staff, and the community in a continuing quest to build the most effective learning environment for all students. Teachers are constantly making decisions, and those who are most effective at teaching are those who reflect upon and learn from their decisions. Good teachers are good learners and thinkers; they think reflectively upon their experiences.

An important strategy for effective instruction is the way students are grouped for positive interaction and quality learning. During any given week, depending on the course and learning activity, a student might experience a succession of group settings. Such teaching proves most effective when the climate of the group is positive—when the students and the teacher know and accept one another and work harmoniously toward common group goals. A positive climate works because feelings of personal worth, belonging, and security tend to support learning. This classroom condition is mostly likely to occur when the group is cohesive and diffusely structured. Diffusely structured groups are those that are free from in-group concerns—self-esteem is spread evenly throughout rather than concentrated in a few stars or favorites. Communications in diffusely structured groups are generally open, and the class norms allow for a wide range of behavior, thus creating an atmosphere of tolerance and good feeling. Groups with these characteristics tend to develop feelings of cohesiveness and togetherness. In such an atmosphere, teaching and learning usually progress smoothly and efficiently. (Ways of grouping students for instruction is a topic of Module 6.)

Mastery (Quality) Learning

Learning is an individual experience. Yet the teacher is expected to work effectively with students on other than an individual basis—more likely thirty-five to one, or even higher. Much has been written of the importance of individualizing the instruction. We know of the individuality of the learning experience. And we know that some students are verbal learners, whereas others are better visual, tactile, or kinesthetic learners (these four learning modalities are discussed in Module 2). As the teacher, though, you find yourself in the difficult position of simultaneously "treating" thirty-five separate and individual learners with individual learning styles and preferences. Each comes to your class with unique experiences and preconceived notions

[31]Bruce Watson and Richard Konicek, "Teaching for Conceptual Change: Confronting Children's Experience," *Phi Delta Kappan* 71(9):680–685 (May 1990), p. 685.

about most everything. To individualize instruction in such circumstances seems an impossible expectation—yet occasionally teachers do succeed. This book will help you maximize your efforts and minimize your failures.

Quality Time on Task

Student achievement in learning is related to both the quality of attention and the length of time given to learning tasks. In 1968, Benjamin Bloom, building upon a model developed earlier by John Carroll, developed the concept of individualized instruction called mastery learning, saying that students need sufficient time-on-task (i.e., engaged time) to master content before moving on to new content.[32] From that concept Fred Keller developed an instructional plan called the Keller plan, or personalized system of instruction (PSI), which by the early 1970s enjoyed popularity and success at many colleges. The Keller plan involves the student's learning from printed modules of instruction (similar to the modules of this book), which allow the student greater control over the learning pace. The instruction is mastery oriented; that is, the student demonstrates mastery of one module before proceeding to the next.

Today's emphasis is on mastery of content, or quality learning, rather than coverage of content or quantity of learning.[33] Because of that emphasis, the importance of the concept of quality learning, **mastery learning**, has resurfaced. For example, in today's efforts to restructure schools, two popular approaches, outcome-based education (OBE) and Coalition of Essential Schools (CES), are both built on the premise that each student can learn and focus on the construction of individual knowledge through mastery.[34] In some instances, however, attention may only be on the mastery of minimum competencies, and thus students are not encouraged to work and learn to the maximum of their talents and abilities.

Mastery of content means that the student demonstrates use of what has been learned. As explained by Horton:

> Mastery learning may be broadly defined as the attainment of adequate levels of performance on tests that measure specific learning tasks. Mastery learning also describes an instructional model whose underlying assumption is that nearly every student can learn everything in the school curriculum at a specified level of competence if the learner's previous knowledge and attitudes about the subject are accounted for, if the instruction is of good quality, and if adequate time on task is allowed to permit mastery.[35]

Assumptions about Mastery Learning

Mastery (quality) learning is based on certain assumptions:

1. Mastery learning is possible for all students.
2. For mastery and quality learning to occur, it is the instruction that must be modified and adapted, not the students. Tracking and ability grouping do not fit with the concept of mastery learning.[36]
3. Although all students can achieve mastery, some may require more time than others to master a particular content. The teacher and the school must provide for this difference in the time needed to complete a task successfully.
4. Most learning outcomes can be specified in terms of observable and measurable performance.

---

[32]Benjamin Bloom, *Human Characteristics and School Learning* (New York: McGraw-Hill, 1976); and John Carroll, "A Model of School Learning," *Teachers College Record* 64(8):723–733 (May 1963).

[33]See, for example, Frank N. Dempster, "Exposing Our Students to Less Should Help Them Learn More," *Phi Delta Kappan* 74(6):433–437 (February 1993).

[34]Cheryl T. Desmond, *A Comparison of the Assessment of Mastery in an Outcome-Based School and a Coalition of Essential Skills School* (paper presented at the Annual Meeting of the American Educational Research Association, San Francisco, April 20–24, 1992).

[35]Lowell Horton, *Mastery Learning*, Fastback 154 (Bloomington, IN: Phi Delta Kappa Educational Foundation, 1981), p. 9.

[36]See, for example, Susan Black, "Derailing Tracking," *Executive Educator* 15(1):27–30 (January 1993), for a review of recent research on student achievement, self-concept, and curriculum and on instruction showing the ineffectiveness of tracking and ability grouping. Alternatives suggested are cooperative learning, mastery learning, peer tutoring, accelerated learning, and computer-aided instruction.

5. Most learning is sequential and logical.
6. Mastery learning can ensure that students experience success at each level of the instructional process. Experiencing success at each level provides incentive and motivation for further learning.[37]

Components of a Mastery Model for Learning

An instructional model designed to teach toward mastery will contain the following components:

1. *Objectives* that are stated in specific behavioral terms. (This topic is discussed in Module 3).
2. *Preassessment* of the learner's present knowledge. (Preassessment strategies will be an important element of your unit and lesson planning, as discussed in Module 4).
3. *Implementation* of the instructional component, with coached practice, reinforcement, frequent comprehension checks (i.e., diagnostic or formative assessment), and corrective instruction at each step to keep the learner on track. (The instructional components are the essentials presented in Modules 6 and 7).
4. *Postassessment* to determine the extent of mastery of the objectives. (Assessment is the component presented principally in Module 10).

Notice that this instructional model was used in the sequence of modules of this book (with the exception of the preassessment component).

Direct versus Indirect Teaching

To properly select and effectively implement a particular teaching strategy to teach specific content to a distinctive group of students, you must make a myriad of decisions along the way. Selection of a particular strategy depends in part upon your decision whether to deliver information directly—direct or expository or didactic teaching—or to provide students with access to information—indirect or facilitative teaching. **Direct teaching** tends to be teacher-centered (see Module 7), whereas **indirect teaching** is more student-centered (see Module 6).

Caution: professional education is rife with a jargon that can be confusing to the neophyte. The terms *direct teaching*, its synonyms, *direct instruction*, *expository teaching*, and *teacher-centered instruction*, and its antonym, *direct experiences*, are examples of how confusing the jargon can be. The term *direct teaching* can also have a variety of definitions, depending on who is doing the defining. The point here now is that you must not confuse *direct instruction* with *direct experiences*. The two terms indicate two separate (although not entirely incompatible) instructional modes.

Reflective Decision Making and the Locus of Control

During any school day, a teacher makes hundreds of decisions, many of which must be made instantaneously. In addition, in preparation for the day, the teacher will have already made many decisions. Thus, during one school year a teacher makes literally thousands of decisions, many of which can and will affect the lives of students for years to come. For you this should seem an awesome responsibility—which it is.

To be an effective teacher, you must become adept at decision making. You must make decisions developed through careful thinking over time, as well as decisions on the spot that arise from unforeseen circumstances. To be adept in making decisions that affect the students in the most positive kinds of ways, you need: (1) common sense; (2) intelligence; (3) a background of theory in curriculum and instruction, with extended practical experience in working with young people; and (4) the willingness to think about and reflect upon your teaching and to continue learning all that is necessary to become an exemplary secondary school teacher.

Initially, of course, you will make errors in judgment, but you will also learn that young people are fairly resilient. And you will find experts to guide you and help you ensure that the

---

[37]Adapted from Horton, *Mastery Learning*, p. 15–18.

students are not damaged severely by errors in judgment that you make. You can learn from your errors. Keep in mind that the sheer number of decisions you make each day will mean that not all of them will be the best ones that could have been made had you had more time to think and had you better resources for planning.

Although effective teaching is based on scientific principles, good classroom teaching is as much an art as it is a science—few rules apply to every teaching situation. In fact, the selection of content, of instructional objectives, of materials for instruction, of teaching strategies, of responses to inappropriate student behavior, and of techniques for assessment are all the result of subjective judgments. Although many decisions may be made unhurried, such as when you plan the instruction, many others must be made on the spur-of-the-moment. Once the school day has begun, you may lack the time for making carefully thought-out judgments. At your best, you will base decisions on your knowledge of school policies and your teaching style, as well as on pedagogical research, the curriculum, and the nature of the students in your classroom. You will also base your decisions on instinct, common sense, and reflective judgment.

The better your understanding and experience with schools, the content of the curriculum, and the students—and the more time you give for thinking and careful reflection—the more likely it will be that your decisions will result in the student learning that you had planned. You will reflect upon concepts developed from one teaching experience and apply them to the next. As your classroom experiences accumulate, your teaching will become more routinized, predictable, and refined.

Decision-Making and Thought-Processing Phases of Instruction

Teaching has been defined as "the process of making and implementing decisions before, during, and after instruction—decisions that, when implemented, increase the probability of learning."[38] Instruction, then, can be divided into four decision-making and thought-processing phases: (1) the preactive (planning), (2) the interactive (teaching), (3) the reflective (analyzing and evaluating the teaching), and (4) the projective (application of that reflection).[39]

The preactive phase consists of all those intellectual functions you make prior to actual instruction. The interactive phase includes all the decisions made during the immediacy and spontaneity of the teaching act. Decisions made during this phase are likely to be more intuitive, unconscious, and routine than those made during the planning phase. The reflective phase is the time you take to reflect on, analyze, and judge the decisions and behaviors that occurred during the interactive phase. As a result of your reflection, you make decisions about what to use in subsequent teaching actions. At that point, you are in the projective phase, abstracting from your reflection and projecting your analysis into subsequent teaching actions.

Locus of Control

During the reflective phase, you have a choice of whether to assume full responsibility for the instructional outcomes or to assume responsibility only for the positive outcomes of the planned instruction, placing the blame for the negative outcomes on outside forces (e.g., parents and guardians, student peer pressure, other teachers, administrators, textbooks). Where the responsibility for outcomes is placed is referred to as locus of control. Competent teachers tend to assume full responsibility for the instructional outcomes, regardless of whether or not those outcomes were intended.[40]

Developing a Teaching Style

Every teacher develops a personal style of teaching with which she or he feels most comfortable. This style develops both from the teacher's personal traits and from the expertise the

[38]Madeline Hunter, *Enhancing Teaching* (New York: Macmillan, 1994).

[39]Arthur L. Costa, *The School as a Home for the Mind* (Palatine, IL: Skylight, 1991).

[40]Costa, p. 105.

teacher has in methodology, subject matter, and pedagogical theory. A teaching style can be defined as the way a teacher teaches, including the teacher's distinctive mannerisms complemented by his or her choices of teaching behaviors and strategies. The most effective teachers can vary their styles—that is, their styles are flexible enough to encompass many and various strategies. Those teachers, therefore, are prepared to address the great variety of situations that may develop in a classroom.

Effective teachers can modify their styles by selecting the strategy that is most appropriate for the situation, thus securing active student involvement and the greatest amount of student achievement. Highly effective teaching of this sort requires expertise in a wide variety of methods. It also requires a good command of the subject matter and an understanding of the students being taught. This may sound like a large order, but many beginning teachers become adept at this kind of teaching style and do so surprisingly quickly.

Thus, to be an effective teacher you should: (1) develop a large repertoire of techniques—both direct and indirect—in order to be prepared for many contingencies; (2) learn as much about your students and their preferred styles of learning as you can; and (3) develop an eclectic style of teaching, one that is flexible and adaptable.

A Model for Teaching

Into your teaching style you should incorporate the following five-step model for effective teaching:

1. Diagnosis or preassessment.
2. Preparation.
3. Guidance of student learning.
4. Assessment of the learning.
5. Follow-up.

The diagnosis is an initial assessment (or preassessment) of the situation. In this step, you assess the students' present knowledge as well as their needs and desires. Through such diagnosis, you can determine what should be accomplished and how it can best be done.

Next, you prepare for the instruction. Preparation includes planning the units and lessons and the corresponding motivational strategies, gathering materials and equipment, and arranging the setting for instruction.

Guidance of student learning includes the actual instruction—showing students how, making information available to students, and providing constructive feedback to students about their work.

In the fourth step, you and the students assess the progress of their learning and, in so doing, the success of the instruction. Assessment, an ongoing process, provides information to both the teacher and the students about where they have made progress and where they have not. Those data provide a basis for determining the follow-up.

In the final step, you follow up the instruction by helping students fill in what they have missed and by building on what they have learned.

These five steps tend to merge together. For example, the assessment and follow-up for one unit or lesson may become the diagnosis, preparation, and guidance phases for the next one. But even when truncated, this five-step model is always evident in good teaching.

SUMMARY

It is indeed today a challenge to teach middle and secondary school students, whether ten- to fourteen-year-olds (students of the middle school and junior high school grades) or teenagers (students of high school). To help you meet the challenge, there is a wealth of information and resources available about teaching and working with young people. You will likely not have to go it alone.

As you build broader frameworks of understanding of teaching and learning, as you practice the development of your teaching skills, and as you reflect upon that experience, you will be well on your way to becoming the most effective teacher you can be by developing your own personal style of teaching. This teaching style will develop from a combination of personal traits and the expertise you have in methodology, subject matter, and pedagogical theory.

As noted in this module, the most effective teachers can vary their styles—that is, their styles are flexible enough to encompass a great number of strategies and tactics and are therefore readily adaptable to the different sorts of situations that may develop. Effective teachers can modify their styles by selecting and using the strategy that is most appropriate, thus securing active student involvement and the greatest amount of student achievement. Highly effective teaching of this sort requires both expertise in a wide variety of methods and a feeling for the appropriate situation in which to use each method. Such teaching also demands a good command of the subject matter and an understanding of the students being taught. Many beginning teachers become adept at this kind of teaching style and do so surprisingly quickly.

To be an effective teacher you should: (1) develop a large repertoire of techniques—both direct and indirect—in order to be prepared for the many possible contingencies; (2) learn as much about your students and their preferred styles of learning as you can; (3) develop an eclectic style of teaching, one that is flexible and adaptable; and (4) build into your teaching use of the five-step model of diagnosis, preparation, guidance of student learning, assessment of learning, and follow-up.

In deciding which methods to use, you will be influenced by a number of factors, each of which is explored further in subsequent modules (beginning with Module 2). In essence, though, your primary focus will be on organizing your curriculum and instruction to support *authentic learning* in which the students not only learn by doing but think about what they are learning and doing.

Now, to learn more about strategies available and a teacher's decision-making process, do Exercises 1.1 and 1.2.

EXERCISE 1.1
Methods of Instruction

• • • • • •

Instructions: The purpose of this exercise is for you to reflect on how you have been taught (throughout your schooling) and share those reflections with your classmates, looking for differences as well as commonalities.

1. The following is a list of methods of instruction. Rate each according to your familiarity and experiences with it, using this rating scale: *A* = very familiar and with good learning experiences *B* = somewhat familiar *C* = never experienced *D* = familiar but with bad learning experiences

___ Assignment	___ Laser videodisc
___ Audiovisual equipment	___ Lecture
___ Autotutorial	___ Library/resource center
___ Coaching	___ Metacognition
___ Collaborative learning	___ Mock up
___ Cooperative learning	___ Multimedia
___ Compact disc	___ Panel discussion
___ Computer-assisted	___ Periodicals
___ Debate	___ Problem solving
___ Demonstration	___ Project
___ Discovery	___ Questioning
___ Drama	___ Review and practice
___ Drill	___ Role play
___ Expository	___ Self-instructional module
___ Field trip	___ Simulation
___ Game	___ Study guide
___ Group work	___ Symposium
___ Guest speaker	___ Telecommunication
___ Homework	___ Term paper
___ Individualized instruction	___ Textbook
___ Inquiry	___ Think-pair-share
___ Laboratory investigation	___ Tutorial

2. Now list the methods in four columns according to the rating you gave to each.

A Methods	*B Methods*	*C Methods*	*D Methods*

3. In small groups (3 or 4 per group), share your columns with your classmates. Are there methods that seem to show up consistently in certain columns? If so, try to analyze why. Questions that you might discuss in your groups are:

- Were certain methods more consistently used at any one level of your education, such as college, high school, junior high, etc.?

- In what what ways have your teachers' teaching styles differed?

- Which have appealed to you most?

- What qualities did they have that you would most like to emulate? Avoid?

- Did they seem to rely more on certain strategies, tactics, and techniques?

EXERCISE 1.2
The Teacher as Reflective Decision Maker

• • • • • •

Instructions: The purpose of this exercise is to learn more about the nature of the decisions and the decision-making process used by teachers. To accomplish this, you are to talk with and observe one middle school or secondary school teacher for one class period, tabulate the number of decisions the teacher makes for that class period, and then share the results with your classmates. Obtain permission from a cooperating teacher by explaining the purpose of your observations. A follow-up thank you would be appropriate.

School, teacher, and class observed:

1. Use the following format for your tabulations. You may first want to make your tabulations on a separate blank sheet of paper and then organize and transfer those tabulations to this page. Tabulate and identify each decision. To tabulate the decisions made before and after class, confer with the teacher after class.

Decision Made before Class
Examples:

- objectives
- amount of time to be devoted to particular activities
- classroom management procedures

Decisions Made during Class
Examples:

- called on Juanita to answer a question
- teacher remained silent until students in back row got quiet
- talk with tardy student

Decisions Made after Class

Examples:

- to review a particular concept at beginning of class tomorrow
- to arrange a conference with Juanita to talk with her about her hostility during class
- to make a revision in tomorrow's homework assignment

2. What was the total number of decisions made by this teacher before class? _____
   During class? _____ After class? _____
   Compare your results with those of others in your class.

3. Did you see any evidence that this teacher assumed full responsibility for the learning outcomes of this class session? Describe the evidence.

4. What percentage of all decisions by this teacher were planned? _____ Spontaneous? _____

5. Did you share your results of this exercise with the cooperating teacher? His or her reaction?

6. Your conclusions from this exercise?

SUGGESTED READING

Bracey, G. W. "Why Can't They Be Like We Were?" *Phi Delta Kappan* 73(2):105–117 (October 1991).

Brobeck, J. K. "Teachers Do Make a Difference." *Journal of Learning Disabilities* 23(1):11 (January 1990).

Canady, R. L., and Reina, J. M. "Parallel Block Scheduling: An Alternative Structure." *Principal* 72(3):26–29 (January 1993).

Carnegie Council on Adolescent Development. *Turning Points: Preparing American Youth for the 21st Century*. Report of the Task Force on Education of Young Adolescents. New York: Carnegie Corporation, 1989.

Cawelti, G., ed. *Challenges and Achievements of American Education*. 1993 ASCD Yearbook. Alexandria, VA: Association for Supervision and Curriculum Development, 1993.

Darling-Hammond, L. "Reframing the School Reform Agenda." *Phi Delta Kappan* 74(10):753–761 (June 1993).

Dayton, C., et al. "The California Partnership Academies: Remembering the Forgotten Half." *Phi Delta Kappan* 73(7):539–545 (March 1992).

Evans, K. M., and King, J. A. "Research on OBE: What We Know and Don't Know." *Educational Leadership* 51(6):12–17 (March 1994).

Friedland, S. "Building Student Self-Esteem for School Improvement." *National Association of Secondary School Principals (NASSP) Bulletin* 76(540):96–102 (January 1992).

George, P., et al. *The Middle School—And Beyond*. Alexandria, VA: Association for Supervision and Curriculum Development, 1992.

Glasser, W. *The Quality School*. New York: Harper & Row, 1990.

Glasser, W. "The Quality School." *Phi Delta Kappan* 71(6):424–435 (February 1990).

Holt, M. "The Educational Consequences of W. Edwards Deming." *Phi Delta Kappan* 74(5):382–388 (January 1993).

Hunter, M. *Enhancing Teaching*. New York: Macmillan, 1994.

Jasa, S., and Enger, L. "Applying OBE to Arts Education." Educational Leadership 51(6):30–32 (March 1994).

Kellough, R. D.; Kellough, N. G.; and Hough, D. L. *Middle School Teaching: Methods and Resources*. New York: Macmillan, 1993.

Louis, K. S., and Miles, M. B. *Improving the Urban High School: What Works and Why*. New York: Teachers College Press, 1990.

Muncey, D. E., and McQuillan, P. J. "Preliminary Findings from a Five-Year Study of the Coalition of Essential Schools." *Phi Delta Kappan* 74(6):486–89 (February 1993).

Newman, F. M. "What Is a Restructured School?" *Principal* 72(3):5–8 (January 1993).

Olthoff, R. J. "The Principal as Instructional Coach—Providing Quality Education." *National Association of Secondary School Principals* (NASSP Bulletin 76(542):6–12 (March 1992).

Schmoker, M., and Wilson, R. B. "Transforming Schools Through Total Quality Education." *Phi Delta Kappan* 74(5):389–395 (January 1993).

Tye, K. A. "Restructuring Our Schools: Beyond the Rhetoric." *Phi Delta Kappan* 74(1):8–14 (September 1992).

Wheeler, L. M. "New Designs for American Schools." *Principal* 72(3):17, 19–21 (January 1993).

Wiles, J., and Bondi, J. *The Essential Middle School*. 2nd ed. New York: Macmillan, 1993.

POSTTEST

Multiple Choice

_____ 1. A school that houses students of grades 6 through 8 is most likely to be called a(n)
   a. middle school
   b. junior high school
   c. elementary school
   d. intermediate school

_____ 2. One of the following is *not* synonymous with the others. Which one is different?
   a. direct instruction
   b. expository teaching
   c. didactic teaching model
   d. student-centered teaching

_____ 3. Transecence is a period of
   a. change.
   b. stability.
   c. self-confidence.
   d. independence from peer pressure.

_____ 4. According to this text, teaching style should be
   a. eclectic.
   b. indirect.
   c. student-centered.
   d. teacher-centered.

_____ 5. You should develop a large repertoire of teaching strategies so that you can
   a. cover the subject matter more easily.
   b. utilize more fully strategies of direct instruction.
   c. utilize more fully strategies of indirect instruction.
   d. better adapt your teaching to particular teaching-learning situations.

_____ 6. *Time on task* refers to
   a. the length of a lesson.
   b. time allotted for a learning activity.
   c. estimated time to complete one unit of study.
   d. time students spend actually working at a learning activity.

_____ 7. A *core curriculum* includes what subject areas?
   a. English/language arts, mathematics, science, and history/social studies
   b. English/language arts and history/social studies
   c. Physical education, music, and art
   d. Mathematics and science

_____ 8. In the five-step model for teaching, which step(s) are analogous to the preactive phase of decision making and thought processing?
   a. first step
   b. first two steps
   c. third step
   d. fourth step
   e. fifth and first steps

_____ 9. Which one of the four decision-making and thought-processing phases of instruction occurs at the time the lesson is being taught?
   a. preactive
   b. reflective
   c. projective
   d. interactive

_____ 10. At which decision-making and thought-processing phase of instruction are decisions made by the teacher most likely to be intuitive or unconscious?
   a. preactive
   b. reflective
   c. projective
   d. interactive

_____ 11. Learning skills are
   a. innate.
   b. learned.
   c. inherited.
   d. instinctive.

_____ 12. The real test of your teaching is
   a. your classroom control.
   b. the quality of your planning.
   c. how well your students have learned.
   d. the degree that the lesson interests people.

_____ 13. True middle schools are
   a. no longer in existence in the United States.
   b. those schools designed for students ranging in age nine to fourteen
   c. those schools that used to be known as junior high schools.
   d. those schools that house departmentalized seventh and eighth grades.

Short Explanation

1. Clearly distinguish these types of schools: middle school, junior high school, high school, secondary school.
2. Distinguish between the terms *teaching team* and *team teaching*.
3. Describe the "school-within-a-school" concept and its advantages and disadvantages from an educational standpoint.
4. Define *school restructuring*, describe its purpose, and exemplify some of the results at restructuring.
5. Describe the philosophy that drives the middle school movement.
6. Describe the constructivist philosophy of learning.
7. Describe what is meant by a mastery learning instructional model and explain why you agree or disagree with it.
8. Explain the difference between direct instruction and indirect instruction and when, if ever, it is most appropriate to use each type of instruction.
9. Describe when, if ever, a middle school is not a secondary school.
10. Identify the steps that comprise the five-step model for effective teaching.

Essay

1. Do you agree that when starting a unit of instruction you should assess what students already know or think they know about it? If not, explain why. If you do agree, explain why and describe ways you could go about finding out what they already know.
2. From what you now know about middle schools and secondary schools, at which do you believe you would most like to teach? Explain why.
3. Do you agree or disagree with the statement that the teacher's style must be eclectic? Explain what is meant by an eclectic style and why you agree or disagree with the position.
4. Explain why you agree or disagree with the conclusion that the organization of groups of students according to age, grade level, scores on achievement tests, or ability is detrimental to the education of most children.
5. Explain why you do or do not favor the use of instructional grouping within the classroom.
6. From your current observations and field work (related to your teacher-preparation program), clearly identify one specific example of an educational practice that seems contradictory to exemplary practice or theory as presented in this module. Present your explanation for the discrepancy.
7. Describe any prior concepts you held that changed as a result of your experiences with this module. Describe the changes.

Middle and Secondary School Students: Meeting the Challenge

RATIONALE

No one is exactly like anyone else. Even identical twins are not identical in all respects; in spite of the similarity in their genetic background, environmental factors beginning even before birth shape each twin differently. And for most people, the differences in genetic material eliminate the chances of anyone's being an exact duplicate of anyone else. Brothers and sisters may have family resemblances; tenth graders may have some traits in common. African Americans share some common characteristics, as do members of honors sections, teacher credential candidates, and university professors. Yet each one is an individual who looks and behaves differently from everyone else and brings to a learning situation his or her unique background of experiences and perceptions.

The ways in which individuals differ are innumerable. Not only are there differences in physical appearance but also in personality traits and cultural backgrounds. Some students will be quick, whereas others will be slow; some will demonstrate academic talents, whereas others will not; some will be friendly, whereas others will not; some will be from socioeconomic, religious, or cultural backgrounds similar to yours, whereas others will be from backgrounds that are quite different from yours.

Some of these differences may be of no importance as far as school is concerned: whether a student's eyes are blue, grey, or brown does not really matter. Other differences are extremely important for teaching, because what is good education for one person may not be so good for another. Thus, in this module we present some of the characteristics and differences in students that you need to consider, as well as guidelines for working with particular groups of students.

There is no one best method of teaching that will always generate a high degree of student learning. Rather, there are any number of methods that may or may not be effective in a particular situation.

To be an effective teacher you must select the teaching method that best suits each situation. In deciding which method to use, you will be influenced by a number of factors, some of which are: (1) the students and how they learn, (2) the content and objectives of the instruction, and (3) the availability of equipment, materials, and other resources. In this module we explore the first, the nature and diversity of students and how they learn.

SPECIFIC OBJECTIVES

At the completion of this module, you should be able to:

1. Demonstrate an understanding of the characteristics of middle and secondary school students today.
2. Describe the role of the teacher in facilitating student learning.
3. Describe the unique characteristics of students of middle school age and how their needs differ from older students of high school age.
4. Describe the contributions of Jean Piaget to today's understanding of teaching and learning.
5. Describe how students develop their understandings of concepts.
6. Describe the contributions of Robert Gagné to today's understanding of teaching and learning.
7. Differentiate between the definitions of *learning* as used by behaviorists and by constructivists, and describe how each definition could prove useful in your work.
8. Describe the contributions of Benjamin Bloom to today's understanding of teaching and learning.
9. Describe the contributions of Jerome Bruner to today's understanding of teaching and learning.

10. Define *discovery learning* and describe the benefits of learning by discovery.
11. Describe the contributions of David Ausubel to today's understanding of teaching and learning.
12. Exemplify the use of an advance organizer in your subject field.
13. Describe a concept map, how it is used by students, and its benefit to their learning.
14. Identify the characteristics of intelligent behavior and how you can use those characteristics in your teaching.
15. Define *thinking*, identify skills involved in good thinking, and describe ways you can help students become better thinkers.
16. Describe how the characteristics of students influence the choice of teaching methods.
17. Describe how the workings of the human brain affect the choice of teaching methods.
18. Describe how our knowledge of learning modalities and student learning styles affect the choice of teaching methods.
19. Demonstrate your knowledge of guidelines for working with exceptional students.
20. Demonstrate your knowledge of guidelines for working with students who have limited English proficiency.
21. Demonstrate your awareness of the value of student journal writing and of the two types of journals described in this module.
22. Demonstrate your awareness of the value in the use of multilevel teaching.
23. Demonstrate your knowledge of guidelines for working with students of ethnically and culturally diverse backgrounds.
24. Demonstrate your knowledge of guidelines for working with students who are academically talented and with those who are academically slower.
25. Demonstrate your knowledge of specific techniques for positive attitude development.
26. Demonstrate your understanding of important principles of learning and how you will incorporate those in your teaching.

MODULE TEXT

Middle and Secondary School Students Today

Middle and secondary school students are in the process of changing from children to young adults. In a dramatic growth spurt during the early years of middle-level schools, children begin changing from little boys and girls to gawky adolescents with new secondary sex characteristics and all the problems that come with new life roles. This growing up continues until the adolescent becomes a young adult—a process not complete until the post–high school years.

During transecence (ages ten through fourteen) and the rest of adolescence, individual differences in physical, intellectual, social, and emotional growth are striking. Individuals seem to change markedly from day to day, for this is not only a period of growth but also a period of instability and insecurity. Becoming an adult is not an easy task (but then, neither is being an adult). Although boys and girls desire opportunities to act independently, they generally need and want security and support. Because of these contrasting needs for both security and for escape from adult domination, young people tend to band together for mutual support as they experiment with new sociosexual roles. To find security, they often become conformists, extremely susceptible to peer pressure. Nevertheless, adolescents normally are self-motivated, active, and interested in novelty. Their intellectual growth causes them to be interested in ideas and eventually allows them to cope with formal intellectual operations and abstract ideas. These desires compel some adolescents to adopt idealistic causes and others to try adventures and roles that get them into trouble.

Adolescence is a period of change, of new experiences, of learning new roles, of uncertainty and instability—undoubtedly one of the most trying times in life. Schools and teachers should provide opportunities for adolescents to explore and experiment in a stable and supportive atmosphere. As discussed in Module 1, an increasing number of middle schools have recognized that students in those early adolescent years need a special educational experience to nurture them through this unstable period. Educators have learned that to be most effective, school organization and instructional techniques must be quite different from those of the past. The efforts of teachers and administrators today to restructure the school and change instructional techniques has been compared to that of trying to rebuild a 747 jetliner while it's in the air.[1] Middle school and secondary school teaching today is indeed a tremendous challenge.

The Challenge

The bell rings for class to begin, and the students enter your classroom, "a kaleidoscope of personalities, all unique, each a bundle of idiosyncrasies, different strengths, different attitudes and aptitudes, different needs."[2] What a challenge for you—to understand and to teach thirty or so unique individuals, all at once, and to do it six hours a day, five days a week, 180 days a year! What a challenge it is to be a teacher, whether teaching youngsters of middle school and junior high school, or students of high school.

To help you meet the challenge, there is a wealth of information available about teaching and working with young people. As a credentialed teacher, you are expected to know it all (or at least to know where you can find all necessary information) and to review it when needed. Certain information you have learned or are learning and have stored in long-term memory, and this will surface and become useful at the most unexpected times. While concerned about all students' safety and physical well-being, you will want to remain sensitive to each student's attitudes, values, social adjustment, emotional well-being, and cognitive development. You must be prepared not only to teach your subject but also to do it effectively with students of different cultural backgrounds, diverse linguistic abilities, and different learning styles, as well as with students who have been identified as having special needs. A challenge indeed!

The following statistics make clear this challenge:

- Approximately one-half of U.S. students will spend some years being raised by a single parent. The traditional two-parent, two-child family now constitutes only 6 percent of the nation's households. Between one-third and one-fourth of the nation's students go home after school to places devoid of adult supervision. And on any given day there are many young people who have no place to call home.
- In the nation's largest school systems, minority enrollment levels range from 70 to 96 percent. By the year 2010, the school-age population throughout the United States will average about 39 percent minority youths. By the year 2050, the nation's population is predicted to increase to 383 million, from today's 252 million. That population boom will be led by Hispanics and Asian Americans; the nation's white population will play little part in it.
- Presently, nearly a quarter of all preschool children live below the poverty level, the highest percentage in nearly a quarter of a century.
- In just one school district, the Los Angeles School District, more than eighty-one languages are represented, with as many as twenty different ones found in some classrooms. Nationwide, the number of students whose primary language is not English is expected to triple during the next thirty years.[3]

As emphasized by Jacobsen, Eggen, and Kauchak, the language diversity of students poses special problems for teachers who use language as a major vehicle for the transmission of ideas. The overall picture that emerges is of a rapidly changing, diverse student population that challenges the teaching skills of teachers. Such traditional teaching techniques as the lecture, which assume that students are homogeneous in terms of background, knowledge, moti-

[1]Gordon A. Donaldson, Jr., "Working Smarter Together," *Educational Leadership* 51(2):12–16 (October 1993).

[2]Mary Hatwood Futrell, *Education Week*, 3 April 1985, p. 10.

[3]Adapted from David Jacobsen, Paul Eggen, and Donald Kauchak, *Methods for Teaching: A Skills Approach*, 4th ed. (New York: Merrill/Macmillan, 1993), pp. 227–228.

vation, and facility with the English language, are ineffective in classrooms of such student diversity. As a teacher for the twenty-first century you must become knowledgeable about how students develop and learn, and you must become skilled in using teaching strategies that recognize and build upon that diversity.

General Characteristics of Adolescents

If you are to be an effective teacher, then you must be aware of what is known about young people. Knowing and understanding the general characteristics of adolescents will do much to make teaching and learning an enjoyable and rewarding experience for both you and your students. Remember, these are general characteristics of all young people, regardless of their individual genetic or cultural differences.

Egocentrism. Most young people, to some degree or another, are egocentric. To egocentric youth, everything is important to them insofar as it relates to themselves. In young children, this egocentrism is quite natural, because children find themselves in a strange yet wonderful world, filled with events that are constantly affecting them. They tend to interpret the phenomena according to how the phenomena effect them personally—using everything they learn for the purpose of adjusting to the world in which they live, whether for better or for worse. As a teacher you can help students understand this world and to adjust to it in positive ways.

As children develop psychologically, emotionally, and intellectually, they overcome this egocentrism. An important skill needed to accomplish that step is listening to others, with understanding and empathy. But many secondary students—and even many adults—are not very good at listening. Thus, teachers must help their students to develop that skill. One way of doing that is to ask a student to paraphrase what another has said and then ask the first student if, in fact, that is what he or she said. If it isn't, then have the first student repeat what he or she said, and then ask another student to paraphrase that statement. Keep the process going until the original student's statement is correctly understood.

Interpreters. Young people are constantly interpreting their environment, trying to make sense of the phenomena that affect their lives. Very often these interpretations are incomplete, or even incorrect. Yet young people will continue to arrive at interpretations that satisfy them and allow them to function adequately in their daily lives, no matter how objectively incorrect these interpretations are.

Learners try to construct meaning for their experiences by referring to a body of related information stored in long-term memory from past experiences and knowledge. This body of information is referred to as networks, or **schema**. Learning continues by assimilating new information into a schema and then modifying or forming a new schema, a process known as **accommodation**. This process allows the learner to function adequately in a normal setting. Young people's interpretations of phenomena change with increasing maturity. Consequently, students are engaged in a constant process of revising interpretations as they grow in the ability to think abstractly. A technique called concept mapping, (discussed later in this module) is a learning strategy useful in helping students develop interrelated knowledge and understandings that result in useful schemata.[4]

Students come to your classroom with existing schemata about mostly everything—many of which from an adult's point of view may not always be sound. That is, the schemata may sometimes be incongruent with accepted views. Such an incongruent schema is referred to as a **naive theory**, or conceptual **misunderstanding** or **misconception**.

One teaching task is to correct student's misconceptions. Like many adults, young people naturally resist changes in their interpretations, and thus changing their misconceptions often proves to be no easy task. Even after corrective instruction, students will often persist with their misconceptions. But as Haberman says, "Whenever students are asked to think about an idea

[4]Joseph D. Novak, "How Do We Learn Our Lesson?" *The Science Teacher* 60(3):50–55 (March 1993).

in a way that questions common sense or a widely accepted assumption, that relates new ideas to ones previously learned, or that applies an idea to the problems of living, then there is a chance that good teaching is going on."[5]

Regardless of subject or grade level, students come to your classroom with misconceptions, and correcting their misconceptions is often a long and arduous task that demands understanding, patience, and creative instruction. Students are much more likely to modify an interpretation of their experiences to accommodate a schema than they are to change their beliefs as a result of new experiences.[6] This should not be particularly surprising to anyone. Stories abound of reputable scientists, politicians, and attorneys who themselves were tempted to modify data to support their beliefs. Common human attributes include both stubbornness of belief and openness to change, however in conflict those attributes may be.

Persistence.   Young people are tenacious. They like to achieve their objectives, and will spend unusual lengths of time and effort at activities that are important and interesting to them. With those efforts comes a feeling of personal satisfaction and a sense of accomplishment. As a teacher you must take advantage of this persistence and desire to achieve by presenting instruction in the form of interesting and meaningful learning activities.

Curiosity.   Young people are naturally curious. A secondary student's curiosity will vary, depending upon what catches his or her interest. Generally speaking, students are more interested in things that move than in things that do not. They are also more interested in objects that make things happen than in those to which things are happening. Their curiosity reaches a peak with objects or events that appear mysterious and magical. To initiate effective learning in the classroom, good instruction takes advantage of this natural curiosity. For example, the use of "magic" and discrepant events are both popular and successful in motivating student learning in science and social science.

Adventurers.   Young people love to explore. When given an object with which to play, younger children try to take it apart and then put it together again. They love to touch and feel objects. Children are always wondering "what will happen if . . ." and suggesting ideas for finding out. Children are natural questioners. The words *what, why,* and *how* are common in their vocabulary. Most older children retain this attribute. While investigating, young people work and learn best when they experience firsthand. Therefore, you should provide a wide variety of experiences that involve hands-on learning. Hands-on learning engages the learner's mind, causing questioning. When allowed to question and to explore, the learner's mind is engaged. You should encourage rather than discourage students' questions. Hands-on and minds-on learning encourages students to question and then devise ways of investigating tentative but satisfactory answers to their questions.

Abundant energy.   Young people are energetic and would rather not sit for a long time—for some, sitting still seems nearly impossible. They would rather do something than listen. Even while listening, some students may move their bodies restlessly. This difficulty in sitting still has a direct bearing on the student's attention span. As a result, teaching should provide for many activities that give students the opportunity to be physically active.

Social beings.   Young people like to be with and to be accepted by their peers. They like to work together in planning and carrying out activities. They work well together when given proper encouragement, clear direction, and worthwhile opportunity. Furthermore, each stu-

[5]Martin Haberman, "The Pedagogy of Poverty Versus Good Teaching," *Phi Delta Kappan* 73(4):290–294 (December 1991), p. 294.

[6]Bruce Watson and Richard Konicek, "Teaching for Conceptual Change: Confronting Children's Experience," *Phi Delta Kappan* 71(9):680–685 (May 1990), p. 683.

dent forms a self-concept through these social interactions in school. The student will develop a satisfactory self-esteem when given an opportunity to work with others, offer ideas, and work out peer relationships. Your teaching can help foster not only the learning but also the development of each student's self-esteem by incorporating social-interaction teaching strategies, such as cooperative learning, peer tutoring, and cross-age teaching.

Needs for growth of self.   Abraham Maslow postulated a continuum of psychological needs applicable to all people. From the most basic to the highest, these needs are:

- *Physiological* (provision of food, clothing, and shelter)
- *Security* (feeling of safety)
- *Social* (sense of love and belonging)
- *Sense of self-esteem,*
- *Self-actualization* (full use of talents, capacities, abilities, acceptance of self and others).[7]

When children are frustrated because of a lack of satisfaction of one or more of these needs, their classroom behavior is affected and their learning is stifled.[8] Some students become aggressive and disrupt normal classroom procedures, hoping in this way to satisfy a basic need for recognition. Others become antisocial and apathetic and then fail to participate in class activities. This behavior has been well explained by the sociologist D. S. Eitzen:

> Everyone needs a dream. Without a dream, we become apathetic. Without a dream, we become fatalistic. Without a dream and the hope of attaining it, society becomes our enemy. We educators must realize that some young people act in antisocial ways because they have lost their dreams. And we must realize that we as a society are partly responsible for that loss. Teaching is a noble profession whose goal is to increase the success rate for *all* children. We must do everything we can to achieve this goal. If not, we—society, schools, teachers, and students—will all fail.[9]

The wise teacher is alert to any student whose needs are not being satisfied. A student comes to school hungry, and another comes to school feeling insecure because of problems at home. Still another comes to school tired from having to spend each night sleeping and living out of an automobile. As a classroom teacher you cannot solve all the ailments of society, but you do have an opportunity and responsibility to make all students feel welcome, respected, and wanted, at least while they are in your classroom.

Working with Adolescents

Historically, many teachers have found students of ages ten through fourteen to be at a particularly troublesome stage to teach. As a teacher candidate in a program of professional education, you should want part of your field experience (e.g., student teaching) to be with students of this age and part of it to be with older high school students. An understanding of the general characteristics of ten- to fourteen-year-olds provides not only a further understanding of these children, but also, by inference, increased understanding of the differences between children in these grades and the teenagers of high school years.

Through experience and research, experts have come to accept certain precepts about young adolescents. These are presented in Figure 2.1 in five developmental categories: intellectual, physical, psychological, social, and moral and ethical development. With those characteristics as a basis, we next consider what is known about how young adolescents learn and think, and how you can use that knowledge in your teaching.

---

[7]See Abraham H. Maslow, *Motivation and Personality* (New York: Harper & Row, 1970).

[8]See, for example, Sally Reed and R. Craig Sautter, "Children of Poverty: The Status of 12 Million Young Americans," *Phi Delta Kappan* 71(10):K1–K12 (June 1990).

[9]D. Stanley Eitzen, "Problem Students: The Sociocultural Roots," *Phi Delta Kappan* 73(8):584–590 (April 1992), p. 590.

Intellectual Development   Young adolescents tend to:

1. Be egocentric, argue to persuade others, and exhibit independent, critical thought.
2. Be intellectually at-risk; that is, they face decisions that have the potential to affect major academic values with lifelong consequences.
3. Be intensely curious.
4. Consider academic goals as a secondary level of priority, whereas personal-social concerns dominate thoughts and activities.
5. Display broad individual intellectual development as their minds experience change from the concrete-manipulatory stage to the capacity for abstract thought. This change makes possible:
   - Ability to project thought into the future, to anticipate, and to formulate goals.
   - Analysis of the power of a political ideology.
   - Appreciation for the elegance of mathematical logic expressed in symbols.
   - Consideration of ideas contrary to fact.
   - Insight into the nuances of poetic metaphor and musical notation.
   - Insight into the sources of previously unquestioned attitudes, behaviors, and values.
   - Interpretation of larger concepts and generalizations of traditional wisdom expressed through sayings, axioms, and aphorisms.
   - Propositional thought.
   - Reasoning with hypotheses involving two or more variables.
6. Experience the phenomenon of metacognition—that is, the ability to think about one's thinking, and to know what one knows and does not know.
7. Exhibit strong willingness to learn what they consider to be useful, and enjoy using skills to solve real-life problems.
8. Prefer active over passive learning experiences, and favor interaction with peers during learning activities.

Physical Development   Young adolescents tend to:

1. Be concerned about personal physical appearance.
2. Be physically at risk; major causes of death are homicide, suicide, accident, and leukemia.
3. Experience accelerated physical development marked by increases in weight, height, heart size, lung capacity, and muscular strength.
4. Experience biological development five years sooner than adolescents of the nineteenth century—since then, the average age of menarche has dropped from seventeen to twelve years of age.
5. Experience bone growth faster than muscle development—uneven muscle/bone development results in lack of coordination and awkwardness; bones may lack protection of covering muscles and supporting tendons.
6. Experience fluctuations in basal metabolism, which at times can cause either extreme restlessness or listlessness.
7. Face responsibility for sexual behavior before full emotional and social maturity has occurred.
8. Have ravenous appetites and peculiar tastes—may overtax digestive system with large quantities of improper foods.
9. Lack physical health and have poor levels of endurance, strength, and flexibility—young adolescents as a group are fatter and less healthy.
10. Mature at varying rates of speed—girls are often taller than boys for the first two years of early adolescence and are ordinarily more physically developed than boys.
11. Reflect a wide range of individual differences, which begin to appear in prepubertal and pubertal stages of development. Boys tend to lag behind girls at this stage, and there are marked individual differences in physical development for both boys and girls. The greatest variation in physiological development and size occurs at about age thirteen.
12. Show changes in body contour—including temporarily large noses, protruding ears, and long arms—and have posture problems.

Psychological Development   Young adolescents tend to:

1. Be easily offended and be sensitive to criticism of personal shortcomings.
2. Be erratic and inconsistent in their behavior—anxiety and fear are contrasted with periods of bravado; feelings shift between superiority and inferiority.

Figure 2.1   Characteristics of Young Adolescents

3. Be moody, restless—they often feel self-conscious and alienated, lack of self-esteem, and are introspective.

4. Be optimistic, hopeful.

5. Be psychologically at risk—at no other point in human development is a person likely to meet so much diversity in relation to self and others.

6. Be searching for adult identify and acceptance even in the midst of intense peer group relationships.

7. Be searching to form a conscious sense of individual uniqueness—"Who am I?"

8. Be vulnerable to naive opinions and one-sided arguments.

9. Exaggerate simple occurrences and believe that personal problems, experiences, and feelings are unique to themselves.

10. Have an emerging sense of humor based on an increased intellectual ability to see abstract relationships; appreciate the *double entendre.*

11. Have chemical and hormonal imbalances, often triggering emotions that are frightening and poorly understood—they may regress to more childish behavior patterns at this point.

Social Development   Young adolescents tend to:

1. Act out unusual or drastic behavior at times—they may be aggressive, daring, boisterous, and argumentative.

2. Be confused and frightened by new school settings that are large and impersonal.

3. Be fiercely loyal to peer-group values and sometimes cruel or insensitive to those outside the peer group.

4. Be impacted by the high level of mobility in society—they may become anxious and disoriented when peer-group ties are broken because of family relocation.

5. Be rebellious toward parents but still strongly dependent on parental values—they want to make their own choices, but the authority of the family is a critical factor in final decisions.

6. Be socially at risk—adult values are largely shaped conceptually during adolescence; negative interactions with peers, parents, and teachers may compromise ideals and commitments.

7. Challenge authority figures, and test limits of acceptable behavior.

8. Experience low-risk trust relationships with adults who show lack of sensitivity to adolescent characteristics and needs.

9. Experience often-traumatic conflicts because of opposing loyalties to peer group and family.

10. Refer to peers as sources for standards and models of behavior—media heroes are also singularly important in shaping both behavior and fashion.

11. Sense the negative impact of adolescent behaviors on parents and teachers and realize the thin edge between tolerance and rejection—feelings of adult rejection can drive the adolescent into the relatively secure social environment of the peer group.

12. Strive to define sex role characteristics, and search to set up positive social relationships with members of the same and opposite sex.

13. Want to know and feel that significant adults, including parents and teachers, love and accept them—they tend to need frequent affirmation.

Moral and Ethical Development   Young adolescents tend to:

1. Ask broad, unanswerable questions about the meaning of life—they do not expect absolute answers but are turned off by trivial adult responses.

2. Be at risk in the development of moral and ethical choices and behaviors—they depend on the influences of home and church for moral and ethical development, and they explore the moral and ethical issues that are met in the curriculum, in the media, and in the daily interactions with their families and peer groups.

3. Be idealistic, and have a strong sense of fairness in human relationships.

4. Be reflective, introspective, and analytical about their thoughts and feelings.

5. Experience thoughts and feelings of awe and wonder related to their expanding intellectual and emotional awareness.

6. Face hard moral and ethical questions for which they are unprepared to cope.

Source: California State Department of Education, *Caught in the Middle: Educational Reform for Young Adolescents in California Public Schools* (Sacramento, CA: Author, 1987), pp. 144–48.

Intellectual Development: Contributions of Learning Theorists

Jean Piaget, Lev Vygotsky, Robert Gagné, Jerome Bruner, and David Ausubel are four learning theorists who have had significant historical influence on modern pedagogy. Of the several psychologists whose theories of learning made an impact during the last half of the twentieth century, perhaps no other has had such a wide-ranging influence on education than Swiss psychologist Jean Piaget (1896–1980). Although Piaget began to publish his insights in the 1920s, his work was not popularized in the United States until the 1960s.

Piaget's Theory of Cognitive Development

Piaget postulated four stages of mental development, from birth to post-adolescence. Even though you will not have students in all stages, you must understand that mental development is a continuing progress and that children must begin with the first stage and progress developmentally through each succeeding stage. A child cannot skip a stage. Furthermore, because students in your classroom might be at different stages of mental development, it is important to attend to the stage where each child is developmentally. To that end, you can use **multitasking**, or **multilevel teaching**, in which different students are working at different tasks to accomplish the same objective, or are working at different tasks to accomplish different objectives. Consider the following review of Piaget's stages of cognitive development.

Sensorimotor stage (birth to age two).   At this stage, from birth until about age two, children are bound to the present and to their immediate environment. Learning and behaviors are from direct interaction with stimuli that the child can see or feel. Objects that are not seen can be found only by random searching. Through direct interaction the child begins to build mental concepts—associating actions and reactions—and later in the stage begins to label people and objects and to demonstrate an imagination. The child, then, is developing a practical base of knowledge that forms the foundation for learning in the next stage.

Preoperational stage (ages two through seven).   Children at the preoperational stage, through about age seven, can imagine and think before acting, rather than only responding to external stimuli. This stage is called preoperational because the child does not use logical operations in thinking. In this stage the child is egocentric, and the child's world view is subjective rather than objective. Because of egocentrism, the child has difficulty considering and accepting another person's point of view. The child is perceptually oriented—judgments are made according to how things look to the child. The child does not think logically and therefore does not reason by implication. Instead, an intuitive approach is used, and judgments are made according to how things look to the child. When confronted with new and discrepant information about a phenomenon, the child adjusts the new information to accommodate his or her existing beliefs about it. While in this stage, children often make humorous comments, ask many *why* questions, and are quite serious about their play.

At this stage, the child can observe and describe variables (properties of an object or aspects of a phenomenon) but can concentrate on just one variable at a time, usually a variable that stands out visually. The child cannot coordinate variables, so has difficulty in realizing that an object has several properties. Consequently, the child has difficulty combining parts into a whole. The child can make simple classifications according to one or two properties but finds it difficult to realize that multiple classifications are possible. Also, the child can arrange objects in a simple series but has trouble arranging them in a long series or inserting a new object in its proper place within a series. To the child, space is restricted to the child's neighborhood, and time is restricted to hours, days, and seasons.

The child in this stage has not yet developed the concept of conservation. This means the child does not understand that several objects can be rearranged and that the size or shape or volume of a solid or liquid can be changed, yet the number of objects and the amount of solid or liquid will be unchanged, or conserved. For example, if two rows of ten objects are arranged so they take up the same area, the child will say that the two rows are the same and the same number of objects make up each row. But if the objects in one row are spread out, the child is likely to maintain that the longer row now has more objects in it. Similarly, if the child is shown two identical balls of clay, the child will agree that both balls contain the same amount of material. When, in full view of the child, one of the balls is stretched into the shape of a sausage, the child is likely to say the sausage has more clay because it is larger, or less clay because it is thinner. Either way, the child at this stage is "centering" his or her attention on just one particular property (here, length or thickness) to the neglect of the other properties.

In both of the preceding examples, the reason for the child's thinking is that the child does not yet understand *reversibility*. The child's thinking cannot yet reverse itself back to the point of origin. As a result, the child does not understand that since nothing has been removed or added, the extended row of objects can be rearranged to its original length, and the clay sausage can be made back into the original ball. The child does not yet comprehend that action and thought processes are reversible.

Not yet able to use abstract reasoning—and only beginning to think conceptually—students at this stage of development learn best by manipulating objects in concrete situations rather than by verbal learning alone. For children at this stage of development, conceptual change comes very gradually.

For conceptual development and change, Piaget developed a theory of learning that involves children in a three-phase *learning cycle*. The three phases are: (1) an exploratory hands-on phase, (2) a concept development phase, and (3) a concept application phase. When a learner is applying a concept (the third phase), the learner is involved in a hands-on activity. During application of a concept, the learner may discover new information that causes a change in his or her understanding of the concept being applied. Thus, the process of learning is cyclic. You should keep this concept in mind as you read later modules.

Concrete operations stage (ages seven through eleven). This stage seems to have several sub-stages, and a task of schools is to foster the development of children's thinking through those steps. By this stage the learner can perform logical operations. The child can observe, judge, and evaluate in less egocentric terms than in the preoperational stage, and can also formulate more objective explanations. As a result, the learner knows how to solve physical problems. Because the child's thinking is still concrete and not abstract, the student is limited to problems dealing with actual concrete situations. Early in this stage the learner cannot generalize, deal with hypothetical situations, or weigh possibilities.

The child can make multiple classifications as well as arrange objects in long series and place new objects in their proper place in the series. The child can begin to comprehend geographical space and historical time. The child develops the concepts of conservation according to their ease of learning: first, number of objects (ages six to seven), then matter, length, area (age seven), weight (ages nine to twelve), and volume (age eleven or more), in that order. The child also develops the concept of reversibility and can now reverse the physical and mental processes when numbers of objects are rearranged or when the size and shape of matter are changed.

Later in this stage children can hypothesize and do higher-level thinking. Not yet able to use abstract reasoning, and only beginning to be able to think conceptually, students at this stage of development still learn best by manipulating objects in concrete situations rather than by verbal learning alone. At this stage, hands-on, active learning is most effective.

Formal operations stage (age twelve and up). Piaget initially believed that by age fifteen most adolescents reach formal operational thinking, but now it is quite clear that many high school students and even some adults do not yet function at this level. Essentially, students who are quick to understand abstract ideas are formal thinkers. But most middle school and junior high school students are not at this stage. For them, **metacognition**—planning, monitoring, and evaluating one's own thinking—may be very difficult. In essence, *metacognition* is today's term for what Piaget referred to as *reflective abstraction* (reflection upon one's own thinking), without which continued development cannot occur.[10]

---

[10]For attempts to clarify today's concept of metacognition, see I. Braten, "Vygotsky as Precursor to Metacognitive Theory: I. The Concept of Metacognition and Its Roots," *Scandinavian Journal of Educational Research* 35(3):179–192 (1991).

At the formal operations stage, the person's method of thinking shifts from the concrete to the more formal and abstract. The learner, who can now relate one abstraction to another, grows in ability to think conceptually. At this stage, the learner can develop hypotheses, deduce possible consequences from them, and then test these hypotheses with controlled experiments in which all the variables are identical except the one being tested. When approaching a new problem, the learner begins by formulating all the possibilities and then determining which ones are substantiated through experimentation and logical analysis. After solving the problem, the learner can reflect upon or rethink the thought processes that were used.

Rate of cognitive development.   As presented by Piaget, the four stages are general descriptions of the psychological processes in cognitive development. But keep in mind that the rate of cognitive development varies considerably among children. As a teacher, you must be cautious about placing too much reliance on the age ranges assigned to Piaget's stages. For example, about 5 percent of middle school children (children ages ten through fourteen) operate at the preoperational level. Furthermore, evidence indicates that for many learners, including adults, there is a tendency to revert to an earlier developmental stage when confronted with a perplexing situation.

The rate of cognitive development is different in each person. That rate is affected by the child's maturation, which is controlled by (1) inherited biological factors and general health, (2) the richness of the child's experiences, (3) the complexity of social interactions, and (4) the child's equilibration.

Concept development.   To understand concept development, you should be familiar with a few terms. *Assimilation* is the input of new information into existing schemata; *accommodation* is the development of new or modification of old schemata. **Equilibrium** is the balance between assimilation and accommodation, and a person is always internally striving for this balance. *Disequilibrium* is the state of imbalance. **Equilibration**, which affects the rate of cognitive development, is the process of moving from disequilibrium to equilibrium. When disequilibrium occurs (such as with the presentation of a discrepant event) the learner is internally motivated to assimilate and to accommodate. With or without a teacher's guidance, a learner will assimilate information. The task of the teacher is to facilitate the learner's continuing accurate construct of old and new schemata. Concept mapping has been shown to be an excellent tool for facilitating assimilation and accommodation. (We return to these concepts in Module 6 in the discussion of learning by inquiry).

Concept attainment: A continuing process.   You can think of the learner's developing an understanding of a concept, called concept attainment, as being a cyclical (continuing), three-stage process. The first stage is an increasing awareness, which is stimulated by the quality and richness of the child's learning environment. The second stage is disequilibrium. The third stage is reformulation of the concept, which is induced by the learner's process of equilibration.

From recent research on the brain, new principles have been formulated that may have profound effects on teaching and on how schools are organized. For example, according to Caine and Caine, "Because there can be a five-year difference in maturation between any two 'average' children, gauging achievement on the basis of chronological age is inappropriate."[11] Research indicates brain growth spurts for students in grades 1, 2, 5, 6, 9, and 10. If schools were organized solely on this criterion, they would be configured in grade clusters K, 1–4, 5–8, and 9–12.[12] With its increasing use of the 5 through 8 grade span, the middle school may be an indicator of an advance in that direction.[13]

[11]Renate Nummela Caine and Geoffrey Caine, "Understanding a Brain-Based Approach to Learning and Teaching," *Educational Leadership* 48(2):66–70 (October 1990), p. 66.

[12]R. Sylwester, J. S. Chall, M. C. Wittrock, and L. A. Hart, "The Educational Implications of Brain Research," *Educational Leadership* 39(1):6–17 (October 1991).

[13]From 1981 to 1992, the number of middle-level schools using a 5–8 grade span tripled; and when compared with 1981 figures, only about one-third of middle-level schools in 1992 use the 7–9 grade span. See Jerry W. Valentine et al., *Leadership in Middle Level Education* (Reston, VA: National Association of Secondary School Principals, 1993), p. 19.

Many advances are expected in knowledge about neurological processing during the next few years. You should recognize the ramifications of that quest on how children learn and process information. Clearly, if learning is defined as the accumulation of bits and pieces of information, then teachers already know how to teach for that learning to occur. But the accumulation of pieces of information is at the simplest end of a wide spectrum of types of learning. We are still learning about learning, about teaching for understanding, and about the reflective use of that understanding. For higher levels of thinking and learning, brain research supports current methods of teaching, such as the whole-language approach to reading, thematic teaching, and connecting life experiences with the curriculum.[14] Thus, to be most effective in teaching important understandings to the diversity of students in today's schools, learning in each discipline must be integrated with the whole curriculum and made meaningful to the lives of the students, rather than simply taught as an unrelated and separate discipline at the same time each day.

Lev Vygotsky: Cooperative Learning in a Supportive Environment

The Soviet psychologist Lev Vygotsky (1896–1934), a contemporary of Piaget, studied and agreed with Piaget on most points, though he differed on the importance of a child's social interactions. Vygotsky argued that learning is most effective when students cooperate with one another in a supportive learning environment under the careful guidance of a teacher. Cooperative learning, group problem solving, and cross-age tutoring are instructional strategies used today that have grown in popularity as a result of research evolving from the work of Vygotsky.

Robert Gagné and the General Learning Hierarchy

Robert Gagné is well known for his hierarchy of learning levels. According to Gagné, learning is the establishing of a capability to do something that the learner was not capable of doing previously. Notice the emphasis on the learner's "doing."

Gagné postulates a hierarchy of learning levels, or capabilities. Learning at one particular capability usually depends upon having previously learned one or more simpler capabilities. For Gagné, observable changes in behavior comprise the only criteria for inferring that learning has occurred. It follows, then, that the beginning, or lowest, level of a learning hierarchy would include very simple behaviors. These behaviors would form the basis for learning more complex behaviors at the next level of the hierarchy. At each higher level, learning requires that the appropriate simpler, or less complex, behaviors have been acquired in the lower learning levels.

Gagné identifies eight levels of learning in this hierarchy, as shown in Figure 2.2. Beginning with the simplest and progressing to the most complex, these levels are described briefly as follows.

1. *Signal Learning.* At this level, a person learns to make a general conditioned response to a given signal. Examples are a child's pleasure produced by the sight of a favorite pet animal and a child's expression of fright at the sound of a loud noise.

[14]Caine and Caine, p. 67.

Figure 2.2 Gagné's Learning Hierarchy

Level 8:	Problem Solving
Level 7:	Principle Learning
Level 6:	Concept Learning
Level 5:	Multiple Discrimination
Level 4:	Verbal Association
Level 3:	Chaining
Level 2:	Stimulus-Response Learning
Level 1:	Signal Learning

2. *Stimulus-Response Learning.* At this level, a person acquires a precise physical or vocal response to a discriminated stimulus. Examples include a child's initial learning of words by repeating the sounds of adults and the training of a dog to sit.

3. *Chaining.* Sometimes called skill learning, chaining involves the linking together of two or more units of simple stimulus-response learning. Chaining is limited to physical, nonverbal sequences. Examples include winding up a toy, writing, running, and opening a door. The accuracy of the learning at this level depends on practice, prior experience, and reinforcement.

4. *Verbal Association.* This is a form of chaining, but the links are verbal units. Naming an object is the simplest verbal association. In this case, the first stimulus-response link is involved in observing the object, and the second is involved in enabling the child to name the object. A more complex example of verbal chaining would be the rote memorization of a sequence of numbers, a formula, or the letters of the alphabet in sequence. Considered alone, these learned behaviors are not usually seen as important goals of teaching. But viewed as a level in a hierarchy, they may be important first steps in certain higher levels of learning.

5. *Multiple Discrimination.* At this level, a person links individual learned chains to form multiple discriminations. Examples include the identification of the names of students in a classroom, where the learner associates each student with his or her distinctive appearance and correct name; and learning in science the distinction between solids, liquids, and gases.

6. *Concept Learning.* Learning a concept means learning to respond to stimuli by their abstract characteristics (such as position, shape, color, and number), as opposed to their concrete physical properties. A child may learn to call a 2-inch cube a *block*, and to apply this name to other objects that differ from it in size and shape. Later, the child learns the concept *cube*, and by so doing can identify a class of objects that differ physically in many ways (e.g., by material, color, texture, and size). Rather than learning concepts by trial and error, the child learns more systematically. Under the careful guidance of the teacher, a child's learning is sequenced in such a way as to lead to the child's improved conceptual understanding.

7. *Principle Learning.* In simplest terms, a principle is a chain of two or more concepts. In principle learning, the person must relate two or more concepts. An example is the relation of a circle's circumference to its diameter. Three separate concepts (circumference, pi, and diameter) are linked or chained together.

8. *Problem Solving.* According to Gagné, problem solving is the most sophisticated type of learning and thus the highest level on the hierarchy. In problem solving, the individual applies principles learned to achieve a goal. While achieving this goal, however, the learner becomes capable of new performances by using the new knowledge. When a problem is solved, new knowledge has been acquired, and the person's capacity moves forward. The learner is now able to handle a wide class of problems similar to the one solved. What has been learned, according to Gagné, is a higher-order principle, which is the combined product of two or more lower-order principles.

Thus, when a child has acquired the capabilities and behaviors of a certain level of learning, we assume that the child has also acquired the capabilities and behaviors of all the learning levels below this level. Furthermore, if the child were having difficulty in demonstrating the capabilities and behaviors for a certain level, the teacher could simply test the child on the capabilities and behaviors of the lower levels to determine which one or ones were causing the difficulty.

Benjamin Bloom and Mastery Learning

Benjamin Bloom has made numerous important contributions to our understanding of learning. Most significantly, Bloom and his colleagues developed a *taxonomy of educational objectives,* which divides cognitive goals of instruction into a hierarchy of levels of thinking and doing (presented in Module 3). Bloom's taxonomy is similar to Gagné's simple-to-complex hierarchy of types of learning. Like Gagné, Bloom stresses the importance of prior experiences and learning and the effect they have on current learning.

Research has shown that student achievement in learning is related to (1) time and to (2) the quality of attention being given to the learning task. As discussed in Module 1, Bloom developed the concept of individualized instruction called **mastery learning**, based on the premise that students should be given sufficient time on task to master content before moving on to new content.[15] Mastery learning has been defined as "the attainment of adequate levels of performance on tests that measure specific learning tasks. Mastery learning also describes an instructional model whose underlying assumption is that nearly every student can learn everything in the school curriculum at a specified level of competence if the learner's previous knowledge and attitudes about the subject are accounted for, if the instruction is of good quality, and if adequate time on task is allowed to permit mastery."[16]

Jerome Bruner and Discovery Learning

Jerome Bruner, a leading interpreter and promoter of Piaget's ideas in the United States, also made his own significant contributions on how children learn. Some of Bruner's thinking was influenced by the work of the Soviet psychologist Lev Vygotsky.[17] Like Piaget, Bruner maintains that each child passes through stages that are age-related and biologically determined, and that learning will depend primarily on the developmental level that the child has attained.

Bruner's theory also encompasses three major sequential stages, which he refers to as representations. These are *enactive representation* (a knowing that is related to movement, through direct experiencing), *ikonic representation* (a knowing that is related to visual and spatial representations, such as films and still visuals), and *symbolic representation* (a knowing that is related to reason and logic, that depends on the use of words). Bruner's representations correspond to the sensorimotor, concrete operations, and formal operations stages of Piaget. Although Bruner's description of what happens during these three representations corresponds to that of Piaget's stages, he differs from Piaget in his interpretation of the role language plays in intellectual development.

Piaget believed that although thought and language are related, they are different systems. He posited that a child's thinking is based on a system of inner logic that evolves as the child organizes and adapts to experiences. Bruner, however, maintains that thought is internalized language. The child translates experience into language, and then uses language as an instrument of thinking.

Bruner and Piaget differ also in their attitudes toward the child's readiness for learning. Piaget concluded that the child's readiness for learning depends upon maturation and intellectual development. Bruner, however, believes that a child is always ready to learn a concept at some level of sophistication. He holds that any subject can be taught effectively in some intellectually honest form to any child in any stage of development. He supports this concept, for example, by noting that the basic ideas of science and mathematics are simple, and only when these ideas are out of context with the child's life experiences and formalized by equations and complex verbal statements do they become incomprehensible to children (and to adults).

According to Bruner, when a child learns concepts, the child can learn them only within the framework of whichever stage of intellectual development the child is in at the time. In teaching children, then it is essential then that each child be helped to pass progressively from one stage of intellectual development to the next. Schools can do this by providing challenging but usable opportunities and problems for children that tempt them to forge ahead into the next stages of development. As a result, the children acquire a higher level of understanding.

Bruner and the act of learning.   Bruner proposes that the act of learning involves three almost simultaneous processes. The first is the process of acquiring new knowledge. The second is the process of manipulating this knowledge to make it fit new tasks or situations. The

[15]Benjamin S. Bloom, "Learning for Mastery," *Evaluation Comment* 1, No. 2 (May 1968).

[16]Lowell Horton, *Mastery Learning*, Fastback 154 (Bloomington, IN: Phi Delta Kappa Educational Foundation, 1981), p. 9.

[17]Jerome Bruner, "Vygotsky: A Historical and Conceptual Perspective," *in* J. Wertsch (ed.), *Culture, Communication and Cognition: Vygotskian Perspectives* (Cambridge, England: Cambridge University Press, 1985.)

third is the process of evaluating the acquisition and manipulation of this knowledge. A major objective of learning is to introduce the child at an early age to the ideas and styles that will help the child become literate. Consequently, the school curriculum should be built around major conceptual schemes, skills, and values that society considers to be important. These should be taught as early as possible in a manner consistent with the child's stages of development and forms of thought.

Bruner has been an articulate spokesperson for **discovery learning**. He advocates that, whenever possible, teaching and learning should be conducted in such a matter that children be given the opportunity to discover concepts for themselves.

Benefits of discovery learning.   Bruner cites four major benefits that are derived from learning by discovery. First, there is an increase in intellectual potency. By this is meant that discovery learning helps students learn how to learn. It helps the learner develop skills in problem solving, enabling the learner to arrange and apply what has been learned to new situations and thus learn new concepts. Second, there is a shift from extrinsic to intrinsic rewards. Discovery learning shifts motives for learning away from that of satisfying others to that of internal self-rewarding satisfaction, that is, satisfying oneself. Third, there is an opportunity to learn the working heuristics of discovery. By *heuristics*, Bruner means the methods in which a person is educated to find out things independently. Only through the exercise of problem solving and by the effort of discovery can the learner find out things independently. The more adept the learner becomes in the working heuristics of discovery, the more effective the decisions the learner will make in problem solving, with the decisions leading to a quicker solution than any trial-and-error approach would. Fourth, there is an aid to memory processing. Knowledge resulting from discovery learning is more easily remembered, as well as more readily recalled when needed. Bruner's work, strongly supported by recent research on the brain, provides a rationale for using discovery and hands-on activities.

Gagné and Bruner differ in their emphasis upon learning. Gagné primarily emphasizes the product of learning (the knowledge), whereas Bruner primarily emphasizes the process of learning (the skills). For Gagné the important question is, "*What* do you want the child to know?" For Bruner it is, "*How* do you want the child to know?" For Gagné the emphasis is on learning itself, whether by discovery, review, or practice. For Bruner the emphasis is on learning by discovery; it is the method of learning that is important.

Gagné emphasizes problem solving as the highest level of learning, with the lower learning levels prerequisite to this highest level. For Gagné, the appropriate sequence in learning (and teaching) is from these lower levels toward problem solving. The teacher begins with simple ideas, relates all of them, builds on them, and works toward the more complex levels of learning. On the other hand, Bruner begins with problem solving, which in turn leads to the development of necessary skills. The teacher poses a question to be solved and then uses it as a catalyst to motivate children to develop the necessary skills.

Piaget, Bruner, and Gagné also differ in their attitude toward the child's readiness for learning. As noted, Piaget believes that readiness depends upon the child's maturation and intellectual development. Bruner believes that the child is always ready to learn a concept at some level of sophistication. Gagné, however, thinks that readiness is dependent on the successful development of lower level skills and prior understandings.

David Ausubel and Meaningful Verbal Learning

David Ausubel is an advocate of *reception learning,* or the receipt of ideas through transmission.[18] He agrees with other psychologists that the development of problem-solving skills is a primary objective in teaching. Similar to Gagné, however, he thinks that effective problem solving and discovery are more likely to take place after children have learned important and supporting concepts.

[18]David P. Ausubel, *The Psychology of Meaningful Verbal Learning* (New York: Grune & Stratton, 1963).

Ausubel strongly urges teachers to use learning situations and examples that are familiar to the students. This helps students assimilate what is being learned with what they already know, making their learning more meaningful. Ausubel believes that discovery learning is too time consuming to enable students to learn all they should know within the short time allotted to learning. Like Bruner and Gagné, he suggests that children in the primary grades should work on as many hands-on learning activities as possible. For children beyond the primary grades, though, he recommends the increased use of learning by transmission—using teacher explanations, concept mapping, demonstrations, diagrams, and illustrations. Ausubel cautions against learning by rote.

To avoid rote memorization, Ausubel encourages teachers to make the learning meaningful and longer lasting by using **advance organizers**, ideas presented to the students before the new material that mentally prepare students to integrate the new material into previously built cognitive structures. Many textbook programs today are designed in this way.

No doubt, the most effective teaching is when the students see meaning to what is being taught. Yet, danger in expository teaching (listening, reading and memorizing) is that there may be a tendency to rely too heavily upon spoken communication, a form that for many learners is highly abstract and, thus, likely to be ineffective. This danger is especially relevant to classrooms with a diversity of students in terms of language proficiency, cultural backgrounds, and skill levels.

Concept mapping.   A technique based on Ausubel's theory of meaningful learning that has been found useful for helping students in changing their misconceptions is use of the **concept map**. According to Novak, "Concepts are regularities in events or objects designated by some arbitrary label."[19] A concept map typically refers to a visual or graphic representation of concepts with bridges (connections) that show relationships. Figure 2.3 shows a concept map in social studies. Junior high school students have made connections of concept relationships related to fruit farming and marketing.

The general procedure for concept mapping is to have the students: (1) identify important concepts in materials being studied, often by circling those concepts, (2) rank order the concepts from the most general to the most specific, and (3) arrange the concepts on a sheet of paper, connect related ideas with lines, and define the connections between the related ideas. Concept mapping has been found to help students in their ability to organize and to represent their thoughts, as well as to help them connect new knowledge to their past experiences and precepts.[20]

Arthur L. Costa and Teaching for Thinking

Synthesizing what has been learned about learning and brain functioning, Arthur Costa encourages teachers to integrate explicit thinking instruction into the daily lessons and help students develop their thinking skills. According to Costa:

> In teaching for thinking, we are interested not only in what students know but also in how students behave when they don't know. . . . Gathering evidence of the performance and growth of intelligent behavior is difficult through standardized testing. It really requires "kid-watching": observing students as they try to solve the day-to-day academic and real-life problems they encounter in school, at home, on the playground, alone, and with friends. By collecting anecdotes and examples of written, oral, and visual expressions, we can see students' increasingly voluntary and spontaneous performance of these intelligent behaviors.[21]

---

[19]Joseph D. Novak, "Application of Advances in Learning Theory and Philosophy of Science to the Improvement of Chemistry Teaching," *Journal of Chemistry Education* 61(7):607–612 (July 1984), p. 607.

[20]For further information about concept mapping, see Joseph D. Novak, "Concept Maps and Vee Diagrams: Two Metacognitive Tools to Facilitate Meaningful Learning," *Instructional Science* 19(1):29–52 (1990).

[21]Arthur L. Costa, *The School as a Home for the Mind* (Palatine, IL: Skylight Publishing, 1991), p. 19; from original in Arthur L. Costa (ed.), *Developing Minds*, 2d ed. (Washington, DC: Association for Supervision and Curriculum Development, 1991).

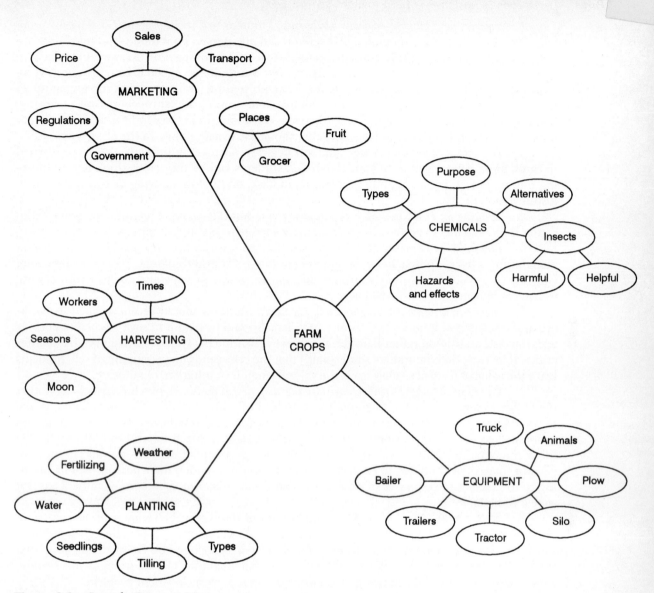

Figure 2.3   Sample Concept Map

Characteristics of Intelligent Behavior

Costa identified and articulated fourteen characteristics of intelligent behavior that teachers can teach for and observe developing in students. They include:

1.   *A Sense of Humor.* The positive effects of humor on the body's physiological functions are well established; these include a drop in the pulse rate, the secretion of endorphins, and an increase of oxygen in the blood. Humor liberates creativity and provides high-level thinking skills, such as anticipation, finding novel relationships, and visual imagery.

The acquisition of a sense of humor follows a developmental sequence similar to that described by Piaget and Kohlberg.[22] Initially, children may find humor in all the wrong things—human frailty, ethnic humor, sacrilegious riddles, ribald profanities. Later, creative children thrive on finding incongruity and will demonstrate a whimsical frame of mind during problem solving.

[22]J. Piaget, *The Psychology of Intelligence* (Totowa, NJ: Littlefield Adams, 1972); and I. Kohlberg. *The Meaning and Measurement of Moral Development* (Worcester, MA: Clark University Press, 1981).

2. *Cooperative Thinking—Social Intelligence.* Humans are social beings. Real-world problem solving has become so complex that seldom can any person go it alone. Not all children—not even all secondary school students—come to school knowing how to work effectively in groups. They may exhibit competitiveness, narrow-mindedness, egocentrism, ethnocentrism, or criticism of others' values, emotions, and beliefs. Listening, consensus seeking, giving up an idea to work on someone else's, empathy, compassion, group leadership, cooperative learning, knowing how to support group efforts, altruism—those are behaviors indicative of intelligent human beings, and and they are the ones that should be learned while in the classroom.

3. *Decreasing Impulsivity.* When students begin to decrease impulsivity, they have learned to think more before acting. In your classroom, students can be trained to think before shouting out an answer, before beginning a project or task, and before arriving at conclusions with insufficient data.

4. *Drawing on Past Knowledge and Applying It to New Situations.* The ultimate goal of education is for students to apply school-learned knowledge to real-life situations.

5. *Flexibility in Thinking.* Intelligent people can approach a new problem from a new angle, using a novel approach. De Bono refers to this as "lateral thinking."[23] In your classroom, you can train your students to consider alternative points of view and to deal with several sources of information simultaneously.

6. *Ingenuity, Originality, Insightfulness, Creativity.* Students should be encouraged to do, or act, and discouraged from saying, "I can't." Students should be taught in such a way that encourages intrinsic motivation rather than relying on extrinsic sources. Teachers should be able to offer criticism in a way that the student understands that the criticism is not a criticism of self. Students learn the value of feedback. They learn the value of their own intuition, of guessing.

7. *Listening to Others—with Understanding and Empathy.* Some psychologists believe that the ability to listen to others, to empathize with and to understand their points of view, is one of the highest forms of intelligent behavior. Piaget refers to this behavior as "overcoming egocentrism." As discussed previously, students can be taught to listen to, and to build upon, the ideas of others. In "think tanks" and in legislative bodies, people from various walks of life convene to share their thinking, to explore their ideas, and to broaden their perspectives by listening to the ideas and responses of others. You can teach your own classroom of students as if it were a think tank.

8. *Metacognition.* An important characteristic of intelligent behavior is an awareness of one's own thinking, through planning, monitoring, and evaluating one's own thoughts. Students can learn this skill. You can help students develop their metacognition by modeling your own thinking processes, such as by thinking aloud about what an author may be saying (while reading aloud to the students) or by thinking aloud when trying to solve a classroom problem.

9. *Persistence.* Persistence is sticking to a task until it is completed. Consider these examples of persistence: Between 1831 and before being elected President in 1860, Abraham Lincoln failed twice in business and was defeated eight times for various political offices, including the vice-presidency in 1858. Thomas Edison tried approximately 3,000 filaments before finding one that worked. For years Babe Ruth had not only the highest number of home runs but also the highest number of strikeouts. Caroline V. Anderson, an African American pioneer in medicine, was refused internship at the Boston New England Hospital for Women and Children the first time she applied, simply because of her color.

10. *Questioning and Problem Posing.* As noted previously, young children are full of questions—and they ask practically every one. We want all students to be alert to discrepancies and problems in their environment and to inquire about their causes.

11. *Risk Taking.* We should encourage students to venture forth and explore their ideas. As a classroom teacher you can provide this opportunity with techniques such as brainstorming, experimenting, and cooperative learning.

12. *Striving for Accuracy and Precision.* You can observe your students growing in this behavior as they (1) take time to check over their work, (2) review the procedures, and (3) use more concise language.

---

[23]de Bono, E., *Lateral Thinking: Creativity Step by Step* (New York: Harper & Row, 1970).

13. *Using All the Senses*. As appropriate, you should encourage students to use all their senses for learning rather than to depend on only one or two.

14. *Wonderment, Inquisitiveness, Curiosity, and the Enjoyment of Problem Solving—A Sense of Efficacy as a Thinker*. Through classroom learning students should be able to develop a feeling of "I can" and express a feeling of "I enjoy." This expression should never be stifled. To encourage the wonderment of learning is every teacher's challenge and within each person's lifetime wonderment should never cease.

Costa gives us fourteen characteristics of intelligent behavior to which we should strive to help students develop. Now, let's review additional research findings that are important considerations in helping young people learn.

Styles of Learning

Teachers who are most effective are those who adapt their teaching styles and methods to their students. Such teachers use approaches that interest the students, that are neither too easy nor too difficult, that match the students' learning styles, and that are relevant to the students' lives. This adaptation process is complicated, because each student is different from every other—all do not have the same interest, abilities, backgrounds, or learning styles. As a matter of fact, students not only differ from one another but each student can change to some extent from day to day. What appeals to a student today may not appeal tomorrow. Therefore, you need to consider both the makeup of each particular student and the nature of students in general (e.g., methods appropriate for a particular senior high school class are unlikely to be the same as those that work best for students of middle school). What follows is a synopsis of what has been learned about aspects of student learning styles.

Brain Laterality

Research has shown that how a person learns is related to differences in the left and right hemispheres of the brain. This theory is sometimes referred to as *brain laterality* or *brain hemisphericity*. Verbal learning, logical and convergent thinking, and the academic cognitive processes are dominated by the left cerebral hemisphere, whereas the affective, intuitive, spatial, emotional, divergent thinking, and visual elements are dominated by the right cerebral hemisphere. Some students are oriented to learning with the right cerebral hemisphere learning, whereas others are oriented to the left. This means that some students learn better through verbal interactions, and others learn better through visual, kinesthetic, and tactile involvement. Yet, "in a healthy person the two hemispheres are inextricably interactive, irrespective of whether a person is dealing with words, mathematics, music, or art."[24]

This concept of brain laterality has implications for teaching. By providing a variety of instructional options, you are more likely to teach effectively to more of the students more of the time. When integrating disciplines in the school curriculum and connecting what is being learned with real life situations, the teacher is most likely to be teaching to both hemispheres.

Learning Modalities

A **learning modality** is the way students prefer to receive sensory reception, called *modality preference*, or the actual way a student learns best, called *modality adeptness* or strength. Some students prefer learning by seeing, referred to as *visual modality*. Some prefer learning through instruction from others or self, referred to as *auditory modality*. Some prefer learning by doing and being physically involved, referred to as *kinesthetic modality*. Finally, some prefer learning by touching objects, referred to as *tactile modality*.

Sometimes a student's modality preference is not that student's modality strength. A student's primary modality strength can often be determined by observing the student. But you

[24]Caine and Caine, p. 67.

should note that students can have a mix of strengths and that modality strength can change as the result of experience and intellectual maturity. Research on modality strengths and learning includes these findings:

- Between the middle school years and adulthood, auditory learning becomes more important than kinesthetic learning, though visual learning remains dominant.
- Modality integration (using several modalities at once) has been found to contribute to better achievement.
- Teachers tend to teach the way they learn best (modality strength), but students may have modality strengths different from the teacher. This difference can affect achievement.

This concept of learning modality has implications for teaching. Most students have neither a preference nor a strength for auditory reception, and therefore middle school and secondary school teachers should limit use of the lecture method of instruction. Furthermore, instruction that uses a singular approach, such as auditory, cheats students who learn better another way. This difference can affect student achievement. Finally, if a teacher's verbal communication conflicts with his or her nonverbal messages, students can become confused, and this can affect their learning as well.

As a general rule, middle school and secondary school students prefer to learn by touching objects, by feeling shapes and textures, by interacting with each other, and by moving things around. In contrast, sitting and listening are difficult for many of these students. This dependence on the tactile and kinesthetic modalities decreases with maturity. Some students are good visual learners; they can read easily and rapidly and can visualize what they are reading about. Other students, though, lack that modality strength.

Because different students have different modality strengths, you should use strategies that integrate the modalities. Combining reception learning and cognitive mapping is an example of modality integration. When well designed, thematic units also incorporate modality integration. In conclusion, when teaching a group of students of mixed learning abilities, mixed modality strengths, mixed language proficiency, and mixed cultural backgrounds, the integration of learning modalities is a must.

Learning Styles

Closely related to learning modality (i.e., sensory portal preference) is **learning style**, the way a student learns best in a given situation. For example, some students are comfortable with beginning their learning with abstractions, whereas others feel the need to begin with the concrete. Some prosper while working in groups, whereas others prefer to work alone. Some are quick in their studies, whereas others are slow and methodical and cautious and meticulous. Some can sustain attention on a single topic for a long time, becoming more absorbed in their study as time passes. Others are slower starters and more casual in their pursuits, but they are capable of shifting with ease from subject to subject. Some can study in the midst of music, noise, or movement, whereas others need quiet, solitude, and a desk or table.

The point is that students vary in not only their skills and modality strengths but also in how they mentally process that information once it has been received, or the person's style of learning. A learning style, then is a person's style of learning, "a gestalt combining internal and external operations derived from the individual's neurobiology, personality, and development and reflected in learner behavior."[25]

Anthony Gregorc, for example, classifies learning styles according to whether students prefer to begin with the concrete or the abstract and according to whether they prefer random or sequential ordering of information.[26] As a result, his classification of learning styles has four categories:

1. *Concrete sequential learners,* who prefer direct, hands-on experiences presented in a logical sequence.

---

[25]James W. Keefe and Barbara G. Ferrell, "Developing a Defensible Learning Style Paradigm," *Educational Leadership* 48(2):57–61 (October 1990), p. 59.

[26]Anthony Gregorc, "Learning and Teaching Styles—Potent Forces Behind Them," *Educational Leadership* (January 1979), pp. 234–36.

2. *Concrete random learners*, who prefer a more wide-open, exploratory kind of activity, such as games, role-playing, simulations, and independent study.
3. *Abstract sequential learners*, who are skilled in decoding verbal and symbolic messages, especially when presented in logical sequence.
4. *Abstract random learners*, who can interpret meaning from nonverbal communications and consequently do well in discussions, debates, and media presentations.[27]

Most secondary school students are better at one of the two categories of concrete learning than at either category of abstract learning.

Although there are probably as many types of learning styles as there are individuals, most classifications focus on four general types, based on the work of Carl Jung in the early part of the twentieth century.[28] David Kolb later described two major differences in how people learn: how they *perceive* situations and how they *process* information.[29] In new situations, for example, some people are watchers and others are doers. It is important to note that learning style is not an indicator of intelligence, but rather an indicator of how a person learns.

More recently, Bernice McCarthy has described the following four major learning styles:

1. *The imaginative learner.* Imaginative learners perceive information concretely and process it reflectively. They learn well by listening and sharing with others, integrating the ideas of others with their own experiences. Imaginative learners often have difficulty adjusting to traditional teaching, which depends relatively little on classroom interactions and students' sharing and connecting of their prior experiences. In a traditional classroom, the imaginative learner is likely to be an at-risk student.

2. *The analytic learner.* Analytic learners perceive information abstractly and process it reflectively. They prefer sequential thinking, need details, and value what experts have to offer. Analytic learners do well in traditional classrooms.

3. *The common-sense learner.* Common-sense learners perceive information abstractly and process it actively. This type of learner is pragmatic and enjoys hands-on learning. Common-sense learners sometimes find school frustrating unless they can see immediate use to what is being learned. In the traditional classroom the common-sense learner is likely to be an at-risk learner.

4. *The dynamic learner.* Dynamic learners perceive information concretely and process it actively. They prefer hands-on learning, and are excited by anything new. Dynamic learners are risk takers and are frustrated by learning if they see it as being tedious and sequential. In a traditional classroom the dynamic learner is likely to be an at-risk students.[30]

With a system developed by McCarthy (called the 4MAT System), teachers employ a learning cycle of instructional strategies that reach each student's learning style. According to McCarthy, learners in the cycle "sense and feel, they experience, then they watch, they reflect, then they think, they develop theories, then they try out theories, they experiment. Finally, they evaluate and synthesize what they have learned in order to apply it to their next similar experience. They get smarter. They apply experience to experiences."[31] And through this process they are likely to be using all four learning modalities.

Finally, in contrast to Jung's four learning styles, Howard Gardner in his Theory of Multiple Intelligences (which grew from his work with gifted children and those with learning problems) introduces seven learning styles. These learning styles, or independent forms of

[27]Adapted from Robert Heinich, Michael Molenda, and James D. Russell, *Instructional Media and the New Technologies of Instruction*, 4th ed. (New York: Macmillan, 1993), p. 38.

[28]See Carl G. Jung, *Psychological Types* (New York: Harcourt Brace, 1923). See also Anthony Gregorc, *Gregorc Style Delineator* (Maynard, MA: Gabriel Systems, 1985); and Rita Dunn and Kenneth Dunn, *Teaching Students Through Their Individual Learning Styles* (Reston, VA: Reston Publications, 1978).

[29]See David Kolb, *The Learning Style Inventory* (Boston, MA: McBer, 1985).

[30]Bernice McCarthy, "Using the 4MAT System to Bring Learning Styles to Schools," *Educational Leadership* 48(2):31–37 (October 1990), p. 32.

[31]McCarthy, p. 33.

knowing and processing information, are exhibited by individuals in differing ways: (1) verbal-linguistic, (2) logical-mathematical, (3) intrapersonal, (4) visual-spatial, (5) musical-rhythmic, (6) body-kinesthetic, and (7) interpersonal.[32]

As implied previously, many educators believe that at-risk students are those who may be dominant in a cognitive learning style that is not in sync with traditional teaching methods. Traditional methods largely apply to McCarthy's analytic style, in which information is presented in a logical, linear, sequential fashion, and to the first three of Gardner's types: verbal-linguistic, logical-mathematical, and intrapersonal.[33] Consequently, to better match methods of instruction with learning styles, some teachers and schools have restructured the curriculum and instruction around Gardner's seven ways of knowing.[34]

As a teacher, you should note two concepts related to learning styles that have implications for teaching:

1. *Intelligence is not a fixed or static reality but can be learned, taught, and developed.*[35] This concept is important for your students to understand, too. When students understand that intelligence is incremental—something that is developed through use over time—they tend to be more motivated to work at learning than when they believe intelligence is a fixed entity.[36]

2. *Not all students learn and respond to learning situations in the same way.* A student may learn differently according to the situation or according to the student's ethnicity, cultural background, or socioeconomic status.[37] A teacher who uses only one style of teaching or who teaches to only one or a few styles of learning, day after day, is short-changing those students who learn better another way.

A trap the teacher must avoid is to regard all students who have difficulty or who have a history of doing poorly in school as being alike. In a culture such as ours, which values quantity, speed, and measurement, it is easy to make the mistake that being a slow learner is the same as being a poor learner. The perceptive teacher understands that slowness may be simply another style of learning, with potential strengths of its own. Slowness can reflect many things—caution, a desire to be thorough or meticulous, a great interest in the matter being studied. To ignore the slow student, or to treat all students who seem slow as though they were victims of some deficiency, is to risk discouraging those who have deliberately opted for slowness and thus limiting their opportunities.

Your obligation is to recognize that students have different ways of receiving information and different ways of processing that information. These differences are unique and important, and they are what the teacher should address in his or her teaching. Thus, you should try to learn as much as you can about how each student learns and processes information. Because you can never know everything about each student, the more you vary your teaching strategies, the more likely you are to reach more of the students more of the time. A specific technique for getting to know more about how your own students prefer to learn can be found in Module 5, in the section "Getting to Know Your Students as People."

Now do Exercises 2.1 and 2.2.

[32]See Howard Gardner and Thomas Hatch, "Multiple Intelligences Go to School: Educational Implications of the Theory of Multiple Intelligence," *Educational Researcher* 18(8):4–9 (November 1989); or Tina Blythe and Howard Gardner, "A School for All Intelligences," *Educational Leadership* 47(7):33–37 (April 1990); or Howard Gardner, "The Theory of Multiple Intelligences," *Annals of Dyslexia* 37:19–35 (1987).

[33]See, for example, Thomas Armstrong, "Learning Differences—Not Disabilities," *Principal* 68(1):34–36 (September 1988).

[34]For teachers see, for example, Launa Ellison, "Using Multiple Intelligences to Set Goals," *Educational Leadership* 50(2):69–72 (October 1992); for schools see for example, Thomas R. Hoerr, "How Our School Applied Multiple Intelligences Theory," *Educational Leadership* 50(2):67–68 (October 1992).

[35]David G. Lazear, *Teaching for Multiple Intelligences*, Fastback 342 (Bloomington, IN: Phi Delta Kappa, 1992), p. 8. See also Gerald W. Bracey, "Getting Smart(er) in School," *Phi Delta Kappan* 73(5):414–416 (January 1992).

[36]Lauren B. Resnick and Leopold E. Klopfer, *Toward the Thinking Curriculum: Current Cognitive Research*, 1989 ASCD Yearbook (Alexandria, VA: Association for Supervision and Curriculum Development, 1989), p. 8.

[37]For relevant discussions about students' cultural differences and learning styles, see Scott Willis, "Multicultural Teaching Strategies," *ASCD Curriculum Update* (Alexandria, VA: Association for Supervision and Curriculum Development, September, 1993), p. 7; and Gene Gallegos, "Learning Styles in Culturally Diverse Classrooms," *California Catalyst* 36–41 (Fall 1993).

• • • • • •

Sources of Motivation

Instructions: The purpose of this exercise is for you to explore your present understanding of what motivates you to learn. Answer the following questions and then share those answers with your colleagues. When answering these questions, don't concern yourself with whether your answers are "right" or "wrong."

1. How do you define what is learning?

2. Do you think there is any difference in the way you personally learn for short-term retention as opposed to the way you learn for long-term retention? If so, explain that difference.

3. Identify and rank order (from most important to least important) what you believe to be at least three sources of motivation for your own learning. For each, identify by writing either *I* or *E* in the blank whether you believe that source is Intrinsic (within yourself) or Extrinsic (grades, rewards, expectations of others, etc.).

_____ a.

_____ b.

_____ c.

_____ d.

_____ e.

4. Did you ever learn something that you previously had thought you could never have learned? Explain, describing what motivated you and helped you to learn it.

My Perceptions of How I Learn

• • • • • •

Techniques Used

Instructions: The purpose of this exercise is for you to explore your present understanding of how you learn best. Answer the following questions and then share those answers with your colleagues. When answering these questions, don't concern yourself with whether your answers are "right" or "wrong."

1. When in a class, how do you study for an examination? Check each of the following techniques you use, then elaborate with an example that will help you explain it to others. For each technique that you use, circle *S* or *L* to indicate that you believe you use this technique primarily for short-term (*S*) or long-term (*L*) retention.

    ____ a. *Outline* material?   S   L

    ____ b. Use *mnemonic* devices?   S   L

    ____ c. Make *connections* (i.e., build bridges) of the new material with your prior knowledge, experiences, attitudes, beliefs, or values (known as elaboration)?   S   L

    ____ d. Write *summaries* of important ideas?   S   L

    ____ e. Construct *visual (graphic) representations* (e.g., charts, graphs, maps, or networks) of verbal material to be learned?   S   L

    ____ f. Participate in *cooperative study* groups?   S   L

    ____ g. *Teach others* what you have learned or are learning?   S   L

    ____ h. Other?   S   L

2. From your selections and descriptions to the first question, do you believe that there is any difference in how you learn, depending on whether you are learning for short-term or long-term retention? If so, in a paragraph describe this difference.

3. Now share your answers to questions one and two with your colleagues, and compare their results with your own. How do they compare?

4. From this exercise, what can you conclude? What have you learned about your own learning? About how others learn?

Recognizing, Celebrating, and Building upon Student Diversity

Assume that you are a high school history teacher and that your teaching schedule includes three sections of U.S. History. Furthermore, assume that students at your school are tracked (as they are, unfortunately, in many schools). One of your classes is a so-called college-prep class with thirty students. Another is a regular-education class with thirty-five students, two of whom have special needs because of physical handicaps. And the third is a sheltered English class with thirteen students, nine Hispanics with limited proficiency in English and four Southeast Asians, two with no ability to use English. Again, for all three sections the course is U.S. History. Will one lesson plan using lecture and discussion as the primary instructional strategies work for all three sections? The answer is an emphatic no! How do you decide what to do? Before you finish this book we hope the answer to that question has become clear to you.

Providing for Student Differences

Students differ in many ways: physical characteristics, interests, intellectual ability, motor ability, social ability, aptitudes of various kinds, experience, ideals, attitudes, needs, ambitions, dreams, and hopes. Having long recognized the importance of these individual differences, educators have made many attempts to develop systematic programs of individualized instruction. In the 1920s there were the "programmed" workbooks of the Winetka Plan. The 1960s brought a multitude of plans, such as IPI (Individually Prescribed Instruction), IGE (Individually Guided Education), and PLAN (Program for Learning in Accordance with Needs). The 1970s saw the development and growth in popularity of individual learning packages and the Individualized Education Program (IEP) for students who are handicapped. Although some of these efforts did not survive the test of time, others met with more success; some have been refined and are still being used. Today, for example, some schools are reporting success in the use of IEPs for all students, not just for students with special needs.

Furthermore, for a variety of reasons (e.g., learning styles, modality preferences, information-processing habits, motivational factors, and physiological factors) all persons learn in their own ways and at their own rates. Interests, background, innate and acquired abilities, and a myriad of other influences shape how and what a person will learn. No two students ever learn exactly the same thing from any particular learning experience.

There is a growing interest in the psychological factors of learning and in the possibility of matching students to instructional treatments. A related need is to increase our knowledge about strategies for teaching the number of students from diverse cultural backgrounds and whose primary language may not be English. Consider this statement, written in 1989 by James A. Banks and Cherry A. McGee Banks:

> Cultural diversity in U.S. schools has deepened considerably during the last two decades. The aging of the mainstream population and the influx of immigrants to the United States since the Immigration Reform Act of 1965 have resulted in a rapid rise in the percentage of ethnic, cultural, language, and religious minorities in the nation's schools. One out of three U.S. students will be an ethnic minority by the turn of the century. The civil rights movement of the 1960s and 1970s and the resulting national legislation have increased cultural diversity within the schools and have also made educators more sensitive to the special educational needs of various groups of students, such as females, the disabled, the poor, and students from various language groups.
>
> Today, most teachers have students in their classroom from various ethnic, cultural, religious, language, and social-class groups. They are also likely to have one or more exceptional students in their classes. Such students may be handicapped, gifted, or both. Teachers should be aware of the many needs of students from diverse groups and also sensitive to the special characteristics and needs of female and male students. It is also important for teachers to keep in mind that most students belong to several of these groups . . . [although] for many students one group identification is much more important than all the others.[38]

---

[38]James A. Banks and Cherry A. McGee Banks (eds.), *Multicultural Education: Issues and Perspectives* (Boston: Allyn & Bacon, 1989), p. xi.

The recognition and acceptance of students from a great variety of backgrounds are central to the concept of **multicultural education**. Multicultural education encompasses at least three aspects: it is (1) a concept, (2) an educational reform movement, and (3) a process whose major goal is to change the structure of educational institutions so that male and female students, exceptional students, and students who are members of diverse racial, ethnic, and cultural groups will have an equal chance to achieve academically in school.[39]

This variety of individual differences among students requires that teachers find teaching strategies and tactics to accommodate those differences. In order to be able to teach students who are different from you, you need skills in:

- Establishing a classroom climate in which all students feel welcome.
- Providing a classroom environment in which all students feel they can learn.
- Building upon students' learning styles.
- Adapting to students' skills levels.
- Using techniques that emphasize cooperative learning and that deemphasize competitive learning.
- Using strategies and techniques that have proven successful for students of specific differences.

The last skill in the list is the focus of the sections that follow.

Working with Students with Special Needs

Students with special needs include those in any of the following categories: autistic, deaf, deaf-blind, hard of hearing, mentally retarded, multihandicapped, orthopedically impaired, other health impaired, seriously emotionally disturbed, speech impaired, traumatic brain injury, and visually handicapped. Such students must, to the extent possible, be educated with their peers in the regular classroom. Public Law 94-142, the Education of the Handicapped Act (EHA) of 1975 (and its amendments) mandates that all children have the right to a full and free public education, as well as to nondiscriminatory assessment.[40]

This legislation, which emphasizes normalizing the educational environment for students with special needs, requires provision of the least-restrictive environment for these students—an environment that is as normal as possible. Students who are identified as having special needs because of handicaps may be placed in the regular classroom for the entire school day, called full **inclusion**, and that is the trend.[41] Those students may also be in a regular classroom the greater part of the school day (partial inclusion) or only for designated periods. This placement concept has also been known as **mainstreaming** (though that term is gradually being replaced by this term *inclusion*).

You will need information and skills unique to teaching special-needs students in your classroom. In effect, this means that you must be, at least for a part of the time, a teacher of students with special needs. Actually, teaching students with special needs is not so different from ordinary teaching, except that it requires more care, better diagnosis, greater skill, more attention to individual needs, and an even greater understanding of the students. Yet the challenges of teaching students with special needs in the regular classroom are great enough that to do it well you need additional specialized training far beyond that which can be provided by this book. At some point in your teacher preparation you should, or may be required to, take one or more courses in working with the mainstreamed special learner.

As a regular classroom teacher, you should keep this important fact in mind: When a student with special needs is placed in your regular classroom, your objective should not be to

---

[39]Banks, p. 1.

[40]Public Law 94-142 was amended by Public Law 99-457 in 1986 and again in 1990 by Public Law 101-476, at which time its name was changed to the Individuals with Disabilities Education Act (IDEA).

[41]See, for example, Anne Wheelock, "The Case for Untracking," *Educational Leadership* 50(2):6–10 (October 1992). For a review of the history of special education reform, see Richard Schattman and Jeff Benay, "Inclusive Practices Transform Special Education in the 1990s," *School Administrator* 49(2):8–12 (February 1992). See also "Special Education Group Weighs in on Full Inclusion," *Teacher Magazine* 4(9):9 (August 1993) and John O'Neil, "Inclusive Education Gains Adherents," *ASCD Update* 35(9):1, 3–4 (November 1993).

make the student normal, but, rather, to deal directly with the differences between this student and other students in your classroom. To deal directly with these differences, you should:

1. Develop an understanding of the general characteristics of different types of special needs students.
2. Identify the student's unique needs relative to your classroom.
3. Design lesson plans that teach to different needs at the same time. As previously noted, teaching to different needs at the same time is called multilevel teaching (or multitasking).

Because of a concern for problems of the special-needs child, Congress stipulated in Public Law 94-142 that an *Individualized Educational Program (IEP)* be devised annually for each special-needs student. According to that law, an IEP for each student is developed each year by a team that includes special education teachers, the child's parents, and the classroom teachers. The IEP contains: (1) a statement of the student's present educational levels, (2) the educational goals for the year, (3) specifications for the services to be provided and the extent to which the student should be expected to take part in the regular program, and (4) the evaluative criteria for the services to be provided.

Consultation by special and skilled support personnel is essential in all mainstream IEP models. A consultant works directly with teachers or with students and parents. As a classroom teacher, you may have an active role in preparing the specifications for the special-needs students assigned to your classes, as well as a major responsibility for implementing the program.

Guidelines for working with students with special needs.   The following are guidelines for working with special-needs learners who are wholly or partially included in regular education classrooms. Although these guidelines are important for teaching all students, they are especially necessary for teaching students with special needs in the regular education classroom.

- *Adapt and modify materials and procedures to the special needs of each student.* For example, a student who has extreme difficulty sitting still for more than a few minutes will need planned changes in learning activities. When assigning student seating in the classroom, give preference to students according to their special needs. Try to incorporate into your lessons activities that engage all learning modalities—visual, auditory, tactile, and kinesthetic. Be flexible in your classroom procedures, such as allowing the use of tape recorders for note taking and test taking, when students have trouble with the written language.
- *Break complex learning into simpler components, moving from the most concrete to the abstract.* Check frequently for student understanding of instructions and procedures, as well as for their comprehension of content. Use computers and other self-correcting materials (e.g., self-instructional packages) for drill and practice and for provision of immediate feedback to the student without embarrassment.
- *Define the instructional objectives in behavioral terms* (discussed in Module 3). This will provide high structure and clear expectations.
- *Exercise your withitness—be aware of everything that is going on in the classroom, at all times, monitoring students for signs of restlessness, frustration, anxiety, and off-task behaviors.* Be ready to reassign individual learners to different activities as the situation warrants.
- *Have students copy assignments for the week into a folder kept in their notebooks.* Post assignments for the week in a special place on the bulletin board and remind students of deadlines.
- *Maintain consistency in your expectations.* Special-needs students, particularly, can become frustrated when they do not understand a teacher's expectations.
- *Maintain consistency in your responses.* Special-needs learners can become frustrated when they cannot depend on a teacher's reactions.
- *Plan interesting learning activities that help the students connect what is being learned with their real world.* Sometimes called "bridging" activities, learning that connects what is being learned with the real world helps to motivate students and to keep them on task.
- *Plan your questions and questioning sequence* (using questions is discussed in Module 7). Plan questions you will ask special-needs students so that they are likely to answer with confi-

dence. Use signals to let students know that you are likely to call on them (e.g., prolonged eye contact, mentioning it to the student before class). After asking a question, give the student adequate time to think and to respond. Build upon the student's response.

- *Provide for and teach toward student success.* Offer students activities and experiences that ensure success and mastery at some level. Use of student portfolios can give evidence of progress and help in building student confidence. Capitalize on students' strengths and provide opportunities for success in a supportive atmosphere to help build student self-esteem.
- *Provide guided or coached practice of what is being learned.* Provide time in class for students to begin work on their assignments. During this time, you can monitor the work of each student, while looking for misconceptions, and assuring that students get started on the right track.
- *Provide help in the organization of students' learning.* For example, give instruction in the organization of notes and notebooks. Have a three-hole punch available in the classroom so that students can put papers into their notebooks immediately, thus avoiding disorganization and the loss of papers. During class presentations use an overhead projector with transparencies. Then those students who need more time can copy material from the transparencies. Ask students to read their notes aloud to each other in small groups, thereby aiding their recall and encouraging them to take notes for meaning rather than for rote learning.
- *Reward approved and appropriate behavior* (discussed in Module 5). Unacceptable behavior, if not too disruptive, can sometimes be ignored.
- *Teach students the correct procedures for everything* (discussed in Module 5).

Working with Students of Diversity and Differences

A teaching credential authorizes you to teach in any public school throughout a state—in some instances, throughout a region that consists of several states. That means you could find yourself teaching in a school that is ethnically, culturally, linguistically, and socioeconomically diverse. The United States is a country of a variety of families, many with different ethnic heritages—African American, Cambodian American, Chinese American, Cuban American, Filipino American, French Canadian American, Hungarian American, Iranian American, Italian American, Jewish American, Laotian American, Mexican American, Native American, Polish American, Puerto Rican American, Russian American, and Vietnamese American, to name but a few. California students, for example, represent more than eighty language groups and dozens of nations. In this country, some inner-city schools have student bodies that represent forty to fifty different languages. It will be important for you to determine the language and nationality groups represented by the students in your classroom.

A major problem for recent immigrant children, as well as some ethnic groups, is learning a second language. In many cities, and even in smaller communities today, it is not uncommon for more than half the children in school to come from homes where the native language is not English. Yet standard English is a necessity in most communities of this country if a person is to become vocationally successful and enjoy a full life. Learning to communicate reasonably well in English can take an immigrant student at least a year, and probably more; some authorities say three to seven years.

To be successful in teaching students who have limited proficiency in English (LEP) includes hands-on learning and cooperating learning groups (discussed in Module 6). Some schools use a *pullout approach,* in which part of the student's school time is spent in special bilingual classes and the rest of the time in regular classrooms. In some schools LEP students are placed in academic classrooms that use a *sheltered English approach.* For example, a section of life science is established especially for students whose primary language is not English but who do have limited proficiency in English (conversational ability). The teacher of that class is one who is trained in techniques suitable for teaching life science to LEP students. Specific techniques include:

1. Speaking clearly and naturally but at a slower pace.
2. Using simplified vocabulary but without "talking down" to students.
3. Giving directions in a variety of ways.

4. Using a variety of examples and observable models.
5. Giving special attention to key words that convey meaning, and writing them on the board.
6. Avoiding jargon or idiomatic phrases that might be misunderstood.
7. Reading written directions out loud, and writing oral directions on the board.
8. Allowing time for translation by an aide or classmate and allowing time for discussion to clarify meaning.
9. Dividing complex or extended language discourse into smaller, more manageable units.
10. Allowing extra time than you would normally.[42]

As a regular-education classroom teacher, you need to know the extent to which your LEP students are in these types of programs. You may be expected to work in conjunction with a bilingual-program teacher in developing an individualized education program for the LEP students.

Additional guidelines for working with students with limited proficiency in English (LEP). To work effectively with students in your classroom who have limited proficiency in English, consider the following additional guidelines.

- *Avoid instruction that is abstract.* With LEP students you should use the most concrete (least abstract), hands-on forms of instruction.
- *Build upon (or connect with) what the students already know.* One way to do this is when introducing a new topic or concept, use a technique called think-pair-share. With this technique, the new topic is introduced by the teacher's writing it on the board. Pairs of students are then asked to think about this new word and discuss what meaning it has to them—any experiences or thoughts they have about it, not worrying about whether they are right or wrong. After sharing their ideas in pairs, the pairs then share their thoughts with the rest of the class. The teacher records these thoughts and experiences on the board (or an overhead transparency) and then builds the lesson from the thoughts and experiences expressed by the students.
- *Encourage student writing.* One way to encourage students to write is through the use of journal writing. Two kinds of journals are appropriate when working with LEP students: dialogue journals and reading-response journals. Dialogue journals are used for students to write anything that is on their mind. Teachers, parents, and other students then respond, thereby "talking with" the journal writer. Reading-response journals are used for students to write (record) their reactions to what they are reading.
- *Help students learn the vocabulary.* Assist the LEP student in learning two vocabulary sets: the vocabulary needed to learn and the vocabulary needed to understand subject content.[43]
- *Involve parents or guardians.* Parents (or guardians) of new immigrants are usually truly concerned about the education of their children, and may be very interested in cooperating with you in any way possible. If their help is solicited, they may do all they can to help, and perhaps can help you to facilitate their children's learning. Students whose primary language is not English may have other differences about which you will need also to become knowledgeable.[44] These differences are related to culture, customs, family life, and expectations. To be most successful as a classroom teacher of LEP students, you should learn as much as possible about each student. To this end it is valuable to solicit the help of each student's parent or guardian.

---

[42]Adapted from Donovan R. Walling, *English as a Second Language: 25 Questions and Answers*, Fastback 347 (Bloomington, IN: Phi Delta Kappa Educational Foundation, 1993), p. 26.

[43]See Daniel L. Watson, Linda Northcutt, and Laura Rydell, "Teaching Bilingual Students Successfully." *Educational Leadership*, 46(5):59–61 (February 1989).

[44]One source of useful resources for teachers of students from Southeast Asia is the Southeast Asia Community Resource Center, Folsom Cordova Unified School District, 2460 Cordova Lane, Rancho Cordova, CA 95670, phone (916) 635-6815, Fax (916) 635-0174. Among that center's currently available resources, and costing less than $5 each, are: *Handbook for Teaching Hmong-Speaking Students; Handbook for Teaching Khmer-Speaking Students; Handbook for Teaching Lao-Speaking Students; and Vietnamese Language Materials Sourcebook.*

- *Use cooperative learning groups.* Use small-group, mixed-ability, cooperative learning groups, with individual rewards for students according to group achievement (techniques for using cooperative learning are presented in Module 6).
- *Use modern technology.* For example, use computer networking to allow the language minority student to write and communicate with peers, as well as to publish their work in the classroom.
- *Plan for and use all learning modalities.* You will need to concentrate on the use of multisensory approaches. Plan learning activities that involve students in auditory, visual, tactile, and kinesthetic learning.

A teacher whose preparation occurs exclusively among students whose backgrounds are similar to his or her own may not be adequately prepared to teach in a classroom of such diversity. You will need to learn as much as you can about each student and to become aware of any student who has difficulties in adjusting or developing at school because of economic factors, racial insensitivity, home environmental conditions, or limited proficiency in English.

Guidelines for working with students of diverse backgrounds.   To be compatible with, and be able to teach, students who come from backgrounds different from yours, you need to believe that all students can learn—regardless of their gender and social class, and their ethnic or cultural characteristics. You also need to develop special skills that include those in the following guidelines, each of which is discussed in detail in subsequent modules.

To effectively work with students of diverse backgrounds, you should:

- Build the learning around students' individual learning styles. For example, different ethnic groups seem to prefer certain ways of learning (though it is dangerous to overgeneralize here). African American students, as a general rule, respond well to collaborative, hands-on approaches. Students from Asian and Native American cultures learn better in a holistic presentation, with emphasis on oral discourse and active learning, than by a linear, step-by-step fashion.[45]
- Communicate positively with every student and with his or her parents or guardians, learning as much as you can about the student and the student's culture and encouraging family members to participate in the student's learning.
- Establish a classroom environment in which each student feels he or she can learn.
- Establish a classroom environment in which each student feels welcomed.
- Hold and maintain high expectations for every student. Both teacher and students must understand that intelligence is not a fixed entity, but a characteristic that—through a feeling of "I can" and with proper coaching—can be developed.
- Involve parents, guardians, and other members of the community in the educational program so that all have a sense of ownership and responsibility and feel positive about the program.
- Involve students in understanding and in making important decisions about their own learning, so that they feel ownership of that learning.
- Personalize learning for each student, much as is done in the use of the IEP with special-needs students.
- Provide learning activities adapted to individual students' skill levels.
- Teach to individual needs by using a variety of strategies to achieve an objective or by using a number of different objectives at the same time (multilevel teaching).
- Use techniques that emphasize cooperative learning and that deemphasize competitive learning.

Working with Students Who Are Academically Talented

Sometimes neglected in the regular classroom are those students with special talents, students whose level of interest, understanding, and past performance in the subject matter is consider-

---

[45]Scott Willis, "Multicultural Teaching Strategies," *ASCD Curriculum Update* (Reston, VA: Association for Supervision and Curriculum Development, September, 1993), p. 7.

ably beyond that of their peers. There is no one accepted method for identification of these students. For placement of students in special classes or in programs for the academically talented in elementary school and middle-level schools, most school districts have traditionally used standard intelligence quotient (IQ) testing. Often, by the time these students reach high school, they have been tracked into "college preparatory" (enrichment and accelerated) classes or selected to attend magnet schools. Otherwise, they generally are expected, and often do, take care of themselves.[46] In contrast, some schools today plan their curriculum around the philosophical assumption that all students have the potential to be gifted and talented learners.

Through evaluation of numerous studies, Rogers and Kimpston conclude that research indicates that bright students benefit academically from a more challenging learning environment. They also conclude that these students are not harmed socially or psychologically when in an environment that is academically challenging.[47] Various methods have been devised to provide a more challenging learning environment. These include: allowing students to skip a grade, setting up a nongraded classroom, developing an accelerated curriculum (or curriculum compacting), shortening the time a student passes through the grades (called "grade telescoping"), allowing students to attend a high school class while still a middle or junior high school student, allowing students to attend one or more college classes while still in high school, providing a program of advanced placement (i.e., student takes a high school class that has been accepted as college level, and receives college credit for it when the student scores well on an advanced placement test), and instituting a mentorship program (e.g., student receives special training from an adult expert in a particular field of study). A student might also consider college admission without having completed high school.

Guidelines for working with students who are academically talented.   A student who has special intellectual talent should be allowed to pursue the subject at an accelerated pace and in more depth and complexity than others in the class. To provide this differentiation in learning, you as a teacher should:

- Become familiar with special programs (local, regional, and national) specially designed for academically talented learners, and encourage parents or guardians to consider involving them in such programs. Perhaps a school counselor can help you identify these programs.
- Emphasize skills in critical thinking, metacognition, problem solving, and inquiry.[48]
- Involve students in choosing and inviting effective guest speakers to class.
- Involve the students in selecting and planning interesting field trips.
- Plan and provide optional and voluntary enrichment activities. Self-instructional packages, learning activity centers, special projects, computer activities, and multimedia programs are excellent tools for provision of enrichment activities.
- Plan assignments and activities that challenge the students to the fullest of their abilities. This does not mean overloading them with homework. Rather, carefully plan so that the students' time spent on assignments and activities is quality time and not merely quantity time. One research-supported strategy for planning assignments and activities that challenge these students is known as curriculum compacting, a three-phase process that can be accomplished by one teacher with a classroom of students or by a team of teachers for a larger group.[49] The three phases are: (1) define the goals and outcomes of a given unit of study,

[46]Since the establishment of the first state academy for the academically gifted in North Carolina, other state-supported, residential schools for academically gifted high school students have developed. For a history and description, see James E. Green, *State Academies for the Academically Gifted*, Fastback 349 (Bloomington, IN: Phi Delta Kappa Educational Foundation, 1993).

[47]Karen B. Rogers and Richard D. Kimpston, "Acceleration: What We Do Vs. What We Know," *Educational Leadership* 50(2):58–61 (October 1992), p. 58. See also, James A. Kulik "An Analysis of the Research on Ability Grouping," *The National Research Center on the Gifted and Talented Newsletter*, pp. 8–9 (Spring 1993).

[48]For example, in English and language arts, the critical thinking skills of bright and gifted students can be challenged with the use of mystery literature. See Jerry Flack, "Sherlock Holmes Meets the 21st Century," *Gifted Child Today* 14(4):15–21 (July/August 1991).

[49]See Sally M. Reis and Joseph S. Renzulli, "Using Curriculum Compacting to Challenge the Above-Average," *Educational Leadership* 50(2):51–57 (October 1992).

(2) identify students who have mastered the objectives or outcomes of the unit, (3) provide acceleration and enrichment options for those students. Finally, a fourth phase can be helpful: complete an individual educational program (IEP) for each student.

- Provide in-class seminars for students to discuss topics and problems they are pursuing individually or as members of a learning team.
- Provide independent and dyad learning opportunities. Students who are intellectually gifted often prefer to work alone or with another gifted student.
- Use preassessments (diagnostic evaluation) for reading level and subject achievement so that you are better able to prescribe objectives and activities for each student.
- Work with individual students in some planning of their own objectives and activities for learning.

Working with Students Who Are Academically Slower

Secondary school students who are slower to learn typically fall into two types: (1) those who try to learn but simply need more time to do it, and (2) those who do not try, referred to variously as underachievers, recalcitrant, or reluctant learners. Teaching strategies that work well with those of the first type are not necessarily the same strategies that work well with those of the second—making life difficult for a teacher of thirty students, half who try and half who don't. It is worse still for a teacher of thirty students who include some who try but need time, one or two who are academically talented, some who are LEP students, and several who seem not only unwilling to try but who are also disruptive to classroom procedures.

Guidelines for working with slower students who are willing to try.   The following guidelines may be helpful when working with a slow-learning student who has indicated a willingness to try:

- Adjust your instruction to the student's preferred learning style, which may be different from yours.
- Vary the instructional strategies, using a variety of activities to engage the visual, verbal, tactile and kinesthetic modalities.
- Emphasize basic communication skills, such as speaking, listening, reading, and writing, to ensure that the student's skills in these areas are sufficient for learning the intended content.
- If necessary, help the student to improve his or her reading skills, such as pronunciation, word meanings, and comprehension.
- Help the student learn content in small sequential steps with frequent comprehension checks (at least four during one 50-minute class period).
- When necessary, use frequent positive reinforcement, with the intention of increasing the student's sense of personal worth.
- If using a single textbook, be certain that the reading level is adequate for the slow-learning student; if it is not, then for that student discard the book and use other more appropriate reading materials.
- Maximize the use of in-class, on-task work and the use of cooperative learning (Module 6), with close monitoring of the student's progress. Do not rely so much on successful completion of out-of-class assignments unless the student gets coached guidance by you before leaving your classroom.
- Be less concerned with the amount of content coverage than with the student's successful understanding of content that is covered.

Guidelines for working with recalcitrant learners.   For working with recalcitrant learners you can use many of the same guidelines, except that you should understand that the reasons for these students' behaviors may be quite different than for the other type of slow learners. Slower-learning students who are willing to try are simply that—slower learning. They may be slow because of their learning style or because of genetic reasons, or a combination of the two. But they can and will learn. Recalcitrant learners, on the other hand, may be quite bright but reluctant even to try because of a history of failure, a history of boredom with school, a poor self-concept, severe personal problems that distract from school, or any variety and combination of reasons, many of which are psychological in nature.

Whatever the case, you need to know that a student identified as being a slow or recalcitrant learner, might, in fact, be quite gifted or talented in some way, but who, because of personal problems, may have a history of increasingly poor school attendance and poor attention to schoolwork. Consider the following guidelines when working with recalcitrant learners:

- Make sure your classroom procedures and rules are understood at the beginning of the school year, and enforce them.
- At the beginning, learn as much about each student as you can. Be cautious in how you do it, though, because many of these students will be suspect of any genuine interest in them shown by you. Be businesslike, trusting, genuinely interested, and patient.
- Early in the school year, preferably with the help of adult volunteers (e.g., mentors), work out an individual education program (IEP) with each student.
- Help students develop their studying and learning skills, such as concentrating, remembering, and comprehension. Mnemonics, for example, is a device these students respond to positively.
- Engage the students in active learning with real-world problem solving.
- Don't try lecturing to these students; it won't work.
- When necessary, use frequent positive reinforcement, with the intention of increasing the student's sense of personal worth. When using praise for reinforcement, however, be sure to praise the deed rather than the student (see Module 5).
- If using a single textbook, be certain that the reading level is adequate; if it is not, then discard the book and use other more appropriate reading materials.
- Maximize the use of in-class, on-task work and the use of cooperative learning (Module 6), with close monitoring of the student's progress. Do not rely on successful completion of out-of-class assignments unless the student gets coached guidance by you before leaving your classroom.
- Be less concerned with the amount of content coverage than with the student's successful understanding of content that is covered.
- Use simple language in the classroom. Be concerned less about the words the students use and the way they use them and more about the ideas they are expressing. Let the students use their own idioms without carping too much on grammar and syntax. Always take care to use proper English yourself, however.
- Forget about trying to "cover the subject being taught," concentrating instead on student learning of some things well. A good procedure is to use thematic teaching and divide the theme into short segments. Because school attendance for these students is sometimes sporadic, try to individualize their assignments so that they can pick up where they left off and move through the course in an orderly fashion even when they have been absent excessively. Make sure that each student experiences learning success.

Attitude Development

In recent years there has been a resurgence in national interest in the development of students' values, especially those of honesty, kindness, respect, and responsibility. This growing interest is in what has been called "character education."[50] Whether defined as ethics, citizenship, moral values, or personal development, character education has long been part of public education in this country.[51] Today, stimulated by a perceived need to act to reduce students' antisocial behaviors (such as drug abuse and violence) and to produce more respectful and responsible citizens, many schools and districts are developing curricula in character education, with the ultimate goal of "developing mature adults capable of responsible citizenship and moral action."[52]

---

[50]Mary Massey, "Interest in Character Education Seen Growing," *ASCD Update* 35(4), 1, 4–5 (May 1993).

[51]Kenneth Burrett and Timothy Rusnak, *Integrated Character Education,* Fastback 351 (Bloomington, IN: Phi Delta Kappa Education Foundation, 1993), p. 10. See also Thomas Lickona, "The Return of Character Education," *Educational Leadership* 51(3):6–11 (November 1993).

[52]Ibid., p. 15.

Teachers can teach attitudes in two ways: (1) by providing a conducive classroom atmosphere where students actively and positively share in the decision making, and (2) by providing models that students can emulate. Acquiring knowledge and developing understanding can enhance the learning of attitudes. Nevertheless, changing an attitude is often a long and tedious process, requiring the commitment of the teacher and the provision of numerous experiences that will guide students to new convictions. These are some specific techniques:

- Use cooperative learning to increase students' abilities to work together toward common goals.
- Have students practice and develop skills in conflict resolution.
- Sensitize students to value issues through role play and creative drama.
- Have students take the opposite point of view in discussions.
- Promote higher-order thinking about value issues through appropriate questioning techniques.
- Arrange action-oriented projects that relate to curriculum themes.
- Involve students in planning and organizing the projects.
- Use parents and community members to assist in projects.
- Highlight examples of class and individual cooperation in serving the school and community.
- Make student service projects visible in the school and community.

SUMMARY

When you have obtained the knowledge and skills necessary to effectively work with students who have special needs, students of cultural, ethnic, or socioeconomic diversity, students of limited proficiency in English, students who are academically talented, and students of adolescent age, you can then effectively teach all students. For that is likely to be the situation in your first classroom.

From years of research, certain important principles of learning have evolved. As summarized from this module, five important principles are:

1. *Students construct their knowledge and develop new skills by connecting their experiences to what is being learned.* Much of this learning takes place through collaboration with others, through shared thinking and doing—that is, through authentic learning.

2. *Thinking is critically important to and inseparable from learning.* Students best acquire new knowledge, develop understanding, and develop new skills when they think about the things being learned, share that thinking with others, become aware of and analyze their own thought processes, and make connections between what is being learned in one discipline with other disciplines, with real life, and with varying cultural situations. Students must be actively and mentally engaged in their own learning and in the assessment of their learning. For greatest achievement in learning to occur, students should receive steady, understandable, and reliable feedback about their learning.

3. *Thinking and learning take time, more time for some students than for others, but all students can learn.* The construction of learning, however, takes effort; students must extend that effort. Good teaching demands effort and gets it by helping students make connections and derive meaning through reading, writing, thinking, and sharing. You should have high expectations for the accomplishments of each student, and you must not waiver from those expectations.

4. *Not all students learn and respond to learning situations in the same way.* A student may learn differently according to the situation or according to the student's ethnicity or socioeconomic status. A teacher who, for all students, uses only one style of teaching, or who teaches only one or a few styles of learning, day after day, is shortchanging those students who learn better another way. Thus, you should:

- Diagnose what students already know or think they know about a topic and help them to build their learning around that.

- Facilitate student learning by helping them see connections between disciplines and by bridging what they are learning with real-life situations.
- Vary your instructional strategies.
- Run your class in an efficient and businesslike way.
- Use techniques for small-group instruction.
- Differentiate student assignments.
- Closely monitor and guide the learning of each student.
- Use a variety of instructional materials.

5.   *Intelligence is not a fixed or static reality, but can be learned, taught, and developed.* This concept is important for students to understand, too. When students understand that intelligence is incremental—something that is developed through use over time—they are more motivated to work at learning than when they believe intelligence is a fixed entity.

You are now ready to begin learning the specifics of how to plan for instruction and to establish and maintain a safe and effective classroom environment.

SUGGESTED READING

Ascher, C. "School Programs for African-American Males . . . and Females." *Phi Delta Kappan* 73(10):777–782 (June 1992).

Banks, C. B. "Harmonizing Student-Teacher Interactions: A Case for Learning Styles." *Synthesis* 2(2):1–5 (May 1991).

Beilin, H. "Piaget's Enduring Contribution to Developmental Psychology." *Developmental Psychology* 28(2):191–204 (March 1992).

Boutte, G. S. "Frustrations of an African-American Parent: A Personal And Professional Account." *Phi Delta Kappan* 73(10):786–788 (June 1992).

Bracey, G. W. "Why Can't They Be Like We Were?" *Phi Delta Kappan* 73(2):105–117 (October 1991).

Bransford, J. D., and Vye, N. J. "A Perspective on Cognitive Research and Its Implications for Instruction." In *Toward the Thinking Curriculum: Current Cognitive Research*, edited by L. B. Resnick and L. E. Klopfer. 1989 ASCD Yearbook. Reston, VA: Association for Supervision and Curriculum Development, 1989.

Brooks, J. G., and Brooks, M. G. *In Search of Understanding: The Case for Constructivist Classrooms*. Reston, VA: Association for Supervision and Curriculum Development, 1993.

Brown, D. E. "Using Examples and Analogies to Remediate Misconceptions in Physics: Factors Influencing Conceptual Change." *Journal of Research in Science Teaching* 29)1):17–34 (January 1992).

Bruner, J. S. *Acts of Meaning*. Cambridge, MA: Harvard University Press, 1990.

Bruner, J. S. *The Process of Education*. Cambridge, MA: Harvard University Press, 1960.

Bruner, J. S. *Toward a Theory of Instruction*. Cambridge, MA: Harvard University Press, 1966.

Burrett, K., and Rusnak, T. *Integrated Character Education*, Fastback 351 (Bloomington, IN: Phi Delta Kappa Educational Foundation, 1993).

Caine, R. N., and Caine, G. *Making Connections: Teaching and the Human Brain*. Alexandria, VA: Association for Supervision and Curriculum Development, 1991.

Carns, A. W., and Carns, M. R. "Teaching Study Skills, Cognitive Strategies, and Metacognitive Skills Through Self-Diagnosed Learning Styles." *School Counselor* 38(5):341–46 (May 1991).

Cooper, J. D. *Literacy: Helping Children Construct Meaning*. 2d ed. Burlington, MA: Houghton Mifflin, 1993.

Costa, A. L. *The School as a Home for the Mind*. Palatine, IL: Skylight Publishing, 1991.

Cuevas, G. J. "Developing Communication Skills in Mathematics for Students with Limited English Proficiency," *Mathematics Teacher* 84(3):186–189 (March 1991).

Curry, L. "A Critique of the Research on Learning Styles." *Educational Leadership* 48(2):50–56 (October 1990).

Darling-Hammond, L. "Reframing the School Reform Agenda." *Phi Delta Kappan* 74(10):753–761 (June 1993).

Dreyfus, A., et al. "Applying the 'Cognitive Conflict' Strategy for Conceptual Change—Some Implications, Difficulties, and Problems." *Science Education* 74(5):555–569 (September 1990).

Eitzen, D. S. "Problem Students: The Sociocultural Roots." *Phi Delta Kappan* 73(8):584–590 (April 1992).

Ennis, C. D. "Discrete Thinking Skills in Two Teachers' Physical Education Classes." *Elementary School Journal* 91(5):473–87 (May 1991).

Ennis, C.D., et al. "The Role of Value Orientations in Curricular Decision Making: A Rationale for Teachers' Goals and Expectations." *Research Quarterly for Exercise and Sport* 63(1):38–47 (March 1992).

Ernest, P. "Constructivism, the Psychology of Learning, and the Nature of Mathematics: Some Critical Issues." *Science and Education* 2(1):87–93 (1993).

First, P.F., and Curcio, J.L. *Implementing the Disabilities Act: Implications for Educators.* Fastback 360. Bloomington, IN: Phi Delta Kappa Educational Foundation, 1993.

Fourgurean, J.M., et al. "The Link Between Learning Style and Jungian Psychological Type: A Finding of Two Bipolar Preference Dimensions." *Journal of Experimental Education* 58(3):225–237 (Spring 1990).

Fowler, C. "Recognizing the Role of Artistic Intelligence." *Music Educators Journal* 77(1):24–27 (September 1990).

Gallegos, G. "Learning Styles in Culturally Diverse Classrooms." *California Catalyst* 36–41 (Fall 1993).

Gamoran, A. "Is Ability Grouping Equitable?" *Educational Leadership* 50(2):11–17 (October 1992).

Gardner, H. *Art, Mind and Brain.* New York: Basic Books, 1982.

Gardner, H. *Frames of Mind.* New York: Basic Books, 1985.

Gardner, H. *The Unschooled Mind: How Students Think and How Schools Should Teach.* New York: Basic Books, 1991.

Gazzaniga, M. *Mind Matters: How the Mind and Brain Interact to Create Our Conscious Lives.* Boston: Houghton Mifflin, 1988.

Grady, M. P. *Whole Brain Education.* Fastback 301. Bloomington, IN: Phi Delta Kappa Educational Foundation, 1990.

Jenkins, J. M. "Learning Styles: Recognizing Individuality." *Schools in the Middle* 1(12):3–6 (Winter 1991).

Jones, B. F., and Fennimore, T. *The New Definition of Learning.* Oakbrook, IL: North Central Regional Educational Laboratory, 1990.

Keefe, J. W. "Learning Style: Where Are We Going?" *Momentum* 21(1):44–48 (February 1990).

Lazear, D. G. *Teaching for Multiple Intelligences.* Fastback 342. Bloomington, IN: Phi Delta Kappa Educational Foundation, 1992.

Leake, D., and Leake, B. "African-American Immersion Schools in Milwaukee: A View From the Inside." *Phi Delta Kappan* 73(10):783–785 (June 1992).

Lickona, T. "The Return of Character Education." *Educational Leadership* 51(3):6–11 (November 1993).

Lombardi, T. P. *Learning Strategies for Problem Learners.* Fastback 345. Bloomington, IN: Phi Delta Kappa Educational Foundation, 1992.

Louis, K. S., and Miles, M. B. *Improving the Urban High School: What Works and Why.* New York: Teachers College Press, 1990.

Novak, J. D. "How Do We Learn Our Lesson?" *The Science Teacher* 60(3):50–55 (March 1993).

Oakes, J., and Lipton, M. "Detracking Schools: Early Lessons from the Field." *Phi Delta Kappan* 73(6):448–454 (February 1992).

Okebukola, P. A., and Olugbemiro, J. J. "Cognitive Preference and Learning Mode as Determinants of Meaningful Learning through Concept Mapping." *Science Education* 72(4):489–500 (July 1988). Publishing, 1991.

Peterson, P. L., and Knapp, N. F. "Inventing and Reinventing Ideas: Constructivist Teaching and Learning in Mathematics." In *Challenges and Achievement of American Education,* edited by Gordon Cawelti. 1993 ASCD Yearbook. Alexandria, VA: Association for Supervision and Curriculum Development, 1993.

Piaget, J. *The Development of Thought: Elaboration of Cognitive Structures.* New York: Viking, 1977.

Rollins, T. J. "Analysis of Theoretical Relationships between Learning Styles of Students and Their Preferences for Learning Activities." *Journal of Agricultural Education* 31(1):64–70 (Spring 1990).

Roth, W-R., and Roychoudhury, A. "The Concept Map as a Tool for the Collaborative Construction of Knowledge." *Journal of Research in Science Teaching* 30(5):503–534 (May 1993).

Samples, B. "Using Learning Modalities to Celebrate Intelligence," *Educational Leadership* 50(2):62–66 (October 1992).

Saunders, W. L. "The Constructivist Perspective: Implications and Teaching Strategies for Science." *School Science and Mathematics* 92(3):136–141 (March 1992).

Shade, B. J. (Ed.) *Culture, Style and the Educative Process.* Springfield, IL: Charles Thomas, 1989.

Shaughnessy, M. F. "Cognitive Structures of the Gifted: Theoretical Perspectives, Factor Analysis, Triarchic Theories of Intelligence, and Insight Issues." *Gifted Education International* 6(3):149–151 (1990).

Stanley, J. C. "A Better Model for Residential High Schools for Talented Youths." *Phi Delta Kappan* 72(6):471–473 (February 1991).

Stevens, L. J., and Price, M. "Meeting the Challenge of Educating Children at Risk." *Phi Delta Kappan* 74(1):18–23 (September 1992).

Strommen, E. F., and Lincoln, B. "Constructivism, Technology, and the Future of Classroom Learning." *Education and Urban Society* 24(4):466–476 (August 1992).

Sylwester, R. "What the Biology of the Brain Tells Us about Learning." *Educational Leadership* 51(4):46–51 (December 1993/January 1994).

Titus, T. G., et al. "Adolescent Learning Styles." *Journal of Research and Development in Education* 23(3):165–171 (Spring 1990).

Vygotsky, L. *Thought and Language.* Cambridge, MA: The M.I.T. Press, 1926.

Walling, D. R. *English as a Second Language: 25 Questions and Answers.* Fastback 347. Bloomington, IN: Phi Delta Kappa Educational Foundation, 1993.

Walling, D. R. *Gay Teens at Risk.* Fastback 357. Bloomington, IN: Phi Delta Kappa Educational Foundation, 1993.

Wang, M. C.; Haertel, G. D., and Walberg, H. J. "What Helps Students Learn?" *Educational Leadership* 51(4):74–79 (December 1993/January 1994).

Watson, B. and Konicek, R. "Teaching for Conceptual Change: Confronting Student's Experience." *Phi Delta Kappan* 71(9):680–685 (May 1990).

Weinstein, C. E., et al. *Learning Styles in Secondary Schools: A Review of Instruments and Implications for Their Use.* Madison: Wisconsin Center for Education Research, 1990.

Wheelock, A. "The Case for Untracking." *Educational Leadership* 50(2):6–10 (October 1992).

Wynne, E. A., and Ryan, K. *Reclaiming Our Schools: A Handbook on Teaching Character, Academics, and Discipline* (New York: Macmillan, 1993).

Yarusso, L. "Constructivism vs. Objectivism." *Performance and Instruction* 31(4):7–9 (April 1992).

POSTTEST

Multiple Choice

_____ 1. Learning is the assimilation of new information into a body of information already stored in memory, bodies or networks of information known as
a. schemata.
b. transecents.
c. naive theories.
d. accommodations.

_____ 2. Students' conceptual misunderstandings are called
a. naive theories.
b. misconceptions.
c. incongruent schemata.
d. all of the above.

_____ 3. A constructivist view of teaching and learning
   a. emphasizes the importance of covering the subject material.
   b. is irrelevant for teaching the diversity of students in today's schools.
   c. relies less on the use of manipulatives and more on the facts of the subject matter content.
   d. emphasizes the importance of preassessing the learners' understandings about the subject matter.

_____ 4. The teacher's use of student interaction as a viable learning strategy is consistent with a learning theory that assumes the learner's development is not entirely fixed by genetics or completely controlled by external environmental factors. Such a learning strategy is consistent with the learning psychologies of
   a. Jean Piaget.
   b. Jerome Bruner.
   c. Arthur L. Costa.
   d. all of the above.

_____ 5. Asking a student to paraphrase what another has said is an important strategy for helping students to develop their skill in
   a. listening.
   b. persistence.
   c. overlapping.
   d. reflective thinking.

_____ 6. Assimilation is the mental process of
   a. forming a new schema.
   b. developing a naive theory.
   c. moving away from an egocentric outlook.
   d. fitting new information into an existing schema.

_____ 7. Regarding Piaget's three-phase learning cycle, which one of the following is *least* like the others?
   a. direct learning
   b. exploratory phase
   c. hands-on learning
   d. expository teaching

_____ 8. The planning, monitoring, and evaluation of one's own thinking is called
   a. overlapping
   b. withitness
   c. metacognition
   d. reflective listening

_____ 9. The rate of a child's intellectual development is not fixed by genetics, but is affected by the child's
   a. experiences.
   b. equilibration.
   c. social interactions.
   d. all of the above.

_____ 10. Bruner's way of knowing that is referred to as "symbolic representations," is analogous to Piaget's
   a. sensorimotor stage.
   b. preoperational stage.
   c. formal operations stage.
   d. concrete operations stage.

_____ 11. The authors of our textbook believe that your teaching style should be
   a. eclectic.
   b. student-centered.
   c. teacher-centered.
   d. curriculum-focused.

_____ 12. To promote higher-order learning it is best to
   a. insist on absolute quiet in the classroom.
   b. make the learning challenging but achievable.
   c. concentrate on right-brain learning.
   d. concentrate on direct instruction.

_____ 13. While teaching middle school children about the water cycle, the teacher has grouped the students. One group is doing an experiment to find out how many drops of water can be held on the side of a penny versus how many can be held on the side of a worn penny; another group is composing a song about the water cycle; another group is creating and drawing a poster about it; another group is reading about the water cycle in supplementary reading materials; and another group is creating a drama about the water cycle. When each group is finished, they share their group work with others in the class. This teacher is using a teaching strategy that is
   a. an example of multilevel teaching.
   b. encompasses what is known about student learning styles.
   c. based on Gardner's Theory of Multiple Intelligences.
   d. all of the above.

Short Explanation

1. Give an example of how you would use multilevel teaching in your subject field. What benefit is the use of multilevel teaching?
2. Explain why knowledge of teaching styles and student learning styles is important for a teacher in your subject field.
3. Describe the relationship among awareness, disequilibrium, and reformulation in learning.
4. Explain why integration of the curriculum is important for learning in the middle and secondary school.
5. Identify some techniques used in middle and secondary schools to integrate the learning.
6. For a concept usually taught in your subject field (your choice), demonstrate specifically how you might help students bridge their learning of that concept with what is going on in their lives and with other disciplines.
7. Could the technique of concept mapping be used as an advance organizer? Explain your answer.
8. Explain any danger inherent in the use of expository teaching.
9. Identify behaviors that you can watch for and observe in your students that demonstrate that they are behaving intelligently. Have you ever observed teachers squelching student behaviors that are intelligent? Explain.
10. Do you believe student journals should be evaluated by the teacher? Explain why or why not.
11. Do you believe that middle and secondary school teachers should be concerned about student character development? Explain why or why not. If you believe in the affirmative, explain some specific ways you would address it in your own teaching.
12. Identify and explain five important principles of learning as presented in this module. For each principle give one specific example of how you would address it while teaching your subject.
13. Colleen, a social science teacher, has a class of thirty-three eighth graders. During her lectures, teacher-led discussions, and recitation lessons, these students are restless and inattentive, creating a major classroom management problem for her. At Colleen's invitation, the school psychologist tests the children for learning modality and finds that twenty-nine of the thirty-three are predominately kinesthetic learners. Of what use is this information to Colleen?

Essay

1. Identify the topic of a lesson for middle school or secondary school students in your subject field. Describe how you would teach that lesson from a behaviorist viewpoint; then describe

how you would teach the same lesson from a constructivist viewpoint. Compare your response with the response that you gave for the same question in the posttest of the first module. How are your responses similar? How are they different?

2. Do you accept the view that learning is the product of creative inquiry through social interaction with the students as active participants in that inquiry? Explain why you agree or disagree.

3. Assume that you are a high school teacher and that your teaching schedule includes three sections of U.S. History. Furthermore, assume that students at your school are tracked (as they are, unfortunately, in many schools) and that: one of your classes is a so-called college prep class with thirty students; another is a regular education class with thirty-five students, two of whom have special needs because of physical handicaps; and the third is a sheltered English class with thirteen students, nine of whom are Hispanics with limited proficiency in English and four of whom are Southeast Asians, two with no ability to use English. Will one lesson plan using lecture and discussion as the primary instructional strategies work for all three sections? If so, explain why. If not, explain what you will have to do and why.

4. From your current observations and field work as related to this teacher preparation program, clearly identify one specific example of educational practice that seems contradictory to exemplary practice or theory as presented in this module. Present your explanation for the discrepancy.

5. Describe any prior concepts you held that changed as a result of your experiences with this module. Describe the changes.

Part II

PLANNING FOR INSTRUCTION

After several years of intensive work on these matters, the improvements in students' higher mental process learning and achievement became very pronounced. These and other approaches made it clear that most students could learn the higher mental processes if they became more central in the teacher-learning process.
— Benjamin Bloom

There is probably only one person's behavior we have the power to control, train, and modify: our own!
— Art Costa

Progressing from one cover of the textbook to the other during one school term is not necessarily indicative of good teaching.
— Callahan, Clark, and Kellough

On the clarity of your ideas depends the scope of your success in any endeavor.
— Horace Greeley

Part II, consisting of three modules, assists with your understanding of the:

- Reasons for thoughtfully and thoroughly planning for effective instruction.
- Levels of planning.
- Components of a complete instructional plan.
- Documents available as resources for the selection of content.
- Value and limitations of student textbooks.
- Guidelines for using the student textbook.
- Procedures for preparing a course content sequence.
- Types of instructional objectives.
- Process of preparing instructional objectives.
- Types of unit and lesson plan formats.
- How to prepare an effective teaching unit.
- Place and role of each of the four decision-making and thought-processing phases in unit planning and lesson plan implementation.

- Guidelines for planning and implementing an efficient and effective classroom management system.
- Guidelines for dealing with inappropriate student behaviors.
- Guidelines for planning and establishing a supportive classroom environment.
- Techniques for getting to know your students as people.
- The importance of providing positive modeling behaviors.
- The concept of classroom control.
- Guidelines for planning and establishing procedures and rules for appropriate behavior.

Module 3

Selecting Content and Preparing Objectives

RATIONALE

Planning the instruction constitutes a large part of a teacher's job. The teacher is responsible for planning at three levels: (1) courses for a semester or academic year, (2) units of instruction, and (3) lessons. Throughout your career, you will be engaged almost continually in planning at each of these three levels. Planning for instruction is a steady and cyclic process that involves the preactive and reflective thought-processing phases (discussed in Module 1). The importance of mastering the process at the very beginning of your career cannot be overemphasized.

We begin this module by emphasizing the importance of planning. Then we take you through the process of selecting content for a course and preparing the specific learning outcomes expected as students learn that content. From that content outline, and the related and specific learning outcomes, a teacher prepares units and daily lessons (discussed in Module 4). Let us begin the discussion by clarifying a few relevant terms.

A **course** can be defined as a complete sequence of instruction that presents a major division of a subject matter or discipline. Courses are laid out for a year, a semester, a quarter, or, in the case of minicourses, a few weeks (minicourses are common to the exploratory programs found in some exemplary middle schools). Each course is composed of units. A **unit** is a major subdivision of a course, comprising planned instruction about some central theme, topic, issue, or problem for a period of several days to several weeks. Units that take much longer than three weeks (with the exception of interdisciplinary units) tend to lose their effectiveness as recognizable units of instruction. Each unit is composed of lessons. A **lesson** is a subdivision of a unit, usually taught in a single class period or, on occasion, for two or three successive periods.

Although planning is a critical skill for a teacher, a well-developed plan will not guarantee the success of a lesson or unit or even the overall effectiveness of a course. But the lack of a well-developed plan will almost certainly result in poor teaching. Like a good map, a good plan helps you reach your destination with more confidence and with fewer wrong turns.

The heart of good planning is decision making. For every plan, you must decide what your goals and objectives are, what specific subject matter should be taught, what materials of instruction are available and appropriate, and what methods and techniques should be employed to accomplish the objectives. Making these decisions can be complicated because there are so many choices. Therefore, you must be knowledgeable about the principles that undergird effective course, unit, and lesson planning. That the principles of all levels of educational planning are much the same makes mastering the necessary skills easier than you might think.

SPECIFIC OBJECTIVES

At the completion of this module, you should be able to:

1. Explain the relationship of planning to the preactive and reflective thought-processing phases of instruction.
2. Identify at least eight reasons a teacher should plan the instruction thoughtfully and thoroughly.
3. Identify the eight components of a complete instructional plan.
4. Explain the value of various types of documents that can be helpful in instructional planning.
5. Explain the scope and status of national curriculum standards for your subject field.
6. Explain the value and limitations of student textbooks for your subject field.
7. Identify multicultural components that should be present in any instructional planning.
8. Identify the value of cooperative and collaborative planning.
9. Demonstrate an ability to plan the long-range sequence of content for teaching in your subject field.

10. Explain the difference between resource units and teaching units.
11. Describe the basic components of the daily lesson plan and their functions.
12. Construct a standard teaching unit complete with daily lessons.

MODULE TEXT

Reasons for Planning Thoughtfully and Thoroughly

Thoughtful and thorough planning is vital for effective teaching to occur. Such planning helps produce well-organized classes and a purposeful classroom atmosphere and reduces the likelihood of problems in classroom control. A teacher who has not planned or who has underprepared will have more problems than imaginable. While planning, a teacher should keep in mind these two important goals: (1) not to waste anyone's time and (2) to select strategies that keep students physically and mentally on task and that ensure student learning.

Careful planning has several other benefits as well. Planning well helps guarantee that you know the subject, for in planning you will more likely become master of the material and the methods to teach it. No one can know everything about a subject matter, but careful planning can save you from fumbling through half-digested, poorly understood content, making errors along the way. Thoughtful planning is likely to make your classes more lively, more interesting, more accurate, and more relevant, and thus make your teaching more successful.

Another important reason for careful planning is to ensure program coherence. Periodic lesson plans constitute an integral part of a larger plan, represented by course goals and objectives. The students' learning experiences should be thoughtfully planned in sequence and then orchestrated by a teacher who understands the rationale for their respective positions in the curriculum—not precluding, of course, an occasional diversion from planned activities.

Unless your course stands alone, following nothing and leading to nothing (which is unlikely), there are prerequisites to what you want your students to learn, and there are learning objectives to follow that build upon this learning. Good planning addresses both the scope (breadth and depth of the content coverage) and the sequence of the content.

Another important reason for careful planning is that the diversity of students in today's schools demands that the teacher consider those individual differences—such as diverse cultural experiences, different learning styles, and various levels of proficiency in the use of English. Still another reason for planning is to ensure program continuation. In case a substitute teacher is needed or other members of the teaching team must fill in, the program continues without you.

Careful and thoughtful planning is important for teacher self-assessment. After an activity, a lesson, or a unit, as well as at the end of a semester and the school year, you will assess what was done and the effect it had on student achievement (the reflective phase of instruction, discussed in Module 1).

Finally, administrators expect you to plan well. Your plans represent a criterion recognized and evaluated by administrators—the experienced know that inadequate attention to planning is usually a precursor to incompetent teaching.

Components of Instructional Planning

Eight components should be evident in a complete instructional plan:

1. *Statement of philosophy*. This is a general statement about why the plan is important and how students will learn its content.
2. *Needs assessment*. The wording of the statement of philosophy should demonstrate an appreciation for the cultural diversity of the nation and of the school, with a corresponding perception of the needs of society, of the learners, and of the functions served by the school.

The statement of philosophy and needs assessment should be consistent with the school's mission or philosophy statement. (Every school or school district has such a statement, usually posted in the office and in several classrooms.)

3. *Aims, goals, and objectives*. The plan's stated aims, goals, and objectives should be consistent with the school's mission or philosophy statement.

4. *Sequence*. The sequence of a plan refers to its relationship to the preceding and subsequent curricula. A presentation of the sequence, or the vertical articulation, shows the plan's relationship to the learning that preceded and the learning that follows, from kindergarten through twelfth grade (in some instances, to the learning that follows high school graduation).

5. *Integration*. The integration component concerns the plan's connection with other curriculum and co-curriculum activities across the grade level. For example, the language arts curriculum at a middle school may be closely integrated with that school's social studies curriculum; or, at a high school, the curriculum of the courses that juniors take in history may be integrated with courses taken in English. The integration component is also referred to as the horizontal articulation of a plan. The activity "writing across the curriculum," used in many schools, is an example of integration across grade level.

6. *Sequentially planned learning activities*. This is the presentation of the organized and sequential units and lessons, which must be appropriate for the subject and grade level and for the age and diversity of the students.

7. *Resources needed*. This is a listing of resources, such as books, speakers, field trip, and audio-visual materials.

8. *Assessment strategies*. These strategies, which must be consistent with the objectives, include procedures for diagnosing what students know or think they know prior to the instruction (preassessment) as well as the evaluation of student achievement during (formative assessment) and at completion of the instruction (summative assessment).

Planning a Course

When planning a course, you must decide exactly what is to be accomplished in that time period for which students take the course, whether for an academic year, a semester, or some lesser time period. To do this, you should:

- Probe, analyze, and translate your own convictions, knowledge, and skills into behaviors that foster the intellectual development of your students.
- Review school and other public documents for mandates and guidelines.
- Talk with colleagues and learn of common expectations.

Documents That Provide Guidance for Content Selection

Curriculum publications of your state department of education, district courses of study, and school-adopted printed and nonprinted materials are all valuable sources you will use in planning the school year. Your college or university library may have some of these documents. Others may be obtained from cooperating teachers in your local schools. Many of these documents are generated through the process of state accreditation.

To receive accreditation (which normally occurs every three to six years), a high school is reviewed by an accreditation team. Prior to the team's visit, the school prepares self-study reports, for which each department reviews and updates the curriculum guides that provide information about the objectives and content of each course and program offered. In some states, middle schools and junior high schools also are accredited by state or regional agencies. In other states, those schools can volunteer to be reviewed for improvement. The accreditation process, which can be expensive, is paid for with school or district funds.

National Curriculum Standards

Until recently, national curriculum standards did not exist in the United States. The National Council on Education Standards and Testing has recommended that national standards for subject content in education be developed for all core subjects—the arts, civics/social studies, English/language arts/reading, foreign languages, geography, history, mathematics, physical education, and science. Such standards provide specifics about what students should know and be able to do. For the subjects and grade level of interest to you, you will want to follow the development of national curriculum standards. For example, in 1989 the National Council of Teachers of Mathematics (NCTM) issued standards for mathematics for grades K through 12. By 1992, more than forty states, usually through state curriculum frameworks, were following those standards to guide what and how mathematics is taught as well as how student progress is assessed.[1] At the time of preparation of this book, other projects are in various states of development. Those projects (with addresses for additional information) include:

1. *Arts*. With a grant from the U.S. Department of Education, standards for visual and performing arts are being developed jointly by the American Alliance for Theater and Education, the National Art Education Association, the National Dance Association, and the Music Educators National Conference. Standards for the arts were completed in 1994. For information, contact John Mahlmann, Music Educators National Conference (MENC), 1902 Association Drive, Reston, VA 22091.[2]
2. *Civics/social studies*. With grants from the U.S. Department of Education and the Pew Charitable Trust, the Center for Civic Education and the National Center for Social Studies are in the process of developing standards for civics and for social studies. Standards for social studies were expected by 1994. For information, contact the National Council for the Social Studies (NCSS), 3501 Newark St., NW, Washington, DC 20016. Standards for civics, which focus on the values and principles of the U.S. Constitution, were expected to be completed in 1994. For information, contact Charles Quiqley, Center for Civic Education, 5146 Douglas Fir Road, Calabasas, CA 91302.
3. *English/language arts/reading*. Standards for English are being developed jointly by the International Reading Association, the National Council of Teachers of English, and the University of Illinois Center for the Study of Reading. These standards were expected to be completed by 1995. For information, contact Jean Osborn, the Center for the Study of Reading, 174 Children's Research Center, 51 Gerty Drive, Champaign, IL 61820.
4. *Foreign languages*. The American Council on the Teaching of Foreign Languages (ACTFL) is developing outlines for three levels of language proficiency based on the number of years a language is taken. For information, contact ACTFL, Six Executive Plaza, Yonkers, NY 10701.
5. *Geography*. With a grant from the U.S. Department of Education, the Association of American Geographers, the National Council for Geographic Education, and the National Geographic Society are developing standards for geography education. Geography standards were expected to be completed in 1994. For information, contact Anthony de Souza, Geography Standards Project, 1600 M St., NW, Washington, DC 20036.
6. *History*. The U.S. Department of Education and the National Endowment for the Humanities provided funding to the National Center for History in the Schools to develop standards for history education, expected to be completed in 1994. For information, contact Charlotte Crabtree, National Center for History in the Schools at UCLA, 231 Moore Hall, 405 Hilgard Ave., Los Angeles, CA 90024.
7. *Mathematics*. To order *Curriculum and Evaluation Standards for School Mathematics* (item number 398E1; ISBN 0-87353-273-2; cost, $25), write to the National Council of Teachers of Mathematics, Order Processing, 1906 Association Drive, Reston, VA 22091.
8. *Physical Education*. For a definition of the characteristics of physically educated students, as well as the desirable outcomes of a physical education program, see *Outcomes of Quality Physical*

---

[1] For an account of an alternative mathematics program (K–12)—that is, one that does *not* follow NCTM guidelines—see David Hill, "Math's Angry Man," *Teacher Magazine* 5(1):24–28 (September 1993). See also three informative articles on mathematics education in the February, 1994, issue of *Phi Delta Kappan* 75 (6).

[2] See also the several informative articles in the "arts in education" theme issue of *Phi Delta Kappan* 75 (6) (February 1994).

Education Programs, published in 1992 by the National Association of Sports and Physical Education (NASPE). For information, contact NASPE, 1900 Association Drive, Reston, VA 22091.

9. *Science*. With a grant from the U.S. Department of Education, the National Research Council's National Committee on Science Education Standards and Assessment (with input from the American Association for the Advancement of Science and the National Science Teachers Association) is developing standards for science education. Science standards were expected to be completed in 1994. For information, contact Ken Hoffman, National Academy of Sciences, National Research Council, 2101 Constitution Avenue, NW, Washington, DC 20418.

Once the new standards have been completed (as with the mathematics standards), they will be used by state and local school districts for the revision of their curriculum documents. Guided by these standards and the content of state frameworks—especially those of the larger states such as California, Florida, and Texas—publishers of student textbooks and other instructional materials will develop their new or revised printed and nonprinted instructional materials. By the year 2000, these new standards will likely be in place in a way to be having a positive effect upon student achievement in classroom learning.

Proceed now to Exercises 3.1, 3.2, and 3.3, through which you will explore both local curriculum documents and national standards.

EXERCISE 3.1
Examining State Curriculum Documents

• • • • • •

Instructions: The purpose of this exercise is to become familiar with curriculum documents published by your state department of education. You must determine if that department publishes a curriculum framework for various subjects taught in schools. State frameworks provide valuable information about both content and process, and teachers need to be aware of these documents.* You may want to duplicate this form so you can use it to evaluate several documents. After examining documents that interest you, use the following questions as a guideline for small or large group class discussion.

1. Are there state curriculum documents available to teachers for your state? If so, describe them, and explain how they can be obtained.

Title of document:

Source:

Most recent year of publication:

Other pertinent information:

2. Examine how closely the document follows the eight components presented in this module. Are any components omitted? Are there additional components? Specifically, check for these components:

	Yes	No
2.1. Statement of philosophy?	_____	_____
2.2. Evidence of a needs assessment?	_____	_____
2.3. Aims, goals, and objectives?	_____	_____
2.4. Schemes for vertical articulation?	_____	_____
2.5. Schemes for horizontal articulation?	_____	_____
2.6. Recommended instructional procedures?	_____	_____
2.7. Recommended resources?	_____	_____
2.8. Assessment strategies?	_____	_____

Other:

3. Are the documents specific as to subject-matter content for each grade level? Describe evidence of both vertical and horizontal articulation schemes.

*For example, for the state of California there are frameworks for English, foreign language, health instruction, mathematics, physical education, reading, science, social science, and visual and performing arts.

4. Do the documents offer specific strategies for instruction? If yes, describe.

5. Do the documents offer suggestions and resources for working with students who are culturally different, for students with special needs, and for students who are intellectually gifted and talented? Describe.

6. Do the documents offer suggestions or guidelines for dealing with controversial topics? If so, describe.

7. Do the documents distinguish between what shall be taught (mandated) and what can be taught (permissible)?

8. Do the documents offer suggestions for specific resources?

9. Do the documents refer to assessment strategies? Describe.

10. Anything else about the documents you would like to discuss in your group?

EXERCISE 3.2
Examining Local Curriculum Documents

• • • • • •

Instructions: The purpose of this exercise is to become familiar with curriculum documents prepared by local school districts. A primary resource for what to teach is referred to as a *curriculum guide*, or *course of study*, which normally is developed by teachers of a school or district. Samples may be available in your university library or in a local school district resource center. Or perhaps you could borrow them from teachers you visit. Obtain samples from a variety of sources and then examine them using the format of this exercise (you may duplicate this form for each document examined). An analysis of several documents will give you a good picture of expectations. If possible, compare documents from several schools districts, and states.

Title of document:

District or school:

Date of document:

1. Examine how closely the documents follow the eight components. Does the document contain the following components?

	Yes	*No*
1.1. Statement of philosophy?	———	———
1.2. Evidence of a needs assessment?	———	———
1.3. Aims, goals, and objectives?	———	———
1.4. Schemes for vertical articulation?	———	———
1.5. Schemes for horizontal articulation?	———	———
1.6. Recommended instructional procedures?	———	———
1.7. Recommended resources?	———	———
1.8. Assessment strategies?	———	———

2. Does the document list expected learning outcomes? If so, describe what they are.

3. Does the document contain detailed unit plans? If so, describe them by answering the following questions:
   3.1. Do they contain initiating activities (how to begin a unit)?
   3.2. Do they containing specific learning activities?
   3.3. Do they contain suggested enrichment activities (as for gifted and talented students)?
   3.4. Do they contain culminating activities (activities that bring a unit to a climax)?

3.5. Do they contain assessment procedures (for determining student achievement)?

3.6. Do they contain activities for learners with special needs? or for learners who are different in other respects?

4. Does it provide bibliographic entries for:

- The teacher?

- The students?

5. Does it list audiovisual and other materials needed?

6. Does the document clearly help you understand what the teacher is expected to teach?

7. Are there questions not answered by your examination of this document? If so, list them for class discussion.

Examining National Curriculum Standards

• • • • • •

Instructions: The purpose of this exercise is to become familiar with the status of national curriculum standards being developed for your subject field. Use the addresses of sources provided in the section on national curriculum standards as well as other sources, such as professional journals and the suggested readings at the end of this module. Discover the status of the development of standards and their implementation in your teaching field. The questions in this exercise should serve as a guideline for small- or large-group class discussions within your subject field. Following subject-area group discussion, share the developments in your field with the rest of the class.

Subject area:

1. Status of the national curriculum standards:

2. Standards developed by:

3. Specific goals as specified by the new standards:

4. Are the standards specific as to subject-matter content for each grade level? Explain.

5. Do the standards offer specific strategies for instruction? Describe.

6. Do the standards offer suggestions for teaching students who are culturally and intellectually different as well as students with special needs? Describe.

7. Do the standards offer suggestions or guidelines for dealing with controversial topics? Describe.

8. Do the standards offer suggestions for specific resources? Describe.

9. Do the standards refer to assessment? Describe.

10. In summary, compared with the traditional content and teaching methods in this field, what is new with the standards?

11. Anything else about the standards you would like to discuss in your group?

Student Textbooks

Traditionally, class time for many students has largely been devoted to use of the textbook and other printed materials. Often a gap exists between what is needed in textbooks and what is available for student use. As you may have discovered, considerable national attention has lately been given to finding ways of improving the quality of student textbooks, with particular attention to the need for developing student skills in critical thinking.

For several reasons—the recognition of different individual learning styles of students, the increasing costs of textbooks and a decreasing availability of funds, and the availability of non-printed learning materials—textbook appearance, content, and use has changed considerably in recent years. Still, "ninety percent of all classroom activity is regulated by textbooks."[3]

School districts have textbook adoption cycles, usually every five or so years; the books purchased are then used for several years, until the next adoption cycle. For you, if you are a student teacher or a first-year teacher, this means that most likely someone will say, "Here are the textbooks you will be using." Starting now, you should become familiar with the textbooks you may be using, as well as how you may be using them.

How a Textbook Can Be Helpful to Students

How can textbooks be of help? Textbooks can help students in their learning by providing:

- A base for building higher-order thinking activities (e.g., inquiry discussions and student research) that help develop critical thinking skills.
- A basis for selecting subject matter that can be used for deciding content emphasis.
- An organization of basic or important content for the students.
- Information about other readings and resources that could enhance the learning experiences of students.
- Previously tested activities and suggestions for learning experiences.

Problems with Reliance on a Single Textbook

The student textbook, despite its value, should never become the "be all and end all" of the instructional experience. The textbook is only one of many teaching tools and should not be cherished as the ultimate word. Of the many methods by which teachers use student textbooks, perhaps the least acceptable is to depend completely on a single book, requiring students simply to memorize content from it. That is the lowest level of learning; furthermore, complete dependence on a textbook implies that the teacher is unaware of other significant printed and nonprinted instructional materials and has nothing more to contribute to student learning.

Another problem can occur by reliance upon a single textbook. Textbook publishers prepare books for use in large markets, that is, for national or statewide use.[4] The textbook adopted by your state or district may not, in the minds of some members of your school community, adequately address issues of special interest and importance to your community of children and their parents or guardians. For that reason, some teachers and schools, as well as many textbook publishers, provide supplementary printed and nonprinted instructional materials.

Another important reason to provide supplementary reading materials is to ensure multicultural balance. A single textbook may not provide the balance needed to make sure traditional cultural and ethnic biases are not continued. Such biases, which we want to correct in our schools and in our teaching, include (1) a linguistic bias caused by the overuse of masculine terms and pronouns, (2) the use of gender and ethnic stereotypes, (3) the relative invisibility of

---

[3]J. Starr, "The Great Textbook War," in *Education and the American Dream: Conservatives, Liberals and Radicals Debate the Future of Education* edited by H. Holtz, I. Marcus, J. Dougherty, J. Michaels, and R. Peduzzi (Grandy, MA: Bergin and Garvey, 1989), p. 106.

[4]At least twenty-four states use statewide textbook adoption review committees to review books and then provide public school districts with lists of recommended books, from which a district may select its books and purchase them with funds provided by the state.

women, minorities, and disabled persons on printed pages, and (4) the imbalance created by glossing over controversial topics, such as avoiding discussions of discrimination and prejudice.[5]

Still another problem brought about by reliance upon a single source is that for many students the adopted textbook may just not be at the appropriate reading level. In today's heterogeneous classrooms (containing students with mixed abilities), the reading range can vary by as much as two-thirds of the chronological age of the students in the classroom. That means that if the chronological age is fifteen years (typical for tenth-grade students) then the reading-level range would be ten years; that is, the class may have some students reading only at the fifth-grade level and other students reading at the college level. That is a reason why many teacher education programs today require a course in teaching reading for all secondary school credential candidates: teachers in most fields and grade levels necessarily must devote time to helping students develop their reading skills. All teachers need to know about the kinds of problem readers, and all share in the responsibility of seeing that those students get help in reading.

General Guidelines for Textbook Use

Using a textbook as a learning tool may not be as straightforward as you think. Consider the following general guidelines for the use of a textbook in the classroom:

1. Provide students with their own copies of a textbook whenever possible. For most courses in middle and secondary schools, students can benefit from having their own copy, especially when the textbook is the current edition. Because of a school's budget constraints, however, the textbook may not be the latest edition. In some schools there may be only classroom sets, which students are allowed to use only while in the classroom. In such cases, students may not be allowed to take the books home or can only occasionally check them out. In other classrooms there may be no textbook at all.

2. Maintain supplementary reading materials for students to use in the classroom. School and community librarians usually are delighted to cooperate with teachers in the selection and provision of such materials.

3. Supplement the textbook with materials provided by modern technology. Some students benefit from drill, practice, and reinforcement afforded by accompanying workbooks, but this does not mean that all students necessarily benefit from such work, nor do all benefit from doing the same activity. In fact, the traditional workbook, now nearly extinct for use in many courses taught in middle and secondary schools, is being replaced by computer software, videodiscs, compact discs, and other materials provided by modern technology. As the cost of hardware and software become more realistic for schools, the use of programs by individual students is also becoming more common. Computers provide students with a psychologically safe learning environment. With computer programs and interactive media, the student has greater control over the pace of the instruction, can repeat instruction if necessary, and can ask for further clarification, without the fear of having to publicly ask for help or admit that help is needed.

4. Provide vocabulary lists to help students learn meanings of important words and phrases.

5. Teach students how to study from a textbook, perhaps by using the **SQ4R** method: *s*urvey the chapter, ask *q*uestions about what was read, *r*ead to answer the questions, *r*ecite the answers, *r*ecord important items from the chapter into their notebooks, and then *r*eview it all. Or, you could use the **SQ3R** method—*s*urvey the chapter, ask *q*uestions about what was read, and then *r*ead, *r*ecite, and *r*eview.

6. Encourage students to search other sources for information that will update that found in the textbook, especially when the textbook is several years old. This task is especially important in certain disciplines, such as science, where there is such a tremendous growth in the amount of new information, or geography, where there have been so many recent developments. And other sources are also important whenever a multicultural balance is needed.

[5]Myra Sadker, David Sadker, and Lynette Long, "Gender and Educational Equality," in Chapter 6 of *Multicultural Education: Issues and Perspectives*, edited by J. A. Banks and C. A. McGee Banks (Boston: Allyn and Bacon, 1989), p. 107–108. See the other excellent chapters in this book for ideas and resources on bringing multicultural balance to your curriculum.

7. Encourage students to be alert for errors in the textbook, including content errors, printing errors, and discrepancies or imbalances in the treatment of minorities, women, and persons with special needs. Perhaps you could give students some sort of credit reward, such as points, when they bring an error to your attention. Encouraging students to be alert for errors in the textbook encourages critical reading, critical thinking, and healthy skepticism.

8. Progressing from one cover of the textbook to the other during one school term is not necessarily an indicator of good teaching. The emphasis in instruction should be on mastery of content rather than simply on coverage of content. The textbook is only one resource among many; to enhance learning, students should be encouraged to use a variety of resources.

9. Individualize the learning for students according to their reading and learning abilities. Consider differentiated reading and workbook assignments, in the textbook and in supplementary materials. When using supplementary materials, consider using several rather than just one. For today's typical classroom, with its diversity of students, there is no advantage in having all students working out of the same workbook and doing the same workbook exercises (except for making life a bit easier for the teacher). When students use workbooks not designed to accompany their text, you should cut and edit the exercises so they relate well to your course.

10. Encourage students to respect their books, by covering and protecting them and by not making permanent marks in them. In many schools at the end of the term students who have damaged or lost their books are charged a fee. In some schools, students have a choice of purchasing their books, and in that case they are usually free to mark in the books any way they want.

The Future for School Textbooks

Within the span of your professional career, you likely will take part in a revolution of the design of school textbooks. Already some school districts and states allow teachers in certain disciplines (where the technology is available) to choose between traditional student textbooks and interactive videodisc programs.[6]

One prediction is that with the revolution in microcomputer-chip technology, student textbooks may soon take on a whole new appearance. That will produce dramatic changes in the importance and use of student texts, as well as new problems for the teacher, some of which are predictable. Student "texts" may become credit-card size, increasing the chance of students' "losing" their books. On the positive side, the classroom teacher will probably have available a variety of "textbooks" to better address the variety of reading levels, interests, learning styles, and abilities of individual students. Distribution and maintenance of reading materials could create an even greater demand on the teacher's time. Regardless, dramatic and exciting changes have begun to occur in a teaching tool that previously had not changed much throughout the history of education in the United States. As an electronic, multimedia tool, the textbook of the twenty-first century may be "an interactive device that offers text, sound, and video."[7]

Proceed now to Exercise 3.4, through which you examine student textbooks and accompanying teacher's editions.

[6]For example, for elementary school science the state of Texas allows its schools to adopt Optical Data's *Windows on Science* videodisc-based program. The program comes with a Curriculum Publishing Kit that allows teachers to design their own curriculum from the *Windows on Science* program, and users periodically receive updated discs. Texas, Utah, and West Virginia were the first states, for specific curriculum areas, to allow schools to choose between a textbook-centered program and one that is videodisc-centered. By the time you read this, other states have probably instituted similar policies.

[7]Bernard R. Gifford, "The Textbook of the 21st Century," *Syllabus*, no. 19 (October/November 1991), p. 15–16. See also Elizabeth Greenfield, "Evolution of the Textbook: From Print to Multimedia," *T. H. E. Journal* 20(10):12, 14, 16, and 19 (May 1993).

Instructions: The purpose of this exercise is to become familiar with textbooks that you may be using in your teaching. Student textbooks are usually accompanied by a teacher's edition that contains specific objectives, teaching techniques, learning activities, assessment instruments, test items, and suggested resources. Your university library, local schools, and cooperating teachers are sources for locating and borrowing these enhanced textbooks. For your subject field of interest, select a textbook that is accompanied by a teacher's edition and examine the contents of both using the following format. If there are no standard textbooks available for your teaching field (such as might be the case for art, home economics, industrial arts, music, and physical education), then select a field for which there is a possibility you might teach. Beginning teachers are often assigned to teach in more than one field—sometimes, unfortunately, in fields for which they are untrained or have only minimal training. After completion of this exercise, share the book and your analysis of it with your colleagues.

Title of book:

Author(s):

Publisher:

Date of most-recent publication:

1. Analyze the teacher's edition for the following elements.

		Yes	No
a.	Are its goals consistent with the goals of local and state curriculum documents?	_____	_____
b.	Are there specific objectives for each lesson?	_____	_____
c.	Does the book have scope and sequence charts for teacher reference?	_____	_____
d.	Are the units and lessons sequentially developed with suggested time allotments?	_____	_____
e.	Are there any suggested provisions for individual differences?	_____	_____
	for reading levels?	_____	_____
	for students with special needs?	_____	_____
	for students who are gifted and talented?	_____	_____
	for students who have limited proficiency in English?	_____	_____
f.	Does it recommend specific techniques and strategies?	_____	_____
g.	Does it have listings of suggested aids, materials, and resources?	_____	_____
h.	Are there suggestions for extension activities (to extend the lessons beyond the usual topic or time)?	_____	_____
i.	Does the book have specific guidelines for assessment of student learning?	_____	_____

2. Analyze the student textbook for the following elements.

    a.   Does it treat the content with adequate depth?   _____ _____

    b.   Does it treat ethnic minorities and women fairly?*   _____ _____

    c.   Is the format attractive?   _____ _____

    d.   Does the book have good quality binding with suitable type size?   _____ _____

    e.   Are illustrations and visuals attractive and useful?   _____ _____

    f.   Is the reading clear and understandable for the students?   _____ _____

3. Would you like to use this textbook? Give reasons why or why not.

---

*For a detailed procedure that is more specific to subject areas, see Carl A. Grant and Cristine E. Sleeter, *Turning on Learning: Five Approaches for Multicultural Teaching Plans for Race, Class, Gender, and Disability* (New York: Macmillan, 1989), pp. 104–109.

Students and the Textbook Reading Level

A frequent concern of many teachers is with the reading level of their students. How can a teacher select books that are neither too easy nor too difficult for their students to read? To determine a textbook's reading level you can use any of several techniques, such as the Cloze procedure, the Fry readability formula, or the Forecast readability formula.[8] Since these techniques give only the technical reading level of a book, you have to interpret the results by subjectively estimating the book's conceptual reading level. To do so, the teacher must consider the students' experience in light of the content, the number of new ideas introduced, and the level of the abstraction of the ideas.

As a teacher, you could conduct your own silent and informal reading inventory. First, have students read four or five pages of the text; then give them a ten-item quiz on what was read. You should consider that the text is too difficult for any student who scores less than 70 percent on the quiz. Another way you can conduct an informal reading inventory is by having a student read aloud a 100-word passage. The text may be too difficult if the student stumbles over or misses more than 5 percent of the words.[9]

Cooperative Planning

As noted, the textbook is only one resource for determining content to be studied. Your students and teaching colleagues are resources, too. Much of your instructional planning will be done by you, alone. But many secondary and middle school teachers also do a considerable amount of shared planning in instructional teams, at either the department level and between departments, and involve their students in phases of the planning as well.

Team Planning

In some schools, teachers plan together in teams (as discussed in Module 1). Planning procedures are much the same as recommended previously in this module, the difference being that the team members might split the planning responsibilities. Coming back together to share their individual planning, the team members work cooperatively to develop a final plan.

Teacher-Student Collaboration in Planning

Many teachers today encourage students to participate in the planning of some phase of the learning activities, units, and courses. Such participation tends to give students a proprietary interest in the activities, thereby increasing their motivation. What students have contributed to the plan often seems more relevant to them than what others have planned for them. And students like to see their own plans succeed. Thus, teacher-student collaboration in planning can be a very effective motivational tool.[10]

Preparing for the Year

You have reviewed the rationale and the components for instructional planning and examined state and local curriculum documents, and student reading materials. While doing so you undoubtedly have reflected on your own biases regarding content you believe should be included in a subject at a particular grade level. Now it is time to obtain practical experience in long-range planning.

[8]See J. Bormuth, "The Cloze Readability Procedure," *Elementary English* 45:429–436 (April 1968); Edward Fry, "A Readability Formula That Saves Time," *Journal of Reading* 11:587 (April 1968); and Novella M. Ross, "Assessing Readability of Instructional Materials," *VocEd* 54:10–11 (February 1979), respectively, for an explanation of the three techniques.

[9]See M. S. Johnson and R. A. Kress, *Informal Reading Inventories* (Newark, DE: International Reading Association, 1965).

[10]For a report of a study of a seventh-grade class in which students designed their own course of study for an integrated unit, see J. Lea Smith and Holly A. Johnson, "Control in the Classroom: Listening to Adolescent Voices," *Language Arts* 70(1):18–30 (June 1993). For a report about the use of a "student-negotiated curriculum," with eleventh-grade students in an integrated social studies and English block course, see Katy Smith, "Becoming the 'Guide on the Side,'" *Educational Leadership* 51(2):35–37 (October 1993).

Some authors believe that writing objectives should be the first step in preparing to teach. It is our contention that a more logical first step is to prepare a sequential topic outline. From that outline, you then write the instructional objectives—the final focus of this module. Once you have decided the content and objectives, you are ready to create the subdivisions known as units of instruction and then prepare those units with their daily lessons (the topics of Module 4).

For most beginning teachers, topic outlines and instructional objectives are presented in the course of study or the teacher's edition of the student textbook, with the expectation that these will be used in teaching. Yet someone had to have written those outlines and objectives, and that someone was one or several teachers. As a teacher candidate, you should know how it is done, for someday you will be concentrating on it in earnest.

The next step, then, is for you to experience preparing a year-long (or, in some instances, a semester-long) content outline for a subject and grade level that you intend to teach. Please be cautioned that beginning teachers often have unrealistic expectations about the amount of content that middle and secondary students can study, comprehend, and learn over a given period of time. These teachers often fail to consider that learning by those students is influenced by special needs and diverse cultural and language backgrounds. Reviewing school and other public documents and talking with experienced teachers in your local schools can be very helpful in developing a realistic selection and sequencing of content, as well as the time frame for teaching that content. Keeping that caution in mind, now work on preparing a content outline by doing Exercise 3.5.

EXERCISE 3.5
Preparing a Content Outline

• • • • • •

Instructions: The purpose of this exercise is for you to organize your ideas about subject content and the sequencing of content. Unless instructed otherwise by your instructor, you should select the subject (e.g., algebra I, biology, English, U.S. history) and the grade level (7–12).

With *three levels of headings*, prepare a sequential topic outline (on a separate piece of paper) for a subject and grade level you intend to teach. Identify the subject by title, and clearly state the grade level. This outline is of topic content only, and does *not* need to include student activities associated with the learning of that content (i.e., do not include experiments, assignments, or assessment strategies).

Share your completed outline to obtain feedback from your colleagues and university instructor. Because content outlines are never to be "carved into stone," make adjustments to your outline when and as appropriate.

Here are some content outline evaluation guidelines:

• Does the outline follow a logical sequence, with each topic logically leading to the next?
• Does the content assume prerequisite knowledge or skills that the students are likely to have?
• Is the content inclusive, and to an appropriate depth?
• Does the content contain relevant multicultural components?
• Are there serious content omissions?
• Is there content that is of questionable value for this level of instruction?

Now that you have analyzed various curriculum documents and you have prepared a content outline (Exercise 3.5), you are ready to write specific instructional objectives, known also as **behavioral** or **performance objectives**.[11] Behavioral objectives are statements that describe what the student will be able to do upon completion of the instructional experience.

Aims, Goals, and Objectives

As a teacher, you will often encounter this compound: *goals and objectives*. A distinction needs to be understood. The easiest way to understand the difference between the two words *goals* and *objectives* is to look at your intent.

Goals are ideas that you intend to reach—that is, what you ideally would like to have accomplished. Goals may be stated as teacher goals, as student goals, or as course goals. In all three, the goal is the same. If, for example, the goal is to improve students' knowledge of U.S. history, it could be stated as follows:

Teacher course or goal	To help students improve their knowledge of how a democratic legislative body works.
Student goal	To improve my knowledge of how the legislature works.

Goals are general statements of intent and thus should be prepared early in course planning.[12] Goals become useful when planned cooperatively with students and/or shared with students as advance organizers (see Module 2). The students, knowing what to expect, begin to prepare mentally to learn the appropriate material. From the goals, specific objectives are prepared, and these should be written in behavioral terms.[13] Objectives are not intentions. They are the actual behaviors teachers intend to cause students to display. In short, objectives are what students do.

There has not been a standardization of the terminology used for designating the various types of objectives. In the literature, the most general educational objectives are often called *aims*; the general objectives of schools, curricula, and courses are called *goals*; the objectives of units and lessons are called *instructional objectives*. Aims are more general than goals, goals are more general than objectives. Instructional objectives are quite specific.

As implied in the preceding paragraphs, goals guide the instructional methods, whereas objectives drive student performance. Goals are general statements, usually not even complete sentences (often beginning with the word *to*). They identify what the teacher intends the students to learn. Objectives, stated in performance (behavioral) terms, are specific actions. Thus, they should be written as complete sentences in the future tense (using the word *will*) that indicate what each student is expected to be able to do as a result of the instructional experience.

Whereas instructional goals may not always be quantifiable—that is, readily measurable— behavioral objectives *should* be measurable. Those objectives, then, become the essence of what is measured for in instruments designed to assess student learning.

Consider the following examples of goals and objectives.

Goals

1. To develop an appreciation for music.
2. To provide reading opportunities for students.
3. To demonstrate the relationship between mathematics and the natural environment.

---

[11]The terms *performance objective* and *behavioral objective* are synonymous.

[12]Some writers use the phrase "general goals and objectives," but that is incorrect usage. Goals *are* general, whereas objectives are specific.

[13]The value of stating learning objectives in behavioral terms and in providing advance organizers is well documented by research. See Thomas L. Good and Jere E. Brophy, *Looking in Classrooms*, 6th ed. (New York: HarperCollins, 1994), p. 244.

Objectives

1. Each student will correctly identify ten different musical instruments by listening to a tape recording of the Boston Pops orchestra and orally tell the class which instrument is being played at different times, as specified by the teacher.
2. The student will read two books, three short stories, and five newspaper articles at home, within a two-month period. The student will maintain a daily written log of these activities.
3. Using a sheet of graph paper, the student will plot the diagonals formed by Fibonacci numbers, forming an Archimedian spiral. The student will list at least three different forms in nature that resemble the Archimedian spiral formed by the drawing on the graph paper.

Behavioral Objectives and Their Relationship to Instruction and to Assessment of Student Learning

One purpose for writing objectives in specific, behavioral terms is to be able to assess (evaluate) with precision whether the instruction has resulted in the desired terminal behavior. In most school districts the educational goals are established as competencies that the students are expected to achieve. This is known variously as **competency-based, performance-based**, or **outcome-based education**. These goals are then divided into specific performance objectives, sometimes referred to as goal indicators. When students perform the competencies called for by these objectives, their education is considered successful. Expecting students to achieve one set of competencies *before* moving on to the next set is called mastery learning (discussed in Module 2). The success of school curricula, teacher performance, and student achievement may each be assessed according to these criteria.

Assessment is not difficult to accomplish when the desired performance is **overt behavior**—that is, when it can be observed directly. Each of the three sample objectives of the list above is an example of an overt objective.

Assessment is more difficult to accomplish when the desired terminal behavior is **covert behavior**—that is, when it is not directly observable. Terminal behaviors of "understanding" or "appreciation," for example, are not directly observable because they occur within a person, and so are covert behaviors. Since covert behavior cannot be observed directly, the only way to tell whether the objective has been achieved is to observe overt behavior that may be indicative of that achievement. The objective, then, must be written in terms of overt behaviors. Evaluators can only assume or trust that the observed behavior is, in fact, indicative of the expected learning outcome.

Behaviorists—those who believe in the theory of **behaviorism**—assume a definition of learning that deals only with changes in observable (overt) behavior. In contrast, constructivists—those who believe in the theory of cognitivism—hold that learning entails the construction or reshaping of mental schemata and that mental processes mediate learning. As a consequence, constructivists are concerned with both overt and covert behaviors (see Module 2).

When assessing whether an objective has been achieved, the assessment device must be consistent with the desired learning outcome. When the measuring device and the learning objective are compatible, the assessment is referred to as **authentic assessment**. For example, a person's competency to teach history to ninth grade students is best measured by directly observing that person doing that very thing—teaching history to ninth grade students. In such a case, the assessment is referred to as being authentic. Using a standardized paper-and-pencil test to determine a person's ability to teach history to ninth graders is not authentic assessment. (Assessment is the topic of Module 10.) For now, the point is that when writing instructional objectives you should write most or all of them in overt terms.

Writing Behavioral Objectives

When writing behavioral objectives you should ask yourself: How is the student to demonstrate that the objective has been reached? The objective must include an action that demonstrates the objective has been achieved. That portion of the objective is sometimes referred to as the **terminal behavior** (or the *anticipated measurable performance*) and is especially important in what is called an outcome-based educational program.

The ABCDs of Writing Behavioral Objectives

When completely written, a behavioral objective has four components. To aid in your understanding and remembering, you can refer to this as the ABCDs of writing behavioral objectives.

One of these components is the *a*udience—the student for whom the objective is intended. To address this component, teachers sometimes begin their objectives with the phrase "The student will be able to . . ." or, to personalize the objective, "You will be able to. . . ."

The second component of a behavioral objective is the expected *b*ehavior—the expected performance. The behavior should be designated by using verbs that indicate measurable actions, that is, with action verbs. The reason for using action verbs is so that the terminal behavior is measurable (directly observable) and thus the teacher knows the objective has been reached. Some verbs are vague or ambiguous, suggesting covert behaviors that are not clearly measurable.

When writing behavioral objectives, you should avoid verbs that are not clearly measurable, verbs such as those listed in Figure 3.1. Notice that for the three examples of objectives given earlier, the behaviors (two for each objective) are (1) "will *identify* and orally *tell*," (2) "will *read* and *maintain*," and (3) "will *plot* and *list*." These are all action verbs. To check your understanding, do Exercise 3.6.

Figure 3.1   Verbs to Avoid When Writing Behavioral Objectives.

Appreciate	Familiarize	Learn
Believe	Grasp	Like
Comprehend	Indicate	Realize
Enjoy	Know	Understand

A Self-Check Exercise

Instructions: The purpose of this exercise is to check your recognition of verbs that are suitable for use in overt behavioral objectives. From the list of verbs below, circle those that *should not* be used in overt behavioral objectives—that is, those verbs that describe covert behaviors that are not directly observable and measurable. Check your answers against the answer key that follows. Discuss any problems with your classmates and instructor.

1. apply

2. appreciate

3. believe

4. combine

5. comprehend

6. compute

7. create

8. define

9. demonstrate

10. describe

11. design

12. diagram

13. enjoy

14. explain

15. familiarize

16. grasp

17. identify

18. illustrate

19. indicate

20. infer

21. know

22. learn

23. name

24. outline

25. predict

26. realize

27. select

28. solve

29. state

30. understand

Answer Key

The third component of a behavioral objective is the *c*onditions—the setting in which the behavior will be demonstrated by the student and observed by the teacher. Consider sample Objective 1. For students to be able to "correctly identify ten different musical instruments," the conditions are: "by listening to a tape recording of the Boston Pops orchestra." And, for "orally tell . . . which instrument is playing," the conditions are: "specified times as determined by the teacher." In Objective 2, for "the student will read . . ." the conditions are: "at home within a two-month period." In Objective 3, the conditions are: "using a sheet of graph paper."

The fourth component—though not always included in objectives written by teachers—is the *d*egree or level of expected performance. This is the component that allows for the assessment of student learning. When mastery learning is expected (achievement of 85 to 100 percent), the level of expected performance is usually omitted from the written objective (because it is understood).[14] Now reinforce your learning by doing Exercise 3.7.

---

[14]In teaching for mastery learning, the performance-level expectation is 100 percent. In reality, however, the performance level will most likely be between 85 and 95 percent, particularly when working with a group of students rather than with an individual student. The 5 to 15 percent difference allows for human error, as can occur with written and oral communication.

Recognizing the Parts of Criterion-Referenced Behavioral Objectives

• • • • • •

A Self-Check Exercise

Instructions: The purpose of this exercise is to practice your skill in recognizing the four components of a behavioral objective. In the following two objectives, identify the parts of the objectives by underlining once the *audience*, twice the *behavior*, three times the *conditions*, and four times the *performance level* (degree or standard of performance). Check against the answer key that follows; discuss any problems with your classmates and instructor.

1. You will write a 500-word account of the battle between the forces of Gondor and its allies against those of Mordor and its allies, as related in *The Lord of the Rings*, completely from memory. This account will be accurate in all basic details and include all the important incidents of the battle.

2. Given an interurban bus schedule, at the end of the lesson the student will be able to read the schedule well enough to determine at what time buses are scheduled to leave randomly selected points, with at least 90-percent accuracy.

Answer Key

	Objective 1	*Objective 2*
Audience	You	The Student
Behavior	will write a 500-word account of the battle between the forces of Gondor and its allies against those of Mordor and its allies	will be able to read the schedule
Conditions	completely from memory	given an interurban bus schedule
Performance level	This account will be accurate in all basic details and include all the important incidents of the battle.	well enough to determine (and) with at least 90-percent accuracy

The degree component of an objective—the performance level—is used to evaluate student achievement, and sometimes it is used to evaluate the effectiveness of the teaching. Student grades might be based on performance levels; the evaluation of teacher effectiveness might be based on the level of student performance. In recent years there has been a rekindling of interest in performance-based (outcome-based, competency-based) assessment. Now try your skill at recognizing objectives that are measurable by doing Exercise 3.8.

Recognizing Objectives That Are Measurable

• • • • • •

A Self-Check Exercise

Instructions: The purpose of this exercise is to assess your skill in recognizing measurable objectives—those stated in behavioral terms. Place a check before each of the following that is a student-centered behavioral objective, or a learning objective that is clearly measurable. Although the audience, conditions, and degree of the ABCD structure may be absent, ask yourself, "As stated, is it a student-centered and measurable objective?" If it is, then place a check in the blank. An answer key follows. After checking your answers, discuss any problems with your classmates and instructor.

_____ 1. The students will understand that the basic issue that resulted in secession was the extension of slavery.

_____ 2. Digestion is the chemical change of foods into particles that can be absorbed.

_____ 3. To explain what an acid is and what an acid's properties are.

_____ 4. Introduction to vector qualities and their use.

_____ 5. The students will be able to convert Celsius temperatures to Fahrenheit.

_____ 6. The students will understand that vibrating bodies provide the source of all sounds and sound waves.

_____ 7. At the end of the lesson, with at least 90-percent accuracy, the students will be able to read a bus schedule well enough to determine at what time buses are scheduled to arrive and leave at designated stations.

_____ 8. Given a number of quadratic equations with one unknown, the students will be able to solve the equations correctly in 80 percent of the cases.

_____ 9. The students will appreciate the problems faced by those who have emigrated from Southeast Asia to the United States.

_____ 10. A study of the external features and internal organs of the frog through video films of dissections.

_____ 11. To discuss the reasons why the field of philosophy was well developed by the ancient Greeks.

_____ 12. Animals' physical adaptation to their environments.

1. This is a behavioral objective. Although another verb might be more appropriate (e.g., *recognize*), understanding is a kind of behavior. In this case, understanding that slavery was the basic issue that brought about secession is the terminal behavior the teacher expects of the students.

2. This is not a behavioral objective. Rather, it is a description of a concept and does not describe an expected terminal behavior.

3. This is not a behavioral objective. It describes teacher behavior rather than student terminal behavior. It is more a teaching procedure than an objective.

4. This is not a behavioral objective—or even an objective of any type. It is a topic or title.

5. This is a behavioral objective. It describes clearly what the students will be able to do as a result of the instruction; it describes their expected terminal behavior.

6. This is a behavioral objective. The objective is rather broad, and another verb might have been more useful. *Understanding* is a kind of terminal behavior, but the objective might have been more measurable had the teacher used a verb other than *understanding*. A better formulation would have been: "The students will be able to recall that . . ." or "The students will be able to demonstrate that . . ."

7. This is a behavioral objective. It is specific and very clear about the teacher's expectation of student behavior at completion of the lesson.

8. This is a clearly written behavioral objective.

9. This is a behavioral objective. Although the terminal behavior described is vague and general, it is nevertheless a terminal behavior. Perhaps a clearer formulation would have been: "The students will demonstrate an appreciation of the problems faced by those who have emigrated from Southeast Asia to the United States by recalling the many problems the people faced before, during, and following that emigration."

10. This is not a behavioral objective. It describes no behavior of any kind. It is the title of a topic with a mention of methods.

11. This is not a behavioral objective. It is not an objective at all, but rather a description of the teaching procedure to be used.

12. This is not a behavioral objective. Again, this is a title of a topic. It describes no behavior and no objective.

Classification of Behavioral Objectives

Three domains of learning are useful in classifying behavioral objectives:

- **Cognitive domain**. This is the domain of learning that involves mental operations, from the lowest level of simple recall of information to high-level and complex evaluative processes.
- **Affective domain**. This domain of learning involves feelings, attitudes, and values, from lower levels of acquisition to the highest level of internalization and action.
- **Psychomotor domain**. This domain of learning involves locomotor skills, from the low-level simple manipulation of materials to the higher level of communication of ideas, and finally to the highest level of creative performance.

Schools attempt to provide learning experiences designed to meet the needs of the total child. Specifically, five areas of developmental needs have been identified: (1) intellectual, (2) physical (3) psychological, (4) social, and (5) moral and ethical (see Module 2). You should include learning objectives that address each of these developmental needs. These needs can be related to the domains of learning: the intellectual is primarily within the cognitive domain, the physical is within the psychomotor domain, and the psychological, social, and moral and ethical are within the affective domain.

Too frequently, the teacher's attention is focused on the cognitive domain while assuming that the psychomotor and affective domains will take care of themselves. Effective teachers direct their planning and sequence their teaching so that students are guided from the lowest to highest levels of operation within each of the three domains.

A description of three developmental hierarchies follow; these should guide your understanding of how you can address each of the five areas of needs. Take special note of the verbs listed for each level of each domain. These verbs should help you fashion your behavioral objectives for the lesson plans you will soon be developing.

Cognitive Domain Hierarchy

In a taxonomy (classification) of objectives that is widely accepted, Bloom and his associates arranged cognitive objectives into a system according to the complexity of the skills and abilities embodied in the objectives.[15] The resulting taxonomy portrays a ladder, or hierarchy, ranging from the simplest to the most complex intellectual processes.[16] Prerequisite to a student's ability to function at one level of the hierarchy is the student's ability to function at the preceding level or levels. In other words, when a student is functioning at the third level of the cognitive domain, then that student is automatically also functioning at the first and second levels. (This concept holds true regardless of the domain.)

The six major levels (or categories) in Bloom's taxonomy of cognitive objectives are:

1. *Knowledge*. Recognizing and recalling information.
2. *Comprehension*. Understanding the meaning of information.
3. *Application*. Using information.
4. *Analysis*. Ability to dissect information into component parts and see relationships.
5. *Synthesis*. Putting components together to form new ideas.
6. *Evaluation*. Judging the worth of an idea, notion, theory, thesis, proposition, information, or opinion.

Although space does not allow elaboration here, Bloom's taxonomy includes various sublevels under each of these six major levels. It is less important that you can classify an objective

[15]Benjamin S. Bloom, ed., *Taxonomy of Educational Objectives, Book I: Cognitive Domain* (White Plains, NY: Longman, 1984).

[16]Rather than an orderly progression from the simple to the complex, as illustrated by Bloom's taxonomy, other researchers prefer an identification of cognitive abilities that range from simple information storage and retrieval, through a higher level of discrimination and concept attainment, and to the highest cognitive ability to recognize and solve problems, as organized by Robert M. Gagné, Leslie Briggs, and Walter Wager, *Principles of Instructional Design*, 3rd ed. (New York: Holt, Rinehart and Winston, 1988).

absolutely than it is that you understand levels of thinking and doing. Also important is that you recognize the necessity of attending to each student's cognitive development and intellectual behavior, from lowest to the highest levels of operation in all three domains.

A discussion of each of Bloom's six major levels follows.

Knowledge.   The basic element in Bloom's taxonomy concerns the acquisition of knowledge—the ability to recognize and recall information. (This is similar to the input level of thinking and questioning, as discussed in Module 7.) Although this is the lowest of the six levels, the information to be learned may not itself be of a low level. In fact, the information may be of an extremely high level. Bloom includes at this level knowledge of principles, generalizations, theories, structures, and methodology, as well as knowledge of facts and ways of dealing with facts.

Action verbs appropriate for this level include: *choose, complete, define, describe, identify, indicate, list, locate, match, name, outline, recall, recognize, select,* and *state.* (You will note that some verbs may be appropriately used at more than one cognitive level.)

The following are examples of objectives at this cognitive level (note especially the verb used in each example):

- From memory, the student will recall and define the principal parts of speech.
- The student will state the Pythagorean theorem.
- Beginning with prophase, the student will list in order the stages of mitosis.
- The student will name the positions of offensive players on a football team.

Once past this first level, knowledge, the remaining five levels of Bloom's taxonomy of the cognitive domain deal with the use of knowledge. They encompass the educational objectives aimed at developing cognitive skills and abilities, including comprehension, application, analysis, synthesis, and evaluation of knowledge. The last three—analysis, synthesis, and evaluation—are considered higher-order thinking skills.

Comprehension.   Comprehension includes the ability to translate or explain knowledge, to interpret that knowledge, and to extrapolate from it to address new situations.

Action verbs appropriate for this level include: *change, classify, convert, defend, derive, describe, estimate, expand, explain, generalize, infer, interpret, paraphrase, predict, recognize, summarize,* and *translate.*

Examples of objectives at this level are:

- In her or his own words, the student will describe each of the principal parts of speech.
- The student will derive the Pythagorean theorem.
- The student will generalize about each stage of mitosis.
- The student will explain the responsibility of the player of each offensive position on a football team.

Application.   Once students understand information, they should be ready to apply it. This is the level of operation above comprehension.

Action verbs appropriate at this level include: *apply, compute, demonstrate, develop, discover, discuss, modify, operate, participate, perform, plan, predict, relate, show, solve,* and *use.*

Examples of objectives at this level are:

- In complete sentences, the student will demonstrate the listed principal parts of speech.
- The student will solve a problem using the Pythagorean theorem.
- The student will discuss each stage of mitosis, demonstrating her or his comprehension of how a cell's chromosome number remains constant despite the cell's duplication of itself.
- The student will relate how the different positions of offensive members of a football team depend upon each other.

Analysis.   This level includes objectives that require students to use the skills of analysis.

Action verbs appropriate for this level include: *analyze, break down, categorize, classify, compare, contrast, debate, deduce, diagram, differentiate, discriminate, identify, illustrate, infer, outline, relate, separate,* and *subdivide.*

Examples of objectives at this level include:

- The student will analyze a paragraph, illustrating how the principal parts of speech are related.
- Using the mathematics of the Pythagorean theorem, the student will illustrate the theorem's use and importance in the modern world of everyday living.
- The student will diagram each stage of mitosis to illustrate what is happening to the nuclear material of the original parent cell.
- For a given offensive play, the student will illustrate by diagram the responsibilities and relationships of the offensive players for that play.

Synthesis.   This level includes objectives that involve such skills as designing a plan, proposing a set of operations, and deriving a series of abstract relations.

Action verbs appropriate for this level include: *arrange, categorize, classify, combine, compile, constitute, create, design, develop, devise, document, explain, formulate, generate, modify, organize, originate, plan, produce, rearrange, reconstruct, revise, rewrite, summarize, synthesize, tell, transmit,* and *write.*

Examples of objectives at this level are:

- With correct usage of the principal parts of speech listed, the student will write an essay on a given topic.
- The student will produce a plan that uses the mathematics of the Pythagorean theorem for solving a real-life problem.
- The student will design an experiment related to the concept of mitosis that is suitable for testing a hypothesis.
- The student will create and illustrate on the chalkboard an original offensive play that uses the different positions of players on a football team.

Evaluation.   The highest cognitive level of Bloom's taxonomy is evaluation. This includes offering opinions and making value judgments.

Action verbs appropriate for this level include: *appraise, argue, assess, compare, conclude, consider, contrast, criticize, decide, discriminate, evaluate, explain, interpret, judge, justify, rank, rate, relate, standardize, support,* and *validate.*

Examples of objectives at this level are:

- The student will listen to and critique other students' oral essays for their proper use of the principal parts of speech.
- The student will assess a proposition presented by another student of a plan to use the mathematics of the Pythagorean theorem for solving a real-life problem.
- While observing living plant cells, the student will justify his or her interpretation that specified nuclei are in certain stages of mitosis.
- The student will judge for feasibility another student's original offensive play that uses the different positions of players on a football team.

Now gain further understanding of behavioral objectives by doing Exercise 3.9.

EXERCISE 3.9
Classifying Cognitive Objectives

●●●●●●

A Self-Check Exercise.

Instructions: The purpose of this exercise is to assess your ability to recognize the level of cognitive objectives. For each of the following cognitive objectives, identify by appropriate letter the *highest* level of operation that is called for. Check your answers with the answer key, and then discuss the results with your classmates and instructor. Your understanding of the concept involved is more important than whether you score 100 percent against the answer key.

Use the following codes for your answers: 1 = knowledge; 2 = comprehension; 3 = application; 4 = analysis; 5 = synthesis, 6 = evaluation.

_____ 1. The student will be able to detect faulty logic in advertising propaganda.

_____ 2. The student will be able to differentiate fact and opinion in news stories.

_____ 3. Given the facts of the political situation, the student will be able to draw reasonable hypotheses concerning the causes of the Persian Gulf War.

_____ 4. The student will be able to devise a workable plan for investigating a social phenomenon.

_____ 5. The student will write an original short story.

_____ 6. At the end of the lesson, the students will perceive the moods of melancholy and retreat in Byron's *The Ocean*.

_____ 7. You will be able to define *corporation* in your own words.

_____ 8. Given the requisite tools and materials—electric drill and bit, knife, screw-driver, ruler, soldering gun, wire strippers, solder, and flux—the student will construct a portable testing device for repair of motors and sealed-in units.

_____ 9. Given a list of five solids, five liquids, and five gases, students will be able to describe the physical and chemical properties of each.

_____ 10. You will be able to devise a method to prove a ray to be the bisector of an angle.

Answer Key

5. level 5	10. level 5
4. level 5	9. level 1
3. level 4	8. level 3
2. level 4	7. level 2
1. level 6	6. level 2

Affective Domain Hierarchy

Krathwohl, Bloom, and Masia developed a useful taxonomy of the affective domain.[17] The following are their major levels (or categories), from least internalized to most internalized:

1. *Receiving.* Awareness of the affective stimulus and the beginning of favorable feelings toward it.
2. *Responding.* Taking an interest in the stimulus and viewing it favorably.
3. *Valuing.* Showing a tentative belief in the value of the affective stimulus and becoming committed to it.
4. *Organizing.* Organization of values into a system of dominant and supporting values.
5. *Internalizing values.* Beliefs and behavior are consistent and have become a way of life.

Although there is considerable overlap from one level to another, the hierarchy does give a basis by which to judge the quality of objectives and the nature of learning within this domain.

Receiving.   At this level, which is the least internalized, the student exhibits a willingness to give attention to particular phenomena or stimuli, and the teacher is able to arouse, sustain, and direct that attention.

Action verbs appropriate for this level include: *ask, choose, describe, differentiate, distinguish, hold, identify, locate, name, point to, recall, recognize, reply, select,* and *use.*

Examples of objectives at this level are:

- The student pays close attention to the directions for enrichment activities.
- The student listens attentively to the ideas of others.
- The student demonstrates sensitivity to the concerns of others.

Responding.   At this level, students respond to the stimulus they have received. They may do so because of some external pressure, or they may do so voluntarily because they find it interesting or because responding gives them satisfaction.

Action verbs appropriate for this level include: *answer, applaud, approve, assist, comply, command, discuss, greet, help, label, perform, play, practice, present, read, recite, report, select, spend* (leisure time in), *tell,* and *write.*

Examples of objectives at this level are:

- The student reads for enrichment.
- The student discusses what others have said.
- The student willingly cooperates with others during group activities.

Valuing.   Objectives at the valuing level have to do with students' beliefs, attitudes, and appreciations. The simplest objectives concern a student's acceptance of beliefs and values. Higher objectives concern a student's learning to prefer certain values, finally becoming committed to them.

Action verbs appropriate for this level include: *argue, assist, complete, describe, differentiate, explain, follow, form, initiate, invite, join, justify, propose, protest, read, report, select, share, study, support,* and *work.*

Examples of objectives at this level include:

- The student protests against racial discrimination.
- The student supports actions against gender discrimination.
- The student argues for or against abortion rights for women.

---

[17]David R. Krathwohl, Benjamin S. Bloom, and Bertram B. Masia, *Taxonomy of Educational Goals, Handbook II: Affective Domain* (New York: David McKay, 1964).

Organizing.   This fourth level within the affective domain concerns the building of a personal value system. At this level the student is conceptualizing values and arranging them into a value system that recognizes priorities and the relative importance of various values held.

Action verbs appropriate for this level include: *adhere, alter, arrange, balance, combine, compare, defend, define, discuss, explain, form, generalize, identify, integrate, modify, order, organize, prepare, relate,* and *synthesize.*

Examples of objectives at this level are:

- The student forms judgments concerning proper behavior in the classroom, school, and community.
- The student forms and adheres to a personal standard of work ethic.
- The student defends the important values of his or her own culture.

Internalizing values.   This is the last and highest level within the affective domain. At this level the student's behaviors are consistent with his or her beliefs.

Action verbs appropriate for this level include: *act, complete, display, influence, listen, modify, perform, practice, propose, qualify, question, revise, serve, solve,* and *verify.*

Examples of objectives appropriate at this level are:

- The student behaves according to a well-defined and ethical code of behavior.
- The student is accurate in his or her verbal communication.
- The student works independently and diligently.

Psychomotor Domain Hierarchy

Whereas classification within the cognitive and affective domains is generally agreed upon, there is less agreement on classification within the psychomotor domain. Originally, the goal of classifying within this domain was simply that of developing and categorizing proficiency in skills, particularly those dealing with gross and fine muscle control. Today's classification of this domain, as presented here, follows that lead but includes at its highest level the most creative and inventive behaviors, thus coordinating skills and knowledge from all three domains.

Consequently, the objectives are arranged in a hierarchy from simple gross locomotor control to the most creative and complex, requiring originality and fine locomotor control—for example, from simply threading a needle to designing and making a piece of clothing. Harrow developed the taxonomy of the psychomotor domain used here.[18] The following are the major levels:

1. *Movement.*
2. *Manipulating.*
3. *Communicating.*
4. *Creating.*

A discussion of the four levels follows, with possible action verbs for each level.

1. Movement.   This involves gross motor coordinations.
Action verbs appropriate for this level include: *adjust, carry, clean, locate, obtain,* and *walk.*
Sample objectives at this level are:

- The student demonstrates jumping a rope ten times without missing.
- The student correctly grasps the driving club used in golf.
- The student correctly grasps and carries the microscope to the work station.

---

[18]A. J. Harrow, *Taxonomy of the Psychomotor Domain* (White Plains, NY: Longman, 1977).

2. Manipulating. This level involves fine motor coordination.

Action verbs appropriate for this level include: *assemble, build, calibrate, connect,* and *thread.*
Sample objectives at this level are:

- The student will build and fly a kite with the materials on the table.
- The student will play the C scale on the clarinet.
- The student will focus the microscope correctly.

3. Communicating. This level involves the communication of ideas and feelings.

Action verbs appropriate at this level include: *analyze, ask, describe, draw, explain,* and *write.*
Sample objectives at this level are:

- The student demonstrates active listening skills.
- The student describes his or her own feelings about the use of animals for medical research.
- The student accurately draws what is depicted while observing a slide through the microscope.

4. Creating. This is the highest level of this domain—and of all domains—and represents the student's coordination of thinking, learning, and behaving in all three domains.

Action verbs appropriate for this level include: *create, design, perform,* and *invent.*
Sample objectives at this level are:

- The student will write and perform a musical composition.
- The student will choreograph and perform new dance patterns.
- From materials that have been discarded in the environment, the student designs an environment for an imaginary animal that he or she has created.

Using the Taxonomies

Theoretically, the taxonomies are so constructed that students achieve each lower level before being ready to move to the higher levels. But because categories overlap, this theory does not always hold in practice. The taxonomies are important in that they emphasize the various levels to which instruction must aspire. For learning to be worthwhile, you must formulate and teach to objectives from the higher levels of the taxonomies as well as from the lower ones. Student thinking and behaving must be moved from the lowest to the highest levels of thinking and behavior.

In using the taxonomies, remember that the point is to formulate the best objectives for the job to be done. The taxonomies provide the mechanism for assuring that you do not spend a disproportionate amount of time on facts and other learning that are relatively trivial. Writing objectives is essential to the preparation of good items for the assessment of student learning. As noted many times before in this book, clearly communicating your behavioral expectations to students and then specifically assessing student learning against those expectations makes the teaching most efficient and effective—and it also makes the assessment of the learning closer to being authentic. We do not mean to imply that you will always write behavioral objectives for everything taught, nor will you always be able to accurately measure what students have learned. Learning that is meaningful to students is not as easily compartmentalized as the taxonomies of educational objectives would imply. As said by Caine and Caine, "The bottom line is that thoughts and feelings are inextricably interconnected—we 'think' with our feelings and 'feel' with our thoughts."[19]

---

[19]Geoffrey Caine and Renate Nummela Caine, "The Critical Need for a Mental Model of Meaningful Learning," *California Catalyst* (Fall 1992, 18–21), p. 19.

Using a Response Journal to Assess for Meaningful Learning

With learning that is most important and that has the most meaning to students, the learning domains are inextricably interconnected. Consequently, when assessing for student learning you must look for those connections. One way of doing that is to have students maintain a journal in which they reflect on and respond to their learning using five categories.[20] Those categories are:

1. "I never knew that." In this category, student responses are primarily to factual information—to their new knowledge and to the bits and pieces of raw information, often expected to be memorized, regardless of how meaningful to students it might be. Because this is only fragmented knowledge, merely scratching the surface of meaningful learning, it must not be the end-all of student learning. Learning that is truly meaningful goes beyond the "I never knew that" category. It expands upon and connects the bits and pieces, allowing the learner to make sense out of what he or she is learning. Learning that does not extend beyond this category is dysfunctional.

2. "I never thought of that." Here, student responses reveal an additional way of perceiving. Their responses may include elements of "I never knew that" but also contain higher-level thinking as a result of their reflection on that knowledge.

3. "I never felt that." In this category, student responses are connected to the affective, eliciting more of an emotional response than a cognitive one. Learning that is truly meaningful is much more than intellectual understanding—it includes a "felt" meaning.[21]

4. "I never appreciated that." Responses in this category reflect a sense of recognition that one's own life can be enriched by what others have created or done, or that something already known can be valued from an additional perspective.

5. "I never realized that." In this category, student responses indicate an awareness of overall patterns and dynamic ways in which behavior is holistic, establishing meaningful and potentially useful connections among knowledge, values, and purposes.

Now, with Exercise 3.10, try your hand at recognizing objectives according to which domain they are in. Then, with Exercise 3.11, write your own objectives for use in your teaching.

---

[20]Adapted from Seymour Fersh, *Integrating the Trans-National/Cultural Dimension* (Bloomington, IN: Fastback 361, Phi Delta Kappa Educational Foundation, 1993), pp. 23–24. By permission of Phi Delta Kappa Educational Foundation.

[21]Geoffrey Caine and Renate Nummela Caine, "The Critical Need for a Mental Model of Meaningful Learning," *California Catalyst* (Fall 1993), p. 19.

EXERCISE 3.10

Assessing My Recognition of Cognitive, Affective, and Psychomotor Objectives

• • • • • •

A Self-Check Exercise

Instructions: The purpose of this exercise is to assess your ability to recognize objectives according to their domain. Classify each of the following instructional objectives by writing in the blank space the appropriate letter according to its domain: *C* - cognitive, *A* - affective, *P* - psychomotor. Check your answers with the key at the end; then discuss the results with your classmates and instructor.

____ 1. The student will continue shooting free throws until the student can successfully complete 80 percent of the attempts.

____ 2. The student will identify on a map the mountain ranges of eastern United States.

____ 3. The student will summarize the historical development of the Democratic party of the United States.

____ 4. The student will demonstrate a continuing desire to learn more about using the classroom computer for word processing by volunteering to work at it during free time.

____ 5. The student will volunteer to tidy up the storage room.

____ 6. After listening to several recordings, the student will identify the respective composers.

____ 7. The student will translate a favorite Cambodian poem into English.

____ 8. The student will accurately calculate the length of the hypotenuse.

____ 9. The student will indicate an interest in the subject by voluntarily reading additional library books about earthquakes.

____ 10. The student will write and perform a piano concerto.

Answer Key

1. *P*		6. *C*	
2. *C*	7. *C*	
3. *C*	8. *C*	
4. *A*	9. *A*	
5. *A*	10. *P*	

Preparing My Own Behavioral Objectives

• • • • • •

Instructions: The purpose of this exercise is to begin the construction of objectives for your own teaching. For a subject content and grade level of your choice (perhaps from your content outline, Exercise 3.5), prepare ten specific behavioral objectives. (Audience, conditions, and performance level are not necessary unless requested by your course instructor.) Exchange completed exercises with your classmates; then discuss and make changes where necessary.

Subject field: Grade Level:

1. Cognitive knowledge:

2. Cognitive comprehension:

3. Cognitive application:

4. Cognitive analysis:

5. Cognitive synthesis:

6. Cognitive evaluation:

7. Affective (low level):

8. Affective (highest level):

9. Psychomotor (low level):

10. Psychomotor (highest level):

SUMMARY

As you reviewed curriculum documents and student textbooks, you probably found most of them well organized and useful. In your comparison and analysis of courses of study and the teacher's editions of student textbooks, you probably discovered that some are accompanied by sequentially designed resource units from which the teacher can select and build specific teaching units. A resource unit usually consists of an extensive list of objectives, a large number and variety of kinds of activities, suggested materials, and extensive bibliographies for teacher and students, from which the teacher will select those that best suit his or her needs to build an actual teaching unit.

As you also may have discovered, some courses of study contain actual teaching units that have been prepared by teachers of that particular school district. An important question often asked by beginning teachers, as well as by student teachers, is this: How closely must I follow the school's curriculum guide or course of study? You need the answer before you begin teaching. To obtain that answer, you talk with teachers and administrators of that particular school.

In conclusion, your final decisions about what content to teach are guided by all of the following:

- Articles in professional journals.
- Discussions with other teachers.
- Local courses of study.
- State curriculum documents.
- The differences, interests, and abilities of your students.
- Your own personal convictions, knowledge, and skills.

After discovering what you will teach comes the process of preparing the plans. The next module will guide you through the planning process. Although teacher's textbook editions and other curriculum documents make the process easier, they should never substitute for your own specific planning.

Attempting to blend the best of behaviorism and constructivism, many teachers do not bother to try to write specific objectives for all the learning activities in their teaching plans. Clearly, though, when teachers do prepare specific objectives (by writing them or borrowing from other sources) and teach toward those objectives, student learning is better.

Most school districts require teachers to use objectives that are specifically stated. There is no question that clearly written instructional objectives are worth the time, especially when the teacher teaches toward those objectives and evaluates students' progress and learning against them—that is called performance-based teaching or outcome-based or criterion-referenced assessment. It is not imperative that you write all the instructional objectives that you will need. In fact, many of them are usually already available in textbooks and other curriculum documents.

As a teacher, you should plan specifically that which you intend your students to learn, convey your expectations to your students, and then assess their learning against that specificity. There is a danger inherent in such performance-based or criterion-referenced teaching, however. Because it tends toward high objectivity, it could become too objective and thus have negative consequences. The danger is this: if students are treated as objects, then the relationship between teacher and student is impersonal and counterproductive to real learning. Highly specific and impersonal teaching can be discouraging to serendipity, creativity, and the excitement for real discovery and meaningful learning. It can also have a negative impact on the development of students' self-esteem.

Performance-based instruction works well when teaching toward mastery of basic skills, but mastery learning often assumes that there is some foreseeable end point to learning—an assumption that is obviously erroneous. With performance-based instruction, the source of student motivation tends to be mostly extrinsic. Teacher expectations, grades, society, and peer pressures are examples of extrinsic sources that drive student performance. To be an effective teacher, you must use performance-based criteria but simultaneously use a teaching style that encourages the development of intrinsic sources of student motivation. Your teaching style must allow for, provide for, and encourage coincidental learning—learning that goes beyond the predictable and immediately measurable and that represents minimal expectations. Part III is designed to assist you in meeting that challenge.

Now, with your content outline (Exercise 3.5) and instructional objectives (Exercise 3.13) in hand, you are ready for preparation of detailed instructional plans, discussed in the next module.

SUGGESTED READING

Ahlgren, A., and Rutherford, F. J. "Where is Project 2061 Today?" *Educational Leadership* 50(8):19–22 (May 1993).

Aldridge, B. G. "Project on Scope, Sequence, and Coordination: A New Synthesis for Improving Science Education." *Journal of Science Education and Technology* 1(1):13–21 (March 1992).

Barba, R. H., et al. "User-Friendly Text: Keys to Readability and Comprehension." *The Science Teacher* 60(5):15–17 (May 1993).

Battista, M. T. "Teacher Beliefs and the Reform Movement in Mathematics Education." *Phi Delta Kappan* 75(6):462–463, 466–468, 469 (February 1994).

Bradley Commission on History in Schools. *Building a History Curriculum: Guidelines for Teaching History in School.* Westlake, OH: Bradley Commission, 1988.

Brandt, R. S., ed. *Content of the Curriculum.* 1988 ASCD Yearbook. Alexandria, VA: Association for Supervision and Curriculum Development, 1988.

Brandt, R. S. "On Outcome-Based Education: A Conversation with Bill Spady." *Educational Leadership* 50(4):66–70 (December-January 1992–93).

Caine, G., and Caine, R. N. "The Critical Need for a Mental Model of Meaningful Learning." *California Catalyst* 18–21 (Fall 1993).

Chiappetta, E. L., et al. "Do Middle School Life Science Textbooks Provide a Balance of Scientific Literacy Themes?" *Journal of Research in Science Teaching* 30(7):787–797 (September 1993).

Cuban, L. "The Lure of Curricular Reform and its Pitiful History." *Phi Delta Kappan* 75(2):182–185 (October 1993).

Darling-Hammond, L. "Reframing the School Reform Agenda." *Phi Delta Kappan* 74(10):753–761 (June 1993).

Dempster, F. N. "Exposing Our Students to Less Should Help Them Learn More." *Phi Delta Kappan* 74(6):433–437 (February 1993).

Down, A. G., and Mitchell, R. "Shooting for the Moon: Standards for the Arts." *Educational Leadership* 50(5):32–35 (February 1993).

Eisner, E. "Why Standards May Not Improve Schools." *Educational Leadership* 50(5):22–23 (February 1993).

English-Language Arts Model Curriculum Guide. Sacramento: California Department of Education, 1988.

Ennis, C. D., et al. "The Role of Value Orientations in Curricular Decision Making: A Rationale for Teachers' Goals and Expectations." *Research Quarterly for Exercise and Sport* 63(1):38–47 (March 1992).

Gagnon, P. ed. *Historical Literacy: The Case for History in American Education.* New York: Macmillan, 1989.

Gollnick, D. M., and Chinn, P. C. *Multicultural Education in a Pluralistic Society*, 4th ed., New York: Merrill-Macmillan, 1994.

Grafton, T., and Suggett, M. "Resources for Teaching Astronomy." *Physics Education* 26(1):58–65 (January 1991).

Haynes, C. *Religion in American History: What to Teach and How.* Alexandria, VA: Association for Supervision and Curriculum Development, 1990.

Hernández, H. *Multicultural Education: A Teacher's Guide to Content and Process.* New York: Macmillan, 1989.

Hoffman, K. M., and Stage, E. "Science for All: Getting it Right for the 21st Century." *Educational Leadership* 50(5):27–31 (February 1993).

Jacobs, H. H. *Interdisciplinary Curriculum: Design and Implementation.* Alexandria, VA: Association for Supervision and Curriculum Development, 1989.

National Association for Sport and Physical Education. *Outcomes of Quality Physical Education*. Reston, VA: National Association for Sport and Physical Education, 1992.

O'Neil, J. "Can National Standards Make a Difference?" *Educational Leadership* 50(5):4–8 (February 1993).

Parker, W. C. *Renewing the Social Studies Curriculum*. Alexandria, VA: Association for Supervision and Curriculum Development, 1991.

Physical Best: *The AAHPERD Guide to Physical Fitness Education and Assessment*. Reston, VA: The American Alliance for Health, Physical Education, Recreation, and Dance, 1989.

Pollock, J. E. "Blueprints for Social Studies." *Educational Leadership* 49(8):52–53 (May 1992).

Ravitch, D. "Launching a Revolution in Standards and Assessments." *Phi Delta Kappan* 70(10):767–772 (June 1993).

Resnick, L. B., and Klopfer, L. E., eds. *Toward the Thinking Curriculum: Current Cognitive Research*. 1989 ASCD Yearbook. Alexandria, VA: Association for Supervision and Curriculum Development, 1989.

Romberg, T. A. "NCTM's Standards: A Rallying Flag for Mathematics Teachers." *Educational Leadership* 50(5):36–41 (February 1993).

Rényi, J. "The Arts and Humanities in American Education." *Phi Delta Kappan* 75(6):438–445 (February 1994).

Singer, H., and Donlan, D. *Reading and Learning from Text*. Hillsdale, NJ: Lawrence Erlbaum, 1990.

Tchudi, S. *Planning and Assessing the Curriculum in English and Language Arts*. Alexandria, VA: Association for Supervision and Curriculum Development, 1991.

Tate, W. F. "Race, Retrenchment, and the Reform of School Mathematics." *Phi Delta Kappan* 75(6):477–480, 482–484 (February 1994).

Toward Civilization: A Report on Arts Education. Washington, DC: National Endowment for the Arts, 1988.

Walstad, W. B., and Soper, J. C. (Eds.) *Effective Economic Education in the Schools*. Reference and Resource series. Washington, DC: Joint Council on Economic Education, 1991.

Wiggins, G. "Assessment: Authenticity, Context, and Validity." *Phi Delta Kappan* 75(3):200–214 (November 1993).

Willoughby, S. S. *Mathematics Education for a Changing World*. Alexandria, VA: Association for Curriculum and Supervision Development, 1990.

Wiske, M. S., and Levinson, C. Y. "How Teachers are Implementing the NCTM Standards." *Educational Leadership* 50(8):8–12 (May 1993).

With History—Social Science for All: Access for Every Student. Sacramento: California Department of Education, 1992.

Zabaluk, B. L., and Samuels, S. J. *Readability: Its Past, Present, and Future*. Newark, DE: International Reading Association, 1988.

POSTTEST

Multiple Choice

_____ 1. Which one of the following is *least* likely to be an appropriate source of content for what you are expected to teach in middle or secondary schools?
   a. public school curriculum documents.
   b. the common expectations of your colleagues.
   c. your own convictions, knowledge, and skills in the subject.
   d. lecture notes from your college or university courses in your academic major.

_____ 2. The textbook authors believe that the first step in preparing to teach content is to
   a. write the course objectives.
   b. prepare a sequential topic outline.
   c. write the course examination questions.
   d. develop a list of resources and audiovisual needs.

_____ 3. When developing your curriculum, you need to consult
    a. a variety of textbooks, courses of study, and other public documents.
    b. your own convictions.
    c. other colleagues.
    d. all of the above.

_____ 4. A course that is articulated with other courses being taken concurrently (e.g., the mathematics teacher helping students to develop their writing skills as coordinated with grade-level English teachers) is an example of a program
    a. with vertical articulation.
    b. with horizontal articulation.
    c. with built-in self-evaluation.
    d. that demonstrates appreciation for the nation's cultural plurality.

_____ 5. The difference between SQ4R and SQ3R study methods is that in SQ4R the students also
    a. read.
    b. write.
    c. recite.
    d. review.

_____ 6. Statements that describe what the student will be able to do upon completion of an instructional experience are called
    a. course goals.
    b. instructor goals.
    c. covert objectives.
    d. behavioral objectives.

_____ 7. When writing behavioral objectives, which one of the following is the only acceptable verb?
    a. *know*
    b. *write*
    c. *appreciate*
    d. *understand*

_____ 8. Which one of the following sets of verbs describe behaviors at the highest cognitive level?
    a. *match, list, define*
    b. *show, predict, use*
    c. *rank, assess, argue*
    d. *describe, infer, explain*

_____ 9. Development of character, acceptable values, and ethics is at the highest level of the ___ domain.
    a. affective
    b. cognitive
    c. psychomotor
    d. none of the above

_____ 10. The purpose of the taxonomies, according to this module, is to establish
    a. proper teaching strategies.
    b. standards for curriculum improvement.
    c. levels to which instruction should aspire.
    d. standards for assessment of student learning.

Short Explanation

1. When you have prepared a course topic outline, how will you know if the content of that outline is appropriate content for the subject and grade level for which the outline is intended?
2. Explain the relationship of planning to the preactive and reflective thought-processing phases of instruction.

3. Explain two important goals a teacher needs to keep in mind when planning the instruction.
4. Explain the intent of having national standards for each subject taught in public schools. Who prepares these standards?
5. Explain how a textbook can be helpful to a student's learning in your discipline. How might reliance on a single textbook be a hindrance to student learning?

Essay

1. From your current observations and field work as related to this teacher preparation program, clearly identify one specific example of educational practice that seems contradictory to exemplary practice or theory as presented in this module. Present your explanation for the discrepancy.
2. Describe any prior concepts you held that changed as a result of your experiences with this module. Describe the changes.

Module 4

Preparing Unit and Lesson Plans

Rationale
Specific Objectives
Module Text

RATIONALE

As noted in Module 3, the teacher's edition of a student textbook and other resource materials can expedite your planning but should not substitute for it. You must know how to create a good instructional plan. Having prepared a topic content outline (Exercise 3.5) and related instructional objectives (Exercise 3.11), you have begun development of a complete instructional plan, which you will complete in this module.

Seldom can a teacher enter a classroom of students unprepared or underprepared and yet teach effectively. Spur-of-the-moment teaching rarely results in forceful, meaningful, logically presented lessons from which students develop clear understanding of knowledge, skills, or concepts. Such lessons require careful thought and preparation. The teacher must decide which aspects of the subject should be the focus of each lesson, how a topic should be adapted to a particular group of students, how a lesson should build upon preceding lessons, and how a lesson should prepare students for lessons to come. Without careful attention to these matters, lessons tend to be dull, drifting aimlessly toward no good purpose.

This module is designed to acquaint you with the basic components and procedures necessary for developing effective units and lessons. It includes both examples and suggestions that should prove helpful. Ultimately, however, you as the teacher will have to adapt, alter, and adjust these suggestions to meet the needs of your own particular groups of students. You will have to develop a lesson-plan style that is comfortable for you, usable in your teaching, and effective in facilitating student learning.

SPECIFIC OBJECTIVES

At the completion of this module, you should be able to:

1. Describe the eight steps in planning.
2. Prepare a course syllabus.
3. Identify the value in using a course syllabus in teaching.
4. Explain the value in dividing the course content into units of instruction.
5. Differentiate among introductory activities, developmental activities, and culminating activities, and identify how and when each is useful.
6. Prepare a standard teaching unit complete with daily lesson plans.
7. Describe several multicultural components that might be included in any unit of instruction.
8. Explain what kind of assessment can be described as authentic.
9. Differentiate among preassessment, formative assessment, and summative assessment, and describe how each is useful.

10. Explain the characteristics and usefulness of an interdisciplinary thematic unit of instruction.
11. Explain the procedures for developing an interdisciplinary thematic unit of instruction.
12. Describe the various formats for lesson planning.
13. Describe the basic components of any daily lesson plan, and their functions.
14. Explain the role of the daily lesson plan.
15. Construct a daily lesson plan.
16. Explain the reason that lesson planning is a continual process.
17. Explain the place and role of each of the four decision-making and thought-processing phases in unit planning and implementation.

MODULE TEXT

Processes in Instructional Planning

Complete planning of your instruction comprises an eight-step process. Certain steps have previously been addressed, but they are discussed again in this module so you will understand where they fit in the planning process. The eight steps are:

1. *Course and school goals.* Consider and understand your course goals and their relationship to the goals and the mission of the school. Your course is not an isolated event; rather, it is an integral part of the total school curriculum, of both the vertical curriculum (grades K through 12) and the horizontal curriculum (across the grade level).

2. *Expectations.* Consider topics and skills that you are expected to teach, such as ones that may be found in the course of study (Module 3.)

3. *Academic year-long calendar plan.* You must consider where you want the class of students to "be" months from now. Working from your tentative topic outline (Exercise 3.5) and with the school calendar at hand, you begin by deciding approximately how much class time should be devoted to each topic, penciling those times onto the subject outline.

4. *Course schedule.* This schedule becomes a part of the course syllabus presented to students during the first week of school. The schedule must remain flexible, however, to allow for the unexpected, such as a cancellation or interruption of a class meeting or an unpredictable extended study of a particular topic.

5. *Class meeting lessons.* Working from the course schedule, you prepare lessons for each class meeting, keeping in mind the abilities and interests of your students while making decisions about appropriate strategies and learning experiences (strategies are the focus of Part III of this text). Preparation of daily lessons takes considerable time, and it continues throughout the year and throughout your career, as you arrange and prepare: instructional notes, demonstrations, discussion topics and questions, classroom exercises, guest speakers, the use of audiovisual equipment and materials, field trips, and tools for assessment of student learning.

Because one class meeting is often determined by accomplishments of the preceding meeting (especially if you are teaching toward mastery), your lessons are never "set in concrete" but need steady revisiting and evaluation by you.

6. *Instructional objectives.* As you prepare the daily lessons, you complete your preparation of the instructional objectives (begun in Exercise 3.11). These instructional objectives are critical for development of Step 7.

7. *Assessment.* This important step deals with how assessment of student achievement is to be accomplished and how you will preassess student understanding. Included in this step are your decisions about assignments, diagnostic tools (such as tests), and the procedure by which grades will be determined. (Assessment is the topic of Module 10.)

8. *Classroom management.* This final and important step in planning involves your decisions about providing for a safe and effective classroom environment so that the most efficient learning will occur. (Classroom management is the topic of Module 5).

Those are the eight steps of the planning process. Later, you will proceed step by step toward the development of your first instructional plan. First, though, let's consider the nature of the course syllabus.

The Course Syllabus

A course syllabus is a written statement of information about the working of a particular class. As a college or university student, you have seen a variety of syllabi written by professors, each with individual ideas about what general and specific logistic information is most important for students to know about a course. Some instructors make the mistake of thinking that a course outline constitutes a course syllabus. But a course outline is just one component of a syllabus.

Related to the development and use of a course syllabus are three issues:

1. *Why?* What value is it? What use can be made of it? What purpose does it fulfill?
2. *How?* How do I develop a course syllabus? When do I begin? Where do I start?
3. *What?* What information should be included? When should it be distributed to students? How rigidly should it be followed? Let's consider each of those three issues.

Reasons for a Course Syllabus

The course syllabus is printed information about the course, which is usually presented to students on the first day or during the first week of school. It should be designed so that it:

- Helps establish a rapport among students, parents (or guardians), and the teacher.
- Helps students feel at ease by providing an understanding of what is expected of them.
- Helps students organize, conceptualize, and synthesize their learning experiences.
- Provides a reference, helping eliminate misunderstandings and misconceptions about the nature of the class—its rules, expectations, procedures, requirements, and other policies.
- Provides students with a sense of connectedness (often by allowing students to work in cooperative groups and actually participate in fashioning the syllabus).
- Serves as a plan to be followed by the teacher and the students.
- Serves as a resource for members of a teaching team. Each team member should have a copy of every other member's syllabus.
- Stands as documentation for what is taking place in the classroom, for those outside the classroom (i.e., parents or guardians, administrators, other teachers and students).

Development of a Course Syllabus

The course syllabus is usually prepared by the classroom teacher long before the first class meeting. If you maintain a syllabus template on your computer, then you can easily customize a syllabus for each class you teach. Some teachers have found it more useful if students participate in the development of the syllabus, thereby gaining an ownership in it and a commitment to it. Figure 4.1 provides you with a step-by-step procedure to involve your students in the process. This can be seen as a cooperative-learning experience, where students spend approximately 30 minutes during the first (or an early) class meeting brainstorming the content of their syllabus.

Content of a Course Syllabus

The course syllabus should be concise, matter-of-fact, uncomplicated, and brief—perhaps no more than two pages. It should include the following information:

1. *Descriptive information about the course.* This includes the teacher's name, course title, class period, beginning and ending times, and room number.
2. *Explanation of the importance of the course.* The teacher should describe the course, cite how students will profit from it, and tell whether the course is a required course, a part of a col-

1. Sometime during the first few days of the course, arrange students in heterogeneous groups (mixed abilities) of three or four members.* Each group will brainstorm the development of the course syllabus.

2. Instruct the members of each group to spend 5 minutes listing everything they can think of that they would like to know about the course. For each group, a *recorder* must be chosen by members to write their list of ideas on paper. When directed to do so, the recorder will transfer these ideas to the writing board or to sheets of butcher paper (to be hung in the classroom for all to see), or to an overhead transparency (a transparency sheet and pen is made available to each group). Each group must also select a *spokesperson* who will address the class, explaining the group's list. Each group could also appoint a *materials manager,* whose job it is to see that the group has the necessary materials (e.g., pen, paper, transparency, chalk), and a *leader* whose job is to keep the group on task and to report to the teacher when each task is completed.

3. After 5 minutes, have the recorders prepare their lists. The lists can be prepared by using a transparency or butcher paper, while recorders remain with their groups. If using the writing board, recorders, one at a time, write their lists on areas of the board that you have designated for each group's list.

4. Have the spokesperson of each group explain the group's list. As this is being done, you should make a master list. If transparencies or butcher paper are being used, you can ask for them as backup to the master list you have made.

5. After all spokespersons have explained their lists, you ask the class collectively for additional input: "Can anyone think of anything else that should be added?"

6. You then take the master list and design a course syllabus, being careful to address each question and to include items of importance that students may have omitted. Your guidance during the preceding five steps should ensure that all bases have been covered.

7. At the next class meeting, give each student a copy of the final syllabus. Discuss its content. (Duplicate copies should be made to distribute to colleagues on your teaching team, interested administrators, and parents at Back-to-School Night.)

* Experience has shown that groups larger than three or four result in some students contributing little or nothing to the topic at hand, and that often results in no possibility of compromise among divergent views.

Figure 4.1 Steps for Involving Students in the Development of Their Course Syllabus.

lege prep program, a core curriculum, a cocurriculum course, an exploratory or elective, or some other arrangement.

3. *Materials required.* The teacher should explain what materials are needed, such as a textbook, a notebook, a portfolio, supplementary readings, safety goggles, and so on. The list should identify which are supplied by the school, which must be supplied by each student, and which must be brought to class each day.

4. *Statement of goals and objectives.* This should include a few of the general goals and some of the specific objectives.

5. *Types of assignments that will be given.* These should be clearly explained in as much detail as possible this early in the course. There should also be a statement about where daily assignments will be posted in the classroom (a regular place each day) and about the procedures for completing and turning in assignments. (Assignments are statements of what students will accomplish—what they will *do;* procedures are statements of how they will do it).

6. *Assessment criteria.* The teacher should explain the evaluation procedures. Will there be quizzes, tests, homework, projects, and group work? What will be their formats, coverage, and their weights in the grading procedure?

7. *Special information specific to the course.* Will there be field trips, special privileges, or class projects? Classroom procedures and rules for expected behavior (as discussed in Module 3) should be included here.

Now further explore developing a course syllabus by doing Exercises 4.1 and 4.2.

EXERCISE 4.1
Content of a Course Syllabus
••••••

Instructions: The purpose of this exercise is to begin your thinking about preparing a syllabus for use in your teaching. From the following list of items that might appear on a course syllabus, identify (by circling) all those you would include in your own course syllabus. And, for each, explain why or why not you would include that item. Then share the syllabus with your classmates. After sharing, you might want to make revisions in your own list.

1. Name of teacher (my name):

2. Course title (and/or grade level):

3. Room number:

4. Beginning and ending times:

5. Time when students could schedule a conference with teacher:

6. Course description:

7. Course philosophy or rationale (underline which).

8. Instructional format (such as lecture-discussion, student-centered learning groups or laboratory-centered):

9. Absence policy:

10. Tardy policy:

11. Classroom procedures and rules for behavior:

12. Goals of course:

13. Objectives of course:

14. Policy about plagiarism:

15. Name of textbook and other supplementary materials:

16. Policy about use and care of textbook and other reading materials:

17. Materials to be supplied by student:

18. Assignments:

19. Policy about homework assignments (due dates, format, late assignments, weights for grades):

20. Course relationship to advisor-advisee program, core, cocurricular, exploratories, or some other aspect of the school curriculum:

21. Grading procedure:

22. Study skills:

23. Themes to be studied:

24. Field trips and other special activities:

25. Group work policies and types:

26. Other members of the teaching team and their roles:

27. Tentative daily schedule:

28. Other (specify):

29. Other (specify):

30. Other (specify):

EXERCISE 4.2
Preparing a Course Syllabus

••••••

An Exercise in Collaborative Thinking

Instructions: The purpose of this exercise is to prepare (in a group) a syllabus for a course that you intend to teach. Using your results from Exercise 4.1, work in groups of three or four members to develop one syllabus for a course you and other group members may someday teach. Each group should produce one course syllabus that represents that group's collaborative thinking; the finished product should be duplicated and shared with the entire class. Discuss within your group the pros and cons of having student input into the course syllabus (see Figure 4.1). Share the results of that discussion with the entire class.

Unit Planning

Organizing the entire year's content into units makes the teaching process more manageable than if no plan or only random choices are made by a teacher. Whether in a self-contained middle school classroom or in a course taught in junior or senior high school, the content you intend to present to students must be organized and carefully planned well in advance. The teaching (or instructional) unit is a major subdivision of a course (for one course or self-contained classroom there are several or many units of instruction). Each teaching unit is composed of instruction planned around a central theme, topic, issue, or problem.[1]

The teaching unit can be an interdisciplinary thematic unit or a stand-alone, standard, subject unit—not unlike a chapter in a book, an act or scene in a play, or a phase of work when building a house. Breaking down information or actions into component parts and then grouping the related parts makes sense out of learning and doing. The unit brings a sense of cohesiveness and structure to student learning and avoids the piece-meal approach that might otherwise unfold. You can learn to articulate lessons within, between, and among unit plans, focusing on important elements while not ignoring tangential information of importance. Students remember "chunks" of information, especially when those chunks are related to specific units.

Types of Units

Although the steps for developing any type of a unit are essentially the same, units can be organized in four basic ways:

1. *Standard unit*. This type of unit consists of a series of lessons centered on a topic, theme, major concept, or block of subject matter. A standard unit plan is the kind most commonly described for beginning teachers (unless instructed otherwise by your course instructor, you will develop a standard unit plan for Exercise 4.5 later in this module). In a standard unit, each lesson builds on the previous lesson by contributing additional subject matter, providing further illustrations, and supplying more practice or other added instruction, all aimed at bringing about mastery of the knowledge and skills on which the unit is centered.

2. *Laboratory unit*. This type of unit consists of a variety of learning experiences built around long-term assignments rather than a series of separate (daily or near-daily) lessons. In a laboratory unit (sometimes called a *true unit*) most of the instruction is by small-group, problem-solving, or laboratory-inquiry activities, as opposed to daily lessons planned for the entire class. With a standard unit, instruction can be student-centered or teacher-centered or both; with a laboratory unit, instruction is clearly student-centered. Thus, during much of the unit the student is engaged in active research, alone or in small groups.

In a laboratory unit, not all activities are completed by every student. The ones that are may be called *core* or *basic activities*; the ones that are not are called *optional related activities*. In a laboratory unit, under some guidance from the teacher, the students do a considerable amount of the planning. For the students to have the freedom to proceed at their own speed and in their own directions, they may be provided a study guide that allows them to begin and carry out activities—under supervision—without being heavily dependent on the teacher.

3. *Learning activity packet or module*. This type of unit is designed for individualized or modularized self-instruction. A learning-activity packet (also called a learning packet, learning activity package, or instructional package) is designed for independent, individual study. The packet consists of instructions, references, exercises, problems, self-correcting materials, and all the other information and materials that a student needs to carry out a unit of work independently. Consequently, students can work on learning packets individually at their own speeds, and different students can be working on different packets at the same time. Students who successfully finish a packet can move on to another unit of work without waiting for the other students to catch up. Such packets are essential ingredients of continuous-progress courses.

---

[1]Note that a *teaching unit* is not the same as a *resource unit*. A resource unit is a general plan for a unit or a particular topic, and is designed to be used as a basis for building a teaching unit. Resource units, often found in curriculum centers and curriculum libraries, although often rich in resources, are not comprised of sequentially planned lessons, as are teaching units.

Whether for purposes of remediation, enrichment, or make-up, learning activity packages work especially well when done at and in conjunction with a learning activity center.

4. *Contract unit*. This type of unit is an individualized unit plan for which a student agrees (contracts) to carry out certain activities during the unit. Some contract units have a variable-letter-grade agreement built into them. For example, the contract may contain information such as the following:

- To pass with a *D* grade, you must complete activities 1–10 and pass the posttest.
- For a grade of *C*, you must complete activities 1–10, receive at least a *C* on the posttest, and satisfactorily complete two optional related activities.
- For a grade of *B*, you must complete activities 1–10 plus satisfactorily complete four of the optional related activities, and receive a grade of no less than B on the posttest.
- For a grade of *A*, you must complete activities 1–10 plus satisfactorily complete six of the optional activities, and receive no less than a *B* on the posttest.

Planning and Developing Any Teaching Unit

Although the four types of units can differ significantly, the steps in planning and developing any type is essentially the same. When planning and developing a unit, you should:

1. *Select a suitable topic or theme*. Often topics or themes may already be laid out in your course of study or textbook, or already have been agreed to by members of the teaching team.
2. *Select the goals of the unit*. The goals should be written as an overview or rationale, covering what the unit is about and what the students are to learn. In planning the goals, you should:
    - Become as familiar as possible with the topic and materials used.
    - Consult curriculum documents (such as courses of study), state frameworks, and resource units for ideas.
    - Decide the content and procedures (i.e., what the students should learn about the topic and how).
    - Write the rationale or overview, in which you summarize what you hope the students will learn about the topic.
    - Be sure your goals are congruent with those of the course.
3. *Select suitable specific learning objectives*. In doing this, you should
    - Include understandings, skills, attitudes, appreciations, and ideals.
    - Be specific, avoiding vagueness and generalizations.
    - Write the objectives in behavioral terms.
    - Be as certain as possible that the objectives will contribute to the major learning described in the overview.
4. *Detail the instructional procedures*. These procedures include the subject content and the learning activities, established as a series of lessons. Proceed with the following steps in your initial planning of the instructional procedures:
    - Gather ideas for learning activities that might be suitable for the unit. Refer to curriculum documents, resource units, and other teachers as resources.
    - Check the learning activities to make sure that they will actually contribute to the learning designated in your objectives, discarding ideas that do not.
    - Make sure that the learning activities are feasible. Can you afford the time, effort, or expense? Do you have the necessary materials and equipment? If not, can they be obtained? Are the activities suited to the intellectual and maturity levels of your students?
    - Check resources available to be certain that they support the content and learning activities.
    - Decide how to introduce the unit. Provide *introductory activities*, ones that:

      Arouse student interest.

      Inform students of what the unit is about.

      Help you learn about your students—their interests, their abilities, and their experiences and present knowledge of the topic.

Provide transitions that bridge this topic with what students have already learned.

Involve the students in the planning.

- Plan *developmental activities*, ones that:

Sustain student interest.

Provide for individual student differences.

Promote the learning as cited in the specific objectives.

- Plan *culminating activities,* ones that:

Summarize what has been learned.

Bring together loose ends.

Apply what has been learned to new and meaningful situations.

Provide transfer to the unit that follows.

5. *Plan for preassessment and assessment of student learning.* Preassess what students already know, or think they know. Assessment of student progress in achievement of the learning objectives (formative assessment) should permeate the entire unit. Plan to gather information in several ways, including informal observations, observation of student performance, and paper-and-pencil assessments. Assessment must be consistent with the specific learning objectives.

6. *Provide for the materials of instruction.* The unit cannot function without materials. Therefore, you must plan long before the unit begins for media, equipment, references, reading materials, reproduced materials, and community resources. Materials that are not available to the students are of no help to them.

Those are six steps to follow for developing any type of unit.

Preparing a Standard Unit

In addition to the six steps given for developing a teaching unit, there are two general points that should be made. First, there is no single format that works best for all grades and all subject fields, though particular formats may be best for specific disciplines or topics. During your student teaching, your college program for teacher preparation will probably have a form that you are expected to follow.

Second, there is no set time duration for a unit plan, though for specific units curriculum guides will indicate suggested time durations. Units may extend for a minimum of several days or, as in the case of interdisciplinary thematic units, for several weeks. Be aware, however, that when standard units last more than two or three weeks they tend to lose their identity as clearly identifiable units. The exact duration will depend on the topic or theme, the grade level, and the interests and abilities of the students.

Model Unit Plan with Daily Lessons

The Model Unit Plan with daily lessons has been provided as an exemplary plan for you to study. Note that this plan is more extensive than most would be, because of the narrative format, instructive information within the unit, and the addition of many resources for your use. Please do not be overwhelmed with the thought that your unit plan must be as exhaustive as this one; this is a model rather than a sample unit.

As you read through the unit, notice the use of an abbreviated format for presenting the eleven daily lessons, but with an extended narrative presentation of how the teacher might actually conduct each lesson. Notice also how the students' reading responses are varied from day to day, throughout the unit. For additional suggestions about daily variation to meet individual student differences, some ideas are listed at the end of the unit. Also at the end, resources are listed to assist you in the preparation of a similar unit. After reviewing the Model Unit Plan, do Exercise 4.3, which should help you better understand the plan.

MODEL UNIT PLAN

Course: <u>Social studies/language arts block</u>

Topic: <u>Early English Settlers in North America</u>

Teacher: _____   Duration: <u>10–11 days</u>

Introduction

This unit can be an adventurous one. It is a multidisciplinary unit (principally social studies and language arts) and can readily be developed into an interdisciplinary thematic unit for use at any grade level. As presented here, it is designed for use at the middle or junior high school level. Specifically, in this unit the students:

1. Learn about early English settlers in North America.
2. Develop skills in reading.
3. Develop skills in studying.
4. Develop skills in thinking.

These outcomes are assessed during and at completion of this unit by use of a behavior checklist.

This unit can present sailing ships, English and Spanish sea battles, golden treasurers, hearty sea dogs (captains), brave women and men, stockades at riverbank settlements, and trading with the Native Americans for food. Bulletin boards should be designed to interest the students in this exciting part of North America's history. They could feature colorful illustrations of early explorers, captured treasure from Spanish ships, maps showing routes of their explorations, pictures of early settlements and their leaders, and selected focus questions to develop the students' understanding of the early settlers' adjustments to their new environment.

Goals of the Unit

This unit is part of the social studies program about understanding the development of the United States of America. Through selected learning materials, the students will develop a better comprehension of the United States as they study about people with different backgrounds, different ideas, and different ways of life. In this unit the students become acquainted with the early settlement of the colonies and the people who lived there, as well as with some of the reasons why they came to North America from England. As students learn about this period of U.S. history, they should compare (with the teacher's guidance) that time with present-day events, thereby developing new insights about life in the United States today.

Day One

Objective.   Given assigned reading and student discussion about how English activity began in North America, students will identify some of the explorers who first traveled from England to North America, their reasons for exploring, and their contributions to the development of the colonies.

Materials to Begin Unit.   Arrange an attractive bulletin board to display pictures of early English explorers, with a caption such as "Why did Settlers and Explorers travel to North America?" Possible pictures include: John Cabot (Italian sea captain of the *Matthew* who sailed for North America from Bristol, England, in 1497), Sir Francis Drake (first English person to sail around the world), Sir Humphrey Gilbert (who attempted to begin a colony in Newfoundland), and Sir Walter Raleigh (who started a colony on Roanoke Island). On a learning resource table near the bulletin board, place books to accommodate a variety of reading interests and levels, as well as maps, and supplementary materials that contain information about the early settling of the colonies. At the front of the classroom, have a world globe and a large pull-down map that can be marked on with chalk. Also, prepare Charts 1, 2, and 3.

Activities.   Discussing and locating information.

The teacher begins (anticipatory set; transition from previous unit of study): "Yesterday, some of you mentioned reasons why the leaders of France sent explorers to North America. What were some of the reasons you mentioned?" Discussion. "The leaders of another country, England, also had reasons for sending explorers to North America. As we read about the early English explorers, we'll be introduced to some new words." The teacher turns to the chart stand and draws attention to Chart 1, which contains eight terms with pictures to illustrate the meaning of each term:

Vocabulary

Newfoundland	colony
Nova Scotia	settlement
treasure	colonist
sea dog	stockade

The teacher continues: "Let's turn to the table of contents to find the chapter we need, the one entitled Early English in North America. Let's skim the contents to find the page information it contains about the chapter we need." The teacher turns to the chart stand again and displays Chart 2:

We Read at Different Speeds

When we want to find out if the page or book has information we can use, WE READ RAPIDLY.
When we want to find an answer to a question, WE READ AT A MODERATE SPEED.
When we are studying to understand information, WE READ SLOWLY.

The teacher continues: "When we want to find out if the table of contents has the information we can use, what is our reading speed?" Students respond, the chapter page number is identified, and the students locate the beginning of the chapter in their textbooks. "Let's read silently for the first three paragraphs on page _____ to find out the name of one of England's first explorers and his reason for exploring near North America. Since we will be studying to understand information, what reading speed should we use?" Students respond. After the silent reading, a discussion about John Cabot begins. "In reading these paragraphs, we've seen that John Cabot wanted to find a short northern all-water route to Asia." One student is asked to trace the route with chalk on the globe. Another is asked to identify Cabot's reason for exploration. Still another is asked to record Cabot's reason on a strip of construction paper and then attach the strip under Cabot's illustration on the classroom bulletin board. Giving reasons for silent and oral reading, the teacher guides additional reading about more early English explorers. To emphasize the importance of reading slowly when the students are studying for information, the teacher again turns to the chart stand and reviews these study skills from Chart 3:

When We Study to Understand Information

We concentrate.
We have a question in mind.
We look at the pictures and read captioned information.
We read maps, charts, tables, and graphs.
We discuss and review what we have learned.

The teacher brings a closure to this day's lesson and unit introduction, encouraging student thinking by asking higher-order questions: "Having completed our reading today about some of the early English explorers, you know some interesting information about them. Why do you think John Cabot wanted to travel a northern route across the Atlantic Ocean? What might have changed if Cabot had found a short, all-water route to Asia? What can we say about Raleigh and how he tried to help the English acquire land in North America? What might have changed if these early attempts to start colonies had been successful?"

Day Two

Objective.   Given a class discussion about early English explorers, the students will identify reasons these explorers traveled to North America and will evaluate the success or lack of success of the employers in starting colonies.

Activities.   Discussing, defining, and evaluating.

The teacher provides a transition review statement: "Yesterday we were talking about early English explorers, and I want to pick up where we left off. In review, we said several English explorers came to North America during the 1400s and 1500s. Let's name some of these explorers again." Students respond. "Fine, you remembered some of the people we talked about yesterday. Now let's use these explorers as examples of reasons why people travel and explore." This provides a connection with what students already know. "What can we say are reasons these explorers traveled to North America?" Discussion. "Good thinking. Now, let's move away from this topic for a minute. Gretchen, you mentioned Sir Francis Drake was a sea dog. How does your textbook define *sea dog*?" Gretchen responds with definition. "We can always define a term by reading a definition from a dictionary, a glossary, or a textbook. But there are other ways of defining a term. We can define a word or term by demonstrating something about it. Who will define a sea dog by demonstrating something?" Students respond. "We can also define by describing. Who can define sea dog by describing something about the term?" Students respond. "And then, we can define by displaying an illustration. Who will find a picture to help us define sea dog?" Students respond.

"Good. We have several definitions of *sea dog*. Now, let's return to our main topic for today. We were talking about the reasons why early explorers came to North America. Considering their reasons and the rest of our reading about the explorers, would you say the early explorers were successful or unsuccessful in starting colonies in North America?" Discussion continues as students respond and are asked to clarify and to support their opinions with evidence. The lesson is ended with a summary closure.

Day Three

Objective.   Given selected reading and a class discussion, the students will identify the name of the first permanent settlement, identify the settler's reasons for traveling to North America, and record some of the problems the settlers encountered.

Activities.   Discussing, classifying, categorizing, and evaluating.

The teacher begins with a transition review statement: "In contrast to the unsuccessful attempts we talked about yesterday, there were some early English settlements that were successful. We want to discover the name of the first permanent settlement, the reason or reasons the settlers traveled to North America, and some of the problems they encountered." Students read and discuss. The teacher records students' contributions of settlers' problems on the writing board. Then, the teacher and the students review the list, grouping similar problems together under student-selected headings, such as shelter problems, food problems, and so on. The teacher then asks the students to evaluate the problems by ranking them in the order of the greatest hardship—number-one problem, number-two problem, and so on. Students are asked to justify their choices for these rankings. When the rank ordering and the discussion of the rank ordering is completed, the lesson is closed with an introduction to tomorrow's study of the settlement at Plymouth.

Day Four

Objective.   Given an audio-filmstrip cassette presentation entitled "Thanksgiving Day," the students will become familiar with the Pilgrims' settlement at Plymouth, their reason for settling, and the problems they encountered.

Activities.   Gathering information.

After viewing and listening to "Thanksgiving Day," the students turn to the activity page at the end of the chapter and identify all of the questions they can answer with information from the filmstrip. If there is a textbook question for which they have no information, the text will be used as a reference source from which to locate the required information. Focus questions for review are: "What do we know about the Pilgrims' settlement at Plymouth?" "What was their main reason for traveling to North America?" "What were some of the problems they encountered?" "How do those problems compare with our lists from yesterday?"

Day Five

Objective.   Given information about dissatisfaction in the colonies, the students will recognize how additional English colonies developed.

Activities.   Cooperative learning groups.

The teacher provides an opening to this lesson: "Yesterday some of you mentioned religious freedom as a reason why England began to start colonies along the eastern coast of North America. After the colonies began, some of the people in the colonies became dissatisfied with their way of life. For today, Anthony's group will find out why one person, Roger Williams, was unhappy with his life and left the colony of Massachusetts. Anne Hutchinson was also dissatisfied with the leaders of the Massachusetts Bay Colony. Robyn's group will discover Hutchinson's reason for leaving the colony. Now, during the period of dissatisfaction, additional settlers came to North America. Merribeth's group will investigate who settled in New Amsterdam, the land now known as New York City." Students divide into their cooperative learning groups, select group leaders, managers, recorders, and so on, and make their assignments to collect the needed information for reports to the entire class. This work continues for days 6 and 7, if needed.

Days Six and Seven (as needed)

Cooperative-learning groups continue working.

Day Eight

Objective.   Given the group assignments, the students will become familiar with the beginnings of selected colonies.

Activities.   Organizing and summarizing.

The groups report to the entire class. The teacher helps to summarize: "This week we've been discussing early English settlers. Now I want to find how we can pull our reports together. Using the information you have from the group reports, from the filmstrip, and from our readings and discussion, I would like you now to identify the colony that a selected settler is associated with and to identify the main reason the settler (or group) traveled to North America."

A worksheet study guide to help the students organize and summarize information about early settlers is distributed to the students for their completion:

CAN YOU ORGANIZE AND SUMMARIZE?

Scan your reading material, review your notes about the filmstrip "Thanksgiving Day," and recall what you learned from the group reports in order to organize the material on this worksheet. Write the missing information in the blanks provided.

Date	Settler	In What Colony	Reason for Settling
1583	Sir Humphrey Gilbert	_____	_____
1585	Sir Walter Raleigh	_____	_____
1607	John Smith	_____	_____
1620	Pilgrims	_____	_____
1630	Puritans	_____	_____
1681	William Penn	_____	_____
1733	James Oglethorpe	_____	_____

To help you summarize, consider the following: Give a reason why the colonies of Rhode Island, Connecticut, and New Hampshire were started. Were the Middle colonies started for the same reason or for different reasons? How were the Southern colonies started? What is the main idea or statement you can make from this information?

Day Nine

Objective. Given a map-skills worksheet, the students will demonstrate their skills in locating places, determining distance, identifying latitude, and reading map symbols and color codes.

Activities. Map skills.

The teacher introduces this lesson: "Yesterday you summarized the main idea you developed after organizing the information about the different reasons the colonies were started." Time taken to review those summaries. "Today, we want to gather additional information about the colonies from reading our maps correctly. We'll locate some major places. We'll use our rulers to measure selected distances. We'll review map symbols to locate latitude lines and match a color code to locate specific colonies." To review these map skills, the teacher distributes a worksheet for individual student activity, similar to the one that follows. While students individually work on their map skills, the teacher roams the room and guides students who need assistance.

MAP SKILLS

Map I

Find the map on page _____ of your text. Complete the following items:
1. Locate the English colony on Roanoke Island. Write the name of the ocean that surrounds the island. _____
2. Calculate the miles to inch with your ruler and measure the distance from the colony on Roanoke Island across the ocean to Raleigh Bay. _____

Map II

Find the map on page _____ of your text. Complete the following items:

3. Locate the colony on Roanoke Island. Between which two lines of latitude was this colony located? _____ and _____

4. Study your map symbols to find out which group had the rights to the land where this colony started. _____

Map III

Find the map on page _____ of your text. Complete the following items:

5. Review the color code on the map and write the names of the colonies that were known as the New England colonies.

_____ _____ _____ _____

6. Which colonies were known as the Middle colonies?

_____ _____ _____ _____

7. Which colonies were known as the Southern colonies?

_____ _____ _____ _____

Congratulations! You have completed your map skills work for today. Now it is time to talk about what you learned.

Day Ten

Objective. Given a quiz-show game format, the students will describe an activity in a colony, identify the name of a settlement leader, and identify a reason why that colony's settlers traveled to North America.

Activities. Concluding.

The students, with the teacher's guidance, will use their notes from the worksheet entitled "Can You Organize and Summarize?" to provide information for a quiz show about the early English settlers. One student describes an activity, provides information, or gives other clues about a particular colony. A second student tries to identify the name of the prominent leader of the colony. A third student identifies the main reason for those colonists traveling to North America. Points may be awarded for appropriate responses. The highest number of points determines the winner of the quiz game review.

Day Eleven

Objective. Given a worksheet on which names of prominent colony leaders and descriptions of colony activities are mismatched, the students will match leaders with descriptions and then identify each leader with a reason for settling in North America.

Activities. Assessment.

The students receive a worksheet on which the names of the colony leaders and certain descriptions of colony activity are mismatched. The students are asked to match the leaders with the descriptions. After the matching, the students will identify each leader with a reason for settling in North America.

UNIT EXTENSION AND RESOURCE IDEAS

Reading Assignments (including provisions for individual differences)

Gifted students.   Extensive reading from a unit bibliography (culminating in class reports), independent inquiry, and biographical research about the following:

- Sir George Carteret
- Pocahontas
- Squanto
- Peter Stuyvesant
- John Winthrop

Regular education students.   Reading from text and selected trade books to respond to questions in the unit study guide.

Less-able students.   Reading from easy-to-read books, viewing filmstrips, working with peers in cooperating learning groups, accomplishing short assignments.

Language minority students.   Reading from bilingual materials as needed; emphasis on bicultural materials.

Blind and visually impaired students.   Use of Braille materials, talking books, raised relief maps, projection magnifiers and large-type printed materials.

Deaf and hearing-impaired students.   Assistance from interpreter as needed; use of visuals and overhead projector to write questions and responses.

Physically impaired students.   A buddy system to assist in use of reference materials and other equipment and resources.

Teaching Resources

Books

Brown, Margaret Wise, ed. *Homes in the Wilderness: A Pilgrim's Journal of Plymouth Plantation in 1620 by William Bradford et al.* Reprinted, 1939. Hamden, CT: Linnet, 1988.

Clapp, Patricia. *Constance: A Study of Early Plymouth.* New York: Lothrop, 1966.

Fleischman, Paul. *Saturnalia.* New York: HarperCollins, 1990.

Fritz, Jean. *The Doublelife of Pocahontas.* Illustrated by Ed Young. New York: Putnam, 1983.

Fritz, Jean. *Who's That Stepping on Plymouth Rock?* Illustrated by J. B. Handelsman. New York: Coward, McCann & Geoghegan, 1975.

Lenski, Lois. *Puritan Adventure.* Illustrated by the author. New York: Lippincott, 1944.

Lobel, Arnold. *On the Day Peter Stuyvesant Sailed Into Town.* Illustrated by the author. New York: Harper, 1971.

Petry, Ann. *Tituba of Salem Village.* New York: HarperCollins, 1991.

Pilkington, Roger. *I Sailed on the Mayflower: The True Story of a Pilgrim Youngster.* New York: Vantage, 1990.

Speare, Elizabeth George. *The Witch of Blackbird Pond.* New York: Dell, 1978.

Waters, Kate. *Sarah Morton's Day: A Day in the Life of a Pilgrim Girl.* Illustrated by Russ Kendall. New York: Scholastic, 1989.

Zinner, Feenie. *Squanto.* Reprinted, 1965. Hamden, CT: 1988.

Films, Filmstrips, and Audio-filmstrip Cassettes
Random House School Division, Department 9036, 400 Hahn Road, Westminster, Maryland 21157. *Thanksgiving Day,* produced by Westport Communications Group.

Organizations for Students with Special Needs

American Foundation for the Blind, Consumer Products Department, 15 West 16th Street, New York, NY 10011 (products, reports, films, and publications).
C. C. Publications, Inc., P. O. Box 23699, Tigard, OR 97223 (materials for learning disabled and educable mentally retarded).
Gryphon House, 3706 Otis House, P. O. Box 217, Mount Rainier, MD 20822 (multiethnic books).
National Clearinghouse for Bilingual Education, 1300 Wilson Blvd., Suite B2–11, Rosslyn, VA 22209 (materials for teachers of bilingual students).
National Library Service for the Blind and Physically Handicapped, Library of Congress, Washington, DC 20542 (free reading program for blind and physically handicapped that includes Brailled materials).
Telesensory Systems, Inc., 3408 Hillview Avenue, P. O. Box 10099, Palo Alto, CA 94304 (equipment for handicapped students).

Suppliers of Reading Aids for the Special Student
Magnifiers
Best Visual Products Ltd., 65 Earle Avenue, Lynbrook, NY 11563.

Print to Braille
Curzweil Computer Products, Inc., 185 Albany Street, Cambridge, MA 02139.

Talking Books
Books on Tape, Inc., P. O. Box 7900, Newport Beach, CA 92660.
Hendershot Individualized Instruction, 4114 Ridgewood, Bay City, MI 48706.
Lexicon, Inc., 60 Turner St., Waltham, MA 20154.

Cassettes
Cassette House, Inc., 530 W. Northwest Highway, Mount Prospect, IL 60056.
Listen for Pleasure, Ltd., 417 Center St., Lewistown, NY 14092.
Live Oak Media, P. O. Box 34, Ancramdale, NY 12503.
Mind's Eye, 4 Commercial Blvd., Novato, CA 94947.

Recorded Books
Listening Library Inc., 1 Park Avenue, Greenwich, CT 06970.
Recorded Books, P. O. Box 79, Charlotte Hall, MD 20622.
Spoken Arts, Inc., 310 North Avenue, New Rochelle, NY 10801.

General School Supplies

Baily School Supply Inc., 520 South Walnut, Casper, WY 82601.
Creative Educational Materials, P. O. Box 18127, West St. Paul, MN 55118–0127.
Get Smart, 13724 SW 84 Street, Miami, FL 33186.
The Learning Stop, 3220 New Stine Road, Bakersfield, CA 93309.
Swenson Scholastic Supply, 5138 W. Greenwood, Skokie, IL 60077.
Southwest Teacher Supply, 7497 Southwest Freeway, Houston, TX 77074.
Western School Supply, 3154 N. 34th Drive, Phoenix, AZ 85017.

Assessment Strategies for Unit

A unit checklist, developed from information gained through the unit, can serve as a record of each student's participation, behavior, skills, and knowledge. If a checklist is used from unit to unit, the teacher may observe different behaviors and skills contributed by a student and will have a record of each student's individual differences.

UNIT CHECKLIST

Date _____ Student _____

Objectives	*Achieved*
1. Identifies explorers, reasons for exploration, and initial contributions to colony development.	_____
2. Identifies settlements and problems.	_____
3. Recognizes how early English colonies developed.	_____
4. Develops skills:	
Discussing	_____
Locating information	_____
Reading at different speeds	_____
Studying	_____
Evaluating	_____
Making decisions and justifying choices	_____
Independent work	_____
Group work	_____
Classifying and categorizing	_____
Gathering information	_____
Reporting to class	_____
Organizing information	_____
Summarizing	_____
Reading and understanding maps	_____
Applying information	_____
Testing situations	_____
Other	_____

Additional teacher comments:

EXERCISE 4.3
Studying the Model Unit Plan

• • • • • •

Instructions: The purpose of this exercise is to study the Model Unit Plan in detail. Use the following questions as a guide to that study. Then share and compare your responses with those of your classmates.

1. Identify and state the central theme of this unit.

2. What is the intended duration of this unit?

3. Identify and list the educational goals of this unit.

4. Are the learning objectives for this unit clearly stated? Explain.

5. Do the objectives appear to contribute to the learning goals of the unit? Explain why or why not.

6. Are the instructional procedures clearly spelled out? Explain.

7. Do the learning activities appear feasible? Explain why or why not.

8. Does the unit have an introductory activity that will accomplish the purposes as spelled out in the six steps for unit planning? Explain.

9. Does the unit include developmental activities? If so, identify them.

10. Does the unit include culminating activities? If so, identify them.

11. Describe the unit's strategies for learning assessment.

12. Does the unit clearly identify the materials needed for implementation of the unit? Does it appear that the materials are readily available?

13. Could this unit plan be adaptable and used as an interdisciplinary unit? If yes, explain several changes that could be made to make it an interdisciplinary thematic unit.

14. Are there multicultural components to this unit plan? If so, identify them.

15. Does this unit plan take into account student differences in learning styles and learning modalities? If so, explain how.

16. Identify by day the various teaching strategies used in the narrative discussion of implementation of this unit. (For example: Day 1—teacher led discussion; visuals; silent reading; teacher use of questioning; and so on.)

17. Describe how this unit plan addresses student:

    Reading skills

    Study skills

    Thinking skills

18. Concerning the questions used by the teacher, identify several questions at the:

    Recall or input level

    Processing level

19. Does this unit make any attempt at helping students make connections in their learning with real life today? If it does, explain where and how.

20. Regarding the suggested assessment procedure for this unit, would you label it as being "authentic"? Explain.

21. Are the assessment procedures summative (after instruction is completed) or formative (during instruction) or both? Explain and give examples.

The Daily Lesson Plan

Effective teachers are always planning. For the long range, they plan the scope and sequence of courses and develop content for courses. Within the courses they develop units, and within the units they design the learning activities and assessment strategies to be used. They familiarize themselves with textbooks, materials, media, other resources, and innovations in the field. Yet—despite all this planning—the daily lesson plan remains pivotal to the planning process.

Not all teachers need elaborate written plans for every lesson. Sometimes effective and skilled teachers need only a sketchy outline. Sometimes they may not need written plans at all. Old hands who have taught the topic many times in the past may need only the presence of a class of students to stimulate a pattern of instruction that has often been successful before (though frequent use of old patterns may lead one into the rut of unimaginative teaching).

Assumptions

Considering this apparent diversity among teachers, certain assumptions might be made before exploring lesson planning further:

1. Not all teachers need elaborate written plans for all lessons.
2. Beginning teachers need to prepare detailed written lesson plans.
3. Some subject fields and topics require more detailed planning than others do.
4. Some experienced teachers have clearly defined goals and objectives in mind even though they have not written them into lesson plans.
5. The depth of knowledge a teacher has about a subject or topic influences the amount of planning necessary for the lessons.
6. The skill a teacher has in following a trend of thought in the presence of distraction will influence the amount of detail necessary when planning activities.
7. A plan is more likely to be carefully plotted when it is written out.
8. There is no particular pattern or format that all teachers need to follow when writing out plans. (Some teacher-preparation programs have agreed on certain lesson-plan formats for their student teachers; you need to know if this is the case for your program.)
9. All effective teachers have a planned pattern of instruction for every lesson, whether that plan is written out or not.

Written Plans

Well-written lesson plans have many uses. They give a teacher an agenda or outline to follow in teaching a lesson. They give a substitute teacher a basis for presenting appropriate lessons to a class. They are certainly very useful when a teacher is planning to use the same lesson again in the future. They provide the teacher with something to fall back on in case of a memory lapse, an interruption, or some distraction, such as a call from the office or a fire drill. Above all, they provide beginners security, because with a carefully prepared plan a beginning teacher can walk into a classroom with a confidence gained from having developed a sensible framework for that day's instruction.

Thus, as a beginning teacher you should make considerably detailed lesson plans. Naturally, this will require a great deal of work for at least the first year or two, but the reward of knowing that you have prepared and presented effective lessons will compensate for that effort. Since most teachers plan their daily lessons only a day or two ahead, you can expect a busy first year of teaching.

Some prospective teachers are concerned with being seen using a written plan in class—they think it may suggest that the teacher has not mastered the field. On the contrary, a lesson plan is a visible sign of preparation on the part of the teacher. A written lesson plan shows that thinking and planning have taken place and that the teacher has a road map to work through the lesson no matter what the distractions. Most experienced teachers agree that there is no excuse for appearing before a class without evidence of careful preparation.

A Continual Process

Experienced teachers may not require plans as detailed as those necessary for beginning teachers (after all, experienced teachers often can develop shortcuts to lesson planning without sacrificing effectiveness). Yet lesson planning is a continual process even for them, for there is always a need to keep materials and plans current and relevant. Because no two classes are ever exactly the same, today's lesson plan will probably need to be tailored to the peculiar needs of each class. Also, because the content of a course will change as new developments occur or new theories are introduced, your objectives and the objectives of the students, school, and teaching staff will change.

For these reasons, lesson plans should be in a constant state of revision. Once the basic framework is developed, however, the task of updating and modifying becomes minimal. If you maintain your plans on a computer, making necessary changes from class to class and from year to year becomes even easier.

The daily lesson plan should provide a tentative outline of the class period but should always remain flexible. A carefully worked-out plan may have to be set aside because of unforeseen circumstances, such as a delayed school bus, an impromptu assembly program, or a fire drill. A daily lesson planned to cover six aspects of a given topic may end with only three of the points having been considered. These occurrences are natural in the school setting, and the teacher and the plans must be flexible enough to accommodate this reality.

The Problem of Time

A lesson plan should provide enough materials and activities to consume the entire class period. Since planning is a skill that takes years to master, a beginning teacher should overplan rather than run the risk of having too few activities. When a lesson plan does not provide enough activity to occupy the entire class period, a beginning teacher often loses control of the class and discipline problems develop. Thus, it is best to prepare more than you likely can accomplish in a given class period. Students are very perceptive when it comes to a teacher who has finished the plan for the period and is attempting to bluff through the remaining minutes. If you ever do get caught short—as most teachers do at one time or another—one way to avoid embarrassment is to spend the remaining time in a review of material that has been covered that day or in the past several days.

The Daily Plan Book

At this point, a distinction should be made between actual lesson plans and the book of daily plans that many schools require teachers to maintain and even submit to their supervisors a week in advance. A daily-plan book is most assuredly not a daily lesson plan. Rather, it is a layout sheet on which the teacher shows what lessons will be taught during the week, month, or term. Usually the book provides only a small lined box for each class period for each day of the week. These books are useful for outlining the topics, activities, and assignments projected for the week or term, and supervisors sometimes use them to check the adequacy of teachers' course plans. They can also be useful for substitute teachers, who must try to fill in for you when you are absent. But they are not daily plans. Teachers who believe that the notations in the daily-plan book are lesson plans are fooling themselves. Student teachers should not be allowed to use these in place of real lesson plans.

Constructing A Daily Lesson Plan

Each teacher perhaps should develop a personal system of lesson planning—the system that works best for that teacher. But a beginning teacher probably needs a more substantial framework from which to work. For that reason, this module provides a preferred lesson-plan format as well as several alternative formats. Nothing is sacred about any of these formats, however. Each has worked for some teachers in the past. As you review them, determine which appeals to your style of presentation and use it with your own modifications until you find a better model.

Whatever the format, however, all plans should be written out in an intelligible style. There is good reason to question teachers who say they have no need for a written plan because they have their lessons planned "in their heads." The periods in a school day are many, as are the numbers of students in each class. When multiplied by the number of school days in a week, a semester, or a year, the task of keeping so many things in one's head becomes mind-boggling. Until you have considerable experience behind you, you will need to write and keep detailed daily plans for guidance and reference.

Components of a Daily Lesson Plan

As a rule, your written lesson plan should contain the following basic elements. These components need not be present in every written lesson plan, nor must they be presented in any particular format. As a beginning teacher, however, you would be wise to consider the suitability of each format before attempting to construct a plan. The basic elements are:

1. Control and identification data
   a. Name of course and grade level
   b. Unit
   c. Topic within unit
2. General objectives (the course or unit objective to which this lesson contributes)
3. Specific objectives of this lesson
4. The subject-matter content
5. Key points
6. The procedure (the learning activities)
   a. Introduction
   b. Lesson development
   c. Conclusion
   d. Timetable
7. Materials and equipment to be used
8. Assignment
9. Special notes and reminders
10. Comprehension checks
11. Evaluation of lesson

The following sections consider in some detail each of these elements. As you read about them, remember these three reasons for writing detailed lesson plans: (1) to clarify to yourself what you wish to accomplish, (2) to set forth what you plan to do to achieve your objectives, and (3) to remind yourself what it was you intended so that you will not forget, make mistakes, and omit important details.

Control and Identification Data

Control and identification data are presented as the heading of the lesson plan both for the benefit of supervisors who may check over your work and for your own benefit if you save the plan for future use. These data include:

1. *Name of course and grade level.* These merely serve as headings for the plan, and facilitate orderly filing of plans. Examples are:

   United States History I   Grade 11

   Science   Grade 7

2. *Name of the unit.* Inclusion of this facilitates the orderly control of the hundreds of lesson plans a teacher constructs. For example:

   United States History I   Grade 11   Unit: The Civil War

   Science   Grade 7   Unit: Science and Measurement

3. *Topic to be considered within the unit*. This is also useful for control and identification. For example:

United States History I   Grade 11   Unit: The Civil War
Topic: Main Causes

Science   Grade 7   Unit: Science and Measurement
Topic: Metric Scavenger Hunt

General Objectives

Ordinarily the general objective noted in the daily lesson plan is a broad unit objective that is supported by the lesson, though sometimes the general objective may apply only for two or three days' work rather than for a two- or three-week unit. A lesson usually supports only one general objective, but a lesson occasionally may contribute to more than one broad unit objective. You should state general objectives in your daily lesson plans to guarantee that specific lesson goals are consistent with your major overall goals. Remember that general objectives are often not stated in behavioral terms and are more closely related to concept development. Examples include:

- To develop an understanding of the reasons for the division between the strict constructionists and loose constructionists points of view at the Philadelphia Convention in 1787.
- To understand the concepts of length, area, volume, mass, and time.
- To appreciate the effect that the lifestyle of Edgar Allan Poe had on his writing.

Specific Objectives

Specific objectives should identify the major aims of the daily lesson plan. Ordinarily, these objectives should be specific enough to be accomplished within a class period, though sometimes the development of a specific objective must occur over time. When writing these objectives you should consider them as outcomes, understandings, appreciations, attitudes, special abilities, skills, and facts. Remember that you need to keep in mind how you will evaluate whether your objectives have been achieved. These specific objectives are your expectations of what students will be able to do as a result of this lesson—not what the teacher will do. As discussed earlier, your specific objectives might be covert or overt or a combination of both. Examples include:

- The student will be able to add, subtract, multiply, and divide two-digit numbers using a hand calculator. [overt, cognitive]
- The student will be able to identify the major internal organs of *Rana pipiens*. [overt, cognitive]
- The student will demonstrate appreciation for the symbolism in *Lord of the Flies*. [covert, affective]
- The student will demonstrate an understanding of the underlying cause of the Civil War as it relates to the stated causes. [covert, cognitive]
- The student will be able to list and define the steps in the scientific method. [overt, cognitive]

Setting specific objectives is a crucial step in any lesson plan. It is at this point that many lessons go wrong. In writing specific objectives teachers sometimes mistakenly list what they intend to do—such as "cover the next five pages" or "do the next 10 problems"—and fail to focus on just what their objective in these activities truly is. When you approach this step in your lesson planning, ask yourself, "What do I want my students to learn from these lessons?" Your answer to that question is your objective!

Content

To make sure your lesson actually covers what is intended, you should write down just what content you want covered. This material may be placed in a separate section or combined with the procedure section. The important thing is to be sure that your information is written down so you can refer to it quickly and easily when you need to.

If, for instance, you are going to introduce new material using the lecture method, you will want to outline the content of that lecture. The word *outline* is not used casually—you need not have pages of notes to sift through; nor should you read declarative statements to the class. You should be familiar enough with the content so that an outline (in detail, if necessary) will be sufficient to carry on the lesson as in the following example. (Note: Detailed information about using the lecture as a teaching strategy is found in Module 7.) This is an example of a content outline:

1. Causes of Civil War
   A. Primary causes.
      1. Economics.
      2. Abolitionist pressure.
      3. Slavery.
      4. _____
   B. Secondary causes.
      1. North-South friction.
      2. Southern economic dependence.
      3. _____

If you intend to conduct the lesson through discussion, you should write out the key discussion questions. For example:

- What do you think Golding had in mind when he wrote *Lord of the Flies*?
- What did the conch shell represent? Why did the other boys resent Piggy?

Since it is unlikely that you could remember all aspects of a topic while responding to student discussion, be sure that these aspects are well noted in your content section. If there are opposing sides to topics, for instance, your plan should include the pros and cons of each in order to prompt student discussion. For example:

III. Capital punishment

Pro	*Con*
A. Deterrent	A. Not a deterrent
B. Saves money	B. Rehabilitation
C. Eye for eye	C. Morally wrong

Similarly, if activities such as debates or simulations are to be used, your plan should spell out the details of the activity. For example:

IV. Simulation: War and Peace
   A. Read directions
   B. Break class into nation groups
   C. Elect spokesperson
   D. Read directions for Phase I
   E. Begin Phase I

Key Point

Not every lesson has a key point, though most probably do. Ask yourself if there were one thing in the lesson that you most want the students to retain, could you identify it? If not, there is no need to include this component in the plan. On the other hand, if there is a pivotal point around which the entire lesson revolves, you may wish to identify that point—not only for yourself, but for the class as well. This key point could be effectively used as an introduction or as a conclusion or as both. It could also be emphasized in the content of the lesson. Examples include:

- Key Point: Although there were many causes, primary and secondary, for the Civil War, the main cause for this war (as for all wars) was economics.
- "Today we shall see that. . . . " [Used as an introduction]
- "Today we have seen. . . . " [Used as a conclusion]

The Procedure

The procedure is the section in which you establish what you and your students will do during the lesson. Ordinarily, you should plan this section of your lesson as an organized entity having a beginning, a middle, and an end to be completed during the lesson. This structure is not always needed, because some lessons are simply parts of units or long-term plans and merely carry on activities spelled out in those long-term plans. Still, most daily lessons need to include in their procedure:

- An introduction
- A lesson development
- A lesson conclusion
- A timetable (probably)

Because a written lesson plan can serve as a ready reference, not only should the procedure section of your plan be written down, but it should also be written in a format you can easily follow. Therefore, write down your lesson development so you can read it easily and find your place quickly. This usually means write in large print and in an outline format. (Note: With the increasing use of personal computers many teachers find it helpful to put their lesson plans onto a computer disk; for this portion of their lesson plan they use a large font.)

Introduction to the Lesson.   Like any good performance, a lesson needs an effective introduction. In many respects the introduction sets the tone for the rest of the lesson by alerting the class that the business of learning is to begin. After all, you must have students' attention before you can teach them anything. The introduction should be an attention-getter. If it is exciting, interesting, or innovative, it can create a favorable mood for the class. In any case, a well-done introduction serves as a solid indication that you are thoroughly prepared.

Although it is difficult to develop an exciting introduction to every lesson, there is always a variety of options available by which to spice up the launching of a lesson. You might, for instance, begin the lesson by briefly reviewing yesterday's lesson, showing how it relates to today's lesson. This serves two purposes—introducing today's lesson and reviewing yesterday's. Another possibility is to review vocabulary words from previous lessons and to introduce new vocabulary. A third approach might be to review a concept developed in the previous day's lesson. Still another possibility is to use the key point of the day's lesson as an introduction and then again as the conclusion. Brief examples of introductions are:

- "As we have seen by yesterday's demonstration, the gravitational pull on the earth's surface affects the tides. Today we will consider different types of tides. . . ."
- "Juan, what is meant by *factor*? Suzy, what do we mean when we say *interpolate*?"
- "We have seen that, despite the claims of national unity, the period of the 1820s was actually a time of great regional rivalry."

In short, you can use the introduction of the lesson to review past learning, tie the new lesson to the previous lesson, introduce new material, point out the objectives of the new lesson, or—by showing what will be learned and why the learning is important—induce in students a mindset favorable to the new lesson.

The Lesson Development.   The developmental activities, which comprise the bulk of the lesson plan, are the ways by which you hope to achieve your lesson objectives. They include activities that present information, demonstrate skills, provide reinforcement of previously learned material, and provide other opportunities to develop understanding and skill. These activities should be described in some detail so you will know exactly what it is you plan to do. At this point in the plan, generalities usually do suffice. Teachers often think that they need only determine the principal line of the lesson development. Yet, simply to decide that in a certain lesson you will "discuss the XYZ affair," for instance, will not be sufficient. You will also need to know what principal points should be considered, what key questions should be used, what sequence should be followed, and what conclusions the discussion should focus on. Otherwise the class will likely drift aimlessly.

To ensure that plans for these activities are clearly laid out, they should ordinarily be carefully written out—and in some detail. This will guarantee that you have a firm plan of action (too often, plans not written out are dreams without substance). Writing the plan down will also serve as a reminder or reference. During the stress of a class it is easy to forget details of your plan and your subject, and for this reason you should note the answers to the questions you intend to ask and the solutions to problems you intend your students to solve.

Lesson Conclusion.   Having a clear-cut conclusion—also known as closure or culminating activity—is as important as having a strong introduction. The lesson closure complements the introduction. The closing activity should summarize and bind together what has ensued in the developmental stage and should reinforce the principal point. One way to accomplish these ends is to restate the key point of the lesson. Another is to briefly outline the major points of the lesson development. Still another is to repeat the major concept that was your objective. No matter what the way, this concluding activity should be brief and to the point.

The Timetable.   To estimate the time factors in any lesson can be difficult. A good procedure is to gauge the amount of time needed for each learning activity and note that time alongside the activity and strategy in your plan. For example:

1. Introduce film (10 min)
   a. Why do you suppose Ghandi was so popular?
   b. What do you think Ghandi was trying to do?
   c. Why do you think his methods were so successful?
2. Show film (25 min)
3. Review film's major points (10 min)
4. Comments about tomorrow's assignment (5 min)

Placing too much faith in your time estimate may be foolish—an estimate is more for your guidance in planning than for anything else. Beginning teachers frequently find that their discussions and lectures do not last as long as was expected. To avoid being embarrassed by running out of material, try to make sure that you have planned enough work to consume the entire class period. If you plan too much, you can use the remainder for the next day's lesson. Sometimes, you might plan an extra activity to use if the lesson runs short. Also, as mentioned earlier, if your lesson runs short, you can spend time on review or on introducing the next day's lesson. In any case, remember that to overplan is better than to underplan.

Materials and Equipment

This section of your lesson plan is a reminder that you will need to have certain materials ready for the lesson. For instance, for a certain lesson you may need an opaque projector and some pictures. There is no need to list items that are already or constantly in your classroom—the purpose of this section of the plan is simply to guarantee that you know what is needed for the lesson and that you have it ready when needed. Audiovisual equipment and materials may need to be ordered well in advance of the day you want to use them.

Assignment

If a homework assignment is to be given, you should make note of it somewhere in your lesson plan. When to present the assignment to the class is optional—except that it should never be verbally given as an afterthought as the students begin exiting the room at the end of the period. Many teachers like to write the day's assignment at a regular place on the board at the beginning of the class or an entire week's assignments on the board each Monday, drawing student attention to this early in the class or regularly each Monday. Others prefer to wait until the end of the lesson each day. Either method is acceptable, though mentioning the assignment each Monday or regularly at the beginning of each period (or both) minimizes the chance of your forgetting about it. Still other teachers prefer to write out the assignments for a period of a week or more, distributing copies to the students at regular intervals.

Whatever way you present assignments, you must allow enough time to explain the assignment clearly and to ensure that the students understand what they must do and how they should do it. In preparing an assignment, you should ensure that it:

- Is clear
- Is definite
- Is reasonable, neither too long nor too difficult
- Gives students background necessary for them to complete it successfully
- Shows students how to do it sufficiently well that they will not flounder needlessly
- Provides for individual student differences

In the written plan you usually need only include a short notation concerning the assignment, such as: *Assignment*: Read pp. 234–239, and answer questions 1, 5, 8.

Special Notes

You should provide a place in your lesson plan for special notes and reminders to yourself. Most of the time you will not need such reminders, but when you do, it helps to have reminders in a special place so you can refer to them readily. In this section you can place reminders concerning such things as announcements to be made, school programs, makeup work for certain students, and so on. These things may or may not be important, but they do need to be remembered.

Comprehension Checks

You must include in your lesson details of how you will evaluate how well students are learning and how well they have learned. Comprehension checks for determining how well they are learning can be in the form of questions you ask and the students ask during the lesson. Questions you intend to ask should be built into the developmental section.

For determining how well they have learned, teachers typically use review questions at the end of a lesson (as a closure) or the beginning of the next lesson (as a review or transfer introduction), independent practice at the completion of a lesson, and tests. Again, questions for checking for comprehension should be detailed in your lesson plan.

Evaluation of the Lesson

This section is reserved for the teacher to make notes or comments about the lesson. It can be particularly useful if you plan to use the lesson again. When you look at the lesson the following year, you likely will not recall if the lesson went well or not, so jotting down some notes at the conclusion of a taught lesson will help you make the next presentation more effective. Criteria for evaluating a lesson plan are listed in Figure 4.2.

Figure 4.2 Lesson Plan
Checklist

Does your lesson plan:
- Provide a tie-in to previous lessons?
- Provide an adequate introduction?
- Clearly identify the objectives for the students?
- Provide for a clear presentation of the learning content?
- Provide an adequate demonstration or illustration?
- Provide for checking for student comprehension during the lesson?
- Provide for checking for student comprehension after the lesson?
- Provide for preparing students for their homework assignment?
- Provide an adequate summary and follow up?
- Provide for the elimination of dead spots during the class period?
- Make adequate provisions for individual and small-group activities?
- Provide for student individual differences?
- Provide adequately for materials and equipment for instruction?
- Provide a lead-in for the next lesson?

Lesson Plan Formats

There is no mandatory basic lesson plan format and no irreplaceable list of lesson plan components. You should select a format that you find easy to work with, adapting it to the various lessons you teach. The format preferred by the authors of this text is the outline format that follows. In this format the content of the lesson is incorporated into the procedure, though the major concept or key point is listed separately.

PREFERRED LESSON PLAN FORMAT

Class: United States History   **Grade**: 11
Unit: The New Nation
Topic: Hamilton's Financial Plan
Unit objective: The students will understand the major problems faced by the new nation.
Specific objective: The students will be able to explain the financial dilemma faced by the new nation.
Key point: The diversity of means of exchange helped confuse financial matters in the United States during the Revolution and under the Articles of Confederation.
Procedure:

1. Introduction by teacher to set scene. Make following points and show samples of each. (8 minutes)
    a. Backcountry and West—barter system.
       (1) Put word *barter* on board.
       (2) Ask "What does it mean"?
    b. After 1764 no paper money could be printed but some still in circulation.
    c. British, French, and Spanish coins in demand.
    d. Virginia—tobacco warehouse receipt used as money.
    e. IOUs to soldiers from Continental Congress.
    f. Promissory notes to European creditors.
    g. Each state had own paper money under Articles of Confederation.
2. Role Play. (20 minutes)
    a. Have students play parts of:
       (1) Merchants (3 sts.)
       (2) Soldiers (3 sts.)
       (3) Continental Congress officials (6 sts.)
       (4) European creditors (3 sts.)
       (5) Residents of different states (10 sts.)
    b. Merchants sell to Continental Congress.
    c. Soldiers receive pay from Continental Congress.
    d. Continental Congress goes to European creditors (who sit at a distance).
    e. Residents of different states go back and forth trying to buy and sell.
    f. Easterners go to Kentucky and try to use cash where only barter is used and vice versa.
    g. In all cases—each uses own money and much trouble develops over various forms of currency.
3. Enter Alexander Hamilton [select responsible student] (5 minutes)
    a. Speech outlining financial policy.
       (1) Debts of previous government ($12 million foreign, $44 million domestic, $25 million state).
       (2) Where get money for new government?
       (3) How to strengthen credit?
4. Discussion (12 min.)
    a. Ask individuals what they learned from role playing.
    b. What were characteristics of system? (List on board.)
       Elicit from class:
         confusion

         diversity

         separateness of each political entity

         animosity among people

         much debt

    c. What effect would Hamilton's program have on these characteristics? (List on board.)
       Elicit from class:
         clear up confusion

         unify nation

         sound credit

Materials: play coins; play paper money; replicas of colonial and Revolutionary currency; handmade IOUs; promissory notes; tobacco warehouse receipt; objects for trade.

Assignment: Read Thomas Jefferson's reaction to Hamilton's plan. What was his position and why?

Note: Speak to "Alexander Hamilton" before class.

Evaluation of lesson:

Alternative Format 1

You or the school system for which you work may require other formats. Other commonly used lesson-plan formats are illustrated in the following pages. The first of these alternative formats follows the outline of the preferred format, except that it lists the content and procedures separately.

Lesson Topic_____ **Date**_____
Unit_____**Grade**_____

1. Lesson Objective

2. Content

3. Procedure

4. Instructional Materials

5. Evaluation

Alternative Format 2

The second alternative format is virtually the same as the first, except that it provides a column for notes about the items in the content and procedure sections. It also has a special section for evaluation and questions. In this format, *Evaluation* refers to a test or some other evaluative devices of the students' work, whereas *Questions* refers to the questions the teacher would use in the class recitation or discussion.

Teacher_____Course Topic_____Date_____
Unit _____
Objectives

Content   *Notes*

Procedures

Evaluation and Questions

Assignment

Materials of Instruction

Evaluation

Alternative Format 3

The third alternative format is most suited to a recitation or lecture-question lesson. In this format, following a space for noting the introductory activities, the teacher writes the content in outline form in one column. In a second column, the teacher writes the key questions to be asked in connection with the items in the content column. This section is followed by a space for a summary. Although the word *procedure* is not mentioned, this format provides for a procedure section of three parts: introduction, development, and conclusion.

Unit_____**Course**_____**Date**_____

Lesson Topic_____

Objective_____

Introduction

Content   *Key Questions*

Summary

Materials

Assignment

Evaluation

Alternative Format 4

A fourth alternative format commonly used lists the objectives in one column and the activities that are to bring about these objectives in another column. This format has the advantage of pointing out which activity is designed to bring about each objective, and thus incidentally guarantees that each activity is designed to address some objective. But this format may be difficult to use in class because it does not lend itself to a step-by-step outline of the procedure, as in the Preferred Lesson Plan Format.

Lesson_____ Course_____ Date_____

Objectives	*Activities*
1. Bargain and compromise were the principal methods of solving political difficulties about 1850.	1. Map study. Review the new territory added to United States.
2. etc.	2. What was slave? What free?
	3. On map find slave states.
	4. etc.

Materials of Instruction Needed

Assignment

Evaluation

Alternative Format 5

The fifth alternative format is often used partly as a supervisory device. It provides spaces for detailed identification data, aims, understandings, special notes, and assignments, as well as columns for the teacher's timetable, outline of content, and the methods to be used to teach the content. Although the form may appear complicated, the fact the the three columns of the "procedure" are listed according to time sequence makes the format easy to follow during class.

School _____ Teacher _____	
Grade _____ Date _____ Day _____	
Period(s) or Module(s) _____ Room(s) _____ Week Ending _____	

Daily Lesson Plan

Day's Aims and Objectives Major Understandings: Skills to be Developed: Attitudes:	Routines(general housekeeping reminders) Student Assignment(s) (for one or more days)

Chronological Time Sequence (minute by minute or number of minutes to be used in each part of outline)	Outline of Content to Focus upon in Order to Achieve Aims and Objectives	Teaching Methods, Techniques (and needed materials)

Evaluation

Sample Lesson Plans

The preceding pages have presented the fundamental components in the development of a daily lesson plan. It is important for the beginning teacher to note that some components will bear more strikingly on certain subject fields. Some can be modified to relate more specifically to a given subject, topic, or class of students. The essential point to remember, however, is that a daily lesson plan should be a flexible instrument that can be effectively used by the classroom teacher. A plan is valueless if simply prepared to meet an administrative requirement that plans be filed in the main office. Similarly, a plan is valueless if constructed so rigidly that departures are impossible. Examples of lesson plans in various formats follow.

SAMPLE LESSON PLAN 1—ALGEBRA

1. **Course**: Algebra 1, Grade 9, Average Group
2. **Topic**: Factoring polynomials having common factors.
3. **Content**:

   a. Vocabulary: *Old*   Factor, product, polynomial, monomial.

   New   Common factor, greatest common factor.

   b. Concepts: *Old*   Distributive law.

   New   Factoring polynomials that have common factors is the inverse process of multiplying a polynomial by a monomial.

   c. Skills: *Old*   Using the distributive law, multiplying a polynomial by a monomial.

   New   Finding the greatest common factor.

4. Method of presentation: Teacher-student discussion

   Time schedule: 10 min—review homework.

   15 min—present new material.

   15 min—guided practice and supervised study.

   Assignment: Read pp. 244–245; p. 245, 1–29: all odd numbered problems.

5. Objectives:

   a. Students will be able to demonstrate that factoring polynomials having common factors is the inverse process of multiplying a polynomial by a monomial.

   b. Students will be able to find the greatest common factor.

6. Evaluation:

7. Materials: none

Procedure

1. Review:

   a. What is a product?

   b. What is a factor?

2. Given the problem:

   $3a + 4b$ what are the factors?

   $\times 4a$ how do we find the products?

   what is the product?

3. Can we write this problem another way?

   $4a(3a - 4b) = 12a^2 - 16ab$.

   What gives us the right to do the problem this way? (Dist. Law)

   What is the Distributive Law?

4. Give examples: $2a(m + 3n)$; $3x(2x - 1)$; $a^2(a^2) + b^2)$.

5. $a(x + y + z) = ax + ay + az$.

What law is this?

When multiplying a polynomial by a monomial, what may be said about the product? (The monomial is seen in each term of the product.)

We may say that a is what to each term in the product? (common).

6. In $2ax + 2ay =$ what is the common factor? ($2a$).

Where do you think we would put the common factor?

What do we do to each term in the product? (divide it by the common factor and put quotient in parentheses).

Just as division is the inverse of multiplication, what can we say the relationship between factoring polynomials and the process of multiplying a polynomial by a monomial is? (the inverse).

7. $6m + 6n = 6(m + n)$

$mn + m = m(n + 1)$

$3a^2 - 3a = 3a(a - 1)$

For each problem, what is its common factor?

Where do I put it?

What do I do to each term in the product?

8. $4a^2 + 12a = 4a(a + 3)$

Could I write $4a^2 + 12a = 4(a^2 + 3a)$? Why?

What is $4a$ called? (greatest common factor).

9. What is the greatest common factor in these problems?

Where do I put it?

What do I do to each term in product?

$6xy - 3x^2 = 3x(2y - x)$.

$2a + 4ab + 2ac = 2a(1 + 2b + c)$.

10. Given the example: $6a^2b - 15ab^2 = ?$ [$? = 3ab(2a - 5b)$]

This check could still be valid if G.C.F. had not been chosen, ex. $3a$ instead of $3ab$. Therefore, what should we do to check for G.C.F.? (Inspect each term in the polynomial to make sure no single number or letter is seen in each term.)

SAMPLE LESSON PLAN 2—SOCIAL STUDIES

Social Studies II: United States History and Problems.
Unit: Evolving a Foreign Policy.
Topic: The Changing Relationship of Puerto Rico to the United States in the Twentieth Century.

Objectives

Students will be able to:

1. Outline the evolution of the political and economic ties between Puerto Rico and the United States over a specified period of time.
2. Demonstrate an appreciation for the unique role of Puerto Rico in current inter-American affairs.
3. Relate current problems to their historical antecedents.

Procedure

1. Conclude unfinished business: an oral report comparing life in Maryland suburbia with life in rural North Dakota.
2. Review by means of puzzle.
3. Establish purposes for listening to oral reports by offering listening guide questions. Present reports sequentially to trace the changing relationship of Puerto Rico to the United States.
   a. The Island of Puerto Rico Before 1898.
   b. Political and Economic Change, 1898–1940.
   c. Luis Muñoz Marin and Operation Bootstrap.
   d. Puerto Rico: The Cultural Bridge Between the Americas.
   e. Teodoro Muscoso and the Alliance for Progress.
4. Summarize by means of special assignment, which the students will copy from the board upon entering the classroom.

Assignment

Read "Crisis in Latin America," a speech made by the governor of Puerto Rico. Keep these questions in mind:

1. Why does the author caution us about the use of political "labels"?
2. In what ways is the term *Latin America* really an unsuitable expression?
3. What are the particular problems that Latin America faces?
4. In the Alliance for Progress, what roles does the author hope the United States will play?
5. Why is there stress on the phrase "Operation Seeing-Is-Believing"?
6. What unique function does the governor feel his own island can play in the Alliance for Progress?

Evaluation

Materials   Copies of puzzle for review

SAMPLE LESSON PLAN 3—SCIENCE

Physical Science, Grade 7.
Unit: Science and Measurement
Topic: The Metric Scavenger Hunt
Objectives: Students will estimate length in metric units within a 10 percent accuracy.
Materials: Metric Scavenger Hunt worksheet; metric rulers.

Procedure

1. Introduction: Introduce this as a great activity. (5 min)
    How many have ever gone on a scavenger hunt?
2. Give instructions, rules for Metric Scavenger Hunt. (5 min)
3. Check for understanding. (5 min)
4. Divide class into groups of four (cooperative learning groups) and embark on hunt. (5 min)
5. During hunt, check individuals for understanding. (20 min)
6. Check for group results. Debrief. (10 min)

Evaluation for future use:

Now that you have read through the sample lesson plans, study them more closely by working through Exercise 4.4. Then proceed to Exercise 4.5 to prepare your first complete unit plan.

EXERCISE 4.4

Examination of Sample Lesson Plans

• • • • • •

Instructions: The purpose of this exercise is to provide an in-depth study of the sample lesson plans. First, examine the three sample lesson plans presented in this module. Answer the following questions about them, and share your responses with others in your class.

1. What is your opinion about each of them?

2. Do they measure up to the criteria listed in Figure 4.2?

3. Would a substitute teacher be able to follow each one?

4. Specifically how could each be improved?
   a. Algebra lesson plan:

b. Social studies lesson plan:

c. Science lesson plan:

EXERCISE 4.5

Preparing a Two-Week Unit Plan, Complete with a Sequence of Ten Daily Lesson Plans

• • • • • •

Instructions: The purpose of this exercise is to provide the opportunity to practice what you learned in this and previous modules about planning—putting it all together to make a complete unit plan. Select a topic that you are likely to teach and then prepare a two-week unit plan, complete with a ten-day sequence of daily lesson plans. Your unit plan should include the components for a unit plan as presented in this module. Your daily plans should follow the guidelines presented in this module, but over the period of ten days they should include a variety of teaching strategies, such as lecture, discussion, simulation, inquiry, and the use of audiovisuals. You may need to refer to later modules of this text as you plan the development and phases of the daily lessons and the evaluation tools for the unit.

Upon completion of your unit plan, share it with your classmates for their feedback, make appropriate modifications, and then hand it in for your instructor's feedback and evaluation.

Your course instructor may have additional guidelines or requirements for this exercise.

The Interdisciplinary Thematic Unit

Of special interest to many middle school and secondary school teachers today are units built around interdisciplinary themes rather than content topics that are single-subject specific. Interdisciplinary thematic teaching helps students bridge disciplines and connect school learning with real-life experiences. The Model Unit Plan presented earlier in this module could be used either as a stand-alone, single-subject unit—though one that bridges disciplines—or it could be used as the beginning of an interdisciplinary thematic unit taught by a teaching team. (The length of complete interdisciplinary thematic units makes it impractical to include a sample in this book.)

The six steps given previously are essential for planning any type of teaching unit, and, as mentioned, there are several types. Of increasing interest to many middle school and secondary school teachers is the interdisciplinary thematic unit, which is composed of smaller subject-specific or standard units.

For example, in 1991, four ninth-grade teachers at York High School in Yorktown, Va., decided to make connections for their students in these subjects—science, algebra, geography, and English:

> Using a common planning period to collaborate, the teachers began modestly with an assignment to summarize earth science articles that strengthened students' knowledge of science as well as their writing skills. Later in the year, the teachers launched an interdisciplinary project focused on the Winter Olympics in Albertville, France. In small groups, students were presented with a problem related to one aspect of hosting the Olympics—providing transportation, food, lodging, entertainment, or security. The groups wrote proposals setting forth their solutions, drawing on what they had learned about the geography of the region and applying science knowledge and math skills.[2]

In the York High School project, the English teacher taught vocabulary that students would encounter in their algebra and earth science classes. Primary responsibility for the development of interdisciplinary thematic units often depends upon the cooperation of several teachers, who, in the case of secondary schools, usually represent several disciplines. Remember, as discussed in Module 1 and as exemplified by the York High School project, this interdisciplinary team of teachers may meet daily during a common planning time. Flexible scheduling allows for instructional blocks of time so team members have common planning time. And unit lessons can, likewise, be more flexible and less constrained by time.

Some teaching teams develop one interdisciplinary thematic unit each year, semester, trimester, or quarter—that is, from one to four a year. Over time, then, the team will have developed several units that are available for implementation. The most effective units, however, are often the most current, because they are the most meaningful to students. This means that ever-changing global, national, and local topics provide a smorgasbord from which to choose. And teaching teams must constantly be aware of the changes in the world and society, as well as in the interests of students, in order to update old units and develop new and exciting ones.

One teaching team's unit should not conflict with another's at the same or another grade level. If a school has two or more seventh-grade teams, for example, the teams may want to develop units on different themes and share their products. As another example, a junior high school team may want to share their units with high school teams, and perhaps even feeder schools. The lines of communication within, between, and among teams and schools are critical to the success of thematic teaching.

Because developing interdisciplinary thematic units has increasingly been becoming an essential task for many teachers, you should learn now the process that you may be practicing later as an employed teacher (as well as when student teaching). One other point needs to be made: an interdisciplinary thematic unit can be prepared and taught by one teacher (as in the Model Unit Plan) but more often these units are prepared by and taught by a team of teachers. When the latter is the case, then that instructional strategy is referred to as *interdisciplinary the-*

---

[2]Scott Willis, "Interdisciplinary Learning: Movement to Link Disciplines Gains Momentum," *ASCD Curriculum Update* (November 1992): 1 (Alexandria, VA: Association for Supervision and Curriculum Development).

matic team teaching. Most often (as discussed in Module 1) the team comprises teachers from at least four areas: social studies or history, language arts or English, mathematics, and science. But a thematic unit and teaching team might also consist of fewer than four, say math and science, for example, or history and English, or, as in the model unit, social studies and language arts.

Procedure for Planning and Developing an Interdisciplinary Thematic Unit
The following are nine steps for developing an interdisciplinary thematic unit:

1. *Agree on the nature or source of origin for the interdisciplinary thematic unit.* Team members should view the interdisciplinary approach as a collective effort in which all team members (and other faculty) participate somewhat equally. Discuss how the team wants students to profit from the interdisciplinary instruction. Trouble shoot possible stumbling blocks.

2. *Discuss subject-specific frameworks, goals and objectives, curriculum guidelines, textbooks and supplemental materials, and units already in place for the school year.* This discussion should focus on what each teacher must teach, and it should cover both scope and sequence so that all team members share an understanding of constraints and limitations.

3. *Choose a topic and develop a time line.* From the information provided by each subject specialist teacher (i.e., Step 2), start listing possible topics that can be drawn from within the existing course outlines. Give and take is essential at this step, because some topics will fit certain subjects better than others. The chief goal, here, is to find a workable topic—one that can be adapted to each subject without detracting from the educational plan already in place. This may require choosing and merging content from two or more other units previously planned. The theme is then drawn from the topic. When considering a theme, the team should consider these questions:

- Can this theme lead to a unit that is of proper duration, not too short and not too long?
- Is it worth the time needed to create and implement it? Do we have sufficient materials and resources to supply information we might need?
- Is the theme within the realm of understanding and experience of the teachers involved? Is the theme topic one with which teachers are not already too familiar so they can share in the excitement of the learning? Will the theme be of interest to all members of the teaching team? Does it apply broadly to a wide range of subject areas?
- What is so important about this theme that it will promote future learning? Does the theme have substance and application to the real world? Does it lend itself to active learning? Will it be of interest to students; will it motivate them to do their best? Will it fascinate students once they are into it?[3]

4. *Create two time lines.* The first time line, for the team only, is to ensure that given dates for specific work required in developing the unit will be met by each member. The second time line, for both students and teachers, shows how long the unit will be, when it will start, and in which classes.

5. *Develop the scope and sequence for content and instruction.* Follow the six steps for planning and developing any unit of instruction when developing an interdisciplinary thematic unit. Those steps should be kept in mind by each team member and also by the group during common planning time, so that team members can coordinate dates and activities in logical sequence and depth. This organic process will generate ideas but also produce some anxiety. Members of the team, under the guidance of the team leader, should strive to maintain anxiety at a level conducive to learning, experimenting, and arriving at group consensus.

6. *Share goals and objectives.* Each team member should have a copy of the goals and objectives of every other member. This helps refine the unit and lesson plans and prevent unnecessary overlap and confusion.

[3]See also Scott Willis, "Choosing a Theme," *ASCD Curriculum Update* (November 1992): 4–5 (Alexandria, VA: Association for Supervision and Curriculum Development).

7. *Give the unit its name.* The unit has been fashioned based on a common topic and is being held together by the theme you have chosen. Giving the theme a name and using that name lets the students know that this unit of study is integrated, important, and meaningful to school and to life.

8. *Share subject-specific units, lesson plans, print and nonprint materials.* After teachers have finalized their units, exchange them for review comments and suggestions. Keep a copy of each teacher's unit(s) and see if you could use it to present a lesson from your own subject area. If you can, the plan is probably workable. If you can't, some modification may be necessary.

9. *Check the thematic unit by field testing.* Beginning on the agreed-upon time, date, and class(es), present the lessons. Team members may trade classes from time to time. Team teaching may take place when two or more classes can be combined for instruction, such as can be done with flexible and block scheduling.

After field testing, there is, of course, one final step—the thematic unit must be evaluated and perhaps adjusted and revised. Team members discuss successes and failures during their common planning time and determine what needs to be changed, how, and when, in order to make the unit successful. Adjustments to the unit can be made along the way, called formative evaluation, and revisions of it for future use can be made after the unit is completed, called summative evaluation.

The nine steps are not absolutes and should be viewed only as guides. Differing compositions of teaching teams and levels of teacher experience and knowledge make strict adherence to any modus operandi less productive than group-generated plans. For instance, many teachers recommend that the topic for an interdisciplinary thematic unit be one that the team already knows well. In practice, the process that works for the team—one that results in meaningful student learning and in students feeling good about themselves, about learning, and about school—is the appropriate process.

Now explore interdisciplinary thematic units further by doing Exercises 4.6 and 4.7.

EXERCISE 4.6

Themes for Interdisciplinary Thematic Units

• • • • • •

Generating Ideas

Instructions: The purpose of this exercise is to brainstorm a list of potential theme topics that would be suitable as interdisciplinary units. Divide your class into groups of three to five. Each group should decide the grade level for which its unit ideas are generated. If the group chooses, cooperative learning can be used, and group members are assigned roles (such as facilitator, recorder, reporter, monitor of thinking processes, on-task monitor, and so on). Within each group, generate as many potential topics as possible. One member of each group should record all ideas. Reserve discussion of ideas until no further ones are generated. Lists can be shared in the large group.

Grade level interest of group:

1. Existing subject area content units (as the group knows them to be from your study of existing curriculum documents):

2. Topics of current interest:

    Of global interest

    Of national interest

    Of statewide interest

    Of local interest

Of interest to the school

Of interest to students

Instructions: The purpose of this exercise is to practice weaving interdisciplinary themes into curricula. In groups of three to five, choose one idea that was generated during Exercise 4.6 and derive a list of suggestions about how that theme could be woven into the curricula of various school classes, programs, and activities. Possibly, not all areas listed in this exercise are relevant to the grade level to which your group is addressing its work. Cooperative learning can be used, with roles assigned to group members. One person in the group should be the recorder. Upon completion, share the product of your group's work (the process and product of which will be much like that of an actual interdisciplinary teaching team) with the rest of your class. For those who want a copy, copies should be made of the work of each group.

Unit/Topic/Theme:

1. In core classes:

   English

   Social studies

   Mathematics

   Science

   Reading

Physical education

Art

Music

2. In cocurricular programs and activities:
Electives

Clubs

School functions

Assemblies

Study skills

3. In exploratory courses (noncredit, short courses on specific job skills, hobbies, or occupations):

4. In the homeroom (homebase or advisor-advisee) program:

5. Explain how multicultural components could be incorporated.

6. As individuals, and as a group, how productive was this exercise? Explain why or why not you think it was productive.

SUMMARY

Developing units of instruction that integrate student learning and that provide a sense of meaning for the students requires coordination throughout the curriculum—which is defined here as consisting of all the planned experiences students encounter while at school. Hence, for students learning is a process of discovering how information, knowledge, and ideas are interrelated—learning to make sense out of self, school, and life. Molding "chunks" of information into units, and units into daily lessons, helps students process and make sense out of knowledge. Having developed your first unit of instruction, you are well on your way to becoming a competent planner of instruction.

There is no single best way to organize a daily plan, no fool-proof formula that will guarantee a teacher an effective lesson. With experience and the increased competence that comes from reflecting on that experience, you will develop your own style, your own methods of implementing that style, and your own formula for preparing a lesson plan. Like a map, your lesson plan charts the course, places markers along the trails, pinpoints danger areas, highlights areas of interest and importance along the way, and ultimately brings the traveler to the successful completion of the objective.

The best-prepared units and lessons, though, will go untaught or only poorly implemented if presented in a poorly managed classroom. In the next module, you learn how to provide a supportive classroom environment—to effectively manage the classroom for the most efficient instruction and student achievement.

SUGGESTED READING

Boling, A.N. "They Don't Like Math? Well, Let's Do Something." *Arithmetic Teacher* 38(7):17–19 (March 1991).

Bomeli, C.L. "Mathematics and Meteorology: Perfect Partners." *School Science and Mathematics* 91(1):31–33 (January 1991).

Boyer, M.R. "The Challenge of an Integrated Curriculum: Avoid the Isolated Road." *School Administrator* 50(3):20–21 (March 1993).

Brutlag, D., and Maples, C. "Making Connections: Beyond the Surface." *Mathematics Teacher* 85(3):230–235 (March 1992).

Dolan, D. "Implementing the Standards: Making Connections in Mathematics." *Arithmetic Teacher* 38(6):57–60 (February 1991).

Easterday, K.E., and Bass, D.T. "Using Environmental Issues to Integrate Science and Mathematics." *School Science and Mathematics* 93(5):234–236 (May–June 1993).

Erb, T.O., and Doda, N.M. *Team Organization: Promise—Practices & Possibilities.* Washington, DC: National Education Association, 1989.

Farivar, S. "Continuity and Change: Planning an Integrated History–Social Science/English–Language Arts Unit." *Social Studies Review* 32(2):17–24 (Winter 1993).

Fogarty, R. *How to Integrate the Curricula.* (Palatine, IL: Skylight, 1991).

Gehrke, N.J. "Explorations of Teachers' Development of Integrative Curriculum." *Journal of Curriculum and Supervision* 6(2):107–17 (Winter 1991).

Hunter, M. *Enhancing Teaching.* New York: Macmillan, 1994.

Jacobs, H.H., et al. *Interdisciplinary Curriculum: Design and Implementation.* Alexandria, VA: Association for Supervision and Curriculum Development, 1989.

Kentta, B. "The Challenge of an Integrated Curriculum: Moving With Cautious Velocity." *School Administrator* 50(3):17, 19 (March 1993).

LaPorte, J., and Sanders, M. "The T/S/M/ Integration Project: Integrating Technology, Science, and Mathematics in the Middle School." *Technology Teacher* 52(6):17–21 (March 1993).

Palmer, J., et al. "Teaching Location and Some Characteristics of Place: Using South Africa." *Social Education* 55(1):58–60 (January 1991).

Roth, W.M. "Problem-Centered Learning for the Integration of Mathematics and Science in a Constructivist Laboratory: A Case Study." *School Science and Mathematics* 93(3):113–122 (March 1993).

Schubert, B. "Literacy: What Makes It Real: Integrated, Thematic Teaching." *Social Studies Review* 32(2):7–16 (Winter 1993).

Slay, J.V., and Pendergast, S.A. "Infusing the Arts Across the Curriculum." *School Administrator* 50(5):32–35 (May 1993).

POSTTEST

Multiple Choice

_____   1. The written document explaining the workings of a class, given to students (and parents) during the first few days of the school year, is the
   a. syllabus
   b. textbook
   c. course of study
   d. curriculum guide

_____   2. Which follows a unit of instruction as an assessment of student learning of that unit?
   a. preassessment
   b. formative evaluation
   c. summative evaluation
   d. diagnostic assessment

_____   3. When the teacher monitors student work during a lesson by using guided practice and questioning, and when the teacher assigns independent practice at the completion of the lesson, that teacher is
   a. shifting interaction.
   b. implementing an orientation set.
   c. checking for student comprehension.
   d. assessing student achievement for grading purposes.

_____   4. The lesson plan format that works best is
   a. Hunter's model.
   b. the format that the teacher can most effectively implement.
   c. the lesson plan that includes details of all six common steps.
   d. different for a middle school teacher than it is for a secondary school teacher.

_____   5. From the following, the first step in preparing to teach a course should be to
   a. plan the lessons.
   b. select a textbook.
   c. prepare the course objectives.
   d. select the instructional strategies.

Short Explanation

1. Explain the rationale for organizing course instruction into units.
2. For your subject field, identify and describe criteria for selecting a topic for a unit of study.
3. Explain three reasons why a student teacher or a first-year teacher needs to prepare detailed lesson and unit plans.
4. Explain why you should know how to prepare detailed plans even when the textbook program you are using provides them.

5. When, if ever, during instruction can or should you divert from the written plan?
6. Explain the importance of preassessment of student learning. When do you do a preassessment? How can it be done?
7. Explain why lesson planning is or should be a continual process.
8. Explain why supervisors of student teachers expect student teachers to plan and prepare their classroom management systems in writing and to do very detailed and written unit and lesson planning.
9. Explain some differences between planning a standard unit and planning an interdisciplinary thematic unit.
10. Explain the concept of a "student-negotiated curriculum." Is it used today in middle school and secondary school teaching? Why or why not?

Essay

1. From your current observations and field work as related to this teacher preparation program, clearly identify one specific example of educational practice that seems contradictory to exemplary practice or theory as presented in this module. Present your explanation for the discrepancy.
2. Describe any prior concepts you held that changed as a result of your experiences with this module. Describe the changes.

Module 5

Planning and Maintaining a Supportive Classroom Environment

RATIONALE

No matter how well prepared your plans are, those plans will go untaught or poorly taught if presented to students in a classroom that is nonsupportive and poorly managed. Thoughtful and thorough planning of your procedures for classroom management is as an important part of your preactive-phase decision making as is the preparation of units and daily lessons. And for that reason we include it as one of the important steps for instructional planning. Indeed, a recent analysis of fifty years of research studies concluded that classroom management is the single most important factor influencing student learning.[1] Just as is true for unit and lesson plans, your management system should be planned and written down by you long before you meet your first class of students. You will begin doing that in this module.

In this, the final module of Part II, you learn how to provide a supportive classroom environment and to manage the classroom effectively, for the most efficient instruction will result in the best student achievement.

SPECIFIC OBJECTIVES

At the completion of this module, you should be able to:

1. Describe student perceptions about the classroom and about their learning that are necessary for the expected learning to occur.
2. Describe resources and devices you can use to learn more about your students.
3. Describe various approaches that you might use for improving students' desire to learn.
4. Describe how you can use positive reinforcement to enhance student learning.
5. Describe the concept of effective classroom control.
6. Demonstrate by examples how each of the following contributes to effective classroom control: a positive approach, well-planned lessons, a good start of the school year, classroom procedures and rules, consistent enforcement of procedures and rules, correction of student misbehavior, and classroom management.
7. Describe specific procedures for establishing the conditions and carrying out the actions necessary to establish and maintain classroom control.
8. Plan and write down your own classroom management system.

[1]Margaret C. Want, Geneva D. Haertel, and Herbert J. Walberg, "What Helps Students Learn?" *Educational Leadership* 51(4):74–79 (December 1993/January 1994).

MODULE TEXT

Importance of Perceptions

Unless you, as the teacher, believe that your students can learn, they will not. Unless you believe that you can teach them, you will not. Unless your students believe they can learn and want to learn, they will not. We all know of teachers who get the very best from their students, even from students many teachers would find most difficult to teach.[2] Regardless of individual circumstances, characteristics common to successful teachers are that: (1) they *know* that all students can learn; (2) they *expect* the very best from each student; (3) they establish a classroom climate that is conducive to student learning and motivates students to do their very best; and (4) they effectively manage their classrooms so class time is most efficiently used with the least amount of disturbance to the learning process.

Successful teachers know that the effort a student is willing to spend on a learning task is a product of two factors: (1) the degree to which the student believes he or she can successfully complete the task and achieve the rewards of that completion, and (2) the degree of value the student places on that reward. This has been called the expectancy × value theory.[3] In this theory, for student learning to occur both factors must be present—the student must see value in the experience and must feel that he or she can achieve the intended outcome.[4] A student is less likely to try to learn when he or she perceives no value in the material, and the student is unlikely to try to learn when he or she feels incapable of learning it. In other words, before students do, they must feel they can do; and before students do, they must perceive an importance for doing it.

Therefore, good planning is not enough. Students must also have certain perceptions for successful implementation of those plans to occur:

- Students must feel that the classroom environment is supportive of their efforts.
- Students must feel welcomed in your classroom.
- Students must perceive the expected learning to be challenging but not impossible to achieve.
- Students must perceive achievement of the expected learning outcomes as being worthy of their time and effort.

In this module we provide strategies for setting up and managing your classroom in a way that demonstrates to students that they can learn, and therefore they will learn. We suggest strategies that can help you instill the perceptions that students must hold in order that maximum learning will occur.

Regardless of the effectiveness with which you do these things, classroom management problems are likely to occur. We close the module by focusing your attention on specific ways to manage the classroom effectively and to handle various problems that might occur.

A Supportive Classroom Environment

Teachers whose classes are pleasant and positive find that their students learn and behave better than students in classes that are harsh, repressive, and negative. Thus, as a teacher you

[2]See, for example, the many publications and videos made available by Harry Wong, who for many years was a most successful secondary school teacher and who is now sharing his techniques through writing, filming, and speaking engagements. For information write Harry K. Wong Publications, 1030 W. Maude Ave., Ste. 507, Sunnyvale, CA 94086, Phone (408) 732-1388 or Fax (408) 732-2206. Or see the film *Stand and Deliver*, the story of mathematics teacher J. Escalante while a teacher at Garfield High in Los Angeles. Mr. Escalante is now successfully teaching at Hiram Johnson High School, Sacramento, CA. See also Mike Rose, *Lives on the Boundary: A Moving Account of the Struggles and Achievements of America's Educational Underclass* (New York: Penguin, 1990).

[3]Norman T. Feather (ed.), *Expectations and Actions* (Hillsdale, NJ: Erlbaum, 1982).

[4]Thomas L. Good and Jere E. Brophy, *Looking in Classrooms*, 4th ed. (New York: HarperCollins, 1994), p. 225.

should "accentuate the positive" and "catch them being good." The suggestions in this module can be used to make your classroom atmosphere supportive for student learning.

Getting to Know Students as People

For classes to move forward smoothly and efficiently, they should accommodate the students' abilities, needs, interests, and goals. As emphasized in Module 2, you must plan your instruction with your students' interests and perspectives in mind. You need to know your students well in order to provide learning activities they will find interesting, valuable, motivating, and rewarding. There are a number of specific steps you can take to get to know your students as people.

Prepare and use a seating chart to assist you in quickly learning student names.   Like everyone else, students appreciate being recognized and addressed by name. Quickly learning and using their names is an important motivating strategy. One technique for learning names quickly is to use a seating chart. A way to do this is to prepare slips of paper bearing the names of your students, and then as you call your roll, place the name slips into the proper spots in a pocket-type seating chart. Some schools provide these pocket-type charts; if not, you can easily make one yourself. You can also make a blank seating chart on which you write in the names during roll call or when students are doing seat work. Many teachers prefer to assign permanent seats and then make seating charts from which they can unobtrusively check the roll while students are doing seat work. It is usually best to get your students into the lesson before taking roll and doing other housekeeping chores.

Many teachers assign permanent seats in this way: on the first day of school tell your students that they can sit wherever they want but by Friday of that first week they should be in a permanent seat, from which you will make a permanent seating chart. Other teachers prefer to assign permanent seats on the first or second day of school so they can begin learning student names even more quickly. Whichever way you proceed, a seating chart assists in your quickly learning names and in taking daily roll unobtrusively.

Addressing students by name every time you speak to them will also help you remember their names. (Be sure to learn to pronounce their names correctly; that helps in making a good impression.) Another way to learn student names is to return their papers each day yourself, calling their names and then handing the papers to them, paying careful attention to look at each student and making mental notes that may help you to associate names with faces.

Get to know your students as people.   None of us is motivated when we feel recognized only as a statistic or a number. Each of us is a distinct person, and we feel much more positive about a formal setting (such as a classroom and a doctor's office) when we feel recognized as being important and unique individuals. With your own students, learn about each as much and as quickly as you can—about their personalities, characters, ability levels, interests, and home life. The best way to learn about a person is to spend a great deal of time with that person, talking together, socializing together, and working together. Unfortunately, the structure of high schools (and to a lesser extent middle schools) makes it difficult to know students well. The daily teacher load is often quite heavy (100–150 students per teacher) and the teacher's time is limited. Consequently, teachers must utilize various shortcuts, tips, clues, and other techniques to get to know their students. The most useful techniques for learning about your students include:

- *Classroom sharing.* One technique that is not only motivating during that first week of school but also helpful in getting to know more about each of your students is to spend some time during the first week of class asking each student to share a bit about him- or herself. These are the kind of questions you might ask:

  What name would you like us to call you by?

  Where did you attend school last year?

  What are your out-of-school interests or hobbies?

  What is one thing you would especially like us to know about you?

How the student answers such questions may be as revealing about the student as is the information (or the lack thereof) that the student does share. From what is revealed during this sharing, you sometimes get clues about additional information you would like to solicit from the student in private or to find out from school sources.

- *Observations.* Observing the students in class, on the athletic field, and at lunch may give additional information about their personalities, friendships, interests, and potentialities. For instance, you may find that a student who seems phlegmatic, lackadaisical, or uninterested in the classroom is a real fireball on the playing field or at some other student gathering.

- *Conversations.* Conversations between you and individual students before, during, and after class, as well as at other times in school, can be helpful in conveying the important message that you are interested in each student as a unique and valued individual. Keep in mind that students who feel they have been betrayed by prior adult associations may at first be distrustful of your sincerity. Be patient, but do not hesitate to take advantage of the opportunity afforded by talking with individual students outside of class time. Investing a few minutes of time in a positive conversation between you and a student, during which you indicate a genuine interest in that student, can pay real dividends when it comes to that student's learning in your classroom.

- *Conferences with students.* Conferences with a student, with that student's parent or guardian, and with that student's other teachers can also be useful for data gathering. Conferences with students can be formal, structured, one-on-one interactions scheduled by you for the purpose of learning more about each individual student. In such a setting, it is helpful if you follow these suggestions:

  1. Ask only open-ended questions. Encourage the student to talk freely. Listen to what the student says.
  2. Don't moralize, judge, or condemn, but accept a student's opinions and values as what they are—his or her opinions and values.
  3. Let the student do most of the talking.
  4. As soon as possible after the conference, record your observations. Your personal file concerning the students you teach should by year's end contain hunches about actions you have seen as well as direct quotations of statements you have heard that seem to have some bearing on the student's behavior. Failure to record such revelations quickly may result in your forgetting them or, worse yet, remembering them incorrectly.

Remember, your purpose is to try to learn more about each individual student so you can better facilitate the learning of each student in your class. When a student is aware that you are genuinely interested in him or her as a person, that student is likely to be better motivated to learn in your class.

- *Conferences with parents or guardians.* Parent or guardian conferences can reveal a lot about the student and that student's interests, abilities, goals, and support from home. This information may be volunteered directly by the parent or be gleaned through answers to your questions. Just as often, though, you may be able to draw inferences from unintentional clues. A parent's speech pattern, for example, may reveal the source of a student's mispronunciations. Aggressive or meek behavior by a parent or guardian may suggest reasons for the child's behaviors.

- *Student writing.* What a student writes for your class can be as revealing as what the student says and does. You should read everything a student writes for your class and ask for clarification whenever you need it.

- *Questionnaires.* Some teachers find valuable the use of interest-discovering and autobiographical questionnaires. In an interest-discovering questionnaire the student is asked to answer questions such as:

  When talking to your friends at lunch, what do you usually discuss?

  Do you like to read?

  What kind of books do you read in your spare time?

  Do you read the daily newspaper?

  If so, which section do you read first?

What kind of movies do you enjoy seeing?

Do you watch television often?

If so, what are your favorite shows?

Do you have any hobbies?

If you had free choice, what course would you most like to take at this school?

In an autobiographical questionnaire the student is asked to answer questions such as:

What do you plan to do when you finish high school?

Do you have a job? If so, what is it? Do you like it?

How do you like to spend your leisure time?

Do you like to read? What do you like to read?

Do you have a hobby? What is it?

Answers to student questionnaires can provide ideas about how to tailor assignments for individual students.

- *Cumulative record files.* These record files are held in the school office or counseling department. They include data recorded annually by teachers, administrators, and counselors and contain information about the student's academic background, standardized test scores, and extracurricular activities. Use caution with any conclusions that may have been drawn by others—a student's past should not be held against that student.

Learning styles.   Identifying student learning styles is another important way of getting to know your the people in your classes. In particular, students who are exceptional or culturally different from you may prefer to learn in ways that differ from your preferred way of learning. As noted by Grant and Sleeter, "Learning styles overlap somewhat with cultural background and gender. Although not all members of a cultural or gender group learn in the same way, patterns exist in how members of different groups tend to approach tasks."[5] However, "rather than generalizing about your own students based on the research on group differences, it is much more useful to investigate directly your own students' learning style preferences." A learning styles record sheet, on which you record data, can be helpful for this purpose. Figure 5.1 shows a sample record sheet with five categories, described as follows.

1. *Working alone vs. working with others.* Many students work best cooperatively with a partner or small group, whereas others work best individually. The student's preference should be respected, although those who have not learned to work cooperatively may enjoy and benefit from the experience.
2. *Preferred learning modality.* As discussed in Module 2, the term *preferred learning modality* refers to the sensory channels or processes that students prefer to use for acquiring new information or ideas. They can be investigated in the following ways:

   Give students choices and record which ones they choose most often.

   Record the success with which students have learned under each condition.

   Ask students which they prefer to use for gaining or expressing new ideas or information.
3. *Content about people vs. content about things.* Students' interest in content can be investigated in the following ways:

   Offer students choices (e.g., a story topic or math story problems) and observe which one they select most often.

   Ask students which topic they usually prefer (but do not force them to choose—for some people, it makes no difference).
4. *Structured vs. nonstructured assignments.* Some students prefer tasks that are structured, whereas others prefer to create their own structure. The best way to investigate this prefer-

---

[5]Carl A. Grant and Christine E. Sleeter, *Turning on Learning* (New York: Merrill/Macmillan, 1989), pp. 12–13.

Learning Styles Record Sheet

Directions: For each student, record data you collect about the following items related to the
student's preferred style of learning.

Student's name _____

		Method of Data Collection	Findings
1. Style of working:	Alone With others		
2. Learning modality:	Watching Reading Listening Discussing Touching Moving Writing		
3. Content:	People Things		
4. Need for structure:	High Low		
5. Details versus generalities			

Figure 5.1   A Sample Learning Styles Record Sheet

Source: Reprinted with the permission of Macmillan College Publishing Company from TURNING ON LEARN-
ING: FIVE APPROACHES FOR MULTICULTURAL TEACHING PLANS FOR RACE, CLASS, GENDER, AND DIS-
ABILITY by Carl A. Grant and Christine E. Sleeter. Copyright © 1989 by Macmillan College Publishing Company, Inc.

ence is to give the student choices between highly structured work and open-ended work,
and then determine which is chosen most often. Sometimes the teacher may simply ask students, particularly older students, but certain students may not completely understand the
purpose of your question. Students who seem lost or do poorly on open-ended assignments
probably need structured work. In contrast, those who seem bored with structured assignments probably need open-ended work.

5. *Details vs. the big picture.* Some students do meticulous work well, are attentive to details, and
can work through small steps to arrive at the larger idea. Other students need to view the
larger, more general picture first and may become bored or lost with details or small steps.
For instance, when writing stories, some students use grammar and mechanics correctly, but
their stories may not have much point; whereas other students may produce good overall
story ideas but their first drafts are weak in grammar and mechanics. Students' preferences
for details or generalities are best investigated through observation. Although all students
eventually need to work on both details and generalities, some will have trouble learning
these concepts if the teacher emphasizes one or the other prematurely.

Grant and Sleeter emphasize that after analyzing the data collected you may notice certain learning-style patterns based on gender and ethnic background, but that you should avoid
stereotyping whole groups as preferring one style over others. Instead, you should use the patterns you discover as guides for planning the lessons and selecting teaching strategies.

Students' experiential background.   Another way of getting to know your students is to spend
time in the neighborhoods in which they live, observing and listening. Then, you can use

familiar places or events as examples in your lessons. To keep track of your observations, use a record sheet such as the one shown in Figure 5.2.

Creating a Positive Classroom Atmosphere

The classroom should be a pleasant place to be and in which to learn. All students should feel welcomed in the classroom and accepted by the teacher. The following are suggestions for making your classroom a place where all of your students want to be.

Guarantee that all students feel welcomed into your classroom.   The academic classroom is no place for prejudice of any sort. You should personalize the teaching by demonstrating to each student that he or she is welcomed and accepted into your classroom. You can do this by being positive in your comments and mannerisms to each and every student and by modeling behaviors that represent trust and respect and that are characteristic of an open, accepting classroom environment. You may need to learn how to demonstrate dislike for a specific student behavior without demonstrating nonacceptance of that student as a person. Students sometimes need help in understanding that denial of a specific behavior is not denial of them as worthwhile persons. To increase a student's feelings of self-worth and acceptance in your classroom, you might want to consider each of the following:

- Mark the number right instead of the number wrong.
- Use correcting pens with colors other than red.
- Reward positive behaviors rather than punish negative behaviors.
- Send positive notes home.

	Observations	Related Academic Concepts	Ideas for Using Observations
1.			
2.			
3.			
4.			
5.			
6.			
7.			

Figure 5.2   Sample Record Sheet to Record Observations in Neighborhoods

Source: Reprinted with the permission of the Macmillan College Publishing Company from TURNING ON LEARN-ING: FIVE APPROACHES FOR MULTICULTURAL TEACHING PLANS FOR RACE, CLASS, GENDER, AND DIS-ABILITY by Carl A. Grant and Christine E. Sleeter. Copyright © 1989 by Macmillan College Publishing Company.

- Teach students cooperative learning procedures.
- Check the roll at the end of each week and ask yourself if there are students that you should give some special positive attention to during the next week.

Try to emphasize the "dos" rather than the "don'ts," the rewards rather than the punishments, the joy of learning and knowing rather than the pain of studying and the fear of failure. Let the students know that you want them to do their best. Give them time and support their efforts. Reward their successes and honest attempts. This may mean modifying your own concept of what a success actually is. Especially avoid punishing a student who is trying but has not yet succeeded.

Pay attention to your classroom's physical appearance.   This is easier for teachers who have their own classroom for the entire day than for those who move from one classroom to another. Nevertheless, there are things that all teachers can do to create a hospitable classroom environment. A pleasant, neat, comfortable, and bright classroom helps provide a climate favorable to learning—when the room looks nice, the tendency for everyone is to keep it that way. Therefore, make the classroom as attractive as possible. It is surprising how much you and your students can do to make even the most drab classroom a pleasant place.

An initial step in improving a classroom's appearance—and student attitudes—is to keep the classroom neat and orderly. Provide a place for everything and try to keep everything in its place. Tidy up, clean up, and put things away after using them. Improve the classroom atmosphere by brightening it up. Use displays, murals, bulletin boards, posters, and pictures. If you lack tackboards or display areas, be creative: use adhesives that allow you to fasten things directly to the wall without marring its finish, or cover the wall with murals drawn on wrapping paper. You might cover the walls with wrapping paper and let your graffiti artists decorate them (be sure not to use paint or ink that will stain through and mark the walls). Use a lot of pictures. Preferably, these should all be pertinent to what you are teaching and should be changed for each unit in order to keep the classroom bright, interesting, and up-to-date. But purely decorative pictures are better than no pictures at all.

Pay attention to your students' creature comforts.   Students find studying difficult when they are physically uncomfortable. To the extent possible, attend to the lighting, heating, cooling, and ventilation in the classroom. A hot and stuffy classroom can destroy motivation and control; so too can classrooms that are too dark or in which students are facing a glare. Young adolescents in particular cannot sit for long periods of time. Try to vary the instruction so that they will not have to sit and listen quietly for long periods of time.

Teachers, students, and staff must realize that classroom instruction is an important school activity.   Unfortunately, the behavior of some schools seems to teach students that the least important thing happening in the school is the classroom instruction. Classes are too often interrupted by announcements or by students arriving with unimportant messages from the office, or they are dismissed for last-minute pep rallies and other assemblies and activities. Noises and activities from outside the classroom often distract students, and you may not have much control over such things. The weather may be too warm to close doors and windows to eliminate the sounds and sights of these distractions. For example, it is all too common to visit schools and hear loud noises from lawn maintenance crews operating hedge clippers and lawn mowers right outside of classroom windows—noises so loud that classroom discussions and activities have to be suspended. Teachers should appeal to their administrators that class disruptions, interruptions, and outside distractions must be kept to a minimum. Why can't lawn crews do those things before or after school? Why can't schools enact policies that announcements and messages be delivered only during the first or last five minutes of each class period? A school that seems to place little importance on the teacher's classroom instruction diminishes student motivation for learning.

Try to run a happy ship.   Try to make what you have to teach seem attractive to learn. Fun and humor both relaxes tension and enhances student motivation and learning. A teacher who can admit to mistakes, and even laugh at them, is more motivating than one who never admits to a mistake, never laughs when appropriate, and never seems to enjoy having fun with the students. Of course, fun and humor should not ever be at the expense of an individual student in the class.

Encourage students' high levels of aspiration and self-esteem.   Success raises aspirations, whereas failure lowers them. Therefore, try to see that each student experiences success in your class. Provide creative, interesting, and challenging but reasonable assignments. Treat mistakes positively, and use them as opportunities to teach the students the value of errors. Students need successes so they will not become discouraged and give up. Set high standards, however. Be certain that your students know what your standards are and that you are confident of their ability to meet those standards. Take time to make your expectations clear, and help the students meet these expectations by showing them what they do well and what they could do differently to improve their work.

Diffusely structure your class.   Try to build group cohesiveness in your class by encouraging cooperative student involvement and participation. Cooperative learning procedures get all students into the act of learning, disallowing any in-group from dominating the class. Your class should act as a group working for a common cause with shared responsibilities rather than as a bunch of competing individuals. Rewards for progress can be given to teams on the basis of the team's achievement rather than given to individual students.

Use interesting strategies and tactics.   Today's students have been growing up in an electronic age saturated with multimillion-dollar television, stage, and screen productions; with fast-paced, computer-controlled arcade games; and with instant communication and information retrieval systems made available by modern electronics—an age unlike any previous generation of school children. When these young people step into your classroom and experience something short of a high-budget production—without an eyecatching and sensory-stimulating "commercial break"—it may seem difficult to motivate them or maintain their attention for longer than 10 minutes. By the time these students have reached middle school, however, they are aware of the realities of school teaching and have experienced past teachers and classes that were not particularly motivating. Because of that awareness and their prior experiences, you will have ample opportunity to plan courses that will stimulate and motivate your students into productive learning. The following is a list of some teaching strategies that can be used to arouse interest and increase motivation:

- Building real things.
- Creative introduction of topics, such as the use of "magic" to introduce topics, especially in mathematics, science, and social science.
- Discussion and decision-making on real topics and problems.
- Education games.
- Imaginative assignments, both for individual and group work.
- Imaginative use of traditional audiovisual equipment, such as the chalkboard and the overhead and opaque projectors.
- Modern audiovisual equipment, such as laserdiscs, interactive computer programs, multipurpose writing boards, and telecommunications.
- Real-life examples that the students can relate to.
- Real-life situations in which students do real things.
- Simulations and role-playing.
- Solving real problems, perhaps those of the school or community.
- Special projects, both individual and group.

Providing Positive Modeling and Examples

Students learn behavior by imitating others. If teachers can provide students with good and honorable models from which they can pattern themselves, then the conditions are right for them to achieve the kind of behavior teachers seek. It may be possible to use students' admiration for older students, highly regarded students, natural peer-group leaders, and such personalities as sports stars, movie stars, and world figures. Yet, such personalities are not always reliable as good models of behavior. Fictional and historical characters, however, are always available in books and other media, and it may be possible to use such characters to advantage in your teaching.

Perhaps the most reliable and influential model is a pleasant teacher whose classroom personality is characterized by empathy, warmth, and genuineness. Such a teacher does not take him- or herself too seriously. Self-centered teachers—those who worry about how they will appear and how classroom incidents will affect them—are much more likely to have difficulty than teachers whose interests center on their students and on how classroom incidents will affect their students. Therefore, go in there and teach the very best you can. Act with confidence but without arrogance, and everything will probably go well. If you concentrate on teaching well and if your plans and procedures are reasonably good, you will less likely experience problems in classroom control. As mentioned before, you would do well to develop an active interest in your students, a friendly attitude, an interesting personality, and a healthy sense of humor. Above all, demonstrate that you enjoy teaching, studying, and working with your students. Attitudes are contagious. If you demonstrate that you are enthusiastic about what you teach and teach joyously, your students may become enthusiastic too. Approach your teaching with pleasure and with confidence. If you concentrate on teaching in a businesslike, confident manner, you will probably be well on the road to having the kind of classroom control you desire.

A word of caution is necessary: although every teacher should be friendly with students, becoming too chummy could be detrimental to the classroom atmosphere. Avoid the kind of friendliness that might be misperceived. Teachers should behave as responsible adults and socialize with adults—students will often like and respect them more that way. And keeping the proper distance diminishes the danger of being accused of playing favorites or of a student's attempting to take advantage of or being hurt by a friendship.

In the final analysis, you should set a good example and be a good model. Your behavior should be consistent with that expected of your students. For example, the teacher should return homework papers in a timely fashion when timeliness is expected of students. The teacher should arrive promptly to class meetings when such promptness is expected of students. The teacher should spell correctly and write clearly and legibly when those things are expected of students. If the students realize that you are trying to serve them well and that you really care about them as persons of dignity, they will be more likely to respond positively to your teaching.

Making the Learning Perceived as Worthwhile

Be sure the learning and activities seem worthwhile. Show the students how the material they are studying can be useful to them now as well as in the future. Provide an assortment of activities, materials, and content that will appeal to the variety of interests and learning styles present in the class. Find special projects for special individual students. Encourage students to cooperate with you in the planning of their own learning activities. Above all, select content that is relevant to their lives and the needs of the community, and be sure they know why that content is important and relevant for them personally. Never start them on an activity without being certain they know why they are going to do it.

Take advantage of the students' motives and natural curiosity. Use their interests, ideals, goals, and attitudes. Appeal to their curiosity, pride, desire for fun, need for achievement, and social interests. Try to use the concerns of your students as vehicles of teaching. Focus on the present and future more than on the past. Utilize job-related applications of the content being taught. Take advantage of situations that occur outside the classroom. In this connection remember that intrinsic sources of motivation (i.e., incentives that come from within the learner) are usually more powerful than extrinsic sources (i.e., sources from without, external rewards). Students will usually work harder to learn something because they want to learn it than they will merely to earn some extrinsic prize or reward.

Building Trust

Try to build students' trust in you. Careful preparation, hard work, enthusiastic teaching, empathy, respect for your students, fairness, and justice will help you in developing a trusting relationship with your students. Trust is something you cannot force; it is given when deserved. Trust is probably the greatest resource you can have when it comes to generating desirable student motivation and furthering their learning.

Reinforcing Positive Behaviors

One theory of psychology holds that people tend to behave in ways that have rewarded them in a way they find valuable. This is called reinforcement theory, because it is based on the belief that rewards or gratifying results strengthen a tendency to behave in a certain fashion, and lack of reward weakens the tendency to act in that fashion. For instance, if a student is promised free time for his or her own purposes when that student has worked well for a certain period, the student may work toward that reward and develop higher standards for work in the future. In disagreeing with this theory, some argue that once the extrinsic reward is removed, the student's motivation dampens and the student ceases the desired behavior. Perhaps the real truth lies somewhere in between. Teaching in a classroom is less than ideal. Not all activities are going to be intrinsically motivating. But activities that are interesting and intrinsically rewarding will not be further served by the addition of external rewards. Evidence indicates that to add external incentives to activities that are already highly interesting tends to reduce motivation. In the development of skills, where much repetition is needed and boredom is likely to ensue, the use of rewards is probably particularly useful.

The reinforcement theory seems to hold many implications for the motivation and control of student behavior. Unfortunately, teachers often unintentionally reinforce the wrong behavior. When the student who is seeking attention (that student's immediate goal) misbehaves (that student's goal-seeking behavior), the teacher might reprimand the student, thus giving the student the attention desired. But when the same student behaves well, the teacher ignores that behavior. Thus, the teacher reinforces the student's negative behavior and neglects the positive behavior. As a result, the teacher strengthens the student's tendency to misbehave and weakens the student's inclinations to behave well. Therefore, take care to reinforce the type of activity you want to encourage. Try not to reinforce negative behavior; rather, "accentuate the positive." Catch students being good! Look for successful efforts to commend rather than failures to berate.

There is no need for you to place much faith in grades and marks for student reinforcement. They are undependable for several reasons:

1. Not all students place great value on high grades.
2. Not all students can expect to receive high grades or marks. High-ability students who try usually receive high grades, but low-ability students who try seldom do.
3. Because the efforts of low-ability students so seldom pay off in high marks no matter how hard they try, those students who need to try hardest are given the least incentive to do so.

Rather than depending on grades to provide motivation, it would ordinarily be more profitable to adjust the lessons and the curriculum, making them appeal more to students' intrinsic motives.

Now reinforce your understanding of rewards by doing Exercise 5.1.

Rewards as Reinforcement

• • • • • •

Instructions: The purpose of this exercise is to learn more about the use of rewards as reinforcement. There are several types of rewards that can be used to reinforce desirable student behavior, including tangible rewards (such as athletic passes), recognition rewards (such as a certificate for achievement), material rewards (such as food or script money), social rewards (such as being assistant coach or teacher), activity rewards (free time), and intrinsic rewards (deriving pleasure from doing an activity).

1. For the subject and grade level you intend to teach, list examples of rewards in each category that you think would be appropriate:

   a. Tangible rewards:

   b. Recognition rewards:

   c. Material rewards:

   d. Social rewards:

   e. Activity rewards:

f. Intrinsic rewards:

2. Now, observe a class (or think back on your own classroom experiences) and answer the following:
   a. What behaviors were rewarded? How were those behaviors rewarded?

   b. What behaviors were not rewarded?

   c. Were there examples of students being rewarded for being quiet, for being cooperative, and so on?

   d. Were there examples of students being rewarded for misbehaving?

   e. Remember, sometimes a punishment can be a reward. From your observations or experiences, were there examples of this?

Effective Classroom Management

Effective teaching requires a well-organized, businesslike classroom in which motivated students work diligently at their learning tasks, free from distractions and inappropriate behavior. Providing such a setting for learning is called effective **classroom management**.

Essential for effective classroom management is the maintenance of **classroom control**, the process of controlling student behavior in the classroom. Classroom control involves:

* Steps for preventing student misbehavior
* Ideas for handling student misbehavior

The control aspect of teaching is frequently the most worrisome to beginning teachers—and they have good cause to be concerned. Even experienced teachers sometimes find control difficult, particularly at the secondary-school level, where teachers have so many students and where many students have already been alienated by bad experiences in their lives.

Another part of effective classroom management is good organization and administration of activities and materials. In a well-managed class students know what to do, have the materials to work with, and stay on task. In such a classroom, the atmosphere is supportive, the assignments and procedures for doing those assignments clear, the materials of instruction current, interesting, and readily available, and the classroom proceedings businesslike. At all times, the teacher is in control, seeing that students are spending their time appropriately. For your teaching to be effective, you must be skilled in classroom-management procedures.

Effective classroom management is the process of organizing and conducting a class so that it results in maximum student learning. To manage your class successfully, you need to plan your lessons thoughtfully and thoroughly and provide students with a pleasant, supportive atmosphere. You need to instill a desire and the confidence to learn and achieve. You also need to prevent distractions and disturbances, dealing quickly and quietly with any unavoidable distractions and disturbances. In addition, you need to develop control procedures, which will help promote effective student learning. If this sounds like a tall order, don't fret: if you adhere to the guidelines set forth in this book, you will be successful.

Getting Organized

In classroom management a good beginning may make all the difference in the world. Therefore, you should appear at your first class, and every class thereafter, as well prepared and as confident as possible. Perhaps you feel nervous and apprehensive? Being ready and well prepared at least will help you look confident. Then, if you proceed in a businesslike, matter-of-fact way, the impetus of your well-prepared beginning will cause the day to proceed as desired.

Planning

Because a good beginning is so important, you must take great care with your planning. The importance of planning has been emphasized in preceding modules, especially for developing units and lessons. The following suggestions reiterate some points made before, but now consider them in terms of how planning well can promote effective classroom management:

* Furnish students with enough purposeful activities that they are kept busy and active throughout the class period. Avoid dead spots, periods of time when some or all of the students have nothing to do. Plan ahead so all materials are available and ready for distribution and student use.
* Limit the time spent in teacher talk (lectures). As a general rule, no more than one-fifth of class time should be devoted to such activity. If you must lecture—and sometimes it may be the only practical procedure—then plan your lecture with key questions, audiovisuals, and other interest-catching activities. (Details on the use of the lecture and other specific strategies follow in the next modules of this text.)

- Provide for individual differences and for instruction in how to study the particular lesson, how to use the equipment or materials, and how to do the assignment.
- Provide enough flexibility in your plan so that you can make minor last-minute adjustments when what you had planned does not seem to fit the class predisposition for that day.
- Be reasonable in your expectations. For example, absolute quiet from students who are excited about the learning activity is not a reasonable expectation.
- Provide for good motivation. The lesson planned should seem interesting, challenging, and valuable to the students. Avoid planning lessons that repeat the same deadly routine day after day after day.
- Understand that not all of your lessons can be exciting and stimulating. Your students need to understand that, too. For less-than-exciting lessons you may want to consider the use of awards for appropriate behavior and for jobs done well or on time.
- Spice up your assignments. Assignments should be worthwhile, interesting, relevant, and challenging. Sometimes, by necessity, assignments are drills, which tend to be dull and boring. For those you may want to increase student motivation by the use of rewards for jobs well done. Be sure that you explain clearly what is to be done and how to do it. Sometimes, you will have to go into detail, giving examples and demonstrating proper procedures, to make everything clear. When students are not clear on what to do or how to do it, they tend to give up.
- Routinize the organizational and administrative details of classroom management in order to eliminate dead spots and avoid disorderly breakdowns in classroom decorum. Students respond better when they know what to expect, when these housekeeping tasks are routinized. These routines should be part of your lesson plan.
- To make your planning and management easier on yourself, have a standard plan or ritual for your lesson organization. This does not mean that you should use the same strategies and tactics in all your classes—quite the contrary. But you should check to see which of your standard sections are necessary for a particular lesson and whether you have adequately provided for each of these necessary sections.

Various lesson plan formats were discussed in Module 4. The following is a restatement of the basic sections that should be considered when you are organizing your lesson:

1. Set introduction (your introduction of the lesson or activity, designed to motivate and to stimulate a mind set)
2. Clarification of objectives for the students (what they are to learn and why)
3. Tie-in with prior lessons
4. Presentation of the new content
5. Presentation follow-up (checking for understanding, guided practice, independent practice)
6. Small-group and independent laboratory-type study
7. Closure (culminating activity that ties together the set, the presentation, the follow-up activities, and sometimes a transfer to the next day's lesson)
8. Materials and equipment of instruction (to be certain that you have these things ready for the lesson)
9. Assignment
10. Notes and reminders (including evaluative items and suggestions for next use of this lesson)

Establishing Classroom Procedures and Rules of Acceptable Behavior

Part of your preparation for the first day of school should be to decide on your classroom procedures and your rules for student behavior. Your procedures and rules must seem reasonable to your students, and you must be consistent in enforcing them. Sometimes, procedures and rules, designed to prevent problems, can be a cause of trouble. To avoid difficulty, it is best at first to establish only the minimum number of procedures and rules necessary. Too many procedures and rules at the beginning only confuses students and makes the classroom seem repressive. By establishing and sticking to a few well-explained procedures and rules, you can leave yourself some room for maneuvering. Those procedures and rules should be quite specific, so that students know exactly what is expected and what is not, as well as what the consequences are for breaking the rules and for not following procedures.

On the first day of class you should explain those initial procedures and rules to your students. You will want to do this in a positive way. Figure 5.3 should give you some ideas about what rules and procedures to establish as well as how to present them to the class. Students work best when teacher expectations are clear to them and when procedures are clearly understood.

After reading Figure 5.3, do Exercises 5.2 and 5.3, in which you are asked to talk with experienced teachers about their classroom management systems and to begin thinking about your own management system.

Establishing Classroom Behavior Rules and Procedures

When establishing behavior rules and procedures for your classroom, keep in mind that the learning time needs to run efficiently (i.e., with no "dead spots"), smoothly (i.e., routine procedures are established and transitions between activities are smooth), and with minimum disruption. When you announce your expectations for student classroom behavior, try to do so in a positive manner, emphasizing procedures and desired behaviors, stressing what students should *do* rather than what they should *not do*.

As you prepare your rules for classroom behavior, you should consider what students need to know from the first day of class. Then, during the first week of school, the rules should be reviewed and procedures rehearsed with the students several times. Thereafter, you should make sure that the rules are followed consistently throughout the school year. What students need to know from the start include:

1. *How to obtain the teacher's attention and help.* Most teachers who are effective classroom managers expect students to raise their hands to gain the teacher's attention and to keep the hands raised only as long as necessary—until the teacher acknowledges (usually by a nod) that a student's hand has been seen. With that acknowledgement, the student should lower his or her hand. To prevent the student from becoming bored and restless from waiting, you should attend to the student as quickly as possible. Expecting students to raise their hands before speaking allows you to control the noise and confusion level, as well as who speaks. During the use of questioning and discussion strategies especially, controlling who speaks is important if you are to manage a classroom with equality—that is, with equal attention to individuals regard-

less of gender, ethnicity, proximity to the teacher, or any other personal characteristic.

2. *How to enter and leave the classroom.* From the time the class is scheduled to begin and until the time it officially ends (some schools do not rings bells at passing time), teachers who are effective classroom managers expect students to be in their assigned seats or at their assigned learning stations. And during that period, students are expected to be attentive to the teacher or to the learning activity.

3. *How to maintain, obtain, and use personal items as well as learning materials.* Students need to know where, when, and how to store, retrieve, and care for such personal items as coats, books, pencils, and medicines. They also need to know how to get papers, laboratory or shop items, and similar learning materials. Finally, they also need to know when they may use the pencil sharpener and wastebasket. Classroom control is easiest to maintain (1) when items that students need for class activities and for their personal use are neatly arranged and located in places that require minimum foot traffic, (2) when there are established routine procedures that students clearly expect and understand, (3) when there is the least amount of student off-task time, and (4) when students do not have to line up for anything. Therefore, you will want to plan the room arrangement, equipment and materials storage, preparation of equipment and materials, and transitions between activities in order to avoid needless delays and confusion.

4. *When they can go to the drinking fountain and the bathroom.* Normally, secondary school students should be able to take care of getting drinks of

Figure 5.3   Establishing Classroom Behavior Rules and Procedures

water and going to the restroom between classes, but sometimes they either do not or can not (such as for medical reasons). Reinforce the notion that they should do those things before coming into your classroom; be flexible enough, however, for the occasional student who has an immediate need.

5. *How to behave during a class interruption.* Unfortunately, class interruptions do occur—and in some schools they occur far too often. For an important reason, the principal or some other person from the school's office may need to interrupt the class to see a teacher or student or to make an announcement of importance to the entire class. Students need to know what behavior is expected of them during those interruptions.

6. *What to do when they arrive late to class or when they must leave a class early.* You need to understand and reinforce school policies on tardies and early dismissals. Routinize your own procedures so students clearly understand what they are to do when they arrive late or when they must leave your class early (e.g., for a medical appointment). The procedures should be such that such students disturb neither the teacher nor the lesson in process.

7. *What the consequences are for inappropriate behavior.* Most teachers who are effective classroom managers routinize their procedures for handling inappropriate behavior, thus assuring that the students understand the consequences for misbehavior. The consequences should be posted in the classroom. Here is one model you might consider:

- *First offense* results in a reminder (verbal or nonverbal, though when nonverbal there must be no doubt that the student received the message).

- *Second offense* results in both a warning and a note to parent or guardian.

- *Third offense* results in both detention and a phone call home.

- *Fourth offense* results in a three-day suspension from class, a note home, and a conference among parent or guardian, student, teacher, and principal or vice-principal.

- *Fifth offense* results in permanent suspension from school.

Marlene and Lee Canter recommend the following five-step model for rules infraction:

- *First offense* results in a warning to the student.

- *Second offense* results in the student's being given a 10-minute time-out in an isolation area.

- *Third offense* results in a 15-minute time-out (in isolation).

- *Fourth offense* results in a phone call to the student's parents or guardian.

- *Fifth offense* results in the student's being sent to the principal's office.*

8. *Rules for behavior and procedures to follow during emergency drills—real or practice.* Students need to know what to do, where to go, and how to behave in emergency conditions, such as might occur because of a fire, storm, earthquake or because of a disruptive campus intruder.

---

* See Eleanor B. Baron, *Discipline Strategies for Teachers,* Fastback 344 (Bloomington, IN: Phi Delta Kappa Educational Foundation, 1992), p. 14. For additional ideas, see Jack Blendinger et al., *Win-Win Discipline,* Fastback 353 (Bloomington, IN: Phi Delta Kappa Educational Foundation, 1993).

Figure 5.3, *continued*

Teachers' Behavior Management Systems

• • • • • •

Instructions: The purpose of this exercise is to interview two teachers, one middle or junior high and the other from a high school, to discover how they manage their classrooms. Use the outline format that follows, conduct your interviews, and then share the results with your classmates, perhaps in small groups.

1. Teacher interviewed:

2. Date: 4. School:

3. Grade level: 5. Subject(s):

6. Please describe your classroom management system. Specifically, I would like to know your procedures for the following:
   a. How are students to signal that they want your attention and help?

   b. How do you call on students during question and discussion sessions?

   c. How and when are students to enter and exit the classroom?

   d. How are students to obtain the materials for instruction?

   e. How are students to store their personal items?

   f. What are the procedures for students' going to the drinking fountain or bathroom?

g. What are the procedures during class interruptions?

h. What are the procedures for tardies or early dismissal?

i. What are the procedures for turning in homework?

7. Describe your expectations for classroom behavior and the consequences for misbehavior.

In discussion with classmates following the interviews, consider the following.

Many modern teachers advocate the use of a highly structured classroom, and then, as appropriate over time during the school year, they share more of the responsibility with the students. Did you find this to be the case with the majority of teachers interviewed? Was it more or less the case in middle schools, junior highs, or high schools? Was it more or less the case with any particular subject areas?

Beginning the Development of My Classroom Management System

• • • • • •

Instructions: The purpose of this exercise is to begin preparation of the management system that you will explain to your students during the first day or week of school. Answer the questions that follow, and share those answers with your peers for their feedback. Then make changes as appropriate. (Upon completion of this module, you may want to revisit this exercise to make adjustments to your management plan, as you will from time to time throughout your professional career.)

1. My teaching subject area and anticipated grade level:

2. Attention to procedures. Use a statement to explain your procedural expectation for each of the following:

   a. How are students to signal that they want your attention and help?

   b. How do you call on students during question and discussion sessions?

   c. How and when are students to enter and exit the classroom?

   d. How are students to obtain the materials for instruction?

   e. How are students to store their personal items?

   f. What are the procedures for students' going to the drinking fountain or bathroom?

   g. What are the procedures during class interruptions?

   h. What are the procedures for tardies or early dismissal?

i. What are the procedures for turning in homework?

3. List of student behavior expectations that I will present to my class (no more than five):

    Rule 1:

    Rule 2:

    Rule 3:

    Rule 4:

    Rule 5:

4. Explanation of consequences for broken rules:

5. How procedures, rules, or consequences may vary (if at all) according to the grade level taught, or according to any other criteria, such as in team teaching:

Organizing and Arranging the Classroom

When it is time for class to start, you should be ready to go. Get together all the instructional materials you will need ahead of time. Have the room and materials arranged for orderly and efficient use. Be sure the bulletin boards are set, any boardwork ready, all needed equipment set up and working, and any necessary supplies at hand.

In most classrooms the seats are arranged in rows. This linear arrangement is fine for lectures and most audiovisual presentations, but rows do not encourage discussion and student involvement. You may find it more satisfactory to arrange your class in a hollow square, a double horseshoe, or a circle (see Figure 5.4). If you plan to use committee or small-group work, small circles usually work best. Although adjusting classroom seating arrangements to the type of activity is generally a good idea, it may be better to go along with an existing arrangement rather than cause a large commotion by moving furniture once a class has started.

Conducting the Class

The effective teacher starts the class immediately with a greeting and an assignment, not roll taking. As the class period begins, you should initiate learning activities posthaste. When there are no announcements or other administrative matters to attend to, you should begin the day's regular lesson immediately and then, within a few minutes after the students have begun their lesson activities, attend to attendance matters. To take attendance and attend to other routine administrative matters, most teachers require students at first to be in their assigned seats. Once administrative matters are completed—usually in a matter of a minute or two—the day's regular lesson should begin, which could mean that students will move to other work stations within the classroom. But remember, movement of students (i.e., foot traffic) within the classroom should be purposeful and minimal.

Other teachers begin the day's lesson immediately themselves, giving a reliable classroom teaching aide the responsibility of taking attendance and dealing with other routine administrative tasks. The classroom teaching aide might be a paid or volunteer adult aide, or a responsible student assigned to work with the teacher as a student assistant, or a reliable and responsible student periodically selected from students within a particular class period. Whichever the case, when another person performs the daily attendance routines it is still your responsibility to check and sign the relevant attendance forms. Once the class period has begun, routines and lesson activities should move forward briskly and steadily until the official end of the class period.

Bell Activity

If you are in a school where you must take attendance at the beginning of each class, an effective management procedure is to have the overhead projector on each day when students arrive to class, with the day's agenda and immediate assignment clearly written on a trans-

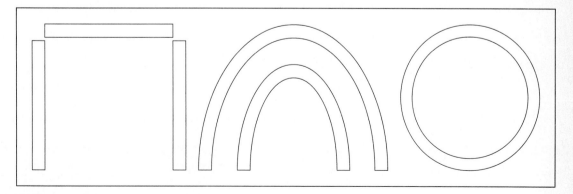

Figure 5.4   Possible Seating Arrangements

parency and displayed on the screen. After you greet your students, you direct their attention to the assignment on the screen. This initial activity is often referred to as the bell activity (though some schools use no bells).

Bell activities can include any variety of activities, such as:

- A specific topic or question to which each student responds by writing in his or her journal.
- A specific topic or question to which pairs (dyads) of students respond by discussing and then writing in their journals.
- A problem to be solved by each student or by student pairs.
- The exchange and discussion of a homework assignment.
- The completion of a report on a laboratory activity.
- Textbook questions to which each student responds by writing the answers, individually or in dyads.

Keeping Things Moving

Once the class has started, it should move forward briskly and steadily. The pace should be vigorous enough to keep students alert, but not so brisk as to lose those who are trying. Each student should feel some pressure to do well. This pressure should not be oppressive, but everyone should realize it exists. Let it be known by word and action that you expect everyone to be on task and to do his or her best, and that you do not tolerate dawdling, disturbances, time wasting, or other inappropriate behavior. To promote this businesslike atmosphere, try to make sure that everyone has something worthwhile to do, that the students all know how to do what they are supposed to be doing, and that the students all have the materials they need. At no time should any student be standing around with nothing to do or be kept waiting for equipment, materials, or attention. Be alert for any student who has a hand raised for your attention, acknowledge that student, and attend to the question as quickly as possible.

Movement Management

To keep things moving smoothly and to minimize distractions, utilize the principles of movement management, the process of keeping the class moving forward at a brisk pace without side trips or interruptions.[6] The first of these principles is that by starting your class the moment the bell rings, you can eliminate the fooling around and time wasting that often occurs before a lesson begins. The second is that the class should move forward steadily and purposefully. Transitions from one activity to the next should be natural and unobtrusive. Each activity should start promptly without confusion and continue briskly to a definite, planned conclusion. Movement around the class should be controlled, orderly, and routinized. In short, movement management is keeping the class on track. To ensure that your movement management is effective, be careful that not even you interrupt the smooth progress of the class. Here are ten rules to follow:

1. When your students are busy and on task, avoid interrupting them with instructions, statements, or announcements.
2. When you do have announcements, instructions, or statements to make, be sure that the students are ready to hear you. A class of twenty-eight students always needs mental time to prepare for any transition.
3. Be sure an activity is finished before you start a new one. Students should not be left dangling on an unfinished activity while the teacher starts off on a new direction. Be sure they know when you end one activity and begin the next, and make the transitions smooth and logical.
4. Avoid interrupting yourself. Avoid getting off the topic. If you start discussing one thing, keep to it until you are finished. Avoid jumping around from one topic or activity to

[6]Jacob S. Kounin, *Discipline and Group Management in the Classroom* (New York: Holt, Rinehart and Winston, 1970), pp. 102–8.

another and then back again. A class of twenty-eight students cannot be expected to make those kinds of cognitive leaps.

5. Try not to be distracted by the irrelevant. Never interrupt the class's progress by harping on matters not pertinent to the task at hand. Avoid public harangues. Admonishments to individual students should always be done quietly and privately, without interrupting the rest of the class.
6. Avoid making mountains out of molehills. Avoid talking an activity to death. Once you have said what is necessary, stop.
7. Avoid providing too much detail. If something can be done in a few steps or explained in a few words, then so explain.
8. Maintain a logical sequence. An outline on a transparency on the overhead or on the writing board is often helpful to teacher and students both.
9. Involve your students in your teaching.
10. Avoid the overuse of workbooks and other humdrum seat work. Activities afforded by workbooks and quiet seat work are best reserved for reinforcing and assessing knowledge and skills that have already been taught.

The teacher should not breach any of these ten rules, otherwise the teacher's infraction will cause student misbehavior to occur and impede the efficiency of that class's movement management. Pay particular attention when planning and implementing small-group work.

Clarifying by Routinizing

Routinizing the humdrum day-after-day tasks will ease movement management. Students are more likely to do things without argument or disruption when they are used to doing them and doing them in a certain way. If you establish routines for various everyday functions, students will always know what they are supposed to do. In this way, you can reduce fuss and confusion. Just what routine you select matters little as long as it is reasonably efficient.

Among the common tasks that need routinizing are: taking attendance, distributing equipment and supplies, collecting and passing papers, starting and stopping class, attending to interruptions caused by a classroom visitor, requesting the teacher's attention, leaving the room for an emergency, arriving to class late, and needing to sharpen a pencil or go to the wastebasket (see Figure 5.3). Therefore, take time to see that your students understand the classroom rules and procedures expected of them. Ordinarily the time to teach such routines occurs when the routine is first introduced. Soon the routines should become so automatic that students follow them without prompting or interruptions.

Withitness and Overlapping

Two teaching skills important for effective classroom management are: (1) **withitness** (as Kounin called it), the teacher's knowing at all times what is going on everywhere in the classroom, and (2) **overlapping**, the teacher's ability to attend to more than one matter at a time.

Withitness might be thought of as "having eyes in the back of your head." In addition to being aware of everything going on in the classroom at all times, there are two other characteristics of the teacher who is "with it." One is the teacher's timing, and the other is the teacher's ability to attend to the right culprit. It is important that you attend to potentially disruptive student behavior quickly and with the least amount of class disturbance, and it is important that you attend to the right student. In effectively managing your classroom, your movement and nonverbal behaviors in the classroom are important. Disrupting the entire class with a reprimand to two misbehaving students (and perhaps only one of those is guilty) is a poor teaching technique—perhaps an even more disrupting behavior than that of the two students being reprimanded.

To develop your withitness skills, you should:

1. Keep the entire class under surveillance all the time. Look around the room frequently. Move around the room. Be on top of potential misbehavior and redirect student attention before the misbehavior occurs or gets out of control.

2. Keep students alert by calling on them randomly, asking questions and then calling on an answerer, circulating from group to group during team learning activities, and frequently checking on individual progress.
3. Keep all students in the act. Avoid becoming too involved with any one student or group. Avoid the temptation to concentrate only on those students who seem most interested or responsive.
4. Quietly redirect the behavior of a misbehaving student.
5. If two or more errant behaviors are occurring simultaneously but in different locations in the classroom, treat the most serious first.
6. Above all, maintain a high level of student interest by introducing variety and sparkle into your teaching.

The teacher's ability to attend to more than one matter at a time is referred to as the teacher's overlapping ability. Overlapping is a prerequisite to effective withitness. The teacher who can effectively attend to more than one matter at once uses body language, body position, and hand signals to communicate with students. Consider the following examples of overlapping ability:

• While working with a small group of students, a student in another part of the room has his hand raised wanting the teacher's attention. While continuing to work with the group of students, the teacher signals with her hand to the student, an acknowledgment that she is aware that he wants her attention and will get to him quickly.
• While attending to a visitor who has walked into the room with a written message from the office and while reading the message, the teacher demonstrates verbally or by gestures to the class that she expects them to continue their work.
• Without missing a beat in his lecture, by gesture, eye contact, or moving closer to the student, the teacher stops the behavior of a potentially disruptive student.
• Rather than being seated at the teacher's desk and allowing students to come to the desk with their papers and problems, the teacher expects students to remain seated and raise their hands, while the teacher moves around the room monitoring and attending to individual students.

Effective classroom management depends on the teacher's constant awareness and monitoring of all students and class activities. Monitoring requires constant checking and feedback. Among the things to check are:

Is everyone attending to business?

Does everyone have something purposeful to do?

Does everyone understand the assignment?

Does everyone understand how to proceed?

Does everyone have the materials to work with?

Are teacher directions clear?

Is the content too difficult?

Is the work challenging enough?

Are the physical conditions all right?

Does everyone understand the expected standards of behavior and workmanship?

Are the students progressing as well as they should? Are they using the proper procedures?

It is absolutely imperative that you continually check students' work and provide feedback. By so doing you can catch and correct errors before they become a problem, as well as find opportunities to provide specific praise for good work. Careful monitoring can prevent problems now and in the future, and it also helps guarantee a businesslike learning climate.

In summary, you need to make sure that your class moves briskly from the first to the final ringing of the bell. To achieve this goal, you must pay particular attention to your preparation, organization, movement management, withitness, and overlapping, and, perhaps above all, to your monitoring.

Maintaining Control

Most beginning teachers find group control their most worrisome problem. As a rule, however, teachers who establish good motivation and classroom management are not greatly troubled by problems with classroom control. Even in the "worst" schools in the "worst" neighborhoods, some teachers run efficient, effective classrooms with hardly any control problems at all.

Why Students Misbehave

Misbehavior is any behavior considered inappropriate in the classroom or school setting. Students misbehave for many reasons. One is the sheer fun of it. Another is for the attention received as a result of the misbehavior. Classrooms are usually somewhat unnatural and restrictive, so students like to relieve the tension. Other reasons for misbehavior may stem from a student's family and community background or from a student's emotional well-being. Some misbehavior is simply an unrestrained outburst of the restlessness, rowdiness, and exuberance of youth. On the other hand, much student misbehavior is school-caused or teacher-caused. Classes may be tedious and boring. The curriculum may seem worthless and irrelevant to anything that is important to youth. When their schooling is far removed from their lives, they can lose interest and become inattentive, the resolution of which is to direct their energies into what seems to them more fulfilling activities.

Some teachers never have discipline problems; others have constant problems. The guidelines presented in this book, if followed, can provide you with the skills necessary to prevent discipline problems from occurring in your classroom—though no teacher can avoid the occasional discipline problems. That being the case, in addition to guidelines for preventive discipline, the guidelines here will assist you in knowing what to do at the first sign of potential misbehavior and how you can positively redirect misbehavior that has occurred.

Sometimes a teacher is confronted at school with major problems of misbehavior that have ramifications outside of the classroom or that start outside and spill over into the classroom. Those types of control problems will be addressed later in this module.

In other instances a misbehavior is so minor and of such short duration that the teacher is advised to ignore it, because not to ignore it would create an even greater distraction from the lesson. From Emmer, examples of behaviors of this type include "occasional callouts during discussions; brief whispering among students during a lesson; or short periods of inattentiveness, perhaps accompanied by visual wandering or daydreaming. There is no point in worrying about such trivial behaviors as long as they are not disruptive; they do not significantly affect student cooperation or involvement in learning activities. To attempt to react to them would consume too much of your energy, interrupt your lessons constantly, and detract from your classroom's climate."[7]

Types of Misbehavior

From Charles are these five broad types of misbehavior that teachers may have to contend with, listed here in declining order of seriousness:

1. *Aggression.* Occasionally, aggressive students physically or verbally attack teachers or other students. By law this can be a punishable offense, and you are best advised to find out what your own state and local laws are with respect to physical and verbal attacks by students upon teachers and students. A teacher should never have to put up with this type of student misbehavior. Whenever you are in doubt about what action to take, you should discuss your

---

[7]Edmund T. Emmer et al., *Classroom Management for Secondary Teachers*, 2nd ed. (Englewood Cliffs, NJ: Prentice Hall, 1989), p. 105.

concern about a student's aggressive behavior with the school counselor or an administrator. In some instances you may need to send for help immediately.

2. *Immorality.* This type of misbehavior includes cheating, lying, and stealing. A student who habitually exhibits such behavior may need to be referred to specialists. Whenever you have good reason to suspect immoral behavior of a student, you should discuss your concerns with that student's school counselor.

3. *Defiance of authority.* This is when a student refuses, perhaps hostilely, to do what the teacher tells that student to do. Defiance is worthy of temporary or permanent removal from the class—at least until there has been a conference about the situation, a conference perhaps that involves the student, the teacher, a parent or guardian, and a school official.

4. *Class disruptions.* This type includes talking loudly, calling out, walking about the room, clowning, and tossing objects, all of which the student knows are unacceptable behaviors in the classroom. In dealing with these kinds of misbehaviors it is important that the teacher has communicated to students the consequences of such inappropriate behaviors, and then deals promptly and consistently with the misbehavior. You must not ignore minor infractions of this type, for if you do they will escalate beyond your worst expectations.

5. *Goofing off.* This least serious type includes those misbehaviors that are most common to the classroom: fooling around, not doing the assigned tasks, daydreaming, and just generally being off task. Fortunately, in most instances, with this type of misbehavior all it takes to get the student back on task is a quiet redirection from the teacher.[8]

Gauge your understanding of student misbehaviors and how teachers should react by doing Exercises 5.4 and 5.5.

---

[8]C. M. Charles, *Building Classroom Discipline: From Models to Practice*, 3rd ed. (New York: Longman, 1989), p. 2.

EXERCISE 5.4
Identifying Teacher Behaviors That Cause Student Misbehavior

• • • • • •

Instructions: The purpose of this exercise is for you to become aware of the kinds of teacher behaviors to avoid because they tend to reinforce or cause student misbehavior. Place a check next to each of the following situations you believe are indicative of teacher behaviors that cause student misbehavior. Then identify what the teacher should do instead. Share your responses with your classmates. An answer key follows.

____ 1. The teacher is always late in arriving to the classroom, and class never begins until at least 5 minutes past the ring of the tardy bell.

____ 2. The teacher ignores brief whispering between two students during a quiet classroom activity.

____ 3. The teacher ignores brief talking between two students during a teacher lecture.

____ 4. During a classroom discussion one student appears to be daydreaming and just staring out the window.

____ 5. During quiet study time the teacher stops all activity and reprimands two students for their horsing around, and then writes out a referral for each of the two students.

____ 6. The teacher advises the students to pay attention during the showing of the film or else he will give them a quiz over the film's content.

____ 7. The teacher tells a student that because he has disturbed the class today he must come in after school and remain with that teacher for the same amount of time that he disturbed the class.

_____ 8. The teacher observes a student cheating on a test, so the teacher walks over to the student, picks up the student's test paper and tears it up.

_____ 9. While delivering a lecture, the principal walks into the classroom. The teacher stops the lecture and walks over to see what the principal wants.

_____ 10. The teacher begins a conversation with several students in the rear of the room while a student learning team is giving its oral report to the class.

Answer Key

Situations 1, 3, 5, 6, 7, 8, 9, and 10 should be checked as teacher behaviors that reinforce or cause student misbehavior for reasons explained below. You may not agree, particularly since specific circumstances might vary. But you should talk about these and arrive at understandings within your group.

1. The teacher must model his or her expectations of students; in this case, arriving and starting class on time.
2. Minor infractions are sometimes best ignored.
3. This should not be ignored. Students are expected to give attention to the teacher or whoever has the floor at the moment—that is common courtesy. By not attending to these students (perhaps by eye contact, proximity control, or use of name dropping during the lecture) the teacher is saying it is okay to talk when the teacher is lecturing.
4. Minor infractions are sometimes best ignored.
5. By disrupting the class learning activity, the teacher is reinforcing the very kind of behavior that the teacher finds unacceptable from the students.
6. Threats are unacceptable behaviors, from the students or the teacher. And tests should never be administered as punishment.
7. By giving the student even more individual time after school, the teacher is likely reinforcing and rewarding the student's misbehavior that caused the student problem in the first place. Besides, this is not a safe thing for the teacher to do. Detention hall, run by someone other than this teacher, is a better alternative.
8. This teacher, who has taken no time to diagnose and prescribe, is reacting too hastily and with hostility. This kind of teacher behavior reinforces the notions that you are guilty until proven innocent and that the process is more important than the individuals.
9. The teacher's lesson is more important; otherwise, the lesson learned is that disruptions are okay.
10. This is disrespectful, and the teacher and class should be giving full attention to the students giving their report.

Resolving a Discipline Problem
• • • • • •

Brainstorming Ideas

Instructions: The purpose of this exercise is to assist you in developing a repertoire of ideas about what you might do in a situation where a student is misbehaving. You can work on this exercise in small groups, or alone whenever you have a student that is causing problems in your classroom. Completion of this exercise will generate ideas about what you might do in certain situations. Follow each step closely.

1. *Statement of the problem.* Identify a specific discipline problem that you have experienced as a student, or one that you are now having as a teacher. State as clearly as you can what the problem is, such as the student is disruptive to classroom learning, the student just sits and does nothing, the student is ridiculed by others in the class, and so on.

2. *Identification of what you have observed about, or that is related to, this student.* List everything you know and have observed about this student, whether you believe it to be relevant or not. Include student behaviors, physical characteristics, grade level, subject, grades, attendance, hobbies, special talents, disabilities, how the student is getting along with other teachers, and so on.

3. *List of things tried.* List everything you have tried with this student and their results, such as isolation in the classroom, referrals, talks with parent or guardian, rewards, discussions with the student in or out of class, discussions with the student's other teachers, the student's counselor, and so on.

4. *Share steps one through three with your colleagues.* During the sharing discussion you may get new ideas about the student, the student's behavior, and things that you might try in order to work more positively with the student. As the ideas are generated, write them down—that is the next step.

5. *New things to try with this student.* As you complete the previous steps you will almost certainly gain ideas about new ways to work with this student. As those ideas are generated, write them down.

6. *Follow-up report of new strategy that was tried and the results.* At some later date, perhaps in a week or two, list here (and perhaps report to your group) what you tried and describe the results.

1. Statement of problem:

2. Observations about the student:

3. Things I have tried and results:

4. Sharing:

5. New ideas:

6. New strategy tried and results:

Preventive Discipline

The most fruitful steps you can take to achieve well-disciplined classes are preventive steps. These steps were considered in the earlier discussion of motivation and classroom management. Basically, the premise is that when motivation and classroom management are well taken care of, problems in classroom control are minimal.

Encouraging Self-Control

Generally students want to behave properly and acquire the approval of the teacher. Usually, a student misbehaves for some specific reason, and the task for the teacher is to understand that reason and help the student regain self-control. The best control of student behavior is self-control. If you help students learn to take responsibility for their own learning and to carry out this responsibility, you will have accomplished much. Some of the ways teachers work to help students with their self-control include the following.

1. *Help students establish a code of conduct for themselves.* Doing so has the advantage of acquainting students with what acceptable behavior is and why such behavior is necessary for the success of the group or of society. To be successful, this code should not be dictated by the teacher, but worked out together to the mutual satisfaction of all concerned.

2. *Help students improve their own standards of conduct.* This must be a slow process. It is accomplished by making students aware of optional behaviors, of high standards, and of the disadvantages of the lower standards. Classroom discussions of behaviors can be helpful in the process. Teachers have had success by talking out behavior problems with the students, so the students can see why a particular behavior is unacceptable, what the students should do about it as penance, and what actions could remedy the fault.

3. *Use the enforcement of rules as a tool.* Sometimes, enforcing rules helps students learn to discipline themselves. Both enforcing the rules fairly and making students follow the rules tend to support the habit of desirable behavior. In some classes students enforce many of the rules themselves. Although this procedure works well for mature groups, it is likely to throw too much burden on younger students. In most cases, the teacher should probably assume the responsibility for rule enforcement.

4. *Support student self-control.* When a teacher assumes control over a student's behavior—by using aggressive verbal orders or punitive measures—the teacher may momentarily cease a disruptive behavior, but such action is usually counterproductive to the encouragement of self-control. Techniques that can be used by a teacher to encourage and support student self-control are those whereby the teacher quietly refocuses student attention to an on-task behavior, with techniques such as the following:

- Use of nonverbal signals sent to the student. These signals can be sent by eye contact, the hand, or facial expressions. They indicate the teacher's withitness and communicate to the student that the teacher wants the student behavior back on task.
- Use of proximity control. When a teacher moves closer to a misbehaving student, the student will usually get back on task.
- Showing interest in a student's work when the student begins to lose interest in the class activity. The teacher can simply walk over to the restless student and ask to see the student's work. Making a positive statement about that work as well as suggesting further improvement will usually redirect the student's behavior.
- Humor and a smile will usually redirect student off-task behavior. This communicates two important things to the student: (1) the teacher is aware and uncomfortable with the student's inattentive behavior and wants the student back on task, and (2) while not being entirely happy with the student's inattentive behavior the teacher still accepts the student as a worthwhile individual.
- Use of academic time-outs. Sometimes, when a student has become bored and inattentive, the student's misbehavior can be redirected by giving the student a minor responsibility, such as delivering materials to the office or doing some paper work for you in the class-

room. However, a word of caution is in order: the student's time-out activity must not be seen by the student as an incentive for future misbehavior. Upon completion of the time-out activity, a quiet word from the teacher to the student is in order, such as, "Thank you for helping me. Now I would like you to finish your work and show it to me when it is done." In that way the student gets back on task after the brief time-out.

Enforcing Rules

No matter how well motivated, managed, and self-controlled your classes are, problems will arise. Therefore, you should be particularly attentive to rule enforcement. What you do when someone breaks the rules is more important than the rule breaking itself.

Reasonably strict enforcement of rules can have a good effect on the class and the classroom atmosphere, because enforcement has a positive ripple effect. When students see that you take swift, fair but firm action against infractions by other students, they are less likely to misbehave. The ripple effect is especially powerful when you show that you can control students who have high status in their peer group. Conversely, when students see that others are getting away with breaking the rules, they lose respect for both the rules and the teacher—and that can have a negative ripple effect. To gain the most advantage of a positive ripple effect, you must start a policy of strict enforcement on the very first day. Being lax in the beginning courts disaster. It is much easier to relax a policy of strict enforcement later than it is to turn a class around.

In any case, rule enforcement should be fair and consistent. Fairness and consistency in enforcement does not mean mindless conformity to an enforcement pattern. Justice should sometimes be tempered with mercy, and the nature of the punishment should sometimes be adjusted to the nature of the offender, as well as to the nature of the offense. But when this is done, the action taken should seem reasonable to all concerned. Ordinarily, measures such as the following, many of which have been previously discussed, will be more effective than negative ones:

- Let students know what you expect of them.
- Correct inappropriate behavior at once.
- Use nonintensive corrective measures, such as movement toward the source of trouble, hand signals, eye contact, and frowns.
- Handle all minor problems and punishments yourself.
- Treat the problem rather than the person.
- If at all possible, use alternatives rather than punishment. If necessary, punishment should be swift, sure, impressive, and appropriate to the "crime."
- Try to relieve tensions. Talk things over with the students. Show them how to improve. Emphasize what they are doing well. Inject a bit of humor and good feeling.
- When the class begins to become restless, switch activities.
- When you foresee that a student is about to get into trouble, attend to that student and redirect the student's attention, such as with the techniques previously discussed on student self-control.
- Plan periodically to make new seating assignments, perhaps on a regular basis, though not too often.
- If you must deny a student request, explain why.
- Keep student movement in the classroom to a minimum.
- Avoid dead time during the period, time when individual students have nothing to do.
- Have an alternative lesson plan in case the original plan is not working.

On the whole, negative methods of rule enforcement are not effective. You should avoid the following:

- *Nagging.* Continual or unnecessary scolding or criticizing of a student succeeds only in upsetting the student and arousing the resentment of other students.

- *Threats and ultimatums.* Avoid painting yourself into a corner. Once you have made a threat or given an ultimatum, you are stuck if the students call you on it. In maintaining control, threats become promises. Once made, they must be carried out or you will lose control. If students learn that your threats are empty, they will disregard them and you. In addition, a threat such as "If you do not pay attention to this film I will give you a quiz on it" is unacceptable in effective teaching. If you are going to give a quiz on the film, then you should prepare the quiz, announce it, and give it, regardless of the students' behavior during the film. They are two separate matters. A test should never be used as a form of punishment. And, in this particular instance, the teacher is threatening punishment of the entire class, though some students, threat or no threat, may well pay attention to the film and not cause any trouble.
- *Hasty judgments and actions.* Although your responses to behavior problems should be prompt, do not be overly hasty. Impulsive reactions on your part could lead to greater problems than you can even imagine.
- *Overreaction to minor incidents.* Avoid treating minor incidents as major ones. Otherwise they may develop into real problems. Minor problems of misbehavior can usually be resolved by the use of the techniques previously discussed about student self-control. When those don't work, then the teacher may need to assume control, using punishment, removal of rewards, detention, or even referral to a counselor or some school authority.
- *Arbitrary, capricious, inconsistent enforcement of rules.* If a teacher is inconsistent, students will test that teacher to see what they can get away with. Inconsistency also causes student resentment, confusion, and mistrust.
- *Loud talk, yelling, and screaming.* Never try to talk over your class. Yelling and screaming simply add to the commotion. Teachers who yell and scream or try to talk over their class are part of the problem; loud talk, yelling, and screaming never solve anything.
- *Harsh, unusual, and inconsistent punishment.* Flogging, beating, tongue-lashing, and humiliation are both ineffective and indicative of a teacher who has lost control. Although some students may occasionally need to be reprimanded, hurting or humiliating them may do much more harm than good. Punishment is discussed in more detail in the next section.

Correcting Misbehavior

The goal of classroom control is to motivate and shape the students in such a way that they do not create discipline problems. Thorough planning, positive motivation, and efficient classroom management are preventive measures that are the real keys to classroom control. When students are working well, control and discipline take care of themselves. Nevertheless, even in the best of classroom situations, the behavior of some students will be less than desirable and will need to be turned into more positive directions.

Theoretically, there are five basic methods to stop anyone from behaving in an undesirable way. One method is to keep the offender at it until he or she gets sick of it (the satiation principle). A second method is to make sure that the undesirable behavior is not rewarded in any way and in that way dies out (the extinction principle). A third method is to provide an alternative that is incompatible with the undesirable behavior, and to see to it that the alternative behavior is rewarded while the undesirable behavior is not (the incompatible alternative principle). A fourth method is to create an aversive situation that the person can relieve only by giving up the undesirable behavior (the negative reinforcement principle). A fifth method calls for punishment or results supposedly so unpleasant that the person will not willingly repeat the misbehavior again (the punishment principle).

Satiation and extinction are not practical measures for correcting misbehavior in the classroom. Therefore, teachers can depend only on incompatible alternatives, negative reinforcement, and punishment to correct misbehavior. The incompatible-alternative and the negative-reinforcement methods are usually more successful than punishment.

In the incompatible-alternative method, the teacher establishes an alternative behavior that is so rewarding the student forsakes the misbehavior. To find extremely strong, usable rewards suitable to the classroom situation is not always easy, but it can be done. The catch, of course, is that the reward for the alternative behavior must be so powerful that it overshadows the reward derived from the misbehavior.

The negative-reinforcement method is much more subtle. In this method, the teacher sets up an aversive situation designed to plague the student as long as he or she misbehaves. As soon as the student stops misbehaving, the plaguing stops. The student who stops misbehaving is rewarded by relief from pain or annoyance. This approach is a more effective way to correct student misbehavior than punishment.

At times a teacher must fall back on punishment in an attempt to cure misbehavior. When this time comes, a teacher should attempt to make the punishment appropriate to the misdeed and also swift, sure, and impressive—definitely a punishment and not a reward. The student should have no doubt about the severity of the punishment, why the punishment has been inflicted, and the types of behavior that will prevent future punishment. Among the punishments often used are isolation, reprimands, extra work, deprivation of privileges, and detention. None is very effective in the long term. In the short term, however, they may shake up the student enough so that more positive measures can be applied with greater chances of success. Now consider some of the punishments used by teachers and the recommendations for their use or disuse.

Verbal Punishment

You will often have to reprimand a student. As often as possible, your reprimand should be a declarative statement that is brief and to the point, and as private as possible. Redirecting student attention with the use of questions such as "Katrina, why are you doing that?" is seldom effective. Also, verbal reprimands that the entire class can hear are disruptive to student concentration and work and thus are counterproductive to an effective learning atmosphere. Loud, public, and frequent reprimands do not create a favorable learning environment, and they may do more harm than good. When you must call a student to task, quietly point out the inappropriate behavior and spell out the corrective behavior. There is no point in hurting the student's feelings, in causing resentment, and in building an unpleasant atmosphere with harsh words. The consequences of misbehavior should already be well understood, so if the student persists in the inappropriate behavior, then you proceed to step two of your consequences, which might be a detention.

Detention

Although detention has not proven to be particularly effective, keeping students after school is one of the most common types of punishment. Since it does have a mildly unpleasant effect on students, it is of some value as a deterrent. For many students, however, detention is such a mild inconvenience that they take it in stride as part of the regular responsibilities of being a student. In contrast, for students who work after school, detention may cause distress out of proportion to the misbehavior. And if the students just sit around during the detention period, detention becomes another complete waste of time for everyone concerned, reinforcing their concept of school as being a waste of time.

Detention after school, alone with the teacher in that teacher's classroom, is not recommended for several reasons. First, such detention might be perceived by the student as a reward rather than a punishment for the student's misbehavior. Second, such detention creates safety and liability problems for the teacher. Third, such detention is often more a punishment for the teacher than for the student.

To be profitable, detention probably should be combined with individual conferences, makeup work, tutoring, or some other educational activity. In some schools, being assigned to detention means to be assigned to a schoolyard clean-up detail. Liability could be an issue in such instances. What if the student is injured while serving on the work detail?

Loss of Privileges

Loss of privileges seems to be one of the most effective forms of punishment. It probably works best when combined with a system that grants rewards for good behavior. Then, if the privileges lost seem valuable to the student, loss of privileges demonstrates to the student that inappropriate behavior is costly while appropriate behavior pays off.

Examples of privileges that have worked for teachers are a trip to a pizza parlor with the teacher as host, a trip to an ice cream parlor with the teacher as host, and free-choice time in class each Friday.

Restitution and Reparation

A time-honored belief in the American tradition is that "the punishment should fit the crime." This notion is the basis for the use of restitution and reparation as punishment. Punishment of this type has several advantages. It associates the punishment with the offense in a natural way. It teaches misbehaving students that they are responsible for their misdeeds and that willful damage should be compensated for. It can be administered fairly and with impartiality. Most importantly, it teaches offenders that their actions affect the welfare of others and that they must accept the responsibility for making things right, by paying back others for the inconvenience and expense caused by the inappropriate behavior.

Punishing the Group

A teacher should never punish—nor threaten to punish—the entire class for the misbehavior of a few. Doing so only aligns the class against the teacher, creating a hostile atmosphere that is counterproductive to the establishment of a positive and effective climate for learning.

Assigning Extra Work

Assigning extra class work to offenders is another punishment you should avoid using. It has no worthwhile advantages, and furthers the notion that schoolwork is just that, work.

Lowering Academic Marks

To lower students' academic marks as a punishment is a misuse of the grading system. Academic marks should be only an indicator of academic achievement. To mark a student down for his or her behavior when the student has learned well gives a false index of that student's academic progress. Schools have separate marks for classroom behavior—the citizenship grade. Citizenship marks represent the teacher's subjective opinion of the student's behavior in that teacher's classroom.

Physical Activity as Punishment

Except perhaps for physical education classes, where the punishment clearly fits the subject matter and can be carefully supervised, physical punishment (e.g., doing push-ups or running around the track) should not be used by the classroom teacher.

Writing as Punishment

Academic work should never be used as punishment or seen by students as being punishment for their misbehavior. Requiring students to write sentences on the board or in their notebooks as a punishment is unacceptable in effective teaching. Writing should never be assigned as punishment. Note well: using writing as punishment will also alienate you from the teachers of the English department.

Corporal Punishment

A teacher should never strike, push, shove, or manhandle a student in any way for any reason. Corporal punishment (e.g., spanking) is now illegal in many states. Physical handling of a student is disallowed in many school districts. There are many instances where physical punishment has resulted in student injury and in subsequent legal action against the teacher and school. In other cases students have reacted violently, injuring the administering teacher or administrator. A good rule of thumb is that if you get really angry at a student, back off until you have cooled off. If you want the student temporarily out of your sight, you can send the student to the vice-principal's office for a cooling-off period. Find out what the policy is in your own school for sending a student to the office for such a time out.

When a Class Is Out of Control

That a class would get totally out of your control is very unlikely if you carefully follow the guidance presented in this book. But if a class does get out of control, the following tactics should help:

1. Get help if you feel the situation is potentially dangerous—from a teacher nearby or from the office—but do not leave the room yourself.
2. Remain calm. If you feel a bit panicky, keep quiet for a while.
3. Try to get the students' attention, but without shouting. Do not add to the confusion. Different tactics may help here. For instance, one teacher sat on the floor in the middle of the room until the class got quiet. Another flicked the light switch a few times. Another blew a whistle.
4. Ask that all students take their seats (or remain standing quietly).
5. Redirect the activity of individual students, one at a time. Try to start with those students you know will respond positively to your request.
6. As soon as things have come under better control, quietly begin a lesson.

Handling Major Offenses

If you are ever confronted with a major offense, such as students' carrying weapons, using drugs, vandalizing property, leaving the room without authorization, or fighting, first try to stop the misbehavior, though without putting yourself in even more danger. Then report it immediately to the principal's office.

Remember, you are neither a law-enforcement officer nor a psychiatrist. Major problems require outside assistance from professionals. As a professional teacher, you have the right to request and receive assistance from principals, parents, and other school personnel.

Check your understanding of measures of control by doing Exercises 5.6 and 5.7.

EXERCISE 5.6
Applying Measures of Control

• • • • • •

Instructions: The purpose of this exercise is for you to determine when you might use each of the various options available when there is a student behavior problem in your classroom. For each of the following, as specifically as possible identify a situation in which you would and you would not use that measure. Then share your responses with those of others in your class.

1. Eye contact and hand signal to the student.

   Would:

   Would not:

2. Send student immediately to the office of the vice-principal.

   Would:

   Would not:

3. Ignore the student.

   Would:

   Would not:

4. Assign the student to detention.

   Would:

   Would not:

5. Send a note home to parent or guardian about the student's misbehavior.

   Would:

   Would not:

6. Touch a student on the shoulder.

   Would:

   Would not:

7. Provide candy as rewards.

   Would:

   Would not:

8. Provide a time-out from academic time.

   Would:

   Would not:

9. Verbally redirect the student's attention.

   Would:

   Would not:

10. Use a verbal reprimand.

    Would:

    Would not:

EXERCISE 5.7
Selecting Measures of Control

• • • • • •

Instructions: The purpose of this exercise is to provide situations to help you in determining which measures of control you would apply in similar situations. For each of the following, write what you would do in that situation. Then share your responses with your colleagues.

1. A student reveals a long knife and threatens to cut you.

2. During a test a student appears to be copying answers from a neighboring student's answer sheet.

3. Although you have asked a student to take his seat, he refuses.

4. While talking with a small group of students, you observe two students on the opposite side of the room tossing paper airplanes at each other.

5. During small-group work one student seems to be aimlessly wandering around the room.

6. Although chewing gum is against your classroom rules, at the start of the class period you observe a student chewing what appears to be gum.

7. During band rehearsal you (as band director) observe a student about to stuff a scarf down the saxophone of another student.

8. During the viewing of a film two students on the side of the room opposite you are quietly whispering.

9. At the start of the period, while about to take her seat, a boy pulls the chair from beneath the student. She falls to the floor.

10. Suddenly, for no apparent reason, a student gets up and leaves the room.

Student Misbehavior: Fifty Mistakes Commonly Made by Beginning Teachers

Often, the misbehavior of a student is the direct result of something that the teacher did or did not do. Each of the following represents a mistake commonly made by student teachers and beginning teachers, though not every teacher makes every one of these mistakes. Read and understand each for its relevancy to your teaching—if the shoe fits, wear it.[9]

1. *Inadequately attending to long-range planning.* Long-range unit planning is important for reasons discussed in the preceding module. A beginning teacher who inadequately plans ahead is heading for trouble.

2. *Using sketchy lesson plans.* Sketchy, inadequate daily lesson planning is a precursor to ineffective teaching and, eventually, to teaching failure. Many beginning teachers plan their lessons carefully at the beginning of the semester, and the students initially respond well. Then, after finding a few strategies that seem to work, their lesson planning becomes increasingly sketchy, and they fall into a rut of doing pretty much the same thing day after day—lecture, discussion, videos, and worksheets are common in these instances. They fail to consider and plan for individual student differences. By mid-semester they have stopped growing professionally, and they begin to experience an increasing number of problems, with students and with parents.

3. *Emphasizing the negative.* Too many warnings to students for their inappropriate behavior—and too little recognition for their positive behaviors—does not help to establish the positive climate needed for the most effective learning to take place. Reminding students of procedures is more positive than is reprimanding them when they do not follow procedures.

4. *Allowing students' hands to be raised too long.* When students have their hands raised for long periods before you recognize them and attend to their questions or responses, you are providing them with time to fool around. Although you don't have to call on every student as soon as he or she raises a hand, you should acknowledge them quickly, such as with a nod or a waive of your hand, so they can lower the hand and return to their work. Then you should get to the student as quickly as possible. Procedures for this should be clearly understood by the students and consistently followed by you.

5. *Spending too much time with one student or one group and not monitoring the entire class.* Spending too much time with any one student or a small group of students is, in effect, ignoring the rest of the class. For the best classroom management you must continually monitor the entire classroom of students. How much time is too much? A rule of thumb is anything over 30 seconds is approaching too much time.

6. *Beginning a new activity before gaining the students' attention.* A teacher who consistently fails to insist that students follow procedures and who does not wait until all students are in compliance before starting a new activity is destined for major problems in classroom control. You must establish and maintain classroom procedures. Starting an activity before all students are in compliance is, in effect, telling the students that they don't have to follow expected procedures. You cannot afford to tell students one thing and then do another. A teacher's actions always speak louder than words.[10]

7. *Pacing teacher talk and learning activities too fast.* Students need time to disengage mentally and physically from one activity before engaging in the next. You must remember that this takes more time for a classroom of thirty students than it does for just one person, you.

8. *Using a voice level that is always either too loud or too soft.* A teacher's voice that is too loud day after day can become irritating to some students, just as one that cannot be heard or understood can become irritating.

9. *Assigning a journal entry without giving the topic careful thought.* If the question or topic about which students are supposed to write is ambiguous or obviously hurriedly prepared—without your having given thought to how students will interpret and respond to it—students

---

[9]Copyright 1994 by Richard D. Kellough.

[10]See Mary M. Williams, "Actions Speak Louder Than Words: What Students Think," *Educational Leadership* 51 (3):22–23 (November 1993).

will judge that the task is simply busywork (e.g., something for them to do while you take attendance). If they do it at all, it is with a great deal of commotion and much less enthusiasm then if they were writing on a topic that had meaning to them.

10. *Standing too long in one place.* In the classroom you must be mobile in order to "work the crowd."

11. *Sitting while teaching.* As a beginning teacher, there is no time to sit while teaching. You cannot monitor the class while seated. You cannot afford to appear that casual.

12. *Being too serious and no fun.* No doubt, good teaching is serious business. But students respond best to teachers who obviously enjoy working with students and helping them learn.

13. *Falling into a rut by using same teaching strategy or combination of strategies day after day.* This teacher's classroom becomes boring to students. Because of the multitude of differences, students respond best to a variety of well-planned and meaningful classroom activities.

14. *Inadequately using silence (wait time) after asking a content question.* When expected to think deeply about a question, students need time to do it.

15. *Poorly or inefficiently using the overhead projector and the writing board.* The ineffective use of the overhead projector (see Module 9) and writing board (see Module 8) says to students that you are not a competent teacher. A competent teacher, like a competent surgeon or automobile mechanic, selects and effectively uses the best tools available for the job to be done.

16. *Ineffectively using facial expressions and body language.* Your gestures and body language say more to students than your words do. For example, one teacher didn't understand why his class of middle school students would not respond to his repeated expression of "I need your attention." In one class, he used that expression eight times in less than 15 minutes. Studying a videotape of his teaching helped him understand the problem. His dress was very casual, and he stood most of the time with his right hand in his pocket. At five foot, eight inches, with a slight build, a rather deadpan facial expression, and a nonexpressive voice, he was not a commanding presence in the classroom. Once he had seen himself on tape, he returned to the class wearing a tie, and he began using his hands, face, and voice more expressively. Rather than saying "I need your attention," he waited in silence for the students to become attentive. It worked.

17. *Relying too much on teacher talk for classroom control.* Beginning teachers have a tendency to rely too much on teacher talk. Too much teacher talk is deadly, (see Module 7). Unable to discern between the important and the unimportant verbiage, students will quickly tune you out. In addition, useless verbalism, such as global praise and verbal fill-ins, causes students to pay less attention when you have something important to say.

18. *Inefficiently using teacher time.* Think carefully about what you are going to be doing every minute, and then plan for the most efficient and therefore the most effective use of your time in the classroom. Consider the following example. A middle school teacher is recording student contributions on a large sheet of butcher paper taped to the writing board. She solicits student responses, acknowledges those responses, holds and manipulates the writing pen and writes on the paper. Each of those actions requires decisions and movements that consume valuable time and can distract her from her students. An effective alternative would be to have a reliable student helper do the writing while she handles the solicitation and acknowledgment of student responses. That way she has fewer decisions and fewer actions to distract her. And she does not lose eye contact and proximity with the classroom of students.

19. *Talking to and interacting with only half the class.* When leading a class discussion, too many beginning teachers favor (by their eye contact and verbal interaction) only 40–65 percent of the students, sometimes completely ignoring the others for an entire class period. Feeling ignored those students will, in time, become uninterested and perhaps unruly. Remember to spread your interactions throughout the entire class. Try to establish eye contact with every student about once a minute.

20. *Not requiring students to raise their hands and be acknowledged before responding.* You cannot be in control of your interactions with students if you allow students to shout out responses and questions whenever they feel like it. In addition, indulging their natural impulsivity is not helping them to grow intellectually.

21. *Collecting and returning homework papers before assigning students something to do.* If, while turning in papers or waiting for their return, students have nothing else to do they get restless and inattentive. Avoid any kind of dead time. Students should have something to do while papers are being collected or returned.

22. *Verbally or nonverbally interrupting students once they are on task.* Avoid doing or saying anything once students are working on a learning task. If there is an important point you must make, write it on the board. If you want to return some papers while they are working, do it in a way and when they are least likely to be interrupted from their learning task.

23. *Using "Shhh" to try to obtain student attention or to quiet them.* When doing that you simply sound like a balloon with a slow leak. That sound and the overuse of verbal fill-ins, such as "okay," should be eliminated from your professional vocabulary.

24. *Overuse of verbal efforts to stop inappropriate student behavior.* Beginning teachers have a tendency to rely too much on verbal interaction and not enough on nonverbal intervention techniques. Verbally reprimanding a student for his or her interruptions of class activities is reinforcing that very behavior you are trying to stop. Develop your indirect, silent intervention techniques.

25. *Poor body positioning in the classroom.* Always position your body so you can continue visually monitoring the entire class.

26. *Settling for less when you should be trying for more—not getting the most from student responses.* Don't hurry a discussion; "milk" student responses for all you can, especially when discussing a topic they are obviously interested in. Ask a student for clarification or reasons for his or her response. Ask for verification or data. Have another student paraphrase what a student said. Pump students for deeper thought and meaning. Too often, the teacher will ask a question, get an abbreviated (often one word) response from a student, and then move on to new content. Instead, follow up a student's response to your question with a sequence of questions, prompting and cueing to elevate the student's thinking to higher levels.

27. *Using threats.* One middle school teacher, for example, told her class that if they continued with their inappropriate talking they would lose their break time. She should have had that consequence as part of the understood procedures and then taken away the break time if student behavior warranted it. Avoid threats of any kind. In addition, be cautious about ever punishing the entire class for the misbehavior of some of the students. Although the rationale behind such action is clear (i.e., to get group pressure working for you), often the result is opposite of that intended—students who have been behaving well become alienated from the teacher because they feel they have been punished unfairly for the misbehavior of others. Those students expect the teacher to be able to handle the misbehaving students without punishing those who are behaving well, and perhaps they are right.

28. *Global praise.* An instance would be: "Your rough drafts were really wonderful." This says nothing and is simply another instance of useless verbalism from the teacher. Be specific—tell what it was about their drafts that made them so wonderful.

29. *Meaningless use of color.* The use of color, such as varying color pens for overhead transparencies and colored chalk for chalkboard writing, can be nice but will lose its effectiveness over time unless the colors have meaning. If you color code everything in the classroom so students understand the meaning of the colors, then use of color is helpful to their learning.

30. *Verbally reprimanding a student across the classroom.* This is needless interruption of all students. In addition, it simply increases the "you versus them" syndrome, because of peer pressure. Reprimand, when necessary, but do it quietly and privately.

31. *Interacting with only a "chosen few" students rather than spreading interactions around to all students.* As a beginning teacher it is easy to fall into a habit of interacting only with a few students, especially those who are vocal and who have "intelligent" contributions. Your job, however, is to teach all students. To do that you must be active, not reactive, in your interactions.

32. *Not intervening quickly enough during inappropriate student behavior.* Inappropriate student behavior usually gets worse, not better, if allowed to continue. It won't go away by itself. It's best to nip it in the bud quickly and resolutely. A teacher who ignores inappropriate

behavior is, in effect, approving it. In turn, that approval reinforces the continuation of those inappropriate behaviors.

33. *Not learning and using student names.* A teacher who does not know or use names when addressing students is, in effect, seen by the students as being impersonal and uncaring. You want to quickly learn the names and then refer to students by their names when you call on them in class.

34. *Reading student papers only for correct answers and not for process and student thinking.* Reading student papers only for "correct" responses reinforces the notion that the process of arriving at answers or solutions is unimportant and that alternative solutions or answers are impossible.

35. *Not putting time plans on the board for students.* Yelling out how much time is left for an activity, such as a quiz or cooperative learning activity interrupts student thinking. Rather, you should write on the board before the activity begins how much time is allowed for it. Write the time the activity is to end. If during the activity a decision is made to change that end time, then write the changed time on the board. Avoid interrupting students once they are on task.

36. *Asking global questions that nobody likely will answer.* Examples of this type of question are: "Does everyone understand how that was done?" "Are there any questions?" and "How do you all feel about . . . ?" If you want to check for student understanding or opinions, then do a spot check by asking specific questions, allow some time to think, and then call on students (the questioning strategy is discussed in Module 7).

37. *Failing to do frequent comprehension checks (every few minutes) to see if students are understanding.* Too often, teachers simply plow through their lesson, assuming students are understanding it.

38. *Using poorly worded, ambiguous questions.* Plan your questions. Write them out. Ask them to yourself, and try to predict how students will respond to a particular question.

39. *Failing to balance interactions with students according to student gender.* Many teachers (experienced as well as beginning) interact more often with male than with female students (see Module 7). Avoid that.

40. *Trying to talk over too much student noise.* This simply tells students that their making noise while you are talking is acceptable behavior. All that you will accomplish when trying to talk over a high student noise level is a sore throat by the end of the school day.

41. *Wanting to be liked by students.* Forget it. If you are a teacher, then teach. Respect will be earned as a result of your good teaching. Liking you may come later.

42. *Allowing students to be inattentive to an educationally useful video or movie.* This usually happens because the teacher has failed to give the students a written handout of questions or guidelines for what they should acquire from watching the audiovisual. Sometimes students need an additional focus. Furthermore, an audiovisual is exactly that—audio and visual. To reinforce the learning, add the kinesthetic, such as the writing aspect when questions are used. This provides the hands-on and minds-on learning that you want.

43. *Stutter starting.* A stutter start is when the teacher begins an activity, is distracted, begins again, is distracted again, tries again to start, and so on. During stutter starts students become increasingly restless and inattentive, making the final start almost impossible for the teacher to achieve. Avoid stutter starts. Begin an activity clearly and decisively.

44. *Failing to give students a pleasant greeting on Monday or following a holiday or to remind them to have a pleasant weekend or holiday.* Students are likely to perceive such a teacher as uncaring or impersonal.

45. *Sounding egocentric.* Whether you are or are not egocentric, you want to avoid sounding so. Sometimes the distinction is subtle, such as when a teacher says "What *I* am going to do now is . . ." rather than saying "What *we* are going to do now is. . . ." If you want to strive for group cohesiveness—a sense of "we-ness,"—then teach not as if you are the leader and your students are the followers, but rather in a manner that empowers your students in their learning.

46. *Taking too much time to give verbal directions for a new activity.* Students get impatient and restless during long verbal instructions from the teacher. It is better to give brief instructions (2 or 3 minutes should do it) and get your students started on the task. For more

complicated activities you can teach three or four students the instructions for the activity and then have those students do "workshops" with five or six students in each workshop group. This frees you to monitor the progress of each group.

47. *Taking too much time for an activity.* Whether lecturing or providing for group work, think carefully about how much time students can effectively attend to the activity. Here is a general rule of thumb for most classes: when only one or two learning modalities are involved (e.g., auditory and visual), the activity should not extend beyond about 15 minutes; when more than two senses are involved (e.g., add tactile or kinesthetic) then the activity might extend longer, say for 20 or 30 minutes.

48. *Being uptight and anxious.* Students quickly, consciously or unconsciously, detect a teacher who is afraid that events in the classroom will probably not go well. And it's like a contagious disease—if you are uptight and anxious, your students will likely become the same. To prevent such emotions, at least to the extent that they damage your teaching and your students' learning, you must prepare lessons carefully, thoughtfully, and thoroughly. Unless there is something personal going on in your life that is making you anxious, you are more likely to be in control and confident in the classroom when you have lessons that are well prepared. If you do have a personal problem, you need to concentrate on ensuring that your anger, hostility, fear, and other negative emotions do not negatively effect your teaching and your interactions with students. Regardless of your personal problems, your classes of students will face you each day expecting to be taught mathematics, history, science, physical education, or whatever it is you are supposed to be helping them learn.

49. *Overusing punishment for classroom misbehavior—jumping to the final step without trying alternatives.* Many beginning teachers mistakenly try either to ignore inappropriate student behavior or to skip steps, resorting too quickly to punishment. They immediately take away PATs (preferred activity time) or break time, or they quickly assign detention (an ineffective punishment). In-between steps that they should consider include the use of alternative activities in the classroom. By their instruction too many teachers unrealistically seem to expect success having all thirty-three students doing the same thing at the same time rather than having several alternative activities simultaneously occurring in the classroom (multilevel teaching). For example, a student who is not responding well (i.e., being disruptive) to a class discussion might behave better if given the choice of moving to a quiet reading center in the classroom or to a learning center to work alone or with one other student. If, after trying an alternative activity, the student continues to be disruptive, then you may have to try another alternative activity. You may have to send the student to another supervised location (out of the classroom, to a place previously arranged by you) until you have time (after class or after school) to talk with him or her about the problem.

50. *Using negative language.* Too often, beginning teachers try to control their students with negative language, such as: "There should be no talking." "No gum or candy in class or else you will get detention." and "No getting out of your seats without my permission." Negative language from the teacher does not help instill a positive classroom environment. As emphasized in this module, students need to know what is expected of them and to understand classroom procedures. Therefore, to encourage a positive classroom atmosphere you should use concise, positive language. Tell students exactly what they are supposed to do rather than what they are not supposed to do.

SUMMARY

Students are more likely to learn when they feel that the learning is important or worth the time. In this module we described factors important for learning to occur.

As a classroom teacher you should not be expected to solve all the societal woes that can spill over into the classroom. Yet as a professional you have certain responsibilities, including: to prepare thoughtfully and thoroughly for your classes; to manage and control your classes;

and to be able to diagnose, prescribe, and remedy those learning difficulties, disturbances, and minor misbehaviors that are the norm for classrooms and for the age group with whom you are working. If you follow the guidelines provided in this book, you will be well on your way to developing a teaching style and management system that, for the most part, should provide teaching that runs smoothly and effectively, without serious problems.

It is important to select the most appropriate strategies to accompany your teaching plans and that compliment your management system. Modules that follow in Part III present guidelines for doing that.

SUGGESTED READING

Baron, E. B. *Discipline Strategies for Teachers*, Fastback 344. Bloomington, IN: Phi Delta Kappa Educational Foundation, 1992.

Black, S. "In Praise of Judicious Praise." *Executive Educator* 14(10):24–27 (October 1992).

Blendinger, J., et al. *Win-Win Discipline*. Fastback 353. Bloomington, IN: Phi Delta Kappa Educational Foundation, 1993.

Chance, P. "Sticking Up for Rewards." *Phi Delta Kappan* 74(10):787–790 (June 1993).

Chance, P. "The Rewards of Learning." *Phi Delta Kappan* 74(3):200–207 (November 1992).

Cleary, L. M. "The Fragile Inclination to Write: Praise and Criticism in the Classroom." *English Journal* 79(2):22–28 (February 1990).

Dreikurs, R.; Grunwald, B.; and, Pepper, F. *Maintaining Sanity in the Classroom*. New York: Harper & Row, 1982.

Froyen, L. A. *Classroom Management: The Reflective Teacher-Leader*, 2d ed. New York: Macmillan, 1993.

Grant, C. A., and Sleeter, C. E. *Turning on Learning: Five Approaches for Multicultural Teaching Plans for Race, Class, Gender, and Disability*. New York: Merrill-Macmillan, 1989.

Hunter, M. *Enhancing Teaching*. New York: Macmillan, 1994.

Jones, F. *Positive Classroom Discipline*. New York: McGraw-Hill, 1987.

Kounin, J. *Discipline and Group Management in Classrooms*. New York: Holt, Rinehart and Winston, 1977.

Merrett, F., and Wheldall, K. "Teachers' Use of Praise and Reprimands to Boys and Girls." *Educational Review* 44(1):73–79 (September 1992).

Sprick, R. S. *Discipline in the Secondary Classroom: A Problem-by-Problem Survival Guide*. West Nyack, NY: The Center for Applied Research In Education, 1989.

Tingley, S. "Negative Rewards." *Educational Leadership* 50(1):80 (September 1992).

Williams, M. M. "Actions Speak Louder Than Words: What Students Think." *Educational Leadership* 51(3):22–23 (November 1993).

Wolfgang, C., and Glickman, C. *Solving Discipline Problems*. Boston: Allyn & Bacon, 1980.

POSTTEST

Multiple Choice

_____   1. If your class of students is getting too noisy, you can try any of the following *except*
        a. remain quiet until the class is quiet.
        b. change the lesson strategy to a distinctly different activity.
        c. hold your hand in the air, thereby nonverbally asking for quiet.
        d. talk louder or, if necessary, yell over their noise, asking them to be quiet.

_____ 2. *Least* recommended of the following, though sometimes necessary for the teacher's intervention of student misbehavior, is the use of
    a. eye contact.
    b. physical contact.
    c. a voice command.
    d. teacher proximity to the offending student.

_____ 3. Effective classroom management should rely on
    a. calm and silence.
    b. fear and subordination.
    c. orderliness and control.
    d. warning and punishment.

_____ 4. An important rule of thumb about the establishment of classroom behavior rules is that
    a. established rules are not necessary.
    b. the more established rules the better.
    c. only the minimum number of rules necessary should be established.
    d. a list of twelve rules is the minimum required to cover basic behaviors.

_____ 5. Which one of the following is a true statement about behavior problems in the middle school and secondary school classroom?
    a. Students are unruly by nature.
    b. Administrators do not adequately support teachers.
    c. Most student misbehavior is preventable.
    d. The occasional use of corporal punishment is absolutely necessary to maintain classroom control.

_____ 6. When assigning a written paper, which one of the following is a desired teacher verbal command?
    a. Don't plagiarize your assignment.
    b. I will know if you have copied someone else's paper.
    c. Please try and use your own ideas, and credit others whenever you do use theirs.
    d. If you try to turn in your first writing draft without rewriting, I guarantee you will get a poor grade.

_____ 7. Which one of the following is *not* recommended?
    a. Routinize ordinary administrative matters.
    b. Individualize the instruction as much as possible.
    c. Punish the entire class of students whenever you are unsure who the guilty party is.
    d. Start and end class meetings immediately when they are supposed to begin and end.

_____ 8. Which one of the following is *not* recommended?
    a. Keep foot traffic in your classroom to a minimum.
    b. Constantly be aware of all activity in the classroom.
    c. When necessary, punish by lowering the student's academic grade.
    d. Maintain the pacing of lessons so that all students feel some pressure.

_____ 9. Two elements necessary for maintaining classroom control are
    a. warning and anxiety.
    b. consistency and fairness.
    c. isolation and suspension.
    d. detention and suspension.

_____ 10. A usually effective safeguard against disruptive student behavior in the classroom is
    a. support from the administration.
    b. the threat of the use of corporal punishment.
    c. a thoughtfully and carefully prepared lesson plan.
    d. a teacher who is physically intimidating to the students.

_____ 11. When showing a video to your class, you are advised to
   a. use that time to grade papers at your desk.
   b. stand behind the class and watch the movie.
   c. stand behind the class and monitor student behavior.
   d. leave the students watching the video and go to the faculty room.

Short Explanation

1. Identify at least four guidelines for your use of praise for a student's appropriate behavior.
2. Explain why it is important to prevent behavior problems before they occur. Describe at least five preventative steps you will take to reduce the number of management problems that you will have.
3. Too many teachers attempt to resolve problems with individual students within the regular class period. Describe two recommendations for what you can do if you have a problem with the classroom behavior of a specific student.
4. Explain the rationale for the phrase "catch them being good."
5. Explain why many learning psychologists (e.g., Montessori and Piaget) oppose the teacher's use of extrinsic reinforcement for managing student behavior.
6. Explain how and why your classroom management procedures and expectations might differ depending upon the nature of the students, the grade level you are teaching, and the activities in your classroom.
7. Explain why supervisors of student teachers expect student teachers to prepare written classroom management plans.
8. Explain the difference between reprimanding a student for his or her inappropriate classroom behavior and reminding that student of classroom procedures.
9. Explain why stopping your lecture or a class discussion to verbally reprimand a student for his or her inappropriate behavior is an inappropriate teacher behavior.
10. Sean, an English teacher, has a class of thirty-three eighth graders who during his lectures, teacher-led discussions, and recitation lessons are restless and inattentive, creating a major classroom management problem for him. At Sean's invitation, the school psychologist tests the children for learning modalities and finds that thirty of them are predominately kinesthetic learners. Explain how this information may be useful to Sean.

Essay

1. Some experts say that 90 percent of control problems in the classroom are teacher caused. Do you agree or disagree? Why or why not?
2. Some supervisors of student teachers prefer that the student teacher never conduct a class while seated. Is it ever appropriate for a teacher to sit down while teaching? Can a teacher effectively monitor a classroom while seated?
3. From your current observations and field work as related to this teacher preparation program, clearly identify one specific example of educational practice that seems contradictory to exemplary practice or theory as presented in this module. Present your explanation for the discrepancy.
4. Describe any prior concepts you held that changed as a result of your experiences with this module. Describe the changes.

SELECTING AND IMPLEMENTING INSTRUCTIONAL STRATEGIES

You can not put the same shoe on every foot.

—Publius Syrus

When teaching a group of students of mixed learning abilities, mixed modality strengths, mixed language proficiencies, and mixed cultural backgrounds, the integration of learning modalities is a must. A teacher who uses only one style for teaching for all students in the same classroom setting, day after day, is short-changing the achievement of students who could learn better if another way of teaching were used.

—Callahan, Clark, and Kellough

Be not the first by whom the new is tried,
Nor yet the last to lay the old aside.

—Alexander Pope

I desire that there be as many different persons in the world as possible; I would have each one be very careful to find out and pursue his own way.
—Henry David Thoreau

Part III, consisting of two modules, facilitates your selection and implementation of particular instructional strategies by:

- Reviewing important principles of instruction and learning.
- Comparing two instructional modes: student-centered instruction and teacher-centered instruction.
- Providing an important rule for planning and selecting learning activities.
- Providing skill development in the use of questioning.
- Providing guidelines for teaching thinking skills.
- Providing descriptions of problem solving, inquiry, and discovery methods.
- Providing guidelines for using teacher talk strategies.

- Providing guidelines for your use of discussion, demonstrations, the textbook, recitation, review, projects, group work, and other strategies.
- Providing guidelines for ensuring equality in the classroom.
- Providing guidelines for using assignments and homework.

Module 6

Student-centered Instructional Strategies

Rationale
Specific Objectives
Module Text
    Principles of Instruction and Learning
    Indirect versus Direct Instruction
    Planning and Selecting Learning Activities
    The Total Class as a Group Enterprise
    Dyad Grouping
    The Learning Activity Center
        Types of Learning Activity Centers
        Purposes of a Learning Activity Center
        Guidelines for Setting Up a Learning Activity Center
    Small Groups
        Purposes for Small Groups
    Cooperative Learning Groups
        Roles in Cooperative Learning Groups
        What Students Do in Cooperative Learning Groups
        Outcomes of Using Cooperative Learning
        Additional Guidelines for Using Cooperative Learning
    Problem Solving
        Thinking
    Discovery and Inquiry
        The Process of Inquiry
        Teacher's Role in Discovery and Inquiry Teaching
        Facts, Concepts, and Understandings
        The Use of Thought Questions
        Springboards
        Suitability of Problems
    Student Presentations
    Projects, Papers, and Oral Reports
        Purposes for Using Projects, Papers, and Oral Reports
        Guidelines for Using Projects, Papers, and Oral Reports
        Projects
        Research Projects
        Surveys
        Case Study Method
    Field Trip
    Action Learning

RATIONALE

As professionals, competent teachers know what they want and ought to do, as well as how to do it. Therefore, if you are to become a professional, you must have well-defined educational goals at which to aim. Basically, those goals should be to: (1) arouse your students to think critically, (2) awaken their power to observe, remember, reflect upon, combine, and use information, and (3) help them to feel good about themselves and about others.

To achieve these basic goals, you must develop skill in teaching, for most effective teachers are made, not born. The cliché is that aptness for teaching is a native endowment, an instinct like a robin's ability to build a perfect nest the first time it needs one. Nonsense! The ability to teach, like most other human abilities, is primarily an acquired power derived from a correct knowledge of what needs to be done. If there are exceptions to this rule, they are quite uncommon. Of course, teachers vary in the skill in which they execute instructional plans effectively, and to some extent these variations derive from differences in innate ability. But many seeming variations in innate ability are really the product of the skills and personality traits a teacher has developed during the normal course of maturing. Therefore, the way to become a competent teacher is to study carefully the how and why of the educational processes and to practice diligently and reflectively, implementing the best that research has to offer. Every teacher can effectively harness whatever innate abilities she or he may possess through following a logical process: carefully defining objectives and developing plans (the preactive phase of instruction); studying the best of research findings about instructional strategies; practicing the implementation of those strategies (the interactive phase of instruction); thoughtfully assessing the results (the reflective phase of instruction); and then making adjustments and doing it over again, but better (the application of the reflection, or projective phase of instruction). Knowledge of effective strategies can be learned. The necessary skills can be developed. Thus, you can master the skills required for the most effective teaching, which will result in the highest achievement in learning by students.

To properly select and effectively implement a particular teaching strategy in order to teach specific content to a distinctive group of students, you must make a myriad of decisions along the way. Selection of a particular strategy depends in part on your decision whether to deliver information directly, known as direct or expository or didactic instruction, or to provide students with access to information, known as indirect or facilitative instruction. Direct instruction tends to be teacher-centered, whereas indirect instruction is more student-centered. The two modules of Part III have been organized with that distinction in mind: this module focuses on instructional strategies that tend to be more student-centered; Module 7 focuses on those that tend more to be teacher-centered.

A note of caution is in order. Professional education is rife with its own jargon, buzzwords that can sometimes be quite confusing to the beginning teacher (and to experienced teachers as well). For an example of how confusing the terminology can be, the term *direct teaching* is synonymous with *direct instruction*, whereas the term *direct experiences* indicates the opposite.

Other synonyms of direct teaching include *direct instruction, expository teaching,* and *teacher-centered instruction.* In addition to the blizzard of terms, note that each can have a variety of definitions, depending on who is doing the defining.

For purposes here, you should make sure you do not confuse *direct instruction* with *direct experiences,* the latter of which is discussed early in this module. The two terms indicate two separate (although not incompatible) instructional modes. *Direct experiences* indicates student-centered instruction (indirect instruction).

Rather than focusing your attention on the selection of a particular model of teaching, our preference is to emphasize the importance of an eclectic model—selecting the best from various models. For example, there are times when you will want to use a direct, expository approach, such as lecturing. Then there are times when you will want to use an indirect, social-interactive approach, such as cooperative learning. The two modules of Part III will help you make decisions about when each approach is most appropriate, and will provide guidelines for their use.

As discussed in Part I, what goes on in each classroom should be consistent with the reality of the world outside the classroom. Today's theory of effective instruction urges teachers to give recognition to the various skills needed to function as a human being, a worker, a citizen, a consumer, and a parent. Teachers must help students to develop a more sophisticated awareness of the uses of knowledge, as well as to become concerned not only with knowing about but also in knowing how.

Teachers are urged to accept the principle that learning is an active process. They are told that the goals of education encompass not only the acquisition of knowledge but also the guidance of every person to her or his fullest potential. Such guidance involves development of a multitude of skills, such as the skills of critical thinking, of independent inquiry and problem solving, and of active participation in group endeavors.

Group activity is a part of life—in the circles of family and friends, as well as in the civic, religious, economic, governmental, and social recreational realms. At one time or another, everyone is involved in activities with others, either as a participant or an observer. These activities include legislative committees, collective negotiations in business and labor, radio and television talk shows, round-table discussions, religious and club activities, various symposia and panels, and Town Hall meetings. Group participatory skills are learned skills, not innate skills. The school has a role to play in the development of those skills, both by encouraging awareness and analysis and by experiential approaches. Therefore, teachers need to add to their repertoire of strategies a variety of techniques that provide students with opportunities to interact with one another.

In this module we present and discuss a number of teaching strategies that all have two common elements: (1) social interaction and (2) problem solving. These teaching strategies require students to interact with one another and to draw conclusions, learn concepts, and form generalizations through induction, deduction, and observation, or application of principles. The premises underlying these methods are that (1) a person learns to think by thinking and sharing his or her thoughts with others, and (2) knowledge gained through active learning and self-discovery is more meaningful, permanent, and transferable than knowledge gained through expository techniques.

SPECIFIC OBJECTIVES

At the completion of this module, you should be able to:

1. Discuss the advantages and disadvantages of direct and indirect instructional strategies.
2. Explain in your own words at least three important principles of teaching and learning.
3. Explain why knowledge and thinking are inseparable.
4. Explain in your own words the difference and relationship between *hands-on* and *minds-on* learning.

5. Give examples in your subject field of learning experiences from each of these categories, and when and why you would use each one: verbal, visual, vicarious, simulated, and direct.
6. Demonstrate how and why in one class period you would combine direct and indirect instructional strategies.
7. Recall several examples of the use of dyad teaching and the value of each.
8. Describe reasons and methods for using a learning activity center in your subject field.
9. Describe the difference between small-group learning and a cooperative learning group.
10. Describe the reasons for using cooperative learning as an instructional strategy.
11. Differentiate between and discuss the relationships among problem solving, inquiry, and discovery.
12. Describe the various techniques for using group work for instruction.
13. Analyze the advantages and disadvantages of each technique.
14. Demonstrate how to conduct each of these techniques.
15. Describe the roles of the teacher and various participants in group activities.
16. Discuss the advantages and disadvantages of the use of various types of student presentations.
17. Discuss important guidelines for using student projects, papers, and oral reports.
18. Discuss the advantages and disadvantages of using role playing and simulations for instruction.
19. Describe ways you can help students develop their thinking skills.
20. Identify guidelines for the introduction and study of controversial issues during instruction.

MODULE TEXT

Principles of Instruction and Learning

To make a decision about what mode of instruction to use, you must keep in mind certain principles of instruction and learning, principles that have evolved from studies of recent years (see Module 2). In summary, these are:

1. *Students construct their knowledge and develop new skills by connecting their experiences to what is being learned.* Much of this learning is through collaboration with others, through shared thinking. To a great degree, it is the mode of instruction that determines the learning.
2. *Thinking is critically important to and inseparable from learning.* Students best acquire new knowledge and develop their skills when they think about the things being learned, share that thinking with others, analyze their own thought processes, and make connections between what is being learned in one discipline with other disciplines, with real-life, and with various cultural situations. Students must be actively and mentally engaged in their own learning as well as in the assessment of their learning. For greatest achievement in learning to occur, students should receive steady, understandable, and reliable feedback about their learning.
3. *Thinking and learning take time, more time for some students than for others, but all students can learn.* Learning takes effort, though, and students must extend that effort. Good teaching demands that students make meaningful connections through reading, writing, thinking, and sharing those things. You should hold high expectations for the learning of each student, and you must not waiver from those expectations.
4. *Intelligence is not a fixed or static reality but can be learned, taught, and developed.* When students understand that intelligence is incremental—something that is developed through use over time—they are more motivated to work at learning, to extend the necessary effort.
5. *Not all students learn and respond to learning situations in the same way.* A teacher who, for all students, uses only one style of teaching, or who teaches to only one or a few styles of learning day after day, is short-changing those students who learn better another way.

As first emphasized in Part I, a student does not learn to write by learning to recognize grammatical constructs, just as a person does not learn to play soccer by listening to a lecture on soccer strategy. School learning is superficial unless the instructional methods are appropriate for the understanding, skills, and attitudes desired. Memorizing, for instance, is not the same as understanding. Yet far too often, memorization seems all that is expected of students. The result is mere verbalism, the mouthing of poorly-understood words and sentences. Requiring that material be memorized is *not* teaching, but merely the orchestration of short-term memory exercises. To make learning real to students, you should use direct experiences as often as possible. Vicarious experiences are sometimes necessary to provide students with otherwise unattainable knowledge, but direct experiences that engage all the student's senses and all their learning modalities are more powerful. Students learn to write by writing and then receiving coaching and feedback about their progress in writing. They learn to play soccer by playing soccer and then receiving coaching and feedback about their developing skills and knowledge in playing it. They learn these things best when they are actively (hands-on learning) and mentally (minds-on learning) engaged in doing them.

Direct versus Indirect Instruction

When planning your instruction and selecting an instructional strategy (the preactive phase of teaching as presented in Module 1) you must make a decision: whether you should use direct instruction or indirect instruction. The traditional mode is to directly deliver information, and thus it is called the delivery mode. Knowledge is passed on from those who know (the teacher and the textbook) to those who do not (the students). Within the delivery mode, time-honored strategies are textbook reading, the lecture (formal teacher talk), questioning, and teacher-led discussions (each of which is addressed in Module 7).

In contrast to the delivery mode is the access mode. Instead of direct delivery of information and direct control over what is learned, your instruction is indirect. That is, you provide students with access to information by working with the students in the designing of experiences that help in building schemata and in obtaining new knowledge and skills. Indirect instruction tends to be more student-centered. Learning often is better when students are taught by the access mode, especially learning at the higher levels of the learning domains. Within the access mode two important instructional strategies are cooperative learning and inquiry learning. Both certainly use questioning, which is associated with the delivery mode, but in these strategies the questions more frequently come from the students than from you or the textbook. Discussions and lectures on particular topics also may be involved, but when used in the access mode those strategies follow or occur during, rather than precede, hands-on learning by the students.

You probably are more experienced with the teacher-centered delivery mode than the student-centered access mode, and Module 7 provides guidelines for the use of the strategies of direct instruction. But to be most effective as a teacher, you must also become knowledgeable and skillful in the use of indirect instruction, or access strategies. The intent here is not to imply that one mode is unquestionably *always* better, only to emphasize that student-centered strategies (strategies within the access mode) do facilitate the positive learning of students. They have a greater tendency to empower the students with responsibility for constructing their knowledge. Regardless of your intended subject or grade level, to be most effective you should be eclectic in selecting strategies; that is, you should appropriately select and effectively use strategies from both modes, but with a strong preference for student-centered (access) strategies.

In this module and the next, you should become knowledgeable about using techniques within each mode. In that way you can make intelligent decisions for choosing the best strategy for particular goals and objectives for your own discipline or grade level and unique group of students. Figures 6.1 and 6.2 provide an overview of the specific strengths and weaknesses of each mode.

Figure 6.1 Strengths and Weaknesses of the Delivery Mode, Teacher-centered Instruction

DELIVERY MODE

Strengths
- Much content can be covered within a short span of time, usually by formal teacher talk, which then may be followed by an experiential activity.
- The teacher is in control of what content is covered.
- The teacher is in control of time allotted to specific content coverage.
- Student achievement of specific content is predictable and manageable.

Potential Weaknesses
- The sources of student motivation are mostly extrinsic.
- Students have little control over the pacing of their learning.
- Students make few important decisions about their learning.
- There may be little opportunity for divergent or creative thinking.
- Student self-esteem may be inadequately served.

As you can see, the strengths and weaknesses of one mode are nearly mirror opposites of the other. Why should most teachers concentrate more on the use of student-centered strategies? Strategies within that mode are more hands-on and concrete—students actually do what they are supposed to be learning to do. Also learning that occurs from use of the access mode is longer lasting (fixes into long-term memory). Finally, as the students interact with one another and with their learning, they develop a sense of "can do," an attitude that enhances self-esteem.

Planning and Selecting Learning Activities

Can you imagine a soccer coach teaching students the skills and knowledge needed to play soccer without ever letting them play the game? Can you imagine a science teacher instructing students on how to read a thermometer without ever letting them handle one? Can you imagine a geography teacher teaching students how to read a map without ever letting them put their eyes and hands on a map? Historically, too many teachers have done almost those exact things—teaching kids to do something without letting them practice doing it.

In planning and selecting learning activities, an important rule to remember is to select activities that are as direct as possible. The reason is that when students are involved in direct

Figure 6.2 Strengths and Weaknesses of the Access Mode, Student-centered Instruction

ACCESS MODE

Strengths
- Students learn content, and in more depth.
- The sources of student motivation are more likely intrinsic.
- Students make important decisions about their own learning.
- Students have more control over the pacing of their learning.
- Students develop a sense of personal self-worth.

Potential Weaknesses
- Content coverage may be more limited.
- Strategies are time-consuming.
- The teacher has less control over content and time.
- The specific results of student learning are less predictable.
- The teacher may have less control over class procedures.

experiences, they are using more of their sensory input channels, their learning modalities (i.e., auditory, visual, tactile, kinesthetic). And when all the senses are engaged, learning is most effective and longest lasting. This is "learning by doing"—commonly called hands-on, minds-on learning. Note that this is Bruner's enactive learning (see Module 2).

In contrast to direct experiences in the classroom are abstract experiences, where the learner is exposed only to symbols (i.e., words and numbers) and use only one or two senses (auditory or visual). The teacher lectures while the students sit and watch and hear. Visual and verbal symbolic experiences, though impossible to avoid when teaching, are less effective for ensuring that planned learning occurs, especially with students with special needs, learners with limited proficiency in English, and intellectually immature learners. This type of learning is even less effective for many adults. Thus, when planning learning experiences and selecting instructional materials, you should select activities that engage the students in the most direct experiences possible and that are appropriate for your specific group of students.

Figure 6.3 shows the Learning Experiences Ladder, which depicts a range of experiences. The most direct are at the bottom of the ladder, forming the first and most basic step. The most abstract experiences are at the top of the ladder.

As can be inferred from the Learning Experiences Ladder, when teaching about tide pools (the first example in each of the steps), the most effective mode is to take the students to a tide

Figure 6.3   The Learning Experiences Ladder

ABSTRACT ↑

Verbal Experiences
Teacher talk, written words; engaging only one sense; using the most abstract symbolization; students physically inactive. *Examples:* (1) Listening to the teacher talk about tide pools. (2) Listening to a student report about the Grand Canyon. (3) Listening to a guest speaker talk about how the state legislature functions.

Visual Experiences
Still pictures, diagrams, charts; engaging only one sense; typically symbolic; students physically inactive. *Examples:* (1) Viewing slide photographs of tide pools. (2) Viewing drawings and photographs of the Grand Canyon. (3) Listening to a guest speaker talk about the state legislature and show slides of it in action.

Vicarious Experiences
Laser videodisc programs; computer programs; video programs; engaging more than one sense; learner indirectly "doing"; may be some limited physical activity. *Examples:* (1) Interacting with a computer program about wave action and life in tide pools. (2) Viewing and listening to a video program about the Grand Canyon. (3) Taking a field trip to observe the state legislature in action.

Simulated Experiences
Role-playing; experimenting; simulations; mock-up; working models; all or nearly all senses engaged; activity often integrating disciplines; closest to the real thing. *Examples:* (1) Building a classroom working model of a tide pool. (2) Building a classroom working model of the Grand Canyon. (3) Designing a classroom role-play simulation patterned after the operating procedure of the state legislature.

Direct Experiences
Learner actually doing what is being learned; true inquiry; all senses engaged; usually integrates disciplines; the real thing. *Examples:* (1) Visiting and experiencing a tide pool. (2) Visiting and experiencing the Grand Canyon. (3) Designing an elected representative body to oversee the operation of the school-within-the-school program, and patterned after the state legislative assembly.

CONCRETE ↓

Earlier versions of this concept were: Charles F. Hoban, Sr., et al., *Visualizing the Curriculum* (New York: Dryden, 1937), p. 39; Edgar Dale, *Audio-Visual Methods in Teaching* (New York: Holt, Rinehart & Winston, 1969), p. 108; and, Jerome S. Bruner, *Toward a Theory of Instruction* (Cambridge: Harvard University Press, 1966), p. 49.

pool (at the bottom of the ladder). This is the most direct experience, in which students can see, hear, touch, smell, and perhaps even taste (if not toxic) the tide pool. The least effective mode is for the teacher to merely talk about the tide pool (at the top of the ladder). This is the most abstract experience, with its reliance on symbols, and engages only one sense—the auditory.

Of course, for various reasons—matters of safety, lack of resources for a field trip, location of your school, presence of toxic pollution, and so on—you may not be able to take the students to a tide pool. Not always is it appropriate to use the most direct experience, and thus sometimes you must select an experience higher on the ladder. And self-discovery teaching is not always the best approach for the material. Sometimes it is more appropriate to build upon what others have discovered and learned. Nevertheless, keep in mind that the most effective and longest-lasting learning is learning that engages most or all of a person's senses. On the Learning Experiences Ladder, those are the ones that fall on the bottom three steps—the direct, simulated, and vicarious experiences. This is true with adult learners or with primary-grade children, or with children of any age group in between.

Another value of direct, simulated, and vicarious experiences is that they tend to be interdisciplinary, for they cross subject boundaries. That makes those experiences especially useful for teachers who want to help students connect the learning of one discipline with that of others, and to bridge what is being learned with the students' life experiences. Direct, simulated, and vicarious experiences are more like real life.

Implicit in our emphasis on the student-centered activities is the assumption that students should actively seek out knowledge rather than receive it through teacher-centered activities, such as the lecture. Generally, methods that are student-centered have several advantages over those that are not. Foremost, perhaps, they better motivate students to learn. They also give students opportunities to learn and practice intellectual skills, to learn how to think, to seek out relationships and structure, to understand cognitive processes, and to learn better how to learn. In addition, retention from these kinds of instructional strategies is superior to that from those that are more teacher-centered, and the highly personal and active involvement of the students contributes to feelings of self-worth.

Student-centered activities can also have some disadvantages. They are usually time consuming, though, because many teachers believe less coverage of content can be better. That should not necessarily be seen as a true disadvantage. Another disadvantage in student-centered instructional activities is that classroom control can be a riskier proposition than when using teacher-centered activities. When students are actively learning, they are just that—active. Active students are usually noisy students, and for some teachers noise can be a problem, especially if it gets out of control. Furthermore, the outcomes of student-centered activities can be far removed from those the teacher originally had in mind when planning the lessons. You should consider these potential advantages and disadvantages of student-centered instruction as you study the activities described in this module.

One important strategy for effective instruction is the way that students are grouped for positive interaction and quality learning. During any given week of school, depending on the course and the specific learning activity, a student might experience a succession of group settings. These may include individual activities, student pairs, small groups, and large whole-class interactions. Ways of grouping students to maximize the instruction for each student is the initial focus of this module.

To begin your thinking about student-centered instructional activities, reflect on your personal experience by doing Exercise 6.1 and Exercise 6.2.

EXERCISE 6.1

A Reflection on My Past Involvement with Student-Centered Instructional Activities

• • • • • •

Instructions: The purpose of this exercise is for you to reflect on your past involvement in participatory activities and then to share those thoughts with your colleagues. To that end, this exercise contains a list of such activities.

1. For each activity write *F* if you are *familiar* with it, *E* if you have observed it *effectively* used by a teacher, and *L* if as a student it was an activity that you *liked*. You may use any one, two, or all three of the letter codes in your response to each activity.

<table>
<tr><td>___ Brainstorming</td><td>___ Inquiry</td></tr>
<tr><td>___ Buzz session</td><td>___ Jury trial</td></tr>
<tr><td>___ Case study</td><td>___ Learning activity center</td></tr>
<tr><td>___ Committee</td><td>___ Panel discussion</td></tr>
<tr><td>___ Cooperative learning</td><td>___ Project or independent study</td></tr>
<tr><td>___ Debate</td><td>___ Role playing</td></tr>
<tr><td>___ Discovery</td><td>___ Round table discussion</td></tr>
<tr><td>___ Discussion, whole-class</td><td>___ Simulation</td></tr>
<tr><td>___ Field trip</td><td>___ Sociodrama</td></tr>
<tr><td>___ Fishbowl</td><td>___ Symposium</td></tr>
<tr><td>___ Forum</td><td></td></tr>
</table>

2. Share your marks and experiences with your classmates in small groups of three or four per group.

3. As you study this module, try to engage in various group activities with your classmates. Assume the various roles discussed. Keep records of involvement and interaction. Perhaps ask someone to serve each time as observer to help you analyze the process and its effectiveness. As you gain knowledge and experience about these various student-centered activities, consider how you might use them in your own teaching.

EXERCISE 6.2

Recalling My Own Learning Experiences in School

• • • • • •

Instructions: The purpose of this exercise is to recall and share learning experiences from your own school days. You should reflect upon those with respect to their relationship to the Learning Experiences Ladder and the discussion of the access and delivery modes of instruction.

1. Recall one vivid learning experience from each level of your schooling and identify its position on the Learning Experiences Ladder.

   Secondary School Experience:

   Position on Ladder:

   College Experience:

   Position on Ladder:

2. Share with classmates in small groups. After sharing your experiences with others of your group, what, if anything, can your group conclude? Write those conclusions here and then share them with the entire class.

The Total Class as a Group Enterprise

To start your thinking about processes of participation and group interaction, it may be helpful to view the whole class as a group. In efforts to provide experiences for learners, teachers sometimes overlook the opportunity to make sessions with the total class more interactive.

Consider for a moment the major characteristics of the traditional—and prevalent—teacher-centered, recitation-type strategy:

- Teacher-led and teacher-dominated sessions.
- Questions of a relatively superficial, information-seeking nature.
- Repeating or restating (reciting) what has previously been learned, studied, read, or memorized.
- The "hearing" of lessons to detect right and wrong answers.
- Checking to see if students have done their work.
- A one-to-one relationship between the questioner and hearer and between teller and answerer.
- All decision making in the hands of the teacher regarding purpose, content, process, and participation.

A flowchart of participation in such a session would probably reveal a significant number of tallies for the teacher, with a smaller number distributed over a relatively small number of students selected by the teacher to participate. The major mode of operation would tend to be a question and an answer, with an occasional comment about the accuracy or character of student responses. There also might be the occasional lecture or minilecture.

Figure 6.4 is a diagram showing the flow of interaction found in a typical recitation. Note that the interaction is between the teacher and individual students only. There is no cross flow between student and student.

In contrast, consider the possibilities inherent in the concept of such total-class activity viewed as genuine discussion, with student interactive participation. The focus is not on hearing lessons but on inquiry and discovery. Figure 6.5 is a diagram showing the flow of interaction in a whole-class discussion. In that class, students have been arranged in a hollow square. Arrows pointing to the center of the square indicate that the person was speaking to the group as a whole. Arrows pointing to individuals indicate the person the speaker was addressing. Note that the conversation includes much cross talk between student and student and much talk addressed to the group as a whole. The teacher's role in the discussion is minimal.

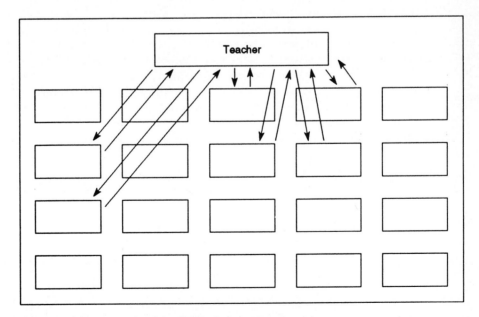

Figure 6.4   Diagram of a Traditional Recitation-type Strategy

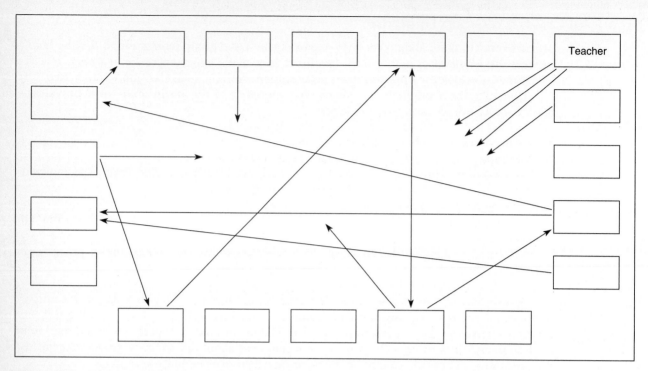

Figure 6.5   Diagram of an Interactive, Whole-class Discussion

In contrast to the traditional strategy, an interactive, whole-class discussion is characterized by:

- Probing exploration of ideas, concepts, and issues.
- Building upon student responses in a developmental flow.
- Interaction among class members.
- Shifting leadership among participants.
- Questioning, sharing, differing, conjecturing on the part of all.
- Student participation in decision making.
- Hypothesizing and problem solving.

The essential difference between the two types of classrooms is that the first (the teacher-centered discussion) is based on the view that knowledge consists of a series of correct answers, with students as more-or-less passive participants, whereas the second is based on the view that knowledge is the product of creative inquiry through social interaction, with the students as active participants in that inquiry. Only through genuine student involvement and interaction can the contributions and thinking of each participant be seen as being welcomed and accepted. And only with such interaction can hypotheses be tested, views expressed and analyzed, questions raised, controversies examined, and insights developed, along with other desirable cognitive and affective processes and outcomes.

What is your recent experience with group activities? Reflect on them by doing Exercise 6.3.

A Reflection on My Own Participation Within Groups

• • • • • •

Instructions: The purpose of this exercise is to reflect on your own participation in groups in order to become more effective in managing group activities. After answering each of the following questions, share your responses with others in your class.

1. List the groups to which you currently belong (in which you have been active during the past several weeks) and the skills needed to function effectively in each group.

Name of Group   *Skills Needed*

2. Select one of the groups you listed and analyze your own participation in a recent activity of that group.

   a. Describe the nature of your own participation.

b. What role(s) did you perform?

c. How effective was your participation?

d. Is there any way your participation could have been made more effective? If so, describe it.

A whole-class discussion is not the only strategy you have at your disposal to promote interactive learning. Many other strategies will provide the opportunity for students to participate interactively in the learning process. For our purposes here, the tactics and strategies are broadly classified into four categories: (1) dyad groups, (2) cooperative learning groups, (3) the relatively formal, planned, short-term, presentation-type technique, and (4) those group strategies that involve more student interaction and work of a long-term nature with varied purposes, including the analysis of the group process itself.

Dyad Grouping

Sometimes pairing students into dyads can be advantageous for studying and learning. Examples include:

- *Peer tutoring*, where one classmate tutors another. Peer tutoring is useful, for example, when one student helps another who has limited proficiency in English, or where a student skilled in math or chemistry helps another who is less skilled.
- *Cross-age coaching*, where one student is coached by another from a higher grade level. Cross-age coaching is similar to peer tutoring, except that the coach is from a higher grade level than the student being coached. It is not uncommon in many school districts, for example, for high school students to coach junior high or middle school students in specific skills and content.
- *Think-pair-share*, where two students examine a new concept about to be studied. The students of each dyad discuss what they already know or think they know about the concept, and then each dyad presents its perceptions to the whole group. This is an excellent technique for discovering students' misconceptions (or naive theories, as discussed in Module 2). A modification of this technique is *think-write-pair-share*, where the students of each dyad think together and write their ideas before sharing with the larger group.
- *Team learning*, where students study and learn in teams of two. Specific uses for paired team learning include the following: *drill partners*, *reading buddies*, *book-report pairs*, *summary pairs*, and *elaborating-and-relating pairs*.

The Learning Activity Center

Another significantly beneficial way of pairing students for instruction (as well as of individualizing the instruction) is through use of a learning activity center (LAC). A learning activity center, which can both integrate and individualize the learning, is a special station located in the classroom where one student (or two, if student interaction is necessary for the center) can quietly work and learn at his or her own pace. All materials needed are provided at that station, including clear instructions for operation of the center. A familiar example is the personal computer station. Long popular in elementary schools, the learning activity center can be an effective instructional device for use at any grade level and for any subject.

The value of learning centers as instructional devices undoubtedly lies with the following two characteristics: (1) while working at the center, the student is giving time and quality attention to the learning task (learning toward mastery); and (2) while working at the center, the student is likely to be engaging her or his most effective learning modality, or integrating several modalities or all of them.

Types of Learning Activity Centers

Learning activity centers are of three types:

1. *Direct-learning center.* Performance expectations for cognitive learning are quite specific, and the focus is on mastery of content.
2. *Open-learning center.* The goal is to provide opportunity for exploration, enrichment, motivation, and creative discovery.

3. *Skill center.* As in a direct-learning center, performance expectations are quite specific, but the focus is on the development of a particular skill or process.

Purposes of a Learning Activity Center

Although in all instances, the primary reason for using a learning center is to individualize the learning, there are additional reasons. These are to provide:

- A mechanism for learning that crosses discipline boundaries.
- A special place for a student with special needs.
- A special place for students to review or to make up work.
- An opportunity for creative work.
- Enrichment experiences.
- Multisensory experiences to enhance learning.
- Opportunities for students to learn from learning packages that utilize special equipment or media of which only one or a limited supply may be available for use in your classroom (e.g., science materials, a computer, or a laserdisc player, or a combination of these).

Guidelines for Setting Up a Learning Activity Center

To set up a LAC you can be as elaborate and as creative as your time and resources allow. Here are some guidelines:

1. Materials used in the center should be safe for student use.
2. Specific instructional objectives and instructions for use of the center should be clearly posted and understandable to the student. An audio or video cassette is sometimes used for this purpose.
3. The center should be easily supervised by you or an adult aide.
4. The purpose of the center should be understood by the students.
5. Centers should *never* be used for punishment.
6. Topics for the center should be related to the instructional program, for review, remediation, or enrichment.
7. The center should contain a variety of activities geared to the varying abilities and interest levels of the students. A choice of two or more activities at each center is one way to provide for this.
8. Materials to be used at the center should be readily available, with descriptions for use provided to the students.
9. Centers should be attractive, purposeful, and uncluttered.
10. The center should be designed with a theme in mind, one that integrates the student's learning by having activities that cross discipline boundaries.

Small Groups

Small groups are those involving three to eight students, depending on the purpose, complexity, and duration of the activity. The use of small groups for learning enhances the opportunities for students to assume greater control over their own learning, sometimes referred to as *empowerment*.

Purposes for Small Groups

Small groups can be formed for a variety of purposes. They might be useful for a specific *learning activity* (e.g., reciprocal reading groups where students take turns asking questions, summarizing, making predictions about, and clarifying a book). They might also be formed to complete a *work project*, only lasting as long as the project does. Teachers may have various rationales for assigning students to groups. Groups can be formed by:

- *Personality type* (sometimes less-assertive students are teamed together to give them the opportunity for greater management of their own learning).
- *Social pattern* (e.g., sometimes it may be necessary to break up a group of rowdy friends or it may be desirable to broaden the association among students).
- *Common interest.*
- *Ability* in a particular skill.[1]

Useful for accomplishing any of these purposes is the cooperative learning group.

Cooperative Learning Groups

Cooperative learning encompasses strategies that use heterogeneous groups of three or four students working together and that emphasize support rather than competition among members of the group. Most often, a cooperative learning group consists of four students of mixed ability, gender, and ethnicity, with each member of the group assuming a particular role. Normally, the group is rewarded on the basis of group achievement, though individual members within the group can later be rewarded for individual contributions. Teachers usually change the membership of each group a few times during the year.[2]

The theory of cooperative learning is that when small groups of students of mixed backgrounds and capabilities work together toward a common goal, members of the group increase their friendship and respect for one another. As a consequence, each individual's self-esteem is enhanced and academic achievement is improved.[3]

Roles in Cooperative Learning Groups

With cooperative learning groups it is advisable to assign roles (specific functions) to each member of the group, and then to rotate roles, either during the activity or from one time to the next. Although titles may vary, typical roles are:

- *Group facilitator*, whose role is to keep the group on task.
- *Materials manager*, whose role is to obtain, maintain, and return materials needed for the group to function.
- *Recorder*, whose role is to record all group activities and processes, and perhaps to evaluate how the group is doing.
- *Reporter*, whose role is to report the group's processes and accomplishments to the teacher and to the rest of the class.
- *Thinking monitor*, whose role is to identify and record the sequence and processes of the group's thinking. This role encourages metacognition and the development of thinking skills.

What Students Do in Cooperative Learning Groups

Typical cooperative learning strategies involve student teams in which students work on group projects that emphasize analysis and evaluation. Normally, the students together study what

---

[1]The reasons listed were adapted from *It's Elementary* (Sacramento, CA: State Department of Education, 1992), p. 32.

[2]Some parents, resenting the grouping of students of mixed abilities, request that teachers not use "cooperative learning groups." To avoid controversy, teachers sometimes use an alternative term, such as *collaborative learning* or *team learning*. These terms are not synonymous with *cooperative learning*, however. In cooperative learning, there is much more individual student accountability than there is in ordinary collaborative or team learning. Some authorities use the term *collaborative learning* for when the teacher is working with the students as a learning partner, and *cooperative learning* when only students are working together.

[3]See, for example, Phillip E. Duren and April Cherrington, "The Effects of Cooperative Group Work versus Independent Practice on the Learning of Some Problem-Solving Strategies," *School Science and Mathematics* 92(2):80–83 (February 1992). See also Stephen Balkcom, "Cooperative Learning," *Education Research Consumer Guide* 1 (June 1992).

has been previously taught and then are later tested individually. And usually each member of the group learns about a specific part of a general topic assigned to the group.[4]

Outcomes of Using Cooperative Learning

The educational value of the use of cooperative learning groups has been well documented by many research studies. The outcomes of cooperative learning include:

- Increased academic achievement.
- Improved communication and relationships between students with learning disabilities and other students.
- Improved communication and relations among students of different ethnic groups.[5]
- Quality learning with fewer off-task student behaviors.[6]

In addition, researchers have compared the use of independent practice with the use of cooperative learning groups in mathematics; students who practice in cooperative groups demonstrate greater long-term memory of problem-solving strategies.[7]

Additional Guidelines for Using Cooperative Learning

Because peer support needs to be stronger than peer pressure, you must be cautious about the use of group grading. For grading purposes, bonus points can be given to all members of a group; individuals can add to their own scores when everyone in the group has reached preset standards. The preset standards must be appropriate for all members of a group. Lower standards or improvement criteria could be set for students with lower ability so everyone feels rewarded and successful. To determine each student's quarter and course grades, individual student achievement is measured later through individual student results on tests, as well as through each student's performance in the group (discussed further in Module 10).

There are several techniques for using cooperative learning.[8] Yet the primary purpose of each is for the groups to learn—which means, of course, that individuals within a group must learn. Group achievement in learning, then, is dependent upon the learning of individuals within the group. Rather than competing for rewards for achievement, members of the group cooperate with one another by helping one another learn so that the group reward will be a good one.

Problem Solving

Learning encompasses much more than simply the learner's acquiring information and developing an understanding of concepts. At its highest, learning involves transferring and applying that knowledge to new situations. The processes of transfer and application are accomplished through what is known as problem solving, or the ability "to define or describe a problem, determine the desired outcome, select possible solutions, choose strategies, test trial solutions, evaluate the outcome, and revise these steps where necessary."[9] Thus, problem solv-

---

[4]See, for example, Stephen Balkcom, "Cooperative Learning," *Education Research Consumer Guide*, number 1, June 1992, p. 3.

[5]See, for example, Balkcom, p. 3; and Gail Oberholtzer Sutton, "Cooperative Learning Works in Mathematics," *Mathematics Teacher* 85(1):63–66 (January 1992).

[6]Kelly Phoenix, *Cooperative Learning: How Does It Affect Discipline?* (unpublished Master's thesis, University of Virginia, 1992).

[7]Phillip E. Duren and April Cherrington, "The Effects of Cooperative Group Work versus Independent Practice on the Learning of Some Problem-Solving Strategies," *School Science and Mathematics* 92(2):80–83 (February 1992).

[8]Of interest to many teachers are general methods of cooperative learning, such as "student team—achievement division" (STAD) and "teams-games-tournaments" (TGT), or methods for particular subjects, such as "team assisted individualization" (TAI) for mathematics and "cooperative integrated reading and composition" (CIRC) for reading and writing. See Robert E. Slavin, *Cooperative Learning: Theory, Research, and Practice* (Englewood Cliffs, NJ: Prentice Hall, 1990). See also Robert E. Slavin et al., "Putting Research to Work: Cooperative Learning," *Instructor* 102(2):46–47 (September 1992).

[9]Arthur L. Costa (ed.), *Developing Minds: A Resource Book for Teaching Thinking* (Alexandria, VA: ASCD, 1985), p. 312.

ing is not a teaching strategy but a behavior that facilitates learning. What a teacher can and should do is to provide opportunities for students to solve problems.

Providing students with activities that develop their problem-solving skills is certainly not a new idea. In 1938, John Dewey stressed the importance of providing students with opportunity and skills in identifying and solving problems that are real and relevant to them.[10] For Robert Gagné problem solving is at the top of the scale of intellectual activity. Gagné stresses that the ability to solve problems is dependent upon prior knowledge and skill development (see Module 2).[11]

As emphasized before in this text, teachers should help students develop cognitive skills in order for them to operate at higher levels of cognition. The question is how to do it. Expository methods—the use of receptive learning—may or may not do an adequate job. The techniques presented here will. Teaching strategies a teacher can use to encourage the development of problem-solving skills are explained in the sections that follow.

When presenting students with the opportunity to solve problems, some problems are closed, or convergent, because there is only one right solution or answer. Other problems are open-ended, or divergent; they have many possible answers or solutions.

Thinking

One of the principal goals of education is to develop skill in thinking. Among other definitions, thinking can be thought of as the mental process by which a person makes sense out of experience.[12] Beyer divides the process into two categories—the cognitive and the metacognitive (both of which have been discussed in previous modules).

In young people, thinking skills are not yet fully developed. They must be instilled and cultivated. Consequently, educators have created numerous programs for instilling and cultivating thinking skills. Many of these programs are set apart from the standard school curriculum and teachers who want to use them may need special training in the techniques and strategies of the individual program.[13]

Fortunately, thinking skills can and should be taught in regular classes. Skillful use of discovery, inquiry, and problem-solving approaches allows teachers to teach students to learn and practice basic thinking skills, such as:

- Recognizing, identifying, and defining problems.
- Finding evidence.
- Observing accurately and without prejudice.
- Interpreting and reporting correctly.
- Detecting faulty arguments, polemics, bias, prejudice, poor logic, and other evidences of faulty reasoning.
- Detecting relationships, seeing parts in relationship to the whole, tying elements together, and recognizing similarities and differences.
- Choosing between alternatives.
- Making inferences and drawing conclusions.
- Analyzing.
- Separating fact from fiction.
- Using knowledge as a departure point for building new knowledge, ideas, and thought.

[10]John Dewey, *Experience and Education* (New York: Macmillan, 1938).

[11]Robert M. Gagné, *The Conditions of Learning* (New York: Holt, Rinehart and Winston, 1977).

[12]Barry K. Beyer, *Practical Strategies for the Teaching of Thinking* (Boston: Allyn & Bacon, 1987).

[13]Examples of such programs for middle school, junior high school, or high school students include Building Thinking Skills (Midwest Publications, P.O. Box 448, Pacific Grove, CA); ICE (Institute for Creative Education, 700 Hollydell Ct., Sewell, NJ 08080); CoRT (Cognitive Research Trust, 2030 Addison St., Suite 400, Berkeley, CA 94794); IE (Instrumental Enrichment, 1211 Connecticut Ave., NW, Washington, DC 20036); SOI (Structure of Intellect, 45755 Goodpasture Rd., Vida, OR 97488); California Writing Project (Office of Teacher Education, University of California at Irvine, Irvine, CA 92717); and Creative Problem Solving (437 Franklin St., Buffalo, NY). For a review of programs and a listing of additional programs, see Robert Baum, "10 Top Programs," *Learning 90*, 18(6): 51–55 (February 1990); and "Programs for Teaching Thinking," in Arthur L. Costa's (ed.), *Developing Minds: A Resource Book for Teaching Thinking* (Alexandria, VA: ASCD, 1985).

Unless students develop their thinking skills, they are doomed to be impulsive, prejudiced, ill-informed, and narrow-minded. If students are to become good thinkers, courses should not only include thought-provoking content but direct interaction in various teaching techniques as well.

To teach thinking skills, the teacher should begin by teaching them directly. First, the teacher should both explain and demonstrate the skill. Second, the teacher should provide examples of the skill well done. For instance, a teacher might point out an excellent use of the technique employed by one of the students or show an example of proper execution of the skill in a film.

Teachers might also use such techniques as probing questions to shape students' abilities to think logically and to recognize, define, and solve problems. If possible, the teacher should stimulate the students to think about both their thought processes and their behavior, encouraging the students to try different and more effective ways to proceed. An example of a cooperative learning activity that can be useful is having pairs of students examine each other's thinking processes listing the strategies and tactics used and describing changes that might improve thinking.

Once students have understood the how and why of the thinking skills, they should then have plenty of practice in using those skills. At first, this practice should be limited to comparatively easy problems with plenty of instructional aids to help them remember what to do and how to do it. Here the teacher can take advantage of timely moments to prompt students into selecting and executing improved thinking procedures. For this purpose many teachers recommend the use of dyads or small groups in which one student goes through the process while the other(s) provides feedback. If students take the opportunity to examine their own thinking and behavior—especially in the light of feedback from their peers or teachers—they should be able to sharpen their thinking skills considerably.

Finally, students should reinforce their learning by applying their thinking skills to a variety of assignments and life situations, both to increase their proficiency and to enhance their ability to transfer thinking skills. In this phase of learning, as in the practice phase, the students need plenty of feedback to capitalize on their successes and errors.

To introduce the teaching of specific thinking skills, some teachers recommend the following approach:

1. *Select the skill to be taught.* Presumably, as in the teaching of any other skill, the teacher should build the "greater skills" on "lesser skills." Thus, the inclusion of thinking skills in any curriculum or course should follow a definite sequence. When you teach thinking skills in your courses, you should make sure that the students in your classes are equipped with the skills and knowledge necessary to provide a foundation for the new skill.
2. *Identify the main attributes of the skill to be taught.* You should make sure that you understand what the skill is, what its purpose is, what skills and knowledge are prerequisite, how to carry out the skill step by step, and so on. This task may require of you some hard thinking and studying.
3. *Introduce the skill.* The skill should be introduced when it will be a meaningful addition to the course content—if the skill is not relevant to the course at a certain point, introducing it at that point will not be fruitful. When the time is right to introduce the skill, first explain what the skill is and why it should be learned. When you are sure they understand, explain how to implement the skill step by step, and then demonstrate the whole procedure and its steps. Once students have caught on to what is expected and how to do it, put them to work using the skill. As they work, let them analyze their procedures and provide them with feedback on their progress.
4. *Provide practice.* Students should have opportunity to practice until they attain mastery. At first, practice sessions should be guided and rather carefully monitored. At this stage, peer criticism as well as teacher guidance may be beneficial. Later, as soon as students seem ready, independent practice should prove profitable.
5. *Continue review and practice sessions throughout the course.* After a skill has been mastered, it should be used as the occasion demands throughout the school year. Skills that are not

practiced from time to time will soon disappear. Such practice sessions should be closely tied to normal course content.[14]

Discovery and Inquiry

Problem solving can be distinguished from discovery and inquiry in this way: whereas problem solving is a way of thinking and behaving, discovery and inquiry are teaching strategies that utilize active student thinking and problem solving. Within discovery and inquiry strategies, the teacher incorporates student problem recognition, problem definition, problem solving, and decision making.

Discovery learning can be thought of as the *result* of seeking knowledge. **Inquiry learning** can be thought of as an open-ended and creative *way of* seeking knowledge.

In education, there is no singular definition of discovery learning. As discussed in Module 2, for Bruner discovery is the act of finding out for one's self.[15] For Gagné, discovery results from problem solving and is the final step in a hierarchy of learning steps that combines previously learned rules into a new and higher order.[16] Whereas Bruner placed emphasis on the importance of inductive learning, Gagné placed greater emphasis on the importance of deductive learning. For true inquiry, both are undoubtedly important, though induction is given high priority.

Both discovery learning and inquiry learning actively involve students in two important activities—problem solving and decision making. To distinguish strategies for inquiry teaching from those of discovery teaching, the teacher should use these two criteria: (1) who recognizes and identifies the problem and (2) the amount of decision making done by students.

Table 6.1 identifies three levels of inquiry according to how much is expected of the student. What is referred to as Level I inquiry is traditional, didactic, "cookbook" teaching, in which a problem is defined for the student, who then works through the problem to an inevitable solution. If the "program" is well designed, the end result is inevitable because the student "discovers" what was intended. This level of inquiry is also referred to both as guided inquiry and as discovery, because the students are carefully guided through the investigation to "discovery."

Level I inquiry is highly manageable, and the learning outcome is predictable. It is probably best for teaching fundamental concepts and principles. But students who never experience learning beyond Level I are missing an opportunity to engage their highest mental operations, and they never get to experience more motivating, real-life problem solving. Furthermore, those students may come away with the false notion that problem solving is a linear process, which it is not. True inquiry is cyclic rather than linear. The inquiry cycle is illustrated in Figure 6.6. One enters the inquiry cycle whenever a discrepancy or problem is observed and recognized, and that can occur at any point in the cycle.

[14]Roberta M. Jackson, "Thumbs up for Direct Teaching of Thinking Skills," *Educational Leadership* 43:33–36 (May 1986) describes how teachers in a Virginia middle school are using this type of approach to teach thinking skills directly.

[15]Jerome Bruner, "The Act of Discovery," *The Harvard Educational Review* 31(1):21 (1961).

[16]Robert Gagné, "Varieties of Learning and the Concept of Discovery," in *Learning by Discovery: A Critical Appraisal*, edited by L.S. Shulman and E.S. Keislar (Chicago: Rand McNally, 1968).

Table 6.1   Levels of Inquiry

	Level I (not true inquiry)	Level II	Level III
Problem identification	Identified by teacher or textbook	Identified by teacher or textbook	Identified by student
Process of solving problem	Decided by teacher or textbook	Decided by student	Decided by student
Identification of tentative solution to problem	Resolved by student	Resolved by student	Resolved by student

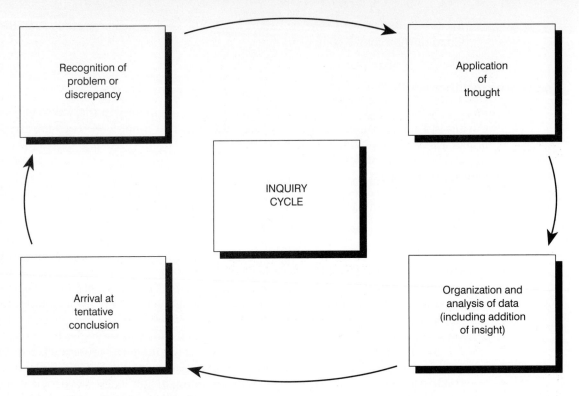

Figure 6.6 The Inquiry Cycle

By the time students reach junior and senior high school, they should be provided experiences for true inquiry, which begins with Level II, where students actually design the processes for their inquiry. In true inquiry teachers emphasize the tentative nature of conclusions, which makes an activity more like real-life problem solving, where decisions are always subject to revision.

In Level III inquiry, students identify the problem as well as decide the processes and reach a conclusion. When using individual projects and independent study as instructional strategies, teachers are usually engaging their students in this level of inquiry.

The Processes of Inquiry

In true inquiry, the students generate ideas and then design ways to test those ideas. The various processes students use represent the many critical thinking skills. Some of these skills are concerned with generating and organizing data, whereas others are concerned with building and using ideas. Figure 6.7 provides four main categories of these thinking processes and their place within the inquiry cycle.

Some processes in the cycle are discovery processes and others are inquiry processes. Inquiry processes include the more complex mental operations (including all of those in the idea category). Adolescents, who are in the process of developing their thinking capabilities, should be provided experiences that require the more complex, higher-level inquiry skills. Such is certainly the case for secondary school students.

Inquiry learning is a higher-level mental operation that introduces the concept of the discrepant event, or using the element of surprise to help learners develop skills in observing and being alert for discrepancies. This strategy provides opportunities for students to investigate their own ideas about explanations. Inquiry, like discovery, is a problem-solving strategy; the difference between the two is in the amount of decision-making responsibility given to the students. Inquiry also helps students understand the importance of suspending judgment and the tentativeness of "answers" and "solutions." Students eventually are better able to deal with ambiguity.

For centuries educational theorists have thought that learning is more meaningful, thorough, and usable when students actively seek out and discover knowledge rather than just being receivers of knowledge. This position is implicit in the strategies of such master teachers as Socrates and Jesus of Nazareth, in the theories of such thinkers as Rousseau and Pestalozzi, and in the ideas of twentieth-century educational philosophers such as John Dewey. Many practitioners today are convinced that this position is correct, and they use discovery and inquiry teaching as the heart of their teaching approaches. But students also learn from being shown, told, or conditioned. It is neither necessary nor wise for teachers to insist that students rediscover all the knowledge encompassed by the curriculum. Some of that knowledge is best learned from expository methods and some by discovery and inquiry. Effective teachers use the teacher-centered or student-centered strategy that seems best suited to a particular learning-teaching situation.

There are many ways to introduce student-centered techniques into your teaching. Among the more common examples are Socratic and guided discussions, research and other student projects, case studies, and the various types of action learning and community involvement activities.

Teacher's Role in Discovery and Inquiry Teaching

Since discovery and inquiry imply problem solving and decision making by students, your role becomes that of guiding their learning rather than that of dictating and giving them direct instruction. In this role you must propose problems, raise issues, and ask questions designed to catch student interest, to start them thinking, and to encourage their own investigation. In addition, you must establish a classroom environment that encourages guessing, skepticism, and intuitive thinking. This kind of classroom environment requires planning, self-control, cooperation, and trust; allows for serendipity; and places a value on mistakes and on diversity. It takes conviction, careful planning, practice, and skill for a teacher to effectively use discovery and inquiry. To get you started in the use of these techniques, keep the following guidelines in mind:

1. Be supportive and accepting.
2. Accentuate the positive.

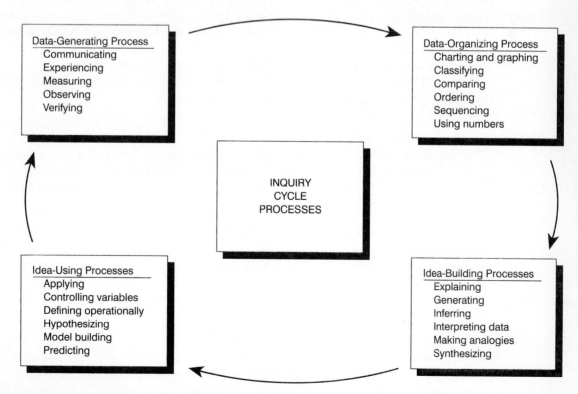

Figure 6.7   Processes of Inquiry Cycle

3. Provide clues.
4. Encourage the exchange of ideas.
5. Encourage students to hypothesize.
6. Provide opportunity for students to investigate their hypotheses.
7. Provide assistance when students seem to lose their way.
8. Help students analyze and evaluate their ideas, interpretations, and thinking.
9. Foster free debate and open discussion, and urge students to try to think things out with no threat of reprisals when their thinking does not conform to the expected or to the norm.

Facts, Concepts, and Understandings

Except for playing a parlor game such as *Trivial Pursuit*, factual knowledge is useful only when it leads to general understanding (principles, theories, and laws). Concepts, major ideas that share a common set of attributes, are the essential building blocks of understanding within a discipline. Although concepts cannot be taught directly, factual knowledge and generalizations can, and learning these things adds to the student's developing understanding of the major themes of a discipline. For example, the United States is a democracy. That statement is an example of a fact. *Democracy* is an example of a concept—in this instance, a rather abstract one. Whereas facts and generalizations take the form of statements, concepts may often take the form of just one word. This is an example of a generalization about democracy: "In a democracy, such as the United States, the decision-making power is placed in the hands of the majority, while at the same time the rights of the minority are protected." A generalization often binds two or more concepts.

Inquiry and discovery are valuable strategies for helping students understand major concepts, especially abstract ones, because with these strategies students can, in some degree or another, actually live what they are learning about. In contrast, students might better learn about a generalization through knowledge of the generalization's component parts—the facts and notions about the concepts. Often such knowledge is best taught by an expository technique.

A person develops an understanding of a notion or concept by becoming familiar both with the ideas, beliefs, artifacts, or objects that are examples and with those that are not examples. A child, for instance, learns by observation that certain characteristics signify that an animal is not a dog by observing both dogs and animals that are not dogs. A child learns that certain characteristics signify being free and others signify not being free by seeing and hearing about instances when people or animals are free and not free. The teacher's job, in these instances, is to provide students with the opportunities to observe, name, classify, and practice, as well as to ask appropriate probing questions in the process.

The Use of Thought Questions

Teaching through use of discovery and inquiry depends on the skillful use of thoughtful and probing questions. You should practice these questions until their use becomes second nature. Students also need to develop their skills in questioning. The techniques (described in Module 7) essentially include:

1. Emphasizing how and why.
2. Following up leads and developing ideas through additional probing, clarifying questions.
3. Encouraging students to acquire facts before venturing too far into flights of fancy.
4. Asking divergent questions.
5. Encouraging students to discuss one another's thinking and thinking processes.
6. Utilizing Socratic questioning.

Springboards

Springboard techniques are excellent for launching problem solving. Springboards include anything that lends itself to such questions as: "How come?" "So what?" "If so, then what?" Examples of such techniques are role playing, movies, dramatizations, pictures, and models. The great teachers of ancient and modern times have used parables to stimulate original thought. In this method those teachers told a simple story, such as that of the good Samaritan, and then asked their students to use the story as a springboard or jumping-off point for building conclusions or generalizations. Springboards are helpful in setting the stage for problem recognition.

Suitability of Problems

When students have recognized and identified problems they want to investigate, the teacher then has the responsibility to approve the problem's suitability for student investigation. Among the criteria you can use are:

- Is it pertinent to the course objectives?
- Is it relevant to students' lives and to community life?
- Is it feasible? Do we have the necessary resources? Can we complete it in the time available? Can the student handle it?
- Is it worth the effort?

When students have identified a problem they want to investigate and you do not believe that it fits these criteria, you can usually guide them in reidentifying or narrowing the problem so that it does fit these criteria.

Student Presentations

You can encourage students to be presenters for discussion of the ideas, opinions, and knowledge gained from their own independent and small-group study. Several techniques, adaptable to a variety of subject areas, encourage the development of certain skills, such as studying and organizing material, discovery, discussion, rebuttal, listening, analysis, suspending judgment, and critical thinking. Possible forms of discussions involving student presentations include:

1. *Debate.* The debate is an arrangement in which formal speeches are made by members of two opposing teams, on topics preassigned and researched. The speeches are followed by a rebuttal from each team.
2. *Jury trial.* The jury trial is a discussion approach in which the entire class simulates a courtroom, with class members playing the various roles of judge, attorneys, jury members, and court recorder.
3. *Panel.* The panel is a setting in which from four to six students, with one designated as the chairperson, discuss a topic about which they have studied, followed by a question-and-answer period involving the entire class. The panel usually begins by each panel member giving a brief opening statement.
4. *Research report.* One student or a pair of students gives a report on a topic that has been investigated, followed by questions and discussions by the entire class.
5. *Round table.* The round table is a small group of three to five students, who sit around a table and discuss among themselves (and perhaps with the rest of the class) a problem or issue that they have studied. The rest of the class members make up the round table's audience.
6. *Symposium.* Similar to a round-table discussion but more formal, the symposium is an arrangement in which each student participant presents an explanation of his or her position on a pre-assigned topic researched by the student. After the presentations, questions are accepted from the rest of the class.

To use these techniques effectively your students will need to be coached by you, individually or in whole class sessions, on procedures: how and where to gather information; how to take notes, to select major points, to organize material, to present a position succinctly, and to listen; how to play roles; and how to engage in dialogue and debates with one another. Be patient, and the results will be worth it.

Now do Exercise 6.4, which should give you a better understanding of student presentations.

EXERCISE 6.4

Investigation of Types of Student Presentations

• • • • • •

Instructions: The purpose of this exercise is for you and your classmates, in groups of four, to use your university library to research in detail the distinctive characteristics for using (1) student reports, (2) debates, (3) forums, (4) round-table discussions, (5) symposa, and (6) any other types of activities that you find.

Following your research, compile your findings within your group. Then through your small group discussion derive examples of appropriate uses for each type of activity, relative to teaching-specific content in your subject field. As a panel of experts, share your findings and examples with the entire class.

Projects, Papers, and Oral Reports

Regardless of the subject being taught, individual writing and small-group projects should be major features of most instruction. The project is a form of independent or small-group study in which students produce something, such as a paper, an investigation, a model, a skit, or a report.

Purposes for Using Projects, Papers, and Oral Reports

The purposes for using this type of student-centered instructional strategy include:

- Such a strategy can be important in teaching gifted and talented students.
- A student can become especially knowledgeable and experienced in one area of subject content or in one process skill, thus adding to the student's knowledge and sense of importance and self-worth.
- A student can develop skill in communication through sharing this special knowledge and experience with the teacher and with the class.
- Students can learn to work independently or work together, cooperatively, and somewhat independently in small groups.
- Students can practice and develop independent learning skills.
- Students can develop skills in writing and in higher-level thinking.
- Students can become intrinsically motivated to learn when working on topics that have personal meaning, with outcomes and even time lines that are relatively open ended.
- By considering and accommodating individual interests, learning styles, and life experiences, personal meaning to the learning can be optimized.

Unless students are given guidance, projects can often be a frustrating experience, for both the teacher and the students. Students should do projects because they want to and because the project seems important to do. Therefore, students should decide what project to do, and how to do it. The teacher's role is to advise and guide students so they experience success. If a project is laid out in too much detail by the teacher, then that project is a procedure rather than a project assignment.

Guidelines for Using Projects, Papers, and Oral Reports

For the experience of a project, paper, or an oral report to be an educationally beneficial experience the teacher should:

1. *Help students generate ideas.* Stimulate ideas for independent study by providing lists of things students might do, by mentioning each time an idea comes up in class that this would be a good idea for an independent project, by having former students tell about their projects, by showing the results of other students' projects, by suggesting readings that are likely to give students ideas, and by using class discussions to brainstorm ideas.

2. *Provide options but insist that writing be a part of the student's work.* Allow students to choose whether to do a project, a paper, or an oral report, or some combination of these three types of assignments. Regardless of whether the student selects a project, paper, or oral report, and regardless of your subject or grade level, insist that writing be a part of the student's work.

Research examining the links among writing, thinking, and learning has helped emphasize the importance of writing. Writing is a complex intellectual behavior and process that helps the learner to create and record his or her understanding—to construct meaning.

Allow students to choose whether they will work alone or in small groups. If they choose to work in groups, then help them delineate job descriptions for each member of the group. Groups of four or less students seem to work better than groups of more than four.

3. *Provide coaching and guidance.* Work with each student or student team in topic selection, as well as in the processes of writing and oral reporting. Allow students to develop their own procedures, but guide their preparation of work outlines and preliminary drafts, giving

them constructive feedback along the way. Help students in identifying potential resources and in the techniques of research.

Frequent drafts and progress reports from the students are a must. With each of these stages, provide students with constructive feedback. Provide written guidelines and timelines for the outlines, drafts, and the completed project.

4. *Evaluation.* The final project, paper, or oral report should be graded. The method of determination of the grade should be clear to students, as well as the weight of the project grade toward the term grade. Provide students with clear descriptions of how evaluation and grading will be done. Evaluation should include meeting deadlines for drafts and progress reports. The final grade for the study should be based on four criteria: (a) how well it was organized, including meeting draft deadlines; (b) the quality and quantity of knowledge gained from the experience; (c) the quality of the student's sharing of that learning experience with the rest of the class; and (d) the quality of the student's final written or oral report.

5. *Sharing.* Insist that students share the progress and the results of their study with the rest of the class. The amount of time allowed for this sharing will, of course, depend upon many variables. The value of this type of instructional strategy comes not only from individual contributions but also from the learning that results from the experience and the communication of that experience with others.

Projects

A project can be any activity, individual or group, involving the investigation and solution of problems that is planned and carried to a conclusion by students under the guidance and coaching of the teacher. In other words, to be a project the activity should be a problem-solving activity. In a true project the student plans, executes, and evaluates the entire undertaking. The teacher's role is simply to help, advise, and guide the learning.

A project may be an undertaking of an entire class, with various portions of that project pursued by smaller groups of students. For example, a high school class in government decides to design and paint a politically oriented mural on a hallway in the school building. Through several interactive class discussions the students list what tasks will be involved and then sort those into categories of responsibilities that will lead to completion of the project. The categories lead to committees (small groups) of students assuming those responsibilities. These categories include such responsibilities as: deciding the theme of the mural; planning the design of the mural; obtaining permission from the administration to paint the mural,[17] assigning artists and helpers to paint it, procuring materials, organizing the work time and clean up, and so on. Students volunteer or are selected in some manner to form the groups that will work on the particular tasks that lead to completion of the total project—that is each group assumes one category of responsibilities.

Although projects ideally should derive from students' interest, students sometimes have trouble finding and selecting suitable projects. You can help them in this several ways. You might provide lists of suggestions or try to stimulate ideas by class discussion. You could tell students about what others have done in the past, or you could have last year's students come to the class on a consulting basis to describe their successful projects. No matter how students get the ideas, when they finally choose their projects, they will need to analyze them for suitability. The criteria that should be considered are that the project should: (1) make a real contribution to a worthwhile learning objective; (2) result in a worthwhile end; and (3) be reasonable insofar as time, effort, cost, and availability of resources are concerned.

To conduct a project requires a combination of restraint and guidance from the teacher. Students need to accept most of the responsibility for their projects, but they should not be allowed to flounder too much. As the teacher of students doing projects, you must make yourself available to assist the students when necessary and must from time to time check their

---

[17]In a high school in California, in a project that began in 1991 and was not completed until late 1993, students actually had to go to court to obtain a court ruling before they were allowed to paint a mural that depicted a burning flag. In the process the students learned much more than was originally expected or intended, especially about constitutional rights, school law, and civil processes.

progress without interfering. Taking the middle course between too much and too little requires both tact and good judgment.

Research Projects

The research project, another type of project, is when a student or a small group investigates some matter and then reports on it. The process used in a research project is that of any problem-solving activity:

1. Identify the problem to be investigated.
2. Define the problem so that it is manageable in the time available and with the materials and personnel available.
3. Identify both the tasks that must be done to get the necessary data and the students who will perform each task.
4. Identify and gather the materials and resources needed.
5. Prepare a data-gathering instrument.
6. Gather the data.
7. Compile and analyze the data.
8. Draw inferences from the data.
9. Prepare the findings and conclusion.
10. Report the findings and conclusion.

Those steps of a problem-solving activity may seem simple and straightforward to you, but when applied to research projects for middle school and secondary school students they may need considerable explanation. For example, you will discover that many students experience great difficulty in selecting a problem on which they can really focus and then pursue successfully. To be worthwhile, the research must be aimed at a very specific problem. Large, diffuse, ill-defined topics seldom result in anything worthwhile. You will need to help students select research topics of manageable proportions.

Gathering the information requires that the students have obtained certain skills and are aware of materials and resources. Make sure students avoid research projects that entail simply cribbing data and information from an encyclopedia. Help students develop skill in finding and identifying pertinent references.

Students generally need help in developing research techniques, and they often need instruction in the art of taking notes. You will also find that they need instruction in using scientific equipment, sampling, analyzing data, testing for fact, and interpreting statistical information. Research is not easy, and proficiency in the use of scholarly procedures and intellectual tools is difficult to attain unless students are carefully instructed and coached in their use.

Students also will need help in seeing the significance of their data and in drawing valid conclusions and generalizations from their research. Special class sessions for teaching these intellectual skills are helpful and should be utilized, but most of the skill development in this area will happen when you are coaching individuals and small groups.

Research projects usually are best conducted as individual or small-group activities. Seldom are they successful when conducted as whole-class activities, though sometimes projects such as a community survey or the preparation of a report on a community problem can be successful and rewarding. Students in one New Jersey high school class, for instance, were concerned about racial prejudice in that school and the surrounding community. As a class, they studied a number of references on the problem of prejudice, developed a questionnaire, gave it to citizens in the community, analyzed the findings, and published the results. Some of the data and conclusions from this study was suspect in several ways (after all, the study was the work of beginners), but the students discovered much about race prejudice and their community and developed some skills in research techniques. Because the teacher carefully supervised the project and coached the students when necessary, errors were kept to a minimum. Remember that students learn through their mistakes as well as their successes.

Learn more about what projects are suitable for students by doing Exercise 6.5.

EXERCISE 6.5
Projects Suitable for Student Investigation

• • • • • •

Instructions: The purpose of this exercise is to start your thinking about projects suitable for middle school and high school students. Identify by title five projects in your field that would be suitable for middle school students as well as five for high school students. The questions to keep in mind are: Would the projects be valuable to students who do them? Are they practicable in time, costs, materials, and abilities of the students? Share your lists with your colleagues for their feedback.

My subject field:

Middle School Student Projects

1.

2.

3.

4.

5.

High Schools Student Projects

1.

2.

3.

4.

5.

Surveys

Surveys of the community or of the school population are among the most interesting types of research projects. If well planned and well conducted, they can teach the students much, but if poorly conceived and executed, they can lead to confusion, miseducation, and an upset community. Before launching into a community survey, be sure that the students know well both the topic they are to investigate and the procedure they are to use. This can be achieved by direct teaching and practice in the class.

Gathering the information.   There are many ways to gather data, such as interviews, questionnaires, or observation. It is, of course, important to pick the right data-gathering technique and to aim it directly at the correct goal. To be sure that the technique is suitable and well aimed, you and your students must carefully examine the problem to see exactly what data are needed for its solution. Then the students, under your guidance, must design a strategy to obtain that information. If this strategy involves a questionnaire or opinion sampling, then the students must design the instrument. Although the development of an instrument may not be so necessary if the strategy adopted involves interviewing or observation, probably the results will be more profitable and dependable if a data-gathering instrument such as a rating scale or checklist is used. The students must be instructed and practiced in the use of these instruments so they will not waste the time of the respondents and also so the data gathered will be what was wanted.

Processing the data.   Once the data have been gathered, they must be interpreted. This part of the research can be somewhat tricky. Most persons are tempted to make generalizations and conclusions that are not justified by the data. You should help students set up criteria by which to distinguish between significant and insignificant data. In some cases, to interpret the data, students may have to use simple statistics, but usually for class use careful inspection will suffice. The important point is to extrapolate cautiously. It is much safer to say that of the people we asked, 10 percent said yes, 70 percent said no, and 20 percent did not answer, than to say that the people of the community reject the proposition. In this regard, students should be made aware of the difficulties of sampling, the need of an adequate sample, and techniques for analyzing and interpreting their data. It is probably best to record the data in tabular form without comment. For example: Question 1. Do you prefer Plan *A* or Plan *B*? Total, 50 (100 percent). *A*, 5 (10 percent). *B*, 30 (60 percent). No Answer, 15 (30 percent).

Publishing the results.   Publishing the results of a survey usually should be reserved for classroom use only. Only exceptionally good surveys rate publishing more widely, and even they should not be published until cleared by school officials. There is no reason to publish anything that will not enhance the school's image or reputation as a scholarly institution.

Building the instrument.   As many college and university graduate students have found out to their sorrow, to build an effective questionnaire is not an easy task. The following suggestions may help students who attempt to use questionnaires or opinion samplings in research projects:

1. Be sure to include in the questionnaire only those things that are needed. If you can find the information in another way with reasonable ease, do so.
2. Be sure the questions are clear. Check them for ambiguities. To be sure that they are unambiguous, try them out on other students and teachers. You may find that you ought to rewrite many of them or explain the terms or references you are using.
3. Be sure the questions are easy to answer. Yes-no, one word checklists, or multiple-choice questions are the easiest and quickest both to answer and to interpret. Be sure, however, to give the respondent a chance to comment. It is maddening to a respondent not to be able to say that the answer is "yes, but . . ." or "well, it depends on. . . ." Forced-choice items

have no place in questionnaires written by public school students; they should be reserved for use by professionals or by graduate students.

4. Be sure to set up the questionnaire so that it will be easy to tally the answers. For instance, if the answers can be arranged so that they appear in a column on the right (or left) side of the sheet, it makes tabulating much easier. Additional remarks and comments cannot be made easy to tabulate, but space should be provided for them. Be sure to give the respondent room enough to write a reasonably long, but not too long, comment.

Interview procedure.   To be sure that students conducting interviews ask the questions they should without taking up too much of the interviewee's time, or garbling the questions, or omitting necessary questions, the interview questions should be planned and written out before the interview. A written plan is necessary also because, if one hopes to get comparable data from the interviews, the students must ask all the respondents the same questions in the same way. Therefore, it is wise to develop a formal procedure, such as the following suggested by Popkewitz:[18]

> My name is _____. My class is doing a survey about student participation. I will be speaking to many students in your school and other schools. I would like to ask you a few questions.
>
> A. Do you often discuss school issues with
>   1. Friends?
>   2. Class officers?
>   3. School officials?
> B. Have you ever attended a meeting (church, school board, union, etc.) in which school policy was discussed?
> C. Have you ever taken an active part regarding school issues, such as writing a letter or presenting a petition?

This format makes it easy for students to record answers to their questions. They should record the answers of the respondent immediately. If they try to depend on memory, they will get mixed up, forget, and, therefore, bring in incorrect data.

Observation techniques.   If research involving the use of observation techniques is to be successful, the students must be well prepared to observe carefully and profitably. The observation must be planned and the observers trained so that they see and report the data in the same way. For this purpose, the students should decide exactly what it is they must look for. In some instances, this means that they will have to decide upon the standards for establishing the presence or absence of the phenomenon, or for deciding the criteria for such categories as *much*, *some*, and *little*. They will also need to devise an instrument on which to record their observations. Frequently this instrument should be a checklist in which the observers merely note the presence or absence of phenomena, as in the following:

> 1. Check the applicable item.
>   a. Student selected a hot dish.
>   b. Student selected a dessert.
>   c. Student selected a coke.

Or the instrument may be a rating scale in which the student records his or her judgment of the amount or quality of the phenomenon present, as in the following:

> The students' conduct in the cafeteria line was
> _____ very orderly   fairly orderly   disorderly
>
> The students' conduct at their tables was
> _____ very orderly   fairly orderly   disorderly

---

[18]Thomas S. Popkewitz, *How to Study Political Participation*, How to Do It Series, no. 27 (Washington, D.C.: National Council for the Social Studies, 1974), p. 5.

In the constructing of these devices, teachers should try to help students concoct procedures that make observing, recording, and interpreting the data as simple and as easy as possible. When observing, recording, or interpreting becomes unnecessarily complicated, the devices are usually accompanied by unnecessary errors.

Case Study Method

The case study is a special type of problem-solving method. It consists of a searching, detailed study of a particular situation, institution, decision, or issue from which students draw generalizations concerning the type. The case study can give students considerable understanding of difficult, complex matters.

Although the procedures for conducting case studies are quite simple, they are usually difficult to carry out. In general, they include the following steps:

1. *Select and define a topic or problem to investigate.* The topic should be a specific case so typical of a larger subject that studying it would throw light on that entire subject.
2. *Identify, collect, and make ready the materials needed for an in-depth study.* Usually, most will be reading material, but do not forget that sometimes films, pictures, or audio and video tapes may be better for your purpose. So may laboratory or field work.
3. *Start with a good introduction.* Now that you have the things to work with, you are ready to begin the case study. In the introduction, the students should get an understanding of the problem or issue before them, what they are attempting to find out, and the method of attack. This is the time when you sell the case study to the students, so make your introduction persuasive. At this point, it may be wise to give out a study guide that the students can use as they investigate the case. The bulk of the study of the case can be done individually by students investigating individually with the study guide for a base. If you wish, it is possible to proceed on a group or whole-class basis through the use of discussions and the like. But the really important part of this phase of the case study approach is to study the particular case in depth, learn as much as one can about it, and draw conclusions.
4. *Share findings and conclusions.* They can do this in many ways; perhaps the most profitable is the free discussion. Role playing, panels, and symposia may also prove very useful. In these discussions, the students should be encouraged to draw inferences from the case study, as they have been doing right along about the class of things the case study represents.

Gain practice in preparing a case study by doing Exercise 6.6.

EXERCISE 6.6
Preparing a Case Study
• • • • • •

Instructions: The purpose of this exercise is to practice writing a case study. Prepare a case study for use in your teaching. Upon completion share it with your colleagues for their reactions and input.

My teaching field:

1. Topic or problem of case study:

2. Listing of materials needed:

3. The case study (identification of type):

    Grade level for which the case can be used:

4. Prepare the case study.

Field Trip

One of the very best ways to make instruction real is to take the students out in the field to see and do things, such as to go to the theater to see a production of *Macbeth*, to go to a wetlands area to see ecological problems firsthand, to go to the museum to see the works of great art, or to visit the site of a battle. Field trips, carefully planned and executed, can pay off in increased motivation and meaningful learning, but they require careful planning. In fact, of all the possible instructional activities, they probably require the most careful planning. To prepare for a particular field trip, you should:

1. Talk over the trip with your principal and department head.
2. Take the trip yourself, if feasible, to see how to make it most productive and to see what arrangements should be made.
3. Arrange for details at the place to be visited. These arrangements include: a schedule; the briefing of the host, or tour personnel, on what you want and what type of group you are; provisions for eating and rest rooms; and so on. Obtain clear information about fees.
4. Arrange for permissions from the school authorities and parents.
5. Arrange for schedule changes, excuses from other classes, and so on.
6. Arrange for transportation.
7. Arrange for the collection of funds, payments, and so on.
8. Arrange for the safety of students.
9. Arrange the itinerary, including all stops—rest stops, meals, and so on. Do not plan to rush. Allow plenty of time. Figure that someone will get lost, or be late, or something!
10. Establish rules of conduct.
11. Brief the students. Give them directions: what to do if lost or left behind, what to take along, what they are going to do, what they should look for, what notes they should take, what materials they should bring back. Give them a copy of the study guide.
12. Provide for follow-up activities. Taking along tape recorders and cameras will allow you to bring back a record of what you did and saw. Tape record interviews, talks, questions and answers, and take pictures of the people, places, and things seen as the basis of a class follow-up.
13. Take steps to see that no one is left out because of lack of money, race, religion, or ethnic background.
14. Arrange for other teachers and parents to help you.

Figure 6.8 is a worksheet used for planning and reporting field trips at a New Jersey junior high school. Notice the meticulous detail that the board of education expects of teachers who conduct field trips. As you examine this form, ask yourself why the school board and school administrators have required each of the items they have listed.

Another type of field trip is when students go into the field (as in life science, biology, or earth science class, for instance) to record observations, or generally to gather data useful for their class assignments. Field work of this type tends to tie instruction to reality as well as make learning more active and interesting.

Action Learning

Field trips and surveys are examples of community involvement activities. Such activities allow students to observe and study realities outside the schoolroom. Action learning activities tend to carry such learning a step further. In these activities students actually become involved in community affairs or community service projects. In Jersey City (NJ), for instance, students participated in a local political campaign; and in a Vermont village a science class investigated and brought to the attention of the local officials a problem concerning water pollution. Such activities effectively extend the classroom into the community. By so doing they quite often get at objectives that other learning activities fail to reach. In action learning, what in the classroom is academic becomes real and vivid. To prepare students for such activities, use the technique suggested for projects discussed in the preceding section.

Date _____

Teacher's Worksheet on Field Trip

This worksheet is intended both as a teacher's guide and a report. It should be handed in after the completion of the trip. Check applicable items as completed.

Trip to _____

Teacher _____ Subject _____ Date of trip _____

Group or section _____ Alternate date _____

Planning on Part of Teacher

_____ Are the educational values of the proposed trip definite and clear? State them briefly:

_____ Figure the cost

Transportation	$	_____
Admissions	$	_____
Meals	$	_____
Total	$	_____

_____ Is the total cost figure sufficient, reasonable, and within the reach of most of the group?

_____ Secure approval of the principal and turn in Permission for School Excursion.

_____ Check school calendar with vice-principal and sign for date.

_____ Make arrangements with bus company, after securing at least two bids.

_____ Have the places you intend to visit been "scouted," either by you or someone you know?

_____ Chaperones to be secured: two adults per bus, one of whom must be a licensed teacher.

_____ If the trip takes two hours or more, is a bathroom stop available en route?

_____ Have teachers made arrangements with the vice-principal for students left behind or for teachers' duties left "uncovered"?

Preparation of the Class

_____ Discuss purposes of trip with the class.

_____ Each student who is going must have Field Trip Permit signed by parents (Form 126).

_____ Discuss proper clothes to be worn by students.

_____ Discuss conduct on bus, including:

　_____ No arms or heads to be out of windows.

　_____ Remain in seats except by permission.

　_____ Trash to be placed in paper bags.

Figure 6.8 Worksheet for Field Trip

Writing Across the Curriculum

Writing instruction received attention in the *Writing Report Card: Writing Achievement in American Schools*.[19] That report indicated that students who use process-writing techniques (where both students and the teacher focus on the process of writing rather than on the products of the writing) produce superior products. In process writing, the emphasis is on planning or rehearsing, drafting and redrafting based on feedback from other students, and revising and editing. With students of all ability levels, it appears that diagnosis and prescription by the teacher, based on actual student errors, are superior to sequences in workbooks and expository teach-

[19]Arthur N. Applebee et al., *The Writing Report Card: Writing Achievement in American Schools* (Princeton, NJ: National Assessment of Education Progress, 1986).

_____ Nothing to be thrown out of bus windows.

_____ Students remain in seats on bus at destination until teacher gets off first.

_____ Listen to teacher's directions for dismounting at destination.

_____ Discuss the method of control which is to be used during the trip:

    _____ "Buddy System"—students are paired up and given numbers (1A-1B, 2A-2B, etc.). The pair must remain together. If they leave the main group, they must tell another pair where they are going. Students must immediately report the loss of a "buddy." Each chaperone will supervise so many sets of buddies.

    _____ Or "Group system"—divide a busload into two or three squads, with a student leader *and* a chaperone in charge of each. Attendance to be taken by each group frequently.

    _____ Or other system of control as planned by teacher and approved by principal.

_____ Eating arrangements to be explained to pupils. Need for staple foods, rather than a day of candy and soda, should be discussed.

_____ On day before trip, class should make a list of things to be looked for on trip.

On the Morning of the Trip

_____ Proper attendance taken in homeroom or classroom.

_____ Correct absentee cards sent to office.

_____ Correct list of those remaining behind turned in to office.

_____ Permission slips filed in main office.

_____ Students reinstructed on bus safety rules.

_____ Take first-aid kit; also empty paper bags for car sickness.

_____ Check attendance *on the bus* immediately before leaving. Teacher in charge reports discrepancies to the attendance secretary in main office.

Follow-Up

_____ Has the trip been followed up by the class with evaluation—either written or oral—of ideas and facts learned?

_____ Write a brief explanation of the trip: What were its values? Would you take a group on it next year? Other comments. Use space below.

_____

Signature of Teacher

---

ing. Also helpful in revising the writing of students are word processors and computers and accompanying word-processing programs. With these tools, a student can make revisions without copying material by hand. This freedom from hand copying allows a student to focus on revising and not on the labor of recopying.

As noted, research examining the links among writing, thinking, and learning has helped emphasize the importance of writing across the curriculum. Writing is a complex intellectual task that helps the learner create and record his or her understanding—to construct meaning. In exemplary secondary schools, student writing is encouraged in all disciplines—that is, across the curriculum.[20]

---

[20]One resource for specific ideas about how writing can be used in various disciplines in secondary school (e.g., business, electronics, English, foreign languages, home economics, mathematics, science, social studies, and vocational education) is Deborah Hightshue et al., "Writing in Junior and Senior High Schools," *Phi Delta Kappan* 69(10):725–728 (June 1988).

Student Journals

Many teachers, across the curriculum, have students maintain journals in which the students write their thoughts about what it is they are studying.[21] These are referred to as response journals. Actually, commonly used are two types of journals: dialogue journals and reading-response journals. Dialogue journals are used for students to write anything that is on their minds; teachers, parents or guardians, and other students respond, thereby "talking with" the journal writer. Reading-response journals are used for students to write their reactions to what is being studied.

Purpose and Evaluation of Student Journal Writing

The purpose of journal writing is to encourage students to write, to think about their writing, and to record their creative thoughts. Students are encouraged to write in their journals about personal experiences, both in school and out, that are related to the subject being studied. They should be encouraged to write down their feelings about what and how they are learning. Journal writing provides practice in expression and thus should be not be graded by the teacher. Negative comments and evaluations from the teacher will discourage creative and spontaneous expression by students. Teachers should read the journal writing and offer constructive and positive feedback, but should avoid negative comments or grading the journals. For grading purposes, most teachers simply record whether or not a student does, in fact, maintain the required journal.

Resources for Writing Across the Curriculum

Additional resources on writing across the curriculum include:

Illinois Writing Project, National Louis University, 2840 Sheridan Road, Evanston, IL 60201.

International Reading Association, 800 Barksdale Road, Newark, DE 19711.

National Center for the Study of Writing and Literature, School of Education, University of California–Berkeley, Berkeley, CA 94720.

National Council of Teachers of English, 1111 Kenyon Road, Urbana, IL 61801.

National Writing Project, 5627 Tolman Hall, University of California–Berkeley, Berkeley, CA 94720.

Whole Language Umbrella, Unit 6-846, Marion St., Winnipeg, Manitoba, Canada R2J0K4.

Writing to Learn, Council for Basic Education, 725 15th St., NW, Washington, DC 20005.

Role Playing and Simulation

Role Playing

Role playing and simulation can be used effectively in inquiry and discovery teaching. By attempting to act out a real problem, students may get real insight into the nature of a problem situation. Role playing may be used to clarify attitudes and concepts; demonstrate attitudes and concepts; deepen understandings of social situations; prepare for real situations (such as practicing the interview procedures to be used in a survey); plan and try out strategies for attacking problems; test out hypothetical solutions to problems; and practice leadership and other skills. Role playing has a number of drawbacks, however. Role playing is slow; is often not realistic enough, so that false concepts result; and although serious business, is often thought of as entertainment.

---

[21]For example, see Christine J. Gordon and Dorothy Macinnis, "Using Journals as a Window on Students' Thinking in Mathematics," *Language Arts* 70(1):37–43 (January 1993); and Cyrene M. Wells, "At the Junction of Reading and Writing: How Dialogue Journals Contribute to Students' Reading Development," *Journal of Reading* 36(4):294–302 (December–January 1992–93), and Jim Anderson, "Journal Writing: The Promise and the Reality," *Journal of Reading* 36(4):304–309 (December–January 1992–93).

As you know, role playing is an unrehearsed dramatization, in which the players try to clarify a situation by acting out the roles of the participants in the situation. To carry out a role-playing session, the following procedures are recommended:

1. Pick a simple situation, not a complicated one, to role-play. Two to four characters usually are quite enough.
2. Select a cast who will do the job. Use volunteers, if feasible, but only if the volunteers are equal to the task. It is preferable to sacrifice self-selection for effectiveness. Sometimes it is helpful to select several casts and run through the role-playing several times, each time with a different cast. Different interpretations of the parts should give the audience more data from which to draw their inferences and make their discoveries.
3. Be sure that the characters in the cast understand the situation, the purpose of the role playing, and their roles. To this end, brief the players well and then discuss their roles with them. Sometimes it is helpful to outline the general line they should follow and to rehearse the first few lines. However, too much direction and too much warmup can ruin the role playing by stereotyping the interpretations.
4. Brief the audience. Be sure everyone understands what the players are supposed to be trying to do.
5. Stage the role playing. Let the role players interpret freely. However, if they get hopelessly lost, it may be necessary for you to stop the role playing and reorient the players.
6. If it seems desirable, repeat the role playing with reversed roles or with different role players.
7. Follow up the role playing with a discussion about what happened in the role playing and its significance. At this point, the teacher should encourage students to come to some conclusions and make some generalizations (although it may be more satisfactory to leave the discussion open-ended). Sometimes the discussion may reveal new or different interpretations and concepts that warrant a replaying of the roles and further discussion and analysis.

Simulation

A simulation differs from role playing in that the former is an enactment of a make-believe episode as much like the real thing as possible, but with some of the dangerous and complicating factors removed. The beginning truck driver does not suffer dire results from a mistake if he or she pulls in front of a speeding bus when driving the driver education simulator, the beginning aviator crashes with impunity when the plane stalling is simulated, and the soldier who mishandles a new weapon in a dry run without live ammunition kills no one. Simulations of this sort, although in our examples largely aimed at developing skills, can be useful for helping students gain insights into difficult matters. The young, aspiring lawyer who tries a case in a simulated courtroom not only gains skill in legal practice but also gains insight into the law of the case being tried. In the social studies classroom, the students simulating the management of a business are learning what happens when they overbuy, overprice, and make strategic errors.

In these simulations, students go through the process in what they were learning in a real way. That is the value of simulation. By taking roles in the simulated activity, the students may come to understand the real situation and how to act in it.

Simulations differ from role playing in that the scenarios must be carefully drafted. In these scenarios the students are assigned definite roles that require them to take specific action in a well-defined situation, and the students are confronted by simulated, real-life situations that require them to take actions just as they would have to in real life (or at least as close to real life as feasible). These actions may lead to new predicaments that require new actions. In taking actions, the players are not free but must stay in character and keep their actions within the limits prescribed by the roles they have assumed and by the realities of the simulated situation.

If you are to produce a simulation, the following procedure may prove useful:

1. Prepare the material, equipment, and props that will be needed.
2. Introduce the plan to the students. Explain the purpose of the simulation. Give the directions for playing it.

3. Assign roles. Probably it is best to pick the players yourself. Accepting volunteers or selecting students by chance may result in disastrous miscasting.
4. Brief the students in their roles. Be sure they understand them.
5. Conduct the simulation. Follow the scenario to the letter.
6. Follow up with a critique in which students have a chance to discuss what they have done and to draw generalizations.

Controversial Issues

The content of topics most suitable for the methods described in this module may sometimes be controversial. Teaching controversial issues can be something of a problem. Students, parents, and the local public often feel very strongly about them. It is wise to treat them gingerly or your teaching may do more harm than good.

In the first place, because controversial issues can be so touchy, you should be careful to select topics that will throw more light than heat. There is no point in introducing into your courses topics so controversial that they inhibit your effectiveness. Therefore, before you commit yourself to any controversial topics, consider the following criteria:

1. Is the topic pertinent to your course and your course goals?
2. Are you knowledgeable enough and neutral enough to handle it fairly and impartially?
3. Is it worth the time and effort?
4. Are the students sufficiently mature and informed to cope with it?
5. Is there sufficient material available to allow students adequate consideration of the various points of view?
6. Can it be discussed without overemotionalism? Will it be upsetting to the people in the community?

After you select a controversial topic, you must be careful to teach it fairly and honestly. Controversial issues are open-ended questions and should be treated as such. Ordinarily they do not have "right answers" or "correct solutions"—otherwise there would be no controversy. Therefore your focus, when teaching controversial matters, should be on process rather than content. Your goal should be to show students how to deal with controversial issues so as to make wise decisions on the basis of carefully considered information.

To achieve this end you should teach your students what the issues are, how to sort out facts from propaganda and myth, how to evaluate the positions of the various sides, and how to draw their own conclusions. To do this you will have to teach students how to check out sources of information and facts, to identify sources of information, and to test these sources for authority, accuracy, objectivity, and timeliness by using such questions as: "What is the basis for this statement?" "Is this 'authority' really in a position to know?" "Is it corroborated by other evidence?" "Is the information current?" To build reasoning skills, provide pupils with questionable statements and show them how to prove or disprove them. To help students separate fact from opinion, keep a fact-opinion table on the chalkboard (Figure 6.9). You should also help students from getting hung up on the meaning of words. Often the emotional connotations of words obscure their meaning and prevent logical evaluation of facts and arguments. So do students' values. Such techniques as value-clarifying responses, value sheets, and value discussions help students discover and evaluate their own values. So that the students may understand just what community value conflicts are involved in the issue being studied, it is sometimes helpful for students to conduct an opinion survey on the topic. In any case you should encourage the students to use research-type activities to dig out facts, opinions, and values, and to place them on the table for all to see and evaluate.

When teaching controversial issues, you should try not to become too involved in the controversy. Certainly you should not advocate one position or another. This is another reason for using research or problem-solving activities as a basis for the study of controversial issues. Nevertheless, at times you may find that in order to give students a chance to look at all sides of

Figure 6.9   Fact-Opinion
Table

Fact	Opinion

the controversy, you may have to present some aspects of the topic yourself. Otherwise students may never understand the complexity of the issue, the variety of positions, the divergence in values, or the moral, ethical, political, financial implications, and the like. Sometimes it may be necessary to play the devil's advocate. When you do, try not to give the impression that you are advocating one side or another. Use expressions such as "some people say," "other people believe," and so on.

Everyone in a class should have the right to express an opinion on the issue to be studied. Problem-solving, research-type activities followed by discussion activities provide good ways for obtaining nearly universal student involvement. Debates, panels, dramatics, role playing, and simulations are other examples of activities that let students present their points of view. Simulated town meetings, jury trials, council meetings, legislatures, or party conventions can be especially useful.

When using such discussion modes for teaching controversial issues, you should first establish some ground rules. For example:

- All facts must be supported by authority.
- Everyone must be given an opportunity to be heard.
- No one should interrupt (except perhaps the leader to keep the discussion on track).
- Personal remarks are forbidden.

To get the study of the issue started and to arouse interest, sometimes a free-for-all introductory discussion in which students may express themselves without restraint is helpful, but ordinarily you should apply the ground rules so as to promote orderly thinking and to keep the discussion from getting too hot. To keep rash opinion statements under control, sometimes teachers ask students to present arguments contrary to their own point of view. Doing so may help students to understand and respect the opinions of others and to realize the complexity of the issue.

In short, to teach controversial issues well, you must see to it that students learn how to identify what is the basis for the controversy, what is at stake, what value conflicts are involved, what the facts are, and what their own values and beliefs are so that they can make informed decisions and take intelligent stands now and in the future.

Exercise 6.7 will help you explore how you might teach a controversial issue.

Teaching About Controversial Issues

• • • • • •

Instructions: The purpose of this exercise is for you to discover controversial issues that you may face as a teacher, and to consider what you can and will do about them. After completing this exercise, share it with members of your class.

1. By studying current periodicals and talking with colleagues in the schools you visit, list two or three potentially controversial topics that you are likely to encounter as a teacher. (An example is given for you.)

   Issue   *Source*

   [Use of chimpanzees for medical research]   *[National Geographic, March 1992]*

2. Take one of these issues, and identify opposing arguments and current resources.

3. Identify your own position on this issue.

4. How well can you accept students (and parents or guardians) who assume the opposite position?

5. Share the preceding with other teacher candidates. Note comments that you find helpful or enlightening.

SUMMARY

You have learned about the importance of learning modalities, enactive learning, and instructional modes, as well as about middle and secondary school students, their needs, and the importance of providing an accepting and supportive learning environment. You have learned important principles of teaching and learning.

This module has initiated the development of a repertoire of teaching strategies necessary for you to become an effective teacher. As you know, many students can be quite peer-conscious, have relatively short attention spans, and prefer active learning experiences that engage many of their senses. Most are intensely curious about things of interest to them. Cooperative learning, independent study, and teaching strategies that emphasize shared inquiry and discovery within a psychologically safe environment encourage the most positive aspects of thinking and learning. Central to your strategy selection should be those strategies that encourage students to become independent thinkers and skilled learners who can help in the planning, structuring, regulating, and assessing of their own learning and learning activities.

In this module we presented and discussed a number of teaching strategies that all have two common elements: (1) social interaction and (2) problem solving. These teaching strategies require students to interact with one another and to draw conclusions, learn concepts, and form generalizations through induction, deduction, and observation, or application of principles. The premises underlying these methods are (1) that a person learns to think by thinking and sharing his or her thoughts with others, thereby obtaining feedback and doing further thinking, and (2) that knowledge gained through active learning and self-discovery is more meaningful, permanent, and transferable than knowledge obtained through expository techniques.

The strategies that have been presented in this module are not easy to implement. To use them effectively and without problems of classroom control requires conviction and careful preparation. Even with firm conviction and careful preparation there may need to be a period of trial and error before you perfect your skills in their implementation. Yet, techniques that use cooperative learning, problem solving, and discovery are important teaching tools. They are absolutely worth the effort, time, and potential frustrations that can occur for the beginning teacher who deviates from the traditional, teacher-centered strategies. Such expository methods of instruction are presented next, in Module 7.

SUGGESTED READING

Alvino, J., ed. "Building Better Thinkers." *Learning 90* 18(6):40–55 (February 1990).

Artzt, A. F., and Newman, C. M. *How to Use Cooperative Learning in the Mathematics Class*. Reston, VA: National Council of Teachers of Mathematics, 1990.

Barell, J. *Teaching for Thoughtfulness*. White Plains, NY: Longman, 1991.

Bowser, J. "Structuring the Middle-School Classroom for Spoken Language." *English Journal* 82(1):38–41 (January 1993).

Carson, L., and Hoyle, S. "Teaching Social Skills: A View From the Classroom." *Educational Leadership* 47(4):31 (December/January 1989–90).

Costa, A. L., ed. *Developing Minds: A Resource Book for Teaching Thinking*. Rev. ed. Alexandria, VA: Association for Supervision and Curriculum Development, 1991.

Costa, A.L., ed. *Developing Minds: Programs for Teaching Thinking*. Rev. ed. Alexandria, VA: Association for Supervision and Curriculum Development, 1991.

Costa, A. L. *The School as a Home for the Mind*. Palatine, IL: Skylight, 1991.

Ellis, S. S. "Introducing Cooperative Learning." *Educational Leadership* 47(4):34–37 (December/January 1989–90).

Evans, P., et al. "Cooperative Learning: Passing Fad or Long-Term Promise?" *Middle School Journal* 24(3):3–7 (January 1993).

Ferguson, P. "Cooperative Team Learning: Theory into Practice for the Prospective Middle School Teacher." *Action in Teacher Education* 11(4):24–28 (Winter 1989–90).

Good, T. L., et al. "Using Work-groups in Mathematics Instruction." *Educational Leadership* 47(4):56–62 (December/January 1989–90).

Hagaman, S. "The Community of Inquiry: An Approach to Collaborative Learning." *Studies in Art Education* 31(3):149–157 (Spring 1990).

Johnson, D. W., and Johnson, R. T. "Social Skills for Successful Group Work." *Educational Leadership* 47(4):29–33 (December/January 1989–90).

Johnson, D. W., and Johnson, R. T. *Learning Together and Alone: Cooperative, Competitive, and Individualistic Learning*. Englewood Cliffs, NJ: Prentice Hall, 1991.

Johnson, D. W., et al. *Circles of Learning: Cooperation in the Classroom*. Edina, MN. Interaction, 1990.

Kemp, S. G., and Sadoski, M. "The Effects of Instruction in Forming Generalizations on High School Students' Critical Thinking in World History." *Reading Research and Instruction* 31(1):33–42 (Fall 1991).

Lyman, L., and Foyle, H. C. "The Constitution in Action: A Cooperative Learning Approach." *Georgia Social Science Journal* 21(1):24–34 (Spring 1990).

Lyman, L., and Foyle, H. C. "Teaching Geography Using Cooperative Learning." *Journal of Geography* 90(5):223–226 (September-October 1991).

Margolis, H., et al. "Using Cooperative Learning to Facilitate Mainstreaming in the Social Studies." *Social Education* 54(2):111–114 (February 1990).

Marzano, L. "Connecting Literature with Cooperative Writing." *Reading Teacher* 43(6):429–430 (February 1990).

McClure, M. F. "Collaborative Learning: Teachers' Game or Students' Game?" *English Journal* 79(2):58–61 (February 1990).

McKenzie, F. D. "Equity: A Call to Action." In *Challenges and Achievements of American Education*, edited by Gordon Cawelti. 1993 ASCD Yearbook. Alexandria, VA: Association for Supervision and Curriculum Development, 1993.

Resnick, L. and Klopfer, L., eds. *Toward the Thinking Curriculum: Current Cognitive Research*. 1989 ASCD Yearbook. Alexandria, VA: Association for Supervision and Curriculum Development, 1989.

Resnick, L. *Education and Learning to Think*. Washington, DC: National Academy Press, 1987.

Rich, Y. "Ideological Impediments to Instructional Innovation: The Case of Cooperative Learning." *Teaching and Teacher Education* 6(1):81–91 (1990).

Ross, J. A., and Raphael, D. "Communication and Problem Solving Achievement in Cooperative Learning Groups." *Journal of Curriculum Studies* 22(2):149–164 (March–April 1990).

Sapon-Shevin, M., and Schneidewind, N. "Selling Cooperative Learning Without Selling it Short." *Educational Leadership* 47(4):63–65 (December/January 1989–90).

Schultz, J. L. "Cooperative Learning: Refining the Process." *Educational Leadership* 47(4):43–45 (December/January 1989–90).

Slavin, R. E. "Research on Cooperative Learning: Consensus and Controversy." *Educational Leadership* 47(4):52–54 (December/January 1989–90).

Slavin, R. E. *Cooperative Learning*. Englewood Cliffs, NJ: Prentice Hall, 1990.

Slavin, R. E., et al. "Putting Research to Work: Cooperative Learning." *Instructor* 102(2):46–47 (September 1992).

Totten, S., and Sills, T. M. "Selected Resources for Using Cooperative Learning." *Educational Leadership* 47(4):66 (December/January 1989–90).

POSTTEST

Multiple Choice

_____ 1. Which one of the following is *not* the same as the others?
   a. student-centered teaching
   b. direct learning experience
   c. expository teaching
   d. indirect instruction

_____ 2. If you are a physical education instructor and you want your students to learn how to shoot a free throw in basketball, the best teaching technique from the following would be to
   a. lecture to the class about how to shoot a free throw.
   b. have cooperative learning groups discuss how to shoot a free throw.
   c. have a guest speaker discuss with the students about how to shoot free throws.
   d. demonstrate to the students how to shoot a free throw and follow that with having the students practice shooting free throws.

_____ 3. Which one of the following includes learning modalities that tend to rely more on abstract symbolization?
   a. visual and auditory
   b. tactile and auditory
   c. tactile and kinesthetic
   d. kinesthetic and visual

_____ 4. If a high school government class takes a field trip to observe the state legislature in session, for the students this is
   a. an abstract verbal experience.
   b. a concrete visual experience.
   c. a simulated experience.
   d. a direct experience.

_____ 5. Which steps of the Learning Experiences Ladder correspond to Bruner's concept of enactive learning (refer to Module 2)?
   a. top
   b. middle
   c. bottom
   d. none of them.

_____ 6. While teaching middle school children about the water cycle, the teacher has grouped the students. One group is doing an experiment to find out how many drops of water can be held on the side of a new one-cent coin versus how many can be held on the side of a worn one-cent piece; another group is composing a song about the water cycle; another group is creating and drawing a poster about it; another group is reading about the water cycle in supplementary reading materials; and another group is creating a drama about the water cycle. When each group is finished they share their group work with others in the class. This teacher is using a teaching strategy that is
   a. an example of multilevel teaching.
   b. based on what is known about student learning styles.
   c. based on Gardner's theory of multiple intelligences.
   d. all of the above.

_____ 7. Bruner's symbolic representation (see Module 2) is analogous to
   a. the top steps of the Learning Experiences Ladder.
   b. the middle steps of the Learning Experiences Ladder.
   c. the bottom steps of the Learning Experiences Ladder.
   d. none of the steps of the Learning Experiences Ladder.

_____ 8. To promote student inquiry, which one of the following is *least* useful?
   a. the use of dogmatism

        b. an open classroom environment

        c. encouraging guessing and intuitive thinking

        d. encouraging skepticism and the suspension of judgment

_____   9. All else considered equal, which one of the following transitions in learning activities is probably best during the same instructional period?

        a. teacher talk to student discussion

        b. teacher talk to student investigation

        c. cooperative learning to student oral reports

        d. video presentation to a 35-mm slide presentation

_____   10. A major justification for helping students develop skills in discussion and group process is

        a. the inclusion of speech in the language arts curriculum.

        b. the failure of parents to accept responsibility for teaching these skills.

        c. the necessary respite that such activities provide from the more cognitive aspects of the instructional program.

        d. the prevalence of group activity and human interaction in everyday life and experience.

_____   11. A major value in role-playing activities lies in

        a. promoting the creative instincts of students.

        b. enhancing the acting skills of talented students.

        c. permitting ego gratification on the part of some students.

        d. deepening insights/understandings about the issues and personalities involved.

_____   12. One virtue of group instructional techniques is that they

        a. save time.

        b. are teacher centered.

        c. present facts more vividly.

        d. tend to foster an openness to ideas and an acceptance of others.

_____   13. Which of these roles should the teacher assume when conducting discussions and group activities?

        a. guide

        b. mediator

        c. resource person

        d. all of the above

Short Explanation

1. Explain when and why vicarious student learning experiences are appropriate.
2. Describe the steps to critical thinking and problem solving. Describe a situation in your own teaching where you would engage your students in critical thinking and problem solving.
3. Explain the differences and similarities between Bruner's three stages of learning (Module 2) and the Learning Experiences Ladder of this module.
4. Identify the pros and cons of using direct eye contact with your students.
5. Explain the concept of hands-on, minds-on learning.

Essay

1. Is a student's ability or style for inquiry effected by the student's gender or by the student's cultural, linguistic, or ethnic background? What do you think? What evidence do you have for your conclusion? Is the question even fair or relevant?
2. From your current observations and field work as related to this teacher preparation program, clearly identify one specific example of educational practice that seems contradictory to exemplary practice or theory as presented in this module. Present your explanation for the discrepancy.
3. Describe any prior concepts you held that changed as a result of the experiences of this module. Describe the changes.

Teacher-centered Instructional Strategies

Rationale
Specific Objectives
Module Text
    Teacher Talk: Formal and Informal
        Cautions about Using Teacher Talk
        Teacher Talk: General Guidelines
        Teacher Talk: Specific Guidelines
    Demonstrations
        Purposes for a Demonstration
        Guidelines for Using a Demonstration
    Questioning
        Purposes for Using Questioning
        Types of Cognitive Questions
        Levels of Cognitive Questions
        Guidelines for Using Questioning
        Preparing Questions
        Implementing Questions
        Student Textbook Questions
        Handling Student Questions
    Recitation
        Open-Text Recitation
    Equity in the Classroom
        Ensuring Equity
    Assignments and Homework
        Purposes for Assignments
        Guidelines for Using Assignments
    Memorizing
    Reviewing
Summary
Suggested Reading
Posttest

RATIONALE

In this module we consider teaching methods that are basically expository in nature, such as lecturing, whole-class discussion and recitation, questioning, and demonstrating. All are largely teacher-centered; their basic purpose is to deliver information to students. Although strategies presented in this module are somewhat easier to implement than student-centered strategies, because classroom control is more easily managed, they are no less difficult to master. As a consequence, there are, perhaps, more boring classes taught by ineffective teachers using teacher-centered approaches than there are by ineffective teachers using student-centered approaches.

Consider again the potential strengths and weaknesses of teacher-centered instruction, as presented in Figure 6.1 of Module 6. The strengths include that much content can be covered within a short span of time, that the teacher has great control over the content covered and the time allotted, and that student achievement of specific content is predictable and manageable. The weaknesses include that the sources of student motivation are mostly extrinsic, that students have little control over pacing and make few important decisions about their learning, that opportunity for divergent or creative thinking is lacking, and that student self-esteem may be inadequately served.

Thus, to use teacher-centered instructional strategies effectively, it is advisable for you to do two things: (1) become skilled in their use, and (2) either mix them with strategies that are more student-centered or make the strategies themselves more student-centered. To help you in these tasks, in this module the guidelines for using teacher-centered instructional strategies have been prepared to make such strategies more student-centered.

In addition, in this module we discuss the importance of ensuring equality in the classroom, present guidelines for the use of assignments and homework, and discuss the significance of students memorizing and reviewing material that is being studied.

SPECIFIC OBJECTIVES

At the completion of this module, you should be able to:

1. Demonstrate your skill in the use of teacher talk, formal and informal.
2. Recognize the inherent dangers in using teacher talk.
3. Demonstrate your skill in the preparation and use of questioning as an instructional strategy.
4. Describe techniques for using student recitations effectively.
5. Effectively use the classroom demonstration.
6. Help students decide what and how to memorize.
7. Effectively handle questions from students.
8. Describe procedures for conducting review sessions.
9. Demonstrate your awareness of the importance of equality in the classroom and of ways of ensuring it.
10. Demonstrate your knowledge of why and how assignments and homework are important tools for learning.

MODULE TEXT

Perhaps no other strategy is used more by teachers than teacher talk, both formal and informal. Therefore, we begin this module with a presentation of guidelines for use of that indispensable and significantly important instructional strategy.

Teacher Talk: Formal and Informal

Teacher talk encompasses both lecturing *to* students and discussions *with* students. A lecture is considered formal teacher talk, whereas a teacher-led discussion is considered informal teacher talk.

Cautions about Using Teacher Talk

Whether formal or informal, teacher talk has several risks associated with it. Perhaps the most important is from talking too much. If a teacher talks too much, the significance of his or her words may be lost, because some students will tune the teacher out.

Another risk is from talking too fast. Students can hear faster than they can understand what is heard. It is a good idea to remind yourself to talk slowly and to check for student comprehension, frequently.

A third risk is not being heard or understood. Sometimes teachers talk in too low a pitch, or use words that are not understood by many of the students, or both. You should vary the pitch of your voice, and stop and help students with their understanding of new vocabulary.

A fourth risk is believing that students have learned something just because you told them about it. From the Learning Experiences Ladder (Module 6, Figure 6.3), remember that although verbal communication is an important form of communication, it is the least effective form because of its reliance on abstract symbols. Teacher talk relies on words, as well as on listening, a skill not mastered by many students.

Related to that risk is yet another one, believing that students have attained a skill or have learned something that was taught previously, by you or by another teacher. During any talk (formal or informal), rather than assuming that your students know something, you should make sure they know it. For example, if the discussion and a student activity that follows involves a thinking skill, then you will want to make sure that students know how to use that skill.

Still another risk is when a teacher speaks in a humdrum monotone. Students need teachers whose voices exude enthusiasm and excitement about the subject and about teaching and learning. Enthusiasm is contagious. With a voice that demonstrates enthusiasm for teaching and learning, you will do better at motivating your students.

Keep these cautions in mind as you study the general and specific guidelines for productively and effectively using teacher-talk strategies.

Teacher Talk: General Guidelines

Certain principles should be followed whether your teacher talk is formal or informal:

1. Begin the talk with an advance organizer. Advance organizers (discussed in Module 2) are introductions that mentally prepare students for a study by helping them make connections with material already learned—a comparative organizer—or by providing students with a conceptual arrangement of what is to be learned—an expository organizer. For example, an advance organizer can be a brief introduction or statement about the main idea you intend to convey and how it is related to other aspects of the students' learning, or it can be a conceptual map of the topic, or it can be a presentation of a discrepancy. Preparing an organizer helps you plan and organize the sequence of ideas, and its presentation helps students organize their own learning and become motivated to learn. An advance organizer can also make their learning meaningful by providing important connections between what they already know and what is being learned.

2. Plan your talk so that it has a beginning and an end, with a logical order between. During the process of your talk, you should reinforce your words with visuals. These visuals may include writing unfamiliar terms on the board and using prepared graphs, charts, photographs, and various audiovisuals.

3. Consider the pacing of your talk. It should move briskly, but not too fast. The ability to pace your instruction will improve with experience. Until you have perfected your skill in pacing lessons—the tendency among many beginning teachers is to talk too fast and too much—you should constantly remind yourself during lessons to slow down and provide silent pauses and frequent checks for student comprehension. Specifically, your talk should:

- Be brisk, though not too fast, but with occasional slow downs to change the pace and to check for student comprehension.
- Be adequately paced to allow students time to make notes and to ask questions.
- Have a time plan. A talk planned for 10 minutes, if interesting to students, will probably take longer. If not interesting to them, it will probably take less than the planned time. When that is the case, problems in classroom control can be expected.

4.   Encourage student participation during your talk. Their active participation enhances their learning. This encouragement can be planned as questions that you ask, or as time allowed for students to comment and ask questions, or as a conceptual outline or concept map that students complete during the talk.

5.   Make sure your talk has a clear ending, followed by another activity (during the same or next class period) that will help secure the learning. As for all lessons, you want to strive for planning a clear and mesmerizing beginning, an involving lesson body, and a firm and meaningful closure.

Teacher Talk: Specific Guidelines

Specific guidelines for the use of teacher talk are:

1.   *Purposes for teacher talk*. Teacher talk, formal or informal, can be useful to:

- Discuss the progress of a unit of study.
- Explain an inquiry.
- Introduce a unit of study.
- Present a problem.
- Promote student inquiry or critical thinking.
- Provide a transition from one unit of study to the next.
- Provide information otherwise unobtainable to students.
- Share the teacher's experiences.
- Summarize a problem.
- Summarize a unit of study.
- Teach a thinking skill.

2.   *Objectives of the talk*. Your talk should focus on one central idea. The learning objectives, not too many for one talk, should be made clear to the students; otherwise, they may never know what you are talking about.

3.   *Informal vs. formal talk*. Although an occasional formal "cutting edge" lecture may be appropriate for some high school classes, spontaneous interactive informal talks of 5 to 12 minutes are preferable for most classes. A teacher should never give period-long lectures with no teacher-student interaction. Remember also, today's students are of the "video generation" and are used to commercial breaks. After about 10 minutes into many lessons, student attention is likely to begin to stray. You need to have elements planned that will recapture their attention. These include:

- Analogies to help connect the topic to students' experiences.
- Verbal cues, such as voice inflections.
- Planned pauses to allow information to sink in.
- Humor.
- Visual cues, such as the use of slides, excerpts from videodiscs, real objects (realia), or body gestures.
- Sensory cues, such as eye contact and proximity, (as in moving around the room, or casually and gently touching a student on the shoulder without interrupting your talk).

Perhaps most useful as a strategy for recapturing student attention is to change to an entirely different strategy or modality. For example, from teacher talk (teacher-centered strategy) you would change to a student activity (student-centered strategy). Notice that changing from a lecture (mostly teacher talk) to a teacher-led discussion (mostly more teacher talk) would not be changing from an entirely different modality. Figure 7.1 provides a comparison of two different changes. As a generalization, with most classes you will want to plan to change the learning activities about every 10 to 15 minutes. This means that in a 60-minute class period, for example, you should probably plan three or four learning activities, with some that are teacher-centered and others that are more student-centered. You could have several activities concurrently being performed by individuals, dyads, and small groups of students (i.e., multitasking or multilevel instruction).

4.   *Using notes as a guide for your talk.* Planning your talk and preparing notes to be used during formal and informal teacher talk is important—just as important as is implementing the talk with visuals. There is nothing wrong with using notes during your teaching. You can carry them on a clipboard as you move around the room. Your notes for a formal talk can first be prepared in narrative form; for class use, though, they should be reduced to an outline form. Talks to students should always be from an outline, never read from prose. (The only time that the teacher's reading from prose is appropriate is when reading aloud to the class for the purpose of helping the students with their language arts skills.)

Figure 7.1   Comparison of Efforts to Recapture Student Attention by Changing the Instructional Strategy

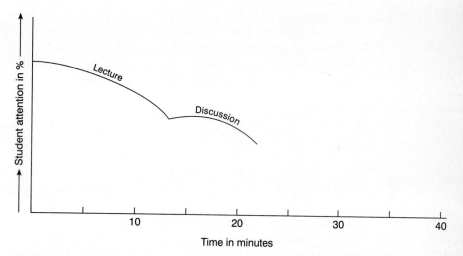

Example 1: Changing teacher talk (lecture) to more teacher talk (teacher-led discussion)

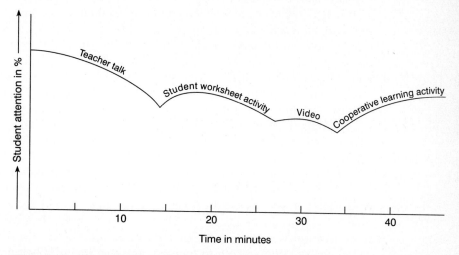

Example 2: Changing from teacher talk (teacher-centered activity) to cooperative learning activity (student-centered activity)

In your outline, use color coding with abbreviated visual cues to yourself. You will eventually develop your own coding system—though whatever coding system you use, keep it simple or else you may forget what the codes are for. Consider these examples of coding:

- Where transitions of ideas occur or where you want to allow silent moments for ideas to sink in, mark *P* for *pause*, or *T* for *transition*, and *S* for moments of *silence*.
- Where a slide or other visual aid will be displayed, mark *AV* for *audiovisual*.
- Where you intend to stop and ask a question, mark *TQ* for teacher questions and *SQ* or *?* where you want to stop and allow time for *student questions*.
- Where you plan to have a discussion, mark *D*, and mark *SG* where you plan *small-group* work and *L* where you plan to switch to a *laboratory activity*.
- For *summaries*, *reviews*, and *comprehension checks*, mark *R* or *CS*.

5. *Rehearsing the talk*. Rehearse your talk using a camcorder or an audiorecorder, or rehearse it while talking into a mirror. Remember to allow more time for implementation than it takes for rehearsal. You may want to include a time plan for each subtopic to allow you to gauge your timing during implementation of the talk.

6. *Avoiding a race through your talk solely to complete it by class dismissal time*. It is more important that students understand some of your talk than that you cover it all and they understand none of it. If you don't get finished, continue it later.

7. *Augmenting your talk with multisensory stimulation*. Your presentation should not overly rely on verbal communication. When using visuals, such as videodisc excerpts or overhead transparencies, do not think that you must be constantly talking; after clearly explaining the purpose of a visual, give students sufficient time to look at it, to think about it, and to ask questions about it. The visual is new to the students, so give them time for it to sink in.

8. *Content of your talk*. Rather than simply rehashing content from the textbook, the content of your talk should supplement and enhance that found in the student textbook. Students may never read their book if you tell them in an interesting and condensed fashion everything that is in it.

9. *Your voice*. Your voice should be pleasant and interesting to listen to, rather than a steady, boring, monotone or a constantly shrieking, irritating, high pitch. On the other hand, it is good to show enthusiasm for what you are talking about. Use dramatic voice inflections to emphasize important points and meaningful body language to give students a visual focus.

10. *Vocabulary of the talk and opportunity to help students with word morphology*. Words used should be easily understood by the students, though you should still model professionalism and help students develop their vocabulary. During your lesson planning, predict when you are likely to use a word that is new to most students, and plan to stop to ask for a student to help explain its meaning and perhaps demonstrate its derivation. Help students with word meaning. This helps students with their remembering. Remember, regardless of grade level or your teaching field, all teachers are language arts teachers. Knowledge of word morphology is an important component of skilled reading; this includes the ability to gain information about a word's meaning and pronunciation, as well as the ability to generate new words from prefixes, roots, and suffixes. For example, when introducing to students the word *hermaphrodite*, the biology teacher has the opportunity to teach a bit of Greek mythology in the process of helping students with the meaning of that important term in biology, through showing students the origin of the word's prefix (Hermes, or Mercury, the messenger of the gods) and suffix (Aphrodites, or Venus, goddess of love and beauty). And taking time to teach a bit of Greek mythology affords the biology teacher an opportunity to capture the interest of a few more students.

For some students, each subject in the school schedule is like being in a foreign language class. That is certainly true for students who have limited proficiency in English. For those students, teacher talk, especially formal teacher talk, should be used sparingly, if at all. General biology, as typically taught at the ninth or tenth grade, for example, has been said to contain more new words than does a course in beginning French. Every teacher has the responsibility of helping students learn how to learn, and that includes helping students develop their word comprehension skills, reading skills, and thinking skills.

11.   *Lecturing only when appropriate.* You may not need to lecture—sometimes a handout will do. Some students can read and understand faster than they can listen and understand. For other students, however, talking to them may be better insurance that they "got" the information than is expecting them to read a handout. Remember, though, a formal period-long non-interactive lecture, common in some college teaching, is inappropriate when teaching middle school and secondary school students. While student teaching, if you have doubt or questions about your selection and use of a particular strategy, discuss your concern with your cooperating teacher or your university supervisor or both.

12.   *Providing students with a conceptual outline or a study guide.* An outline of major ideas of the talk, with lines connecting them (the beginning of a concept map, which students can complete), or a study guide (an expository organizer) can facilitate students' understanding and organization of the content of your talk. Note that the outline should be a skeletal one—not a complete copy of the talk.

13.   *Using familiar examples and analogies to help students make relevant connections (bridges).* Connect the talk with ideas and events with which the students are already familiar. The most effective talk is one that makes frequent and meaningful connections between what students already know and what they are learning, and that bridges what they are learning with what they have experienced in real life.

14.   *Considering student diversity.* While preparing your talk, consider students who are culturally and linguistically different and who have special needs. Personalize the talk for them by planning meaningful analogies and examples, and relevant audio and visual displays.

15.   *Establishing eye contact frequently.* Your primary eye contact always should be with your students. Only momentarily should you look at your notes, your visuals, the writing board, and any other objects in the classroom. With practice, you can learn to visually scan a class of thirty students, establishing eye contact with each student about once a minute. To "establish" eye contact means that the student is aware that you are looking at him or her. Frequent eye contact can have two major benefits. First, as you "read" a student's body posture and facial expressions, you obtain clues about that student's attentiveness and comprehension. Second, eye contact helps to establish rapport between you and a student. Be alert, though, for students who are from cultures where eye contact is infrequent or unwanted and could have negative consequences.

Frequent eye contact is easier when using an overhead projector than when using the writing board. When using a writing board, you have to turn at least partially away from your audience, and you may also have to pace back and forth, moving from writing on the board to a position nearer to the students.

Now, to review this information about the use of the lecture and to practice your skill in its use, do Exercise 7.1.

EXERCISE 7.1
The Lecture

• • • • • •

Summary Review and Practice

Instructions: The purpose of this exercise is to provide a summary review to check your comprehension of this important, often used, and often abused teaching strategy. Answer each of the following questions and then share your responses with your classmates.

1. How does the lecture differ from informal teacher talk?

2. Although sometimes a useful technique, lecturing should be used sparingly in high school classes and even less for junior high and middle school classes. Why is it not as useful as some other strategies?

3. Specifically, when might you use a formal lecture?

4. What can a lecturer do to arouse and maintain interest in the lecture?

5. While planning a lecture, what principles should be kept in mind?

6. Identify at least five things you can do to make a lecture successful.

7. Thinking back to the classes given by the best lecturer in your college experience, what did that professor do that made his or her lectures better than average?

8. Thinking of a lecture or informal talk given by one of your current professors or colleagues, what use of aids did the lecturer use to spice up the lecture? What devices might have been used that were not? If you were the lecturer, would you have done it differently? If so, explain how.

9. For a specific grade level (identify) prepare a major behavioral objective for a topic in your field. Identify the major points that you would try to make and how you would try to get those points across in a lecture designed to support that major objective.

    Field:

    Grade level:

    Topic:

    Major objective:

    Major points: *Method of achieving:*

Estimate of amount of time needed to present this lecture:

10. Now, implement the lecture of the previous item (number 9) to a group of your peers and obtain their feedback, using the criteria of number 8 for that feedback. If the equipment is available, you may wish to videotape your lecture so you can watch it and evaluate it yourself. Upon completion of implementing the lecture and obtaining evaluative feedback about it, prepare a self-evaluation of the lecture, again using the criteria of number 8. Share this self-evaluation with your course instructor.

Demonstrations

Students like demonstrations, especially ones that are performed by the teacher or by a guest speaker. They like them because the demonstrator is actively engaged in a learning activity rather than merely verbalizing about it. Demonstrations can be used in teaching any subject, at any grade level, and for a variety of purposes. A role-playing demonstration can be used in a social studies class. A mathematics teacher demonstrates the steps in using the Pythagorean theorem. An English teacher demonstrates clustering to students ready for a creative writing assignment. A science teacher demonstrates what happens when a weak acid and a weak base are combined.

Purposes for a Demonstration

A demonstration can be designed to serve any of the following purposes:

- To introduce a lesson or unit of study in a way that grabs the students' attention.
- To review.
- To bring an unusual closure to a lesson or unit of study.
- To assist in the recognition of a solution to an existing problem.
- To demonstrate a thinking skill.
- To establish problem recognition.
- To give students opportunity for vicarious participation in active learning.
- To illustrate a particular point of content.
- To reduce potential safety hazards (where the teacher demonstrates, using materials that are too dangerous for student use).
- To save time and resources (as opposed to the entire class doing that which is demonstrated).
- To set up a discrepancy recognition.

Guidelines for Using a Demonstration

When planning a demonstration, you should consider each of the following:

1. *Mode.* Decide what is the most effective way to conduct the demonstration (e.g., as a verbal or a silent demonstration; by a student or by the teacher; by the teacher with a student helper; to the entire class or to small groups).
2. *Visibility.* Be sure that the demonstration is visible to all students. For this purpose some schools have installed overhead mirrors. Where demonstrations are more frequent and financial resources are available, classrooms use overhead videocameras with large screen television monitors.
3. *Practice.* Practice with the materials and procedure before demonstrating to the students.
4. *Murphy's Law.* Consider what might go wrong, because if anything can, it probably will.
5. *Pacing.* Consider your pacing of the demonstration, allowing for enough student wait-see and think time.
6. *Beginning and ending.* At the start of the demonstration, explain its purpose and the learning objectives. Remember this adage: tell them what they will see, show them, and then tell them what they saw. As with any lesson, plan your closure, and allow time for questions and discussion.
7. *Comprehension checks.* During the demonstration, as in other types of teacher talk, use frequent stops to check for student understanding.
8. *Lighting.* Consider the use of special lighting to highlight the demonstration. For example, a slide projector can be used as a spotlight.
9. *Safety considerations.* Be sure that the demonstration table and area are free of unnecessary objects that could distract, be in the way, or pose a safety hazard. With potentially hazardous demonstrations, such as might occur in teaching science or shop, you should model proper safety precautions: wear safety goggles, have fire-safety equipment at hand, and place a protective shield between the demonstration table and nearby students.

Questioning

An instructional strategy of fundamental importance to both the access and delivery modes is questioning. You will use questioning for so many purposes that to teach effectively you must become skilled in its use.

Purposes for Using Questioning

You should always adapt the type and form of each question to the purpose for which it is asked. The purposes of questions can be divided into five categories:

1. *To politely give instructions.* For example, "Anthony, would you please turn out the lights so we can show the slides?" You can also use rhetorical questions to regain student attention and maintain classroom control. For example, "Juan, would you please attend to your own work?"
2. *To review and remind students of classroom procedures.* For example, if students continue to talk without first raising their hands and being recognized by you, you can stop the lesson and ask, "Class I think we need to review the procedure for answering my questions. What is the procedure for talking?"
3. *To gather information.* For example, "How many of you have finished the exercise?" To find out whether a student knows something, you might ask, "Yvonne, can you please tell us what a thesaurus is?"
4. *To discover student interests or experiences.* For example, "How many of you would be interested in going on a field trip to the state legislature?" or "How many of you have already been to the marine aquarium?"
5. *To guide student thinking and learning.* This category of questioning is the primary focus of our attention in this module. Questions in this category are used to:
   - Clarify a student response.
   - Develop appreciation.
   - Develop student thinking.
   - Diagnose learning difficulty.
   - Emphasize major points.
   - Encourage students.
   - Establish rapport.
   - Evaluate learning.
   - Give practice in expression.
   - Help students in their own metacognition.
   - Help students interpret materials.
   - Help students organize materials.
   - Probe deeper into a student's thinking.
   - Provide drill and practice.
   - Provide review.
   - Show agreement or disagreement.
   - Show relationships, such as cause and effect.

Types of Cognitive Questioning

Before we go further, let's define, describe, and provide examples for each type of cognitive question you will use in teaching. Then, in the section that follows, we focus your attention on the levels of cognitive questions. The types of cognitive questions include the following.

Clarifying question.   A clarifying question is used to gain more information from a student to help the teacher better understand a student's ideas, feelings, and thought processes. Examples of clarifying questions are: "Would you please explain to us what you mean by your statement that the 'the author was hypocritical'?" "What I hear you saying is that you would rather work alone than in your group. Is that correct?" Research has shown there to be a strong and positive correlation between student learning and development of metacognitive skills and the teacher's use of questions that ask students for clarification.[1] In addition, by seeking clarification the teacher is likely to be demonstrating an interest in the student and her or his thinking.

Convergent-thinking question.   Convergent-thinking questions (also called narrow questions) are low-order thinking questions that have a singular answer (such as recall questions). Examples of convergent questions are: "If the radius of a circle is 20 feet, what is the circle's circumference?" "What is the subject of this sentence?"

Cueing question.   If you ask a question to which, after sufficient wait-time, no students respond or to which their inadequate responses indicate they need more information, then you can ask a question that cues the answer or response you are seeking. In essence, you are going backward in your questioning sequence in order to cue the students. For example, if a biology teacher asks her students "How many legs do crayfish, lobsters, and shrimp have?" and there is no accurate response, then she might cue the answer with the following information and question: "The class to which those animals belong is class Decapoda. Does that give you a clue about the number of legs they have?"

Divergent-thinking question.   Divergent-thinking questions (also known as broad, reflective, or thought questions) are open-ended (i.e., usually having no singularly correct answer) questions of high-order thinking. They require students to think creatively, to leave the comfortable confines of the known, and to reach out into the unknown. Examples of questions that require divergent thinking are: "What measures could be taken to improve the traffic problem at King High School?" "In view of the arguments presented by Senator Merlino and the National Rifle Association, do you think that the government should ban Saturday night specials?"

Evaluative question.   Some types of questions, whether convergent or divergent, require students to place a value on something, and these are sometimes referred to as evaluative questions. If the teacher and the students all agree on certain premises, then the evaluative question would also be a convergent question. If original assumptions differ, then the response to the evaluative question would be more subjective, and therefore that evaluative question would be divergent. Examples of evaluative questions are: "Should the United States send ground forces to Bosnia?" "Should women be allowed to choose to have abortions?"

Focus question.   This is any question that is designed to focus student thinking. For example, the evaluative question "Should women be allowed to choose to have abortions?" becomes a focus question when the teacher asking it is attempting to focus student attention on the social issue involved.

Probing question.   Similar to a clarifying questions, the probing question requires student thinking to go beyond superficial "first-answer" or single-word responses. Examples of probing questions are: "Why, John, do you think that every citizen has the right to say what he or she believes?" "Could you give us an example?"

Levels of Cognitive Questions

As the teacher, questions posed by you are cues to your students about the level of thinking expected of them—ranging from the lowest level of mental operation, requiring simple recall of knowledge (convergent thinking), to the highest, requiring divergent thought and application of that thought. It is important that you (1) are aware of the levels of thinking, (2) under-

---

[1] Arthur L. Costa, *The School as a Home for the Mind* (Palatine, IL: Skylight 1991), p. 63.

stand the importance of attending to student thinking from low to higher levels of operation, and (3) understand that what may be a matter of simple recall of information for one student may require a higher-order mental activity for another student, such as figuring something out by deduction.

You should structure and sequence your questions in a way that is designed to guide students to higher levels of thinking. Consider these three levels of questioning and thinking:

1. *Lowest level (the data-input phase): gathering and recalling information.* At this level, questions are designed to solicit from students concepts, information, feelings, or experiences that were gained in the past and stored in memory. Key words and desired behaviors include: *complete, count, define, describe, identify, list, match, name, observe, recall, recite,* and *select.*
2. *Intermediate level (the data-processing phase): processing information.* At this level, questions are designed to draw relationships of cause and effect, as well as to synthesize, analyze, summarize, compare, contrast, or to classify data. Key words and desired behaviors include: *analyze, classify, compare, contrast, distinguish, explain, group, infer, make an analogy, organize, plan,* and *synthesize.*
3. *Highest level (the data-output phase): applying and evaluating in new situations.* Questions at this level encourage students to think intuitively, creatively and hypothetically, to use their imaginations, to expose a value system, or to make a judgment. Key words and desired behaviors include: *apply a principle, build a model, evaluate, extrapolate, forecast, generalize, hypothesize, imagine, judge, predict,* and *speculate.*[2]

You should use the type of question that is best suited for the purpose and also use a variety of different levels of questions. Remember, you must structure questions in a way intended to move student thinking to higher levels. When teachers use higher-level questions, their students tend to score higher both on tests of critical thinking and on standardized tests of achievement.[3]

Developing your skill in the use of questioning requires attention to detail. The guidelines that follow provide that detail, and the exercises should prove useful for developing your skill in the use of this important instructional strategy.

Guidelines for Using Questioning

As we have emphasized many times, your goals are to help your students learn how to solve problems, to make decisions and value judgments, to think creatively and critically, and to feel good about themselves and their learning. You are not there simply to fill their minds with bits and pieces of information. How you construe your questions and how you carry out your questioning strategy are important to the realization of these goals.

Preparing Questions

When preparing questions, consider the following:

1. *Cognitive questions should be planned, thoughtfully worded, and written into your lesson plan.* Thoughtful preparation of questions helps to ensure that they are clear and specific, that the vocabulary is appropriate, and that each question matches its purpose. Incorporate

[2]Arthur L. Costa, *The Enabling Behaviors* (Orangevale, CA: Search Models Unlimited, 1989). This three-tiered model of thinking has been described variously by others. For example, in Elliot Eisner's *The Educational Imagination*, 3rd ed. (New York: Macmillan, 1994), the levels are referred to as "descriptive," "interpretive," and "evaluative." For a comparison of thinking models, see Arthur L. Costa, *The School as a Home for the Mind* (Palatine, IL: Skylight, 1991), p. 44. You probably recognize the similarity between these three levels of questions and the six levels of thinking from Bloom's taxonomy of cognitive objectives. For your daily use of questioning, it is probably more practical to think and behave in terms of these three levels.

[3]See, for example, B. Newton, "Theoretical Basis for Higher Cognitive Questioning—An Avenue to Critical Thinking," *Education* 98(3):286–290 (March–April 1978). See also D. Redfield and E. Rousseau, "A Meta-analysis of Experimental Research on Teacher Questioning Behavior," *Review of Educational Research* 51(2):237–245 (Summer 1981).

questions into all of your lessons as instructional devices, welcomed pauses, attention grabbers, and checks for student comprehension. Thoughtful teachers even plan questions to ask specific students.

2. *Questions should be matched with their purposes.* Carefully planning the questions allows them to be sequenced and worded to match the levels of cognitive thinking expected of students.

To help students in developing their thinking skills, you need to demonstrate higher-level thinking. To demonstrate, you must use terminology that is specific and that provides students with examples of experiences consonant with the meanings of the cognitive words. You need to demonstrate this every day, so that students learn the cognitive terminology.[4] Here are three examples:

Poor	*Better*
"How else might you do it?"	"How could you *apply* . . . ?"
"Are you going to get quiet?	"If we are going to hear what Mark has to say, what do you need to do?"
"How do you know that is the case?"	"What *evidence* do you have that that is the case?"

Implementing Questions

Careful preparation of questions is one part of the skill in questioning. Implementation is the other part. Here are guidelines for effective implementation of this strategy:

1. *Avoid bombarding students with too much teacher talk.* Sometimes teachers talk too much. This could be especially true for teachers who are nervous, such as might be the case for many during the initial weeks of student teaching. Knowledge of the guidelines presented here will be helpful in avoiding that syndrome. Remind yourself to be quiet after you ask a question that you have carefully formulated. Sometimes, especially when a question hasn't been carefully planned by the teacher, the teacher asks the question and then, with a slight change in wording, asks it again, or asks several questions one after another. That is too much verbiage—"shotgun" questioning only confuses students, while allowing too little time for students to think.

2. *After asking a question, provide students with adequate time to think.* Too many teachers, knowing the subject better than the students and having given thought to it before class, fail to allow students sufficient time to think after asking a question. And, by the time the students have reached the middle grades (or sooner), they have learned pretty well how to play the "game"—they know that if they remain silent long enough the teacher will probably answer his or her own question. After asking a well-worded question, you should remain quiet for awhile, allowing students time to think and respond. If you wait long enough, they usually will.

After asking a question, how long should you wait before you do something? You should wait at least 2 seconds, and as long as 9. Stop reading now to look at your watch or a clock to get a feeling for how long 2 seconds is. Then observe how long 9 seconds is. Did 9 seconds seem a long time? Because most of us are not used to silence in the classroom, 2 seconds of silence can seem quite long, and 9 seconds can seem like an eternity. If, for some reason, students have not responded after a period of 2 to 9 seconds of this **wait time** (think time), then you can ask the question again (but don't reword an already carefully worded question, or else students are likely to think it is a new question). Pause for several seconds. Then if you still have not received a response you can call on a student, then another, if necessary, after sufficient wait time. Soon you will get a response that can be built upon. Never answer your own question!

3. *Practice calling on all students, not just the bright or the slow, not just the boys or the girls, not just those in the front of the room, but all of them.* To call on all students takes concentrated effort on your part, but the practice is extremely important.

[4]Costa, 1991, p. 110.

4.   *Give the same amount of wait time to all students.* This, too, will require concentrated effort on your part, but it also is important to do. A teacher who waits for less time when calling on a slow student, or students of one gender more than the other, is showing a prejudice or a lack of confidence in certain students, both of which are detrimental to a teacher striving to establish a positive, equal, and safe classroom environment for all students. Show confidence in all students, and never discriminate by expecting less or more from some than from others.

5.   *When you ask questions, don't let students randomly shout out their answers; instead, require them to raise their hands and be called on before they respond.* Establish that procedure and stick with it. This helps to ensure that you call on all students equally, fairly distributing your interactions with all the students. This procedure also ensures that girls are not given less attention than boys, a common tendency because boys usually are more outgoing. Even at the college level, male students tend to be more vocal than female students and, when allowed by the instructor, tend to outtalk and interrupt their female peers. Every teacher has the responsibility to guarantee a nonbiased and equal distribution of interaction time in the classroom.

6.   *Use strong praise sparingly.* Use of strong praise is sometimes okay, especially when working with students who are different and when asking questions of simple recall. But when you want students to think divergently and creatively, you should be stingy with your use of strong praise for student responses. Strong praise from a teacher tends to terminate divergent and creative thinking.

One of your goals is to help students find intrinsic sources of motivation, that is, an inner drive or desire that causes them to want to learn. Use of strong praise tends to build conformity because it causes students to depend on outside forces (i.e., the giver of praise) for their worth rather than upon themselves. An example of a strong praise, called active acceptance, is when a teacher responds to a student answer with "That's right! Very good." On the other hand, a response such as "Okay, that seems to be one possibility," called passive acceptance, keeps the window open for further thinking, particularly for higher-level, divergent thinking.

Another example of passive acceptance is one used in brainstorming sessions, when the teacher says, "After asking the question and giving you some time to think about it, I will hear your ideas and record them on the board." Only after all student responses have been heard and recorded does the class begins its consideration of each. In the classroom that kind of nonjudgmental acceptance of all ideas will generate a great deal of high-level thought.[5]

7.   *Encourage students to ask questions about content and process.* There is no such thing as a dumb question. Sometimes students, like everyone else, ask questions that could have just as easily been looked up. Those questions can consume precious class time. For a teacher, it can be frustrating. A teacher's initial reaction might be to brush off that type of question with sarcasm, assuming that the student is too lazy to look up an answer. In such instances, you are advised to think before responding and then respond kindly and professionally—though in the busy life of a classroom teacher that may not always be so easy to do. Be assured, however, that there is a reason for a student's question. Perhaps the student is signaling a need for recognition.

In large schools, it is sometimes easy for a student to feel alone and insignificant (although this seems less the case with schools that use a school-within-a-school plan, discussed in Module 1). When a student makes an effort to interact with you, that can be a positive sign. So, gauge carefully your responses to those efforts. If a student question is really off track, out of order, and out of context with the content of the lesson, a possible response could be: "That is an interesting question [or comment] and I would very much like to talk with you more about it. Could we meet at lunchtime or before or after school?" (Note: Some teachers conduct a brown-bag lunch session each day in which students are welcomed to come to their classrooms to share lunch and talk about anything.)

Student questions can and should be used as springboards for further questions, discussion, and investigations. Students should be encouraged to ask questions that challenge the

---

[5]For further discussion of research findings about the use of praise and rewards in teaching, see B. Joyce and B. Showers, *Student Achievement through Staff Development* (New York: Longman, 1988); and M. Lepper and D. Green (eds.), *The Hidden Cost of Rewards: New Perspectives on the Psychology of Human Motivation* (New York: Erlbaum, 1978). See Module 5, Suggested Reading, for several articles about the use of praise versus encouragement.

textbook, the process, or another person's statements, and they should be encouraged to seek the facts or evidence behind a statement.

8.   *Being able to ask questions may be more important than having right answers.* Knowledge is derived from asking questions. Being able to recognize problems and formulate questions is a skill as well as the key to problem solving and critical thinking skill development. You have a responsibility to encourage students to formulate questions, and to help them word their questions in such a way that tentative answers can be sought. That is the process necessary to build a base of knowledge that can be called upon over and over as ways to link, interpret, and explain new information in new situations.[6]

9.   *Questioning is the cornerstone to critical thinking and real-world problem solving.* With real-world problem solving, there are usually no absolute right answers. Rather than "correct" answers, some are better than others. Generally, a person with a problem first recognizes the problem and then formulates a question about that problem (e.g., "Should I buy a house or rent?" "Should I date this person or not?" "Should I take this job or not?" "Which car should I buy?" "Should I abuse drugs or not?"). The next step is to collect data. Finally, the person arrives at a temporarily acceptable answer to the problem, while realizing that at some later time new data may dictate a review of that answer. For example, if an astronomer believes she has discovered a new galaxy, there is no textbook (or teacher) to which she may refer to find out if she is right. On the basis of her self-confidence in identifying the problem, asking questions, collecting enough data, and arriving at a tentative conclusion based on those data, she assumes that for now her conclusion is safe.

10.   *Avoid bluffing an answer to a question for which you do not have an answer.* Nothing will cause you to lose credibility with students any quicker than when you fake an answer. There is nothing wrong with admitting that you do not know. It helps students realize that you are human. It helps them maintain an adequate self-esteem, realizing that they are okay. What is important is that you know where and how to find possible answers and that you help students develop that same knowledge and those same skills.

Exercises 7.2 through 7.7 are designed to aid your understanding and to develop your skill in the use of questioning. Do those exercises now.

---

[6]Lauren B. Resnick and Leopold E. Klopfer (eds.), *Toward the Thinking Curriculum: Current Cognitive Research*, 1989 ASCD Yearbook (Alexandria, VA: Association for Supervision and Curriculum Development, 1989), p. 5

EXERCISE 7.2
Identifying the Cognitive Levels of Questions

• • • • • •

A Self-Check Exercise

Instructions: The purpose of this exercise is to test your understanding and recognition of the levels of questions. Mark each of the following questions with a:

- *1*, if it is at the lowest level—gathering and recalling data.
- *2*, if it requires the student to process data.
- *3*, if it is at the highest level of mental operation, requiring the student to apply or to evaluate data in a new situation.

Check your answers against the key that follows. Resolve problems by discussing them with your instructor and classmates.

____ 1. John, do you agree with Maria?

____ 2. How does the repetition in Bolero affect you?

____ 3. Do you believe that argument will hold up in the case of Swaziland?

____ 4. What must I multiply by in order to clear the fractions in this equation?

____ 5. Did O. Henry's trick ending make the story more interesting?

____ 6. How would you end the story?

____ 7. Who came out of the door, the lady or the tiger?

____ 8. How do the natural resources of the United States compare with those of China?

____ 9. If you were setting up the defenses of the colonies, where would you put the forts?

____ 10. In view of all the information we have, do you believe the union's sending out seventy thousand letters asking voters to defeat the six assemblymen was justified?

____ 11. What difference has an equal rights amendment made?

____ 12. Who was Otto Jespersen?

____ 13. Should a teacher who earns $32,000 a year be entitled to unemployment benefits during the summer months when school is not in session?

____ 14. What would you do in this situation if you were governor?

____ 15. What would have happened if Washington had decided to attack New Brunswick rather than Quebec?

____ 16. What would happen if you used H_2SO_4 instead of HCl?

____ 17. How would you set up the equation?

____ 18. Why did you like this poem better than the previous one?

____ 19. Which type of cell, animal or plant, has a cell wall?

____ 20. When $2N - 10 = 0$, what does N equal?

Answer Key

1. 2 (analyze, compare)	6. 3 (design)	11. 3 (generalize)	16. 3 (predict)
2. 3 (evaluate)	7. 1 (recall)	12. 1 (recall)	17. 2 (explain)
3. 3 (evaluate)	8. 2 (compare)	13. 3 (judge)	18. 3 (evaluate)
4. 1 (recall)	9. 3 (hypothesize)	14. 3 (design)	19. 1 (recall)
5. 3 (evaluate)	10. 3 (evaluate)	15. 3 (hypothesize)	20. 1 (simple recall)

EXERCISE 7.3

Observing the Cognitive Levels of Classroom Verbal Interaction

• • • • • •

Instructions: The purpose of this exercise is to develop your skill in recognizing the levels of classroom questions. Arrange to visit a secondary school classroom. In the spaces provided here, tally each time you hear a question (or statement) from the teacher that causes students to gather or recall information, to process information, or to apply or evaluate data. In the left-hand column you may want to write in additional key words to assist your memory. After your observation, compare and discuss the results of this exercise with your colleagues.

School and class visited: _____

Date of observation: _____

Level	Tallies of Level of Question or Statement
1. Recall level (key words: *complete, count, define, describe,* and so on.)	1.
2. Processing level (key words: *analyze, classify, compare,* and so on.)	2.
3. Application level (key words: *apply, build, evaluate,* and so on.)	3.

An Analysis of Good, Fair, and Poor Questions

• • • • • • •

A Self Check Test

Instructions: The purpose of this exercise is to practice your skill in analyzing questions. Evaluate each of the following questions by checking the Poor, Fair, or Good column for each question. Use the following code in the right column to indicate your reasons why:

A = Calls for no answer and is a pseudo question.
B = Asks for recall but little or no thinking.
C = Challenging, stimulating or discussion-provoking type of question that calls for high-level thinking, including reason and problem-solving.

Upon completion check your responses against the answer key and discuss any problems with your colleagues and instructor.

Questions	Poor	Fair	Good	Why?
1. In what region are major earthquakes located?				
2. According to the theory of isostasy, how would you describe our mountainous regions?				
3. What mineral will react with HCl to produce CO_2?				
4. What kind of rock is highly resistant to weathering?				
5. Will the continents look different in the future? Why?				
6. Who can describe what is a continental shelf?				
7. What caused the Industrial Revolution?				
8. What political scandal involved President Harding?				
9. This is a parallelogram, isn't it?				
10. Wouldn't you agree that the base angles of an isosceles triangle are congruent?				
11. In trying to determine the proof of this exercise, what would you suggest we examine at the outset?				
12. What conclusion can be drawn concerning the points of intersection of two graphs?				

Questions	Poor	Fair	Good	Why?
13. Why is pure water a poor conductor of electricity?				
14. How do fossils help explain the theory of plate tectonics?				
15. If Macbeth had told you about his encounter with the apparitions, what advice would you have offered?				
16. Who said, "If it were done when 'tis done, then 'twere well if it were done quickly"?				
17. In the poem "The Sick Rose," what do you think Blake means by "the invisible worm"?				
18. Should teachers censor the books that students read?				
19. Explain the phrase "ontogeny recapitulates phylogeny."				
20. Name the ten life functions.				
21. What living thing can live without air?				
22. What is chlorophyll?				
23. Explain the difference between RNA and DNA.				
24. Who developed the periodic table based on the fact that elements are functions of their atomic weight?				
25. Johnny, why aren't you in your seat?				

Answer Key

1. F, B	6. P, A	11. G, C	16. F, B	21. F, B
2. G, C	7. G, C	12. G, C	17. G, C	22. F, B
3. F, C	8. F, B	13. F, B	18. G, C	23. G, C
4. F, B	9. P, A	14. G, C	19. G, C	24. F, B
5. G, C	10. P, A	15. G, C	20. B	25. P, A

EXERCISE 7.5
Creating Cognitive Questions

• • • • • •

Instructions: The purpose of this exercise is to provide practice in writing cognitive questions. Read the following example of verse. Then, from that verse, compose three questions about it that would cause students to identify, list, and recall; three that would cause students to analyze, compare, and explain; and three that would cause students to predict, apply, and hypothesize. Share and check questions with your peers.

We Are One

Truth, love, peace, and beauty,
We have sought apart
    but will find within, as our
Moods—explored, shared,
      questioned, and accepted—
Together become one and all.

Through life my friends
We can travel together,
for we now know
each could go it alone.

To assimilate our efforts into one,
While growing in accepting,
and trusting, and sharing the
    individuality of the other,
Is truly to enjoy God's greatest gift—
Feeling—knowing love and compassion.

Through life my friends
We are together,
for we must know
we are one.

R. D. Kellough

Recall Questions

   1. (to *identify*)

   2. (to *list*)

   3. (to *recall*)

Processing Questions

   1. (to *analyze*)

   2. (to *compare*)

   3. (to *explain*)

Application Questions

   1. (to *predict*)

   2. (to *apply*)

   3. (to *hypothesize*)

EXERCISE 7.6

Analyzing the Level of Questions in Course Materials

• • • • • •

Instructions: The purpose of this exercise is to examine course materials for the levels of questions presented to students. Examine a student textbook (or other instructional material) for a subject and grade level you intend to teach, specifically examining questions posed for the students, perhaps found at the ends of chapters. Also examine workbooks, examinations, instructional packages, and any other printed or electronic (i.e., computer-software programs) materials used by students in the course. Complete the exercise as follows, then share your findings with other members of your class.

1. Materials examined (include date of publication and target students):

2. Examples of lowest-level (recall level) questions found:

3. Examples of intermediate-level (processing level) questions found:

4. Examples of highest-level three (application level) questions found:

5. Approximate percentages of questions at each level:

    Lowest = ___%   Intermediate = ___%   Highest = ___%

6. One study reports that "of more than 61,000 questions found in teacher guides, student workbooks, and tests for nine history textbooks, more than 95 percent were devoted to factual recall."[*] In a recent analysis of eight middle-grade science textbooks and their end-of-chapter questions, 87.5 percent of those questions were at the input level, and 78.8 percent of all textbook questions were at the input level.[+] How do your data from this exercise compare with those results?

7. Did you find evidence of question-level sequencing? If so, describe it.

8. After sharing and discussing with your classmates, what do you conclude from this exercise?

[*]California State Department of Education, *Caught in the Middle* (Sacramento, CA: Author, 1987), p. 13.

[+]Edward L. Pizzini et al., "The Questioning Level of Select Middle School Science Textbooks," *School Science and Mathematics* 92(2):74–78 (February 1992).

An Exercise in the Use of Questioning

• • • • • • •

A Self-Check Test

Instructions: The purpose of this exercise is to practice preparing and asking questions that are designed to lead student thinking from the lowest level to the highest. Before class, prepare a 5-minute lesson for posing questions that will guide the learner (one of your peers) from lowest to highest levels of thinking. Teaching will be one-on-one, in groups of four, with each member of the group assuming a particular role—teacher, student, judge, or recorder. Each of the four members of your group will assume each of those roles once, 5 minutes each time. (If there are only three members in a group, the roles of judge and recorder can be combined during each 5-minute lesson; or, if there are five members in the group, one member could sit out each round or two can work together as judge).

Suggested lesson topics:

● A particular teaching strategy
● A skill or hobby
● Assessment of learning
● Characteristics of youngsters of a particular grade level
● Finding a teaching job
● Learning modalities
● Learning styles
● Student teaching and what it will really be like
● Teaching competencies
● Teaching styles

In class, divide into groups of four:

Teacher (sender): Pose recall (input), processing, and application (output)questions related to one of the topics above, or any topic you choose.

Student (receiver): Respond to the questions of the teacher.

Judge: Identify the level of each question or statement used by the teacher and the level of the student's response.

Recorder: Tally the number of each level of question or statement used by the teacher (S = sender) as indicated by the judge; also tally the level of student responses (R = receiver). Record any problems encountered by your group.

Tally Sheet
(You may want to duplicate this so there is a
separate tally sheet for each sender.)

	Minute	Input	Processing	Output
Sender _____	1 S			
	R			
Receiver _____	2 S			
	R			
	3 S			
	R			
	4 S			
	R			
	5 S			
	R			

Student Textbook Questions

When using a textbook that you believe has a disproportionate percentage of its questions at the lowest level, the following suggestions are offered to incorporate higher-order questions and, hence, higher-order thinking:

1. Develop and present higher-level cognitive questions to students prior to textbook reading, requiring students to link prior textual information and student experiences with current textual information.
2. Prior to current text reading, develop and present higher-level statements that require students to prove or disprove the statements through the application of the current textual information.
3. Have students scan chapter subheadings and develop higher-level questions based on the subheadings, which they may answer through reading.
4. Progressively increase the number of higher-level questions inserted into the text from the first chapter to the last chapter. This enables students to become more experienced in responding to higher level cognitive questions.
5. Where appropriate, have students develop higher-level questions from prior textual information that relates to the current textual information.
6. Integrate higher-level questions into chapter activities that require students to think about the information derived from the activity.
7. Require students to defend their answers to lower-level chapter-review and end-of-chapter questions with textual information and experience.[7]

Handling Student Questions

To create the proper atmosphere for productive interaction and involvement, you must be careful in not only how you use questions but also how you respond to students' questions and answers. According to an old proverb, "What I hear, I forget. What I see, I remember. What I say and do, I understand." What students say and do can also cause them to think in an inquiring manner. They may question each other; they may question the teacher, who should be able to respond with other questions that can guide students toward the educational goals. Therefore, try to develop a classroom atmosphere in which students are encouraged to ask questions and seek answers to their questions.

The questions of students present teachers with a persistent dilemma: how much should you as a teacher help the students *versus* how much should you as teacher require students to work things out on their own? The nature of teaching seems to indicate that students should be taught to depend on their own resources. Therefore, it is unwise both to let students acquire the habit of running to you as soon as a slight difficulty presents itself and to discourage students who need assistance and clarification. Often, the best procedure is to suggest clues that will help students solve their problems themselves. Refer the student to principles that have previously been learned but perhaps forgotten. Call the student's attention to some rule or explanation previously given to the class. Go just as far as to enlighten the student and get the student on the right track. There is great satisfaction in discovering the solution to a difficult problem for one's self. Not only is the problem solved, but the process of doing it alone also goes far in adding to the student's self-esteem.

Additional hints on handling student questions and promoting student interaction and the development of individual student self-esteem include:

- Use student questions as springboards for further questions, discussions, and investigations.
- Consider all relevant questions that students ask. Some you may answer yourself, some others you may refer to the class or to specific individuals, and some you may have to look up or have someone look up.

[7]Edward L. Pizzini et al., "The Questioning Level of Select Middle School Science Textbooks," *School Science and Mathematics* 92(2):74–78 (February 1992).

- Encourage students to ask questions that challenge the textbook or other persons' statements, such as "What was the authority or basis for that statement?" or "Can you provide evidence to support that to be the case?"
- Handle trivial and irrelevant questions kindly, courteously, and firmly.
- Avoid allowing particular students to dominate. Counsel privately students who do tend to dominate and take up too much of the time. Let them know that you appreciate their contributions but that you want to give equal time to all students.

Recitation

The old-fashioned recitation method continues to be in vogue, perhaps because it is one of the simplest teaching methods to understand. Theoretically, it should be one of the easiest to conduct, for essentially it consists of only three steps:

1. The teacher assigns students something to study.
2. The students study it.
3. The teacher asks the students (in a whole-class situation ordinarily) about what they have studied in order to see if they have got it right.

The method has merit. Because of its long history, it is pretty well known and accepted by students. The question-and-answer technique both provides reinforcement for what has been learned and gives students feedback about accuracy. The expectation of having to face questions in class has motivational value as well. Finally, recitation provides opportunities for students to learn from each other.

As practiced too frequently, though, the recitation method has more faults than merits. Too much of the questioning, for example, is of simple cognitive recall. As a result, when poorly used the method tends to yield only superficial understanding, even discouraging the development of higher mental processes, including attitudes, appreciations, ideals, and skills. When used by an unskilled teacher, recitation tends to be boring and to create an unfriendly, anti-intellectual class atmosphere.

Recitations, however, need not be stifling. To liven them up, focus them on interesting and thought-provoking questions. Present these questions to the students in the initial assignment so that the questions are before them as they study. Then use the questions as the basis for the recitation. Plan your questioning procedures in advance of the class so that the questions focus on thinking and sharing of ideas rather than only on recall. Because of the de-emphasis on rote memorization and the emphasis on using the higher intellectual processes, students can be—and perhaps should be—allowed to consult their texts as the recitation is carried on. It might sometimes be advantageous for student learning to have students study in teams of three or four, where the teams are made of students of varying abilities and knowledge of the subject.

Open-Text Recitation

The open-textbook recitation is really a discussion in which the students may consult their books and other materials to back up their arguments and justify their opinions. The procedure for conducting an open-text recitation is basically the same as that outlined in the previous section. The teacher first makes a study assignment that includes suggestions and questions designed to encourage students to think and draw inferences about what they are to read and study. Then the recitation is focussed on open-ended, thought-provoking questions of the Socratic, divergent, or evaluative type. Lower-order recall and convergent questions should be used as well, but ordinarily they do not play as important a role as broader, open-ended questions. As the recitation proceeds, the teacher encourages students both to challenge and respond to others' statements and to express their own interpretations, inferences, and conclusions. At any time the students are free to consult their texts, notes, or other materials to support their arguments. Finally, someone, the teacher or a student, provides a summary. In many instances, no final decisions or arguments are necessary or desirable—the summary simply cites the positions and arguments taken. At other times, the facts of the case and the nature of the subject matter may require a definite conclusion.

This technique has many advantages. It frees the class from overemphasis on simple recall of facts and opens it up to higher levels of thinking. It helps students realize that facts are means to ends—the ends being concepts, ideas, understandings, and the ability to think critically. It gives students practice in checking and documenting. In the best of circumstances, it shows them the importance of getting the facts straight, of listening to and respecting the opinions of others, and of suspending judgments until sufficient data are in. All in all, this is an excellent means of teaching students to use their higher mental faculties, because the basic technique is to use broad divergent and evaluative questions and to bounce follow-up questions around the class until the group begins to discuss the question freely.

Equity in the Classroom

To ensure a psychologically safe and effective environment for learning for every person in your class, you must attend to all students and try to involve all students equally in all class activities. You must not fall into the trap of interacting with only the brightest, or only those in the front of the room or on one side, or only the most vocal and assertive. You must not have biased expectations about certain students or discriminate against students according to their gender or some other personal characteristic.

You must avoid the unintentional tendency of all teachers, regardless of their gender, to discriminate on the basis of gender. For example, teachers, along with the rest of society, tend to have lower expectations for girls than for boys in science and mathematics. They tend to call on and encourage boys more than girls. They often let boys interrupt girls, but praise girls for being polite and waiting their turn.[8] To avoid such discrimination may take special effort on your part.

To guarantee equity in interaction with students, many teachers have found it useful to ask someone secretly to tally classroom interactions between the teacher and students during a class discussion. After an analysis of the results, the teacher arrives at decisions about his or her own attending and facilitating behaviors. Another strategy for collecting data about characteristics of classroom interaction is with the Flanders interaction analysis technique (presented in Module 11).

Ensuring Equity

Teachers have found various ways of assuring that students are treated fairly in the classroom. These include:

- Have and maintain high expectations for all students.
- Insist on politeness in the classroom. For example, a student can be shown appreciation—such as with a sincere "thank you" or "I appreciate your contribution," or a whole-class applause, or with a genuine smile—for her or his contribution to the learning process.
- Insist that students be allowed to finish what they are saying, without being interrupted by others. Be certain you model this behavior yourself.
- Insist that students raise their hands and be called on by you before they are allowed to speak.
- Keep a stopwatch handy to unobtrusively control the wait time given for each student. Although at first this idea may sound impractical, we assure you it works.
- Use a seating chart attached to a clipboard, and next to each student's name make a tally for each interaction you have with a student.
- Encourage students to demonstrate an appreciation for one another by applauding all individual and group presentations.

---

[8]Betty Vetter, "Ferment: Yes; Progress: Maybe; Change: Slow," *Mosaic* 23(3):34–41 (Fall 1992), p. 34.

Assignments and Homework

An assignment is a statement of *what* the student is to accomplish—to do—and is tied to a specific instructional objective; procedures, in contrast, are statements of *how* to do something. Assignments, whether completed at home or at school, can ease student learning in many ways.

Purposes for Assignments

Purposes for giving homework assignments can be any of the following.

* Constructively extending the time that students are engaged in on-task learning.
* Helping students to develop personal learning.
* Helping students to develop their research skills.
* Helping students to develop their study skills.
* Helping students to organize their learning.
* Individualizing the learning.
* Involving parents and guardians in their children's learning.
* Providing a mechanism where students receive constructive feedback from the teacher.
* Providing students with opportunity to review and practice what is being learned.
* Reinforcing the classroom experiences.
* Teaching new content.

Guidelines for Using Assignments

To use assignments, consider the following guidelines.

1. *Plan ahead.* Plan early the types of assignments you will give (e.g., daily and long-range; minor and major; in class or at home), and prepare assignment specifications. Assignments must correlate with specific instructional objectives and should never be given as "busy-work" or as punishment. For each assignment, let students know what the objectives are.

2. *Parental or guardian permission.* Use caution about giving assignments that could be controversial or that could pose a safety hazard to students. In such cases (especially if you are new to the community) before giving the assignment you may wish to talk it over with members of your teaching team, your department chair, or the principal. Also, for a particular assignment, you may need to have parental or guardian permission for students to do it.

3. *Differentiated assignments.* Provide differentiated assignments—assignment variations given to students or selected by them on the basis of student interests and abilities. To accomplish the same objective, students can select or be assigned different activities, such as read and discuss, or they can participate with others in a more direct learning experience. Afterwards, students share what they have learned. This is an example of the use of multilevel teaching.

4. *Study guide (expository organizer).* Teachers have found it beneficial to prepare individualized study guides with questions to be answered and activities to be done by the student while reading textbook chapters at home. Advantages of a study guide include that it can be individualized for each student and that it can make the reading more than a visual experience. A study guide can help organize student learning by (a) accenting instructional objectives, (b) emphasizing important points to be learned, (c) providing a guide for studying for tests, and (d) encouraging the student to read the homework assignment.

5. *Stimulate thinking.* As a general rule, homework assignments should "arouse student curiosity, raise questions for further exploration, and foster the self-discipline required for independent study."[9]

6. *Resources and their availability.* Determine the resources that students will need to complete assignments, and check the availability of these resources. For this, the school librarian can be an excellent resource.

---

[9]California State Department of Education, *Caught in the Middle: Educational Reform for Young Adolescents in California* (Sacramento, CA: Author, 1987), p. 30.

7. *Announcing assignments*. When giving assignments in class, you should write them on a special place on the writing board, or give a copy to each student or include them in the course syllabus. Take extra care to be sure that assignment specifications are clear to the students. Never yell assignments out as students are leaving your classroom. Be prepared if a parent complains that you never assign homework. To avoid that happening, the written syllabus with assignments—as well as the use of student portfolios—are helpful. It is important that your procedure for giving assignments be consistently followed throughout the school year.

Students should be given sufficient time to complete their assignments. In other words, avoid announcing an assignment to be due the very next day. As a general rule, all assignments should be given at least a week in advance, and for major assignments students should be given much longer than that.

Try to avoid changing assignment specifications after once given. Especially avoid changing them at the last minute. Changing them at the last minute can be very frustrating to students who have already completed the assignment, and shows little respect to those students.

8. *Due dates*. Maintain assignment due dates, allowing, of course, for legitimate excuses. Consider allowing students to select their due dates from a list of options. Without legitimate reasons, late papers should either not be accepted or accepted only with a severe reduction in grade.

9. *Class time*. Allow time in class for students to begin work on homework assignments, so you can give individual attention (guided or coached practice) to students. Being able to coach students is the reason for in-class time to begin work on assignments. Recently, some secondary schools have extended the length of class periods to allow more in-class time for teacher guidance on homework assignments. The benefits of coached practice include being able to: (a) monitor student work so a student doesn't go too far in a wrong direction, (b) help students to reflect on their thinking, (c) assess the progress of individual students, and (d) discover or create a "teachable moment."[10] For example, while observing and monitoring student practice the teacher might discover a commonly shared student misconception. The teacher, taking advantage of this teachable moment, stops and talks about that and attempts to clarify that misconception.

10. *Help from other teachers*. Consider asking a teacher colleague to help a student who may benefit from that teacher's help on certain assignments.

11. *Timely and meaningful response from teacher*. Timely, constructive, and corrective feedback from the teacher on the homework—and grading of homework—raises the positive contributions of homework dramatically.[11] If the homework is important for students to do, then you must give your full and immediate attention to the product of their efforts. Read everything that students write. "Students are more willing to do homework when they believe it is useful, when teachers treat it as an integral part of instruction, when it is evaluated by the teacher, and when it counts as a part of the grade."[12]

12. *Attention to reading, listening, speaking, and writing skills*. Regardless of subject or grade level taught, each teacher must give attention to the development of students' reading, listening, speaking, and writing skills. Attention to these skills must also be obvious in both your assignment specifications and your assignment grading policy. Reading is crucial to the development of a person's ability to write. For example, to encourage high-order thinking, students (in any subject field) can and should be encouraged to write (in their journals) their thoughts about the material they have read.

13. *Teacher comments*. Provide feedback about each student's work, and be positive and constructive in your comments. Always think about the written comments you make, to be relatively certain they will convey your intended meaning to the student. And, when writing com-

---

[10]See John D. Bransford and Nancy J. Vye, "A Perspective on Cognitive Research and Its Implications for Instruction," *Toward the Thinking Curriculum: Current Cognitive Research*, 1989 ASCD Yearbook, edited by L. B. Resnick and L. E. Klopfer (Reston, VA: Association for Supervision and Curriculum Development, 1989), p. 196–198.

[11]Herbert J. Walberg, "Productive Teaching and Instruction: Assessing the Knowledge Base," *Phi Delta Kappan* 71(6):470–478 (February 1990), p. 472.

[12]*What Works: Research about Teaching and Learning* (Washington, DC: United States Department of Education, 1986), p. 42.

ments on student papers, consider using a color other than red. To many people, red brings with it a host of negative connotations (e.g., blood, hurt, danger, stop).

14. *Scoring versus grading.* Rather than grading (i.e., giving a percentage or numerical grade), with its negative connotations, teachers sometimes prefer to score assignments with constructive comments.

Now use these guidelines to do Exercise 7.8.

EXERCISE 7.8
Planning Assignments

• • • • • •

Instructions: Plan the student assignments for a unit you intend to teach. When completed, share your results with your colleagues and ask for their suggestions. Reviewers may need a copy of your unit plan (Exercise 4.5).

1. List all assignments for the unit.

2. Correlate (by code) these assignments with your course objectives.

3. Identify (the best you can) resources students can use to complete the assignments, and where those resources are to be found by students.

4. Indicate the relative weight (grade) of each assignment, showing the percent of the assignment to the total term grade.

Memorizing

Sometimes students must memorize things. There is even a time for memorization without much understanding. For example, to learn a language you must first memorize the alphabet. To learn to play the trumpet you must memorize the fingering. To learn mathematics you must first learn the numbering system. In the study of chemistry, you should know the symbols for the common elements. The alphabet, the fingering on the trumpet, numbers, and symbols are all kinds of tools. In mathematics certain assumptions must be memorized before other concepts can be developed. In fact, in all the disciplines, there are basic points that must be memorized before a learner can understand the major concepts.

When teaching through memorizing, the following guidelines will be helpful:

1. Avoid overuse of memorizing. Be sure there is a purpose for the memorizing and that the students see what that purpose is. Have students memorize only those things that are absolutely essential to memorize.
2. If possible, have students study for meaning before memorizing. Some things must be memorized, meaningful or not, such as German word order or Greek letters, whose shape seem arbitrary. These are tools of the trade, and they must be mastered to move on. But it is much easier to memorize those things that have meaning if you understand the meaning. For instance, for someone who does not know Latin it is probably much easier to remember "There is no accounting for taste" than to remember "*De gustibus non est disputandum.*"
3. Utilize the recall method, where students study and then try to recall without prompting.
4. Encourage the use of mnemonics to aid students in their memorization, devices students invent or ones supplied by you. Examples of common mnemonic devices include:

   a. The notes on a treble staff are *FACE* for the space notes and *Empty Garbage Before Dad Flips* (EGBDF) for the line notes. The notes on the bass staff are *All Cows Eat Granola Bars* and *Grizzly Bears Don't Fly Airplanes.*
   b. The periods of the Paleozoic Era are *Cavemen Object Strenuously During Most Polite Parties* (Cambrian, Ordovician, Silurian, Devonian, Mississippian, Pennsylvanian, and Permian).
   c. The order of the planets from the Sun are *My Very Educated Mother Just Served Us Nine Pizzas* (Mercury, Venus, Earth, Mars, Jupiter, Saturn, Uranus, Neptune, and Pluto).
   d. The hierarchy of the biological classification system is *Kindly Professors—or Doctors—Can Only Fail Greedy students* (Kingdom, Phylum—or Division—Class, Order, Family, Genus, and species).

To review what must be memorized in your discipline, do Exercise 7.9.

EXERCISE 7.9
What Must Be Memorized in My Discipline?

• • • • • •

Instructions: The purpose of this exercise is to begin your thinking about what students will need to memorize when learning in your subject field, as well as ways they could go about it. For your discipline, identify content that must be memorized before a student can proceed in the development of an understanding of major concepts. List these things, identifying some ways you might be able to facilitate student memorization of that content. Then discuss this with colleagues in your discipline.

Content to be memorized   *Suggested ways to memorize it*

Reviewing

In any class of students, frequent reviews are necessary, because memory is aided by repetition and by association and because understanding is improved by review. In the sciences, for instance, many concepts cannot be fully understood in isolation. Neither can all the scientific terms be fully appreciated until they are seen in the context of later topics. Frequently, notions that were understood only dimly the first time they were studied become much clearer when revisited later while studying other topics.

In conducting reviews, the teacher must be aware both of the character of the students and of the discipline being pursued. In mathematics and in foreign languages, where so much depends upon every link in the great chain, frequent reviews are often necessary. It is profitable to recall, almost daily, some principles that were previously studied. In disciplines where the parts have less direct connection, such as geography, the reviews may be given at larger intervals, though daily review helps to keep students on their toes.

Here again the techniques of questioning come into play. As far as possible, the review should lead from facts to concepts to principles applied to practical life. Experience in thinking is often more profitable than the knowledge itself.

It is always advantageous to have a general review at the close of any particular study, such as at the end of a unit or of a semester of study. This enables you to detect any false notions that the students entertained during the study. You now can present the subject as a whole and view one part in the light of another. In human physiology, for instance, much more understanding is gained about the process of growth after a person has studied absorption and secretion. Similarly, the economy of respiration is much clearer when viewed in connection with the circulation of the blood.

A general review can be an enlightening process and is always profitable, with perhaps one exception: when the review is instituted solely as preparation for a written examination. Then, review may degenerate into a mere device for passing the exam. The purpose of reviewing should be to master the subject for its own sake—to unify concepts—and not for the purpose of being able to talk about it on one special occasion.

In summary, a review is an opportunity for the students to look at a topic again. It is a "re-view," a repeat look. It is not the same as drill or practice, though sometimes a teacher can use the same methodology. Review is useful every day as a means for tying the day's lesson to preceding lessons. At this time you can summarize points that should have been made and establish relationships with past and future lessons. End-of-unit and end-of-term reviews are useful, but it is important that reviewing be more frequent than only at the end of a unit or term. Frequent reviews are more effective. Besides, end-of-unit and end-of-term reviews tend to become preparations for examinations.

Almost any technique can be used in review sessions, though the common oral quiz in which the teacher goes around the room asking one fact question after another can become pretty boring. If you do use this type of review, use some scheme to mix up the questions to keep students alert. Tactics that you might want to consider are student summaries, quiz games, dramatizations, student-provided test questions, discussion, broad questioning, and application problems. Techniques that require students to use what they should have learned are good because those techniques may not only serve as review but also provide motivation by opening new vistas for students.

SUMMARY

In this final module of Part III, we have provided guidelines for the use of a number of rather traditional teaching methods that generally are centered on the teacher and involve a lot of teacher talk. Lectures, questioning, discussions, recitations, and so on have all stood the test of time, but unless modified to be more student-centered they are less useful today than in the past, because of the diversity of students in our schools and classrooms and because of what has been learned about learning styles and how children build their knowledge. You are advised to learn well how to use them, however, and to continue to enlarge your repertoire of methods by developing your understanding and skill in the use of strategies of both modes of acquiring knowledge and skills—the access or student-centered mode and the delivery or teacher-centered mode. Remember, you should strive to be eclectic in your teaching style—use the best of each mode to make the learning interesting, meaningful, and lasting for your students.

To help make the learning interesting, meaningful, and lasting, there are many instructional aids and materials from which you may choose for your own situation. That is the topic of Part IV.

SUGGESTED READING

Beatch, D. H., and Stone, H. M. "Provocative Opinion: Survival of the High School Chemistry Lab." *Journal of Chemical Education* 65(7):619–620 (July 1988).

Borich, G. D. "Direct Instruction Strategies." Chap. 6 in *Effective Teaching Methods*. 2d ed. New York: Merrill/Macmillan, 1992.

Caine, R., and Caine, G. *Making Connections: Teaching and the Human Brain*. Alexandria, VA: Association for Supervision and Curriculum Development, 1991.

Carlsen, W. S. "Questions in Classrooms: A Sociolinguistic Perspective." *Review of Educational Research* 61(2):157–178 (Summer 1991).

Clemson, R., and McTighe, J. "Teaching Teachers to Make Connections: A Challenge for Teacher Educators." *Action in Teacher Education* 12(1):55–60 (Spring 1990).

Collins, M. A. J., and Earle, P. "A Comparison of the Effects of Computer-Assisted Testing, Computer-Based Learning and Lecture Approaches on Learning in an Introductory Biology Course." *Journal of Computers in Mathematics and Science Teaching* 9(2):77–84 (Winter 1989-1990).

Heath, S. B. *Ways with Words: Language, Life and Work in Communities and Classrooms*. New York: Cambridge University Press, 1983.

Hunter, M. *Enhancing Teaching*. Chapter 22, "Homework: Asset to Learning or Waste of Time?" New York: Macmillan, 1994.

McLeish, J. "The Lecture Method." Part I of *The Psychology of Teaching Methods—The Seventy-fifth Yearbook of the National Society for the Study of Education*, edited by N. L. Gage. Chicago: The National Society for the Study of Education, 1976.

Perry, R. P.; Abrami, P. C.; and Leventhal, L. "Educational Seduction: The Effect of Teacher Effectiveness and Lecture Content on Student Ratings and Achievement." *Journal of Educational Psychology 71(1): 107–116 (February 1979)*.

Risch, N. L., and Kiewra, K. A. "Content and Form Variations in Note Taking: Effects among Junior High Students." *Journal of Educational Research* 83(6):355–357 (July–August 1990).

Smith, D. C. "Classroom Interaction and Gender Disparity in Secondary Vocational Instruction." *Journal of Vocational Education Research* 16(3):35–58 (November 1991).

Wassermann, S. *Asking the Right Question: The Essence of Teaching*. Fastback 343. Bloomington, IN: Phi Delta Kappa Educational Foundation, 1992.

Wiederhold, C. *Cooperative Learning and Critical Thinking: The Question Matrix*. Palatine, IL: Skylight, 1991.

Wilen, W. W. *Questioning Skills for Teachers*. 3d ed. Washington, DC: National Education Association, 1991.

POSTTEST

Multiple Choice

_____ 1. A very general guideline for middle school and secondary school teaching is that
   a. lectures should not be used.
   b. lectures should be limited to 10–15 minutes.
   c. lectures should be no longer than 30 minutes.
   d. for any class, an occasional full-period lecture is okay.

_____ 2. Which type of question would be best as a set introduction for a new topic?
    a. a low-order question
    b. a close-ended question
    c. a question that causes divergent thinking
    d. a question that causes convergent thinking

_____ 3. Which one of the following is a *false* statement?
    a. Key questions to be used should be written in the lesson plan.
    b. The teacher should ensure that all students are given opportunity to respond to questions.
    c. Questions used by the teacher should be matched with the levels of thinking expected of the students.
    d. After asking a question, you should pause for no longer than 2 seconds before calling upon a student.

_____ 4. Questions that cause students to apply a principle to a new situation are
    a. requiring convergent thinking only.
    b. at the lowest level of mental operation.
    c. at the highest level of mental operation.
    d. at the intermediate level of mental operation.

_____ 5. The classification of questions is closely related to the taxonomy used to classify
    a. learning styles.
    b. cognitive objectives.
    c. instructional media.
    d. instructional strategies.

_____ 6. Which pair of verbs is asking students to apply their knowledge?
    a. *build, evaluate*
    b. *define, analyze*
    c. *count, describe*
    d. *classify, compare*

_____ 7. In number 6, which pair of verbs requires the highest level of mental operation?
    a. *a*
    b. *b*
    c. *c*
    d. *d*

_____ 8. Which set of verbs is most likely to be requiring students to use only their short-term memory?
    a. *judge, predict*
    b. *build, evaluate*
    c. *define, describe*
    d. *classify, compare*

_____ 9. Which pair of verbs is asking students to process information?
    a. *identify, list*
    b. *apply, complete*
    c. *analyze, compare*
    d. *predict, hypothesize*

_____ 10. Which pair of terms represents the highest level of mental activity in inquiry?
    a. *communicating, experiencing*
    b. *comparing, classifying*
    c. *explaining, inferring*
    d. *applying, hypothesizing*

Short Explanation

1. Estella, a high school English teacher, has a class of thirty high-risk sophomores, most of whom are of either Hispanic or Asian ethnicity. On this particular day the students are participating in a 30-minute, four-step prewriting exercise. After explaining the rationale for

the lesson, relating it to the importance of being able to read and to write, Estella tells the students that the first step is for each of them to think of someone whom they admire and to write a three-sentence paragraph that describes that person. She gives them 5 minutes to do this. Her lesson proceeds as follows:

1:00: *Estella:* "Think of a man whom you admire, perhaps a father figure, and write a three-sentence paragraph describing that person." Students begin their writing.

1:00:05: *Estella:* "Only three sentences about someone you look up to. It might be your father, uncle, anyone."

1:00:07: *Student:* "Does it have to be about a man?" *Estella:* "No, it can be a man or a woman, but someone you truly admire."

1:01: Estella works the rows seeing that students are on task.

1:01:10: *Estella:* "Three sentences is all you need to write."

1:01:15: *Estella:* "Think of someone you really look up to, and write three sentences in a paragraph that describes that person."

1:01:30: *Estella:* "Someone you would like to be like."

1:02: Estella continues walking around helping students who are having difficulty. All students are on task.

1:04: *Estella:* "Now I want you to exchange papers with the person behind or beside you, read that person's description of the person they admire, and describe a setting that you see their person in. Write a paragraph that describes that setting."

1:04–1:05: Students exchange papers; teacher walks around seeing that everyone has received another student's paper.

1:05: *Estella:*"Where do you see that person being? Below the paragraph I want you to write a new paragraph describing where you see this person, perhaps in an easy chair watching a ball game, or on a porch, in a car, in the kitchen cooking?"

1:05:10 *Estella:* "Describe a scene you see this person in."

1:05:15: *Estella:* "After you read the description I want you to create a setting for the person described."

1:05:18: Students seem confused either about what they are reading (e.g., asking the writer what a word is or means) or what they are supposed to do.

1:05:19: *Estella:* "Anything is fine. Use your imagination to describe the setting."

1:05:22: *Estella:* "Describe a setting for this person."

1:09: *Estella:* "Now I want you to exchange papers with yet someone else, and after reading the previous two paragraphs written by two other students, write a third paragraph describing a problem you think this admired person has."

Describe what you believe are the good points and weak points of this portion of Estella's lesson and her implementation of it.
2. Identify ways you can recapture student attention during your use of expository teaching.
3. Explain precautions a teacher needs to consider when going from a student-centered activity to an expository, teacher-centered activity during the same class period.
4. Is hands-on learning necessarily minds-on learning as well? Explain.
5. Identify some of the specific strategies you can use to help students develop their critical-thinking and problem-solving skills in your subject field.
6. Explain the principle for using cooperative learning groups in teaching. Do you believe that the use of cooperative learning groups enhances or impedes the learning of students who are identified as being academically gifted and talented. Explain your answer and reason for it.

Essay

1. Assume that you are a high school teacher and that your teaching schedule includes three sections of U.S. History. Furthermore, assume that students at your school are tracked: one

of your classes is a so-called college prep class with thirty students; another is a regular education class with thirty-five students, two of whom have disabilities; and the third is a sheltered English class with thirteen students, nine of whom are Hispanics with limited proficiency in English and four are Southeast Asians, two with no ability to use English. Will one lesson plan using lecture and discussion as the primary instructional strategies work for all three sections? If so, explain why. If not, explain what you will have to do and why. Compare your response here to your response to the same question in Module 2. Identify similarities and differences in your responses? Explain the differences.

2. Do you accept the view that achievement in school learning is the product of creative inquiry through social interaction with the students as active participants in that inquiry? Explain why you do or do not agree.

3. From your current observations and field work as related to this teacher preparation program, clearly identify one specific example of educational practice that seems contradictory to exemplary practice or theory as presented in this module. Present your explanation for the discrepancy.

4. Describe any prior concepts you held that changed as a result of your experiences with this module. Describe the changes.

Part IV

INSTRUCTIONAL AIDS AND RESOURCES

I've finally come to the conclusion that computers are smarter than people. Not once have I ever seen one jogging.

—Bob Orben

Blessed are the censors for they shall inhibit the earth.
—Official Bulletin of England's Guild of Film Critics

Novelty is no substitute for quality.

—Anonymous

Part IV, consisting of two modules, facilitates your selection and use of specific instructional aids by:

- Providing guidelines for the selection and use of audiovisual materials.
- Providing guidelines for the selection and use of printed and display materials.
- Providing resources for teaching materials.

Nonprojected Instructional Aids

RATIONALE

You will be delighted to know that you can draw from a large variety of useful and effective educational materials, aids, and resources as you plan your instructional activities. On the other hand, you could become overwhelmed by the sheer quantity—perhaps as many as 1 million different materials are available for classroom use. They include:

anthologies	newspapers
CD-ROMs, videodiscs	pamphlets
CDs, records, cassettes	paperbacks
classroom periodicals	programmed instructional systems
computer software	realia
dictionaries	reference books
encyclopedias	slides
films	supplementary texts
filmstrips	tests
games	textbooks
globes	transparencies
graphics	videotapes
manipulatives	workbooks

You could spend a lot of time reviewing, sorting, selecting, and practicing with the materials and tools available for your use. Although nobody can make the job easier for you, the information in this module and the next will expedite the process. That is accomplished by the provision of guidelines for the use of nonprojected and projected aids and materials, as well as information about where to obtain additional resources.

Long ago, when humankind was young and writing had not yet been invented, men and women taught their children by means of very simple tools. Telling children what they should know was an important teaching technique, but there were other teaching and learning methods, too. Children learned to hunt by practicing with spears, by throwing sticks, and by simulating hunts of simulated animals. Parents taught geography by maps drawn in the sand and religion by pictures drawn on the walls of caves. The history, customs, and lore of a group were portrayed by dance and drama. From the very earliest times, teachers have depended on diverse teaching tools to make their teaching interesting and effective.

Today, teachers still depend on a variety of teaching tools to make their teaching interesting and effective. In some respects, modern teaching tools are much more sophisticated than those of old. Yet, we use our new tools for the same purposes and in much the same ways that our ancestors did: to make things clear, to make instruction real, to spice up the learning process, and to make it possible for students to teach themselves. Teaching would be impossible without some instructional aids, including printed materials, three-dimensional objects, and flat aids on which to write or display materials. This module is about these kinds of aids, called nonprojected visual aids. The projected visual aids, those that require electricity and that project material onto screens, are presented in the next module.

We begin this module with a discussion of textbooks. Although the most common of all teaching tools used in schools in this country, textbooks are not always chosen wisely or used effectively. Other printed materials, such as workbooks, can be a way to awaken thought and interest when used well but can be a source of tedium when used poorly. Sometimes the most useful of printed materials are teacher-made exercises and study guides. Supplementary reading material can also be quite useful for learning.

If you are to teach effectively, how to get the most out of the various printed materials available will be one of the most pressing problems for you to solve. Similarly, you will have to master the use of display materials. Bulletin boards, pictures, charts, and similar displays often make the difference between students' understanding and not understanding.

When teachers create their own visual aids, audiovisual aids, and teaching devices, they can raise their teaching from the humdrum of dispensing information to the excitement of experimenting with new ideas. This and the module that follows both end with suggestions about where and how to procure materials of instruction—after all, if you do not have it, you cannot use it.

SPECIFIC OBJECTIVES

At the completion of this module, you should be able to:

1. Explain the pros and cons of textbook use.
2. Describe recommended procedures for using textbooks.
3. Describe how to teach with multiple readings.
4. Describe what and how other printed and duplicated materials may be used in your teaching.
5. Explain how to use display devices, including a writing board, a bulletin board, posters, and charts and graphs.
6. Name several sources for procuring free or inexpensive printed materials, and how to evaluate them for usability.
7. Demonstrate your understanding of the community as being a rich resource for your instruction.

MODULE TEXT

Textbooks

Of all the materials of instruction, the textbook has had the most influence on teaching content and method. For many teachers, it has been the "be all and end all" of their instructional life. This is unfortunate because, properly used, the textbook is merely one of many teaching tools. It should not be revered as the ultimate word. As a tool, the textbook is an aid, a means to an end. Do not let it dominate you. You, not the textbook, are supposed to be the master.

Although textbooks are only teaching tools, they can be of great value, particularly to beginning teachers. You will find them very helpful in your planning, because they: (1) provide an organization or structure for the course; (2) provide selection of subject matter that can be used as a basis for determining course content and determining emphases; (3) provide a certain number of activities and suggestions for teaching strategies and tactics; and (4) provide information about other readings, sources of information, audiovisual and other aids, and other teaching materials and teaching tools.

You will also find that a textbook can make an excellent base for building interesting, high-order learning activities (discussion, inquiry, research activities) that call for critical thinking and other higher mental processes. On the other hand, textbooks are far from being the ideal tool some teachers take them to be. They have many faults. As used by many teachers, they assume too large a place in the classroom and in curriculum making. Their construction is often too rigid to allow them to fit in easily in today's enlightened classroom situation: they are sometimes dull, they discourage the reading of more profitable materials, they are often superficial, and above all they do not allow for differences in students' talents, interests, and goals. Uncritical users have a tendency to build their whole course around their text, modifying class activities to conform to the time needed for text analysis.

To get the most out of your textbooks and to avoid their weaknesses, you should:

- Become familiar with the textbook before you use it.
- Use the textbook in your planning as a source of structure if it seems desirable to do so, but do not let yourself become chained to the book.
- Use the text as only one of many materials and activities. Use other readings, simulation, role playing, discussion, films, and pictures.

- Use problem-solving approaches in which the text is but one source of data.
- Use only those parts of the book that seem good to you. Skip the other parts, and rearrange the order of topics if you think it desirable. In other words, adapt the text to your pupils and their needs.
- Use additional or substitute reading to allow for differences in students.
- Provide help for students who do not read well.
- Teach students how to study the text and to use the parts of the text, such as the table of contents, index, headings, charts, graphs, and illustrations.
- Use the illustrations, charts, graphs, and other aids included in the textbook in your teaching. Build lessons around them; study them.
- Encourage critical reading. Compare the text to source materials and other texts. Test it for logic and bias.
- Teach vocabulary.
- Incorporate the textbook into a multiple-text teaching strategy.

Introducing the Textbook

Students seldom know how to use their texts efficiently and effectively. Therefore, on the first day before they begin to read, you might introduce students to the textbook in a lesson in which you and they discuss these elements of the text:

1. *Title page.* What information does it give? When was the book written? Has it been revised? Who is the publisher? Where was it published? Do these indicate any likelihood of bias?
2. *Preface.* What does the author claim he or she intended to do? What was his or her purpose?
3. *Table of contents.* How much weight is given to various topics? How can we use the information contained in the table of contents to help us study the text?
4. *List of maps, charts, and illustrations.* What is the importance of these devices? How can one use them to aid study? Choose examples of each—maps, charts, tables, graphs, illustrations—and have pupils find essential information in them.
5. *Appendix.* What does *appendix* mean? What is it for?
6. *Index.* Use drill exercises to give pupils practice in using the index. These can be made into games or contests.
7. *Glossary.* What is a glossary? Why is it included? Utilize exercises that call for looking up words and then using them in sentences.
8. *Study aids at the ends of chapters.* How can study questions be used? Which are thought questions? Which are fact questions?
9. *Chapter headings, section headings, paragraph leads, introductory overviews, preliminary questions, and summaries.* What are the purposes of each of these? Use exercises that call for getting meaning from aids such as these without reading the entire text.

Selecting a Textbook

In Module 3, we examined student textbooks, gave general guidelines for their use, and discussed textbook reading level. Here, we return to the issue of readability, for the reading level of a textbook is often a major concern of the teacher when selecting a text to use for a class. Sometimes the reading level is supplied by the textbook publisher. If not, you can apply selections to a readability formula to determine the technical reading level of the book. You could also use the simpler method of merely having students read selections from the book aloud, (see Module 3). If they can read the selections without stumbling over many of the words and can tell you the gist of what has been said, you can feel confident that the textbook is not too difficult.

Readability Formulas

As a rule, use of a textbook will be ineffective unless its reading level matches the reading level of the students (see Module 3). Techniques such as the Fry readability formula can be used to estimate the grade level of the text. To use these formulas is not difficult. For instance, the procedure for the Fry technique is to:

1. Determine the average number of syllables in three 100-word selections—one taken from the beginning, one from the middle, and one from the ending parts of the book.
2. Determine the average number of sentences in the three 100-word selections.
3. Plot the two values on the Fry readability graph as shown in Figure 8.1. Their intersection will give you an estimate of the text's reading level at the 50 percent to 75 percent comprehension level.

Practice use of the Fry readability graph by doing Exercise 8.1.

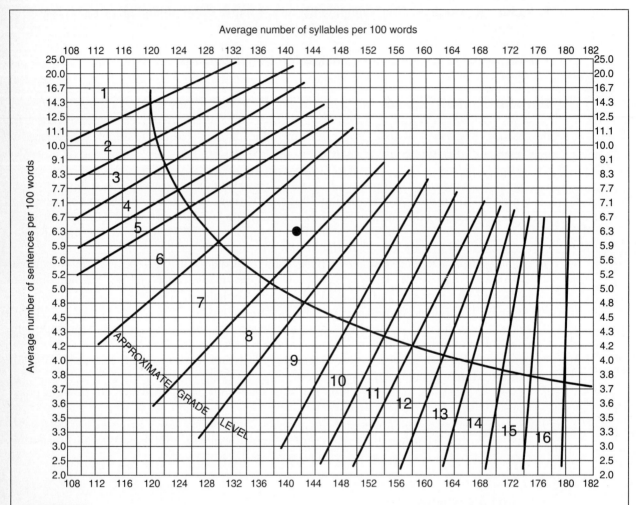

DIRECTIONS:
Randomly select 3 one hundred word passages from a book or an article. Plot average number of syllables and average number of sentences per 100 words on graph to determine the grade level of the material. Choose more passages per book if great variability is observed and conclude that the book has uneven readability. Few books will fall in gray area but when they do grade level scores are invalid.

Count proper nouns, numerals, and initializations as words. Count a syllable for each symbol. For example, *1945* is 1 word and 4 syllables and *IRA* is 1 word and 3 syllables.

EXAMPLE:	SYLLABLES	SENTENCES	
1st Hundred Words	124	6.6	
2nd Hundred Words	141	5.5	
3rd Hundred Words	158	6.8	
AVERAGE	141	6.3	READABILITY 7th GRADE (see dot plotted on graph)

Figure 8.1 Fry Readability Graph

Source: Edward Fry, "A Readability Formula That Saves Times," Journal of Reading (April 1968), 11:587.

Practice Computation of Reading Level Using the Fry Formula

• • • • • •

A Self-Check Exercise

Instructions: The purpose of this exercise is to practice computing textbook reading level using the Fry readability formula. For a text in which you find that three 100-syllable passages contain 130, 145, and 149 words and 7, 9, and 11 sentences, respectively, what would be the reading level?

ANSWER KEY

Your answer should be grade 6, computed in this way:

$$\frac{130 + 145 + 149}{3} = \frac{424}{3} = 141 \text{ syllables}$$

$$\frac{7 + 9 + 11}{3} = \frac{27}{3} = 9 \text{ sentences}$$

By plotting 141 and 9 on the graph, you find that the intersection of the two points falls in the area designated as approximately grade level 6. Presumably, then, the book would be suitable for most sixth graders.

Since these formulas give only the technical reading level of the book, you will have to interpret the results by subjectively estimating the conceptual reading level of the work. To do so, consider your students' experience with the subject, the number of new ideas introduced, the abstraction of the ideas, and the author's external and internal clues. Then raise or lower the estimated level of difficulty.

To tell how well your students can read the text, use the Cloze procedure, or an informal reading inventory. The Cloze procedure that was first described by Bormuth in 1968 has since appeared in a number of versions.[1] From your textbook select several typical passages so that you will have a total of 400 to 415 words or so. Delete every eighth word in the passage except for the words in the first and last sentences, proper names, numbers, and initial words in sentences. It will be helpful if you eliminate 50 words. Duplicate the passages with 10 to 15 space blanks replacing the eliminated words. Pass out these "mutilated" readings to the students. Ask them to fill in the blanks with the most appropriate words they can think of. Collect the papers. Score them by counting all the words that are the exact words in the original text and by dividing the number of correct responses by the number of possibles. (Fifty blanks makes this division easy.)[2]

$$\text{Score} = \frac{\text{Number of correct responses}}{\text{Number of possibilities}}$$

You can assume that students who score better than 50 percent can read the book quite well, students who score between 40 and 50 percent can read the book at the instructional level, and students who score below 40 percent will probably find the book frustrating.

Multitext and Multireadings Approaches

Expressing a dissatisfaction with the single-textbook approach to teaching, some teachers have substituted a multitext strategy, in which they use one set of books for one topic and another set for another topic. This strategy provides some flexibility, though it really is only a series of single texts.

Other teachers—usually the more knowledgeable and proficient—use a strategy that incorporates many readings for a topic during the same unit. This multireading strategy gives the students a certain amount of choice in what they read. The various readings allow for differences in reading ability and interest level. By using a study guide, all the students can be directed toward specific concepts and information, but they do not have to all read the same selections. To implement this type of multireading approach:

1. Select your instructional objectives.
2. Solicit the help of your school librarian. Generally, school librarians are quite willing to help you put a list of readings together.
3. Select a number of readings that throw light on your objectives. Be sure there are several readings for each objective. Provide for variation in students' reading levels and interests as you make your selections.
4. Build a study guide that directs the students toward the objectives, and suggest readings appropriate to each objective.
5. Let the students select what they will read to meet the provisions of the guide.

[1] J. Bormuth, "The Cloze Readability Procedure," *Elementary English* 45:429–436, (April 1968).

[2] Some persons recommend that only exact words be counted; others would allow exact synonyms. We suggest that you not count synonyms or verbs of different tense. See N. McKenna, "Synonymic Versus Verbatim Scoring of the Cloze Procedure," *Journal of Reading* 20:141–143 (November 1976).

Other Printed Materials

Besides the student textbook and maybe an accompanying workbook, a vast array of other printed materials is available for use in teaching—and many are available without cost. Printed materials include books, workbooks, pamphlets, magazines, brochures, newspapers, professional journals, periodicals, and duplicated materials. When thinking about what materials to use, you should be alert for:

- Appropriateness of the material in both content and in reading level.
- Articles in newspapers, magazines, and periodicals related to the content that your students will be studying or to the skills they will be learning.
- Assorted workbooks that emphasize thinking and problem solving rather than rote memorization. With an assortment of workbooks you can have students working on similar but different assignments depending upon their interests and abilities—an example of multilevel teaching.
- Pamphlets, brochures, and other duplicated materials that students can read for specific information and viewpoints about particular topics.
- Relatively inexpensive paperback books that would both provide multiple book readings for your class and make it possible for students to read primary sources.

Cost is always an important consideration in deciding what materials to use. For free and inexpensive printed materials, look for sources in your college, university, or public library, or look in the resource center at a local school district. Figure 8.2 gives you a list of resources through which you can find such materials.

Effective teachers keep a file of printed materials and sources of such materials that might be useful in their teaching. A good idea would be for you to begin your file now. Exercises 8.2 and 8.3 will help you make that beginning.

A Guide to Print and Nonprint Materials Available from Organizations, Industry, Governmental Agencies and Specialized Publishers. New York: Neal Schuman.

Bibliography of Free and Inexpensive Materials for Economic Education. New York: Joint Council on Economic Education.

Civil Aeronautics Administration, *Sources of Free and Low-Cost Materials.* Washington, DC: U.S. Department of Commerce.

Educator's Guide to Free Health, Physical Education, and Recreation Materials. Randolph, WI: Educators Progress Service.

Educator's Guide to Free Home Economics Materials. Randolph, WI: Educators Progress Service.

Educator's Guide to Free Science Materials. Randolph, WI: Educators Progress Service.

Educator's Guide to Free Social Studies Materials. Randolph, WI: Educators Progress Service.

Educator's Guide to Free Materials. Randolph, WI: Educators Progress Service.

Educator's Guide to Free Teaching Aids. Randolph, WI: Educators Progress Service.

Ewing, S. *A Guide to Over One Thousand Things You Can Get for Free.* Lynn, MA: Sunnyside Publishing Company, 1984.

Free and Inexpensive Learning Materials. Nashville, TN: Division of Surveys and Field Services, George Peabody College for Teachers.

Index to Multi-Ethnic Teaching Materials and Teaching Resources. Washington, DC: National Education Association.

Materials List for Use by Teachers of Modern Foreign Languages. New York: Modern Foreign Language Association.

Figure 8.2   Resources for Free and Inexpensive Printed Materials

EXERCISE 8.2

Beginning My Professional Materials Resource File

• • • • • •

Instructions: The purpose of this exercise is to get you started building your own personal file of aids and resources for teaching, a file that will continue throughout your professional career. Begin your file either on a computer program or on 3-by-5 file cards (color coded). You should list:

- Name of resource.
- How to get and when available.
- How to use.
- Evaluative comments.

Organize the file in whatever way that makes the most sense to you. Cross-reference or color code your system to accommodate the following categories of aids and resources:

1. Articles from magazines, newspapers, journals, and periodicals.
2. Compact-disc sources.
3. Computer-software sources.
4. Examination question items.
5. Games and games sources.
6. Guest speakers and other community resources.
7. Media catalogs.
8. Motivational ideas.
9. Multimedia-program sources.
10. Pictures, posters, and other stills.
11. Resources to order.
12. Sources of free and inexpensive items.
13. Student worksheets.
14. Supply catalogs.
15. Thematic unit ideas.
16. Unit and lesson plan ideas.
17. Unit and lesson plans completed.
18. Videocassette titles and sources.
19. Videodisc titles and sources.
20. Other or miscellaneous sources.

EXERCISE 8.3

Collecting and Evaluating Free Materials

• • • • • •

Instructions: The purpose of this exercise is to start your collection and evaluation of free and inexpensive teaching materials. From one of the resources listed in Figure 8.2, select one free material that is offered to teachers, and send for it on official school stationery. When it arrives, share the material with your colleagues. Evaluate all materials using the following criteria.

1. Name of free material:

2. Source of free material:

3. Will the material further your educational objectives?

4. Is the material free from objectionable advertising, propaganda, etc.?

5. Is the material accurate, honest, and free from bias?

6. Is it interesting, colorful, exciting?

7. Does it lend itself to school use?

8. Is it well made?

Professional Periodicals

Figure 8.3 provides you with a sample listing of the many professional periodicals and journals in which you can find useful teaching ideas. They also contain information about instructional materials and how to get them. Most of these periodicals, as well as others of interest to you, are likely to be in your university or college library.

The ERIC Information Network

The Educational Resources Information Center (ERIC) system, established by the United States Office of Education, is a widely used network providing access to information and research in education. Sixteen clearinghouses form the network, each providing information on specific subjects. Addresses for those of particular interest to middle school and secondary school teachers are:

Adult, Career, and Vocational Education. Ohio State University, 1960 Kenny Road, Columbus, OH 43210-1090.

Handicapped and Gifted Children. Council for Exceptional Children, 1920 Association Drive, Reston, VA 22091.

Languages and Linguistics. Center for Applied Linguistics, 1118 22nd St., NW, Washington, DC 20037-0037.

Reading and Communication Skills. Indiana University, 2606 East 10th St., Smith Research Center, Suite 150, Bloomington, IN 47408.

Science, Mathematics, and Environmental Education. Ohio State University, 1200 Chambers Road, 3rd Floor, Columbus, OH 43212-1792.

Social Studies/Social Science Education. Indiana University, Social Studies Development Center, 2805 East 10th St., Bloomington, IN 47408-2698.

Tests, Measurements, and Evaluation. American Institutes for Research, Washington Research Center, 1055 Thomas Jefferson St., NW, Washington, DC 20007-3893.

Figure 8.3   Sample Listing of Professional Periodicals

American Biology Teacher, The	*Language Arts*
American Journal of Physics	*Language Learning*
American Music Teacher, The	*Learning*
American Teacher	*Mathematics Teacher, The*
Arithmetic Teacher, The	*Middle School Journal*
Art Teacher, The	*Modern Language Journal*
Computing Teacher, The	*Music Educator's Journal*
Educational Horizons	*NEA Today*
Educational Leadership	*Phi Delta Kappan*
Educational Researcher	*Physical Education*
English Journal	*Physics Teacher, The*
English Language Teaching Journal	*Reading Teacher, The*
Hispania	*Reading Today*
Instructor	*Science*
Journal of Business Education	*School Arts*
Journal of Chemical Education	*School Musician, The*
Journal of Home Economics	*School Science and Mathematics*
Journal of Learning Disabilities	*School Shop*
Journal of Physical Education and Recreation	*Science Scope*
	Science Teacher, The
Journal of Reading	*Social Education*
Journal of Teaching in Physical Education	*Social Studies*
	Teacher Magazine

Copying Printed Materials

Although still used in some schools, the spirit duplicator (ditto machine) has been replaced with modern dry copiers in many schools. No matter which type of copying machine is available at your school, these are guidelines for its use:

1. You might arrive at the copy room and discover that the copy machine has broken down. Planning ahead is the secret to not becoming frustrated and incapacitated by a broken copy machine. Do your copying well in advance.

2. If permissible at your school, learn to operate the copy machine yourself. Some teachers purchase their own home computers, printers, or copy machines and do their copying at home. That is fine if you have the finances, and is particularly helpful in case of emergencies and times without the lead time that may be necessary for school duplication.

3. When using copyrighted materials, cite the appropriate reference (i.e., author, title, date, source, and publisher) and, when necessary, get permission to copy. When permission is required there usually is no fee for nonprofit, educational purposes.

Every teacher must know the laws about the use of copyrighted materials, printed and nonprinted. Although space here prohibits full inclusion of U.S. legal guidelines, your local school district should be able to provide a copy of current district policies for compliance with copyright laws.

When preparing to make a copy, you must find out whether the copying is permitted by law under the category of "permitted use." If not allowed under "permitted use," then you must get written permission to reproduce the material from the holder of the copyright. When copying printed materials, adhere to the guidelines shown in Figure 8.4.

Permitted Uses—You May Make:

1. Single copies of:
   - A chapter of a book.
   - An article from a periodical, magazine, or newspaper.
   - A short story, short essay, or short poem whether or not from a collected work.
   - A chart, graph, diagram, drawing, cartoon.
   - An illustration from a book, magazine, or newspaper.

2. Multiple copies for classroom use (not to exceed one copy per student in a course) of:
   - A complete poem if less than 250 words.
   - An excerpt from a longer poem, but not to exceed 250 words.
   - A complete article, story, or essay of less than 2,500 words.
   - An excerpt from a larger printed work not to exceed 10 percent of the whole or 1,000 words.
   - One chart, graph, diagram, cartoon, or picture per book or magazine issue.

Prohibited Uses—You May Not:

1. Copy more than one work or two excerpts from a single author during one class term (semester or year).
2. Copy more than three works from a collective work or periodical volume during one class term.
3. Reproduce more than nine sets of multiple copies for distribution to students in one class term.
4. Copy to create or replace or substitute for anthologies or collective works.
5. Copy "consumable" works, such as workbooks, standardized tests, or answer sheets.
6. Copy the same work year after year.

Figure 8.4 Guidelines for Copying Copyrighted Printed Materials
Source: Section 107 of the 1976 Federal Omnibus Copyright Revision Act.

4.   Use varying colors to highlight printed materials. Ditto masters come in standard blue, but also in black, red, and green. If not overly used, multicolored dittos are interesting and the colors can be meaningful. Dry copy machines are available at commercial copy stores for color duplication, but the cost may be prohibitive for the duplication of class sets of materials. Likewise, for computer printers and computer programs with color commands, the cost of duplicating in several colors may be too high for more than an occasional printing of class sets of materials.

The Writing Board

Can you imagine a classroom without a writing board? Teacher talk (discussed in Module 7) can often use help to make it interesting to students. The classroom writing board can be useful as a visual enhancement to verbal communication.

Writing boards used to be slate blackboards. Today's classroom may have a board that is painted plywood (chalkboard), or a magnetic chalkboard (plywood with a magnetic backing), or a white or colored (commonly light green and light blue) multipurpose board on which you write with special marking pens. Multipurpose boards are important for classrooms where chalkdust would create problems—allergies can be caused by chalkdust and dust can interfere with computer maintenance. In addition to providing a surface upon which you can write and draw, the multipurpose board can be used both as a projection screen and as a surface to which figures cut from colored transparency film will stick. It may also have a magnetic backing.

Extending the purposes of the multipurpose board is a board that can transfer whatever information is written on it to a connected computer monitor, which in turn can save the material as a computer file. The board uses special dry-erase markers and erasers that have optically encoded sleeves that enable the device to track their position on the board. The data are then converted into a display for the computer monitor, which may then be printed, cut and pasted into other applications, sent as e-mail or fax message, or networked to other sites.[3]

Guidelines for Using the Classroom Writing Board

Whichever kind of writing board your classroom has, follow these guidelines for its use:

1.   Except for announcements that you place on the board, you should begin each day, each class, and even each new idea with a clean board. At the end of each class clean the board, especially if another teacher follows you in that room—simple professional courtesy.
2.   Use colored chalk (or marking pens) to highlight your "board talk." This is especially helpful for students with learning difficulties.
3.   Print or write neatly and clearly, beginning at the top left of the board.
4.   Position the writing in ways that will indicate content relationships, including categorical, causal, comparative, numerical, and oppositional relationships.[4]
5.   Use the writing board to acknowledge acceptance and to record student contributions.
6.   Print instructions for an activity on the board, rather than giving them orally.
7.   Keep clips for hanging posters, maps, and charts at the top of the board frame.
8.   Maintain a personal supply of chalk (or pens) and an eraser.
9.   Learn to write on the board without having to turn your back entirely to the class or block the students' view of the board.
10.   When you have a lot of material to put on the board, do it before class, and then cover it. Better yet, put the material on transparencies and use the overhead projector rather than the board, or use both.
11.   Be careful not to write too much information. When using the writing board to complement your teacher talk, write only key words and simple diagrams, thereby making it pos-

[3]For more information, contact Microfield Graphics, Inc., Beaverton, OR; (800) 334-4922.

[4]Madeline Hunter, *Enhancing Teaching* (New York: Macmillan, 1994), p. 135.

sible for the student's right brain hemisphere to process what is seen, while the left hemisphere processes the elaboration provided by your words.[5]

Visual Displays

Visual displays include bulletin boards, charts, graphs, flip charts, magnetic boards, realia (real objects), pictures, and posters. As a new or visiting member of a faculty, one of your first tasks is to find out what visual materials are available for your use and where they are kept.

The Classroom Bulletin Board

Bulletin boards are found in nearly every classroom. Although sometimes poorly used or not used at all, they can be relatively inexpensively transformed into attractive and valuable instructional tools. When preparing a bulletin board, it is important to be sure that the board display reflects gender and ethnic equity.

How can you effectively use a classroom bulletin board? Your classroom bulletin board will be most effective if you consider your *CASE*:

C for colorful constructions and captions.

A for attractive arrangement.

S for simple and student prepared.

E for enrichment and extensions of learning.

C—Colorful constructions and captions.   Take time to plan the colors you select for your board and, whenever possible, include different materials for the letters and for the background of the board. For letter variety, consider patterns on bright cloth such as denim, felt, and corduroy. Search for special letters: they might be magnetic or ceramic, or precut letters of different sizes. Or make unique letters by cutting them from magazines, newspapers, posters, or stencils, or by printing the letters with rubber stamps, sponges, or vegetable prints. You may print out the shapes of letters by dabbing colors on letter shapes with sponges, rubber stamps, or with vegetable slices that leave an imprint.

For the background of your board and the borders, consider gift-wrapping paper, wallpaper samples, shelf paper, and remnants of fabric—flowers, polka dots, plaids, solids, or checks. Corrugated cardboard makes sturdy borders: cut out scallops or the shape of a picket fence, or make jagged points for an icicle effect. Other colorful borders can be made with wide braid, wide rickrack, or a contrasting fabric or paper. Constructions for the board may be simple ones made of yarn, ribbon, braid, cardboard pointers, maps, scrolls, banners, pennants, wheels that turn, cardboard doors that open, shuttered windows to peek through, or flaps that pull down or up (to be peered under or over).

If you need more bulletin-board space, prepare large, lightweight screens from the cardboard sides of a tall refrigerator carton, available from an appliance store. One creative teacher asked for, and received without charge, several empty gallon ice-cream containers from a local ice-cream shop. The teacher then stacked five containers on top of one another, fastened them together with wide masking tape, painted them, and prepared her own bulletin board "totem pole" for display in the corner of the classroom. On that circular display space, the students placed their items about a current unit of study.

A—Attractive arrangement.   Use your creative imagination to make the board attractive. Is your arrangement interesting? Did you use texture? Did you consider the shapes of the items selected? Are the colors attractive? Does your caption draw student attention?

[5]*Hunter*, p. 133.

S—Simple and student prepared.   The bulletin board should be simple, emphasizing one main idea, concept, topic, or theme, and captions should be short and concise. Are your students interested in preparing the bulletin board for your classroom? Plan class meeting time to discuss this with them. They have great ideas:

- They can help plan. Why not let them diagram their ideas and share them with each other?
- They can discuss. Is there a more meaningful way to begin to discuss an evaluation of what they see, to begin to discuss the internal criteria that each student brings to class, or to begin to discuss the different values that each student may have?
- They can arrange materials. Why not let them discover the concepts of balance and symmetry?
- They can construct and contribute. Will they feel they are more actively involved and are really participating if it is their bulletin board?

When the bulletin board is finished, your students can get further involved by: (1) reviewing the board during a class meeting; (2) discussing the materials used; and (3) discussing the information their bulletin board is emphasizing.

Additional class projects may be planned during this meeting. For instance, do the students want a bulletin-board group or committee for their class? Do they want a permanent committee, or one in which the membership changes from month to month? Would they prefer that existing cooperative learning groups assume bulletin-board responsibility, with periodic rotation of that responsibility? Do they want to meet on a regular basis? Can they work quietly and not disturb other students who may still be completing their other learning tasks? Should they prepare the board, or should the committee ask everyone to contribute ideas and items for the weekly or monthly bulletin board? Does the committee want to keep a register, guest book, or guest file of students who contribute to the board? Should there be an honorary list of bulletin-board illustrators? Should the authors of selected captions sign their names beneath each caption? Do they want to keep a file binder of all of the different diagrams of proposed bulletin boards? At each class meeting, should they discuss the proposed diagrams with the entire class? Should they ask the class to evaluate which idea would be an appropriate one for a particular study topic? What other records do they want to keep? Should there be a bulletin board medal or a classroom award?

E—Enrichment and extensions of learning.   Illustrations on the bulletin board can accent learning topics, verbs can vitalize the captions, phrases can punctuate a student's thoughts, and alliteration can announce anything you wish on the board. For example:

- *Animals can accent!* Pandas, panthers, and parrots can help present punctuation symbols. A giant octopus can show students eight rules to remember, eight things to remember when preparing a book report, or eight activities to complete when academic work is finished early. A student can fish for anything—math facts, correctly spelled words, or the meanings of science words. A bear character helps students to "bear down" on errors of any kind. A large pair of shoes helps "stamp out" errors, incomplete work, forgotten school materials, or student misbehavior. Dinosaurs can begin a search for any topic, and pack rats can lead one into phrases, prose, or poetry.
- *Verbs can vitalize!* Someone or something (your choice) can "swing into" any curriculum area. Some of the verbs used often are *soar, win, buzz, rake, scurry,* and *race.*
- *Phrases point out!* Some of the short, concise phrases used as captions may include:

Roll into	*All aboard for*	*Race into*
Hop into	*Peer into*	*Grow up with*
Bone up on	*Tune into*	*Monkey with*
Looking good with	*Fly high with*	*Get on track with*

- *Alliteration announces!* Some classroom bulletin boards show Viking ships or Voyages that guide a student to vocabulary words. Monsters monitor Math Madness. Other boards present Surprises of Spring, Fantasies of Fall, Wonders of Winter, and Safety in Summer. Still other boards send messages about Library Lingo, Dictionary Dynamite, and Thesaurus Treats.

Charts, Posters, and Graphs

Charts, posters, and graphs can be used for displays just as bulletin boards can, but as a rule they are better suited for explaining, illustrating, clarifying, and reinforcing specific points in lessons. Charts, posters, and graphs might also be included in a bulletin board display. The guidelines for use of the writing board and bulletin board also apply to the use of charts, posters, and graphs. Clarity, simplicity, and attractiveness are essential considerations. Here are additional suggestions for their preparation and use:

1. Most students enjoy making charts, posters, and graphs. Involve students in finding information, planning how to represent it, and making the chart or poster. Have the author(s) of the chart or poster sign it, and then display it in the classroom. Students should credit their sources on the graphs and charts.
2. When making graphs students may need help in keeping them proportional, and that provides an opportunity for you to help students develop a thinking skill.
3. Students can also enjoy designing flip charts, a series of charts or posters (including graphs) to illustrate certain points or a series of related points. To make a large flip chart, they can use the large pads used by artists for sketching; to make mini–flip charts to use in dyads, they can use small notepads.

The Community as a Rich Resource

One of the richest resources is the local community, and the people and places in it. You will want to build your own file of community resources—speakers, sources for free materials, and field-trip locations. Your school may already have a community resource file available for your use, though it may need updating.

A community resource file should contain information about: (1) possible field-trip locations, (2) community resource people who could serve as guest speakers or mentors, and (3) local agencies that can provide information and instructional materials.

SUMMARY

As should be obvious by now, the selection and use of printed materials and the preparation and sharing of bulletin-board displays, charts, graphs, and posters can be important and integral to effective teaching and learning.

In the next module we provide guidelines and resources for your use of projected visual aids.

SUGGESTED READING

Heinich, R.; Molenda, M.: and Russell, J. D. *Instructional Media and the New Technologies of Instruction*. 4th ed. New York: Macmillan, 1993.

Hunter, M. *Enhancing Teaching*. New York: Macmillan, 1994.

McDermott, C., and Trimble, K. "Neighborhoods as Learning Laboratories." *California Catalyst* 28–34 (Fall 1993).

Murray, K. T. "Copyright and the Educator." *Phi Delta Kappan* 75(7):552–555 (March 1994).

Talab, R. S. *Copyright and Instructional Technologies: A Guide to Fair Use and Permissions.* 2d ed. Washington, DC: Association for Educational Communications and Technology, 1989.

Turner-Egner, J. "Teacher's Discretion in Selecting Instructional Materials and Methods." *West's Education Law Reporter* 53(2):365–79 (July 6, 1989).

POSTTEST

Short Explanation

1. Explain how your effective use of the writing board can help students see relationships among verbal concepts or information.
2. In selecting a textbook, what should you look for?
3. Where could you turn to find out about teaching materials that might be suitable for use in your teaching?
4. Describe what you should look for when deciding whether material that you have obtained free is suitable for use in your teaching.

Essay

1. From your current observations and field work as related to this teacher preparation program, clearly identify one specific example of educational practice that seems contradictory to exemplary practice or theory as presented in this module. Present your explanation for the discrepancy.
2. Describe what you would or could do if you had to teach from a student textbook that you do not like.
3. Describe ways that you could use your school neighborhood and community as a rich resource for learning.
4. Describe any prior concepts you held that changed as a result of the experiences of this module. Describe the changes.

Projected and Recorded Instructional Aids

RATIONALE

Continuing with instructional tools that are available for use in teaching, the focus of this module is on equipment that depends upon electricity to project light and sound and to focus images on screens. These instructional tools include projectors of various sorts, computers, CD-ROMs, sound recorders, video recorders, and laserdisc players. The aim of this module is not to teach you how to operate modern pedagogical technology but to help you develop a philosophy for using it and to provide strategies for using these tools in your teaching.

SPECIFIC OBJECTIVES

Upon completion of this module, you should be able to:

1. Explain the benefits of using audiovisual aids.
2. Explain the virtues and uses of overhead and opaque projectors.
3. Describe the general procedures for using audiovisual aids.
4. Describe uses and resources for classroom computers.
5. Describe uses and resources for CD-ROMs and laserdiscs.
6. Define and describe multimedia presentations.
7. Demonstrate awareness of copyright laws regarding the use of projected visuals.
8. Demonstrate what you would do when equipment malfunctions during instruction.
9. Demonstrate your knowledge of the use of filmstrips, slides, and film loops for teaching.
10. Demonstrate your knowledge of procedures for showing a film.
11. Demonstrate your knowledge of the use of television for instructional purposes.

MODULE TEXT

Audiovisual Aids

Certain teaching tools that rely upon sight and sound fall into the category commonly known as audiovisual aids. Included in this general category are such teaching tools as charts, models, pictures, graphs, maps, mock-ups, globes, flannel boards, writing boards, and all of the tools discussed in the previous module. Also included in the general category of audiovisual aids are those devices that require electricity for their operation—projectors of various sorts, computers, sound recorders, video recorders, laserdisc players, and so forth. This module is about the selection and use of tools of this second group, the ones that require electricity to project sight and sound and that focus images onto screens.

These instructional tools are aids to teaching. It is important to remember that their role is to aid you, not to teach for you. You must still select the objectives, orchestrate the teaching plan, evaluate the results, and follow up the lessons. If you use audiovisual aids prudently, your teaching will benefit.

Uses of Audiovisual Aids

The main effort of any teacher in instruction is to make the message clear—communicate the idea, capture the content, clarify the obscure for the learners. Hence, teachers almost universally rely on the spoken word as their primary medium of communication. Most of the day is filled with explanation and discourse, to the point that the teaching profession has been accused of making words more important than reality—perpetuating a culture of verbalism in the schools. Teachers use definitions, recitations, and—perhaps too often—rote memory in the quest of the goals for the day.

To rely on verbalism is to rely on communication through abstract symbolization. Symbols (in this case, letters and words) may not always communicate what is intended. Audiovisual aids can serve to facilitate communication and understanding by adding depth to the learning, thus making the learning less abstract. Utilizing the concept that one picture is worth a thousand words, such aids attempt to clarify the presentation as well as to intensify the image by doubling the number of senses through which the information is communicated to the learner— that is, sound plus sight. Instead of just description, these aids create visual images to accompany the script. In communicating the definition of the word *escarpment*, for example, imagine how much more vivid, effective, and complete the students' understanding would be when pictures or slides or films are used than if words were used alone. With the addition of visuals, an empathy for the word can be developed; a "eureka" phenomenon can be produced in place of the boredom of memorizing a bare-bones definition that satisfies only the verbal need for understanding. Consider a presentation of the concept of air pressure in lecture form versus an actual demonstration or a visual presentation of the crushing of a vacuumized can by the power of the atmosphere. Consider a recitation by a teacher about the nature of Elizabethan theater versus a graphic illustration with an actual wood model or a computer rendering of London's Globe Theatre.

Aids not only can help clinch the achievement of educational goals but also can be exciting, thus enhancing lessons being taught. When properly utilized, aids can make graphic and thrilling what might have remained pedestrian and routine. They can add color to a presentation, help motivate some students to attend to the instruction, and serve to reinforce the learning that has already taken place.

Sometimes you may hear teachers express the opinion that the use of audiovisual aids sugarcoats learning and thus is educationally undignified. Do not be misled by that opinion. Remember, your job is to teach so that students learn, and any device that will help you achieve that end must be considered. The use of audiovisual aids is an essential for making teaching effective.

General Guidelines for Using Audiovisual Aids

Like any other boon to progress, audiovisual aids must be worked with if they are to yield what is expected. The mediocre teacher who is content to get by without expending additional effort will in all likelihood remain just that, a mediocre teacher, despite the excellent quality of whatever aids he or she chances to use. Because the mediocre teacher fails to rise to the occasion and hence presents poorly, that teacher's lesson results in being less effective and less impressive than it could have been. The effective teacher makes the inquiry about audiovisual aids and expends the effort needed to implement them well for the benefit of the students. The effective teacher will capitalize on the drama made possible by the shift in interaction strategy and enhance the quest for knowledge by using vivid material. Such teaching involves four steps:

1. Selecting the proper audiovisual aid.
2. Preparing for the audiovisual aid.
3. Guiding the audiovisual activity.
4. Following up the audiovisual activity.

Selecting the proper audiovisual aid. Care must be exercised in the selection of an audiovisual aid for use in the classroom. A poor selection, an inappropriate aid, can turn an excellent lesson into a disappointing fiasco. An audiovisual aid that projects garbled sound, outdated pictures, or obscure or shaky images will not be met with delighted response from the class. An aid that is too difficult to present, takes too long to set up, or is not suitable for the age level will dampen the enthusiasm of a class as quickly as a boring lesson.

In the selection process, then, the effective teacher follows an inquiry routine similar to this:

1. Is the contemplated aid suitable? Will it help to achieve the objective of the lesson? Will it present an accurate understanding of the facts in the case? Will the aid highlight the points that the teaching has underscored? Will it work with the equipment used in the school?
2. Is the audiovisual aid within the level of understanding of the class? Is it too mature? too embarrassing? too dated?
3. Is the audiovisual aid lucid in its presentation? Is it clear in its images and sounds?
4. Is the audiovisual aid readily available? Will it be available when needed?

The best response for most of these questions can come after a careful previewing of the aid. Sometimes, because of existing conditions, this dry run is not possible. But the best way to discover how inadequate the catalogue descriptions are of films, filmstrips, videotapes, and records—or the condition in which the product has been left by previous users—is to try them out yourself under practice conditions.

Preparing for the audiovisual aid.   To use audiovisual aids with maximum effectiveness usually will require preparation of two types: psychological and physical. From the psychological standpoint, students have to be prepped for the utilization of the aid and coached on how best to profit from its presentation. Films, filmstrips, recordings, and pictures will require that you spend some time setting the scene. You will need to make clear the purpose of the activity, suggest points to look for, present problems to solve, and, in general, clue your students about potential dangers that may mislead them.

From the physical standpoint, preparation pertaining to the machine to be used, the equipment involved, and the arrangement of the classroom furniture will have to be attended to. Sometimes, as with the use of the chalkboard, the preparation is minimal. All that may be necessary may be the identification of the aid and a brief recitation concerning the use you intend to make of it, other than making sure of a satisfactory supply of chalk and erasers. At other times, however, as when the morning or afternoon sun affects the visibility, each section of the classroom will need to be checked, as well as the focusing dials of the apparatus for appropriate sharpness of images and the amplitude dials for clarity of voice sound. In the absence of preparation, bedlam can ensue. The missing chalk, the borrowing and lending of board erasers among the students, or the absence of an extension cord can spell defeat for even the best audiovisual aid. The double-checking of the action-readiness of the projector and the arrangement in sequence of the slides to be used are vital to success.

Guiding the audiovisual activity.   The purpose of audiovisual teaching tools is not to replace teaching but to make teaching more effective. Therefore, you cannot expect the tool to do all the work. You should, however, make it work for your purposes. You will have to highlight in advance the use of those things that you want to be remembered most completely. You may have to enumerate the concepts that are developed or to illustrate relationships or conclusions that you wish to be drawn. You may have to prepare and distribute a study guide or a list of questions, to stop the presentation periodically for hints or questions, or maybe even to repeat the entire performance to ensure a more thorough grasp of particulars.

Following up the audiovisual activity.   Audiovisual presentations that are allowed just to lie there upon completion squander valuable learning opportunities. Some discussion should ensue that is pointed and directed toward closure. The time for such postmortems should have been a vital part of the preparation for the use of the aid. Upon completion of the use of the aid, students are now permitted to and indeed expected to engage in responding to the sets of questions proposed in the preview activity. Points that were fuzzily made should be clarified. Questions that were not answered should be pursued in depth. Deeper responses that go beyond the present scope of the inquiry should be noted and earmarked for further probing at a later date. Quizzes, reviews, practice, and discussions all can be used to tie loose ends together, to highlight the major concepts, to clinch the essential learnings. The planned, efficient use of the aid helps create the atmosphere that audiovisual presentations are learning opportunities and not purely recreational activities.

When Audiovisual Equipment Malfunctions

When using the tools discussed in this module, it is nearly always best to set up the equipment and have it ready to go before students arrive. That helps avoid problems in classroom management that can occur when there is a delay because the equipment was not ready (an example of dead time, as discussed in Module 5). Of course, delays may be unavoidable, such as when equipment breaks down or videotape breaks.

If anything can go wrong, it will go wrong. That "law" is particularly relevant when using audiovisual equipment. The professional teacher is prepared for such emergencies. Effectively planning for and responding to this eventuality must become a part of your system of movement management (as introduced in Module 5).

Three Principles to Remember

When equipment malfunctions, three principles should be kept in mind: (1) you want to avoid dead time in the classroom, (2) you want to avoid causing permanent damage to equipment, and (3) you want to avoid losing content continuity of a lesson. So, what do you do when equipment breaks down? The answer is to be prepared for any eventuality.

If a projector bulb goes out, quickly insert another. That means you should have an extra bulb on hand. If a tape breaks, you can do a quick temporary splice with cellophane tape. That means that tape should be readily available. And, if you must do a temporary splice, do it on the film or videotape that has already run through the machine rather than on the end yet to go through, in order not to mess up the machine or the film. Then, after class or after school, be sure to notify the person in charge of the tape that a temporary splice was made, so the tape can be permanently repaired before use again.

Go to Plan B

If a fuse blows or for some other reason you lose power, or you can see that there will be too much dead time before the equipment is working again, that is the time to switch to an alternative lesson plan—you "go to Plan B." Without missing a beat, you immediately and smoothly switch to an alternate learning activity, one that will accomplish the same instructional objective or some other objective. For you, the beginning teacher, this doesn't mean that you must plan *two* lessons for every one; rather, when planning a lesson that utilizes audiovisual equipment, you should plan in your lesson an alternative activity, just in case. Then, you move your students into the planned alternative activity quickly and smoothly.

Projectors

Projection machines today are lighter, more energy efficient, and easier to operate than they were a few years ago—they almost have been "defanged." Among the most common and useful to the classroom teacher are the overhead projector, the opaque projector, the slide projector, the filmstrip projector, and the 16-mm film projector. Because limited space disallows presentation of the operating procedures for every model of projector that you may come across, our discussion is limited to general guidelines for their use. Because operations from one projector to the next are quite similar, these guidelines will still be of value to you. At any school there are teachers who will gladly answer questions you may have about a specific projector.

Overhead and Opaque Projectors

The overhead projector is a versatile, effective, and reliable teaching tool. The bulb can burn out, but not much else can go wrong with an overhead projector. There is no film to break or program to crash. And, along with a bulletin board and a writing board, nearly every classroom has an overhead projector. For an opaque projector, you may have to scrounge around the school a bit. Chances are that there is one in the art or science department.

The overhead projector projects light through objects that are transparent, as shown in Figure 9.1. The opaque projector, in contrast, reflects light from objects that are not transparent—that are opaque—as shown in Figure 9.2. To use an opaque projector, room lights must be turned off, but an overhead projector usually works quite well in a fully lit room. An opaque projector (especially older models) may be quite large and bulky; an overhead projector is more portable. Truly portable overhead projectors are available that can be carried from place to place in their compact cases.

Other types of overhead projectors include rear-projection systems, which allow the teacher to stand to the side rather than between students and screen, and overhead video projectors, which use video cameras to send images projected by television monitors.

The opaque projector is useful for showing pages from a book or for showing real objects. But be careful: objects placed in older-model opaque projectors may get quite hot; pages will begin to brown as if they were in an oven. Some schools use overhead video camera technology that assumes, and improves upon, the function of the opaque projector, focusing on an object, pages of a book, or a demonstration, while sending a clear image to a video monitor with a screen large enough for an entire class to clearly see.

In some respects, the overhead projector is more practical than the writing board, particularly for a beginning teacher who is nervous. Use of the overhead projector rather than the writing board can help avoid tension by decreasing the need to pace back and forth to the board. And, by using an overhead projector rather than a writing board, you can maintain both eye contact and physical proximity with students, both of which are important for maintaining classroom control.

Figure 9.1 An overhead projector consists of a glass-topped box that contains a light source and a vertical post mounting a head that contains a lens. To use it, place an acetate transparency on the glass top (some overhead projectors are equipped with acetate rolls to use as transparencies), switch on the light, and adjust the focus by moving the head, which contains the lens, up and down.

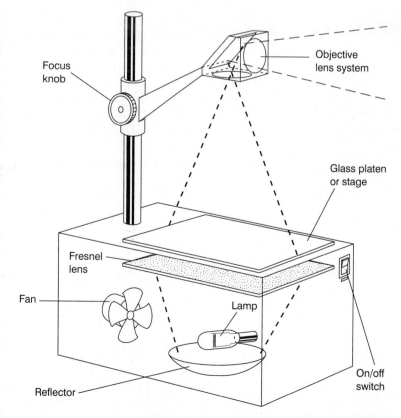

Figure 9.2 Opaque Projector, Cutaway View

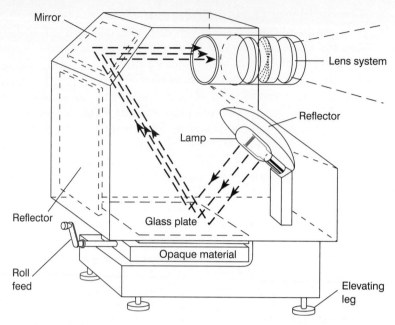

Source: Reprinted with permission of Macmillan College Publishing Company from INSTRUCTIONAL MEDIA AND THE NEW TECHNOLOGIES OF INSTRUCTION, 4/e by Robert Heinich, Michael Molenda, and James D. Russell. Copyright © 1993 by Macmillan College Publishing Company, Inc.

Guidelines for Using Overhead and Opaque Projection
Consider the following specific guidelines when using the overhead and opaque projectors.

1. For writing, when using an overhead projector ordinary felt-tip pens are not satisfactory. Select a transparency marking pen (available at an office supply store). The ink of these pens is water soluble, so keep the palm of your hand from resting on the transparency or you will have ink smudges on your transparency and on your hand. You can use pens that are not water soluble—permanent markers—but if you want to reuse the transparency you must clean it with an alcohol solvent (ditto fluid works, but for safety there must be proper ventilation) or a plastic eraser. With a cleaning solvent you can clean and dry with paper towels or a soft rag. To highlight the writing on a transparency and to organize student learning, use pens in a variety of colors. Transparency pens tend to dry out quickly and they are relatively expensive, so the caps must be taken on and off frequently, which is something of a nuisance when working with several colors. Practice writing on a transparency, and also practice making overlays.

2. You can use either an acetate transparency roll or single sheets of flat transparencies. Flat sheets of transparency come in different colors—clear, red, blue, yellow, and green—which can be useful in making overlays.

3. Some teachers prefer to prepare an outline of a lesson in advance, on transparencies. This practice allows more careful preparation of the transparencies, and they are then ready for reuse at another time. Some teachers prefer to use an opaque material, such as 3-by-5 note cards, to block out prewritten material and then uncover it at the moment it is being discussed. For preparation of permanent transparencies you will probably want to use permanent markers rather than those that are water soluble and can be easily smudged. Heavy paper frames are available for permanent transparencies; marginal notes can be written on the frames.

4. Other transparent materials can be shown on an overhead projector, such as transparent rulers, protractors, Petri dishes, and even objects that are opaque, if you want to simply show a silhouette.

5. With any projector, take time to find the best place in your classroom to place it. If there is no classroom projection screen, you can hang white paper or a sheet, use a white multipurpose board, or use a white or near-white wall.

6.   Have you ever attended a presentation by someone using an overhead projector, but who was not using it properly? It can be frustrating to members of an audience when the image is too small, or out of focus, or partially off the screen, or partially blocked from view by the presenter. To use this teaching tool in a professional manner, follow this procedure: Turn on the projector (the switch is probably on the front), and then place the projector so that the projected white light covers the entire screen and hits the screen at a 90-degree angle. Focus the image to be projected. Remember to face the students while using the projector. That you do not lose eye contact with students is a major advantage of using the overhead projector over using a writing board. What you write, as you face your students, will show up perfectly (unless out of focus, or off the screen). Rather than using your finger to point to detail, or pointing to the screen (thereby turning away from your students), use a pencil—lay the pencil directly on the transparency with the tip of the pencil pointing to the detail being emphasized.

7.   Some teachers suggest you turn the overhead projector off when you want student attention to be shifted back to you, or when changing transparencies.

8.   Personal computers with laser printers and thermal processing (copy) machines (probably located in the teacher's workroom or in the school's main office) can be used to make permanent transparencies.

9.   Calculators are available specifically for use on the overhead projector, as is a screen that fits onto the platform and is circuited to computers, so whatever is displayed on the computer monitor is also projected onto the classroom screen.

10.   Making transparent charts or drawings into larger drawings by tracing them onto paper or onto the writing board is easily done with use of the overhead projector. In the same manner, opaque drawings, such as from a textbook, can be projected by the opaque projector. With both, the image projected onto the screen can be made smaller or larger by moving the projector closer or farther away, respectively, and then traced when you have the size you want.

11.   An overhead projector or a filmstrip projector can be used as a light source (spotlight) to highlight demonstrations by you or your students.

12.   Commercial transparencies are available from a variety of school supply houses. For sources, check the catalogs available in your school office or at the audiovisual and resources centers in your school district. Well-known sources include:

- BJ's School Supplies, 1807 19th Street, Bakersfield, CA 93301.
- Carolina Biological Supply Company, 2700 York Road, Burlington, NC 27215.
- Denoyer-Geppert Audiovisuals, 5235 Ravenswood Ave., Chicago, IL 60640.
- E.M.E., P.O. Box 2805, Danbury, CT 06813-2805.
- Hammond, Inc., 515 Valley Street, Maplewood, NJ 07040.
- Lakeshore Curriculum Materials Co., 1144 Montague Ave., San Leandro, CA 94577.
- Media Associates, Inc., 7322 Ohms Lane, Minneapolis, MN 55435.
- MMI Corporation, 2950 Wyman Parkway, P.O. Box 19907, Baltimore, MD 21211.
- Stasiuk Enterprises, 3150 NE 30th Ave., P.O. Box 12484, Portland, OR 97212.
- 3M Audio Visual, Building 225-3NE, 3M Center, St. Paul, MN 55144.
- United Transparencies, P.O. Box 688, Binghamton, NY 13902.
- Ward's Natural Science, 5100 West Henrietta Rd., P.O. Box 92912, Rochester, NY 14692-9012.

Now explore the use of overhead projectors by doing Exercise 9.1.

EXERCISE 9.1

Competency in Using the Overhead Projector

• • • • • •

Instructions: The purpose of this exercise is to practice writing on the overhead and making transparencies with overlays, including those using colored acetate, until you are proficient with the overhead projector. For this exercise follow the guidelines as presented in the text.

When you feel competent in the use of the overhead projector, your course instructor will certify your competency and provide you with a competency verification certificate for the overhead projector.

Slides and Filmstrips

Slides and filmstrips are variations of the same medium, and most of what can be said about the use of one is true for the other. In fact, one projector may sometimes serve both functions. Filmstrips are, in effect, a series of slides connected on a roll of film. Slides can be made into filmstrips. Relatively inexpensive technology is now available that allows you to take slides or home movies and convert them into videocassettes. Because videocassettes offer more instructional flexibility, cost relatively little, and have greater visual impact, they have generally replaced the once-popular films and filmstrips for school use.

Slides

For teaching purposes, 35-mm slides are still quite useful and are available from school supply houses and, of course, from your own collection and from students and friends. Some schools have the equipment for making slides from computer programs.

Using the slide projector.   For educational purposes, 35-mm slides are available in great abundance. Commercially produced slides can be purchased through school supply houses and photography and other stores. Other slides can be obtained from students, friends, neighbors, and relatives. It is quite possible to make your own slides. With a little practice, you can learn to copy pictures, book pages, documents, and maps with a 35-mm camera. Photographs you take of scenes and events may be excellent teaching aids. You may even find use for your vacation photos. Techniques to use in copying documents and taking other pictures can be found in photographic manuals and works on instructional media.[1]

Slides of flat visuals (magazine pictures, photographs, maps, etc.) can be easily made with a device known as the Kodak Ektagraphic Visualmaker and a Kodak Instamatic camera.[2] With the use of this device no specialized skills are necessary to make perfect 35-mm slides. With the sophistication of computers and specialized equipment, slides can also be generated from computer programs, but the expense of the equipment for this technology is still beyond the means of most school districts.

Slides may be used in a number of ways. An effective technique is to use single slides to illustrate important points or concepts. Another technique is to arrange a series of slides into a slide program, as in a filmstrip. If you wish, you can prerecord your own commentary and sound effects and synchronize them with the slides, although for most class purposes this is not necessary. Slide projection can also be adapted for individual or small-group use, such as in a learning activity center. For individual or small-group viewing, the image can be projected onto a sheet of white cardboard no larger than the projector itself. Some teachers place white paper in a cardboard box and project into it, thereby shielding the image from outside light and keeping it from distracting other students.

Slide projection is excellent for illustrating, clarifying, motivating, and summing up, as well as for introducing study, discussion, or research. Projecting two or more pictures at once makes it possible to show comparisons and contrast. Use slides as springboards. Encourage students to build slide programs and illustrated reports as individual or small-group projects. This technique is an excellent way to make concepts and facts clear and to stimulate thinking.

Slide-loading procedure.   To load slides into slide carriers or trays, position the slides in this way:

1. Face the screen.
2. Hold the slide so that it reads normally. (In most cases, commercially processed slides will carry the company trademark on the side of the slide that faces the projection screen.)

---

[1]*Copying*, Eastman Kodak Publication M1 (Rochester, NY: Eastman Kodak Co., 1969); *How to Make Good Pictures*, Eastman Kodak Publication AW1 (Rochester, NY: Eastman Kodak Co.); *Producing Filmstrips and Slides*, Eastman Kodak Publication S-8 (Rochester, NY: Eastman Kodak Co., 1969); Robert Heinich et al., *Instructional Media and the New Technologies of Instruction*, 4th ed. (New York: Macmillan, 1993).

[2]*Simple Copying Techniques with a Kodak Ektagraphic Visualmaker*, Eastman Kodak Publication S–40 (Rochester, NY: Eastman Kodak Company).

3. Invert the slide, so that the image is upside down, and insert the slide into the tray slot.

Thumb spots help orient slides for projection. Traditionally, the spot is placed in the top right-hand corner of the slide on the side that is away from the screen when the slide is in position for loading.

Preparing a slide program.   Slide programs are quite easy to prepare. Students can and do make excellent programs. Basically, this is the procedure:

1. Decide on your objectives.
2. Decide on the points you want to make.
3. Select slides that will make your points. Use slides that are technically good, though it sometimes is necessary to use a slide that is photographically less than good.
4. Arrange these points into an outline or scenario.
5. Arrange the slides in sequence according to the scenario.
6. Make title and commentary slides, or prepare an oral or written commentary.
7. Place the slides into the projector tray. Be sure they are in proper sequence. If you will be using a single-slot projector, place the slides in order and number them. Even though you will not be using a slide tray, the slide tray is the best place to keep your slides in order.
8. Plan a commentary, if you think one is needed. If you plan a written commentary, make copies so everyone can see it. This type of commentary is good for small-group and individual work. If you plan an oral commentary, you or someone else may read or give the commentary as the slides are shown. This procedure is most common. If you wish, you can tape-record your comments. When you do, be sure to include some sort of signal on the audiotape so that the operator will know when to go to the next slide. If you have the proper equipment, it is quite easy to produce a taped program in which the slides are changed automatically by an electronic signal, but such sophistication is not really necessary.

Filmstrips

Filmstrips are, in effect, a series of slides strung together on a roll of film. They may be used in much the same way as slide programs. In fact, sometimes it may make for more effective teaching if you treat frames as individual slides. Studying an individual frame alone, even for an entire period, has much to recommend it. Studying single frames or short sequences may be more interesting and effective than viewing the entire filmstrip. Many filmstrips come with recorded commentary and sound effects. They may be impressive, but perhaps you would rather provide your own commentary as the filmstrip progresses. To run through an entire filmstrip without stopping for discussion or sharing of ideas usually makes the class monotonous. For this reason, you should be very careful when selecting sound filmstrips. Unless they are unusually well done, they may be boring. In any case, when using the silent filmstrip you should try to involve the students as much as possible. With slower students, allow them to read the captions of silent filmstrips. Stop periodically to discuss the implications of the pictures. You may want to let one of the students run the projector, which would relieve you of that chore and make at least one student interested.

Filmstrips are excellent for small-group and individual work. Use individual screens or screens in boxes. You may, or may not, want to give students study guides to use as they view the filmstrips individually. Such study guides make it possible for students to study completely on their own. With some filmstrips and slide programs, study guides are not really necessary because directions, problems, and other instructional matter that you would expect in a study guide appear on the filmstrip.

Projection procedure for filmstrips.   When ready for showing, the filmstrip should be in a roll with the lead end on the outside and the tail of the film in the center of the roll. Face the screen and hold the filmstrip so that the title reads normally. Keep the same surface toward the screen, invert the filmstrip, and insert the end downward into the threading slot, pushing gently while you turn the film-advance knob slowly until the sprocket wheels engage the perforations along the edges of the filmstrip. When the focus frame or title appears, take time to frame it properly by working the framing lever or knob until you see only one complete frame on the screen. Then focus the picture by moving the lens forward or back.

Making a filmstrip.   It is possible to make filmstrips, but to do so requires special equipment or special skills. Ordinarily, what you must do, in effect, is to make a slide program and then have an audiovisual person turn it into a filmstrip with special equipment. If one has good slide projection equipment, making filmstrips hardly seems worthwhile. The slide program will do almost everything the filmstrip can do. If you wish to make filmstrips, however, you can find detailed instructions in various texts.[3]

Film Loops

The single-concept loop film projector is a simple video device that should not be overlooked. It requires no threading or rewinding. Plastic, self-contained cartridges are inserted into a slot in the rear of this unit and the program is viewer ready. The cartridge is foolproof because it can only be inserted in the correct, ready-to-show position. A focus knob, a framer, and an elevation level are the only controls. Three-to-fifteen minute films are available in most subject areas and at most grade levels. Such films illustrate one concept or idea and often are used to introduce a problem without trying to solve it or to demonstrate a technique or procedure for performing some task.

Loops of this type are commercially prepared on 8-mm film. Local programs, that is, sequences produced by you or someone in your school on this kind of film are easy to make. All that is needed is an easy-to-operate 8-mm camera, normal classroom lighting, and a self-made plan to follow. You can compose and produce film loops that meet with your specifications and are germane to the topic you are teaching in precisely the way you desire.

16-mm Films

Videocassettes and videodiscs are relatively inexpensive to make and offer great instructional flexibility; for those reasons they have generally replaced 16-mm films for use in the classroom. In fact, laserdiscs may eventually replace traditional textbooks as well.[4] Although there are still some effective and new 16-mm films available for instruction, many others are old and sometimes include dated or incorrect information. As with filmstrips, you need to view films carefully and critically before showing them to your class. Many classic films are now available on videocassette or on videodisc. Nevertheless, you should be prepared to deal with the older technology, since you may find yourself teaching in a school that lacks up-to-date equipment.

Instructional films, those designed for instructional use in the classroom, range from presentations of literary masterpieces to short sequences on how to use a certain piece of equipment. Since they are instructional tools, you should usually select films that are pertinent to your teaching objectives, using the films when these objectives are the basis of the content to be shown. The biggest hitch in the utilization of films concerns their availability and your planning. With effective use of long-range planning and early ordering of films, you should be able to make your instruction close to the expected arrival of the film requested.

---

[3]In such texts as Jerold E. Kemp's *Planning and Producing Audiovisual Materials*, or technical manuals such as Eastman Kodak's *Producing Filmstrips and Slides*, Publication S–8.

[4]For example, in 1991 Texas became the first state to allow its schools to use state textbook funds to purchase videodisc programs as an alternative to traditional textbooks in science, and in 1992 Utah adopted a multimedia system for teaching English as a second language. Other states will most certainly follow these precedents.

If you cannot get the film you want when you want it, it is usually better either to adjust your calendar to the related content when you can get the film or to skip the film altogether. In some cases, however, films are of enough general interest that they can be used at almost any time during the year. If possible, the film should be previewed by you before showing it to the class.

Once the projector has been set up and threaded, it is wise to double-check to see that everything is working. Film projectors are quite rugged as a rule, but in the school situation they usually get a maximum of use and a minimum of maintenance. Checking the equipment, therefore, is essential.

You would be wise to learn to troubleshoot the minor difficulties likely to occur in the different machines you have available. With 16-mm projectors many of the common difficulties can be corrected easily and quickly if you are familiar with the equipment. You ought to be able to change the fuses and lamps and to determine when a machine is not threaded properly. With older machines, it is important to understand the type of loops and tension required in threading, though in newer self-threading machines such matters are not so critical.

If a film breaks, wind the film around the takeup reel several times, mark the break with a slip of paper, and continue with the showing. This procedure will allow you to continue with the presentation and yet notify the audiovisual or film library people of just where the break is. Do not try to repair the break yourself. Amateur, extemporaneous, hasty splicing—or attempts to pin, paper clip, or tape broken film together—only make it more difficult for the next user of the film.

Television

Everyone in the United States knows that television is a powerful medium. Its use as a teaching aid, however, may present scheduling, curriculum, and physical problems that some school systems have not been able to handle.

For purposes of professional discussion, television programs can be divided into three categories: instructional television, educational television, and general commercial television. Instructional television refers to programs specifically designed as classroom instruction; educational television, to programs of public broadcasting designed to educate in general, but not aimed at classroom instruction; general commercial television programs include the entertainment and public service programs of the television networks and local stations.

Instructional Television

As just noted, television is not always used well in schools. Probably in utopian circumstances, television should not be used for classroom instruction, but rather should be reserved for supplementing ordinary curricula and instruction. Nevertheless, sometimes instructional television that takes on the role of classroom instruction is necessary in circumstances in which courses cannot be successfully mounted, because they are beyond the capabilities of the local resources, staff, and facilities. By using television well, schools can offer students courses that otherwise would be impossible. In other school systems, because of a desire for economy or in an attempt to bring the students in touch with master teachers and the very best teaching, instructional television courses have been introduced as substitutes for the regular courses.

Where instructional television courses have been introduced, the fact that the television class is taught by a master television teacher does not relieve the classroom teacher of any teaching responsibilities. He or she must plan, select, introduce, guide, and follow up, as in any other course. Otherwise, the television teaching will leave the students with learning gaps and misunderstandings. In spite of the marvels of television and other machines, students still need the personal guidance of all teachers. To use instructional television properly, you should follow a procedure similar to the following:

1. Prepare for the telecast.
   a. Study the advance material. If possible, preview the telecast.
   b. Arrange the classroom.

   c. Prepare and distribute materials and supplies as needed.
   d. Discuss the lesson to be viewed. Fill in any necessary background. Teach any vocabulary necessary.
2. Guide the learning.
   a. Circulate to help students, if necessary.
   b. Observe student response. Note signs of lack of understanding or misunderstanding.
3. Follow up.
   a. Question and discuss.
   b. Reteach and clarify as necessary.
   c. Use the telecast as a springboard to new experiences involving student participation, creativity, problem solving, and critical thinking.
   d. ·Tie to past and future lessons and experiences.

This same procedure also holds for supplementary programs that are used to fill out, deepen, and enrich the day-by-day instruction.

General and Educational Television Programs

In addition to instructional television programs, there are general and educational programs that you can utilize in your teaching: regular commercial programs, special events, and general cultural, educational, informational, and enrichment programs of the Public Broadcasting System and independent educational television stations. Both public broadcasting stations and commercial stations offer a multitude of programs that can be used to supplement and enrich your teaching. Probably the foremost examples include news programs, news specials, and interview programs such as "Nightline" and the "MacNeil-Lehrer Newshour." Such programs can be excellent sources of material for use in all sorts of courses, not only, as you might surmise, for courses in the social studies. For example, every day the weather map and the radar patterns shown on the weather report portion of the local news (or on the cable weather station) give you ammunition for the study of highs, lows, air currents, and the reading of weather maps. Science editors report on new developments in science almost every day and bring attention to important science knowledge in their science news specials. Stock market reports are basic to the study of business and economics courses.

Ordinary commercial programs may turn out to be the best sources of all. All dramas occur in time and place and are subject to dramatic and literary criticism. They can be used to establish historical and literary concepts. What would make a better subject for the study of plot or characterization (or lack of it) than many of the weekly television dramas? Music is omnipresent. Even commercials can be used—they give almost unlimited opportunities for the study of logic, propaganda, and rhetoric.

Educational television courses, such as those given by public broadcasting stations or by colleges and universities on commercial stations, often include lectures, demonstrations, and background information that is usable for high school courses. Although these courses may be aimed at adults pursuing college credit, they are usually not too difficult for many secondary school students.

To find what programs you might use that are telecast locally, you might consult such references as the local newspaper, news and television magazines, the local television guide, professional journals, and television station and network publicity releases. Sometimes you can obtain helpful information about future programs suitable for school use by writing to the stations or networks.

Television studios do not ordinarily adapt their schedules to those of the secondary schools. This problem may be met in several ways. One solution is to tape programs for replay during the class period. Attention should be paid, however, to copyright laws (discussed later in this module). Another solution is to ask students to watch the telecast at home. This solution is fraught with problems because not everyone will be able to watch that television program. Some may not have television sets available (the family may not own one), some may have an adult in the house who wants to watch another show at that time, and some may not have the time available to watch that show. Consequently, you should make such assignments selectively to certain individuals or committees who will report what they have seen and heard. Sometimes, when a major event is to be telecast on several networks, you might do well to ask different students to watch different channels so that they can compare the coverage. For instance, the difference in opinions of various commentators on a presidential message might be quite revealing. In any case, the assignments made to the students must be clear and must be followed up. You might find it helpful to list the assignments, questions, and projects on the bulletin board.

Physical Arrangements for Television Classes

When using television in the classroom, you should make sure that everyone can see and hear sufficiently well. The following are guidelines for the physical arrangement of the classroom:

1. Large-screen (at least 21-inch) television monitors—with front directional speakers— should be used.
2. The monitors should be placed so that each student has an unobstructed line of sight.
3. The screen should not be more than 30 ft. from any student.
4. The set should be about 5½ ft. from the floor (that is, about the same height as the teacher's face).
5. The vertical angle of sight from any student to the set should never be more than 30 degrees; the horizontal angle, never more than 45 degrees.
6. The room should be kept lighted so that students can see to write notes.
7. No glare should reflect from the screen. To reduce glare you can:
   a Move the set away from windows.
   b. Tilt the set downward.
   c. Provide the set with cardboard blinders.
8. The sound should come from front directional speakers.
9. Students should have adequate surface space for writing.
10. To allow for quick, easy transition from the telecast, television classrooms should be fitted with adequate audiovisual equipment, display space, filing and storage space.[5]

Audio Recordings

You will find that tape recordings, CDs, and records are also excellent media for many purposes. In addition to bringing music, speeches, plays, and other dramatic devices to the class, they can be used to support other media. (What would movies and television be like without the background of sound tracks?) Audiotape can also be used to record your own performance so that no one can criticize your work. Such recording is essential in the study of language and speech.

Audiotapes or cassettes can be used as supplements to workbooks and textbooks in any classroom or as powerful primary sources of information within a course. It is possible, for example, to build a language laboratory around a storage and retrieval system of cassette tapes. Stored tapes can also be used as learning resources in: literature or drama courses; laboratory experiments for detailed instruction; learning activity centers, as exciting supplements in the progress of a lesson where opinions of experts in the field under study are needed for decision making; and musical appreciation.

Videos and Videodiscs

Combined with a television monitor, the VCR (videocassette recorder) is one of the most popular and frequently used pieces of audiovisual equipment in today's classroom.[6] Videotaped pro-

---

[5]Clark and Starr, 6th edition, p. 388.

[6]For example, in a teacher survey conducted by *Instructor* the VCR was reported as the most popular technology device used by teachers. See "Teachers Speak Out on Technology in the Classroom," *Instructor* 100(8):71 (April 1991).

grams can do nearly everything that 16-mm films once did. In addition, a camcorder, a VCR combined with a video camera, makes it possible to record student activities, practice, projects, and student demonstrations, as well as your own teaching. This technology gives students a marvelous opportunity to self-assess as they see and hear themselves in action.

Entire course packages, as well as supplements, are now available on videocassettes or on computer programs. The school where you student teach, and where you eventually are employed, may have a collection of such programs. Some teachers make their own.

Laserdisc and players for classroom use are reasonably priced, with an ever-increasing variety of disc topics for classroom use. There are two formats of laserdisc: (1) freeze-frame format (CAV—Constant Angular Velocity, or Standard Play), and (2) non-freeze-frame format (CLV—Constant Linear Velocity, or Extended Play). Both will play on all laserdisc players. Laserdisc players are quite similar to VCRs and just as easy to operate. The discs are visual archives or visual databases that contain large amounts of information, which can be easily retrieved, reorganized, filed, and controlled by the user with the remote control that accompanies the player. Each side of a double-sided disc stores 54,000 separate still-frames of information—whether pictures, printed text, diagrams, films, or any combination of these. Visuals, both still and motion sequences, can be stored and then selected for showing on a television monitor or programmed onto a computer disc for a special presentation. More than 2,000 videodisc titles are now available for educational use. By the time you read this, there may be more than 3,000 titles. Table 9.1 will give you some sample titles, organized by subject. Your school or district audiovisual or curriculum resource center probably has some titles already. For additional titles, refer to the latest (annual) edition of *Videodisc Compendium*.[7]

Carefully selected programs, tapes, discs, films, and slides enhance student learning. For example, laserdiscs offer quick and efficient accessibility of thousands of visuals, thus providing an appreciated boost to teachers of students with limited language proficiency. In science, with the use of still-frame control students can visually observe phenomena that previous students only read about. In art, students can be taken on a personal guided tour of an entire art museum.

Resources for Videodisc Titles
Here are addresses to which you can send for information about available discs.

- ABC News InterActive, 7 West 66th St., 4th Floor, New York, NY 10023.
- CEL Educational Resources, 477 Madison Ave., New York, NY 10022
- Churchill Media, 12210 Nebraska Avenue, Los Angeles, CA 90025.
- Coronet/MTI Film & Video, 108 Wilmot Road, 5th Floor, Deerfield, IL 60015.
- Emerging Technology Consultants, Inc., 2819 Hamline Ave., North St. Paul, MN 55112.
- Encyclopaedia Britannica Educational Corp., 310 S. Michigan Ave., 6th floor, Chicago, IL 60604-9839.
- Friedman & Costello Assoc., 402 Hickory Hollow, Canfield, OH 44406.
- IBM Corp., Multimedia Division, 4111 Northside Pkwy., Atlanta, GA 30327.
- Instructional Video, P.O. Box 21, Maumee, OH 43537.
- Laser Learning Technologies, 120 Lakeside Ave., Suite 240, Seattle, WA 98122-6552.
- MECC, 6160 Summit Drive North, Minneapolis, MN 55430-4003.
- MMI Corporation, 2950 Wyman Parkway, P.O. Box 19907, Baltimore, MD 21211.
- National Geographic Society Education Services Division, 17th & M St., NW, Washington, DC 20036.
- National Science Programs, Inc., P.O. Box 41, W. Wilson St., Batavia, IL 60510.
- Optical Data Corporation, 30 Technology Drive, Warren, NJ 07059.
- Optilearn, Inc., Park Ridge Dr., Ste. 200, Stevens Point, WI 54481
- Pioneer Communications of America, 3255-1 Scott Blvd., Santa Clara, CA 95054.
- Prentice Hall School Group, 113 Sylvan Ave., Englewood Cliffs, NJ 07632.

---

[7]Published and sold by Emerging Technology Consultants Inc., 2819 Hamline Avenue North, St. Paul, MN 55113. Phone (612) 639-3973, Fax (612) 639-0110.

Table 9.1   Sample Videodisc Titles and Sources

Subject	Title	Sample Source
Art	*National Gallery of Art*	Laser Learning Technologies
	Ansel Adams: Photographer	Laser Learning Technologies
	Georgia O'Keefe: Portrait	Ztek
	Homage of Chagall	Ztek
	The Louvre	Ztek
	National Gallery of Art	Ztek
Earth Science	*Earth Science*	Systems Impact, Inc.
	Explore Antartica!	Emerging Technology Consultants
	Gems and Minerals	Smithsonian
	Planet Earth: The Force Within	Coronet/MTI
	Restless Earth	National Geographic
English	*David Copperfield*	Pioneer
	Treasure Island	Pioneer
Environmental Education	*Global Warming: Hot Times Ahead?*	Churchill Media
	Garbage: The Movie—An Environmental Crisis	Churchill Media
	Picture Atlas of Our World	National Geographic
	Planet Earth: The Blue Planet	Coronet/MTI Film & Video
Foreign Languages	*Basic French by Video*	Pioneer
	Basic Spanish by Video	Pioneer
	La Maree et Ses Secrets	Laser Learning Technologies
	Mexico Vivo	Laser Learning Technologies
Geography	*The Explorers: A Century of Discovery*	National Geographic
	Great Cities of Europe	Ztek
	Our Environment	Optilearn
	Regard for the Planet	Voyager
Health	*AIDS/HIV: Answers for Young People*	Churchill Media
	AIDS—What Everyone Needs to Know	Churchill Media
	A Million Teenagers	Churchill Media
	When Your Unborn Child is on Drugs, Alcohol or Tobacco	Churchill Media
	Have a Healthy Baby: Pregnancy	Churchill Media
History	*The American History Videodisc*	Laser Learning Technologies
	The Divided Union	Laser Learning Technologies
	The Holocaust	Friedman & Costello Associates
	Inventors and the American Revolution	Churchill Media
	Set on Freedom: The American Civil Rights Movement	CEL Communications
	Struggles for Justice	Laser Learning Technologies
	The Video Encyclopedia of 20th Century	Laser Learning Technologies

- Sargent-Welch Scientific Co., P.O. Box 1026, Skokie, IL 60076-8026.
- Sony Corp. of America Education System Division, 10833 Valley View St., Cypress, CA 90630.
- Tandy Corp./Radio Shack, 1600 One Tandy Center, Ft. Worth, TX 76102.
- Videodiscovery, Inc., 1700 Westlake Ave., N, Suite 600, Seattle, WA 98109-3012.
- Ztek Co., P.O. Box 1055, Louisville, KY 40201-1055.

Literature	*All Summer in a Day*	Laser Learning Technologies
	Shakespeare in Conversation	Laser Learning Technologies
Life Science	*African Wildlife*	National Geographic
	Atoms to Anatomy: A Multimedia View of Human Systems	Videodiscovery
	The Living Cell	Coronet/MTI
	Dinosaurs	Smithsonian
	Encyclopedia of Animals	Pioneer
	Insects	Smithsonian
	The Living Cell	Coronet/MTI
	The National Zoo	Smithsonian
	Rain Forest	National Geographic
Mathematics	*Adventures in Mathland*	Mindscape, Inc.
	Mastering Fractions	Systems Impact, Inc.
Music	*All that Bach*	Ztek
	Satchmo	Laser Learning Technologies
	Videodisc Music Series	Ztek
Physical Science	*Flying Machines*	Smithsonian
	Physical Science Sides 1–4	Optical Data Corp.
	Physics at Work	Videodiscovery
	Physics: Cinema Classics	Ztek
Social Studies	*A Geographic Perspective on American History*	National Geographic
	America and the World Since WW II	Pioneer
	The First Ladies	Smithsonian
	In the Holy Land	Optical Data Corporation
	Martin Luther King	Optical Data Corporation
	The Video Encyclopedia of the 20th Century	CEL Educational Resources
	Vietnam: Ten-Thousand Day War	Pioneer
Sports	*Michael Jordan's Playground*	Laser Learning Technologies
	Golf My Way: Volumes I and II	Laser Learning Technologies

Movies on Cassette

Thousands of movies are now readily available from libraries and video stores, and movies on cassette can be useful instructional tools. For example, film versions of literary classics are often interesting for students to see, and sometimes a current movie can prompt a classroom discussion about an important social issue. But the teacher's responsibility includes more than just inserting the cassette into the VCR and pushing the play button. Just as with any other teaching strategy, you must plan your objectives as well as your assessment. You must also make sure the VCR is in working order and the tape is ready to play. Finally, you must prepare your students for what they are going to watch. Today's students are used to watching movies on cassette, but they are not used to watching with a critical eye.

Once you are ready to start, introduce the movie. Be sure that the students know what they are supposed to be doing. Unless you make a point of this, they may think of the movie simply as entertainment. Let them know what they should look for and what questions to think about. In some cases, you may want to give them a study guide to follow. Then as soon as everyone is ready, start the movie and keep quiet. Do not make comments while the movie is running. If you must interrupt for some purpose, stop the VCR, say what has to be said, and restart it. To talk while the movie is in progress is silly. All you do is interrupt the story. Besides, no one can hear you. Usually the need for comment can be anticipated and taken care of by your introduction. On the other hand, do not be afraid to stop the VCR for class discussion or explication if it seems advisable. By so doing, you may make instructional videos much clearer. Movies that present a story, however, probably should not be interrupted, because interruptions may destroy the film's impact.

Upon completing the movie, follow it up. Discussion of what was presented is always in order. Written work, tests, problems, reading on the topic, and practice of a skill demonstrated in the film are also useful. The point is to make sure that the students profit from the showing. If there is no adequate follow-up, movies on cassette will become mere recreation. Sometimes the follow-up will show the necessity for seeing the movie again. This is often true when teaching skills. Then you may want to stop the VCR, have the student practice, and then show the video again.

Introducing, setting up, and following up movies, if done well, are likely to be time consuming. Consequently, you should be careful to allow yourself plenty of time for the introduction, showing, and follow-up.

Think about how you would introduce a movie or instructional video by doing Exercise 9.2.

• • • • • •

Critiquing an Introduction

Instructions: The purpose of this exercise is to make you think about how you would introduce a video to your students.

The following description is what actually occurred in a seventh-grade science class. Read the description and write a critique of the procedure (introduction) used by the teacher of that class. After you have written your critique share it with others in your class.

On Monday of the final week of a three-week unit on the planets, the teacher told the class that today they would view a video about the outer planets. The teacher then told the students that the pictures in the video were taken by the *Voyager* spacecraft mission and that the students should take notes during the video, because afterwards they would be given an open-note quiz. The quiz would count toward their grades. After this introduction the VCR was started.

Critique:

Computers

As a teacher of the twenty-first century, you must understand and be able to use computers as well as you can read and write. To complete your teaching credential, your teacher education program and state teacher licensing commission probably require this at some level of competency, or will soon.

The computer can be valuable to you in several ways. For example:

- The computer can be useful as a help in managing the instruction, by obtaining information, storing and preparing test materials, maintaining attendance and grade records, and preparing programs to aid in the academic development of individual students. This category of use is referred to as **computer-managed instruction**, or **CMI**.
- The computer can be used for instruction with the help of various instructional software programs. This is called **computer-assisted instruction**, or **CAI**. Table 9.2 explores various CAI methods.
- The computer can be used to teach about computers and to help students develop their skills in computer use.
- With the help of software programs about thinking, the computer can be used to teach about thinking and to help students develop their thinking skills.

For a student, use of the computer is motivating, exciting, and effective as an instructional tool. Consider the following examples:

- *Computer programs can motivate.* For example, one teacher motivated his students to write by sending their writing work to another class electronically. That was the beginning of the "kids2kids Writing Circle," a national electronic writing project.[8]
- *Computer programs can activate.* For example, in Maine, students prepared maps of local land and water resources from computer analyses of satellite images of the coastline, analyzed those maps, and then advised local authorities on development. Through mixing technology and environmental awareness, the students learned that they could exercise some control over their environment and their future.[9]
- *Computer programs can excite.* Particularly exciting to students are the use of computers with telecommunications systems to connect with other students from around the world, providing an exciting format, for example, for comparing data, sharing ideas, and encouraging students to challenge each other toward better holistic understandings of global environmental problems.[10]

The Placement and Use of Computers in Schools

The way that you use the computer for instruction is going to be determined by the number of computers that you have available, by where computers are placed in the school, and by the software that is available. Despite tight budgets, schools continue to purchase computers. Approximately 50 percent of the computers in schools are found in classrooms; about 40 percent are found in computer labs. However, "the days of a computer in every classroom are still a long way off."[11] Considering the placement, here are some possible scenarios and how classroom teachers work within each:

---

[8]For information on necessary equipment, how to participate, and how to register with the network, see Steven Pinney, "Long Distance Writing," *Instructor* 100(8):69–70 (April 1991).

[9]See Lisa Wolcott, "The New Cartographers: In Maine, Students Are Helping Map the Future," *Teacher Magazine* 2(6):30–31 (March 1991).

[10]For example, many middle and secondary school classrooms have joined the World School for Adventure Learning, one goal of which is to establish and sustain a global telecommunications network of schools for ongoing, interactive environmental studies. For more information about World School, contact University of St. Thomas World School for Adventure Learning, 2115 Summit Avenue, St. Paul, MN 55105. In addition, the National Association of Secondary School Principals has joined the Global Learning Corporation to produce World Classroom, a telecommunications network involving K–12 students and teachers in global educational activities. For more information on World Classroom, call NASSP Partnerships International at 800-253-7746.

[11]National School Boards Association, "Education Vital Signs," *The American School Board Journal* 180(12):A22 (December 1993).

Table 9.2 Utilization of Various CAI Methods

Methods	Description	Role of Teacher	Role of Computer	Role of Student	Applications/Examples
Drill-and-Practice	Content already taught Reviews basic facts and terminology Variety of questions in varied formats Question-answer drills repeated as necessary	Arranges for prior instruction Selects material Matches drill to student Checks progress	Asks questions "Evaluates" student response Provides immediate feedback Records student progress	Practices content already taught Responds to questions Receives confirmation or correction Chooses content and difficulty level	Parts of a microscope Completing balance sheets Vocabulary building Math facts Product knowledge
Tutorial	Presentation of new information Teaches concepts and principles Provides remedial instruction	Selects material Adapts instruction Monitors	Presents information Asks questions Monitors responses Provides remedial feedback Summarizes key points Keeps records	Interacts with computer Sees results Answers questions Asks questions	Clerical training Bank teller training Science Medical procedures Bible study
Gaming	Competitive Drill-and-practice in a motivational format Individual or small group	Sets limits Directs process Monitors results	Acts as competitor, judge, and scorekeeper	Learns facts, strategies, skills Evaluates choices Competes with computer	Fraction games Counting games Spelling games Typing (arcade-type) games
Simulation	Approximates real-life situations Based upon realistic models Individual or small group	Introduces subject Presents background Guides "debriefing"	Plays role(s) Delivers results of decisions Maintains the model and its database	Practices decision making Makes choices Receives results of decisions Evaluates decisions	Troubleshooting History Medical diagnosis Simulators (pilot, driver) Business management Laboratory experiments
Discovery	Inquiry into database Inductive approach Trial and error Tests hypotheses	Presents basic problem Monitors student progress	Presents student with source of information Stores data Permits search procedures	Makes hypotheses Tests guesses Develops principles or rules	Social science Science Food-intake analysis Career choices
Problem Solving	Define problem State hypothesis Examine data Generate solution	Assigns problems Assists students Checks results	Presents problem Manipulates data Maintains database Provides feedback	Defines the problem Sets up the solution Manipulates variables Trial and error	Business Creativity Troubleshooting Mathematics Computer programming

Source: Reprinted with the permission of Macmillan College Publishing Company from INSTRUCTIONAL MEDIA AND THE NEW TECHNOLOGIES OF INSTRUCTION, 4/e by Robert Heinich, Michael Molenda, and James D. Russell. Copyright © 1993 by Macmillan College Publishing Company, Inc.

- *Scenario 1.* Many schools have one or more computer labs where a teacher may schedule to take an entire class or send a small group of students for computer work. In some instances the student computers are networked to the teacher's computer in the lab, in which case the teacher can control and monitor the computer work of each student.[12]
- *Scenario 2.* Some schools have "computer" as an elective course. Students in your classes who are simultaneously enrolled in the computer course may be given special computer assignments by you. They can then share those assignments with the rest of the class.
- *Scenario 3.* Some classrooms have one computer that is connected to a large-screen video monitor. The teacher, or a student, works the computer, and the monitor screen can be seen by the entire class. As students view the screen, they can verbally respond and interact to what is happening on the computer.
- *Scenario 4.* In your classroom, you may be fortunate to have one or more computers, a videodisc player, an overhead projector (one that has light projection from the base), and an LCD (liquid crystal display) projection system. Coupled with the overhead projector, the LCD projection system allows you to project onto your large wall screen (and TV monitor at the same time) any image from computer software or a videodisc. With this system, all students can see and verbally interact with the **multimedia instruction**.
- *Scenario 5.* Many classrooms have one, or perhaps several, computers. When this is the case in your classroom, then you most likely will have one or two students working at the computer while others are doing other learning activities (an example of multilevel teaching).

Computers can be an integral part of a learning activity center within the classroom, and an important aid in your overall effort to individualize the instruction within your classroom.

Computer and Multimedia Programs

When selecting software programs you and your colleagues need, of course, to choose those that are compatible with your brand of computer(s) and with your instructional objectives. According to a recent study of computers in U.S. schools, about half are old computers for which software is no longer made and for which multimedia software and computer networks are not available.[13] As budgets permit, schools will need to replace their old computers.

Like laser videodiscs and compact discs, computer software programs are continually being developed—these are far too many to be listed in this book. Table 9.3 gives you a small sample.

Selecting Computer Software

Computer software available for secondary school instruction is varied and is being developed with ever increasing rapidity. For selection of software programs for your own teaching, your discipline, and the hardware you have available, we suggest that you become acquainted with the many courseware reviews, such as:

- *Courseware Report Card.* 150 West Carob Street, Compton, CA 90220.
- *EPIE Reports.* EPIE (Educational Product Information Exchange) Institute, P.O. Box 839, Water Mill, NY 11976.
- *Journal of Courseware Review.* Apple Education Foundation, 20525 Mariani Avenue. Cupertino, CA 95014.
- *Microcomputers in Education.* Queue, Inc., 5 Chapel Hill Drive, Fairfield, CT 06432.
- *Micro-Scope.* JEM Research, Discovery Park, University of Victoria, P.O. Box 1700, Victoria, BC V8W 2Y2, Canada.
- *MicroSIFT.* Northwest Regional Educational Lab, 300 SW Sixth Street, Portland, OR 97204.

---

[12]For a discussion on how to use cooperative learning groups on computers and a recommended list of science software that works in a cooperative learning environment, see John S. Neal, "The Interpersonal Computer," *Science Scope* 17(4):24–27 (January 1994).

[13]Reported in National Science Teachers Association's *NSTA Reports!* (February/March 1994): 3.

Table 9.3 Sample Computer Software Programs

Topic	Title	Computer*	Company
Fine Arts	*Delta Drawing*	AP/AT/C64/IBM	Spinnaker
Foreign Language	*Anagramas Hispanoamericanos*	AP	Gessler
Language Arts	*The Bank Street Writer*	AP/AT/C64/IBM	Scholastic
	Story Tree	AP/C64/IBM	Scholastic
Math†	*Bumble Plot*	AP/C64/IBM/TRS	The Learning Co.
	Fractions	AP/FR	Encyclopaedia Britannica
	The Quarter Mile Series	AP	Barnum Software
Problem Solving	*Gertrude's Puzzles*	AP/C64/Comp/IBM	The Learning Co.
	The Factory	AP/AT/C64/Comp/IBM/TRS	Sunburst Communications
Science	*Project Zoo*	AP	National Geographic
	The Weather Machine Courseware Kit	AP	National Geographic
Social Science	*The Golden Spike*	AP	National Geographic

* Key to computer brand: AP = Apple; AT = Atari; C64 = Commodore 64 or 128; Comp = Compaq; FR = Franklin; IBM = International Business Machines; MAC = Apple Macintosh; TRS = Radio Shack

† For an excellent listing of computer programs for specific areas of mathematics, refer to James W. Heddens and William R. Speer, *Today's Mathematics,* 7th ed. (New York: Macmillan, 1992).

- *Pipeline*. Conduit Clearinghouse, University of Iowa, Oakdale Campus, Iowa City, IA 55242.
- *Purser's Magazine*. P.O. Box 266, El Dorado, CA 95623.
- *School Microwave Reviews*. Dresden Associates, P.O. Box 246, Dresden, ME 04342.
- *Software Review*. Meckler Publishing, 520 Riverside Avenue, Westport, CT 06880.

In addition to those sources, your professional journal (e.g., *The Science Teachers, Science Scope,* etc.) will likely provide reviews of new software issues. Figure 9.3 gives you an appraisal checklist to use when evaluating computer software for your classroom.

The CD-ROM

Computers have three types of storage disks—the floppy disk, the hard disk, and the **CD-ROM** ("compact disc–read only memory"). Use of a CD-ROM requires a CD-ROM drive. Newer computers may have built-in CD-ROM drives, while older computers must be connected to a CD-ROM drive. As with floppy and hard disks, CD-ROMs are used for storing characters in a digital format, whereas images on a videodisc are stored in an analog format. The CD-ROM is capable of storing approximately 250,000 pages of text—or the equivalent of 1,520 360K floppy disks or 8 70M hard disks—and is therefore ideal for storing large amounts of information such as encyclopedias and other reference books.[14] Videodiscs, in contrast, are ideal for storing video stills and motion images. Like the videodisc, information stored on a CD-ROM disc cannot be erased or modified. With the computer, any information stored on a CD-ROM disk or a videodisc can be found and retrieved within a few seconds. Usually, companies that sell videodiscs also sell CD-ROMs.[15]

---

[14]For example, the complete twenty-six-volume printed version of *Compton's Encyclopedia* is available on CD-ROM. In addition, the disc, titled *Compton's Multimedia Encyclopedia*, contains about an hour of music, plus animated sequences and *Merriam-Webster's Intermediate Dictionary*. The disc is recommended for ages 6–adult, requires a Mac LC computer or higher, with a 40 MB hard disk, a CD-ROM drive, and a 12-inch or larger color monitor. It has a suggested retail price of $795, though it can be purchased for considerably less. For example, in 1993 it was available from MacWarehouse (1720 Oak Street, P.O. Box 3013, Lakewood, NJ 08701-9917) for $595.

[15]For a listing of CD-ROM titles, see *CD-ROM in Print*, published by Meckler, 11 Ferry Lane West, Westport, CT 06880.

❑ APPRAISAL CHECKLIST
Computer-Based Instruction

Title _____ **Format**

Series Title (if applicable) _____ Disk Size

Source _____

Length (completion time) Range: _____ to _____ minutes   Average: _____ minutes

Designed for What System? _____ **Memory Required?** _____

Subject Area _____

Intended Audience _____

Objectives (stated or implied)

Brief Description

Entry Capabilities Required
❑ Prior subject-matter knowledge/vocabulary
❑ Reading ability
❑ Mathematical ability
❑ Other

Rating	High		Medium		Low	Comments
Relevance to objectives	❑	❑	❑	❑	❑	
Accuracy of information	❑	❑	❑	❑	❑	
Likely to arouse/maintain interest	❑	❑	❑	❑	❑	
Ease of Use ("user friendly")	❑	❑	❑	❑	❑	
Appropriate color, sound, graphics	❑	❑	❑	❑	❑	
Frequent, relevant practice (active participation)	❑	❑	❑	❑	❑	
Feedback provides remedial branches	❑	❑	❑	❑	❑	
Free of technical flaws (e.g., dead ends, infinite loops)	❑	❑	❑	❑	❑	
Clear, complete documentation	❑	❑	❑	❑	❑	
Evidence of effectiveness (e.g., field-test results)	❑	❑	❑	❑	❑	

Strong Points

Weak Points

Reviewer _____

Position _____

Recommended Action _____ Date _____

Figure 9.3 Appraisal Checklist to Use for Evaluation of Computer Software

Source: Reprinted with permission of Macmillan Publishing Company from INSTRUCTIONAL MEDIA AND THE NEW TECH-NOLOGIES OF INSTRUCTION, 4/e by Robert Heinich, Michael Molenda, and James D. Russell. Copyright © 1993 by Macmillan College Publishing Company, Inc.

Sources of Free and Inexpensive Audiovisual Materials

For free and inexpensive audiovisual materials, check your college or university library for these sources:

1. Check in professional periodicals and journals for teachers.
2. *An Annotated Bibliography of Audiovisual Materials Related to Understanding and Teaching the Culturally Disadvantaged*. Washington, DC: National Education Association.
3. *Catalog of Audiovisual Materials: A Guide to Government Sources* (ED 198 822). Arlington, VA: ERIC Documents Reproduction Service.
4. *Catalog of Free-Loan Educational Films/Video*. St. Petersburg, FL: Modern Talking Picture Service.
5. From Educator's Progress Service, Randolph, WI: *Educator's Guide to Free Audio and Video Materials, Educator's Guide to Free Films, Educator's Guide to Free Filmstrips, Guide to Free Computer Materials*

Using Copyrighted Video and Computer Programs

You must be knowledgeable about the laws on the use of videos and computer software materials that are copyrighted. Although space here prohibits full inclusion of United States legal guidelines, your local school district undoubtedly can provide a copy of current district policies to ensure compliance with all copyright laws. As noted in the previous module (in the discussion about the use of printed materials that are copyrighted), when preparing to make any copy you must find out whether the copying is permitted by law under the category of "permitted use." If not allowed under "permitted use," then you must get written permission to reproduce the material from the holder of the copyright. Figures 9.4 and 9.5 present guidelines for the copying of videotapes and of computer software. As of this writing, there are no guidelines for fair use of films, filmstrips, and slides.

Figure 9.4 Copyright Law for Off-Air Videotaping

Source: Information from *Instructional Media and the New Technologies of Instruction*, 4th ed., by Robert Heinich, Michael Molenda, and James Russell (New York: Macmillan), p. 431.

Permitted Uses—You May:

1. Request your media center or audiovisual coordinator to record a program for you if you cannot or if you lack the equipment.
2. Keep a videotaped copy of a broadcast (including cable transmission) for forty-five calendar days, after which the program must be erased.
3. Use the program in class once during the first ten school days of the forty-five calendar days, and a second time if instruction needs to be reinforced.
4. Have professional staff view the program several times for evaluation purposes during the full forty-five day period.
5. Make a few copies to meet legitimate needs, but these copies must be erased when the original videotape is erased.
6. Use only a part of the program if instructional needs warrant (but see Prohibited Uses).
7. Enter into a licensing agreement with the copyright holder to continue use of the program.

Prohibited Uses—You May Not:

1. Videotape premium cable services such as HBO without express permission.
2. Alter the original content of the program.
3. Exclude the copyright notice on the program.
4. Videorecord before a request for use—the request to record must come from an instructor.
5. Keep the program, and any copies, after forty-five days.

Figure 9.5 Copyright Law for Use of Computer Software

From the December, 1980, Congressional amendment to the 1976 Copyright Act.

Permitted Uses—You May:

1. Make a single backup or archival copy of the computer program.
2. Adapt the computer program to another language if the program is unavailable in the target language.
3. Add features to make better use of the computer program.

Prohibited Uses—You May Not:

1. Make multiple copies.
2. Make replacement copies from an archival or backup copy.
3. Make copies of copyrighted programs to be sold, leased, loaned, transmitted, or given away.

SUMMARY

From this and the previous module you have learned of the variety of tools available to supplement your instruction. When used widely, these tools will help you to reach more of your students more of the time. As you know, teachers must meet the needs of a diversity of students—many of whom are linguistically and culturally different. The materials presented in these two modules should be of help in doing that. The future will undoubtedly bring technological innovations that will be even more helpful—CDs, computers, and telecommunications equipment have only marked the beginning of a revolution for teaching. Within the next decade, new instructional delivery systems made possible by microcomputers and multimedia workstations will likely fundamentally alter the role of the classroom teacher.

You should remain alert to developing technologies for your teaching field. Laserdiscs and CD-ROMs interfaced with computers (i.e., the use of multimedia) offer exciting technologies for teachers. New instructional technologies are advancing at an increasingly rapid rate.[16] You and your colleagues must maintain vigilance over new developments, constantly looking for those that will not only help make student learning meaningful and interesting, and your teaching effective, but also be cost-effective as well.

To help you analyze and understand the effects of your instructional efforts, and to help students understand the results of their learning efforts, you need to know how to measure and to evaluate those instructional and learning efforts; that is the topic of Part V of this book. The modules that follow will focus your attention on how you can determine how well you and your students are meeting the challenge. They deal with the assessment of learning and the assessment of the instruction.

SUGGESTED READING

Beardslee, E. C., and Davis, G. L. *Interactive Videodisc and the Teaching-Learning Process.* Fastback 294. Bloomington, IN: Phi Delta Kappa Educational Foundation, 1989.

Dalton, D. W. "The Effects of Cooperative Learning Strategies on Achievement and Attitudes During Interactive Video." *Journal of Computer Based Instruction* 17(1):8–16 (Winter 1990).

Dockterman, D. A. "A Teacher's Tools." *Instructor* 100(5):58–61 (January 1991).

[16]For example, in 1993 California, Florida, and Texas jointly awarded a contract to a software developer and to a textbook publishing company to cooperate in the development of a multimedia history and social science curriculum targeted for LEP students. Called Vital Links, the program will consist of an interrelated series of videodiscs, CD-ROMs, and print materials, and is planned for availability in 1995.

Dyer, D. C., et al. "Changes in Teachers' Beliefs and Practices in Technology-Rich Classrooms." *Educational Leadership* 48(8):45–52 (May 1991).

Franklin, S. "Breathing Life into Reluctant Writers: The Seattle Public Schools Laptop Project." *Writing Notebook: Creative Word Processing in the Classroom* 8(4):40–42 (April/May 1991).

Freedman, K. "Possibilities of Interactive Computer Graphics for Art Instruction: A Summary of Research." *Art Education* 44(3):41–47 (May 1991).

Gleason, M., et al. "Cumulative Versus Rapid Introduction of New Information." *Exceptional Children* 57(4):353–358 (February 1991).

Green, L. *501 Ways to Use the Overhead Projector*. Littleton, CO: Libraries Unlimited, 1982.

Gross, B. "Can Computer-assisted Instruction Solve the Dropout Problem?" *Educational Leadership* 46(5):49–51 (February 1989).

Hancock, M. K., and Baugh, I. W. "The New Kid Graduates." *Computing Teacher* 18(7):17–19, 21 (April 1991).

Hedley, C. N. "What's New in Software? TESOL Programs for the Bilingual Special Learner." *Journal of Reading, Writing, and Learning Disabilities International* 7(2):165–70 (April/June 1991).

Huang, S. D., and Aloi, J. "The Impact of Using Interactive Video in Teaching General Biology." *American Biology Teacher* 53(5):281–284 (May 1991).

Hubbard, G., and Greh, D. "Integrating Computing into Art Education: A Progress Report." *Art Education* 44(3):18–24 (May 1991).

Is It Okay for Schools to Copy Software? Washington, DC: Software Publishers Association, 1991.

Johnson, L. N., and Tulley, S. *Interactive Television: Progress and Potential*. Fastback 289. Bloomington, IN: Phi Delta Kappa Educational Foundation, 1989.

Johnson, T. R., and Geller, D. M. "Experimental Evidence on the Impacts of Computer-Assisted Instruction in the Job Corps Program." *Evaluation Review* 16(1):3–22 (February 1992).

Kaplan, N., et al. "The Classroom Manager. Hands-on Multimedia." *Instructor* 101(8):105 (April 1992).

Kehoe, B. P. *Zen and the Art of Internet: A Beginner's Guide to the Internet*. Englewood Cliffs, NJ: Prentice Hall, 1992.

Kemeny, J. G. "Software for the Classroom." *Mathematics and Computer Education* 25(1):33–37 (Winter 1991).

Kernan, M., et al. "Making and Using Audiovisuals." *Book Report* 10(2):16–17, 19–21, 23, 25–35 (September/October 1991).

Kolich, E. M. "Effects of Computer-Assisted Vocabulary Training on Word Knowledge." *Journal of Educational Research* 84(3):177–82 (January/February 1991).

LaQuey, T., and Ryer, J. C. *The Internet Companion: A Beginner's Guide to Global Networking*. Redding, MA: Addison-Wesley, 1992.

Malouf, D. B., et al. "Integrating Computer Software Into Effective Instruction." *Teaching Exceptional Children* 23(3):54–56 (Spring 1991).

Marschalek, D. "The National Gallery of Art Laserdisk and Accompanying Database: A Means to Enhance Art Instruction." *Art Education* 44(3):48–53 (May 1991).

Martorella, P. H. "Harnessing New Technologies to the Social Studies Curriculum." *Social Education* 55(1):55–57 (January 1991).

Maxwell, M. "Writing Centers Offer Personal Touch in the World of Computer Composition." *Communication: Journalism Education Today* 24(4):2–5 (Summer 1991).

Mead, J , et al. "Teaching with Technology." *Teacher Magazine* 2(4):29–57 (January 1991).

Mernit, S. "Black History Month—Let Your Database Set the Stage." *Instructor* 100(6):109–110, 112 (February 1991).

O'Neil, J. "Using Technology to Support 'Authentic Learning.'" *ASCD Update* 35(8):1, 4–5 (October 1993).

Potter, R. L. *Using Microcomputers for Teaching Reading in the Middle School*. Fastback 296. Bloomington, IN: Phi Delta Kappa Educational Foundation, 1989.

Rakow, S. J., and Brandhorst, T. R. *Using Microcomputers for Teaching Science*. Fastback 297. Bloomington, IN: Phi Delta Kappa Educational Foundation, 1989.

Reich, C. F., et al. "Teaching Earth Science Through a Computer Network." *Perspectives in Education and Deafness* 9(5):4–7 (May/June 1991).

Roberts, N., et al. *Integrating Telecommunications into Education*. Englewood Cliffs, NJ: Prentice Hall, 1990.

Sayers, D. "Cross-Cultural Exchanges between Students from the Same Culture: A Portrait of an Emerging Relationship Mediated by Technology." *Canadian Modern Language Review* 47(4):678–96 (June 1991).

Snider, R. C. "The Machine in the Classroom." *Phi Delta Kappan* 74(4):316–323 (November 1992).

Strauss, R. T., and Kinzie, M. B. "Hi-Tech Alternatives to Dissection." *American Biology Teacher* 53(3):154–158 (March 1991).

Talab, R. S. *Copyright and Instructional Technologies: A Guide to Fair Use and Permissions*. 2nd ed. Washington, DC: Association for Educational Communications and Technology, 1989.

ten Brink, B. "New Frontiers With Science Videodiscs." *Educational Leadership* 50(8):42–43 (May 1993).

Tiene, D. "Channel One: Good or Bad News for Our Schools?" *Educational Leadership* 50(8):46–51 (May 1993).

Welch, M., and Jensen, J. B. "Write, P.L.E.A.S.E.: A Video-assisted Strategic Intervention to Improve Written Expression of Inefficient Learners." *Remedial and Special Education* 12(1):37–47 (January–February 1991).

Wishnietsky, D. H. *Using Computer Technology to Create a Global Classroom*. Fastback 356. Bloomington, IN: Phi Delta Kappa Educational Foundation, 1993.

Wohlers, J. "The Multimedia Language Lab." *Media and Methods* 28(3):36, 38–40 (January-February 1992).

Wresch, W., ed. *The English Classroom in the Computer Age: Thirty Lesson Plans*. Urbana, IL: National Council of Teachers of English, 1991.

Yeager, E. A., and Pandiscio, E. A. "Newscasts in the Classroom." *Educational Leadership* 50(8):52–53 (May 1993).

POSTTEST

Multiple Choice

_____ 1. Which type of projector would you use to directly show to an entire class a picture from a book?
   a. opaque
   b. 16-mm
   c. 35-mm
   d. overhead

_____ 2. As an overhead projector is moved farther away from the screen, the image becomes
   a. larger and less brilliant.
   b. larger and more brilliant.
   c. smaller and less brilliant.
   d. smaller and more brilliant.

_____ 3. To project an enlarged image of a real three-dimensional object to an entire class, you should use the
   a. 16-mm projector.
   b. opaque projector.
   c. filmstrip projector.
   d. overhead projector.

_____ 4. The use of laser videodiscs and CD-ROMs interfaced with computers for instructional purposes is called
   a. distance learning.
   b. instruction with multimedia.
   c. computer-managed instruction.
   d. competency-based instruction.

_____ 5. When showing your students a video you should
   a. go to the faculty room and relax.
   b. sit at your desk and correct papers.

    c. stand behind the students and monitor student behavior.

    d. stand in the front of the room and monitor student behavior.

Short Explanation

1. Describe how the use of audiovisual materials helps to reinforce student learning.
2. It has been said that the overhead projector can be one of the teacher's best friends. What is meant by that?
3. Describe two ways that the laserdisc can be used in your teaching.

Essay

1. From your current observations and field work as related to this teacher preparation program, clearly identify one specific example of educational practice that seems contradictory to exemplary practice or theory as presented in this module. Present your explanation for the discrepancy.
2. Describe any prior concepts you held that changed as a result of the experiences of this module. Describe the changes.

Part V

ASSESSMENT OF TEACHING AND LEARNING

Children need models more than they need critics.

—Joseph Joubert

We worship the quantity of practice and ignore the quality.

—Anonymous

The acquiring mind or the inquiring mind? We have a choice.

—Anonymous

The two modules of Part V assist you with:

- Understanding the purposes and procedures of the assessment component of teaching and learning.
- Understanding the relationship between instructional objectives and assessment, furthering your understanding of the importance of an aligned curriculum.
- Understanding the difference between criterion-referenced and norm-referenced assessment.
- Recognizing the importance of authentic assessment.
- Understanding the purposes and procedures for arriving at grades for student achievement.
- Using alternative tools for assessment.
- Understanding the relationship between cooperative learning and assessment of student learning.
- Recognizing the importance of continuous self-assessment.
- Understanding how to prepare various types of assessment items and instruments and to analyze their results.
- Understanding the reasons for and methods of reporting student achievement.
- Recognizing the importance of continued professional development and some ways of doing it.
- Understanding the importance of the field experiences of teacher preparation.

Module 10

Assessing and Reporting Student Achievement

RATIONALE

Assessment, also known as evaluation, is an integral part and an ongoing process of the educational scene. Curricula, buildings, materials, specific courses, teachers, supervisors, administrators, and equipment all must be periodically assessed in relation to student learning, the purpose of any school. When gaps between anticipated results and student achievement are found, efforts are made to eliminate those factors that seem to limit the educational output, or in some other way to improve the situation. Thus, educational progress occurs.

To learn effectively, students need to know how they are doing. Similarly, to be an effective teacher, you must be informed about what the student knows, feels, and can do so that you can help the student build on her or his skills, knowledge, and attitudes. Therefore you and your students need continous feedback on their progress and problems in order to plan appropriate learning activities and to make adjustments to those already planned. If this feedback indicates that progress is slow, you can provide alternative activities; if it indicates that students have already mastered the desired learning, you can eliminate unnecessary activities and practice. In short, assessment provides a key for both effective teaching and learning.

The importance of continuous assessment mandates that you know the principles and techniques of assessment. In this module, we explain some of those and show you how to construct and use assessment instruments. We also define the terms related to assessment, consider what makes a good assessment instrument, relate the criteria to both standardized and non-standardized instruments, suggest procedures to use in the construction of assessment items, point out the advantages and disadvantages of different types of assessment items and procedures, and explain the construction and use of alternative assessment devices.

In addition, we discuss grading and the reporting of student achievement, two responsibilities that can consume much of your valuable time. Grading is time consuming and frustrating for many teachers. What should be graded? Should marks represent student growth, level of achievement in a group, effort, attitude, or general behavior, or a combination of these? What should determine grades—homework, tests, projects, class participation, and group work, or all of these? These are just a few of the questions that plague the teacher and parents—indeed, the profession—when decisions about grades must be made.

In too many schools, the grade progress report and final report card constitute the only consistent communication between the school and the student's home. But unless the teacher and the school have clearly determined what grades represent, and unless such understanding is periodically reviewed with each set of new parents or guardians, these reports may create unrest and dissatisfaction among parents, guardians, and students, and thereby prove to be alienating devices. Thus, the grading system and reporting scheme that purports to inform parents and guardians may instead separate even further the home and the school, despite their having a common concern—the intellectual, physical, and emotional development of the student.

The maturation of the student encompasses growth in the cognitive, affective, and psychomotor domains. Traditional objective paper-and-pencil tests provide only a portion of the data needed to indicate student progress in those domains. Many experts today question the traditional sources of data and for that reason encourage the development and use of alternative means to authentically assess the students' development of thinking and higher-level learning. Although many things remain unclear about assessment, we do know that various techniques must be used to determine how the student works, what the student is learning, and what he or she can produce as a result of that learning. As a teacher, you must develop a repertoire of ways to assess learner behavior and progress.

Although grades have been a part of school for a century or so and seem firmly entrenched—parents, students, colleges, and employers have come to expect grades—some critics suggest that the emphasis in schools is more on getting high grades than on learning, and they argue that the two do not necessarily go hand in hand. As a consequence of such criticism, the trend is to put more emphasis on what the student can do (performance testing) as a result of a learning experience rather than merely on what the student can recall (memory testing) from the experience.

In addition, there have been complaints about subjectivity and unfair practices. As a result of these concerns, various systems of assessment and reporting have evolved and are still evolving, and will likely continue to evolve throughout your professional career.

When teachers become aware of alternative systems, they are more able to develop assessment and reporting processes that are fair and effective for particular situations. The final focus of this module, then, considers today's principles and practices in grading and reporting student achievement.

SPECIFIC OBJECTIVES

At the completion of this module, you should be able to:

1. Describe the purposes of assessment in teaching and learning.
2. Define *assessment* and *measurement*, indicating two specific differences between the terms.
3. List five criteria for selecting a test, and cite a purpose for each.
4. Construct a table of specifications for a unit test, and classify five items in correct cells in the table.
5. Explain the various uses of test results.
6. Cite ten different types of objective test items, and indicate one advantage and one disadvantage of each type.
7. Specify four guidelines for a teacher preparing an essay test.
8. Explain the concept of authentic assessment.
9. Explain the importance of performance assessment.

10. Explain the value of and give an example of performance testing that could be used in your teaching field.
11. Demonstrate two devices by which you might ensure objectivity in your evaluation of a product or process.
12. Diagram a teaching model and indicate where assessment is utilized.
13. Explain the reason that criterion-referenced grading is preferable to norm-referenced grading.
14. Explain the criteria for an effective system for grading.
15. Indicate specific reasons for helping students to participate in self-assessment of their learning.
16. Explain the role of student portfolios and journals in the assessment of teaching and learning.
17. Explain the relationship and difference between grading and the assessment of student learning.
18. Describe any student learning activities or situations that should not be graded but should or could be assessed by the teacher.
19. Differentiate among diagnostic assessment, summative evaluation, and formative assessment, and give examples of when and how you would use each in your teaching.

MODULE TEXT

A Teaching Model

When Bob Hernandez begins his daily trip to his job, his usual route is Lincoln to Main, Main to College, and College to the parking lot beside Central High School. Since construction has started on the new highway, Bob sometimes has to change his route. If the Lincoln-Main intersection is blocked, he drives down Washington to Lake Street and then over to Main. In the fall, when the family is still staying at the cottage, his drive to work takes him in a southeasterly direction instead of the northwest route he takes from home. Occasionally, he has an errand, mailing a package or returning a book to the library. Again he adjusts his trip to the situation. How are such revised routes planned? Often with little conscious effort, since the driver is familiar with the area, knows where he is going, where he is, and what must be accomplished en route.

If Bob Hernandez is driving in a city unfamiliar to him, he plans his route more carefully, using a map or specific directions provided by someone who is acquainted with the area. In such a situation, he may recognize another possibility. Without a street number, sign, or other recognizable clue, he may not know when he reaches his destination. So the final target, which is obvious in a familiar situation (going to work), may not be so easily determined in a strange or unfamiliar setting.

The teacher's plans for the educational journeys of the students in a class require answers to the same basic questions: Where are we going? Where are we now? How do we get where we are going? How do we know when we get there?

These are questions that must be considered in educational assessment. The answers provide the teacher with the basis for working with individual students and with groups. Since in the never-static educational setting the answers are ever-changing, the teacher continuously assesses and adjusts flexible plans to the new situation.

The basic question of goals—or "where are we going"—is in a broad sense determined by society. State requirements and limitations, school board policies, curricula, and courses of study usually evolve with input from all segments of the community. Major factors considered include the society, the students, the school, and the future. The purpose and philosophy of the school distilled from the collected efforts of all of these forces provide the broad objectives for the teacher (the *where*). Guidelines in each course of study provide the framework within which the teacher will make selections of content and strategies (the *what* and *how*). For those who believe that process is a crucial goal of education, the strategies relate to objectives. If one objective is that the student will be able to demonstrate a rational method of attacking a new problem, then a problem-solving approach must be implemented in the classroom. If, however, the objective is the rote memorization of tribal lore or the accumulation and retention of a wide variety of facts about the world in general, a different approach will be called for. The teacher, in selecting specific objectives and activities appropriate for the situation, exerts considerable influence on the learning environment and helps determine where we are going.

"Start where the student is" is a pedagogical cliché. Nevertheless, the statement emphasizes the need to know where we are before we can make reasonable plans for progress. A student who reads at the third-grade level is not going to be able to cope successfully with a social studies text written on the seventh-grade reading level. A student who does not comprehend percentage is not ready for interest problems. A diagnostic test is one tool for determining where we are. Other assessment procedures can also provide information about skills and understanding, such as reading a paragraph and giving an oral summary to indicate comprehension, driving a golf ball to demonstrate the skill, and writing a description of a picture to reveal how well the student can write a paragraph. Students are frustrated and do not progress educationally when they are bored by tasks that they have already mastered as well as by tasks that require skills or knowledge they do not have. Information about a student's achievement provides a basis for appropriate planning to stimulate further development.

Information about where we are going (objectives) and where we start (achievement and attitude of students) enables the teacher to propose several plans for reaching the goals. Students, for example, may work as individuals or in groups on common goals or on specific individualized objectives. Selection and implementation of a plan and of appropriate learning activities require continuing assessment to check on progress and to adopt strategies to promote the desired student behavior. When student feedback indicates satisfactory attainment of objectives, the teacher moves to a new unit, problem, or content area and develops another learning cycle. In the learning cycle (Figure 10.1) assessment is critical. It establishes the starting point, provides data on progress, and indicates arrival at the destination. A teacher must recognize the need for good evaluation and measurement and must develop skill in preparing effective instruments.

Clarification of Terms

When discussing assessment, the terminology can be confusing. To help in your reading and understanding, consider the explanations that follow.

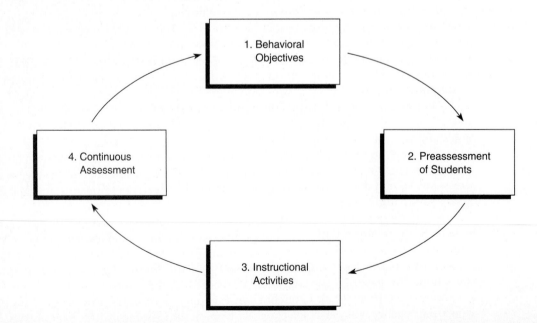

Figure 10.1   Learning Cycle

Measurement and Assessment

Measurement is concerned with quantifiable data about specific behaviors. Examples of measurement include tests and the statistical procedures used to analyze the results. Thus, measurement is a descriptive and objective process, one that is relatively free from human value judgments.

Assessment includes this objective data from measurement, but it also includes other types of information, some of which are more subjective, such as anecdotes in a student's record, teacher observations, and ratings of student performance. Thus, in addition to using objective data (data from measurement), assessment also encompasses arriving at value judgments made on the basis of subjective information.

An example that illustrates the difference in these terms follows. A teacher records the information that Sal Grisso received the top score at East High School on the SAT this year. That is a statement of measurement, only a part of the assessment. The teacher adds that "according to my assessment of his work in my class, he has not been an outstanding English student." That is a statement of evaluation, a subjective judgment that also is part of the assessment of Sal Grisso's work at school.[1]

Validity and Reliability

The degree to which a measuring instrument actually measures what it is intended to measure is called the instrument's **validity**. For example, when we ask if an instrument (e.g., a performance-assessment instrument) has validity, important questions concerning that instrument are:

- Does the instrument adequately sample the intended content?
- Does it measure the cognitive, affective, and psychomotor skills that are important to the unit of content being tested?
- Does it sample all the instructional objectives of that unit?

For example, if a science teacher wants to find out if the students have learned how the position of the fulcrum in a first-class lever will make a difference in the amount of effort exerted, the teacher should carefully select a test question (or performance situation) that will clearly indicate that this is what the item is measuring. The teacher could make a line drawing of a first-class lever, showing a weight at one end of the lever, an effort at the other end, and a fulcrum at a certain position between them. Or, for a performance situation (a more authentic assessment procedure), the teacher could set up an actual working first-class lever, with weights and an application of force (the force could be one of the students and that student's known body weight). The students are then asked to predict the effect of the fulcrum's position on the effort exerted.

The consistency with which a technique measures a quantity or behavior is called its **reliability**. Suppose, for example, you weigh 114 pounds. If a scale consistently records 114 pounds when you stand on it, then you would say that scale has reliability. Notice, though, that if a scale consistently records 100 pounds when you stand on it, you would still say the scale has reliability. This example should make clear to you that an instrument could be reliable (it produces similar results when used again and again) and yet also not be valid (it does not measure what it is supposed to measure). The second scale was consistent but not accurate; so although it had reliability, it did not have validity. A technique might be reliable and yet not be valid. But a technique *must have reliability before it can have validity.*

The need for reliability can be shown clearly with the example of the effect of the fulcrum's position on the effort exerted in a first-class lever. If the teacher asks the students to predict this effect on the basis of just one position of the fulcrum, the answer will give the teacher no assurance that the students know what will happen. To be confident that the students know how the fulcrum's position affects the effort exerted, it is necessary to use several

[1]Note that *assessment* is the preferred term in most circles today, though *evaluation* is also used in some circumstances. For purposes here, the terms are synonymous.

positions of the fulcrum and have the students predict what will happen in each case. Thus, the greater the number of test items or situations on this problem, the higher the reliability. The higher the reliability, the more consistency there will be in student's scores measuring their understanding of this particular concept.

Assessing a Student's Achievement

There are three general approaches for assessing a student's achievement. You can assess (1) what the student says, such as a student's contributions to class discussions; (2) what the student does, such as a student's performance on a task (e.g. setting up a first-class lever); and (3) what the student writes, such as on homework assignments, written tests, and the student's journal. Although your own situation and personal philosophy will dictate the weight you give to each avenue of assessment, you should have good reasons if you weigh the three categories differently than one-third each.

Authentic Assessment

When assessing for student achievement it is important that you use procedures that are compatible with the instructional objectives. This is referred to as **authentic assessment**.[2] For example, in science, "if students have been actively involved in classifying objects using multiple characteristics, it sends them a confusing message if they are then required to take a paper-and-pencil test that asks them to 'define classification' or recite a memorized list of characteristics of good classifications schemes."[3] An authentic-assessment technique would be a performance item that actually involves the students in classifying objects. Thus, for an authentic assessment of the student's understanding of that which the student has been learning, you would use a performance-based assessment procedure.

Assessment: A Three-Step Process

As has been implied in previous modules, assessing a student's achievement is a three-step process, involving: (1) **diagnostic assessment**, or **preassessment**, which is an assessment of the student's knowledge and skills *before* the new instruction; (2) **formative assessment**, the assessment of learning *during* the instruction; and (3) **summative assessment**, the assessment of learning *after* the instruction (ultimately represented by the student's term, semester, or year's achievement grade). Grades shown on unit tests, progress reports, deficiency notices, and six-week or quarter grades (in a semester-based program) are examples of formative-assessment reports. An end-of-chapter test or a unit test, however, is summative when the test represents the absolute end of the student's learning of material of that instructional unit.

Assessing What a Student Says and Does

When assessing what a student says, you should: (1) listen to the student's questions, responses, and interactions with others; and (2) observe the student's attentiveness, involvement in class activities, and responses to challenges.

Notice that we say you should both listen and observe. While listening to what the student is saying, you should also be observing the student's nonverbal behaviors. For this you can use checklists and rating scales, behavioral-growth record forms, observations of the student's performance in classroom activities, and periodic conferences with the student. Figure 10.2 illus-

---

[2]Other terms used for authentic assessment are *accurate*, *active*, *aligned*, *alternative*, and *direct* assessment. *Performance assessment* is also sometimes used, but performance assessment more properly refers to the type of student response being assessed, whereas authentic assessment refers to the assessment situation. Although not all performance assessments are authentic, assessments that are authentic are most assuredly performance assessments. For further elaboration, see Carol A. Meyer, "What's the Difference Between 'Authentic' and 'Performance' Assessment?" *Educational Leadership* 49(8):39–40 (May 1992).

[3]Steven J. Rakow, "Assessment: A Driving Force," *Science Scope* 15(6):3 (March 1992), p. 3.

Student _____	Course _____	School _____
Observer _____	Date _____	Period _____

Objective for Time Period	Desired Behavior	What Student Did, Said, or Wrote

Teacher's (observer's) comments:

Figure 10.2   Sample Form for Evaluating and Recording Student Behaviors

trates a sample form for recording and evaluating teacher observations of a student's verbal and nonverbal behaviors.

Please remember that, with each technique used, you must proceed from your awareness of anticipated learning outcomes (the instructional objectives), and you must evaluate a student's progress toward meeting those objectives. That is referred to as **criterion-referenced assessment**.

Here are guidelines to follow when assessing a student's verbal and nonverbal behaviors in the classroom:

1. Maintain an anecdotal record book or folder, with a separate section in it for your records of each student.

2. List the desirable behaviors for each specific activity.
3. Check the list against the specific instructional objectives.
4. Record your observations as quickly as possible following your observation. Audio or video recordings and computer software programs can help you check the accuracy of your memory. If the use of such technology is inconvenient, you should spend time during school, immediately after, or later that evening recording your observations while still fresh in your memory.
5. Record your professional judgment about the student's progress toward the desired behavior, but think it through before transferring any comments to a permanent record.
6. Write comments that are reminders to yourself, such as:

   "Check validity of observation by further testing."

   "Discuss observations with student's parent."

   "Discuss observations with school counselor."

   "Discuss observations with other teachers on the teaching team."

Assessing What a Student Writes

When assessing what a student writes, you can use worksheets, written homework, student journal writing, student portfolios, and tests. In many schools, portfolios, worksheets, and homework assignments are the tools usually used for the formative assessment of each student's achievement. Tests, too, should be a part of this assessment, but tests are also used both for summative assessment at the end of a unit and for diagnostic purposes as well.

Your summative assessment of a student's achievement, and any other final judgment made by you about a student, can have impact upon the emotional and intellectual development of that student (special attention is given to that point in the section Recording Teacher Observations and Judgments later in the module).

Here are guidelines to follow when assessing what a student writes:

1. Make sure worksheets, homework, and test items correlate with and are compatible with specific instructional objectives.
2. Read everything a student writes. If you think the assignment is important for the student to write, then it is equally important that you give your professional attention to the product of the student's efforts.
3. Provide written or verbal comments about the student's work, and be positive in those comments. Rather than just writing "good" on a student's paper, briefly explain what it was about it that made it good. Try to avoid negative comments. Rather than simply saying or pointing out that the student didn't do it right, tell or show the student acceptable ways and how to get there. For reinforcement, use positive rewards as frequently as possible.
4. Think before writing a comment on a student's paper. Ask yourself how you think the student (or a parent or guardian) will interpret the comment and if that is the interpretation you intend.
5. Avoid writing negative comments or grades in student journals. Student journals are valuable for encouraging students to write, to think about their thinking, and to record their creative thoughts. In journal writing students should be encouraged to write about their experiences in school and out of school, and especially about their experiences related to what is being learned. They should be encouraged to write their feelings about what is being learned and about how they are learning it. Writing in journals gives students practice in expressing themselves in written form and in making thoughtful connections in their learning, and it should provide a nonthreatening medium in which to do so. Comments and evaluations from teachers might discourage creative and spontaneous expression.
6. Talk individually with students about their journals to seek clarification of their written expressions. Student journals are useful to the teacher (of any subject field) in understanding the student's thought processes and writing skills (for diagnostic evaluation). Journals should never be graded. For grading purposes, teachers may simply record whether the stu-

dent is maintaining a journal and, perhaps, a judgment about the quantity of writing in it—but there should be no judgment of the quality.

7. Talk individually with students about any progress in learning shown by materials in their student portfolios (described in a later section). Students should keep in their portfolios all papers related to the course. As with student journals, portfolios should never be graded; also, portfolios of different students should never be compared. The purpose of a portfolio is primarily for student self-assessment—to help a student see progress in his or her learning.

Regardless of the avenue chosen and the relative weight given by you to each, your evaluation must be made with the instructional objectives in mind. Any given objective may be checked by using more than one method, and by using more than one instrument. Subjectivity, inherent in the evaluation process, can be reduced as you check for validity, comparing results of one measuring technique against those of another.

Although assessment of cognitive objectives lends itself to traditional written tests of achievement, the assessment of affective and psychomotor objectives requires the use of performance checklists where student behaviors can be observed in action. Even for cognitive learning, educators today are encouraging the use of **alternative assessment**—that is, authentic assessment procedures that serve as alternatives to traditional paper-and-pencil tests. Alternative assessment strategies include the use of projects, portfolios, skits, papers, oral presentations, and performance tests. One advantage claimed for the use of such authentic assessment includes the direct (performance-based, or criterion-referenced or outcome-based) measurement of what students should know and can do. Another advantage claimed is an emphasis on higher-order thinking. Disadvantages of authentic assessment include higher costs, difficulty in making results consistent and usable, and problems with validity, reliability, and comparability.

Unfortunately, for the teacher who never sees a student again after a given school year is over, any effects the teacher has had on a student's values and attitudes may never be observed by that teacher. Consider, though, schools in which groups or teams of teachers remain with the same cohort of students throughout several years of school ("houses," as discussed in Module 1). Those teachers often do have the opportunity to observe the positive changes in their students' values and attitudes.

Cooperative Learning and Assessment

As discussed in Module 6, the purpose of a cooperative learning group is for the group to learn. But group achievement in learning necessarily depends on the learning of individuals within the group. Rather than competing for rewards for achievement, members of the group cooperate with one another, helping all members learn, so that the group reward will be a good one. Theoretically, when small groups of students of mixed backgrounds, skills, and capabilities work together toward a common goal, the students enhance their liking and respect for one another. As a result, there is an increase both in each student's self-esteem and in academic achievement.

When the achievement of a cooperative learning group is recognized, group achievement is rewarded, but there must be rewards for individuals within the group as well. The emphasis must be on peer support rather than peer pressure, and thus you must be cautious about ever giving group grades. Some teachers give bonus points to all members of the group when everyone in the group has reached preset criteria, and then individuals add those points to individual scores. In establishing preset standards, the standards can be different for individuals within a group, depending on each member's ability and past performance. It is important that each member of a group feel rewarded and successful. Some teachers also give subjective grades to individual students on their role performances within the group.

For determination of students' report card grades, the achievement of individual students is measured through individual results on tests and other assessment instruments. And the final grade is based on those individual results as well as on the student's performance in the group.

Involving Students in Self-Assessment

In exemplary school programs, each student's continuous self-assessment is an important component of the evaluation process. If students are to progress in their understanding of their own thinking (metacognition), as well as in their intellectual development, then they must receive instruction and guidance in how to become more responsible for their own learning (i.e., to be empowered). During that process they learn to think better of themselves and of their individual capabilities. To achieve this self-understanding and improved self-esteem requires the experiences afforded by successes, along with guidance in self-understanding.

Portfolios

To meet these goals, teachers should provide opportunities for students to think about what they are learning, about how they are learning it, and about how far they have progressed. One procedure is for students to maintain portfolios of their work, using rating scales or checklists to assess their own progress periodically. The student portfolio should be well organized and contain assignment sheets, class worksheets, the results of homework, forms for student self-evaluation and reflection on past work, and other class materials thought important by the students and teacher.

Portfolio assessment as an alternative to traditional methods of evaluating student progress has gained momentum in recent years, but setting standards can be very difficult. Thus far, research on the use of portfolios for assessment indicates that the validity and reliability of teacher evaluation is quite low.[4] Before using portfolios as an alternative to traditional testing, teachers must consider and clearly understand the reasons for doing it, carefully decide on portfolio content, consider parent and guardian reactions, and anticipate grading problems.[5] (For additional resources on the use of student portfolios refer to the suggested readings at the end of this module.)

Rating scales and checklists both emphasize the criteria for evaluation and provide students with means of expressing their feelings. They also give the teacher still another source of input data for use in evaluation. To provide students with reinforcement and guidance for their learning and development, teachers meet with individual students to discuss their self-evaluations. Such conferences should provide students with understandable and achievable short-term goals, as well as help them develop and maintain adequate self-esteem.

Although most any of the instruments used for evaluating student work can be used for student self-evaluation, in some cases it might be better to construct specific instruments for that purpose, instruments constructed with the student's understanding of the instrument in mind. Student self-evaluation and reflection should be done on a regular and continuing basis, so comparisons can be made by the student from one time to the next. You will need to help students learn how to make these comparisons. Comparisons should provide a student with information previously not recognized about his or her own progress and growth.

Checklists

One of the items maintained by students in their portfolios should be a series of self-evaluation checklists. Items on a student's self-evaluation checklist will vary depending on subject and grade level. Generic items similar to those in Figures 10.3 and 10.4 can be used. (Another sample checklist is the one presented in the Model Unit Plan of Module 4). Checklist items (1–6 in Figure 10.3) can be used easily by a student in comparing with previous self-evaluations. The open-ended items (7 and 8 in Figure 10.3) allow the student to provide additional information as well as an opportunity to do some expressive writing.

---

[4]John O'Neil, "Portfolio Assessment Bears the Burden of Popularity," *ASCD Update* 35(8):3, 8 (October 1993).

[5]Susan Black, "Portfolio Assessment," *Executive Educator* 15(1):28–31 (February 1993). To assist educators in portfolio assessment are two publications: *Portfolio News*, Portfolio Assessment Clearinghouse, San Dieguito High School District, 710 Encinitas Blvd., Encinitas, CA 92024; and *Portfolio Assessment Newsletter*, Northwest Evaluation Association, 5 Centerpointe Drive, Suite 100, Lake Oswego, OR 97035.

Student Self-Evaluation Form

Student: _____   Date: _____

Teacher: _____   Number: _____

Circle one response for each of the first six items. If you circle the last response of any of the items, you can write a response that is more accurate than the given ones.

1. Since my last self-evaluation, my assignments have been turned in:
    a. always on time
    b. always late
    c. sometimes late; sometimes on time
    d.

2. Most of my classmates:
    a. like me
    b. don't like me
    c. ignore me
    d.

3. I think I am:
    a. smart
    b. the smartest in the class
    c. the slowest in the class
    d.

4. In this course, since my last self-evaluation I think I am:
    a. doing better
    b. doing worse
    c. doing about the same
    d.

5. In this course, I am:
    a. learning a lot
    b. not learning very much
    c. not learning anything
    d.

6. In this course, I am:
    a. doing the best work I can
    b. not doing as well as I can
    c.

7. Describe what you have learned in this class since your last self-evaluation that you have used outside of school. Tell how you used it. (You can refer to your previous self-evaluation.)

8. Describe anything that you have learned about yourself since you completed your last self-evaluation. (You can refer to your previous self-evaluation.)

Figure 10.3   Student Self-Assessment (to be kept in student's portfolio): A Sample Generic Form

Student Self-Evaluation Form

Student: _____ Date: _____

Teacher: _____ Number: _____

Draft Title of Paper: _____

Answer the following questions about the draft of your own paper after all group members have shared their papers by reading them aloud to others in the group.

	Yes	No
1. In my introduction, I put forth my thesis.	____	____
2. In the beginning I orient the reader by providing relevant background information and sources.	____	____
3. I support my interpretive claims by providing (circle those that apply): textual evidence, specific quotations, personal experience, related readings.	____	____
4. I explain how my examples support my claim by using words such as *shows, demonstrates, proves,* and *illustrates.*	____	____
5. My supporting evidence provides the bulk of my composition.	____	____
6. I take a strong, consistent stance and maintain it.	____	____
7. I convince my readers that my interpretation is valid.	____	____

8. What I like best about my paper is:

9. A part where I need more information is:

10. Other revisions I might make are:

Figure 10.4 Student Self-Assessment (to be kept in students portfolio): A Sample Generic Form for an Interpretive Writing Assignment

Source: Adapted from unpublished material by Pam Benedetti, *Using Portfolios to Strengthen Student Assessment in English/Language Arts (Grades 6–12)*, Copyright 1991 by Pam Benedetti, p. 29.

Maintaining Records of Student Achievement

You must maintain well-organized and complete records of student achievement. You may do this in a written record book or on an electronic record book (i.e., a computer software program, one commercially developed or one you develop yourself, perhaps by using a computer spreadsheet as the base). The record book should include tardies and absences as well as all records of scores on tests, homework, projects, and other assignments.

Anecdotal records can be maintained in a separate binder (or separate computer file, a section for each student (organized in alphabetical order). Daily interactions and events occur in the classroom that may provide informative data about a student's intellectual, emotional, and physical development. Maintaining a dated record of your observations of these interactions and events can provide important information that might otherwise be forgotten if not written down. At the end of a unit and again at the conclusion of a grading term, you will want to review your records. During the course of the school year your anecdotal records (and those of other members of your teaching team) will provide important information about the intellectual, psychological, and physical development of each student, and ideas about attention that may need to be given to individual students.

Recording Teacher Observations and Judgments

As noted previously, you must carefully think through any written comments that you intend to make about a student. Students can be quite sensitive to what others say about them—most particularly to negative comments about them made by a teacher.

In addition, anecdotal comments in students' permanent records often say more about the teachers who made the comments than about the recipient students. Comments made carelessly, hurriedly, and thoughtlessly can be detrimental to a student's welfare and progress in school. Teacher comments must be professional. That is, those comments must be diagnostically useful to the continued intellectual and psychological development of the child. This is true for any comment the teacher makes or writes, whether on a student's paper or on the student's permanent school record, or on a note sent home to a student's parent or guardian.

For example, consider this unprofessional comment found in one student's permanent record: "John is lazy." Describing John as "lazy" could be done by anyone; it is nonproductive, and it is certainly not a professional diagnosis. How many times do you suppose are needed for John to receive such negative descriptions of his behavior before he begins to believe that he is just that—lazy—and as a result will act that way even more often? Written comments like that can also be damaging because they may be read by the teacher who next has John in class, and that teacher may simply perpetuate the same expectation of John. To say that John is lazy merely describes behavior as judged by the teacher who wrote the comment. More important, and more professional, would be for the teacher to analyze why John is behaving that way and then to prescribe activities that are likely to motivate John to assume a more constructive charge of his own learning behavior.

For students' continued intellectual and emotional development, your comments should be useful, productive, analytical, diagnostic, and prescriptive. The professional teacher makes diagnoses and prepares prescriptions. A professional teacher does not label students as being "lazy," "vulgar," "slow," "stupid," "difficult," or "dumb." The professional teacher sees the behavior of a student as being goal-directed. Perhaps "lazy" John discovered that that particular behavioral pattern won him attention. John's goal, then, was attention, and he used negative, perhaps even self-destructive, behavioral patterns to reach that goal. The task of any professional teacher is to facilitate the learner's understanding (perception) of a goal, with the identification of acceptable behaviors positively designed to reach that goal.

What separates the professional teacher from just anyone "off the street" is the teacher's ability to go beyond mere description of behavior. Keep that in mind always when you write comments that will be read by students, their parents or guardians, and other teachers.

Grading and Marking Student Achievement

If conditions were ideal (which they are not) and if teachers did their job perfectly well (which many of us do not), then all students would receive top marks (the ultimate in mastery learning) and there would be less need to talk about grading here. Mastery learning implies that some end point of learning is attainable, but there probably isn't an end point. In any case, because conditions for teaching are never ideal and teachers are merely human, this topic (grading) is undoubtedly of special interest to you, to your students, to their parents or guardians, to school counselors, administrators and school boards, and to college admissions offices.

In this module we have frequently used the term *achievement*. What is meant by that term? Achievement means accomplishment, but is it accomplishment of the instructional objectives against preset standards or is it just simple accomplishment? Most teachers would probably endorse the former—the teacher subjectively establishes a standard that must be met in order for a student to receive a certain grade for an assignment, a test, or a quarter, a semester, or a course. In that case, achievement is decided by degrees of accomplishment.

Preset standards are usually expressed in percentages (degrees of accomplishment) needed for marks or *ABC* grades. If no student achieves the standard required for an *A*, for example, then no student receives an *A*. On the other hand, if all students meet the preset standard for an *A*, then all receive *A*s. Determining student grades on the basis of preset standards is referred to as criterion-referenced grading.

Criterion-Referenced vs. Norm-Referenced Grading

Criterion-referenced grading is grading that is based on preset standards. **Norm-referenced** grading, in contrast, is based on the relative accomplishment of individuals in a group (e.g., one classroom of ninth-grade English students) or in some larger group (e.g., all students enrolled in ninth-grade English), established by comparing and ranking students—commonly known as "grading on a curve."

Note well that norm-referenced grading is *not* recommended, because it encourages competition and discourages cooperative learning. Norm-referenced grading, or grading on a curve, is educationally dysfunctional. After all, each student is an individual and should not be converted to a statistic on a frequency-distribution curve. After several years of teaching, you may want to produce frequency-distribution studies of grades you have given in a course you have been teaching. But you should never grade students on a curve. Grades for student achievement should be tied to performance levels and determined on the basis of each student's achievement toward preset standards.

In norm-referenced grading, the aim is to reveal how the individual compares either with other students in the group under instruction or with the larger groups who have taken a particular test. Such grading can sometimes be useful when communicating information about students to parents and colleges or employment agencies. In criterion-referenced grading the aim is to communicate information about an individual student's progress either in knowledge and work skills compared with that student's previous attainment or in the pursuit of an absolute, such as content mastery. Criterion-referenced grading is generally used in continuous-progress curricula, competency-based (outcome-based education) curricula, and other programs that focus on individualized education.

Each of the two approaches is based on a different philosophy. Norm-referenced grading recognizes a competitive social structure. The grade is assigned to indicate how a student compares with other students. The top grade, usually an *A*, generally means that the students receiving that grade have learned the content better than most other students in the comparison group. The lowest grade, *F* or *U* in most scales, shows that the student has done poorly and has achieved less than others in the group. In general, the system assumes that the group of students approximates a normal distribution, or bell-shaped curve. Such a distribution of marks follows a pattern of a similar number of *A*s and *F*s and of *B*s and *D*s, with the largest number of students receiving *C*s.

One problem that frequently occurs when using norm-referenced grading is what to do with students in high academic courses. If an *A–F* grading scale is used for them, will it accurately represent each student's achievement for college entrance purposes? For example, does a *C* in an advanced English class indicate the same level achieved as a *C* in an average English class? The achievement in the advanced section probably represents more complex content and more sophisticated activities by students. To counteract the grade effect of a more difficult curriculum, some schools have special procedures for indicating advanced work on transcripts sent to colleges or to prospective employers. The same kinds of difficulties may arise with students from courses with lower academic expectations. Employers may interpret grades so that expectations for performance are unrealistic. Then, of course, the school is blamed. Grades often have effects that extend beyond the school.

Criterion-referenced or competency-based grading (the recommended method for the determination of student grades) is based on the level at which each student meets the specified objectives (standards) for the course. The objectives must be clearly stated to represent important student learning outcomes. This approach implies that effective teaching and learning result in high grades (As) for most students. In fact, when a mastery concept is used, a student must accomplish the objectives before being allowed to proceed to the next learning task. The philosophy of teachers who favor criterion-referenced procedures recognizes individual potential. Such teachers accept the challenge of finding teaching strategies to help students progress from one level to the next designated level. Instead of wondering how Sally compares with Juanita, the comparison is between what Juanita could do yesterday and what she can do today, and how well these performances compare to the preset standard.

Most school systems use some sort of combination of norm-referenced and criterion-referenced grading. In beginning keyboarding, for example, a certain basic speed and accuracy are established as criteria. Perhaps only the upper third of the advanced keyboarding class will be recommended for the advanced class in computer programming. The grading for the beginning class might appropriately be criterion-based, but grading for the advanced class might be norm-referenced. Sometimes both kinds of information are needed. For example, a report card for a student in the eighth grade might indicate how that student is meeting certain criteria, such as an A grade for addition of fractions. Another entry on the report card might show that this mastery is expected, however, at the sixth grade.

Both criterion- and norm-referenced data may be communicated to the parents or guardians and to the students. Appropriate procedures should be used: a criterion-referenced approach to show whether or not the student can accomplish the task, and a norm-referenced approach to show how well that student performs compared with the larger group to which the student belongs. Sometimes, one or the other is needed; other times, both are required.

Determining Grades

Once entered onto school transcripts, grades have significant impact upon the futures of students. Determining achievement grades for student performance is serious business, for which several important and professional decisions must be made by you. In a few schools, and for certain classes or assignments, only marks such as E, S, and I or *pass/no pass* are used, but for most courses taught in middle schools and secondary schools, percentages of accomplishment and ABC grades are used. Consider the following guidelines for arriving at final grades:

1.   At the start of the school term, first explain your marking and grading policies to yourself. Then explain those policies to your students and their parents or guardians at Back-to-School Night, or by a written explanation sent home, or both.

2.   When converting your interpretation of a student's accomplishments to a letter grade, be as objective as possible.

3.   Build your grading policy around accomplishment rather than failure, where students proceed from one accomplishment to the next. This is continuous promotion, not necessarily from one grade to the next, but within the classroom. (Some schools have done away with grade-level designation and, in its place, use the concept of continuous promotion from the time of student entry into the school through the student's graduation from it.)

4.   For the establishment of criteria for ABC grades, select a percentage standard, such as 92 percent for an A, 85 percent for a B, 75 percent for a C, and 65 percent for a D. The cut-off percentages used are your decision, though the district, school, or program area may have established guidelines to which you are expected to adhere.

5.   *Assessment* and *grading* are not synonymous terms. As you learned earlier, evaluation implies the collection of information from a variety of sources, including measurement techniques and subjective observations. These data, then, become the basis for arriving at a final grade—which, in effect, is a final value judgment. Grades, one aspect of assessment, are intended to communicate educational progress to students and to their parents or guardians. To be valid as an indicator of that progress, you must use a variety of sources of data for determination of a student's final grade.

6.   For the determination of students' final grades, we recommend using a point system, where things that students write, say and do are given points (but not for journals or portfolios, except perhaps simply whether the student does one or not). The point total, then, is the primary factor for grade determination. For example, if 92 percent is the cutoff for an *A* and 500 points are possible, then any student with 460 points or more (500 × .92) has achieved an *A*. Likewise, for a test or any other assignment, if the value is 100 points, the cutoff for an *A* is 92 (100 × .92). With a point system and preset standards, both the teacher and the students, at any time during the year, always know the current points possible and can easily calculate a student's current grade standing. Then, as far as a current grade is concerned, students know always where they stand in the course.

7.   Students will be absent and will miss assignments and tests. Therefore, it is best that you decide beforehand your policy about makeup work. Your policies about late assignments and missed tests must be clearly communicated to students and to their parents or guardians. For makeup work, consider these recommendations:

- *Homework assignments.* For homework assignments, you should strictly adhere to due dates, giving no credit or reduced credit for work turned in late. You may think this is harsh and rigid, but experience has shown it to be a good policy to which students can and should adjust. It is much like the world of work (and of college) to which they must become accustomed, and it is a policy that is sensible for a teacher who deals with many papers each day. Of course, to work well, students must be given their assignments not at the last minute but long before the due dates.
- *Tests.* Sometimes students are absent when tests are given. For those instances, you have several options. Some teachers allow students to miss or discount one test per grading period. Another option is to allow each student to substitute a written homework assignment or project for one missed test. Still another option is to give the absent student the choice of either taking a makeup test or having the next test count double. When makeup tests are given, the makeup test should be taken within a week of the regular test unless there is a compelling reason (e.g., medical problem or family situation problem) why this cannot happen. Some students miss a testing period not because of being absent from school but because of their involvement in other school activities. In those instances, the student may be able to arrange to come into another of your class periods, on that day or the next, and take the test. If a student for some reason is absent during performance testing, the logistics—and possible diminished reliability—of having to readminister the test for one student may necessitate giving the student an alternative written test.

Testing for Achievement

One source of information used in determining grades are the data obtained from testing for student achievement. Competent planning, preparing, administering, and scoring of tests together constitute an important professional skill, for which you will gain valuable practical experience during your student teaching. This section offers helpful guidelines that you can refer to while you are student teaching and again, occasionally, during your first few years as a credentialed teacher.

Purposes for Testing

Textbook publisher's tests, test item pools, and standardized tests are available from a variety of sources. But because schools are different, teachers are different, and children are different, you will likely be designing and preparing many of your tests for your own purposes and your own distinct group of students. Tests can be designed for several purposes, and a variety of kinds of tests and alternative test items will keep your testing program interesting, useful, and reliable. As a university student, you are probably most experienced with testing for measuring achievement. As a middle school and secondary school teacher, you will use tests for other reasons as well. These other purposes include:

- To assess and aid in curriculum development.
- To help determine teaching effectiveness.
- To help students develop positive attitudes, appreciations, and values.
- To help students increase their understanding and retention of facts, principles, skills, and concepts.
- To motivate students.
- To provide diagnostic information for planning for individualization of the instruction.
- To provide review and drill to enhance teaching and learning.
- To serve as a source of information for students and parents.

When and How Often to Test for Achievement

It is difficult to generalize about how often to test for student achievement, but for most situations testing should be cumulative and frequent. That is, the items for each assessment should measure for the student's understanding of previously learned material as well as for the current unit of study, and tests should be given as often as once a week. The advantages of assessment that is cumulative include the review, reinforcement, and articulation of old material with the recent. The advantages of frequent assessment include a reduction in student anxiety over tests and an increase in the validity of final grades.

Test Construction

After determining the reasons for which you are designing and administering a test, you need to identify the specific instructional objectives the test is being designed to measure. (As you learned in Module 3, your written instructional objectives are so specific that you can write test items to measure against those objectives.) So, the first step in test construction is to identify the purpose(s) for the test. The second step is to identify the objectives to be measured. And the third step is to prepare the test items. The best time to prepare draft items is after you have prepared your instructional objectives, while the objectives are fresh in your mind—which means before the lessons are taught. After a lesson is taught you will then want to rework your first draft of the test items for that lesson.

Administering Tests

For many students test taking can be a time of high anxiety. To measure student achievement accurately, you will want to take steps to reduce that anxiety. Students demonstrate test anxiety in various ways. Just before and during testing, some are quiet and thoughtful, while others are noisy and disruptive. To control or reduce student anxieties, consider these guidelines when administering tests:

1. Since students respond best to familiar routine, plan your program so tests are given at regular intervals (same day each week) and administered at the same time and in the same way. In many high schools, days of the week are assigned to departments for administering major tests. For example, Tuesdays might be assigned for foreign language testing, while Wednesday might be the day for science testing.

2. Avoid writing tests that are too long and that will take too much time. Beginning teachers, in particular, sometimes have unreasonable expectations of students, especially those students of junior high and middle school age, about their attention spans during testing. Frequent testing, and frequent sampling of student knowledge, is better than infrequent and long tests that attempt to cover everything.

3.   When giving paper-and-pencil tests, try to arrange your classroom so the room is well-ventilated, the temperature is comfortable, and the seats are well-spaced. If spacing is a problem, then consider the use of alternative forms of the test, where students next to one another have different forms of the same test (e.g., multiple-choice answer alternatives are arranged in different order).

4.   Before test time be certain that you have a sufficient number of copies of the test. Although this may sound obvious, there have been many instances where the teacher started a test with an insufficient number of test copies. Perhaps the test was duplicated for the teacher by someone else and a mistake was made in the number run off. Whatever the method used for copying, always ensure that you have enough copies of the test.

5.   Before distributing the test, explain to students what they are to do upon completion—such as begin a homework assignment for this or another class—because not all will finish at the same time. Rather than expecting students to sit quietly after finishing a test, they should have something to do.

6.   When ready to test, don't drag it out. Distribute tests quickly and efficiently.

7.   Once testing has begun, avoid interrupting the students. Items of important information can be written on the board or held until all are finished with the test.

8.   During testing, remain in the room and visually monitor the students.

9.   If the test is not going to take an entire class period (and most shouldn't), give it at the beginning of the period, if possible, unless you are planning a test review just prior to the test itself.

Cheating

Cheating on tests does occur, but there are ways to reduce the opportunity and pressure to cheat. Consider the following suggestions:

1. Space students, or use alternative forms of the test.
2. Test frequently, which ensures that a single test does not count too much, reduces text anxiety and the pressure that can cause cheating, and increases student learning by "stimulating greater effort and providing intermittent feedback" to the student.[6]
3. Prepare test questions that are clear—that are not ambiguous—thereby reducing student frustration caused by a question or instructions that students do not understand.
4. Avoid tests that are too long and that will take too much time. During long tests, some students get discouraged and restless, and that is when classroom management problems can occur.
5. Provide monitors for performance tests. These tests, by their sheer nature, can exert great pressure on students and can also provide more opportunity for cheating than paper-and-pencil tests. When administering performance tests to an entire class, it is best to have several monitors. If that isn't possible, consider testing groups of students, such as cooperative learning groups, rather than individuals. Evaluation of test performance, then, would be based on group, rather than individual, achievement.
6. Consider using open-text and open-notebook tests. When students can use their books and pages of notes, it not only reduces anxiety but also helps them with the organization and retention of what has been learned.

If you suspect cheating is occurring, move to the area of the suspected student and stand there. Usually that will stop it. When you suspect cheating has occurred (not caught at the time), you are faced with a dilemma. Unless your suspicion is backed by solid proof, you are advised to forget it, but keep a close watch on the student the next time to prevent cheating from happening. Your job is not to catch students being dishonest, but to prevent it. If you do have absolute proof, then you are obligated to proceed with school policy on student cheating,

[6]Herbert J. Walberg, "Productive Teaching and Instruction: Assessing the Knowledge Base," *Phi Delta Kappan* 71(6):470–478 (February 1990), p. 472.

which may call for a session with the counselor or the student and the student's parent or guardian, perhaps an automatic *F* on the test, and even suspension.

Time Needed to Take a Test

Again, avoid giving tests that are too long and that will take too much time. Preparing and administering good tests is a skill that you will develop over time. In the meantime, test frequently, and use tests that sample student achievement rather than try for a comprehensive measure of that achievement.

Some students take more time on a given test than do others. You want to avoid giving too much time, or classroom management problems will result. On the other hand, you don't want to cut short the time needed by students who can do well but need more time to think and write. Use Table 10.1 as a guide for the time needed for different types of test items. This is only a guide for determining the approximate amount of time to allow students to complete a test. For example, a test composed of ten multiple-choice items, five arrangement items, and two short-explanation items should be planned to take about 30 minutes.

Preparing Assessment Items

Writing good assessment items is yet another professional skill, and to become proficient at it takes study, time, and practice. Because of the recognized importance of an assessment program, you should take this professional responsibility seriously. Although poorly prepared items take no time at all to prepare, they will cause you more trouble than you can ever imagine. As a professional you should take the time to study different types of assessment items that can be used, and to find out how best to write them, and to practice writing them. When writing items, you should ensure that they match and sufficiently cover the instructional objectives. In addition, you should write each item carefully enough to be reasonably confident that each item will be understood by the student in the manner that you anticipate its being understood.

Classification of Assessment Items

Assessment items can be classified into three categories:

- *Verbal* (oral or written words).
- *Visual* (pictures and diagrams).
- *Manipulative* or *performance* (handling of materials and equipment).

Written verbal items are traditionally the ones most frequently used in testing. But visual tests are useful, such as when working with students who lack fluency with the written word (i.e., when testing for the knowledge of students who have limited proficiency in English).

Performance items and tests are useful when measuring for psychomotor skill development. Performance testing of locomotor skills are common, such as a student's ability to skip a rope or a

Table 10.1 Time to Allow for Testing, as Determined by the Types of Test Items

Type of Test Item	Time Needed
Matching	1 minute per matching item
Multiple choice	1 minute per item
Completion and Correction	1 minute per item
Completion drawing	2–3 minutes per item
Arrangement and Grouping	2–3 minutes per item
Identification	2–3 minutes per item
Short explanation and Modified true/false	2–3 minutes per item
Essay and Performance	10 minutes or more per item

student's ability to carry a microscope (gross motor skill) and focus a microscope (fine motor skill). Performance testing can also be a part of a wider testing program that includes testing for higher-level affective and cognitive skills and knowledge. An example is when a student or a small group of students are given the task of creating from discarded materials a habitat for an imaginary animal, and then to display and describe their product to the rest of the class. As noted, educators today have taken a renewed interest in performance testing as a means of assessment that is close to measuring for the real thing (i.e., assessment that is authentic).

Alternative Assessment

Both the type of test and the items you use depend upon your purpose and objectives. Carefully consider the alternatives within that framework. A good assessment program will likely include items from all three types, to provide validity checks and to account for the individual differences of students. Those purposes are what writers of articles in professional journals are considering when they discuss alternative assessment. They are encouraging the use of multiple assessment items as opposed to the traditional heavy reliance on objective items, such as multiple-choice questions.

General Guidelines for Preparing Assessment Items

In preparing assessment items you should:

1. Include several types of items.
2. Ensure that content coverage is complete (i.e., that all objectives are being measured).
3. Ensure that each item of the test is reliable (i.e., that it measures the intended objective). One way to check item reliability is to have more than one test item measuring for the same objective.
4. Ensure that each item is clear and unambiguous.
5. Plan the item to be difficult enough for the poorly prepared student but easy enough for the student who is well prepared.
6. Maintain a bank of assessment items. Because writing good assessment items is time consuming; you should keep a bank of your items, with each item coded according to its matching instructional objective and according to its domain (cognitive, affective, or psychomotor). Also indicate whether it requires low-level recall, processing, or application, and perhaps the level within the hierarchy of its particular domain. Computer software programs are available for such purposes.[7] When preparing items for your own test bank, use your best creative writing skills—prepare items that match your objectives, put them aside, think about them, then work them again.

The test you administer to your students should represent your best professional effort—it should be clean and without spelling and grammar errors. A quickly or poorly prepared test can cause you more grief than you can imagine. A test that obviously had been hurriedly prepared—one rife with spelling errors, for instance—will be frowned upon by discerning parents or guardians. If you are a student teacher, such a test will certainly bring about a strong admonishment from your university supervisor. And if the sloppiness continues, your speedy dismissal from the program will follow.

Attaining Validity

To be sure that your assessment measures what is supposed to be measured, you should construct a table of specifications. This two-way grid indicates behavior in one dimension and con-

---

[7]Ready-made banks of test items are available on computer discs and accompany many programs or textbooks. If you use them, be certain that the items match your course objectives and that they are well written. Just because the items were published does not mean they are well written. Some state departments of education have made efforts to develop test banks for teachers. For example, see John A. Willis, "Learning Outcome Testing Program: Standardized Classroom Testing in West Virginia through Item Banking, Test Generation, and Curricular Management Software," *Educational Measurement: Issues and Practices* 9(2):11–14 (Summer 1990).

tent in the other, as shown in Table 10.2. In this grid, behavior relates to the three domains: cognitive, affective, and psychomotor. The cognitive domain, involving mental processes, is divided, according to Bloom's taxonomy, into six categories: (1) simple memory or knowledge, (2) comprehension, (3) application, (4) analysis, (5) synthesis (usually involves an original product in oral, written, or artistic form), and (6) evaluation. (See Module 3 for a fuller explanation of the domains.)

The teacher examining objectives for the unit decides what emphasis should be given to the behavior and to the content. For instance, if vocabulary development is a concern for this class, then probably 20 percent of the test on vocabulary may be appropriate, but 50 percent would be unsuitable. This planning enables the teacher to design a test to fit the situation, rather than a haphazard test that does not correspond to the objectives either in content or behavior emphasis. Since knowledge questions are easy to write, tests often fail to go beyond that level even though the objectives state that the student will analyze and evaluate. The sample table of specifications for a unit in World Literature on Understanding Others (Table 10.2) indicates a distribution of questions on a test. Since this test is to be an objective test and it is so difficult to write objective-type items to test syntheses and affective and psychomotor behaviors, this table of specifications calls for no test items in these areas. If these categories are included in the unit objectives, some other additional evaluative devices must be used to test learning in these categories. The teacher could also show the objectives tested, as indicated within parentheses in Table 10.2. Then, a check on inclusion of all objectives is easy.

TWELVE TYPES OF ASSESSMENT ITEMS

The sections that follow present the advantages and disadvantages of twelve types of assessment items for your use in alternative assessment of student learning. As you consider each type, notice that some are appropriate for use in direct or performance assessment, whereas others are not.

Table 10.2   Table of Specifications .

CONTENT	BEHAVIORS								TOTAL
World Literature	Cognitive						Affec-tive	Psycho-motor	
Understanding Others	Knowl-edge	Compre-hension	Appli-cation	Analy-sis	Syn-thesis	Evalu-ation			
I. Vocabulary Development		3 (1,2)	2 (2)						5
II. Individual Selections			1 (8)	2 (7)		2 (7)			5
III. Literary Forms and Style	1 (3)		1 (3)	1 (6)		2 (6)			5
IV. Comparison of Culture	2 (4,5)			3 (4)					5
V. Comparison of Values	3 (5)			1 (5)		1 (8)			5
TOTAL	6	3	4	7		5			25

angement

tion. Terms or real objects (realia) are presented and the student arranges them in a
ed order.
xample 1:

om the following list of planets in our solar system, arrange them in order beginning with the one
closest to the sun.

Example 2:

The assortment of balls on the table represents the planets in our solar system. [Note: The balls are
of various sizes, such as marbles, golf balls, tennis balls, and basketballs, and are labeled with their
appropriate planetary names, with a large sphere in the center representing the sun]. Arrange the
balls in their proper order around the sun.

Advantages. This type of item tests for knowledge of sequence and order, and is good for
review, for starting discussions, and for performance assessment. Example 2, a manipulative
(performance) test item, is recommended for observing and assessing the skill and intellectual
development of students.

Disadvantages. Scoring may be difficult, so be cautious and meticulous when using this type
for grading purposes.

Guidelines for Use. When arrangement items are in a paper-and-pencil test, as in Example
1, include instructions to students to write a rationale for their arrangement, thus making the
item a combined arrangement and short-explanation type. Be sure to allow space for explanations on an answer sheet. Such a combination of types enhances reliability.

2. Completion Drawing
Description: An incomplete drawing is presented and the student completes it.
Example 1:

Connect the following items with arrow lines to show the stages from planting of cotton to the distribution of wearing apparel to consumers.

Example 2:

In the following food web, draw arrow lines showing which organisms are consumers and which are
producers.

Advantages. This type takes less time to complete than a whole drawing, which may be
required in an essay item. Scoring is relatively easy.

Disadvantages. Care needs to be exercised in the instructions so students do not misinterpret
the expectation.

Guidelines for Use. Use occasionally for diversion, but take care in preparing. Example 1 is
typical of this type when used in integrated thematic teaching. This type of item can be instructive when assessing for student thinking. Consider making the item a combined completion-
drawing, short-explanation type by having students include their rationales for their drawings.
Be sure to allow space for their explanations.

3. Completion Statement

Description.   An incomplete sentence is presented and the student completes it by filling in the blank space(s).

Example 1:

The name of the author of "The Beggar" is _____.

Example 2:

To test their hypotheses, scientists conduct _____.

Advantages.   This type is easy to devise, to take, and to score.

Disadvantages.   This type tends to emphasize rote memory. It is difficult to write this type of item to measure for higher levels of cognition. You must be alert for a correct response different from the expected one For instance, in Example 2, although the teacher's key has *experiments* as the correct answer, a student might answer the question with *investigations*, which is equally correct.

Guidelines for Use.   Use occasionally for review. Avoid using for grading, unless you can write quality items that extend student thinking beyond that of mere recall. Avoid copying items verbatim from the textbook or workbook. Be sure to provide adequate space for students' answers.

4. Correction

Description.   Similar to completion type, except that sentences or paragraphs are complete, with italicized or underlined words that can be changed to make the sentence correct.

Example:

Photosynthesis in *Alabama* is the breakdown of *kids* into hydrogen and oxygen, the release of *isotopes*, and then the combining of the *arms* with carbon dioxide to make *scarecrows*.

Advantages.   Writing this type can be fun for the teacher when the purpose is review. Students may enjoy this type for the tension relief afforded by the incorrect absurdities.

Disadvantages.   Like the completion type, the correction type tends to measure for low-level recall and rote memory. The italicized incorrect items could be so whimsical that they might cause more classroom disturbance than you want.

Guidelines for Use.   Use occasionally for diversion. Try to write items that measure for higher-level cognition. Consider making it a combined correction, short-explanation type. Be sure to allow space for student explanations.

5. Essay

Description.   A question or problem is presented and the student composes a response in the form of sustained prose, using his or her own words, phrases, and ideas, within the limits of the question or problem.

Example 1:

Explain how one idea can become a law.

Example 2:

Describe the relationship and the difference between these two plant flower processes—pollination, fertilization.

Advantages.   Measures higher mental processes, such as ability to synthesize material and to express ideas in clear and precise written language. Essay items are especially useful in integrated thematic teaching, and they provide practice in written expression.

Disadvantages.   Essay items require a good deal of time to read and to score. They tend to provide an unreliable sampling of achievement and are also vulnerable to teacher subjectivity and unreliable scoring. Furthermore, they tend to punish the student who writes slowly and laboriously but who may have achieved as well as a student who writes faster. Essay items tend to favor students who have fluency with words but whose achievement may be no better than other students. In addition, unless the students have been given instruction both in an item's meaning and in how to respond, the teacher should not assume that students understand key directive verbs, such as *describe* and *explain*, in the two examples here.

Guidelines for Use.

1. When preparing an essay-only test, include many questions, each requiring a relatively short prose response, rather than a smaller number of questions each requiring a long prose response (see type 11, short explanation). Briefer answers tend to be more precise, and including many items provides a more reliable sampling of student achievement. When preparing short-prose-response questions, be sure to avoid using phrases word for word from the student textbook or workbook.
2. Allow students adequate test time for a full response.
3. Require all students to answer the same questions. Different qualities of achievement are more likely comparable when all students must answer the same questions, as opposed to providing a list of essay items from which students may select those they answer.
4. After preparing essay items, make a tentative scoring key, deciding the important ideas you expect students to identify and how many points will be allotted to each.
5. Inform students about the relative test value for each essay item. Point values, if different for each item, can be listed in the margin of the test next to each item.
6. When reading student essay responses, read all student papers for one item at a time and, while doing that, make notes to yourself. Then return to the first paper and read that item again, scoring each student's paper for that item. Repeat the process for the next item. While scoring essay responses, keep in mind the nature of the objective being measured, which may or may not include the qualities of handwriting, grammar, spelling, and neatness.
7. To nullify the "halo effect," use a number code rather than having students write their names on essay papers. Teachers who use this practice make sure they remain unaware of whose paper is being read until the score is given. If you do this, use caution not to misplace or become confused about the identification codes.
8. Be constructive when writing on student papers. Many students may understand a concept and yet not be able to express themselves well. You must remember to be patient, tolerant, positive, and helpful. Mark papers with positive and constructive comments, showing students how they could have explained or responded better.
9. Before using an essay item, give your students instruction and practice in responding to key directive verbs that will be used.[8] These are some common examples:

   Compare asks for an analysis of similarity and difference, but with an emphasis on similarities or likenesses.

   Contrast asks more for differences than for similarities.

---

[8]See, for example, Edward B. Jenkinson, "Practice Helps With Essay Exams," *Phi Delta Kappan* 69(10):726 (June 1988).

Criticize asks for the good and bad of an idea or situation.

Define asks students to express clearly and concisely the meaning of a term, as in the dictionary or in the student's own words.

Diagram asks students to put quantities or numerical values into the form of a chart, a graph, or a drawing.

Discuss asks students to explain or argue, presenting various sides of events, ideas, or situations.

Enumerate asks students to specify one after another or to make a count, which is different than "explain briefly" or "tell in a few words."

Evaluate asks for an expression of worth, value, and judgment.

Explain asks for a description with emphasis on cause and effect.

Illustrate asks for a description by means of examples, figures, pictures, or diagrams.

Interpret asks students to describe or explain a given fact, theory, principle, or doctrine in a specific context.

Justify asks students to show reasons, with an emphasis on the correct, positive, and advantageous.

List asks students to name items in a category or to include them in a tally sheet or inventory, without much description.

Outline asks for a short summary with headings and subheadings.

Prove asks students to present materials as witnesses, proof, and evidence.

Relate asks students to tell how specified things are connected or brought into some kind of relationship.

Summarize asks students to recapitulate the main points without examples or illustrations.

Trace asks students to follow a history or series of events step by step, going backward over the evidence.

6. Grouping

Description.   Several items are presented and the student selects and groups those that are related in some way.

Example 1:

Separate the following list of fabrics into two groups, those that are natural fibers and those that are synthetic.

Example 2:

Circle the one figure that is least like the others: [pictures of a wrench, screwdriver, saw, and a swing.]

Advantages.   This type of item, which tests knowledge of grouping, can be used to measure for higher levels of cognition. If students manipulate actual things, then the item is closer to an authentic assessment. Students like this type of question, which can stimulate discussion. As in Example 2, a grouping item can be similar to a multiple-choice item.

Disadvantage.   The teacher must remain alert for the student who has a valid alternative rationale for grouping.

Guidelines for Use.   To allow for an alternative correct response, consider making the item a combination grouping, short-explanation type. Be certain to allow adequate space for student explanations.

7. Identification

Description.   Unknown specimens are presented and the student identifies it by name or some other criterion.

Example 1:

Identify each of the flowers on the table by its common name.

Example 2:

Identify by name and sport each of the balls on the table.

Advantages.   Verbalization (i.e., the use of abstract symbolization) is less significant, because the student is working with real objects. An identification item should measure for a higher level of learning than simple recall. The item can also be written to measure for procedural understanding, such as in the identification of steps in booting up a computer program. This is another useful type for authentic assessment.

Disadvantages.   To be fair, the "specimens" used should be equally familiar or unfamiliar to all students. Adequate materials must be provided.

Guidelines for Use.   If photographs, drawings, photocopies and copies of recordings are used (rather than actual materials), they must be clear and not confusing to students.

8. Matching

Description.   Students match related entries from a list of numbered entries to a list of lettered entries, or in some way connect those entries that are the same or are related. Or, eliminating the paper-and-pencil aspect and making the item more direct, students match objects on a table, pairing those that are most alike.

Example 1:

In the blank space next to each word in Column A [stem column] put the letter of the best answer from Column B [answer column].

Column A	Column B
_____ 1. $2x + 3 = 7$	A. $x = 9$
_____ 2. $4x = x + 9$	B. $x = 3$
_____ 3. $2x - 1 = 9$	C. $x = 5$
	D. $x = 2$

Example 2:

Match items in Column A [stem column] to those of Column B [answer column] by drawing lines to the matched pairs.

Column A	Column B
snake	worm
eagle	mammal
whale	reptile
praying mantis	insect
	bird

Advantages.   This type can measure for the ability to judge relationships and to differentiate among similar ideas, facts, definitions, and concepts. Items are easy to score and can test a broad range of content. Matching items generally reduces guessing, especially if one group contains more items than the other. They are interesting to students and quite adaptable for performance assessment.

Disadvantages.   Items are not easily adapted to measuring for higher cognition. Because all parts must be homogeneous, it is possible that clues will be given, thus reducing item validity. A student might have a legitimate rationale for an "incorrect" response.

Guidelines for Use.   The number of entries in the answer column should exceed the number in the stem column. The number of entries to be matched should not exceed twelve. Matching sets should have high homogeneity—items in both columns (or groups) should be of the same general category. If entries in the answer column can be used more than once, the directions should so state. Be prepared for the student who can legitimately defend an "incorrect" response.

9. Multiple Choice
Description.   Similar to the completion type, statements are presented, sometimes in incomplete form but with several alternatives, and students choose the correct alternative.
   Example:

_____ Of the following four cylinders, the one that would cause the lowest-pitched sound would be
(a) short and thick
(b) short and thin
(c) long and thick
(d) long and thin

   Example 2:

_____ From the following list of planets, the planet in our system that is farthest from our sun is _____
(a) Earth
(b) Mercury
(c) Pluto
(d) Saturn

Advantages   Items can be answered and scored quickly. A wide range of content and higher levels of cognition can be tested in a relatively short time. These items are excellent for all testing purposes—motivation, review, and assessment of learning.

Disadvantages.   Unfortunately, because multiple-choice items are relatively easy to write, there is a tendency to write items that measure only for low levels of cognition. Multiple-choice items are excellent for major testing, but it takes time to write good questions that measure higher levels of learning.

Guidelines for Use.
   1. If the item is in the form of an incomplete statement, it should be meaningful in itself and imply a direct question rather than merely lead into a collection of unrelated true-false statements.

2. Use a level of language that is easy enough for even the poorest readers to understand, and avoid wordiness.

3. If there is much variation in the length of alternatives, arrange the alternatives in order from shortest to longest—first alternative should be the shortest, last alternative should be the longest.

4. For single-word alternatives, consistent alphabetical arrangement of alternatives is recommended (as in Example 2).

5. Incorrect responses (distracters) should be both plausible and related to the same concept as the correct alternative. Although an occasional humorous distracter helps to relieve text anxiety, they should be avoided (along with absurd distracters). They offer no measuring value.

6. Arrangement of alternatives should be uniform throughout the test, and listed in vertical (column) form rather than in horizontal (paragraph) form.

7. Every item should be grammatically consistent. For example, if the stem (opening statement) is in the form of an incomplete sentence, it should be possible to complete the sentence by attaching any of the alternatives to it.

8. It is not necessary to maintain a fixed number of alternatives for every item, but the use of less than three is not recommended. The use of four or five reduces chance responses and guessing, thereby increasing reliability for the item.

9. The item should be expressed in positive form. A negative form presents a psychological disadvantage to students. Negative items are those that ask what is *not* characteristic of something or what is the *least* useful. Discard the item if you cannot express it in positive terminology.

10. Responses such as "all of these" or "none of these" should be used only when they will contribute more than another plausible distracter. Care must be taken that such responses answer or complete the item. "All of the above" is a poorer alternative than "none of the above" because items that use it as a correct response need to have four or five correct answers; also, if it is the right answer, knowledge of any two of the distracters will cue it.

11. There must be only one correct or best response, although this is easier said than done (see Guideline 19).

12. The stem must have the same meaning for every student.

13. Measuring for understanding of definitions is better tested by furnishing the name or word and requiring choice between alternative definitions than by presenting the definition and requiring choice between alternative words.

14. The stem should state a single and specific point.

15. The stem must not include clues that would clue the correct alternative. For example, "A four-sided figure whose opposite sides are parallel is called _____. (a) an octagon. (b) a parallelogram. (c) a trapezoid. (d) a triangle." The use of the word *parallel* clues the answer.

16. Avoid using alternatives that include absolute terms, such as *never* and *always*.

17. Multiple-choice items need not be entirely verbal. Consider the use of realia, charts, diagrams, and other visuals. They will make the test more interesting (especially to students with low verbal abilities or with limited proficiency in English) and consequently make the assessment more direct (authentic).

18. Once you have composed a multiple-choice test, tally the position of answers to be sure they are evenly distributed, to avoid the common psychological mistake (when there are four alternatives) of having the correct alternative in the third position.

19. Consider providing space between test items for students to include their rationales for their response selections, thus making the test a combination multiple-choice, short-explanation type. This provides for the student who can rationalize an alternative that you had not considered plausible. It also provides for the measurement of higher levels of cognition and encourages student writing.

20. While scoring, tally the incorrect responses for each item on a blank copy of the test. Analyze incorrect responses for each item to discover potential errors in your scoring key. If, for example, many students select *b* for an item that your keys says *a* is the correct answer, you may have made a mistake on your scoring key, or in teaching the lesson.

10. Performance

Description.   Certain conditions or materials are provided, and the student solves a problem or accomplishes some other action.

Example 1:

Given a class of ten students, you are to prepare and teach an effective 15-minute inquiry lesson. [Note: this example is a teacher-education question.]

Example 2:

Show your understanding of diffusion by designing and completing a laboratory experiment using only the chemicals and equipment located at the learning-activity station.

Advantages.   Performance tests come closer to direct measurement (authentic assessment) of certain expected outcomes than do most other types, although, as has been indicated, other assessment types can actually be prepared as performance items—where the student actually does what he or she is being tested for. Learning that is difficult to verbalize can be assessed since little or no verbalization may be necessary. Students who do poorly on verbal tests may do well on performance tests. For example, this is often true for students who have learning disabilities.

Disadvantages.   Performance items can be difficult and time consuming to administer to a group of students. Scoring may tend to be subjective. You may have difficulty in giving makeup tests to students who were absent.

Guidelines for Use.   Use your creativity to design and use performance items, because they tend to measure the most important objectives. To reduce subjectivity in scoring, prepare distinct scoring guidelines, as was discussed in scoring essay items. To set up a performance situation, you should:

• Specify the performance objective.
• Specify the test situation or conditions.
• Establish the criteria for judging the excellence of the process and/or product.
• Make a checklist by which to score the performance or product. (This checklist is simply a listing of the criteria you have established in the previous step. It would be possible to use a rating scale, but ordinarily a rating scale makes scoring too complicated.)
• Prepare directions in writing, outlining the situation, with instructions for the students to follow.

For example, this is a checklist for map work:

Check each item if the map comes up to standard in this particular category.
_____   1. Accuracy
_____   2. Neatness
_____   3. Attention to details

11. Short Explanation

Description.   The short-explanation item is an essay item that requires a shorter answer.
Example 1:

Briefly explain in a paragraph why piano wires are not equal in length.

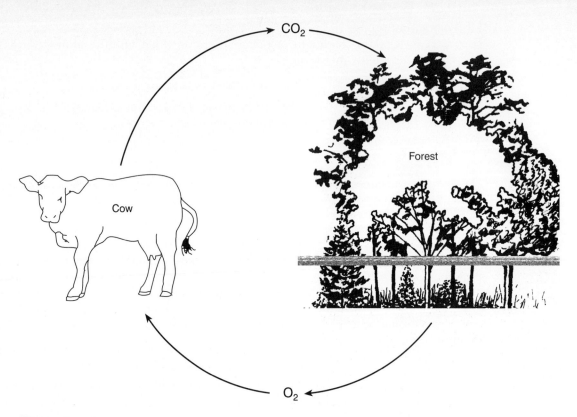

Illustration A

Example 2:

Explain what is incorrect or misleading about Illustration A.

Advantages.   As with an essay item, the student's understanding is assessed, but this type takes less time for the teacher to read and to score. In Example 2, for instance, the diagram of the cow and the forest (similar to drawings seen in some science books) represents a misconception about our own place in nature. The intent of the makers of such a diagram is to illustrate the interdependence of animals and plants; the lesson frequently learned is that plants use carbon dioxide produced by animals and that animals use oxygen produced by plants. Following such a study, teachers and their students were asked, "Do plants use oxygen?" The majority answered "no." A misconception was learned: the teachers and their students did not understand that *all* living organisms need oxygen. The focus was too much on what humans gain from "interdependence" rather than on the nature of "interdependence."

Artificialism is the term used by Piaget to represent the tendency to believe that everything here on earth is for the benefit of humans. Although natural for children in early grades, artificialism does represent a selfish, prejudiced, nonobjective idea that should be corrected and avoided by secondary school teachers. As discussed in Module 2, teachers have an obligation, and an opportunity, to correct student misconceptions—providing the teachers themselves have a correct understanding of the concept. This type of assessment item can be useful in assessing conceptual understanding and critical thinking.

By using several questions of this type, a greater amount of content can be covered than with a fewer number of essay questions. This assessment type is good practice for students to learn to express themselves succinctly in writing.

Disadvantages.   Some students will have difficulty expressing themselves in a limited fashion, or in writing. They need practice and time in doing so.

Guidelines for Use.   These items are useful for occasional reviews and quizzes and as alternatives to other types. For scoring, follow the same guidelines as for an essay item.

12. True-False

Description.   A statement is presented, and students judge it to be accurate or not.
   Example 1:

   Photosynthesis goes on only in green plants. T or F?

   Example 2:

   America was discovered by Christopher Columbus. T or F?

Advantages.   Many items can be answered in a relatively short time, making broad content coverage possible. Scoring is quick and simple. True-false items are good for starting discussions, for review, and for diagnostic evaluation (preassessment).

Disadvantages.   As illustrated by both examples, it is difficult to write true-false items that are purely true or false, or without qualifying them in such a way that clues the answer. Much of the content that most easily lends itself to this type of item is trivial. Students have a 50-percent chance of guessing the correct answer, thus giving this item type both poor validity and poor reliability. Scoring and grading give no clue about why the student missed an item.
   The disadvantages of true-false items far outweigh the advantages; true-false items should never be used for arriving at grades. For grading purposes, you may use *modified true-false items*, where space is provided between items for students to write in explanations, thus making the item a combination true-false, short-explanation type. For instance, as an answer to Example 2 the student might select false and then write an explanation, such as:

   There were people here before Columbus arrived.

   I selected false because I don't know what is meant by "America." Does the question refer to North America, Central America, Latin America, Canada, or what? If I remember correctly, he landed on some islands somewhere.

Guidelines for preparing true-false items.
   1. First write the statement as a true statement, then make it false by changing a word or phrase.
   2. Avoid using negative statements, since they tend to confuse students.
   3. A true-false statement should include only one idea. For more than one reason, Example 1 is a poor item. One is that it measures two ideas: photosynthesis occurs in plants (which is true), and it does so only in plants that are green in color (which is false).
   4. Use close to an equal number of true and false items.
   5. Avoid specific determiners, which may clue that the statement is false (e.g., *always, all,* or *none*).
   6. Avoid words that may clue that the statement is true (e.g., *often, probably,* and *sometimes*).
   7. Avoid words that may have different meanings for different students.
   8. Avoid using word-for-word language from the student textbook or workbook.
   9. Avoid trick items.

10. As noted, for grading purposes you may use modified true-false items, where space is provided between items for students to write in their explanations, thus making the item a combination true-false, short-explanation type. Another form of modified true-false item is the use of "sometimes-always-never," where a third alternative, "sometimes," is introduced to reduce the chance for guessing.

Evaluating the Assessment Item or Instrument

Educational assessment is not complete unless you evaluate the tests and other instruments you use. The variables considered when evaluating an assessment instrument include validity, discriminating power, difficulty, reliability, and usability.

Validity

How well does the test measure what you wanted to measure? Does the content of the test measure the content of the instruction? Does it cover all of the instructional objectives? Is the emphasis on the objectives in the test proportional to that in the instruction?

Discriminating Power

Discriminating power refers to how effectively the item differentiates between the students who did well and those who did poorly on the test. One procedure for determining a test's discriminating power is an item analysis using the upper 25 percent and lower 25 percent of the scores.[9] Perfect discrimination of an item would mean that all the students in the upper quarter answered correctly and all in the lower quarter answered incorrectly. Such precise differentiation between groups seldom occurs. The difference between the number of students in the upper group who answer the test item correctly and the number of students in the lower group who answer the item correctly is divided by the number of students in both groups. For example: Of 100 scores, the top 25 include 20 correct responses on item A; the low 25 include 8 correct responses on the same item.

$$\text{Index of Discrimination} = \frac{20 - 8}{50} = \frac{12}{50} = .22 +$$

The index varies from +1.00 to −1.00. Positive 1 indicates complete differentiation in the desired direction. Any negative value indicates the item discriminates in the wrong direction and is therefore unsatisfactory. Any discriminatory values above +0.40 are considered good. The range +0.40 to + 0.20 is called satisfactory. Teacher-made tests that are norm-referenced should have more than half of the items with an index discrimination of +0.40 or above, and another 40 percent of the items with a satisfactory index. No items should have a negative index.

Difficulty

Another type of item analysis determines item difficulty. Basically, the level of difficulty of an item is determined by the percentage of students who have answered the item correctly. It can easily be calculated. First, tabulate the number of students who correctly answered the question and divide by the number of students who tried to answer. Then, multiply by 100 to change the quotient to a percent. For example, if nineteen of the twenty-five students who responded to a question answered it correctly:

$$\text{Item Difficulty} = \frac{19}{25} \times 100 = 76.$$

[9] Technically it would be better to use the top 27 percent and bottom 27 percent, but for practical purposes in the classroom situation the uppermost and lowest quarters will suffice.

Table 10.3   Checking the
Reliability of a Test

Student	Rank Order in		
	Test I	Test II	Test III
A	1	1	1
B	2	3	2
C	3	4	4
D	4	2	3
E	5	5	6
F	6	6	5

For norm-referenced tests, the items answered correctly or incorrectly by all or most of the students contribute little to determining the norms. In fact, the level of difficulty should be near 50 percent. One recommendation is that only items in the 40 to 70 percent range should be included in a test.

Neither the item difficulty nor discriminating power apply to criterion-referenced tests. Responses on criterion-referenced tests will indicate whether or not individual students know or can do what they are supposed to have learned. If the lesson or unit has been well taught, it is possible that 80 percent or more of the students will have answered all of the items right. Discrimination among students and difficulty factors of items are largely irrelevant for this type of test. If the items show whether or not the objective has been attained, they are good items.

Reliability

Do the test results concur with the results of other tests and evaluations? One way to check is to rank the performance of the students on your various tests. If the results of the new test are consistent with the other tests, presumably the tests are reliable. In the example, Table 10.3, presumably Test III is reliable because its results seem to be consistent with those of Test I and Test II.

Usability

Is the test too long or too short? Is it too hard or too easy? Is it easy to score? Did the students find the directions clear?

General Suggestion: File of Test Items

Tests should be analyzed and revised by the teachers. Reusing the same tests encourages cheating. But using the good questions of a test, eliminating or improving the poor items, and adding new items produce a better test than writing all new items.

Keep a file of your good questions as a convenient way of improving tests. To construct a test item file, put the question on one side of a file card and information about the item on the reverse side. File the question by unit, problem, or some other convenient classification. These cards can then be pulled, sorted, and used as a basis for a new test. Since frequent short tests may be important for feedback to both teacher and student, you can use them to develop the test item file rapidly. Then questions for a unit test or semester examination will be readily available. Objective questions and essay questions from your test file may be combined in the same test. If the equipment is available, test files can be built in a computer data-storage bank as well. The questions could then be pulled from the data bank when it is time to make the test. The computer will randomly select questions from a data bank, or it will make several alternative tests from the data bank using the same data bank of questions. Begin your file of test questions by doing Exercise 10.1.

EXERCISE 10.1
Preparing Assessment Items

• • • • • •

Instructions: The purpose of this exercise is to practice your skill in preparing the different types of assessment items. From your course syllabus (Exercise 4.2) or from your course objectives (Exercise 3.11), select one specific instructional objective and write assessment items for it. When completed, share this exercise with your colleagues for their feedback.

The objective:

Subject and grade level:

1. Arrangement item:

2. Completion-drawing item:

3. Completion-statement item:

4. Correction item:

5. Essay item:

6. Grouping item:

7. Identification item:

8. Matching item:

9. Multiple-choice item:

10. Performance item:

11. Short-explanation item:

12. Modified true-false item (for use in grading):

Reporting Student Achievement

As a classroom teacher, one of your major responsibilities is to report student progress in achievement to parents or guardians. In some schools teachers are required to report student progress and effort as well as student achievement. Reporting is done in at least two and sometimes in three ways: by the grade report, through direct contact, and in conferences and meetings.

The Grade Report

About every six to nine weeks, a grade report (report card) is sent home (from four to six times a year, depending upon the school district). This grade report represents an achievement grade (formative evaluation). The second or third one of the semester also constitutes the semester grade; for courses that are only one semester long, it also is the final grade (summative evaluation). In essence, the first and (sometimes) second reports are progress notices, with the semester grade being the one that is transferred to the student's transcript of records.

In some schools the traditional report card is marked and then sent home either with the student or by mail. In many high schools, reporting is done by computer printouts, often sent by mail directly to the student's home address. (In some schools, as an effort to involve parents, the parents or guardians are expected to come to the school on a given day and pick up the grade report.) These computer printouts ordinarily contain all the subjects or courses taken by the student while enrolled at the school, as well as the student's accumulation of units and current grade-point average.

Whichever reporting form is used, you *must* separate your assessments of a student's social behaviors (classroom conduct) from the student's academic achievement. Academic achievement (or accomplishment) is represented by a letter (sometimes a number) grade: *A* through *E* or *F*; or *E*, *S*, and *U*; or 1 through 5; and sometimes with minuses and pluses. The social behavior is represented by a *satisfactory* or an *unsatisfactory*, or by more specific items. Teacher-written or computer-generated comments may supplement these assessments of social behavior. In some instances there may be a location on the reporting form for the teacher to check whether basic grade level standards have been met in science, language arts, social studies, and mathematics.

Direct Contact with Parents or Guardians

Some teachers make a point to contact parents or guardians by telephone, especially when a student has shown a sudden turn for either the worse or the better in academic achievement or in classroom behavior. Such contact may be an obligation of the job. This initiative and contact by the teacher is usually welcomed by parents and can lead to private and productive conferences with the teacher. A telephone conversation often saves valuable time for both the teacher and the parent.

Another way of contacting parents is by letter. Contacting a parent by letter gives you time to think and to make clear your thoughts and concerns to that parent. A letter also allows you to invite the parent to respond at the parent's convenience by letter, by phone, or by arranging to have a conference with you.

Conferences and Meetings with Parents or Guardians

Teachers meet many parents or guardians early in the school year at Back-to-School-Night and then throughout the year in individual parent conferences. Back-to-School Night is the evening early in the school year when parents can come to the school and meet their child's teachers. Generally, the parents arrive at the child's homebase and then proceed through a simulation of their son or daughter's school day. As a group, the parents meet each class and each teacher for a few minutes. Later, in the spring, there is often an Open House, where parents may have more time to talk individually with teachers. But an Open House is usually a time for the school and teachers to show off the work and progress of the students for that year. At other times during the school year, there are opportunities for teachers and parents to meet and to talk about the children.

For the beginning teacher, these meetings with parents can be anxious times. In the sections that follow, we provide some suggestions that may help you.

At Back-to-School Night.   On this evening parents are anxious to learn as much as they can about their child's new teachers. As one of those teachers, you will meet each group of parents for about 10 minutes. During that brief meeting you should provide them with a copy of the course syllabus, make some straightforward remarks about yourself, and then briefly discuss your expectations of the students.

Although there is usually precious little time for questions from the parents, during your introduction the parents likely will be delighted to learn that you: (1) have your program well planned (2) are a "taskmaster," and (3) are willing to communicate with parents. The parents and guardians will also likely be pleased to find out that you are from the school of the three *F*'s—firm, friendly, and fair.

At this brief meeting parents specifically expect to learn about your curriculum—goals and objectives, about any long-term projects, about when tests will be given and if done on a regular basis, and about your grading procedures. They need to know what you expect of them: Will there be homework? If so, should they help their children with it? How can they contact you?

Try to anticipate other questions. Your principal, department chair, and colleagues can be of aid in helping you anticipate and prepare for these questions. Of course, you can never prepare for the question that comes from left field. Just stay calm and don't get flustered. Ten minutes will fly by quickly, and parents will be reassured to know you are an in-control person.

Parents who have attended many Back-to-School Nights are often both surprised and dismayed that so few teachers seem well-prepared for the few minutes they have with the parents. Considering how often teachers express the desire for more involvement of parents, few seem delighted that parents indeed attend these functions. Few teachers take full advantage of this time with parents to truly celebrate their programs. As with other teacher tasks, planning is essential. Figure 10.5 shows a model handout that demonstrates the kind of planning a teacher should do for Back-to-School Night. Parents like to receive this sort of information from their childrens' teachers early in the school year.

Parent-teacher conference.   When meeting parents for conferences, you should be as specific as possible when explaining the progress of that parent's child in your class. But don't saturate the parent with more information than he or she needs. Resist any tendency to talk too much. Allow time for the parent to ask questions. Keep your answers succinct. Never compare one student with another, or with the rest of the class. If the parent asks a question for which you do not have an answer, tell the parent you will try to find an answer and will phone the parent as quickly as you can. And do it. Have the student's portfolio and other work with you during parent conferences so you can *show* the parent examples of what is being discussed. Also, have your grade book on hand (or a computer printout of it), though protect from the parent the names and records of the other students.

Sometimes it is helpful to have a three-way conference. You might set up a conference with the parent, the student, and you, or a conference with the parent, the principal or counselor, and several or all of the student's teachers.

Ideas for Teacher-Parent Collaboration

A parent often will ask how she or he may help in the child's learning. Here are some ideas you might respectfully suggest the parents consider implementing at home:

- As needed, plan short family meetings after dinner, but while you are still seated at the table. Ask for a "table side" report of what's happening in the school. Ask, "How can I help?" When your child expresses a concern, emphasize ways to solve problems that occur. Help your child develop his or her problem solving skills.
- Ask your child to share with you each day one specific thing learned that day.
- Limit and control your child's television pleasure viewing.
- Set up a regular schedule of reviewing with the child his or her portfolio.
- Set up a regular time each evening for a family discussion about school.

Course:	Honors Precalculus (HP)
Instructor:	Mr. Charles Schwing
Text:	Advanced Mathematical Concepts
Description:	This is an accelerated class designed to prepare the student for calculus. As an Honors class (HP), the course requires a higher level of commitment on the part of the student. Grades of *A, B,* or *C* are awarded an extra grade point by St. Francis High School and by the University of California and California State University systems and are given extra weight by many other public and private colleges and universities. A partial listing of topics covered in this class includes analytic geometry, trigonometry, matrices and determinants, probability and statistics, and an introduction to the calculus, including the epsilon-delta definition of limit.
Homework:	Homework is assigned daily (with very few exceptions) and should require approximately 30 to 40 minutes to complete. Success in this class is virtually impossible unless assignments are done in a timely and conscientious manner.
Grades:	Points are given for homework, quizzes, and major exams. Grades are computed based on total points, with quizzes and exams comprising 75% of those points. The grading scale is: $A = 88\%$ or above, $B = 75\text{--}87\%$, $C = 60\text{--}74\%$, $D =$ below 60%. To earn an *F* requires a special "effort" on the part of the student.
Citizenship:	Students begin this class with an *A* in citizenship. Demerits are earned for tardiness and inappropriate behavior. Three demerits result in a one letter drop in citizenship (e.g., from an *A* to a *B*).
Instructor Availability:	I am available for extra help from 7:45 until 8:10 each morning, during blocks C, D, and F, and after school until 4:00. I can be at school before 7:45 or after 4:00 if arranged in advance. It is your child's responsibility to seek me out—I will not chase after a student to come in for help. If extra help is obtained as soon as the need arises, it is usually only a matter of a 10- or 15-minute session. Hours at a time are rarely needed. There is most definitely a positive correlation between the students who come in for help and the grades they receive. If at any time you are concerned about your child's progress, please feel free to call me at school and leave a message. I will get back to you the same day if at all possible.

Figure 10.5   Handout for Parents at Back-to-School Night

Source: Courtesy of Charles Schwing, teacher, St. Francis High School, Sacramento, California.

You might consider having students take their portfolios home each Friday to share with their parents. The portfolio could have a place where the parent or guardian signs to show they have reviewed their child's work. The form for parent's signature could also have a column for teacher and parent comments to each other—one way to maintain this important line of communication between parent and teacher. Be sure to require that the portfolio returns with the student each Monday.

Helping students become critical thinkers is one of the aims of education and one that parents can help with by reinforcing the strategies being used in the classroom. They can ask *what if* questions. They can think aloud as a model for the child's thinking development. They can encourage their child's own metacognition by asking questions such as: "How did you arrive at that conclusion?" and "How do you feel about your conclusion now?" Have parents ask these questions about the child's everyday social interactions and about topics that are important to the child. Asking a child to elaborate on his or her ideas is something all parents can do. You might suggest to parents that they allow their child to make mistakes while encouraging that child to learn from those mistakes.

Several books are available for parents to use at home. For example, the United States government has a variety of booklets available, most costing less than a dollar. They are ava able from Department 587V, Consumer Information Center, Pueblo, CO 81109. These book-lets include:

> *Helping Your Child Use the Library* (item 465V)
>
> *Becoming a Nation of Readers: What Parents Can Do* (item 459V)
>
> *Help Your Child Do Better at School* (item 412V)

You might also encourage the parent to go to the neighborhood public library and ask for a librarian's help in locating helpful resources. If you and parents are interested in strategies for increasing home-school collaboration, these books may be helpful:

- *Beyond the Bake Sale: An Educator's Guide to Working with Parents*, by Anne T. Henderson, Carl Marburger, and Theodora Ooms (Columbia, MD: National Committee for Citizens in Education, 1985).
- The special section "Parent Involvement" in *Phi Delta Kappan* 72(5) (January 1991).
- *Communicating with Parents*, by Janet Chrispeels, Marcia Boruta, and Mary Daugherty (San Diego: San Diego County Office of Education, 1988).
- *The Evidence Continues to Grow: Parent Involvement Improves Student Achievement* (Columbia, MD: National Committee for Citizens in Education, 1987).
- *Parenting for Education*, by Paula Lowe and Carl Trendler (Seattle: U.S. West Education Foundation, 1989).

Dealing with an Angry Parent or Guardian

A parent or guardian may become angry or hostile towards you and the school. If that occurs, consider these ways for dealing with that hostility:

- Remain calm in your discussion with the parent, allowing the parent to verbalize his or her hostility while you say very little. Usually, the less you say, the better off you'll be. Make sure what you do say is objective and to the point of the child's work in your classroom. The parent may just need to vent frustrations that might have very little to do with you, the school, or even the child.
- Never allow yourself to be intimidated or backed into a corner. If the parent attacks you personally, resist the tendency to press your defense at this time. Perhaps the parent has made a point that you should consider, and now is a good time to arrange for another conference with the parent for about a week later. In a follow-up conference, one agreed to by the parent, you may want to consider bringing in a mediator, such as another member of your teaching team, an administrator, or a school counselor.
- Never talk about other students; rather, keep the conversation focused on this parent's child's progress. The parent is not your rival, or should not be. You both share a concern for the academic and emotional well-being of the child. Use your best skills in critical thinking and problem solving. Try to focus the discussion by identifying the problem(s), defining it, and then arriving at some decision about how mutually to go about solving it. To this end you may need to ask for help from a third party, such as the child's school counselor. If the parent agrees, by all means take that step.
- Parents do not need to hear about how busy you are, or about your personal problems, or about how many other students you are dealing with on a daily basis (unless, of course, a parent asks). Parents expect you to be the capable professional who knows what to do and how to do it.

SUMMARY

The preceding parts of this text addressed the *why*, *what*, and *how* components of teaching. This module focused your attention on one aspect of the fourth and final component—the *how well* component. Because teaching and learning work hand in hand, and because they are reciprocal processes where one depends on and affects the other, the *how well* component deals with the assessment of both how well the students are learning and how well the teacher is teaching. This module addressed the first aspect. In the next, your attention is directed to techniques designed to help you develop and evaluate how well you are teaching and continue your development as a professional teacher.

SUGGESTED READING

Abruscato, J. "Early Results and Tentative Implications from the Vermont Portfolio Project." *Phi Delta Kappan* 74(6):474–477 (February 1993).

Black, S. "Portfolio Assessment." *Executive Educator* 15(1):28–31 (February 1993).

Bracey, G. W. "Assessing the New Assessments." *Principal* 72(3):34–36 (January 1993).

Chambers, D. L. "Standardized Testing Impedes Reform." *Educational Leadership* 50(5):80–81 (February 1993).

Doran, R. L., et al. "Authentic Assessment: An Instrument for Consistency." *The Science Teacher* 60(6):37–41 (September 1993).

Ebel, R. L., and Frisbie, D. A. *Essentials of Educational Measurement.* 5th ed. Needham Heights, MA: Allyn & Bacon, 1991.

Feuer, M. J., and Fulton, K. "The Many Faces of Performance Assessment." *Phi Delta Kappan* 74(6):478 (February 1993).

Goldman, J. P. "Student Portfolios Already Proven in Some Schools." *School Administrator* 46(11):11 (December 1989).

Gronlund, N. F., and Linn, R. L. *Measurement and Evaluation in Teaching.* 6th ed. New York: Macmillan, 1990.

Guskey, T. R. "What You Assess May Not Be What You Get." *Educational Leadership* 51(6):51–54 (March 1994).

Hamm, M., and Adams, D. "Portfolio Assessment." *The Science Teacher* 58(5):18–21 (May 1991).

Hansen, J. "Evaluation: "My Portfolio Shows Who I Am." *Quarterly of the National Writing Project and the Center for the Study of Writing and Literacy* 14(1):5–6, 9 (Winter 1992).

Harmon, J. L.; Aschbacher, P.; and, Winters, L. *A Practical Guide to Alternative Assessment.* Alexandria, VA: Association for Supervision and Curriculum Development, 1992.

Ingalls, B., and Jones, J. "There's a Lot of Things You Can Learn in English That You Can't Really See." *Quarterly of the National Writing Project and the Center for the Study of Writing and Literacy* 14(1):1–4, 9 (Winter 1992).

Kohn, A. "Group Grade Grubbing Versus Cooperative Learning." *Educational Leadership* 48(5):83–87 (February 1991).

Krechevsky, M. "Project Spectrum: An Innovative Assessment Alternative." *Educational Leadership* 48(5):43–48 (February 1991).

LeBuffe, J. R. "Performance Assessment." *The Science Teacher* 60(6):46–48 (September 1993).

Madaus, G. F., and Tan, A. G. A. "The Growth of Assessment." In *Challenges and Achievements of American Education,* edited by Gordon Cawelti. 1993 ASCD Yearbook. Alexandria, VA: Association for Supervision and Curriculum Development, 1993.

Maeroff, G. I. "Assessing Alternative Assessment." *Phi Delta Kappan* 73(4):272–282 (December 1991).

Marzano, R. J. "Lessons from the Field About Outcome-Based Performance Assessments." *Educational Leadership* 51(6):44–50 (March 1994).

Pallrand, G. J. "Multi-media Assessment: Evaluating Your Students' Thinking Skills." *The Science Teacher* 60(6):42–45 (September 1993).

Perrone, V., ed. *Expanding Student Assessment.* Alexandria, VA: Association for Supervision and Curriculum Development, 1991.

Schulz, E. "Putting Portfolios to the Test." *Teacher Magazine* 5(1):36–41 (September 1993).

Simmons, J. "Portfolio as Large-scale Assessment." *Language Arts* 67(3):262–68 (March 1990).

Wiggins, G. "Assessment: Authenticity, Context, and Validity." *Phi Delta Kappan* 75(3):200–214 (November

Wittrock, M. C. and Baker, E. L. *Testing and Cognition*. Englewood Cliffs, NJ: Prentice-Hall, 1990.

Wolf, D. P. "Portfolio Assessment: Sampling Student Work." *Educational Leadership* 46(7):35–39 (April 1989).

Worthen, B. R. "Critical Issues That Will Determine the Future of Alternative Assessment." *Phi Delta Kappan* 74(6):444–454 (February 1993).

POSTTEST

Multiple Choice

_____   1. A criterion-referenced test is constructed so that
   a. each student will attain a perfect score if the student has mastered the objectives.
   b. the student will be compared to other students and his or her position in the group determined.
   c. the test measures what it is supposed to test or meets the criterion established.
   d. the deficiencies of a student are located in a specific area of behavior.

_____   2. Assessment and measurement are defined so that
   a. the terms are synonymous.
   b. assessment includes measurement.
   c. measurement includes assessment.
   d. measurement and assessment are not directly related.

_____   3. The items on a true-false test are *least* likely to
   a. measure complex cognitive behavior.
   b. encourage guessing.
   c. cover a quantity of material in a short time.
   d. take a reasonable amount of teacher time for constructing and checking.

_____   4. Which teacher comment about scoring easy tests will improve the reliability of the test?
   a. "I like to read all the student's answers at one time to get an overview of what he or she knows."
   b. "I can do a better job of scoring when I don't know whose paper I'm reading."
   c. "The time it takes to separate test papers item by item is time I could use more profitably for other purposes."
   d. "I can tell how much a student knows by scanning his paper."

_____   5. In a model of teaching, testing is essential in
   a. preassessment of students.
   b. implementation of instructional plans.
   c. assessment of learning.
   d. both a and c.

_____   6. Multiple-choice items are superior to matching and to true-false items for some purposes because they
   a. save teacher time in construction and grading.
   b. decrease the number of questions the student can answer in a specified time.
   c. measure cognitive processes beyond memory.
   d. increase student choices in the test situation.

_____   7. An effective grading system is *least* likely to
   a. be limited to academic achievement.
   b. include assessment of a variety of student behaviors.
   c. be able to provide criterion- and norm-referenced grades.
   d. provide information about the achievement of objectives.

_____   8. Student products and processes are evaluated by
   a. one of the following devices: a rating scale, checklist, anecdotal record, log.
   b. teacher, student, and peers.
   c. the criterion established in the behavioral objective.
   d. the procedure and individuals appropriate to the intent of the objective.

_____ 9. Homework is an important phase of learning activities in many classes and consequently should be
   a. carefully graded by the teacher.
   b. utilized for learning.
   c. occasionally collected and spot-checked.
   d. considered as a major.

_____ 10. Students learn best when they are
   a. reminded of their shortcomings so that they are more realistic in setting goals.
   b. accepted as worthy individuals and are encouraged to undertake challenging tasks.
   c. homogeneously grouped and are encouraged to work together on similar tasks.
   d. heterogeneously grouped and are encouraged to work together on similar tasks.

Check

A group from the Student Council of Walton High School studied grading systems. Its report to the Advisory Committee included a statement of purpose for grading. Read the following statements and check those that provide valid reasons for grades.

_____ 1. Teachers can control student behavior with grades.
_____ 2. Colleges and employers can get information about students.
_____ 3. Grades give a student information about his or her progress.
_____ 4. Grades replace learning as a motivation for students.
_____ 5. Grades encourage continuous evaluation of student learning.

Analyze

Mr. Taylor decided to use a weight system for six-week grades. The four items selected were class participation, tests, group projects, and assignments. He decided that the most important phase of the learning activities was class participation, which should be half of the grade. The group project and tests were of equal value, but the assignments were half as important as the tests. Set up a system of weights for Mr. Taylor to use. Put the appropriate number in the blank.

_____ 1. Class participation.
_____ 2. Tests.
_____ 3. Group projects.
_____ 4. Assignments.

If the following table of specifications is set up for a unit on short stories in ninth-grade English, indicate the appropriate placement of the tally for each question listed. Put the letter(s) of the correct cell in the blank. Use the highest cognitive level involved.

CONTENT	COGNITIVE BEHAVIOR					
	Knowledge A	Comprehension D	Application G	Analysis J	Synthesis M	Evaluation P
Vocabulary						
Literary Style	B	E	H	K	N	Q
Elements of the Short Story (Plot, Characters, Setting, Theme)	C	F	I	L	O	R

_____ 5. Ten items listing synonyms to be matched with ten of thirteen words given.

_____ 6. What effect on the reader is expected when the author tells the story in the first person?
   a. The reader is an observer of the action.
   b. The reader identifies with the author.
   c. The reader gets a broad insight into the motivation of all characters.
   d. The reader quickly perceives the theme of the story.

_____ 7. Compare the "Tell-Tale Heart" with "The Fugitive" in regard to
   a. point of view.
   b. setting.
   c. plot.

_____ 8. At the end of "Split Cherry Tree," Pa feels that Professor Herbert is a "fine man" because
   a. Professor Herbert had a good education.
   b. Professor Herbert respected the gun Pa carried.
   c. Professor Herbert treated Pa as a worthy individual.
   d. Professor Herbert displayed his intelligence to Pa.

_____ 9. Select the best story you read and defend your selection, using four criteria for a good short story.

Matching

Match the correct test characteristic (a through h below) with the question asked about the test. Use a term only once.

_____ 1. Does the test measure what is supposed to be measured?

_____ 2. Can the test be constructed, administered, and scored conveniently?

_____ 3. Are the results consistent?

_____ 4. Do the test results show the different achievement levels of the students?

_____ 5. Are results affected by the student or the scorer?

a. Comprehensiveness.
b. Correlation.
c. Discrimination.
d. Efficiency.
e. Objectivity.
f. Reliability.
g. Usability.
h. Validity.

Completion Drawing

Complete the model of a learning cycle on page 445 by filling in the blanks.

1. _____
2. _____
3. _____

Completion Statement

List four uses of test results.

1. _____
2. _____
3. _____
4. _____

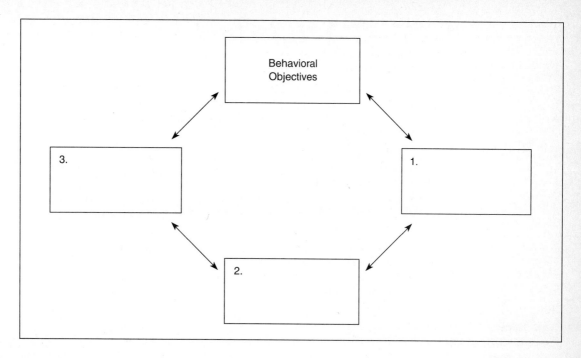

Short Explanation

1. Other than a paper-and-pencil test, identify three alternative assessment techniques for assessing student learning.
2. When using a point system for determining student grades for a course, is it educationally defensible to give a student a higher grade than that student's points call for? A lower grade? Give a rationale for your answers.
3. Explain the dangers in using true-false and completion type items in testing for grading purposes.
4. Explain the concept of authentic assessment. Is it the same as performance assessment? Explain why or why not.
5. Describe any student learning activities or situations that should *not* be graded but should or could be used for assessment of student learning.

Essay

1. For a course that you intend to teach, describe the items and their relative weights that you would use for determining course grades. Explain your rationale for the percentage weight distribution.
2. Explain the value of and give a specific example of a performance test item that you would use in teaching your subject to middle school or secondary school students.
3. From your current observations and field work as related to this teacher preparation program, clearly identify one specific example of educational practice that seems contradictory to exemplary practice or theory as presented in this module. Present your explanation for the discrepancy.
4. Describe any prior concepts you held that changed as a result of the experiences of this module. Describe the changes.

Module 11

Assessment of Teaching and Becoming a Professional

RATIONALE

To become a truly professional teacher you must cultivate a wide repertoire of teaching skills and an understanding of when and how to use them in the teaching-learning situations you encounter.

To master this type of know-how, it will be necessary to learn much more of the theory behind the various methods than we have been able to discuss in these modules. To become more proficient, teachers take many different routes, such as graduate study, workshops, independent study, curriculum committee work, action research, and professional conferences. The essential point is that all of them are working to improve teaching competencies. You are never too old to learn in the teaching profession. And you are never old enough to let yourself become locked into a rigid teaching style. You should always be ready to renew and revamp your style. Who knows, you may find a revised style more comfortable, and new strategies and tactics may make you more interesting. While you are still in training, it would be helpful for you to observe as many different teachers as you can to note the many different styles and strategies in action. You should also avail yourself of every opportunity that presents itself to try out various techniques and examine your performance in them.

Professional laboratory experiences provide an opportunity for you to become familiar with various teaching methods and life in school by actually observing and working with students and teachers in classrooms. It is this portion of the program that gives reality to teacher education.

In a sense, the professional laboratory experiences—particularly student teaching—are the culmination of your teacher education. But teacher education does not stop when you begin to teach. In addition to learning from experiences in school and classroom, you should also upgrade your skills and understandings by professional growth activities of various sorts. It is not too early to become familiar with these opportunities now.

This module briefly examines professional laboratory experiences and suggests ways to make them profitable. It also discusses ways by which you may examine and evaluate your own teaching, both in your laboratory experiences and later in your own classes, so that you can correct your shortcomings and build on your strengths. Finally, the module examines some of the methods you can use to grow professionally, starting now.

SPECIFIC OBJECTIVES

At the completion of this module, you should be able to:

1. Explain the purposes of the laboratory experiences of teacher preparation.
2. Describe the characteristics and roles in teacher preparation of the three types of professional laboratory experiences.
3. Explain what student teachers can do to make their student-teaching experience pleasant and profitable.
4. Describe procedures for analyzing and evaluating your lessons and teaching procedures.
5. Describe the suggestions made in this module for growing in the profession.

MODULE TEXT

Professional Laboratory Experiences

Professional laboratory experiences include the portions of your college or university program in which you observe classroom teachers in the act of teaching, participate in the conducting of classes, teach simulated classes and minilessons, microteach, and teach real classes in the student teaching or internship experience.[1] This module considers observation, participation, and student teaching experiences that occur in secondary and middle schools.

Unless you are different from most persons preparing to be teachers, your professional laboratory experiences will have the greatest impact of all your college experiences. These experiences are real, often exciting, and full of opportunities for creative learning and application of what you have learned. They provide a milieu in which you can experiment with different styles and strategies and develop skills in the various techniques of teaching.

Observation

Most programs for teacher preparation provide opportunities to observe teachers and students in the public schools. Often, a portion of the observation will occur in a middle school, and then in a junior or senior high school, and then sometimes in alternative schools. Programs may also allow students to observe how other students teach, as well as provide demonstration lessons. This variety of observation can give you insights into relations between students and teachers; the various backgrounds of students you will teach; and the effects of different teaching strategies, different instructional materials, and different styles of teaching. The more different styles you observe, the better will be your understanding of the potentials of the various approaches.

Some ways to make your observation profitable include these:

- Concentrate on watching the students in the classrooms. Note the range of differences in appearances, abilities, and interests that appear in a single class. Note how students react to different teaching approaches. Which teaching techniques and materials excite their interest and which engender boredom? Follow a student's schedule all day long. How does it feel to go through the routine of being a middle or secondary school student today? (It may be quite different from what you remember.) Try to think of ways that you as a teacher could make the classes more enjoyable and profitable.
- Observe the ways different teachers handle their classes. How do they get their classes started? How do they bring their classes to a conclusion? How do they develop the important points? How do they create interest? How do they get students involved in their own learning? How do they provide for differences in students? What techniques for motivation, probing, discovery, inquiry, closure, and reinforcement are used? How do students respond to the various tactics? What procedures are used to establish and maintain classroom control?
- Observe the climate of each class. What seems to have created the climate? Is the class teacher-centered or student-centered? Is the class diffusely structured or centrally structured? Is the student morale high or low, and what seems to be the cause for the state of the morale?
- Give particular attention to the manner in which the teachers implement various strategies and the students' responses to each of the strategies.

Participation

In student teaching, after a period of observation and participation, the teacher trainee gradually begins to take over some of the classes and other duties that make up a teacher's load, under the supervision of one or more cooperating teachers as well as a college supervisor. The experience is expected to develop into a genuine simulation of teaching reality. The cooperating teacher, the professional of record, always retains ultimate responsibility for what happens in the classroom, but the intent is for the student teacher to assume as much responsibility as possible—as though the class were fully his or hers to lead. The legal, instructional, and pedagogical ramifications of this activity are such that only a simulation of reality is possible. But the greater the effort to approximate the real thing and the greater the sensitivity to the goals of the activity on the part of everyone concerned, the more rewarding the student teaching

---

[1] *Internship* can sometimes refer simply to student teaching by another name, or it can sometimes refer to a longer or more independent and paid apprenticeship period. In this module, the term *student teaching* refers to both concepts.

experience will be. For most teacher candidates, student teaching is the capstone of their teacher preparation program. It can be both exciting and rewarding. It can also be both difficult and trying.

Student Teaching

Perhaps the first thing to remember about student teaching is that, like observation and participation, it is intended to be a learning experience. It is in student teaching that the beginning teacher first applies the theories and techniques learned in college classes to real teaching situations. Here you will have an opportunity to try out various strategies and techniques so as to begin to build a wide repertoire of teaching skills and to develop an effective, comfortable teaching style.

Student teaching is also a time of trial and error. Do not be discouraged if you make mistakes or your lessons do not go well at first. If you were already a skilled teacher, you would not need the practice. Making mistakes is part of the learning process. Use them as a means for improvement. With the help of your cooperating teacher and supervisor, try to analyze your teaching to find what steps to take to do better next time. Perhaps your execution of the strategies and techniques was faulty; perhaps you used a strategy or technique inappropriate for the particular situation. Such errors can be quite easily remedied as you gain experience.

As a general rule, errors of omission are often worse than errors of commission. The latter generally reflect faulty judgment or inexperience. They do, however, just as often confirm an indication of good will, commendable effort, and a willingness to try. The worst omission errors most often stem from lack of zeal: failure to devote enough time to planning adequately, neglect of previewing audiovisual equipment, lack of research on the topic of presentation, and the like.

In this connection, do not be quick to reject a teaching strategy or technique that fails for you. As you become more skilled in using various strategies and techniques, you will find that all have their uses. Do not allow yourself to become one of those boring teachers who can teach in only one way. Instead, if a strategy or technique does not work for you, examine the situation to see what went wrong. Then try it again in a new situation after brushing up your technique and correcting your faults.

Since student teaching is a time for learning and for getting the mistakes out of your system, it is important not to become discouraged. Many student teachers who do miserably for the first weeks blossom into excellent teachers by the end of the student-teaching period. On the other hand, if things seem to go well at first, do not become overconfident. Many beginners, too soon satisfied with the seeming success of early classes, become complacent and doom themselves to mediocrity. In any case, examine your classes to see what went well and what went wrong. Then try to correct your faults and capitalize on your strengths.

After your initial anxiety and nervousness wear off, use your student teaching as an opportunity to try out new strategies and techniques. Avoid becoming a clone of the cooperating teacher or a replica of the old-time teacher who gave lectures, heard recitations, and sometimes did very little else. But work out the new approaches and techniques you wish to try with your cooperating teacher before you try them. Usually the cooperating teacher can show you how to get the most out of your new ventures and warn you of pitfalls you might encounter.

"Make haste slowly" (ancient advice) as you try new methods and approaches. Things will go more smoothly if you continue with the same strategies and tactics to which the class is accustomed. Students used to a particular style may not readily adapt to innovations. This reluctance is especially bad when the teacher confronts students with quick changes in the length and difficulty of homework assignments or an abrupt switch from prescriptive, didactic methods to discovery and inquiry approaches.

Sometimes the cooperating teacher may think it necessary to veto what seems to you to be your best ideas. Usually there is a sound basis for the veto. It may be, in the cooperating teacher's view, that these ideas will not serve the objectives well, or may require time, money, or equipment not available to you, or violate school policy, or seem unsuited to the age and abilities of the students. Sometimes your ideas may be rejected because they conflict with the cooperating teacher's pedagogical and philosophical beliefs or biases. Whatever the objection, you should accept the decision gracefully and concentrate on procedures the cooperating teacher finds acceptable. After all, the classes and the instruction are the cooperating teacher's responsibility.

Furthermore, you need to become a master of many techniques. If you master the techniques and style your cooperating teacher recommends now, you will have begun to assemble a suitable repertoire of teaching skills. Later, when you are teaching your own classes, you can expand your repertoire by trying out other strategies and styles you find appealing.

To be successful in student teaching requires more study and preparation than most students think possible. To do the job, you must know what you are doing, so pay particular attention to your planning. Bone up carefully on the content of your lessons and units and lay them out carefully step by step. Leave nothing to chance. Check and double-check to be sure you have your facts straight, that your teaching strategies and tactics will yield your objectives, that you have the necessary teaching materials on hand, that you know how to use them, and so on. It is most embarrassing when you find you cannot solve the problems you have given to the students, or cannot answer the students' questions, or cannot find the equipment you need, or cannot operate the projector. So try to be ready for any contingency. As a rule, you should ask your cooperating teacher to approve your plan before you become committed to it. If the cooperating teacher suggests changes, incorporate them into the plan and try to carry them out.

Planning lessons and units for student teaching is no easy task. To become really sure of your subject matter and to think out how to teach it in the short time available during your student teaching is asking a lot of yourself. Therefore, prepare as much as you can before the student teaching period begins. Try to find out what topics you will be expected to teach and master the content before you report for your student teaching. Then when you start student teaching you can concentrate on planning and teaching, confident that you have a firm understanding of the content. Many students have botched their student teaching because they had to spend so much time learning the content they never had time to learn how to teach! Remember, middle and secondary school classes are not replicas of college classes. The content of what you must teach will probably be quite different from what you have been studying in college lately. You will need time to master it. If you take the time before your student teaching starts, you will have a considerable advantage.

Because student teaching is difficult and time demanding, most teacher education institutions recommend that student teachers not combine student teaching with other courses or outside work. If you have to work to eat, you must, but very few people are able both to hold down a job and perform creditably in their student teaching. Outside jobs, additional courses, trying to master inadequately learned subject content, and preparing classes are just too much for one ordinary person to do well at the same time. It is true that many successful teachers have moonlighted on outside jobs or on course work for advanced degrees. It is also true that many undergraduate students have maintained high grades with a full load of college courses and at the same time have worked full time in the evenings. But the student teaching experience is so unique in the many demands that it makes on a student teacher's time as to be virtually impossible for you to perform in a superior fashion if you bog yourself down with outside responsibilities at this crucial early part of your career.

Usually student teaching starts with a few days of observing. This gives you a few days to get ready for actually teaching. Use this time to become familiar with the classroom situation. Get to know the students. Learn their names. Borrow the teacher's seating chart and study it and the students as the class proceeds. In this way you will learn to associate names with faces and also have some inkling of the sort of persons with whom you will soon be dealing. Learn the classroom routines and other details of classroom management. Familiarize yourself with the types of teaching, activities, and assignments that the class is used to so that you can gradually assume the classroom teaching responsibility without too much disruption. Remember, at first students are likely to resent too much deviation from what they have come to expect.

In your observation of the efforts of your cooperating teacher in the act of teaching, keep in mind the following topics and questions:

- *Aims*. What were the aims of the lesson? How did the teacher make the students aware of them? Were the aims achieved?

- *Homework*. Did the teacher make a homework assignment? At what point in the lesson was the assignment made? How did the assignment relate to the day's work? How was the assignment from the previous day handled? How did the teacher deal with students who failed to submit completed work? How much time did the teacher spend on the assignment for the next day? Did the students appear to understand the assignment?
- *Review*. How much of the period was devoted to review of the previous lesson? Did the teacher make any effort to fit the review into the day's lesson? How did the teacher conduct the review—question and answer, student summarization of important points?
- *Methods*. What various methods were used by the teacher in the day's lesson? Did the teacher lecture? For what length of time? How did the teacher shift from one method to the next? How did the teacher motivate the students to attend? Was any provision made for individual differences among the students? Was any provision made for student participation in the lesson? Were the students kept busy during the entire period? Did any disciplinary problems arise? How did the teacher dispose of them?
- *Miscellaneous*. Was the teacher's voice pleasant enough to listen to? Did the teacher have any distracting idiosyncratic habits? Were lighting and ventilation adequate? What system did the teacher use for checking attendance?
- *Evaluation*. How could this lesson have been improved?

Relations in Professional Laboratory Experiences

When you take part in professional laboratory experiences in school, you are in a rather odd position. In a sense, you are neither teacher nor student; yet, in another sense, you are both teacher and student. Many college students have found this position trying. Therefore, included here are a number of suggestions that may make your life a little more pleasant during your laboratory experiences. Although these suggestions apply to observation, participation, and student teaching experience, they are somewhat loaded toward student teaching, the most difficult of the professional laboratory experiences. These suggestions are not meant to be preachy. Rather, they are conclusions drawn from years of observing and trying to help student teachers. It is hoped that they will point out some of the pitfalls in student teaching and ways to make this experience a success.

In professional laboratory experiences your relationship with your cooperating teacher is critical. You should concentrate on keeping these relationships friendly and professional.

Whether you like it or not, student teaching—and to a lesser degree, observation and participation—is a job as well as a learning experience, and the cooperating teacher and college supervisor are your bosses. Ordinarily, you can expect them to be nice bosses who will not only strive to help you in every way they can but will also be tolerant of your mistakes. They are bosses, however, and must be treated as such.

They will have pretty high expectations of you. Not only will they expect you to have an adequate command of the subject to be taught, they will also expect you to have the following:

1. A basic understanding of the nature of learners and learning.
2. A repertoire of teaching skills and some competence in them.
3. A supply of instructional materials.
4. An adequate understanding of the process of assessment and some skill in its techniques.

Do not disappoint them. You should check yourself in each of these areas. If you believe yourself deficient in any of them, now is the time to bring yourself up to par. Student teaching is too hectic to take time out for learning and collecting what you already should have learned and collected.

Your colleagues in the school will also expect you to be a professional—a beginning professional, but a professional just the same. You will be expected to do your job carefully without carping, criticizing, or complaining. Carry out instructions carefully. Keep to the routines of the school. If next week's lesson plans are due at the department head's office before the beginning of school Friday morning, make sure that they are there. Be prompt with all assignments. Never be late or absent unless previous arrangements have been made. Pay attention to details. Fill out reports, requisitions, and so on, accurately and on time. Be meticulous in the preparation of your unit and lesson plans. Never approach a class unprepared. Be sure you know your content and exactly how you plan to teach it. Nothing upsets cooperating teachers more than classes that do not go well because the student teacher was not sufficiently prepared.

Build a reputation for being responsible and dependable by carrying out your assignments faithfully and accurately. Sometimes student teachers fail because they do not understand what their responsibilities are or how to carry them out. Study the teacher's handbook, observe the cooperating teacher, and heed the cooperating teacher's instructions so that you will know just what to do and when and how. If you are uncertain about what to do or how to do it, ask, even though it may embarrass you to admit ignorance. It is much better to admit you do not understand than to keep quiet and reveal it.

Be a self-starter. Teachers, principals, and college supervisors are impressed by evidences of initiative. Volunteer to do things before you have to be asked. Willingly take on such tasks as reading papers and correcting tests. Take part in cafeteria supervision, extracurricular activities, attendance at PTO meetings, and the like. Participating in such activities will give you experience and expertise in these areas of the teacher's job and will also indicate to your colleagues that you are a professionally minded person who does not shun the nitty gritty.

Remember that you are being evaluated all the time that you are student teaching, so try to be just a little more accurate, a little more prompt, a little more precise, a little more dependable, and a little more willing than in other college activities.

During your professional laboratory experiences you are a guest of the school in which you are observing, participating, or student teaching. Your place in the school is not a right, but a privilege. Behave in a way that will make you and succeeding student teachers welcome. As quickly as you can, adapt yourself to the culture of the school and conform to the mores of the school as they apply to teachers. Do not stand on your rights—as a guest of the school you may not have many—but concentrate on your responsibilities. Try as soon as possible to become a member of the school staff and to set up pleasant relationships with your cooperating teacher and other colleagues.

Refrain from criticizing the school, its administration, or its teachers. Be particularly careful about what you say to teachers and other student teachers. If some things in a situation bother you, seek the advice of your college supervisor before you do anything drastic. If there is to be any friction, let the college supervisor absorb the sparks. It is his or her job to see that everything runs smoothly and that you get the best learning experience possible in your laboratory experience.

Do not under any circumstances discuss school personnel with the students. Often students tell student teachers how much better they are than their regular teachers. Do not respond to such bait. To allow yourself to discuss a teacher's performance and personality with a student can lead only to trouble.

Professional laboratory experiences, particularly student teaching, throw students and cooperating teachers into a closeness that can be greatly rewarding and also extremely difficult. From the point of view of the cooperating teacher, the student teaching period presents a threat in several ways. To allow a newcomer to interfere in the smooth running of the class is risky. More than one teacher has had to work extra long hours to repair the damage done to a class by an incompetent student teacher. Teachers who are insecure may find the presence of any other adult in their classes threatening; the presence of a student teacher critically observing the teacher's work can be particularly disturbing. So avoid any appearance of opposing or competing with the cooperating teacher. Consult with him or her before you undertake anything and follow his or her advice and instructions carefully. If you believe those instructions or advice are wrong, your only recourse is to consult with the college supervisor.

Above all, listen to what the cooperating teacher tells you! Many teachers (and college supervisors as well) complain that student teachers do not listen to what they are told. Often student teachers do not listen because they are so caught up in their problems that they find it difficult to concentrate on anything else. They may be too busy justifying their behavior or explaining away what has gone amiss in their classes to hear someone else's criticism. Although it may require some effort, try to hear what the cooperating teacher has to say and follow through on the suggestions. Teachers find it exasperating when student teachers carry on in unwanted ways in spite of the teacher's long and detailed instructions or explanations of what should be done.

As with any public figure in the community, you can expect that you and your performance will be discussed by students as well as the parents in the community. Usually, the students' comments are far removed from the teacher's ears but sometimes chance remarks are caught as you walk through the halls or as students are leaving the room. Let them not turn your head, because often these remarks are quite flattering. At the same time, guard against that feeling of depression that usually follows derogatory statements about your efforts or intentions. Whether you are praised or denounced, try to assume an objective attitude and use the comments for the inherent value they may possess. Remind yourself that you cannot always be all things to all people, nor should you even try to be. Your personality, the school regulations, and the classroom procedures will not let you be equally appealing to or effective with all of your students. You must expect that in the process of upholding your standards you will leave an occasional student dissatisfied. Only by keeping your reactions under control will you be able to preserve a positive feeling for your job.

Relationships with Students

Your relationships with students may make or break you in a laboratory situation, so try to make them as friendly and purposeful as possible. Students like teachers who treat them with respect and whom they can respect. Therefore, treat them courteously and tactfully but at the same time require of them standards of behavior and academic productivity reasonably close to those established by the regular teacher. Show that you have confidence in them and expect them to do well. Let them know you are interested in them and in their activities.

The best way to earn the students' respect and liking is to do a good job of teaching and to treat all students fairly and cordially. Do not, however, become overfriendly. Be friendly, not chummy. Your role is not to be a buddy, but to be a teacher. Seek respect rather than popularity. Remember that you are an adult, not a kid. The students will respect and like you more if you act your age and assume your proper role.

Analysis of Teaching

The examined life is always better than the unexamined life, philosophers tell us. If you know yourself, there is little doubt that the knowledge is beneficial to you as a teacher. Therefore, those who wish to become really professional should examine themselves and their teaching every once in a while. By so doing, it may be possible to detect weaknesses in your classroom behavior and teaching techniques that you can remedy and to discover unrealized strengths on which you can capitalize. This section of the module discusses a number of methods by which to examine your own teaching behavior in the classroom. Most of the procedures you will study here are rather simple methods of analyzing or evaluating teaching. It is hoped that they will not only give you a basis for examining your own teaching but will also serve as a means for reviewing some of the strategies and tactics discussed in earlier modules.

Analyzing Your Lessons

To make the most of your student teaching, you should occasionally stop to examine your lessons. The simplest way to do this is to stop, think back over a lesson, and ask yourself how it went and why. Usually, it is best to pick good lessons to examine so that you can see what you are doing well. The practice is good for the ego and tends to reinforce your good traits. From time to time, you will want to examine classes that failed, to see if you can figure out why they did not go well. If you are having trouble with a class, such an analysis may help you spot the difficulty and correct the errors that you may have been making.

In this type of analysis, as you review your lesson, ask yourself such questions as: What went well? What went badly? Why? What could I have done to improve the lesson? Next time, how should I handle this type of class? A questionnaire, such as that portrayed in Figure 11.1, should prove helpful in this reviewing of your procedures. Rating scales and checklists are also useful, but probably not as useful as the open-ended questionnaire. Figure 11.2 is an example of a rating scale used in rating the teaching experiences of student teachers. Figure 11.3 is a

Figure 11.1   Self-Analysis of
a Lesson

Use this form to analyze the class you thought went best this day.

1. Do you feel good about this class? Why or why not?
2. In what way was the lesson most successful?
3. If you were to teach this lesson again, what would you do differently? Why?
4. Was your plan adequate? In what ways would you change it?
5. Did you achieve your major objectives?
6. Was the class atmosphere pleasant, productive, and supportive?
7. Were there signs of strain or misbehavior? If so, what do you think was the cause?
8. How much class participation was there?
9. Which students did extremely well?
10. Were there students who did not learn? How might you help them?
11. Were the provisions for motivation adequate?
12. Was the lesson individualized so that students had opportunities to learn according to their abilities, interests, and needs?
13. Did the students have any opportunities to think?

rating scale devised by a group of prospective student teachers as a means of rating their teaching during student teaching. Perhaps you could develop a better one yourself.

Another way to check on your teaching is to consider at what level your students have learned. According to Bradfield and Moredock, there are five levels of performance. These levels are set forth in Figure 11.4. Ideally, the students should attain the highest levels of learning in your units. Examine your teaching. Is it the type that should bring students to this high level of learning? Or does it handcuff them to the lower levels?

Another way to upgrade your teaching is to examine your lesson plans. Presumably, the better your lesson plans, the better your teaching will be. Perhaps the form included as Figure 11.5 will help you to evaluate your plans. With a little adjustment, it could be used to evaluate unit and course plans. When using this form, remember that all the characteristics may not be necessary for every lesson plan, but in the long run teachers whose lessons do not meet these criteria cannot be fully effective.

Audio and Video Feedback

Both audio- and videotapes of your classes can be a great help to you as you examine your teaching and personality. Although at first the presence of the tape recorder or camcorder may make you nervous and self-conscious, the feeling will soon wear off. Then you can get a good record of how you look and sound as you teach. You can and should use this record as a basis for detailed analysis of your teaching, but just listening to and seeing yourself may give you important insights into your own teaching behavior. If your self-observation is done thoughtfully and critically, it will, of course, be more rewarding than if it is superficial. Using a simple questionnaire in which you ask yourself such questions as the following may make your self-observation more useful:

- What are my best points?
- What points are fairly good?
- What points are not so good?
- Are my explanations clear?
- Do I speak well and clearly?
- Do I speak in a monotone?

- Do I slur my words?
- Do my sentences drop off so that ends are difficult to hear?
- Do I involve everyone in the class or do I direct my teaching only to a few?
- Are my questions clear and unambiguous?
- Do I dominate class discussions?
- Do I allow certain students to dominate the class?

Figure 11.2 Criteria for an Educational Experience

Column 1 – insert *M* for much, or *S* for some, or *L* for little, or *N* for none.
Column 2 – insert *A* for all students, *M* for most students, *F* for few students, *N* for no students.
Column 3 – list specific next steps the teacher will take to improve the learning experience.

	1	2	3
1. What intellectual experiences were involved?			
a. Information-getting (fact-finding and compiling)?			
b. Organizing facts into own patterns (reasoning)?			
c. Judging, evaluating, applying criteria?			
d. Problem-solving (inventing criteria)?			
e. Creative thinking?(compare with item 9)			
2. Did the learning experience utilize emotional powers?			
a. Wholesome and self-expressive interest in the ideas or end-product of the work?			
b. Wholesome and self-expressive interest in the activity?			
c. Wholesome and self-expressive interest in the persons or group?			
3. Did the learning experience give opportunity for realistic relating by each student?			
a. to individual peers?			
b. to peer groups?			
c. to teacher and other adults?			
4. Did the learning experience promote realistic self-esteem?			
a. Awareness of own feelings?			
b. Recognizing own purposes or goals?			
c. Finding ways to effectively fulfill "a" or "b"?			
d. Realistic awareness of effect of powers and imitations?			
e. Realistic awareness of effect of own words and behavior upon others?			
f. Increased awareness of what he wants from situation to situation (i.e., of own self-expressive interest)?			
g. Realistic viewing of own competences (present and in near future)?			
h. Realistic, independent ideas of self-worth?			
i. Realistic awareness of learnings needed next?			
5. Did the learning experience promote improved behaviors in significant life situations?			
a. Family?			
b. Social groups?			
c. Civic competences?			
(1) Voting			
(2) Study of public problems			
(3) Organizing action groups			

Figure 11.2   *continued*

	1	2	3
6. Did the learning experience involve choosing?			
a. Ability to make critical choice?			
b. Ability to explain and support choice?			
c. Consideration of the consequences of own decision upon self and upon others?			
7. Did the learning experience improve understanding of how own mind works?			
a. Such mind-needs as "who, how, what, why, when, where, so what"?			
b. Basic outlines or structures of ideas into which many future ideas will be organized?			
c. Logical reasoning patterns such as "if..., then..." thinking; or "Are there any alternative answers?"			
d. Examining evidence or making careful generalizations or asking for needed "date"?			
e. Recognizing own bias or error or mistaken idea?			
f. Considering what thoughts, feelings, and actions will be changed in the future?			
g. Applying the new learning or idea to many situations or kinds of ideas?			
h. Increased readiness for "more of the same" ideas or activities?			
8. Did the learning experience promote realistic concepts of others?			
a. Awareness of others' feelings?			
b. Recognizing others' purposes or goals?			
c. Finding ways to effectively fulfill "a" or "b"?			
d. Realistic awareness and acceptance of others' powers and limitations?			
e. Realistic expectations of others?			
f. Realistic awareness of effect of own words and behaviors upon others?			
g. Increased awareness of what he/she "wants" from situation to situation?			
9. What intellectual skills or competences have been forwarded?			
a. Speaking skills?			
b. Writing skills?			
c. Reading skills?			
d. Arithmetical skills?			
e. Eye-hand muscular coordination?			
f. Discriminating discussion skills?			
10. Did each student experience a feeling of achievement?			
11. Did the experience provide for teacher-student conferences and constant re-evaluations?			

Source: J. A. Vanderpol, Jersey City State College, unpublished manuscript.

According to one analysis, there are seven major types of teaching operations: motivating, planning, informing, leading discussion, management, counseling, and evaluating. One way to evaluate your teaching would be to check on a form, such as that shown in Figure 11.6, the type of teaching you were doing every 5 seconds in one of your classes. In this form an eighth category has been added for operations that do not seem to fit into any of the seven listed.

Figure 11.3   Rating Scale
Designed by Teaching
Interns

Rate yourself: 5, 4, 3, 2, 1 (5 is best)
1. Did I look okay?
2. Did I sound okay?
3. Did I make my point?
4. Was I clear?
5. Did I make them think?
6. Is my questioning technique okay?
7. Is my writing-board work okay?
8. Is my audiovisual okay?
9. Did the lesson develop logically?
10. Overall rating:

A usually more profitable use of the recording device is to apply interaction analysis techniques to recording of your own teaching. Such self-evaluation may be more illuminating than simple critical listening to your recordings or hearing the criticisms and comments of an observer.

Interaction Analysis

There are a number of methods by which one can analyze the student-teacher interaction in a class. All of these methods require the services of either an observer or a recording device.

Figure 11.4   Levels of Performance

Level	Performance
I	*Imitating, duplicating, repeating.* This is the level of initial contact. The student can repeat or duplicate what has just been said, done, or read. Indicates that student is at least conscious or aware of contact with a particular concept or process.
II	*Level I, plus recognizing, identifying, remembering, recalling, classifying.* To perform on this level, the student must be able to recognize or identify the concept or process when encountered later, or to remember or recall the essential features of the concept or process.
III	*Levels I and II, plus comparing, relating, discriminating, reformulating, illustrating.* Here the student can compare and relate this concept or process with other concepts or processes and make discriminations. He or she can formulate in his own words a definition, and can illustrate or give examples.
IV	*Levels I, II and III, plus explaining, justifying, predicting, estimating, interpreting, making critical judgments, drawing inferences.* On the basis of understanding a concept or process, the student can make explanations, give reasons, make predictions, interpret, estimate, or make critical judgments. This performance represents a high level of understanding.
V	*Levels I, II, III, and IV, plus creating, discovering, reorganizing, formulating new hypotheses, new questions, and problems.* This is the level of original and productive thinking. The student's understanding has developed to such a point that he or she can make discoveries that are new to him or her and can restructure and reorganize knowledge on the basis of the new discoveries and new insights.

Source: James M. Bradfield and H. Stewart Moredock, *Measurement and Evaluation in Education*, New York: Macmillan Publishing Co., 1957, p. 204

Figure 11.5 Form for Evaluating Lesson Plans

1. The Objective
   a. The objective is clearly stated.
   b. The objective is measurable.
   c. The objective is pertinent to the unit and course.
   d. The objective is worthwhile.
   e. The objective is suitable to the students' age and grade level.
   f. The objective can be achieved in the time allotted.
   g. The objective can be attained in different degrees and/or amounts.
   h. The objective is relevant to the students' lives.

2. The Procedure or Suggested Activities
   a. The suggested activities will stimulate students' thinking.
   b. The suggested activities will produce the objectives.
   c. The procedure is outlined in sufficient detail to be followed easily.
   d. The procedure allows for individual differences.
      (1) choice in required work
      (2) optional work for enrichment
      (3) encouragement of initiative
   e. The activities in the procedure are interesting and appealing enough to arouse student motivation.
   f. The activities relate to
      (1) the aims of the students
      (2) the needs of the students
      (3) work in other courses
      (4) extracurricular life
      (5) out-of-school life
      (6) community needs and expectancies.

Interaction analysis is valuable because it gives you an indication of just who is doing the talking in the class. From it you can learn whether or not the class is teacher-dominated or student-dominated, free and open or repressive, and whether the teaching style is direct or indirect—in short, the classroom atmosphere and type of learning that is going on. As a rule of thumb, you can safely assume that when classes are satisfactory, the following take place:

1. The interaction will show that students actively participate at least half of the time. (Teachers who find themselves to be talking more than half the time should check their procedures.)
2. As far as possible, every student participates in some way. (Classes that are dominated by a few students are not satisfactory.)
3. A good share of the class time is given over to thoughtful, creative activity rather than to mere recitation of information by either teacher or students.

Figure 11.6 Types of Teaching Activities Checklist (5 second interval tallies)

Teaching Operation	Tallies
Motivating	
Planning	
Informing	
Leading discussion	
Management	
Counseling	
Evaluating	
Other	

Interaction analysis schemes vary from the simple to the complex. Some, such as the Flanders system, require that the observation be done by trained observers and that upon completing the observation, the observer arranges findings into a matrix from which one can tell not only what happened but what the atmosphere of the class was. Such systems can give you an excellent picture of the interaction in the classroom that may lead to important insights into your own teaching. If you tape-record the class, it is possible to apply the analysis to the class without the use of an outside observer. Therefore, it would be advantageous for you to learn how to use this system of interaction analysis. Unfortunately, there is not enough space to go into the procedure in detail in this module.

Even though they are not so useful as the more sophisticated methods, simple interaction analysis techniques can be truly helpful. The picture they give is not as clear, but they will show up glaring faults and give indications of more subtle elements of the classroom interaction and atmosphere.

Probably the simplest type of classroom interaction analysis is for an observer to mark down on a sheet of paper every time the teacher talks and every time a pupil talks, such as:

T P T T T P T T T P P T T

This record shows how much the teacher talks as compared to how much the students talk, although it will not show how long they talk. If you tape-record your class, you can do this analysis yourself.

A more complex refinement of this technique is for an observer to sit at the back of the class and to record the number of times each person speaks. This technique gives you a much clearer picture of what is happening in the class. The disadvantage of this technique is that it requires an outside observer. Neither audio- nor videotapes of the type teachers could procure in the ordinary classroom situation would be usable for such an analysis. Figure 11.7 is an illustration of the tallying by this method of interaction analysis. In this figure, the teacher is represented by a circle, and the students by squares. Exercise 11.1 will help you think about this figure.

Figure 11.7   A Form for
Interaction Analysis

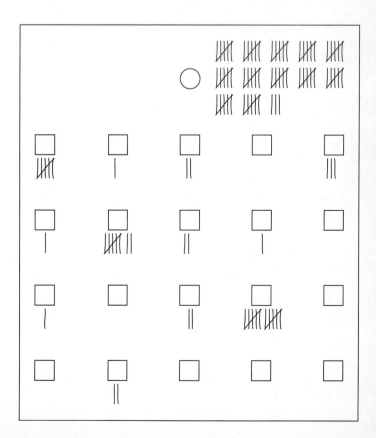

Another version of the form of analysis just described is for the observer to record who is talking every 5 seconds. This variation of the tallying approach has the advantage of showing what persons are interacting and how much they talk, though it does not give as complete a picture as the Verbal Interaction Category System (V.I.C.S.) or Flanders analysis system.

Some supervisors use a simplified version of the Flanders system that does not require the use of a matrix. In this version of the system the observer simply records, at regular intervals, whether the teacher or a student is talking, and the nature of the talk. Flanders has divided the talk into ten categories. Teacher talk he has divided into talk designed to influence students indirectly and talk designed to influence students directly. Under indirect-influence teacher talk, he includes four categories:

1. Talk in which the teacher accepts the student's feelings in a nonthreatening manner.
2. Talk in which the teacher praises or encourages the student's performance or behavior.
3. Talk in which the teacher accepts, uses, or builds on the student's ideas.
4. Talk in which the teacher asks questions designed to elicit ideas.

In direct-influence teacher talk, Flanders includes three categories:

5. Lectures and teacher talks in which the teacher presents information and ideas.
6. Orders, commands, and directions that students are expected to follow.
7. Criticism of student behavior, reprimands, and explanations justifying class procedures.

(Text continues on page 463.)

Reviewing Interaction Analysis

• • • • • •

Instructions: The purpose of this exercise is to check your comprehension of the meaning of interaction analysis. Answer each of the following questions, then compare your responses with your classmates. Resolve any differences.

1. If a classroom analysis of one of your typical classes consists almost entirely of *T*s, what would it show about your teaching?

2. Does this analysis indicate that perhaps you should consider changing your style? Why or why not?

3. Do the tallies in Figure 11.7 give you any inkling about the style of the teacher in that class?

4. Do the tallies in Figure 11.7 tell you anything about class participation?

5. With respect to the tallies in Figure 11.7, what generalizations can you make about that class?

Student talk in this type of instruction analysis is limited to two categories:

8. Student responses to the teacher.
9. Student-initiated talk.

This type of interaction analysis also provides for a tenth category:

10. Times when no one is speaking or if there is a confusing babble as at the beginning or end of a class period or during laboratory or small-group discussion sessions.[2]

To record the interaction according to this simplified version of the Flanders system, use a form such as that shown in Figure 11.8.

Evaluating Specific Teaching Techniques

Evaluating Your Discussions

To improve your skill in using class discussions, you should analyze the discussions that you lead. It is possible to do this in armchair fashion, but it would be more productive to react to a tape recording of the discussion. A self-evaluation form, similar to the one presented as Figure 11.9, should be very helpful for spotting your weaknesses and building your strengths in leading discussions. Flowcharts that depict the course of the discussion may be even more useful. Preparing the flowchart can be entrusted to a student observer since the technique for preparing one is so simple. If the class is arranged in a circle, preparing the flowchart is easier; it is slightly less so if the class is arranged as a hollow square; but when the class is arranged in rows, making the chart becomes quite difficult. (Discussions are difficult to conduct when the students are in rows, too.) All the observer does is to make an arrow from the speaker to the person to whom he or she is speaking each time anyone speaks. A direct reply to a speaker can be noted by a double-headed arrow. Comments or questions that are directed to the group rather than to an individual are indicated by arrows that point to the center of the circle or square. An example of a flowchart showing a portion of a class discussion appears as Figure 11.10.

Figure 11.11 shows another device used to analyze class discussions. In this technique, a recorder simply tallies the number of times each person talks. There is no indication of the conversational interchanges, so this type of record does not give you as complete a picture as the flowchart does.

[2]Edmund J. Amidon and Ned A. Flanders, *The Role of the Teacher in the Classroom* (Minneapolis, MN: Amidon, 1963), p. 15.

Figure 11.8 Interaction
Analysis Record Sheet

	CATEGORY	TALLIES
Teacher Talk	Accepts Feeling Praises or Encourages Accepts or Uses Ideas of Students Asks Questions Lectures Gives Directions Criticizes	
Student Talk	Student Response Student Initiation	
	Silence or Confusion	

Figure 11.9   Self-Evaluation Form for Discussion Leaders

A.

1. Did I have a legitimate objective?
2. Were the objectives suitable for the discussion technique?
3. Did I get good participation?
4. Did I encourage participation or did I tend to cut people off?
5. Did I keep from letting people dominate?
6. Did I encourage the shy, timid, etc.?
7. Did I keep the group to the subject?
8. Was I domineering?
9. In what did I best succeed?
10. In what was I least successful?
11. Did I solicit evocative questions and tentative solutions?
12. Did I summarize conclusions or positions so as to follow through and tie the discussion together?

B.

1. Identify the techniques that seemed to make the discussion effective.
2. Identify the techniques that seemed to detract from the effectiveness of the discussion.

Questions

Questions are among the teacher's most important tools; it is important to learn how to use them well. To check on your questioning technique, you might record and observe yourself (see Module 7). Among the things you might observe are:

- What sorts of questions do I use?
- Are my questions clear?

Figure 11.10   A Sample Flowchart

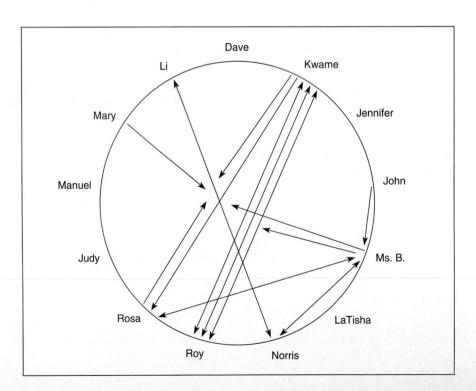

Figure 11.11   Tally Sheet for Class Discussions

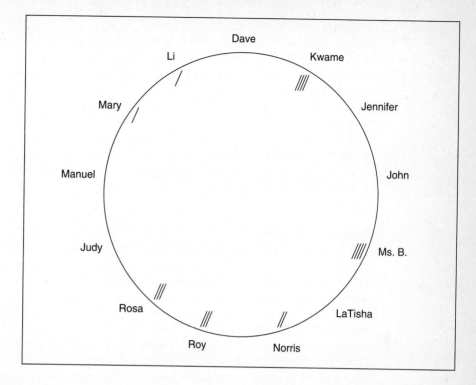

- Do I ask one question at a time or do I confuse students by asking two or more questions as one?
- Do I ask real questions, or are my questions whiplash questions that start out as statements and then suddenly convert into questions, such as: "The point that the author was trying to get across is what?" Whiplash questions are not really fair because they give students the wrong set.
- Do my questions require students to use their knowledge, information, and ideas?
- Do I direct my questions to students or to the class as a whole?
- Do I wait until I have finished asking my question before calling on someone to answer it?
- Do I follow up my questions with probing questions to ferret out ideas, understandings, and thinking?

Most questions in a typical class are aimed at eliciting memorized facts and information. When teachers ask high-order questions, the questions are likely to be convergent questions rather than divergent or evaluative questions. Review Module 7 if you cannot remember what these are. To find out what type of questions you and your students use, forms similar to that presented in Figure 11.12 can be helpful. To use the form, an observer simply checks the appropriate column each time the teacher asks a question. (See also Exercise 7.3 in Module 7.)

Figure 11.12   A Form for Analyzing Questions

	Cognitive Memory Questions	Convergent Questions	Divergent Questions	Evaluative Questions
Teacher Questions				
Student Questions				

Analysis of Test Results

Analysis of students' test results can give one an inkling of the success of your teaching, providing the tests are properly designed and written. For test results to be of value for the analysis of your teaching success, the teaching objectives must be carefully defined and each test item must be aimed at a teaching objective. Once you have given and corrected the test, to analyze the test you must set up a chart that indicates what objective each item tests, and what items each pupil got right, as in Figure 11.13. Such a chart would show you how effectively you taught by indicating how well you achieved each of your objectives. In the example, for instance, if the small sample is any indicator, the teacher evidently was quite successful with Objective 1 and not so successful with Objective 2. This type of analysis is also an excellent tool by which to diagnose the progress of the various students in the class.

Student Evaluation

You can learn much from the students' opinions of your teaching. Just watching their reactions will be enlightening. An eager, enthusiastic, attentive class is a good sign; an apathetic, inattentive, antagonistic class is not. Another method by which to gather student evaluations is to use a simple questionnaire or opinion sampling. Some teachers make a practice of collecting such data at the end of the school year, but if you are to capitalize on the information, perhaps it would be better to collect it earlier in the year. Whenever you do it, make sure that the evaluations are entirely anonymous. To preserve anonymity, use check sheets rather than handwritten comments. Sometimes, however, students will react well to open-ended, free response questions if the questions ask for constructive criticism concerning ways to make the course more effective.

Growing in the Profession

Surveying Employment Prospects

Early in your teacher preparation program you should start thinking about your first job and your career in teaching. If you have not done so already, you should investigate the job market. At the moment this is being written, there appears to be a change settling in regarding the availability of jobs. The decline in student enrollments of the 1970s and early 1980s precipitated a drastic reduction in the number of candidates interested in a teaching career. Of late, however, it appears that the demand has caught up with and in many cases has surpassed the supply of teachers, which had seriously dwindled. Salaries in teaching are rising. Several states have made teaching and teacher preparation items of immediate concern.

Similarly, you should try to pick courses that will prepare you for the subject matter you are likely to have to teach in middle or secondary schools. Courses in writing, composition, and American literature are more likely to be useful to beginning English teachers than Gothic literature, for instance.

Key: + = correct response: 0 = incorrect response

Objective	Item	Joe	Julia	Jamaal	Juanita	Jean	Josie
1.	1	+	+	+	+	+	+
	2	+	0	+	+	+	+
	3	+	0	0	+	+	+
2.	4	+	0	0	0	0	+
	5	+	+	+	0	0	0
	6	0	+	0	+	0	0

Figure 11.13 Example of Test-item Analysis Form

In times of tight employment it may be wise to consider the advisability of seeking a graduate degree or working as a substitute teacher for a year or two. Both of these experiences will make you more hirable. Being a substitute teacher has the added advantage of giving you an inside track when opportunities in the system open up.

Take advantage of the facilities of your college placement service early. You will probably find them anxious to coach you on ways to find, apply for, and obtain jobs, and also to tell you how you can best prepare for the jobs that are becoming available. Similarly, education professors are usually anxious to coach students on such matters as finding job opportunities, writing letters of application, securing favorable recommendations, job interviewing, preparing for the types of jobs available, and so on. The sooner you become knowledgeable in these areas, the better chances you will have of finding congenial employment when the time comes.

You should, as soon as you can, become familiar with the certification requirements of the state or states in which you hope to teach, just as you should become familiar with the college graduation requirements. Usually you can be confident that your college program will meet the local certification requirements for your major. Studying the certification requirements may show you how to become certifiable in more fields and in other parts of the country.

Professional Memberships

Become familiar with the teacher associations in your field as early as you can. Organizations such as The National Council of Teachers of English, The National Council for the Social Studies, and the National Council of Teachers of Mathematics publish journals and monographs that can help you become familiar with what is going on in the teaching field. They also provide opportunities for fellowship with leading teachers and supervisors. As a rule, local affiliates of these organizations welcome teacher education students to their meetings. These meetings provide opportunities to meet important professionals and to learn about the most recent developments in the teaching field.

The local affiliates of the teachers' unions (The American Federation of Teachers and the National Education Association) also provide opportunities for students to become involved in professional activities. You may find joining the union's student affiliate or attending the state or national meetings especially profitable. State and regional conventions in particular can give beginners a superb view of new professional materials and technology available. There is hardly a supplier of educational materials or equipment that does not exhibit at these conventions.

Keeping Up

Once you have begun to teach, do not become complacent. After a period of teaching some teachers become bored, frustrated, and discontented. This phenomenon attacks teachers who do not grow with the profession and so atrophy. Teaching is interesting and exciting if you approach it that way. Try to keep it so by keeping up with what is going on and by becoming active in the professional organizations. Attend workshops, institutes, and conventions that present the new methods and materials of your profession. Take graduate courses that will help you better understand your subject, your pupils, and methods of teaching. Take interest in the students and their activities. Involve yourself in curriculum revision. In short, keep yourself professionally and personally alert and active. You should begin this process now!

Try to grow personally as well as professionally. Keep your mind sharp by staying interested in many things and by becoming more expert in your field. Deepen your appreciation for your work and guard against letting it become a secondary occupation. You may find it necessary to combine your teaching with other work—either part-time work or homemaking—but do not let the other work take away from your teaching. Keep abreast of developments in your field through refresher courses, professional reading, or advanced graduate study. No matter how you do it, keep moving forward with your development of your own personality and your mastery of professional skills. Arrange to visit other teachers and interact with them about what accounts for their success. Keep yourself on the alert for new ways of doing things, new approaches to your students and your subject. Therein lies the excitement of your new profession—reaching a point of competency in your teaching, engaging in activities that bring about successful learning, and finding outlets for your creative juices that will benefit your students. Thus equipped, involve yourself in curricular revision and in short keep yourself professionally alert and alive.

HAIL AND FAREWELL

Working through these modules may have made it seem that teaching is a difficult, arduous profession. Maybe so, but it is also rewarding. Teaching done well is never dull. It can be great fun. Besides, it is important. Working with young minds will keep you on your toes. It also gives you an opportunity to influence the shaping of the future.

Teaching is a profession to be proud of. We welcome you to it!

SUGGESTED READING

Barringer, M. "How the National Board Builds Professionalism." *Educational Leadership* 50(6):18–22 (March 1993).

Black, S. "How Teachers Are Reshaping Evaluation Procedures." *Educational Leadership* 51(2):38–42 (October 1993).

Bullough, R. V., Jr.; Knowles, J. G.; and Crow, N. *Emerging as a Teacher*. London: Routledge, 1992.

Cutler, A. B., and Ruopp, F. N. "Buying Time for Teachers' Professional Development." *Educational Leadership* 50(6):34–37 (March 1993).

Darling-Hammond, L., and Goodwin, A. L. "Progress Toward Professionalism in Teaching." In *Challenges and Achievements of American Education*, edited by Gordon Cawelti. 1993 ASCD Yearbook. Alexandria, VA: Association for Supervision and Curriculum Development, 1993.

Duke, D. L. "Removing Barriers to Professional Growth." *Phi Delta Kappan* 74(9):702–704, 710–712 ((May 1993).

Firestone, W. A. "Why 'Professionalizing' Teaching is Not Enough." *Educational Leadership* 50(6):6–11 (March 1993).

Fullan, M. G. "Why Teachers Must Become Change Agents." *Educational Leadership* 50(6):12–17 (March 1993).

Goddard, R. E. *Teacher Certification Requirements: All Fifty States*. 4th ed. Sarasota, FL: Teacher Certification Publications, 1986.

Havens, B. "Teaching 'Cadet Teachers.'" *Educational Leadership* 50(6):50–51 (March 1993).

Hunter, B. "Linking for Learning: Computer-and-Communications Network Support for Nationwide Innovation in Education. *Journal of Science Education and Technology* 1(1):23–34 (March 1992).

Latham, G. I., and Fifield, K. "The Hidden Costs of Teaching." *Educational Leadership* 50(6):44–45 (March 1993).

Merseth, K. K. "First Aid for First-Year Teachers." *Phi Delta Kappan* 73(9):678–683 (May 1992).

Milner, J. O. "Suppositional Style and Teacher Evaluation." *Phi Delta Kappan* 72(6):464–467 (February 1991).

Poda, J. H. "The Teacher-in-Residence Program." *Educational Leadership* 50(6):52 (March 1993).

Rabbitt, M. "International Recruitment Centers for International Schools." *Phi Delta Kappan* 73(5):409–410 (January 1992).

Vienne, D. T. "Seasoned Pros Give New Teachers a Helping Hand." *Executive Educator* 13(8):32–33 (August 1991).

Walen, E., and DeRose, M. "The Power of Peer Appraisals." *Educational Leadership* 51(2):45–48 (October 1993).

Watts, G. D., and Castle, S. "Electronic Networking and the Construction of Professional Knowledge." *Phi Delta Kappan* 73(9):684–689 (May 1992).

Wilson, M. "The Search for Teacher Leaders." *Educational Leadership* 50(6):24–27 (March 1993).

POSTTEST

Check

In the following, check the appropriate answers according to the module text.

1. Check those of the following that the cooperating teacher will expect you to have when you come to do your student teaching.

   _____   a. A command of the subject to be taught.
   _____   b. Expertise in many teaching skills.
   _____   c. A supply of instructional materials.
   _____   d. An adequate understanding of the evaluation process.
   _____   e. A well-developed teaching style.

2. To make a favorable impression on your cooperating teacher and supervisor,

   _____   a. Prepare very carefully.
   _____   b. Go right ahead with your plans without asking advice.
   _____   c. Show your expertise by criticizing the school's procedures.
   _____   d. Learn and follow the school routines.
   _____   e. Be prompt at all assignments.
   _____   f. Listen to what you are told.
   _____   g. Study the content before the class period begins.

Multiple Choice

Write the letter of the most appropriate answer in the space provided.

_____   1. When you get right down to it, college supervisors and cooperating teachers are your
   a. colleagues.
   b. assistants.
   c. bosses.
   d. collaborators.

_____   2. As a student teacher, you are
   a. a member of the school staff.
   b. only a student.
   c. a guest of the school.
   d. on your own.

_____   3. Most college teacher education students find that the most difficult part of their teacher education program is
   a. Theory courses.
   b. Microteaching.
   c. Participation (practicum).
   d. Student teaching.

_____   4. To make your participation experience profitable, you should
   a. engage in as many types of experiences as you can.
   b. spend the entire period conducting classes.
   c. spend the entire period observing.
   d. focus on getting to know the students.

_____   5. Basically, student teaching is supposed to be
   a. a testing experience.
   b. a learning experience.
   c. a trial experience.
   d. a full-fledged teaching experience.

Short Explanation

1. Suppose you should try out a new teaching technique and it fails miserably for you. What should you do, according to this module?
2. According to Bradfield and Moredock, what is the highest level of teaching?
3. List four of the eight criteria for the objective included in the form for evaluating lesson plans.
4. What is the purpose of recording and playing back your lessons?
5. An interaction analysis shows that most of the class consisted of teacher-initiated talk in which the teacher gave students information and asked narrow memory questions. If this class is typical of this teacher's style:
   a. is she a direct or indirect teacher?
   b. is her style a most effective one?

6. A simple interaction analysis tally shows the following: T T T T T P T P T P T T T P T T P T T P T P T P T P T P.
   a. What does this show about the class?
   b. Is the class good or bad?

7. List six things you would look for in evaluating a discussion.
8. The flowchart of a discussion shows that there are only a few arrows from the teacher's position and all of these point to the center of the diagram. How would you interpret this phenomenon?
9. Why should you avoid using whiplash questions?
10. In what ways are cognitive memory questions, convergent questions, and divergent questions different?
11. In an item analysis, we find the following:

Objective	Item	Student A	B	C	D	E	F
	1	+	+	+	+	+	+
1.	2	+	+	+	+	+	+
	3	+	+	0	+	+	0
	4	0	0	+	0	0	0
2.	5	0	0	0	0	0	0
	6	+	0	+	0	+	0

Assuming that this excerpt is typical of the entire test item analysis, what does it tell you?
12. Identify and explain three ways that you can prepare yourself to be more hirable.
13. Explain why this module recommends that you join a professional organization in your teaching field.

Essay

1. Describe the danger signals that a cooperating teacher needs to be alert for to try and prevent a student teacher from getting into serious teaching trouble.
2. Describe at least five ways you can continue to grow professionally.
3. From your current observations and field work as related to this teacher preparation program, clearly identify one specific example of educational practice that seems contradictory to exemplary practice or theory as presented in this module. Present your explanation for the discrepancy.
4. Describe any prior concepts you held that changed as a result of the experiences of this module. Describe the changes.

Note: For the essay posttest questions there is no answer key. Those questions would be useful as springboard questions for small-group or whole-class discussions.

MODULE 1

Multiple Choice

1. a	2. d
3. a	4. a
5. d	6. d
7. a	8. b
9. d	10. d
11. b	12. c
13. b	

Short Explanation

1.   The primary difference is with grade-level organization. As defined in this book, a secondary school is one that houses students in some combination of grades 7 through 12. A middle school typically is grades 6 through 8 but with variations that might include grades 5 and 9. Junior high schools typically house children in grades 7 through 8 and sometimes grade 9. In addition, other characteristics that distinguish the middle school from the junior high school should be included, as presented in the chapter. High schools typically house students in grades 9 through 12 or 10 through 12.

2.   *Team teaching* refers to two or more teachers simultaneously providing instruction to students in the same classroom. A *teaching team* is composed of one teacher each from two or more disciplines, such as English and history, in order to provide an interdisciplinary approach to learning for a common group of students. Members of a teaching team may participate in team teaching.

3.   In a school within a school, an interdisciplinary team of teachers is assigned each day, for a portion of the school day, or for the entire day and year—and in some instances, for all years that students are at a school—to the same group of from 125 to 150 students. Major advantages include: (1) teachers and students become a family where all get to know, support, and work with one another, and (2) teaching is interdisciplinary and thematic, thus better connecting student learning with the real world. Disadvantages might include complexity of scheduling.

4.   *School restructuring* encompasses activities that change fundamental assumptions, practices, and relationships, both within the organization and between the organization and the outside world, in ways that lead to improved learning outcomes. The general purpose is to design schools that reflect the needs of young people who will be in the work force in the twenty-first century. Restructuring efforts have included site-based management, collaborative

decision making, school choice, personalized learning, school-within-a-school, integrated curricula, and collegial staffing.

5. The middle school movement is driven by the philosophy that children of ages ten through fourteen need an educational program that is specially tailored to their special needs.

6. Constructivism stresses the importance of building conceptual understanding, which implies beginning with the student's existing knowledge.

7. A mastery learning instructional model assumes that every student can learn at a specified level of competence if the learner's previous knowledge and attitudes are accounted for, if the instruction is of good quality, and if adequate time on task is allowed.

8. Direct instruction is where information is delivered to the students (by textbook or teacher such as by a lecture), whereas indirect instruction is where student learning is facilitated by the teacher making information accessible to students.

9. When the middle school includes children of grades below grade 7, such as 5 and 6.

10. The steps of the model are: (1) diagnosis or preassessment; (2) preparation; (3) guidance of student learning; (4) assessment of the learning; (5) and a follow-up.

MODULE 2

Multiple Choice

1.	a	2.	d
3.	d	4.	d
5.	a	6.	d
7.	d	8.	c
9.	d	10.	c
11.	a	12.	d
13.	d		

Short Explanation

1. Any example is okay as long as it demonstrates that different students are working at different tasks to accomplish the same objective, or are working at different tasks to accomplish different objectives. The benefit of multilevel teaching is that it can be used to address the different needs and abilities of students within a classroom.

2. It is important to recognize that students may learn differently from the teacher—that the way an individual teacher learns best may be different from the way many of the students learn. If the teacher is not cognizant of this then that teacher may teach only in the way he or she has learned, thus ineffectively attending to the learning styles, needs, and learning of many of the students.

3. These are the three stages of the continuous or cyclical process of concept attainment.

4. When learning is integrated, it is more meaningful to the lives of the students and is longer lasting. That means the information has been assimilated into the learner's long-term memory.

5. They include: whole-language learning, thematic and interdisciplinary thematic teaching, and team teaching.

6. Concept mapping is one way.

7. Yes. A concept map mentally prepares students to integrate the learning of old material with new.

8. The use of expository teaching (listening, reading, and memorizing) relies heavily upon the use of words (spoken or written); for many students, especially those with limited proficiency in English and with cultural differences, this can be very abstract and difficult learning.

9.   See Costa's fourteen characteristics of intelligent behavior.

10.   For grading purposes the teacher can simply record whether a student keeps a journal or not and, perhaps, the quantity of writing that is in the journal. Beyond that, the teacher should not judge what is in the journal. Otherwise, students begin writing for the teacher rather than for themselves, thereby defeating the purpose of journal writing, which is to encourage students to write, reflect, and make connections in their learning.

11.   The teacher's involvement and influence on character development is unavoidable. As a teacher, you should provide both a conducive atmosphere and a model that students can emulate.

12.   Students construct their knowledge and develop new skills by connecting their experiences to what is being learned. Thinking is critically important to and inseparable from learning. Thinking and learning take time, more time for some students than for others, but all students can learn. Not all students learn and respond to learning situations in the same way. Intelligence is not a fixed or static reality, but can be learned, taught, and developed.

13.   For a class of students composed mostly of students with kinesthetic modality preferences, teacher-centered instructional strategies will be less effective than will be those strategies that are more student-centered. Kinesthetic learners learn better when physically active. Strategies such as sociodrama, skits, bulletin board activities, and making collages will better maintain student interest and motivation.

MODULE 3

Multiple Choice

1. d		2. b	
3. d		4. b	
5. b		6. d	
7. b		8. b	
9. c		10. a	
11. c			

Short Explanation

1.   The content should be compatible with that found in state and local district curriculum documents; obtain input from experienced teachers.

2.   Planning the instruction is the preactive phase; analyzing and assessing the results of the instruction is the reflective phase. An effective teacher does both, plans and reflects on the implementation to improve the instruction the next time around.

3.   Instructional time should not be wasted; students should be engaged mentally and physically in the instructional tasks.

4.   To provide national guidelines represented by standards, that is, definitions of what students should know and be able to do as a result of studying that discipline. Standards are prepared by select committees of professionals in the discipline, including college and university professors and public school teachers.

5.   A textbook can provide important organization of the subject content, resources and readings, and previously tested activities and suggestions for student learning experiences. A textbook cannot or should not become the "be all and end all" of the instructional experiences. Other problems that might be present are those as discussed in the module: lack of multicultural balance; inadequate coverage of specific areas of content; inappropriate reading level for some students.

MODULE 4

Multiple Choice

1. a
2. c
3. c
4. b
5. c

Short Explanation

1. Students learn better when they learn material in meaningful chunks.

2. The criteria should relate to state and local curriculum mandates, as well as to student interests.

3. Reasons include: to prevent ad-lib teaching; to prevent dead time; to make sure that the course of study is being addressed; to make sure that the lessons are related and build from one to the next.

4. To attend to the specific needs and characteristics of your own particular group of students.

5. Many beginning teachers are fearful of diverting from their planned lessons, and that fear is understandable. It is, however, important to recognize when a class is unpredictably "turned on" to a topic, and to know how to take advantage of that teachable moment. For this there are no special guidelines, other than perhaps when in doubt stick with the plan. Later, in reflection on the day's event, you might be able to reorganize your longer-range plan to adjust to the captured student interest. Once lost, however, it is not easy to recapture those precious moments in teaching.

6. Preassessment of student knowledge should be done at the beginning of each unit of instruction, and sometimes even at the beginning of a lesson. If you are to help students construct their knowledge about a subject, then it only makes sense to know what they know or think they know at the start of learning about it. Preassessment can be done in a variety of ways, such as by oral or written questions or by use of the technique called think-pair-share.

7. Recalling the four decision-making and thought-processing phases of instruction, the projective phase is the application of the results of analyzing and evaluating the teaching (the reflective phase). Thus, upon that reflection, changes will occur to a previously taught lesson and then applied in the next application. Because teachers make errors in planning, students differ, situations differ, content changes, and the prior knowledge and misconceptions that one group of students has will differ from another, lesson plans should never be "set in concrete."

8. Not only do supervisors need to know the extent of a student teacher's capability in planning, but they need to know that, in fact, the student teacher is doing the necessary planning. When there are problems during student teaching, the written plans are a good source of data for diagnosing the cause of the problem and for prescribing a solution. Otherwise, everyone involved is more or less in the dark about the student teacher's intent, procedures, and intended outcomes.

9. Although procedures for any sort of unit planning are essentially the same, a standard unit plan is typically prepared by one teacher, whereas an interdisciplinary unit is typically prepared by a team of teachers. In addition, a standard unit may or may not follow a thematic approach (i.e., it may use either a theme or a subject topic), but an interdisciplinary thematic unit does follow a thematic approach and that theme crosses discipline boundaries. Also, the time students study a standard unit is usually shorter than their study of an interdisciplinary thematic unit. Time for preparation is another difference: whereas an ordinary unit can be prepared by a teacher in a relatively short time, it may take a team of teachers as long as a year to complete their preparation of an interdisciplinary thematic unit.

10.   Students play a major role in decision making about what they are going to study and how. Yes, it is used and is becoming more prevalent. For one thing, it fits with the constructivist philosophy; for another, it empowers students and gives them a sense of motivation.

MODULE 5

Multiple Choice

1. d	2. c
3. c	4. c
5. c	6. c
7. d	8. c
9. b	10. c
11. c	

Short Explanation

1.   The praise should be spontaneous, sincere, low-keyed, private, and specific to the deed.

2.   Prevention is so much easier than is treatment. Prevention is positive and productive, while punishment is negative and *ipso facto*. The steps are many, but they should include: planning lessons thoroughly and thoughtfully; planning a variety of activities for any one class period, ensuring that various learning modalities are engaged and all learning styles are attended to; ensuring that students are actively involved in the lesson for the entire class period, with no off-task time; minimizing foot traffic in the classroom; using withitness and overlapping behaviors; using prompt and appropriate intervention; using teacher mobility and proximity as control procedures; using positive cueing and reinforcement.

3.   Recommendations include: spend outside-of-class time collecting data, diagnosing the problem, and planning a strategy; have a personal conference with the student, outside of regular class time; make a phone call to a parent or guardian to solicit that adult's assistance in understanding the problem and prescribing a possible solution; organize a conference with all of that student's teachers and counselors; take an interest in things that interest that student and let the student know about your interest.

4.   It emphasizes the value in reinforcing good behaviors and not bad ones.

5.   Achievement in learning seems better and longer lasting when the student works at it because he or she is intrinsically motivated to learn rather than because of what someone else expects of the student or because of external rewards.

6.   Acceptable answers to this question can vary considerably but should demonstrate your awareness of certain important concepts, such as the following: management procedures might be somewhat tighter when teaching a class of middle school students than were you teaching a college-prep senior high school class; some teachers, when preparing lesson plans, designate certain activities as being relatively high-noise-level expectation activities and designate others as having a much lower noise level or no noise from students, letting students know this at the beginning of each lesson; if a teacher tries during the same class period to make a transition from a social-interactive learning activity to one that is direct instruction (expository) by the teacher, students may have difficulty in making the transition as quickly as the teacher would like.

7.   Writing your classroom management system causes you to think about what your expectations and procedures are going to be, and to reflect on that thinking. Having carefully thought through your expectations and procedures enables you to better communicate them to your students and then to follow through with consistency. Furthermore, when a problem arises

during student teaching the written plan provides a source of data for the supervisor and student teacher to analyze the problem and arrive at a possible solution.

8.   Reprimanding is a form of punishment and is negative; reminding the student of procedures is more positive and consistent with a nonthreatening and positive classroom environment.

9.   By interrupting the content flow to reprimand the student, the teacher is doing the very thing for which he or she is reprimanding the student—that is poor modeling behavior by the teacher.

10.   For a class of students made up mostly of students with kinesthetic modality preferences, teacher-centered instructional strategies will be less effective than will be those strategies that are more student-centered. Kinesthetic learners learn better when physically active. Strategies such as sociodrama, skits, bulletin board activities, and making collages will better maintain student interest and motivation.

MODULE 6

Multiple Choice

1. c	2. d
3. a	4. b
5. c	6. d
7. a	8. a
9. b	10. d
11. d	12. d
13. d	

Short Explanation

1.   When materials, safety, and content disallow direct experiences.

2.   The steps are: recognizing the problem; formulating a question about the problem; hypothesizing a solution; collecting data; analyzing the data; arriving at a tentative solution or resolution of the problem. Answers to second part will vary.

3.   Emphasizing the mental operations of learning, Bruner identified three stages—the enactive (corresponding with the direct learning of the lower steps of the learning experiences ladder), iconic (two-dimensional learning, as with the middle steps), and abstract learning (the visual- and auditory-only learning of the top of the ladder).

4.   The advantages far outweigh the disadvantages.

5.   Learning is most effective when students are learning by doing (hands-on) and mentally engaged in thinking about what they are doing and learning (minds-on).

MODULE 7

Multiple Choice

1. b	2. c
3. d	4. c
5. b	6. a
7. a	8. c
9. c	10. d

Short Explanation

1. In this lesson, there was too much reliance on listening and the use of verbal instructions. The teacher keeps talking, and therefore there is not enough quiet think time. Clear instructions for each step should have been written on chalkboard at the time the step is introduced. The teacher then walks around (as Estella was doing), helping students who are having difficulty but not continuing to address the entire class every few seconds.

2. Ways include: analogies, verbal cues, pauses, humor, visuals, body gestures, sensory cues, proximity, strategy change, voice inflections, and animation.

3. There will be a difference in noise level, and students may not be able to make the transition as quickly as the teacher might expect. The transition needs to be slow but definite. Control problem could occur unless the teacher plans carefully.

4. Students could be doing something but not necessarily thinking about what they are doing. A time-filling activity is not necessarily indicative of good teaching and learning.

5. Strategies include: mental modeling, encouraging metacognition, journal writing, and cognitive mapping.

6. The theory is that when small groups of students of mixed backgrounds and capabilities work together toward a common goal, there is an increase in each individual's self-esteem and academic achievement. Experts tell us that when cooperative learning is used correctly all members of the group benefit both socially and academically. Unfortunately, in many instances it is not used well. Too often, teachers simply tell their class of students to form groups of four and go at some task, and then they call that using cooperative-learning groups. In those instances, it is nothing more than the same sort of traditional group work that teachers have used in the classroom for many decades.

MODULE 8

Short Explanation

1. By careful and thoughtful positioning and diagramming of material on the writing board you can present oral or written language (processed in the left hemisphere) augmented by visual spatial relationships (processed in the right hemisphere), thereby enhancing student learning by encouraging integrated hemispheric processing of information.

2. Basically, a textbook should present the relevant content interestingly, logically, and accurately at a reading level that is compatible with that of the students, and it should give a fair and unbiased treatment to women, minorities, and culturally different students. The module presents a number of other criteria that should be considered (see also Module 3).

3. Among the many sources are curriculum documents, resource units, and educational periodicals.

4. When evaluating the suitability of free materials, you should look for whether the material meets your instructional objectives, whether it treats ethnic, cultural groups, and women fairly, whether it is free from objectionable advertising or propaganda, and whether the material is interesting and attractive for student use, and whether it is generally accurate. Also, you should evaluate the durability of the material.

MODULE 9

Multiple Choice

1. a
2. a

3. b
4. b
5. c

Short Explanation

1. Audiovisual materials make available learning that students may not be able to get in any other way. By seeing the real thing or a representation of it, students both see and hear about it (using two learning modalities), thereby making the learning less abstract than were they to merely read about it.

2. The overhead projector is versatile; use of it rather than the writing board allows you to be closer to the students. Use of an overhead projector also reduces the need to walk back and forth and to turn your back to students, thereby allowing you to maintain eye contact with them.

3. Ways include: simple viewing by small groups of students or an entire class, and interaction with a computer for the development of individualized lessons and the updating of teaching programs.

MODULE 10

Multiple Choice

1. a		2. b	
3. a		4. b	
5. d		6. c	
7. a		8. d	
9. b		10. d	

Check

1.
2. ✔
3. ✔
4.
5. ✔

Analyze

1. 5 ⎫
2. 2 ⎪ any other numbers in ⎧ 10   ⎧ 50
3. 2 ⎬ same relationship, ⎨ 4   or   ⎨ 20
4. 1 ⎭ such as ⎩ 4   ⎩ 20
           2   10

5. A or D
6. K
7. O
8. L
9. R or Q

Matching

1. h
2. g
3. f
4. c
5. e

Completion Drawing

1. Preassessment of students
2. Instructional activities
3. Continuous evaluation

Completion Statement

Choose from the following:

- Placement
- Determine readiness
- Grading
- Diagnosis
- Promotion
- Setting goals
- Determine what to do next
- Judge the effectiveness of one's teaching

Short Explanation

1. Alternative techniques include: conference, discussion, observation of behavior, and observation of product.

2. If teachers were not obligated to make professional judgments, then robots or computers could do much of their work. It *is* professionally responsible for a teacher, as appropriate, to give a grade higher than what points may call for, but *never* lower than the points call for. For example, two students could end a semester with identical point scores. One could have started the semester in high gear with a first quarter grade of *A*, but then ended with total points calling for a *C* grade. That student would get a grade of *C*. Another student, however, could have begun slowly—perhaps even getting an *F* grade the first quarter—but then gone into high gear and earned an *A* the second quarter, though with total points calling only for a grade of *C*. In our opinion, this second student deserves better than the *C* grade because that student's current work is of *A* quality.

3. For true-false questions, reliability is very low—chances of guessing the correct answer are 50 percent. In addition, a student may have a valid reason for selecting the wrong answer. True-false and completion-type questions tend to encourage low-level learning—simple recall and rote memorization.

4. Authentic assessment is the accurate assessment of student learning—that is, by having the student demonstrate (perform) the learning (i.e., show what they know and can do) and then assessing that against preset standards. Authentic assessment *must* be performance assessment, but not necessarily is performance assessment authentic.

5. Journals and portfolios are examples.

MODULE 11

Check

1. a, c, d. Expertise in many teaching skills is asking too much at this stage; you have not had a chance to start developing teaching style yet.
2. a, d, e, f, g. Ask advice to keep from making unnecessary blunders; criticizing the school shows not your expertise, but your boorishness.

Mutliple Choice

1. c
2. c
3. d
4. a
5. b

Short Explanation

1. Examine the incident to see what went wrong and then try again.
2. One that includes all the lower level plus creating, discovering, reorganizing, and formulating new hypotheses, new questions and problems; in short, the level of original and productive thinking.
3. The objective should be clearly stated, measurable, pertinent to unit and course, worthwhile, suitable to age and grade level, achievable, attainable in different degrees and/or amounts, and relevant to the students' lives.
4. So you can get a picture of what you and your teaching are like.
5. a. Direct
   b. Probably not as effective as it would be if it were more indirect.
6. a. Teacher did most of the talking.
   b. Can't tell. Probably the teacher talks too much.
7. Select from good objectives, objectives obtainable by discussion techniques, good participation, teacher drew students out, teacher did not let anyone dominate, teacher kept group on the topic, teacher did not dominate, teacher used evocative questions and tentative solutions, teacher summarized well when needed, and teacher tied the discussion together in summary.
8. Teacher runs a good discussion, does not dominate, and draws out the class.
9. Whiplash questions are really incomplete sentences. They tend to confuse. They do not induce the proper set for answering questions.
10. Cognitive memory questions are narrow memory questions calling only for recall of information. Convergent questions are narrow thought questions that call for coming to a correct solution. Divergent questions are broad, open-ended thought questions for which there are probably no single correct answers.
11. The students seem to have achieved objective 1 but missed objective 2. If objective 2 is important, it probably should be retaught.
12. Choose from:

- Become certifiable in more than one subject.
- Pick courses that will prepare you to teach middle and high school courses.
- Seek a graduate degree.
- Do substitute teaching.
- Take advantage of the college or university placement service.
- Learn the skills of job procurement.

13. Basically so you can learn about new developments in the field at meetings or by reading their journals and monographs and so you can meet leaders and knowledgeable practitioners in your teaching field.

14. Danger signals include: poorly prepared for classes; shows little or no interest in other school activities; not prompt for class meetings and conferences; seems unaware of school clerical responsibilities; poor communication with other adults at the school; poorly organized.

15. Ways you could continue to grow professionally include: advanced academic work; workshops and conferences; off-teaching related experiences; participation in professional associations; communication with other professionals.

Glossary

accommodation. The cognitive process of modifying a schema or creating new schemata.

accountability. The concept that an individual is responsible for his or her behaviors and should be able to demonstrate publicly the worth of the activities carried out.

advance organizer. Preinstructural cues used to enhance retention of materials to be studied.

affective domain. The area of learning related to interests, attitudes, feelings, values, and personal adjustment.

AFT. The American Federation of Teachers, a national professional organization of teachers founded in 1916 and currently affiliated with the American Federation of Labor and Congress of Industrial Organizations (AFL-CIO).

alternative assessment. Assessment of learning in ways that are different from traditional paper-and-pencil objective testing. See *authentic assessment*.

anticipatory set. See *advance organizer*.

assessment. The process of judging the value of results by considering evidence in light of preset standards.

assignment. A statement telling the student what he or she is to accomplish.

assimilation. The cognitive process by which a learner integrates new information into an existing schema.

at-risk learner. General term given to students who show a high potential for not completing school.

authentic assessment. Assessment procedures that are highly compatible with the instructional objectives. Also referred to as *accurate, active, aligned, alternative, direct*, and *performance assessment*.

behavioral objective. A statement of expectation describing what the learner should be able to do upon completion of the instruction, and containing four elements: the audience (learner), the overt behavior, the conditions, and the level or degree of performance. Also referred to as a *performance* or *terminal objective*.

behaviorism. A theory that equates learning with changes in observable behavior.

brainstorming. An instructional strategy used to create a flow of new ideas, during which the judgments of the ideas of others are forbidden.

CD-ROM. (compact disc–read only memory) Digitally encoded information permanently recorded on a compact disc.

classroom control. The process of influencing student behavior in the classroom.

classroom management. The teacher's system of establishing a climate for learning, including techniques for preventing and handling student misbehavior.

clinical supervision. A nonevaluative collegial process of facilitating teaching effectiveness by involving a triad of individuals: the student teacher, the cooperating teacher, and the university supervisor. Sometimes known as *effective supervision*, clinical supervision generally includes: (1) a preobservation conference between the supervisor and the student teacher to specify and agree upon the specific objectives for an observation visit, (2) a data-collection observation, and (3) a postobservation conference to analyze the data collected during the observation and to set goals for a subsequent observation.

closure. In a lesson, the means by which a teacher brings the lesson to an end.

coaching. See *mentoring*.

cognitive disequilibrium. The mental state of not yet having made sense of a perplexing situation.

cognitive domain. The area of learning related to intellectual skills, such as retention and assimilation of knowledge.

cognitive psychology. A branch of psychology devoted to the study of how individuals acquire, process, and use information.

cognitivism.   A theory that holds that learning entails the construction or reshaping of mental schemata and that mental processes mediate learning. Also known as *constructivism*.

compact disc (CD).   A 4.72-inch disc on which a laser has recorded digital information.

competency-based instruction.   See *performance-based instruction*.

comprehension.   A level of cognition that refers to the skill of understanding.

computer literacy.   The ability at some level on a continuum to understand and use computers.

computer-assisted instruction (CAI).   Instruction received by a student when interacting with lessons programmed into a computer system.

computer-managed instruction (CMI).   The use of a computer system to manage information about learner performance and learning-resources options in order to prescribe and control individual lessons.

concept map.   A visual or graphic representation of concepts and their relationships. Words related to a key word are written in categories around the key word, and the categories are labeled.

constructivism.   See *cognitivism*.

convergent thinking.   Thinking that is directed to a preset conclusion.

cooperative learning.   A genre of instructional strategies that use small groups of students working together and helping each other on learning tasks, stressing support for one another rather than competition.

core curriculum.   Subject or discipline components of the curriculum considered as absolutely necessary. These are English/language arts, mathematics, science, and social science.

course.   A complete sequence of instruction that presents a major division of a subject matter or discipline.

covert behavior.   A learner behavior that is not outwardly observable.

criterion.   A standard by which behavioral performance is judged.

criterion-referenced.   When standards are established and behaviors are judged against the preset standards, rather than compared with and judged against the behaviors of others. See *norm-referenced*.

critical thinking.   The ability to recognize and identify problems and discrepancies, to propose and to test solutions, and to arrive at tentative conclusions based on the data collected.

curriculum.   A term derived from a Latin word referring to a race course for the chariots. There still is no widely accepted definition of the term. As used in this textbook, a curriculum is that which is encouraged for teaching and learning. This includes both school and nonschool environments, overt and hidden curriculums, and broad as well as narrow notions of content—its development, acquisition, and consequences.

deductive learning.   Learning that proceeds from the general to the specific. See *expository learning*.

diagnostic assessment.   See *preassessment*.

didactic teaching.   See *direct teaching*.

direct experience.   Learning by doing that which is being learned.

direct intervention.   Teacher use of verbal reminders or verbal commands to redirect student behavior, as opposed to the use of nonverbal gestures or cues.

direct teaching.   Teacher-centered expository instruction.

discipline.   The process of controlling student behavior in the classroom. The term has been largely replaced by the terms *classroom control* or *classroom management*. The term *discipline* is also used in reference to the subject taught (e.g., the disciplines of language arts, science, mathematics).

discovery learning.   Learning that proceeds from identification of a problem, through the development of hypotheses, testing of the hypotheses, to the arrival at a conclusion. See *critical thinking*.

divergent thinking.   Thinking that expands beyond original thought.

eclectic.   Utilizing the best from a variety of sources.

educational goal.   A desired instructional outcome that is broad in scope.

effective school.   A school where students master basic skills, seek academic excellence in all subjects, demonstrate achievement, and display good behavior and attendance.

empathy.   The ability to understand the feelings of another person.

equality.   Considered to be same in status or competency level.

equilibration.   The mental process of moving from disequilibrium to equilibrium.

equilibrium.   The balance between assimilation and accommodation.

equity.   Fairness and justice.

evaluation.   See *assessment*.

exceptional child.   A child who deviates from the average in any of the following ways: mental characteristics, sensory ability, neuromotor or physical characteristics, social behavior, and communication ability. An exceptional child may have multiple handicaps. Also known as a *special-needs child*.

expository learning.   The traditional classroom instructional approach that proceeds as follows: presentation of information to the learners, reference to particular examples, and application of the information to the learner's experiences.

extrinsic motivation.   Rewards for student learning that come from outside of the learner, such as parent and teacher expectations and gifts, certificates, and grades.

facilitating behavior.   Teacher behaviors that make it possible for students to learn.

facilitative teaching.   See *indirect teaching*.

family.   See *school within a school*.

feedback.   Information sent from the receiver to the originator that provides disclosure about the reception of the intended message.

formative assessment.   Evaluation of learning in progress.

goal, course.   A broad generalized statement telling about the expected outcomes of the course.

goal, education.   A desired instructional outcome that is broad in scope.

goal, instructional.   See any of the following: *course goal, educational goal*, and *teacher goal*.

goal, teacher.   A statement telling what the teacher hopes to accomplish.

hands-on learning.   Traditionally referred to as learning by doing, or active learning.

high school.   A school that houses students in any combination of grades 9 through 12.

holistic learning.   Learning that incorporates emotions with thinking.

house.   See *school within a school*.

inclusion.   Refers to the commitment to education of each special-needs learner, to the maximum extent appropriate, in the school and classroom he or she would otherwise attend.

indirect teaching.   Student-centered teaching using discovery and inquiry instructional strategies.

individualized learning.   The self-paced process whereby individual students assume responsibility for learning through study, practice, feedback, and reinforcement, with appropriately designed instructional packages or modules.

inductive learning.   Learning that proceeds from specifics to the general. See *discovery learning*.

inquiry learning.   Like discovery learning, except that the learner designs the processes to be used in resolving the problem, thereby requiring higher levels of cognition.

instruction.   Planned arrangement of experiences to help a learner develop understanding and to achieve a desirable change in behavior.

instructional module.   Any free-standing instructional unit that includes these components: rationale, objectives, pretest, learning activities, comprehension checks with instructive feedback, posttest.

instructional scaffolding.   See *concept map*.

interdisciplinary thematic unit.   A thematic unit that crosses boundaries of two or more disciplines.

internalization.   The extent to which an attitude or value becomes a part of the learner. That is, without having to think about it, the learner's behavior reflects the attitude or value.

intervention.   The teacher interrupts to redirect a student's behavior, either by direct intervention (e.g., by a verbal command) or by indirect intervention (e.g., by eye contact or by physical proximity).

intrinsic motivation.   Rewards for student learning that come from the student's internal sense of accomplishment.

intuition.   Knowing without conscious reasoning.

junior high school.   A school that houses grades 7 through 9 or 7 through 8 and that has a schedule and program of courses that resembles that of the (senior) high school (grades 9 through 12 or 10 through 12) more than it does that of the elementary school.

lead teacher.   The lead teacher is one member of a teaching team who is designated to facilitate the work and planning of that team.

learning.   The development of understanding and the change in behavior resulting from experiences. See *behaviorism* and *constructivism* for different interpretations of learning.

learning modality.   The way a person receives information. Four modalities are recognized: visual, auditory, tactile, and kinesthetic.

learning style.   The way a person learns best in a given situation.

lesson.   A subdivision of a unit, usually taught in a single class period or, on occasion, for two or three successive periods.

magnet school.   A school that specializes in particular academic areas, such as science, mathematics and technology, or the arts, or international relations.

mainstreaming.   Placing an exceptional child in regular education classrooms for all (*inclusion*) or part (partial inclusion) of the school day.

mastery learning.   The concept that a student should master the content of one lesson before moving on to the content of the next.

measurement.   The process of collecting and interpreting data.

mentoring.   One-on-one coaching, tutoring, or guidance to facilitate learning.

metacognition.   The ability to plan, monitor, and evaluate one's own thinking.

micro peer teaching.   Teaching a limited objective for a brief period of time to a small group of peers, for the purpose of evaluation and improvement of particular teaching skills.

middle grades.   Grades 5 through 8.

middle school.   Schools that have been planned and organized especially for students of ages ten through fourteen, and generally have grades 5 through 8, with grades 6 through 8 being the most popular grade-span organization (though many varied patterns exist). For example, a school might include only grades 7 and 8 and still be called a middle school.

minds-on learning.   Learning where the learner is intellectually active, thinking about what is being learned.

misconception.   Faulty understanding of a major idea or concept. Also known as *naive theory* and *misunderstanding*.

modeling.   The teacher's direct and indirect demonstration, by actions and by words, of the behaviors expected of students.

multicultural education.   A deliberate attempt to help students understand facts, generalizations, attitudes, and behaviors derived from their own ethnic roots as well as others. In this process students unlearn racism and prejudices and recognize the interdependent fabric of society, giving due acknowledgment for contributions made by all its members.

multilevel teaching.   See *multitasking*.

multimedia instruction.   The combined use of sound, video, and graphics for instruction.

multipurpose board.   A writing board with a smooth plastic surface used with special marking pens rather than chalk. Sometimes called *visual aid panels*, the boards may have a steel backing and then can be used as a magnetic board as well as a screen for projecting visuals.

multitasking.   When several levels of teaching and learning are going on simultaneously in the same classroom, or when students are working on different objectives, or when different students are doing various tasks leading to the same objective. Also called *multilevel teaching*.

naive theory.   See *misconception*.

NEA.   The National Education Association, the nation's oldest professional organization of teachers, founded in 1857 as the National Teachers Association and changed in 1879 to its present name.

norm-referenced.   When individual performance is judged relative to overall performance of the group. See *criterion-referenced*.

orientation set.   See *advance organizer*.

outcome-based instruction.   See *performance-based instruction*.

overlapping.   A teacher behavior where the teacher is able to attend to more than one matter at once.

overt behavior.   A learner behavior that is outwardly observable.

paraprofessional.   An adult who is not a credentialed teacher, but who works with children in the classroom with and under the supervision of a credentialed person.

performance assessment.   See *authentic assessment*.

performance objective.   See *behavioral objective*.

performance-based instruction.   Instruction designed around instruction and assessment of student achievement against specified and predetermined objectives.

positive reinforcer.   Encouraging desired student behavior by rewarding those behaviors when they occur.

preassessment.   Diagnostic assessment, or assessment of what students know or think they know prior to the instruction.

probationary teacher.   An untenured teacher. After a designated number of years in the same district, usually three, the probationary teacher receives a tenure contract upon rehire.

procedure.   A statement telling the student how to accomplish a task.

psychomotor domain.   The domain of learning related to locomotor behaviors.

realia.   Real objects used as visual props during instruction, such as political campaign buttons, plants, memorabilia, artwork, and so on.

reciprocal teaching.   A form of collaborative teaching, where the teacher and the students share the teaching responsibility and all are involved in asking questions, clarifying, predicting, and summarizing.

reflective abstraction.   See *metacognition*.

reliability.   In measurement, the consistency with which an item or instrument is measured over time.

schema.   A mental construct by which the learner organizes his or her perceptions of situations and knowledge (plural: *schemata*).

school within a school.   Within a school, where one team of teachers is assigned to work with the same group of about 125 students for a common block of time, for the entire school day, or, in some instances, for all the years those students are at that school. A school within a school may also be known as a *house*, a *village*, a *pod*, or a *family*.

secondary school.   Traditionally, any school housing students for any combination of grades 7 through 12.

self-paced learning.   See *individualized learning*.

senior high school.   See *high school*.

sequencing.   Arranging ideas in logical order.

simulation.   An abstraction or simplification of a real-life situation.

special-needs students.   See *exceptional child*.

SQ3R.   A study strategy where students survey the reading, create questions, read to answer the questions, recite the answers, and review the original material.

SQ4R.   Similar to SQ3R, but with the addition of recording—the students survey the reading, ask questions about what was read, read to answer the questions, recite the answers, record important items into their notebooks, and then review it all.

student teaching.   A field experience component of teacher preparation, often the culminating experience, where the teacher candidate practices teaching children while under the supervision of a credentialed teacher and a university supervisor.

summative assessment.   Assessment of learning after instruction is completed.

teacher leader.   See *lead teacher*.

teaching.   See *instruction*.

teaching style.   The way teachers teach, their distinctive mannerisms complemented by their choices of teaching behaviors and strategies.

teaching team.   A team of two or more teachers who work together to provide instruction to the same group of students, either alternating the instruction or simultaneously in team teaching.

team teaching.   Teachers working together to provide instruction to a group of students.

tenured teacher.   After serving a designated number of years in the same school district (usually three) as a probationary teacher, the teacher receives a tenure contract upon rehire, which means that the teacher is automatically rehired each year thereafter unless the contract is revoked by either the district or the teacher and for specific and legal reasons.

terminal behavior.   That which has been learned as a direct result of instruction.

thematic unit.   A unit of instruction built on a central theme or concept.

think time.   See *wait time*.

transescent.   The stage of human development, usually thought of as ages ten through fourteen, that begins before the onset of puberty and extends through the early stages of adolescence. Also referred to as *preadolescent, pre-teen, in-betweenager*, and *tweenager*.

transition.   In a lesson, the planned procedures that move student thinking from one idea to the next, or that move their actions from one activity to the next.

unit.   A major subdivision of a course, comprising planned instruction about some central theme, topic, issue, or problem for a period of several days to several weeks.

validity.   In measurement, the degree to which an item or instrument measures that which it is intended to measure.

village.   See *school within a school*.

wait time.   In the use of questioning, the period of silence between the time a question is asked and the inquirer (teacher) does something, such as repeats the question, rephrases the question, calls on a particular student, answers the question him- or herself, or asks another question.

withitness.   The teacher's ability to timely intervene and redirect a student's inappropriate behavior.

Name Index

Alexander, W., 12, 12n
Allen, H. A., 12n
Amidon, E. J., 463n
Anderson, J., 290n
Anderson, R. H., 15n
Applebee, A. N., 288n
Armstrong, T., 52n
Ausubel, D., 39, 45, 45n

Balkcom, S., 265n, 266n
Banks, C. A. M., 57, 57n, 58n, 88n
Banks, J. A., 57, 57n, 58n, 88n
Baron, E. B., 212
Baum, R., 267n
Benay, 58n
Benedetti, P., 412n
Beyer, B. K., 267n
Black, S., 18n, 410n
Blendinger, J., 212
Bloom, B. S., 18, 18n, 43, 44n, 108, 112n
Blythe, T., 52n
Bormuth, J., 93n, 354n
Bracey, G. W., 52n
Bradfield, J. M., 457
Bransford, J. D., 335n
Braten, I., 40n
Briggs, L., 108n
Brophy, J. E., 97n, 196n
Brown, M. W., 144
Bruner, J. S., 39, 44, 44n, 253, 269n
Burrett, K., 65n

Caine, G., 41n, 42n, 49n, 114n, 115n
Caine, R. N., 41n, 42n, 49n, 114n, 115n
Canady, R. L., 6n
Canter, L., 212
Canter, M., 212
Carroll, J. M., 10n, 18, 18n
Chall, J. S., 41n
Charles, C. M., 222n
Cherrington, A., 265n, 266n
Clapp, P., 144
Combs, A. W., 16n
Conley, D. T., 10n
Costa, A. L., 20n, 46, 46n, 266n, 267n, 315n, 316n, 317n
Crabtree, C., 79

Dale, E., 253
Dayton, C., 6n
de Bono, E., 48n
de Souza, A., 79
Dempster, F. N., 18n
Desmond, C. T., 18n
Dewey, J., 267n
Donaldson, Jr., G. A., 33n
Dougherty, J., 87n
Dunn, K., 51n
Dunn, R., 51n
Duren, P. E., 265n, 266n

Eggen, P., 33n
Eichhorn, D., 12, 12n, 12, 12n
Eisner, E., 316n
Eitzen, D. S., 36n
Ellison, L., 52n
Emmer, E. T., 221n
Escalante, J., 196n

Feather, N. T., 196n
Ferrell, B. G., 50n
Fersh, S., 115n
Flack, J., 63n
Flanders, N. A., 463n
Fleischman, P., 144
Frazer, L., 15n
Fritz, J., 144
Fry, E., 93n, 352n
Futrell, M. H., 33n

Gagné, R. M., 39, 42, 108n, 267n, 269n
Gallegos, G., 52n
Gamoran, A., 14n
Gardner, H., 51, 52n
George, P. S., 12n
Gifford, B. R., 89n
Good, T. L., 97n, 196n
Gordon, C. J., 290n
Grant, C. A., 7n, 92n, 199n, 200, 201
Green, D., 318n
Green, J. E., 63n
Gregorc, A., 50, 50n, 51n

Haberman, M., 35n
Haertel, G. D., 195n
Harrow, A. J., 112n

Hart, L. A., 41n
Hatch, T., 52n
Heddens, J. W., 392n
Heinich, R., 51n, 377n, 390n, 393n, 395n
Hernández, H., 10n, 14n
Hightshue, D., 289n
Hill, D., 79
Hoban, Sr., C. F., 253n
Hoerr, T. R., 52n
Holtz, H., 87n
Horton, L., 18n, 19n, 44n
Hunter, M., 20n, 363n, 364n

Jackson, R. M., 269n
Jacobsen, D., 33n
Jenkinson, E. B., 424n
Johnson, H. A., 93n
Johnson, M. S., 93n
Joyce, B., 318n
Jung, C. G., 51, 51n

Kauchak, D., 33n
Keefe, J. W., 50n
Keislar, E. S., 269n
Keller, F., 18
Kellough, R. D., 237n
Kemp, J. E., 379n
Kimpston, R. D., 63n
Klopfer, L. E., 52n, 319n, 335n
Kolb, D., 51, 51n
Konicek, R., 17n, 35n
Kounin, J. S., 218n
Krathwohl, D. R., 112n
Kress, R. A., 93n
Kulik, J. A., 63n

Lazear, D. G., 52n
Lenski, L., 144
Lepper, M., 318n
Lickona, T., 65n
Lobel, A., 144
Long, L., 88n

Macinnis, D., 290n
Mahlmann, J., 79
Manning, M. L., 12n
Marcus, I., 87n
Masia, B. B., 112n

Subject Index